Business
Plans
Handbook

Business Plans Handbook

A COMPILATION OF ACTUAL BUSINESS PLANS DELEVOPED BY BUSINESS THROUGHOUT NORTH AMERICA

VOLUME

11

**Lynn Pearce,
Project Editor**

THOMSON

GALE

Detroit • New York • San Francisco • San Diego • New Haven, Conn. • Waterville, Maine • London • Munich

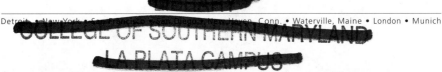

Business Plans Handbook, 11th Volume

Project Editor
Lynn M. Pearce

Product Design:
Jennifer Wahi

Composition and Electronic Capture:
Evi Seoud

Manufacturing
Rita Wimberley

This publication is a creative work fully protected by all applicable copyright laws, as well as by misappropriation, trade secret, unfair competition, and other applicable laws. The authors and editors of this work have added value to the underlying factual material herein through one or more of the following: unique and original selection, coordination, expression, arrangement, and classification of the information.

For permission to use material from this product, submit your request via Web at http://www.gale-edit.com/permissions, or you may download our Permission Request form and submit your request by fax or mail to:

Permissions Department
The Gale Group, Inc.
27500 Drake Rd.
Farmington Hills, MI 48331-3535
Permissions Hotline:
248-699-8006 or 800-877-4253, ext. 8006
Fax: 248-699-8074 or 800-762-4058

Since this page cannot legibly accommodate all copyright notices, the acknowledgments constitute an extension of the copyright notice.

While every effort has been made to ensure the reliability of the information presented in this publication, The Gale Group, Inc. does not guarantee the accuracy of the data contained herein. The Gale Group, Inc. accepts no payment for listing; and inclusion in the publication of any organization, agency, institution, publication, service, or individual does not imply endorsement of the editors or publisher. Errors brought to the attention of the publisher and verified to the satisfaction of the publisher will be corrected in future editions.

LIBRARY OF CONGRESS CATALOGING-IN-PUBLICATION DATA
ISBN 0-7876-6681-5
ISSN 1084-4473

Printed in the United States of America
10 9 8 7 6 5 4 3 2 1

Contents

BUSINESS PLANS

CONTENTS

Highlights

Business Plans Handbook, Volume 11 (BPH-11) is a collection of actual business plans compiled by entrepreneurs seeking funding for small businesses throughout North America. For those looking for examples of how to approach, structure, and compose their own business plans, BPH-11 presents 20 sample plans, including plans for the following businesses:

- Adventure Travel Lodging Company
- Brewpub
- Cigar Company
- Construction Development & Real Estate Firm
- Construction and Home Rehabilitation Company
- Daycare Facility
- Giftware Company
- Handmade Greeting Card Company
- Handyman Service
- Homeless Shelter
- Interior Design Company
- Interior Painting Service
- Internet Loyalty Program
- Internet Services Portal Site
- Massage Therapists
- Mentally Disabled Care Facility
- Motorcycle Dealership and Racetrack
- Online Mortgage Company
- Pizza Restaurant
- Private Investigator

FEATURES AND BENEFITS

BPH-11 offers many features not provided by other business planning references including:

- Twenty business plans, each of which represent an owner's successful attempt at clarifying (for themselves and others) the reasons that the business should exist or expand and why a lender should fund the enterprise.
- Two fictional plans that are used by business counselors at a prominent small business development organization as examples for their clients. (You will find these in the Business Plan Template Appendix.)

- An expanded directory section that includes: listings for venture capital and finance companies, which specialize in funding start-up and second-stage small business ventures, and a comprehensive listing of Service Corps of Retired Executives (SCORE) offices. In addition, the Appendix also contains updated listings of all Small Business Development Centers (SBDCs); associations of interest to entrepreneurs; Small Business Administration (SBA) Regional Offices; and consultants specializing in small business planning and advice. It is strongly advised that you consult supporting organizations while planning your business, as they can provide a wealth of useful information.

- A Small Business Term Glossary to help you decipher the sometimes confusing terminology used by lenders and others in the financial and small business communities.

- A cumulative index, outlining each plan profiled in the complete Business Plans Handbook series.

- A Business Plan Template which serves as a model to help you construct your own business plan. This generic outline lists all the essential elements of a complete business plan and their components, including the Summary, Business History and Industry Outlook, Market Examination, Competition, Marketing, Administration and Management, Financial Information, and other key sections. Use this guide as a starting point for compiling your plan.

- Extensive financial documentation required to solicit funding from small business lenders. BPH-11 contains the most comprehensive financial data within the series to date. You will find examples of: Cash Flows, Balance Sheets, Income Projections, and other financial information included with the textual portions of the plan.

Introduction

Perhaps the most important aspect of business planning is simply doing it. More and more business owners are beginning to compile business plans even if they don't need a bank loan. Others discover the value of planning when they must provide a business plan for the bank. The sheer act of putting thoughts on paper seems to clarify priorities and provide focus. Sometimes business owners completely change strategies when compiling their plan, deciding on a different product mix or advertising scheme after finding that their assumptions were incorrect. This kind of healthy thinking and re-thinking via business planning is becoming the norm. The editors of Business Plans Handbook, Volume 11 (BPH-11) sincerely hope that this latest addition to the series is a helpful tool in the successful completion of your business plan, no matter what the reason for creating it.

This eleventh volume, like each volume in the series, offers genuine business plans used by real people. BPH-11 provides 20 business plans used by actual entrepreneurs to gain funding support for their new businesses. The business and personal names and addresses and general locations have been changed to protect the privacy of the plan authors.

NEW BUSINESS OPPORTUNITIES

As in other volumes in the series, BPH-11 finds entrepreneurs engaged in a wide variety of creative endeavors. Examples include a proposal for an adventure travel lodging company, a brewpub, and a cigar company. In addition, several timely and requested plans are provided, including a daycare facility, interior design company, a massage therapist office, and a private investigator.

Comprehensive financial documentation has become increasingly important as today's entrepreneurs compete for the finite resources of business lenders. Our plans illustrate the financial data generally required of loan applicants, including Income Statements, Financial Projections, Cash Flows, and Balance Sheets.

ENHANCED APPENDIXES

In an effort to provide the most relevant and valuable information for our readers, we have updated the coverage of small business resources. For instance, you will find: a directory section, which includes listings of all of the Service Corps of Retired Executives (SCORE) offices; an informative glossary, which includes small business terms; and a cumulative index, outlining each plan profiled in the complete Business Plans Handbook series. In addition we have updated the list of Small Business Development Centers (SBDCs); Small Business Administration Regional Offices; venture capital and finance companies, which specialize in funding start-up and second-stage small business enterprises; associations of interest to entrepreneurs; and consultants, specializing in small business advice and planning. For your reference, we have also reprinted the business plan template, which provides a comprehensive overview of the essential components of a business plan and two fictional plans used by small business counselors.

SERIES INFORMATION

If you already have the first ten volumes of BPH, with this eleventh volume, you will now have a collection of over 240 real business plans (not including the one updated plan in the second volume, whose original appeared in the first, or the two fictional plans in the Business Plan Template Appendix section of the second, third, fourth, fifth, sixth, and seventh volumes); contact information for hundreds of organizations and agencies offering business expertise; a helpful business plan template; a foreword providing advice and instruction to entrepreneurs on how to begin their research; more than 1,500 citations to valuable small business development material; and a comprehensive glossary of terms to help the business planner navigate the sometimes confusing language of entrepreneurship.

ACKNOWLEDGEMENTS

The Editors wish to sincerely thank the many contributors to BPH-11, including:

- Chelsea L. Aaberg, KHARDS
- Michael G. Erker, E.T. Construction
- Adam Greengrass, AdCon Services, LLC
- Tena Harper, BusinessandMarketingPlans.com
- Patrick Kuyath, KCI
- Eric McMahon, McMahon Interiors
- Gerald Rekve, Corporate Management Consultants
- Zachary David Robinson, The Double Eagle Brewery
- RJ Sak, Andre House Hospitality Center of Phoenix, AZ
- Tony Tecce, RealBusinessPlans.com
- John B. Trautmann, E.T. Construction
- Aaron L. Wappelhorst, Sunrise Care Organization
- Andrew A. Westerfeld, Sunrise Care Organization

The editors would also like to express their gratitude to both Lisa Bastian, CBC, of Bastian Public Relations, and Jerome Katz of the Cook School of Business at Saint Louis University. Both individuals have been instrumental in finding and securing high–quality, successful business plans for inclusion in this publication.

COMMENTS WELCOME

Your comments on Business Plans Handbook are appreciated. Please direct all correspondence, suggestions for future volumes of BPH, and other recommendations to the following:

Managing Editor, Business Product
Business Plans Handbook
The Gale Group

27500 Drake Rd.
Farmington Hills, MI 48331-3535

Phone: (248)699-4253
Fax: (248)699-8052
Toll-Free: 800-347-GALE
E-mail: BusinessProducts@gale.com

Adventure Travel Lodging Company

Cobra Travel Adventure Group

14 Willow Lane
Seattle, WA 98101

Tony Tecce

This business plan raised well over $200,000 for entrepreneurs seeking to build a number of resorts/lodges providing exciting "adventure travel" experiences. Owners housed guests in local hotels for three seasons before finally completing their flagship lodge. Plans are presently on hold for pursuing larger construction dreams.

EXECUTIVE SUMMARY

Cobra Travel Adventure Group (CTAG) is soon to become a leader in the fastest–growing segment of the travel industry: adventure travel. Growing at a solid 15 to 20 percent per year, the demand for adventure travel destinations far outweighs the current supply.

Due to this segment's infancy in the industry, there is no single travel outfitter that offers a broad range of adventure travel options. Yes, there are companies who sell differing packages, but they are the brokers. Somewhat like Hyatt Hotels, CTAG will own and operate a number of adventure travel resorts providing a consistent level of quality and service. An outstanding vacation that the guest can count on whether skiing in Canada or surfing in Costa Rica.

CTAG has 10 resorts/lodges slated for immediate development. These properties include our flagship ski resort in Victoria called Snowfall Lodge. It has taken two years to complete the process for obtaining a perpetual lease on 80+ square miles of pristine forest service land. As of October 2000 it was made official through a country–wide press release, CTAG was granted the land tenure. Snowfall Lodge will be the seventh destination ski lodge in Victoria, which commands most of the world's market share in this industry. These lodges are consistently sold out year after year. *The demand outweighs the supply.*

The other lodges include a fly fishing lodge in Utah, a Brazilian surf and yachting lodge, a mountain bike resort in Montana and a family ecological lodge in Washingon. CTAG is approaching each property on an individual basis. Some will be developed from the ground up, others will be renovations of existing properties.

The CTAG goal is to develop the lodges within the next two years. By our fourth year, CTAG will be prime for DPO (direct public offering) or a buy–out from a larger travel/hotel company looking to expand into the adventure travel market. Either way, the exit strategy looks very profitable.

Cobra Travel Overview

Cobra Travel will act as the branded mother company for all of its adventure properties. Based in Seattle, Washington, the CTAG head office will oversee all functions of the properties including bookkeeping, sales, marketing and reservations. Included in Cobra Travel's responsibilities is the selection of the consultants and professional teams to design and develop each project; entitlement issues, recruitment and training of all personnel (including operations staff) and maintenance.

MARKETING & SALES

Our target market primarily consists of heads of household between the ages of 35 to 54 years old that have high household incomes (averaging $107,000+/yr.). Their trips average about three to six nights, and 72 percent of the time they go on these trips with their children. Secondary markets include the broader, younger enthusiast.

The average market breakdown originates from the following geographical areas:

- 45 percent from North America

- 40 percent from Europe

- 4 percent from Asia

- 3 percent from Victoria

- 8 percent from other countries

The Company's marketing plan will comprise a mix of FAM tours, direct mailings, Internet, print ads plus free film and print publicity.

FAM tours are complimentary packages for industry professionals. We plan to offer these tours to writers from the nation's largest sports and travel publications including *Ski Magazine*, *Mountain Living*, *Snowboarder*, *Couloir*, *Outside*, *Hekler*, *Islands*, *Conde Nast*, *Adventure* and *Powder*. So far, three of the magazines have committed to articles. Publicity generated from such articles has contributed to many bookings for similar resorts in the area.

The direct mailings will be geared for the travel agent market, magazine subscription lists and clubs across the world. The mailings will include a number of brochures and FAM tour invitations for the industry professionals. The travel agent will be our front line for sales, therefore we will offer better than average commissions (15 percent) during our first two seasons of operation. Mailings will include package deals with group discounts.

The direct mailings will be sent worldwide and our brochure will be translated into Italian, German, French, Japanese, and Spanish and sent directly to potential contacts or to distributors. We are working with sporting goods distributors around the world who would be able to provide the starting platform for an international marketing campaign.

The web site will also generate a number of sales. The key to Internet sales is an impressive look with a product targeted to the people surfing the web. Adventure vacation packages are one of the products that generate a lot of interest on the web.

"Seventy percent of downhillers say they have access to the Internet and one–third of those who have that access had visited the homepage of the resort where they were skiing. The majority were between the ages of 25 and 54 with higher than average incomes."

Our Web site will be the most cost–effective form of our advertising campaign. We will build a custom Web site with up–to–the–minute weather conditions, live web cameras, booking availability, and trip details. To pull the potential customer to the site, we will have a unique Web cam for each property. The Web cam takes a picture every 60 seconds and is instantly available for viewing at the site. Our cams will show the view from each resort.

Print ads will be placed in various sports/travel publications. Our target market reads these magazines. These magazines, in most cases, act as a travel organizer for the guest (from accommodations to gear).

Currently, we have had numerous commitments from film and photo professionals to include footage from our resorts in their next projects. Rachel Luevano, one of the most respected sports photographers in the world, will be shooting the Mighty Moose Snowboarding team at our Victoria location in March 2000. Also, Stonecold Films, a ski/snowboard filmmaking company, is filming part of their next feature at our Snowfall Lodge.

MANAGEMENT SUMMARY

Cobra Travel, a Seattle, Washington, limited liability company, is headed by Robert Marians, Ed Macroid and Marcus Stock.

Robert Marians, Chief Operations and Financial Officer

Robert Marians's roots are in sales and the hospitality industry, having run a number of hotels and resorts in the Miami area. He was actively involved with all aspects of the travel business including management, marketing and front–of–house operations. Robert was general manager of Marriott's third–largest timeshare property in the world, as well as two resorts in the Miami area. Strengths lied in budgeting and project management in the hospitality industry. Marians has a strong entrepreneurial background having started four thriving businesses in the South Beach area. He started the companies from their inception, creating the business plan, acting as president reporting directly to the board of directors and shareholders and running day–to–day activities. Marians has started three restaurants, a retail store, prolific Internet mail order company, and an Internet consulting company. His Internet skills include design and marketing, which will prove to be of utmost importance to the success of this project.

With a B.A. in Business Administration and Computer Sciences, Marians and his corporate direction have been truly entrepreneurial. He has participated in the start–up of many companies, acting as the organizer, financial strategist and problem solver. Robert possesses dual citizenship between Canada and the U.S., helping ease the process of foreign investment. His expertise will have a prominent role in the success of CTAG.

Ed Macroid, Chief Project Manager

Ed Macroid serves as the chief project manager for the Lodges. His education includes a B.A. in Restaurant and Hotel Management from Sierra Nevada College at Lake Tahoe. His professional experience includes start–ups of numerous restaurants and hotel management in the Western portion of the United States.

Ed's operations experience has proved to be an invaluable asset to the prosperous future of CTAG.

Marcus Stock, Chief of Marketing and Public Relations

Marcus Stock has extensive sports/resort marketing and public relations. For over 10 years he was marketing manager of a snowboard manufacturing company, spearheading the marketing and promotions of some of the world's most popular snowboards. His education includes a B.A. in Business Administration. He is a member of numerous ski and snowboard industry professional associations.

Stock brings to the company inside contacts within the sports industry and media (print and film) professionals. His extensive sports industry and marketing knowledge is a primary asset to CTAG.

EXIT STRATEGY

There are two possible exit scenarios:

- DPO (Direct Public Offering)

- Buy Out

DPO: If a Direct Public Offering is agreed upon, CTAG will seek new capital to add new properties and cash out investors. Each investor would have the choice of retaining some or all of their ownership. The exact amounts involved would have to be agreed upon at that time.

Buy Out: The buy–out option may present itself even sooner that projected. Currently there is a mass consolidation taking place in the travel/lodging industry. Large hospitality companies like Starwood and Intrawest are acquiring existing properties at an alarming rate. (Starwood has committed to acquiring over 300 properties within the next year.)

Intrawest, dealing mainly in the golf and ski travel industry, has recently closed a deal with CMH (Canadian Mountain Holidays). CMH, the world's largest Heli–Ski outfitter, has sold off 50 percent of its operations to Intrawest for an impressive $40 million. Intrawest also has a stake in resort properties such as Squaw Valley, Mt. Tremblant, Snowbird, etc.

In either scenario, owners of CTAG will be able to cash out handsomely.

SNOWFALL LODGE, VICTORIA

Executive Summary

Snowfall Mountain Lodge (sometimes referred to as the "Resort" or "Lodge") is the vision of Cobra Travel, LLC, (the "Company") a group of private investors from Seattle. Cobra Travel's goal is to develop a first–class backcountry resort, nestled in the pristine wilderness of Victoria, Canada. The Resort will be leading the new trend in tourism called Adventure Travel; created for the traveler who wants more than the run–of–the–mill vacation.

The Lodge will set in the midst of 80+ square miles of mountains, meadows, lakes and streams leased from the Victoria provincial government. Activities to be offered will include ski touring, guided snowcat skiing, mountaineering, rock climbing, hiking, fishing, snow–mobiling, and mountain biking. To add to the experience, the Resort will accommodate only 36 guests personifying the attention to detail, gourmet dining, comfortable rooms and the best in service.

A skilled and creative group of experienced planners, designers, builders and managers has been assembled by Cobra Travel to develop and operate the Lodge. The total project cost will be 4.8 million Canadian dollars (*3.4 million American funds). Management intends to raise all of the total project's costs through this offering. *All currency conversions are based on a 40 percent exchange rate.

Background

The Largetoon region of Victoria has long been the focus of a wide range of outdoor recreational activities. Traditional uses such as hunting, fishing, hiking and mountaineering have been augmented by newer activities such as snowmobiling, telemark skiing, cat–skiing and heli–skiing. In recent years there has been increased interest in the provision of such outdoor recreation opportunities on a commercial basis. This trend is in keeping with the rapid worldwide development of the tourism industry into a segment known as adventure travel.

Adventure travel is the term used to describe a wide grouping of commercial outdoor recreation products from cat–skiing to whale–watching, that currently account for 10 to 20 percent of the U.S.

travel industry. In Victoria adventure travel generated direct revenues exceeding $380 million (CDN) in 1997. As such, Victoria is the adventure travel market leader in North America earning substantially more than any other state or province.

Adventure travel is a relatively new phenomenon. It is experiencing very rapid growth since it is a type of tourism favored by the affluent, activity–conscious "Baby Boom" generation. In Victoria, adventure travel is expanding at a rate of between 15 and 20 percent per year. By the year 2006, it is forecasted to be generating over a half billion dollars in direct revenues.

A study undertaken by Tourism Canada on Adventure Tourism (1996) notes that Victoria currently accounts for a large majority of the Canadian adventure tourism product. This study also identified the geographical criteria necessary for the successful operation of various adventure tourism activities, and revealed that for mountain–related activities (skiing, hiking, etc.) the Largetoon region has the highest quality product in Victoria. It is not surprising, therefore, that substantial interest exists in the development of new adventure tourism activities, particularly snow–based commercial recreation activities on Kopps Lands in the Largetoons.

Snowcat skiing involves the use of caterpillar tracked 12–person vehicles to transport skiers to the top of mountains to access powder skiing. Snowcat skiing represents the intermediate step between the top–end heli–skiing product and lift–serviced skiing.

Snowcat skiing is fast becoming a popular alternative to both heli–skiing and destination ski resorts. The whole idea is simple: Small groups of skiers are chauffeured through the backcountry of a vast mountain range and then guided down wide–open bowls of powder. One can ski for a week without ever waiting in lift lines or worrying about congested runs. All skill levels, beyond beginner, can take advantage of the snowcat experience due to the advent of powder skis that float effortlessly through the deep powder.

Snowcat operations in the United States are becoming popular as off–chutes of established ski areas such as Aspen and Snowbird. These are snowcat–only operations; no lodging or meals are included. Only in Victoria does one see all–inclusive style snowcat resorts. The typical resort charges $500/day (CDN) and includes basic accommodations, meals and guided skiing. Most snowcat packages last from three to six days, allowing for an average of 12,000 vertical feet of skiing per day.

The snowcat resort popularity has been fueled by the rising costs of conventional ski vacations. The average cost for two people to ski and stay in Vail for three days can easily exceed $364 per person/day (including hotel, food and lift ticket). Ski areas are also more crowded due to the explosion of the snowboard market. No longer can a skier enjoy a day on the slopes; each run has to be executed with care to avoid potential collisions with others on the slopes. Quality of service has also diminished in the light of cost cutting and downsizing.

Site Selection

The key for the Resort is to have access to Koops Land. Koops Land is similar to Forest Service Land in the U.S. In Victoria, over 80 percent Koops Land property is available for long–term lease. For our operation, a total of 55 square miles of Koops Land will be needed for the snowcat access area.

Site selection is crucial in many respects, including the right combination of peaks, ridge lines, vertical, streams, meadows and accessibility. But, just finding a suitable area is not enough. Once the area has been located, the process of attaining tenure with the Ministry of Environment, Lands and Parks of Victoria is next. This process takes from one to two years, requiring studies and management plans that satisfy all of the governmental powers involved. Achieving land tenure is key. The process begins by submitting an Expression of Intent (EOI) with the government. Currently, we have been given proponent status to develop a management plan for operations in the Martins area. This means that no other entity can vie for this area.

Continuing the process, the environmental impact studies and overlaid maps detailing use, migration paths, vegetation, roads, precipitation and lodge location have been completed. We expect to complete and redraft the management plan twice before being granted tenure which should be in the fall of 1999. Land tenure gives the company all legal commercial rights to a 55 square mile area with 10– to 20–year leases that can be renewed every three years, in effect an unlimited lease on the land.

This area is conveniently located just north of Jotsey, Victoria. From Jotsey, the area is 10 minutes by car, then 20 minutes by off–road vehicle or a quick seven–minute helicopter ride. The city of Jotsey, incorporated in 1888, located on the East Arm of Largetoon Lake in the heart of the Rachet Mountains in Largetoons. Aircraft access is limited to a small airport in Jotsey with a 2,900 ft. runway accommodating 12 to 15 passenger planes and private jets. The next closest airport is located at Hotts, only 30 minutes from Jotsey, accommodating commuter (Air Canada and Canadian Regional Airlines) and private jet aircraft.

Jotsey is the perfect accentuation for the resort; offering air transportation, nightlife and plenty of turn–of–the–century ambiance.

The resort will be situated on the biggest lake in the center of the land tenure. This area of Canada, averaging 660 inches of snow per season, has many majestic mountain ranges perfectly suited for snowcat skiing, as well as most summer sports.

The Snowfall Mountain Lodge Experience

Winter—Our resort will take advantage of all that is available to create a skiing experience unsurpassed in quality and service. The main lodge will be a 18,000 sq. ft. log cabin with 25 guest rooms, a game room, sundry shop, and dining and meeting facilities.

The skiers' adventure begins with being picked up in town by helicopter which whisks the group to the main lodge. Once settled in, the guests convene in the dining room for the first four–course meal of their vacation. After dinner, everyone heads to the great room for introductions to their guides and basic backcountry tips, instructions, etc. The instructions include information about use of the avalanche transponders, the terrain to be covered during the upcoming days and ski rental fittings. The guests' mornings start with a hearty breakfast, followed by loading the cat for a day in the mountains.

On average, the group will get in three to four runs by lunchtime. Each run is carefully selected, by certified guides, to the ability of the skiers. Lunch is served at the cat, then back to the skiing for another five runs. Once back at the lodge, some apres–ski cocktails in the game–room or hot–tubing to relax the muscles. Soon after, the dinner bell chimes and the group is amazed with another exquisite dining experience. The following days are just like the first; no one goes home unsatisfied.

Now for the skier with a family. We will be the only snowcat resort to provide a daily kid–focused ski camp. Kids between 5 to 16 years old will have the same opportunity for a great ski vacation, without their parents missing a turn. There will be a groomed area, near the lodge, equipped with a tow lift. Under qualified supervision, kids will get to ski, slide, eat and just play while their parents are off tackling the backcountry.

Summer—Our summer guests will have the opportunity to relax or enjoy all of the outdoor sports and recreation they can handle. From the Lodge we will offer hiking and mountain biking; from our day–lodge, guests can go fishing or water skiing in one of our boats, jet skiing, lounging at our sandy beach, swimming, aircraft sight–seeing, golf or enjoying all that the city of Jotsey has to offer.

Our main lodge will be the perfect place to get away from the hustle and bustle of the city. We will offer corporate retreats for play or work in a great atmosphere.

Also, throughout the summer we will host numerous events and seminars in the arts and environment.

The day lodge is located at the entrance to our land, directly on the Largetoon Lake facing Jotsey. This property, to be purchased by the Company, has a private beach, dock and a small log cabin. Equipment at the beach will include a ski boat, fishing boats, jet–skis, sailboards, inflatable air mattresses and shade umbrellas. The log cabin will house the snack bar for the guests.

From the day lodge, our van will take the guest into Jotsey. While in town, guests can shop at some of the many quaint boutiques or soak up some of the old–world charm. Spread throughout Jotsey are more than 200 well–built buildings; some dating back to 1888. The restoration of private residences, churches, businesses and government buildings has given this city a look and feel dating back to the turn of the century. Residential heritage structures, ranging from cottages to mansions, are everywhere in the region. Two of the most striking heritage churches are the Jotsey Congregational Church with it's tall tower and stained glass windows, and the ornate St. Michael the Archangel Cathedral; both were built in the early 20th century.

As for golf, Jotsey is home to the Pinetree Point Golf Course and within 30 minutes of five other courses. Jasper Rock, an 18 hole course (par 72/5,933 yards) with spectacular views of Lookit Glacier, is five minutes from downtown Jotsey.

We also will offer aircraft sight–seeing packages. These packages would include a tour over the area and local glaciers via airplane or helicopter. Other packages will include guided and charter fishing tours, heli–hiking in backcountry glaciers and guided mountain biking.

Objectives

The Company is currently mapping roads and the lodge site; construction and development is to commence by June 2001. By winter 2001/2002 the Lodge will be ready to take on skiers from magazines and film for early publicity. The lodge will be able to take on paying guests in December 2001. Expansion, to be considered in June 2002, will be in the form of adding cats and accommodations at the existing location.

There are two possible exit scenarios:

- DPO (Direct Public Offering)
- Buy Out

The following is the proposed development schedule, to be implemented after financing is secured:

- Design—completed
- Approval/Permit—completed
- Road Mapping—currently underway
- Construction*—180 days - Summer 2001
- Start-up/Trail Cutting—150 days - Summer 2001

*The construction phase will include cutting cat trails along with the building of the Resort.

Competition

Direct competition within the area consists of nine resorts. The snowcat operations vary from ones without lodging to all–inclusive resorts. Our true competition is actually the all–inclusive resorts. These resorts offer lodging, guided snowcat skiing and meals. Currently there are only two heli–ski or cat–ski operations in the Largetoon region and 17 total operations in Victoria.

The following is a list of cat operations in Victora:

- <u>Cougar Paw Skiing, Inc.</u> in Warnerville: 29 maximum occupancy on 39 square miles.
- <u>Fife Lake Lodge</u> in Kit Creek: 5 maximum occupancy on 10 square miles.

- <u>Mike's Northern Skiing</u> at Benjamin Point, 24 maximum occupancy on 45 square miles.

- <u>Cutter Lake Hotel</u> in Boerne: 30 maximum occupancy on 5,000 square acres.

- <u>Carlisle Adventures</u> in Brunswick: 26 maximum occupancy on 55 square miles.

- <u>Wild Bill's Lodge</u> in Yelp: 22 maximum occupancy on 90 square miles.

- <u>Noemi Lake Skiing</u> in Overland: Day operation only, no lodge or food.

All of the resorts run at 90+ percent occupancy throughout the winter season. In 1996, heli and snowcat operations drew over 59,000 visitors spending over 60 million dollars.

Indirect competition includes heli–ski outfits. The helicopter operations are more expensive, up to $1,000/day, and at the mercy of the weather. If conditions are bad, the helicopter can't fly, the skier can't ski!

Our resort will differ in the service. Investigation into our targeted guests has shown that quality service and attention to details far outweighs cost concerns. Some areas of quality service include the food, staff, amenities, and our kids program.

Development Team

The development team that we have assembled insures quality and style. The contractor and designer is Kurt Richie of Richie Design in Jotsey. He has completed over 110 projects in the Jotsey area. He deals in all aspects of construction management, contracting, computer and architectural design. The materials and assembly will be provided by Wilson Lubbock of Quality Post and Beam in Poteet, Victoria. This company has built quality homes and lodges, locally and internationally, since 1972.

Also providing an invaluable service to the company is Luevano Lumber. They have the lumber rights to the tenure area and are currently finishing road access in the area. They are providing us with their maps, projecting roads and cutting areas. They will work with us as to areas to thin out and areas to clear cut.

Also, we have the experience and know–how of Rachel Bastian. Her background includes print communications, local Jotsey and ski industry knowledge. To date, Rachel has helped open the doors of communication between Cobra Travel and the Victoria government and local community groups. Currently she is assistant editor of the *Satureen Weekly Express*, a local newspaper. She has also spent two years on the province's award–winning ski team, experience which has given her invaluable insights into the ski industry from behind the scenes.

Operating Performance

The Company believes Snowfall Mountain Lodge will be one of the most profitable backcountry ski resorts built in North America. Factors such as customer–service driven management, kid programs, gourmet dining, and the opportunity for off–season revenues will contribute to the success of the Lodge.

Brewpub

Hopstreet Brewery

32 Battery Way
Charlotte, NC 28202

Zachary David Robinson

The Hopstreet Brewery is seeking an outlay of $280,000 from investors. This amount will be used to get a loan so The Hopstreet Brewery can purchase everything the brewpub needs to get started. This amount will give The Hopstreet Brewery the 20 percent it needs to acquire a $1.4 million loan from the bank.

EXECUTIVE SUMMARY

The Hopstreet Brewery will be formed to bring patrons a warm and inviting dining experience like no other. The Hopstreet Brewery will feature an eclectic array of homebrewed beers and great food with something for everyone.

The Hopstreet Brewery will be a brewpub incorporated as a limited liability company. The business location will be in Noda in Charlotte and will be completed in spring 2006.

The head of The Hopstreet Brewery management team will be CEO and brewmaster Matt Hanson. Matt has received his brewing certification and has thorough experience of brewpubs. The rest of the management team will consist of a general manager and a kitchen manager/head chef. Aiding the management team are advisors who have restaurant and business experience.

Noda is a residential and commercial area that is being developed just a few miles away from downtown Charlotte. Nearly everything in Noda will be within walking distance. In fact, there will be over 900 residential units within a five–minute walking distance of the Hopstreet Brewery. Ultimately, Noda will be a thriving town of more than 4,000 residents and hundreds of businesses. Noda will be completed in nine phases, with a carefully planned mix of homes in addition to a large town center and four neighborhood centers. 500 homes will be completed in each phase with each phase taking 1–2 years to complete. The project is set to be completed in 2017.

The Hopstreet Brewery will serve a wide selection of homebrewed beers including ales, pilsners, and lagers. The Hopstreet Brewery will also feature a traditional American menu with appetizers, sandwiches, and main and side dishes. There will also be German specials present on the menu. These items are unique and could even be added to the full menu.

There is a lot of competition in food and drink industry. There are a few brewpubs, many bars, and many restaurants in the Charlotte area. However, The Hopstreet Brewery has competitive advantages that will help the brewpub meet or beat the competition.

Brewpubs and microbreweries are growing tremendously in popularity. After meeting all requirements in a site assessment survey, the location of The Hopstreet Brewery should provide a great marketing opportunity. Furthermore, there are many attractions close to The Hopstreet Brewery. From 2003 to 2004, the brewpub industry experienced a growth rate of 4.6 percent. The craft beer industry has become accustomed to growth; the industry has grown every year for the past 35 years. Average beer sales at brewpubs for 2004 were $341,480. Moreover, most brewpubs have a 40:60 alcohol to food sales ratio, meaning it is likely that average food sales was around $512,000.

The marketing strategy of The Hopstreet Brewery is a combination of billboard advertisements, mailings, newspaper ads, kiosks, and promotion at local events. The Hopstreet Brewery will use the services of The Scout Group to help with sales strategy. In addition, The Hopstreet Brewery will use advertisements, a frequent dining program, specials, a happy hour, group events, pub crawls, brewpub tours, and sponsorships to get customers in the door and keep them coming back. Pricing of Hopstreet Brewery products will be based on competition, cost, and demand.

The Hopstreet Brewery is seeking an outlay of $280,000 from investors. This amount will be used to get a loan so The Hopstreet Brewery can purchase everything the brewpub needs to get started.

MISSION

Vision: To bring a warm and inviting atmosphere to Noda and the surrounding Charlotte area.

Mission: The Hopstreet Brewery Brewery in Noda at Charlotte is dedicated to bringing patrons a warm and inviting dining experience like no other. With an eclectic array of homebrewed beers and great food, everyone will be able to find something they like.

Tagline: The Hopstreet Brewery, a place for good beer, good food, and good fun.

ORGANIZATION

Company Name
The Legal Name is: The Hopstreet Brewery, LLC.

Legal Form of Business
The Hopstreet Brewery is incorporated as an LLC located at the address: 32 Battery Way, Charlotte, NC 28202.

The location will move to Noda upon completion.

Management Summary
The Hopstreet Brewery management will primarily be the duty of CEO, Matt Hanson, with the aid of experienced business professionals Jason O'Connor, Richard Vanderburg, Jeff Wolpe. Also, part of the management team will be the Head Chef / Kitchen Manager and a Restaurant / Bar Manager who will be identified later.

Matthew Hanson, CEO and Brew Master BA in German, Duke University, Graduating 1994: Emphasis in Teaching.

The CEO, Matthew Hanson, is from Raleigh, North Carolina. Matt has a brewer's certification from the VLB Berlin three–year program and a teaching certificate from Duke University

Matt's brewing experience is evident from the several years that he spent in Germany. In fall of 1994, he began an apprenticeship for Bierbrauerei in Frankfurt, Germany. Most of his schooling was in Berlin, Germany, but halfway through the three year program, he moved to a smaller brewery that better reflected the kind of operation that he wanted to run. This brewery was in Hamburg, Germany, a part of the Munster Brauhaus.

While at the Brewery in Hamburg, Matt rotated through all aspects of the brewery including: Brewhaus, malting, machine maintenance, filtration, bottling and kegging, bar construction and maintenance, and the laboratory and laggering department. In a one year period, all areas of the brewery were visited twice.

Matt next attended school in Berlin at the Versuchsndashund Lehranstalt fur Brauerei (VLB). This included both theoretical and practical classes in brewing techniques and other related areas to brewing. Schooling was twice a year for a period of 6 to 8 weeks.

In 1996, Matt moved to a family owned pub–brewery in Hamburg, Munster Brauhaus. There, he attended the same kind of school as in Berlin. New responsibilities in Hamburg included all aspects of brewing with a few exceptions (i.e. did not have a laboratory or a maintenance crew). Also, responsibilities included gastronomical aspects such as cooking for the pub, giving small tours, bartending, filling and tapping kegs for guests, working at festivals serving the brewery's beer and working with open fermentation. The final practical examination took place in the Beck's Brewery in Bremen.

In 1997, Matt returned home to receive his teaching certificate. Currently, he is teaching at Charlotte Community College, as well as serving on the Charlotte City Council. On the council he serves on several boards, including: Arts and Culture, Streets, Grant Review Committee, Finance and Audit, Community Center Site Selection Committee, Public Safety, and Technology Committee.

Jason O'Connor Has been running his own businesses for the past 25 years. Currently owns a Subway sandwich restaurant and is on the Board of Directors for the City Planning Committee. Has experience in the restaurant industry.

Richard Vanderburg Has been working as an entrepreneur for most of this life. Has had many successful entrepreneurship relationships in business and politics, has completed marketing plans for businesses and established a number of highly profitable companies from the ground up. Has lots of start–up and business experience.

Jeff Wolpe Developer of Noda, Charlotte. President of Prestwick Homes, one of the largest builders in the state. Lots of business experience and will have major effects on area.

Donald Bilson Sales representative for Food Services LLC. Has 26 years experience in restaurant and food industry.

Matt Hanson, CEO/Brew Master

1. Responsible for maintaining the vision, mission, and philosophy of the company

2. Oversees the brewery as a whole, maintaining the integrity of the operations along with the marketing and sales through advisors

3. Handles all phases of the brewing cycle for the all beer produced on site

4. Responsible for the investor relations of the company

General Manager

1. Handle customers

2. Handle employees—both front of the house and back of the house

3. Prepare paperwork, i.e. count inventory and calculate food cost, complete product ordering, and prepare labor schedules for both FOH

Head Cook/Kitchen Manager

1. Head of the kitchen

2. Handle all aspects of food preparation

3. In charge of kitchen staff, organization, inventory, and orders

General Restaurant Staff

1. Bussers / Dishwashers (2–4)

2. Servers (3–5)

3. Hosts / Hostesses (2–3)

4. Bartenders (1–2)

5. Sous chef (1)

6. Line Cook (1–2)

7. Prep Cook (1–2)

Company Attorney

1. Responsible for establishing an LLC business form

2. Prepare and file necessary legal documentation

3. Responsible for contractual relations with investors and potential investors

4. Responsible for all legal proceedings

Accountant

1. Assist in directing the finances for the brewery

2. Manage all budgets, projections, and all statements necessary for tax filings

3. Assist in preparing financial reports to help make business decisions

BUSINESS OVERVIEW

Brewpub Description

A brewpub is a restaurant and microbrewery combination that makes its own beer and sells the majority of its beer on premise. A brewpub is also referred to as a home–brew house and a house brewery. The first American brewpub opened in 1982. As of July 2003, the Association of Brewers estimated over 1,000 brewpubs in the United States alone. There are brewpubs in many other parts of the world, although not commonly called "brewpubs." Brewpubs are especially popular in European countries, but are growing rapidly in popularity in the United States.

The Hopstreet Brewery will follow these characteristics by offering German craft beers and traditional American food with German specials (if these specials are popular enough, they will be added to the menu).

The Hopstreet Brewery will open in May 2006. For the first couple years, only the bottom floor will be available for business and the second floor will be "white boxed" until further phases of Noda are completed.

Location—Noda at Charlotte

The location of the Hopstreet Brewery is Noda at Charlotte. Noda is a residential and commercial area that is being developed just a few miles away from historic Charlotte. Noda's style is new urbanism and somewhat resembles traditional European architecture. Nearly everything in Noda will be within walking distance. In fact, there will be over 900 residential units within a five minute walking distance of the Hopstreet Brewery.

Ultimately, Noda will be a thriving town of more than 4,000 residents and hundreds of businesses. Noda will be completed in nine phases, with a carefully planned mix of homes in addition to a large town center and four neighborhood centers. 500 homes will be completed in each phase with each phase taking one–two years to complete. Of the 500 homes released for sale, 450 homes have already been sold and the second phase will be released for sale in June 2005. In addition, there are already 26 businesses open. The project is set to be completed in 2017. Developer Carl Knutser's vision is for Noda to be one of the most recognized neighborhoods in the country and this seems possible as sales are more than double original expectation.

Seating

Seating in the first year will include the main floor with approx. 2,280 sq. ft of customer space and a beer garden. The second floor will be "white–boxed" until The Hopstreet Brewery is able to receive adequate customers. The beer garden will consist of 12 tables, but will only be available weather permitting. The bulk (or maybe all) of the kitchen will be off the back of the building. There will be approximately 12 seats along the bar, 18 tables, and additional space. It is estimated that there will be at least 87 seats. There will also be a public swimming pool located beside The Hopstreet Brewery which could be an area where customers could be served. This will allow for more seating. Depending on the season, we are hoping there will be approximately 135 seats in warm months and 87 in cooler months for year one.

The plan is to open the "white–boxed" second floor in year two or three. This area will be approximately 1,500 square feet and should allow for seating of 50 additional customers.

Decorations

The exterior decoration will be painted stucco, 2.5 stories in height, and Central European in design. The interior decor will be warm–natural–stone, wood, and brick in design. There will be wall hangings and memorabilia decorating the walls. The brew system will be shown off in a bay window that runs two stories tall. There will be a lodge–feel upstairs, supported by fire places, a small band stage, and large windows.

Parking

There will be on–street parking in front of The Hopstreet Brewery, a free public parking lot in the back, and on–street parking throughout the community.

PRODUCTS

Alcohol

The Hopstreet Brewery will feature numerous types of beers brewed on–site by Matt Hanson. To suit the tastes of everyone, The Hopstreet Brewery will also serve a few Anheuser–Busch products. Many breweries only serve the beer that is produced on–site, but to maximize business sales and profits, serving other beers and an assortment of liquor is a must.

Craft beers will be brewed in a one–of–a–kind system. The system will be the Kupferversion mit zwei Kupferhauben purchased brand new from SBP Breweries. The Hopstreet Brewery will use a 2500 bbl.

system. This system comes straight from Slovakia and is made of copper giving it a beautiful and unique look. The cost of this system is 323,200 Euro ($417,006 US). The Hopstreet Brewery will make this system easily viewable to anyone in the restaurant, so they can enjoy its beauty and know where the beer they are drinking is coming from.

The Hopstreet Brewery will also make the presentation of beer a highlight. Unlike other drinking places, beers will be presented the way they were meant to be. Beers will not be served in the same simple glass; each beer will be presented in its own unique way according to tradition.

Main beers that will be brewed by The Hopstreet Brewery

- Pilsner (Pils)—Served in a tall, thinner–walled glass, this is the most "elegant" beer. It is bottom–fermented, has the most "bitter" taste (i.e. the most hops content) and is light in color. Ca. 5% alc./vol.

- Lager—Lager is a generic name for bottom–fermented beer. Pilsners are also lagers, but a lager is usually less bitter. The lager can be served in a number of glasses and the beer served by our brewery will be like the German, "Helles" beer: a light colored, somewhat malty beer. Ca.5% alc./vol.

- Dunkeles—A Dunkeles is the same as a lager, however, the color is darker and the beer is a little sweeter due to the residual sugars and caramelized malt. This beer will be served in a round beer glass that is, perhaps, known for being the "typical beer glass". Ca. 5% alc./vol.

- Hefeweizen (a.k.a. Weizen or Weiss)—Hefeweizen is a beer served in a tall, wide–mouthed glass so that the head of the beer can reach a nice three–fingers height. This beer may contain slightly more alcohol at ca. 5.5% alc./vol. and will be made with barley malt and wheat malt (50/50). This is an ale (top fermented beer) and has a stronger flavor. This beer will be served more in summer and offered with banana juice or a slice of lemon. *Instead of brewing separate flavored beers, most of the flavor will be added by syrup to the Hefeweizen after brewing: this allows a wider range of flavoring (and makes the hard–headed brewer feel better about not brewing "candy beer". . .)

- Koelsch—Koelsch is an ale yeast beer known in the Cologne Germany area and served in small, cylinder–style glasses. It is somewhat like a wheat beer. It is lightly colored and will contain a little less alcohol. Ca. 4.5% alc/vol.

- Alt Beer—Beer served in small glasses or special alt glasses that have a curvilinear line to them; darker in color; about 5%, ale yeast.

- Bitter Ales—Such as: Pale Ale (served in "water–style glass"). Ca. 5% alc/vol, light colored.

- Dark Ales/Stouts—These beers are a lot like the brand Guinness, which is an Irish beer. Ca 5% alc./vol. This beer is very dark and black in color and served in a English Pint Glass.

- Berliner Weiss—This beer is close to the Lambic style beers of Belgium. It is an ale yeast, lightly colored and soured with lactic acid. By itself (some like it this way) it may not be a very good tasting beer. This beer is served in a low, very–wide mouthed glass ("Pott" in German) and comes with a "Schuss" or shot of Waldmeister/Woodruff syrup or Himbeer/Raspberry syrup. The beer then takes on a green or red color, respectively.

Additional beers to be served are seasonal, specialty beers:

- Schwarz Beer—"Black" beer, lager yeast (bottom fermented), Ca.5% alc./vol. Served in a large "tulip" styled glass. This beer is a little sweeter than most.

- Doppelbock—A German strong beer that can be light, but is usually dark, and has at least 6% (usually Ca. 6.5% alc./vol). Served in a thick–rimmed glass or stoneware mug.

- Keller Beer—A lager that is unfiltered and cloudy—otherwise is very much like a lager in all ways.

- Hefedoppelbock—A rare wheat beer, ale, but the alcohol content is much higher at around Ca.6.5% alc./vol. Can be dark or light and served from Weizen glass.

- Stein Beer—This is a malty beer that is made by throwing a hot stone into the mash; this helps caramelize it and it becomes sweeter. This beer is considered a lager.

- Vollmond Beer—Really, just a gimmick, this beer is brewed under the full moon to give it mystic powers and make you drunk. It is a lager or really any kind of beer you brew in the middle of the night. We think this would be good for October.

The Hopstreet Brewery will also carry an assortment of hard liquors and wines. The selection of the liquors will be much the same as a standard bar or restaurant.

Food

The Hopstreet Brewery will also be a restaurant serving the general public at lunch, dinner, and after hours. There will be a full menu serving traditional American foods as well as German specialties and other seasonal dishes throughout the year.

Along with sales from the restaurant, we will also sustain revenue with growlers (glass jugs of beer filled on-site), bottled beer, keg beer, and promotional items, such as glasses, hats, key chains, bar towels, golf balls, clothing, and other trinkets.

Concept Menu

As stated, The Hopstreet Brewery will carry traditional American food with German specials. Most of the regular menu items will be similar to other brewpubs, restaurants, and bars. The menu may have a few additions or subtractions in the near future. Also included is non-alcoholic beverages offered.

Menu Items

Appetizers:

- *Nacho Platter*—Nachos topped with ground beef, shredded lettuce, tomatoes, cheese, black olives, chopped green onions, jalapenos and sour cream

- *Buffalo Wings*—One pound of spicy hot wings served with celery and ranch or blue cheese dressing

- *Homemade Giant Onion Rings*—battered in our special beer batter and deep fried to golden perfection

- *Bite-Sized Soft Pretzels*—served with sweet, hot, and horseradish mustard. A way to enjoy the little Kraut in all of us

- *Toasted Ravioli*—This favorite is served with marinara sauce and fresh parmesan cheese

- *Homemade Potato Chips*—Thinly sliced fresh—a basket full

- *Small salad*—Fresh field greens served with fresh Farmers' Bread

- *Chilli*—Our own special recipe served with chic peas, black olives, and topped with shredded cheese

Sandwiches: Served with Fries, Homemade Chips, or Hot German Potato Salad

- *Hamburger*—Thick 1/2 pound hamburger topped with lettuce, tomato, onion, pickles, & lettuce

- *BBQ Hamburger*

- *Swiss and Kraut Burger*—Our hamburger topped with Swiss cheese and finest sauerkraut

- *Steak Sandwich*—Marinated steaks served with grilled onions and grilled to perfection

- *Pulled Pork Sandwich*—Slow-cooked pork roast pulled and covered in bbq sauce

- *Hand–Cut Cod*—battered in our own special beer batter and served on your choice of wheat or white bread
- *Reuben*—Corned beef served on rye bread with Swiss cheese, sauerkraut and Thousand Island dressing

Main Dishes:

- *Chicken Salad with Peanut Sauce Dressing*—Iceberg lettuce covered in our own special peanut dressing and chicken strips
- *Brick Oven Pizzas*—Pizzas served with your favorite toppings including: pepperoni, sausage, chicken, mushrooms, onions, black olives and peppers
- *Schimmelpizza*—Pizza topped with garlic, onions, artichoke hearts and mozzarella cheese
- *Reuben Pizza*—If you like reubens, then you'll love this Italian twist. Thousand Island dressing is the base on this pizza complete with caraway-seed encrusted dough; topped off with corned beef, sauerkraut, and Swiss cheese
- *Sausage Rigatoni*—Lean, fresh sausage in a red or white sauce and topped with fresh parmesan. Served spicy upon request
- *Pork Steak*—Slow grilled served with your choice of two sides. BBQ or dry
- *Pork Cordon Bleu*—Fresh pork chop filled with ham and Swiss cheese, breaded and fried
- *Grilled Chicken Breast*—Served with your favorite two sides and small salad
- *Smoked BBQ Ribs*—Served with your favorite two side dishes
- *Ribeye Steak*—Served with baked potato, broccoli and dinner salad

Sides:

German Cole Slaw; German Potato Salad; Baked Potato; Salad; Chips; Green Beans; Mashed Potatoes; Noodles; Broccoli; Onion Rings; Sauerkraut

Just For Kids:

Chicken Strips; Grilled Cheese; Hamburger; Pizza; PB&J Sandwich

Beverages:

Sodas; Iced Tea; Locally Roasted Coffee; Milk; Apple Spritzers

German Specials (appearing at different intervals)

Appetizers:

- *Landjaeger* with farmer bread and mustard served on wooden board (this is a German Summer Sausage)
- *Cheese and Sausage Platter*
- *German Farmer Bread* served with "hausgemachter braunschweiger" and chives
- *Schupfnudeln Mit Sauerkraut*
- *Pflammkuchen*
- *Radish and Salt*
- *Deutscher Salat*—German Salad

Soups:

Allgauer Cheese Soup; White Asparagus Cream Soup; Dumpling Soup; Chili Con Carne; German Potato Salad Soup

Main Dishes:

- *Bangers and Mash*—Six Nuernberg sausages served on a bed of kraut

- *Schnitzel*—Pork cutlet

- *Rhineland Pork*—Smoked pork chops served on a bed of our special kraut

- *Rinderrouladen Maultaschen*—German–style ravioli stuffed with hamburger and spinach

- *Weisswurst*—served with large soft pretzel and sweet mustard

- *Turkey Leg Dinner*

- *Trout and Boiled Potatoes*—served with German cream sauce

- *Flammkuchen*—pizza base but instead of a tomato sauce, the crust is covered with creme fraiche, bacon, onions, garlic, and cheese

- *White Asparagus*—served wrapped in Black Forest Ham

- *Bratwurst Dinner*

- *Wurstsalat mit Kaese (Schweizer Art)*

Sides:

Spaetzle; German Farmer Bread; German Potato Salad (warm or cold); Schupfnudeln and Kraut; German Salads; Fried Eggs; German Broth

The general menu will remain relatively unchanged throughout the course of business. However, as demand for special dishes are assessed, they might become available on the regular menu. The Hopstreet Brewery is also working on a system where leftover food items can be used in certain dishes the following day. These items might be used to make a soup, side dish, or other dishes. It is estimated that The Hopstreet Brewery will have $20,000 worth of inventory at any one time (includes food, spices, etc.).

The Hopstreet Brewery will audition for a chef who has experience cooking German food. If a German chef is unattainable, The Hopstreet Brewery will find an American chef who is willing to learn.

COMPETITION

Competition can be broken up into three categories: brewpubs, bars, and restaurants. The Hopstreet Brewery will essentially be competing in all three categories which are somewhat related.

Brewpubs

All brewpubs in the Charlotte area are going to present some competition. There are no other planned brewpubs for Noda, so the listed brewpubs are the competition.

Competition: Brewpubs

Name	Distance	Location	Cost	Selection	Presentation	Atmosphere	Food	Beer
Tarheel Tavern	4.60	Very good	Above average	Good	None	Good	Very good	Good, but unoriginal
Charlotte Brewpub	18.72	Very good	Average	Diverse	None	Good	Good	Good
AleHouse	22.41	Good	Above average	Unique	None	Above average	Good	Mediocre at best

The Hopstreet Brewery has some tough competition in this area, especially Tarheel Tavern. All of the brewpubs analyzed have a strong location and convenience. Tarheel Tavern is located in historic Saint Charles; Charlotte Brewpub is located in downtown Charlotte surrounded by huge businesses; and AleHouse sits on the water, attracting passing consumers. The Hopstreet Brewery will have a location that is better than these competitors though. The Hopstreet Brewery will be located in Noda, an area of soon to be some 4,000 residents. As The Hopstreet Brewery is being erected, the amphitheater, public swimming pool and stores will be nearing completion. The Hopstreet Brewery also shares the area of Charlotte with Tarheel Tavern. Charlotte is growing rapidly and contains many attractions such as Wild William's WaterPark and the IMAX theater.

Cost of products will be similar to these brewpubs, above average. The average meal price at these brewpubs is $8 to $10. The selection of foods at The Hopstreet Brewery will be different than competitors' American menu food and German specials will be served. In addition, The Hopstreet Brewery will also feature homebrewed beers different from others. To set itself apart in this category, The Hopstreet Brewery will offer beer with a longer ripening period (a minimum of 21 days versus 14) and a happy hour sampling special. The sampling special will feature a "shot" of every beer to give the customer a taste of everything. The brewing experience of Matt Hanson should also help set Hopstreet Brewery beer apart. Matt spent many years in Germany to receive his brewing certification and worked at numerous German breweries, giving him the knowledge and background to create great beer and run the brewpub.

Notice that no brewpub competitors have unique presentation for their products. This will be a selling point for The Hopstreet Brewery. All beers are meant to be delivered in a certain way. Serving beers in proper drinkware will stick out in the customer's mind. For example, the tall, widemouthed hefeweizen glass and the mini hammer tapped keg will be identifying factors for customers.

The Hopstreet Brewery will use these features to share the Charlotte market with Tarheel Tavern, and capture the Noda market. These features will be attraction points for The Hopstreet Brewery to take customers away from Tarheel Tavern and bring them to the Hopstreet Brewery.

Bars

Of the 26 businesses to open in Noda in phase one, there are no true bars besides The Hopstreet Brewery. This is good news because The Hopstreet Brewery could be one of the few drinking places close and the only within walking distance of many. There are numerous bars/pubs in the Charlotte area, however. Only some of these present competition because most people are not willing to drive long distances to get to a specific bar. There are over 50 bars within a ten mile radius of the Hopstreet Brewery. All of these undoubtedly demonstrate at least some competition. The ten closest bars to The Hopstreet Brewery represent more competition than others. These bars include:

Competition: Bars

Name	Distance	Location	Cost	Selection	Presentation	Atmosphere	Food	Other
Watering Hole	1.73	Okay	Average	Okay	None	Run-down	Average	Locals
Wilson's	2.50	Good	Average	Average	None	Good	Good	Chain rest.
Telly's	3.38	Horrible	Above average	Okay	None	Unfriendly	Average	Inside RV-park
Rottermond	3.97	Poor	Below average	Poor	None	Run-down	Poor	Locals
Hingy's	3.98	Okay	Cheap	Poor	None	Unclean	Poor	$0.25 food
O'Callahan	4.00	Poor	Average	Unique	None	Okay	Average	Irish
Maria's	4.10	Good	Above average	Good	None	Good	Very good	Italian
Brown Brewpub	4.10	Good	Average	Okay	None	Good	Above average	Local favorite
Green Lightpost	4.31	Okay	Average	Okay	None	Okay	Above average	
FlimFlam	4.34	Good	Above average	Good	None	Good	Good	Chain

The only bars that stand out from the crowd in this table are Maria's and FlimFlam. Maria's is, in fact, more of a restaurant than a bar and FlimFlam is part of a restaurant chain. After these two, all of the other bars seem to be average at best. The Hopstreet Brewery will by no means, be an average bar. The food and selection at most of these bars is lackluster and offers nothing unique. This will be an area for The Hopstreet Brewery to capitalize on.

A "beer" heading was not added to this group because none of these bars serve their own beer. They all serve generic products like Bud Light and an occasional microbrewed beer like Charlotte Brew. Therefore, fresh homebrewed beer is another area favoring The Hopstreet Brewery.

In addition, the atmosphere at a lot of these bars was nothing worth noting. Most of them were smoky, unclean, and just not really a fun place to be. However, some of these bars continue to be local hangouts, something that will take time for The Hopstreet Brewery to accomplish. Also, some of these bars have very low prices that will be unmatchable for The Hopstreet Brewery, but the food is not as quality. Furthermore, none of these bars have any unique presentation, giving another advantage to The Hopstreet Brewery.

Restaurants

There are three restaurants that will be completed by the time of the opening of The Hopstreet Brewery. These restaurants are: Tony's BBQ & Grill, Fast Chinese, and Pizza–To–Go. Fast Chinese and Pizza–To–Go sound generic, but Tony's BBQ & Grill could pose as competition. Besides these, there are many restaurants close to The Hopstreet Brewery. Many of these restaurants, though, are considered fast food, and therefore are in a different category than that of The Hopstreet Brewery. More upscale, sit–down restaurants present more competition. Nearly 75 percent of the 50 closest restaurants to The Hopstreet Brewery are fast–food joints. The ten closest, besides those that have already been stated, are listed below.

Competition: Restaurants

Name	Distance	Location	Cost	Selection	Presentation	Atmosphere	Food	Other
Beth's	2.25	Okay	Average	Okay	None	Okay	Average	Locals
Mong Kow	2.34	Poor	Cheap	Okay	None	Poor	Poor	Chinese
Won Ton	2.42	Okay	Cheap	Poor	None	Poor	Poor	Chinese
Main Street Grill	3.34	Okay	Cheap	Poor	None	Poor	Below average	
Pepperoni's	3.40	Good	Average	Okay	None	Okay	Average	Pizza
Washington's Tavern	3.72	Good	Above average	Very good	None	Good	Very good	Very unique
Charbroiled Treats	3.90	Okay	Average	Good	None	Okay	Good	Pizza and burgers
Dim Sum	3.91	Okay	Below average	Poor	None	Poor	Poor	Chinese chain
Le Kabob	3.97	Okay	Average	Okay	None	Run-down	Below average	Locals
El Maguey	4.08	Poor	Below average	Okay	None	Okay	Average	Mexican chain

Similarly to bars in the area, a lot of restaurants located close to The Hopstreet Brewery are just okay or poor. The Hopstreet Brewery should not have much trouble beating out these weak competitors, but will have trouble with some of the better restaurants. The goal of The Hopstreet Brewery will be to achieve equality with these restaurants, because they are local favorites and have been in the area for a long time.

The Hopstreet Brewery will beat out all of the restaurant competition in alcohol category. The Hopstreet Brewery will serve a large selection of homebrewed beers that will be unmatchable by these restaurants. Once again, The Hopstreet Brewery must make use of its delivery and presentation as an advantage to this group. Also, these bars and restaurants will lack the brewpub experience that is evident at The Hopstreet Brewery.

MARKET ANALYSIS

After much research and analysis, The Hopstreet Brewery should have only minor problems in competing in the brewpub, bar/pub, and restaurant industry. There are only three brewpubs in the Charlotte area and the production of craft beers has grown seven percent over the past year. Furthermore, the niche market expanded three percent last year.

The brewpub is not the smoky, dirty bar where you cannot take your family, and it is not the expensive restaurant where you wouldn't take your friends. Brewpubs offer a family oriented atmosphere suitable for family and friends. They offer good food and quality unique beer. This is why brewpubs and small breweries are growing tremendously in popularity (seven percent production growth from 2003 to 2004) with over 1,400 nationwide.

Noda is projected to have annual economic impact of $315 million. This will be cash flow on which businesses in Noda can capitalize on. Other than The Hopstreet Brewery, only three are restaurants and only one of these restaurants is similar to The Hopstreet Brewery (sit–down family restaurant). This means that once phase one is complete (Spring 2006), The Hopstreet Brewery will be one of the main options for the 450 resident homes of Noda.

A site assessment survey was done by the American's Brewers Guild which surveyed successful brewpub operations and identified some important site characteristics that were believed to have contributed to the businesses' success. This assessment follows.

Site assessment

Specification	Recommendation	The Hopstreet Brewery
15-mile radius population	150,000	822,865
Average per capita income	$30,000	$67,904
Percentage of population in target age group	50%	70%
Per capita consumption	Upper 1/3 of nation	Upper 1/10 of nation
Number of successful restaurants in area	5 or more	More than 5
Number of successful bars in area	3 or more	More than 3
Number of taprooms in area	1 to 3	2
Number of brewpubs in area	0 to 3	1
Foot traffic	Moderate to heavy	Heavy
Commerce	A must	Yes
Parking	Ample for pm business	Ample
Proximity to:		
Downtown	Important	Yes
Office	Important during lunch	Yes
Sporting facility	Asset	Yes
College	Post-grads an asset	Yes
Tourist attractions	Asset	Many
Expansion potential	Desirable	Yes
Aesthetics	Moderately important	Strong
Utility requirements	Must meet minimums	Yes
Access	Must be uncomplicated	Uncomplicated
Neighborhood support	Important	Yes

As you notice, The Hopstreet Brewery meets every requirement, and many with ease. Many of these requirements are explained or analyzed throughout the plan. There are some, though, that will be explained here. For instance, University of North Carolina at Charlotte is located close, satisfying the college requirement. There are many sporting facilities including Charlotte Family Club and the Noda YMCA. Furthermore, The Hopstreet Brewery is located in downtown Noda and has an abundance of offices just a few miles away on Battery Way that employs thousands of workers. As Noda grows, The Hopstreet Brewery will beat these requirements with even more ease. The fact that The Hopstreet Brewery more than meets these requirements is in an indication that there is a market for a second brewpub in the area.

Attractions At–Hand

Attractions and amenities close to The Hopstreet Brewery will increase the number of consumers in the area and, therefore, increase the market. The amenities located within a short distance of The Hopstreet Brewery include:

- Wild William's WaterPark

- IMAX Theater

- North Carolina University at Charlotte

- Highway I-85

- Brookfield Mall

- Highway I-77

- Charlotte Airfield

All of these locations are recognizable consumer hot spots. Highways I-85 and I-77are traveled by thousands of people every day. On interstate 85 at Battery Way, 28,506 cars traveling east and 30,849 traveling west pass by per 24 hours on average. Also, according to the Charlotte Department of Transportation, close to 20,000 vehicles travel on Battery Way each day. After the completion of Noda, this number is sure to rise.

The IMAX Theater attracts 54 million people annually. Wild William's WaterPark in Raleigh is the single largest attraction in the state and attracts four million people alone; it has even been called the most visited waterpark in the United States. Judging by the success of the Raleigh–based location, the Charlotte store should continue to gain popularity. As you will learn later, The Hopstreet Brewery already has plans to market there.

Charlotte already has a strong tourism industry; 1,600,000 already visit this historic city annually. These amenities, though, are an extra source of tourism. Take for instance, Ameristar Casino, which attracts over ten million visitors on an annual basis. Moreover, most people who fly into North Carolina travel through Raleigh–Durham International Airport, which is also close to The Hopstreet Brewery and where marketing will take place (see Marketing Strategy).

Brewpub Industry Analysis

The Hopstreet Brewery falls within the brewpub industry. There is no specific "industry" for this category yet, as it is relatively new. Therefore, there is no specific SIC code. For now, it is appropriate to place the brewpub under the drinking place code 5813 and the restaurant code 5812.

The craft beer segment includes brewpubs, microbreweries, and specialty brewers. Craft beer (micro-brewed beer) is the fastest growing segment of the beverage alcohol industry in the United States. There was a seven percent growth rate for craft beer volume in 2004, nearly double the growth rate posted in 2003 of 3.4 percent. More specifically, there was a 4.6 percent growth rate for brewpubs. "Craft beer volume growth outpaced that of imports, large brewers, wine and spirits in 2004," said Paul Gatza, Director of the Brewers Association. "The craft beer segment continues to show healthy and steady growth with many individual brewers enjoying double–digit volume increases," said Charlie Papazian, President of the Brewers Association. For 35 years, the craft beer industry has shown growth each year. "Americans increasingly prefer the flavor and diversity of fresh, locally–made beers," says Papazian. "Many Americans first discovered full–flavored beers at local breweries and now the diverse and exciting choices among those flavorful brews have become a regular part of their lifestyle."

The continuance of the rising growth rate of the craft brew industry means good things for The Hopstreet Brewery. Growth is expected for the 2005 and 2006 years, and The Hopstreet Brewery will benefit from that growth.

Brewpubs have helped revive the beer and drinking places industry. There were a total of 986 brewpubs operating in the United States in 2004. This number includes the 51 brewpubs that opened their doors for the first time in 2004. Listed in the table below are annual beer sales for the brewpub industry.

Annual brewpub sales: Beer

Year	Total industry beer sales	Average brewpub beer sales
2004	$336,700,000	$341,480
2003	$322,000,000	$326,572
2002	$312,800,000	$317,241

Food sales for the brewpub industry were a little harder to come by. Although brewpubs are known more for their beers, food actually accounts for more sales than beer. Brewpubs in the Charlotte area reported a 40:60 ratio of alcohol to food sales. No specific industry food sales were attainable, so the following data was calculated using the previously stated ratio.

Annual brewpub sales: Food

Year	Estimated industry food sales	Estimated average brewpub food sales
2004	$505,050,000	$512,220
2003	$483,000,000	$489,858
2002	$469,200,000	$475,862

End Consumer

The end consumer of The Hopstreet Brewery can be broken down into three groups: locals, brew nuts, and visitors. Locals will be accounting for most of the business, but brew nuts and visitors will make up a respectable proportion. We expect locals to account for at least 80 percent of business, visitors 15 percent and brew nuts 5 percent.

Locals include people living in the Charlotte area, but more specifically citizens of the Noda development. Brew nuts are people who are basically obsessed with microbrewed beer. They will travel long distances just to try out a new beer. After visiting The Hopstreet Brewery, these nuts will forever remember not only our delectable beers, but the presentation of these products the way they were meant to be. Visitors are people visiting the Charlotte area. As you have already learned, there are various attractions close to The Hopstreet Brewery, so there will always be people going in and out of the area.

The majority of Hopstreet Brewery customers will be over the age of 21. However, these adults will bring their family and friends with them who may or may not be 21 and many others will visit who are not 21. In addition, even though people from every income level drink beer, our target group is those with income of more than $30,000. In the end, it should be noted that people may not come to enjoy Hopstreet Brewery beers, they may simply come because they enjoy the food, atmosphere, and company.

As described, our end consumer is made up of three different groups. To determine the amount of locals we may encounter, radial studies must be completed. Within a 1–mile radius of The Hopstreet

Brewery there are 9,732 adults over the age of 21; 64,977 within a 5–mile radius; 253,434 within a 10–mile radius; and 574,995 within a 15–mile radius. Moreover, more than two thirds of these people have an average income of over $30,000.

The demographic of the brew nut is hard to nail down. These are just people who love trying beer. This group is made up of people over 21, but mostly males. Some brew nuts are willing to travel further than others, so the general market is as large as the entire country.

The demographic of the visitor group is just that, a visitor. More than two thirds of adults in the United States aged 21 and older traveled in 2004. That makes visitors a very large group (greater than 125 million). Charlotte alone had over 1.5 million visitors last year, and that was before the construction of Noda.

MARKETING & SALES

Marketing Strategy

The marketing strategy of The Hopstreet Brewery is to uphold to the strictest standards of quality and family fun while serving up excellent food, beer, and atmosphere. This will provide the company with a strong reputation and encourage customers to tell others about their experience. The Hopstreet Brewery must prove itself among the many brewpubs, bars, and restaurants in the Charlotte area. When restaurants and drinking places open, people want to try them out immediately and first impressions can make or break companies in this industry. Therefore, The Hopstreet Brewery will make sure every experience is a positive one. The Hopstreet Brewery will focus on serving the finest beers and delivering them in a fashion unlike any other location. Also, the selection of foods will make sure there is something for everyone and leave the customer craving for more.

The Hopstreet Brewery will use traditional and nontraditional marketing efforts to promote the brewpub. Traditional marketing efforts will include billboard advertisements, direct mailings, and newspaper spots. Nontraditional marketing consists of indirect marketing. The combination of these marketing efforts will be used to create a "buzz" that will generate word–of–mouth marketing in the general public.

In the fall of 2005, billboard advertisements will be done promoting all of Noda. Many of these signs will contain advertisement for The Hopstreet Brewery. These signs will be located on highways 85 and 77, and other major roadways in the Charlotte area. The Hopstreet Brewery will also make use of billboard advertising independently around the same areas. The amount or placement of these billboards will not be assessed until Noda advertising has begun. The Hopstreet Brewery would like to have an advertisement on 370 east and west, 70 east and west, and two on Battery Way/Airport Road in each direction. The plan is to have these advertisements present three months before opening and have them remain until they are inefficient. In addition, Hopstreet Brewery owner, Matt Hanson, has already been in contact about having the brewpub added to the list of restaurants on highways 85 and 77.

There are currently over 5,000 people on the Noda mailing list which keeps interested consumers up to date with what is going on in Noda. It has already been mentioned in this mailer that a brewpub will be open in Noda phase one. Now that more information is available about The Hopstreet Brewery, advertisements and articles will begin appearing in this mailer by summer 2005. This mailer is designed and maintained by Noda development and will cost The Hopstreet Brewery nothing. The Hopstreet Brewery will push to have as many references as possible in this mailer. The Hopstreet Brewery will also begin placing advertisements in the Charlotte newspaper about the brewpub's 2006 opening. An ad or two will be placed in the Sunday newspaper starting a month before opening. These ads will contain a coupon so The Hopstreet Brewery can gauge their effectiveness and determine how long they should use newspaper advertising. Furthermore, the business section of the Charlotte newspaper often features articles about the opening of new businesses, and The Hopstreet Brewery is likely to be featured shortly before opening. There will soon be a daily Noda newspaper and The Hopstreet Brewery will do likewise with this newspaper.

Many different kiosks have been seen at Wild William' WaterPark in Charlotte, marketing and offering samples of products during events. The Hopstreet Brewery is in the process of setting up a kiosk at spring 2006 events. Hopefully, alcohol will be permitted at this event. If not, The Hopstreet Brewery will focus on handing out coupons, fliers, and merchandise. Wild William' WaterPark is a huge attraction and will offer The Hopstreet Brewery a lot of public visibility. Another strong place to advertise is Raleigh–Durham International Airport. The Hopstreet Brewery plans to have advertisements visible to customers as they pick up their luggage and walk out the door.

The Hopstreet Brewery will also participate in local events such as Oktoberfest and parades both before and after opening. At these events, merchandise, coupons, and fliers will be handed out. Moreover, The Hopstreet Brewery will hand out these things as much as possible at as many places as it can to give the brewpub as much promotion as possible.

Sales Strategy

The sales strategy of The Hopstreet Brewery is direct sales to customers from the brewpub. The main selling point will be beer, but food will be the second attraction. Focus, therefore, will be sale of these two groups at the brewpub. All advertising within the brewpub will be endorsement of Hopstreet Brewery products, events, promotions, and specials. There will be no advertising for products like Anheuser–Busch.

Part of The Hopstreet Brewery's sales strategy will be completed by MarketGroup Inc. MarketGroup Inc. specializes in converting first time customers into regular visitors. MarketGroup Inc. will send personalized letters, birthday coupons, emails, web promotions, etc to Hopstreet Brewery customers. The effectiveness of this will be measured by the amount of customers using these coupons or customers noting they received a letter. The cost of this service is $350 a month. The Hopstreet Brewery will begin use of this service a few months after opening, and if it proves not to be cost effective, the brewpub will no longer use the service. MarketGroup Inc. has helped develop customer bases for many prominent Charlotte restaurants like Nook in the Square, Cathy's Cafe, and Dimanto's Italian Eatery.

The Hopstreet Brewery will complete a number of sales strategies on its own too. The brewpub will feature advertisement coupons in newspapers and mailings on a weekly basis. The Hopstreet Brewery will also offer frequent dining programs where after a customers has seven main dish items, he or she will be able to receive a free dish of choice.

The Hopstreet Brewery will have specials within the brewpub. There will be many daily specials that will include German dishes, but many will simply be discounts on regular menu items. The Hopstreet Brewery will also have happy hour specials with half price appetizers and beer from three to six o' clock every weekday. Likewise, a happy hour sampling special will be offered which will incorporate shot size samples of every craft beer.

The Hopstreet Brewery will offer to serve as a meeting place for local groups. The Hopstreet Brewery will contact church groups, senior clubs, tourist groups, and dating services about having events at the brewpub. The groups will receive discounts on all food and beverage items during the meeting, coupons for future use, and a tour of the brewpub.

The Hopstreet Brewery will also encourage pub crawls where people are driven around to different bars/ breweries. These are usually set up by a group of people looking to try out different drinking places. The

Hopstreet Brewery will periodically mention pub crawls in its advertisements and promote it at the brewpub. Moreover, there will be frequent tours of the brewing process where consumers will get a sample of freshly brewed beer at the end. In addition to these strategies, The Hopstreet Brewery will also be available for rental and catering upon request.

The last marketing/sales strategy that The Hopstreet Brewery will take on will be sponsorships. The Hopstreet Brewery will sponsor events at the local amphitheater such as concerts and pageants. The brewpub will try to be active in every event that takes place at the amphitheater because it is located only a few steps from The Hopstreet Brewery. The Hopstreet Brewery will also sponsor local sporting events and teams. This will include charity sporting events, softball leagues, and tournaments. The Hopstreet Brewery will use this form of advertising because it is relatively cheap and can serve as a strong form of advertisement.

Pricing

The pricing of products at The Hopstreet Brewery will be based on three measurements: competition, cost, and demand. All three of these measures will be important for The Hopstreet Brewery to realize its greatest profits.

Pricing of Hopstreet Brewery beer and food will be very similar to competition. If our prices are too high, consumers will choose to take their business elsewhere. If prices are too low, The Hopstreet Brewery's profit margin will not be utilized to the fullest. Much of our pricing will be based on the pricing of items at Tarheel Tavern because they will be a main competitor of The Hopstreet Brewery, and because it too is a brewpub.

Also considered when pricing, will be the cost of the goods sold by The Hopstreet Brewery. All products require different goods, quantities, and effort to be made. Obviously, products with higher priced goods, quantities, and effort are going to command a higher price.

The final factor considered in pricing will be demand. A lot of this demand will be based on consumer input. The Hopstreet Brewery will monitor sales to see which goods are selling better than others. As stated earlier, if some goods are not selling up to standards, they might be removed from the menu. Likewise, The Hopstreet Brewery would like to measure the price sensitivity of its customers. This will be done by making occasional price markups and markdowns on selected menu items. This will survey how much consumers are willing to pay for certain items.

From our research, most sales in the brewpub industry come from food items. However, the greatest profit margin is incurred from alcohol sales, mainly house brewed items. Pricing will change from time to time due to certain conditions, but will remain the same for the most part. Pricing will be reviewed on a monthly basis at a minimum.

Alcohol prices will vary depending upon competitor pricing, size, and cost of goods. The Hopstreet Brewery will price its beers similarly to competitors. Furthermore, larger beers will be more expensive, but will be a better deal per ounce than smaller beverages. The price of ingredients also plays a major role in the price of beer. Labor will not be included in cost of goods, because it will be performed by owner and brewmaster Matt Hanson.

RISK FACTORS

Obviously, there are many risks entering into the drinking place and restaurant industry. Many startups immediately fail and many are still losing money. Possible risks The Hopstreet Brewery faces have been considered and are being planned for. There are also many opportunities that The Hopstreet Brewery can capitalize on.

Risks

1. Lack of business. If The Hopstreet Brewery is not receiving sufficient business, major problems would arise. The outlook, however, looks very strong and there is a healthy market for brewpubs at the moment.

2. Missing inventory. The average alcohol shrinkage of a bar is 20 percent due to too many bartender freebies, mispourings, and incorrect orders. This can cost any business a lot of revenue. If it is noticed that an unreasonable amount of inventory is missing, The Hopstreet Brewery will likely hire PubCo to manage their liquor inventory. PubCo specializes in reducing shrinkage and saving owners plenty of money.

3. Competitors in Noda. After the development of each phase of Noda, there will be more competitors in the area. In phase one, there will only be three other restaurants in Noda, and two are more fast–food type. This leaves Marbella as the only direct competition. As new restaurants open in Noda, The Hopstreet Brewery will already be firmly established and ready to take on new competition.

4. Possible problems with brewing systems. Problems have arisen in other microbreweries with system problems preventing the production of beer. We plan on purchasing new, top–of–the–line equipment to reduce this risk.

5. Overhead costs exceeding sales would pose a problem if it occurred consistently. If the cost to maintain the equipment, building and other overhead costs exceed sales, The Hopstreet Brewery would be in serious disarray. The Hopstreet Brewery will fight this by reviewing finances on a monthly basis at a minimum and hiring an accountant.

6. Management and staff problems. Employees will initially be given a chance to settle disputes and correct mistakes depending on severity. However, some mistakes, such as stealing and harassment will result in immediate firing.

7. Competitive reaction. Competitors in the Charlotte area might react adversely to The Hopstreet Brewery. They might try to undercut pricing or partake in interfering with possible Hopstreet Brewery consumers. The Hopstreet Brewery does not want to go to war with any of its competitors. Actions to prevent this might be forming strategic alliances or supporting competitors.

8. Poor reviews in press. This would pose a major problem for The Hopstreet Brewery because the brewpub is counting on positive reviews to promote business. If this does happen, The Hopstreet Brewery will make greater efforts to improve the brewpub and its products like hiring a new chef or offering more discounts to get consumers back in the door.

9. Liquor related problems. Drunk–driving and other liquor related problems are often troublesome for drinking places. To prevent this, servers will be trained to determine when someone has had too much too drink. The Hopstreet Brewery will also call cabs, family members, or drive people to make sure they get home safely. However, much of The Hopstreet Brewery's customer base will live in Noda, and most residents will be within a ten minute walk.

Opportunities

1. Expansion. If The Hopstreet Brewery is highly successful, another brewpub may be opened in another area.

2. Introduction of new products. It has already been explained that if a German special item is extremely popular, it would be added to the menu. Furthermore, The Hopstreet Brewery will be constantly evaluating sales of items to determine if there is enough demand to add an item to the menu. This could include beer, an American dish, or a German special.

3. Development of surrounding area. The area of Charlotte is growing extremely fast and Noda will eventually have a population of over 10,000. The Hopstreet Brewery is right in the middle of this fast growing area and could see a large increase in customers upon completion of each phase. In addition, The Hopstreet Brewery may be able to sell products to water park guests, amphitheater spectators, and maybe even develop another beer garden.

4. Product sales outside of the brewpub. The Hopstreet Brewery will monitor sales of its products to determine the feasibility of sales at other bars, restaurants, and stores.

5. Strategic alliances with other businesses. The Hopstreet Brewery will try to form alliances with others to promote business. This could be beneficial to both sides. Businesses could advertise for each other, give away coupons, encourage consumers to visit, etc.

Investor Information

The Hopstreet Brewery is seeking an outlay of $280,000 from investors. This amount will give The Hopstreet Brewery the 20 percent it needs to acquire a $1.4 million loan from the bank. Investors will be paid back over a maximum 20–year period on a monthly basis. Please see financials for more details.

Forecasted income statement start-up operations

	Prior to Month 3	Month 3	Month 2	Month 1	Month 0	Total
Net sales	$ 0	$ 0	$ 0	$ 0	$ 0	$ 0
Cost of goods sold	$ 0	$ 0	$ 0	$ 0	$ 0	$ 0
Gross income	$ 0	$ 0	$ 0	$ 0	$ 0	$ 0
Operating expenses (overhead):						
Variable:	$ 0					
Payroll	$ 0	$ 0	$ 0	$ 0	$ 17,794	$ 17,794
Payroll taxes	$ 0	$ 0	$ 0	$ 0	$ 2,135	$ 2,135
Incentives	$ 0	$ 0	$ 0	$ 0	$ 0	$ 0
Advertising	$ 3,000	$ 1,500	$ 1,500	$ 1,500	$ 1,50	$ 9,000
Legal	$ 500	$ 17	$ 17	$ 17	$ 17	$ 568
Accounting	$ 0	$ 0	$ 0	$ 0	$ 0	$ 0
Electric	$ 0	$ 2,027	$ 2,027	$ 2,027	$ 2,027	$ 8,108
Telephone	$ 0	$ 300	$ 300	$ 300	$ 300	$ 1,200
Repair & maintenance	$ 0	$ 0	$ 0	$ 0	$ 1,318	$ 1,318
Gas	$ 0	$ 71	$ 71	$ 71	$ 71	$ 284
Supplies	$ 0	$ 659	$ 659	$ 659	$ 659	$ 2,636
Total variable expenses	$ 3,500	$ 4,574	$ 4,574	$ 4,574	$ 25,821	$ 43,043
Fixed:						
Officer's salaries	NA	NA	NA	NA	NA	NA
Officer's payroll taxes	NA	NA	NA	NA	NA	NA
Insurance	$ 1,318	$ 1,318	$ 1,318	$ 1,318	$ 1,318	$ 6,590
Loan payment	$ 0	$ 0	$ 0	$ 0	$ 0	$ 0
Investor payment	$ 0	$ 0	$ 0	$ 0	$ 0	$ 0
Interest	$ 527	$ 527	$ 527	$ 527	$ 527	$ 2,636
Depreciation	$ 0	$ 2,500	$ 2,500	$ 2,500	$ 2,500	$ 10,000
Licenses & permits	$ 231	$ 231	$ 231	$ 231	$ 231	$ 1,155
Total fixed expenses	$ 2,076	$ 4,576	$ 4,576	$ 4,576	$ 4,576	$ 20,381
Total opearating expenses	$ 5,576	$ 9,150	$ 9,150	$ 9,150	$ 30,397	$ 63,423
Net income before taxes	($ 5,576)	($ 9,150)	($ 9,150)	($ 9,150)	($ 30,397)	($ 63,423)

Forecasted annual income statement

	Year 1	Year 2	Year 3	Assumptions
Food & NA beverages sales	$ 267,750	$ 477,000	$ 592,500	Data from Typical Bar & Restaurant according to Holder Group
Cost of goods sold	$ 85,680	$ 152,640	$ 189,600	unless stated otherwise
Gross food profit	$ 182,070	$ 324,360	$ 402,900	32% of food sales
Alcohol sales	$ 178,500	$ 318,000	$ 395,000	60:40 Ratio of Food to Alcohol (from Saint Louis brewpubs)
Cost of goods sold	$ 35,700	$ 63,600	$ 79,000	20% of alcohol sales (percentage from US Foods)
Gross alcohol profit	$ 142,800	$ 254,400	$316,000	
Merchandise sales	$ 0	$ 7,096	$ 6,876	
Cost of goods sold	$ 0	$ 3,548	$ 3,438	50% of merchandise sales (a guess for now)
Gross merchandise profit	$ 0	$ 3,548	$ 3,438	
Total sales	$ 446,250	$ 802,096	$ 994,376	
Total cost of goods sold	$ 121,380	$ 219,788	$ 272,038	
Total gross profit	$ 324,870	$ 582,308	$ 722,338	
Operating expenses (overhead):				
Variable:				
Payroll	$ 120,488	$ 216,566	$ 268,482	27% of total sales
Payroll taxes	$ 14,459	$ 25,988	$ 32,218	12% of payroll
Incentives	$ 12,000	$ 12,000	$ 12,000	$1,000 average monthly incentives to employees
Advertising	$ 8,925	$ 16,042	$ 19,888	2% of total sales
Legal	$ 200	$ 200	$ 200	Constant
Accounting	$ 4,463	$ 8,021	$ 9,944	1% of total sales
Electric	$ 13,988	$ 24,663	$ 30,431	3% of total sales + $600 for Brewing System Power
Telephone	$ 300	$ 300	$ 300	Constant
Repair & maintenance	$ 8,925	$ 16,042	$ 19,888	2% of total sales
Gas	$ 850	$ 850	$ 850	Constant
Supplies	$ 4,463	$ 8,021	$ 9,944	(Includes bar loss) 1% of total sales
Total variable expenses	$ 189,059	$ 328,692	$ 404,143	
Fixed:				
Officer's salaries	NA	NA	NA	
Officer's payroll taxes	NA	NA	NA	
Insurance	$ 14,000	$ 14,000	$ 14,000	
Loan payment	$ 103,164	$ 103,164	$ 103,164	$1,120,000 Loan; 6%; 20 years
Investor payment	$ 32,424	$ 32,424	$ 32,424	$280,000 Investment; 10%; 20 years
Interest	$ 6,000	$ 6,000	$ 6,000	
Depreciation	$ 30,000	$ 30,000	$ 30,000	$ 600,000 in equipment; Straight Line; 20 years
Licenses & permits	$ 2,772	$ 2,772	$ 2,772	
Total fixed expenses	$ 188,360	$ 188,360	$ 188,360	
Total variable expenses	$ 189,059	$ 328,692	$ 404,143	
Total expenses	$ 377,419	$ 517,052	$ 592,503	
Net income before taxes	−$ 52,549	$ 65,256	$ 129,835	

Forecasted year 1 income statement

	Month 1	Month 2	Month 3	Month 4	Month 5	Month 6
Food sales	$ 7,500	$ 11,250	$ 15,000	$ 19,500	$ 21,000	$ 22,500
Cost of goods sold	$ 2,400	$ 3,600	$ 4,800	$ 6,240	$ 6,720	$ 7,200
Gross food profit	$ 5,100	$ 7,650	$ 10,200	$ 13,260	$ 14,280	$ 15,300
Alcohol sales	$ 5,000	$ 7,500	$ 10,000	$ 13,000	$ 14,000	$ 15,000
Cost of goods sold	$ 1,000	$ 1,500	$ 2,000	$ 2,600	$ 2,800	$ 3,000
Gross alcohol profit	$ 4,000	$ 6,000	$ 8,000	$ 10,400	$ 11,200	$ 12,000
Merchandise sales	$ 0	$ 0	$ 0	$ 0	$ 0	$ 0
Cost of goods sold	$ 0	$ 0	$ 0	$ 0	$ 0	$ 0
Gross merchandise profit	$ 0	$ 0	$ 0	$ 0	$ 0	$ 0
Total sales	$ 12,500	$ 18,750	$ 25,000	$ 32,500	$ 35,000	$ 37,500
Total cost of goods sold	$ 3,400	$ 5,100	$ 6,800	$ 8,840	$ 9,520	$ 10,200
Total gross profit	$ 9,100	$ 13,650	$ 18,200	$ 23,660	$ 25,480	$ 27,300
Operating expenses (overhead):						
Variable:						
Payroll	$ 3,375	$ 5,063	$ 6,750	$ 8,775	$ 9,450	$ 10,125
Payroll taxes	$ 405	$ 608	$ 810	$ 1,053	$ 1,134	$ 1,215
Incentives	$ 1,000	$ 1,000	$ 1,000	$ 1,000	$ 1,000	$ 1,000
Advertising	$ 250	$ 375	$ 500	$ 650	$ 700	$ 750
Legal	$ 17	$ 17	$ 17	$ 17	$ 17	$ 17
Accounting	$ 125	$ 188	$ 250	$ 325	$ 350	$ 375
Electric	$ 425	$ 613	$ 800	$ 1,025	$ 1,100	$ 1,175
Telephone	$ 25	$ 25	$ 25	$ 25	$ 25	$ 25
Repair & maintenance	$ 250	$ 375	$ 500	$ 650	$ 700	$ 750
Gas	$ 71	$ 71	$ 71	$ 71	$ 71	$ 71
Supplies	$ 125	$ 188	$ 250	$ 325	$ 350	$ 375
Total variable expenses	$ 6,068	$ 8,520	$ 10,973	$ 13,916	$ 14,897	$ 15,878
Fixed:						
Officer's salaries	NA	NA	NA	NA	NA	NA
Officer's payroll taxes	NA	NA	NA	NA	NA	NA
Insurance	$ 1,167	$ 1,167	$ 1,167	$ 1,167	$ 1,167	$ 1,167
Loan payment	$ 8,597	$ 8,597	$ 8,597	$ 8,597	$ 8,597	$ 8,597
Investor payment	$ 2,702	$ 2,702	$ 2,702	$ 2,702	$ 2,702	$ 2,702
Interest	$ 500	$ 500	$ 500	$ 500	$ 500	$ 500
Depreciation	$ 2,500	$ 2,500	$ 2,500	$ 2,500	$ 2,500	$ 2,500
Licenses & permits	$ 231	$ 231	$ 231	$ 231	$ 231	$ 231
Total fixed expenses	$ 15,697	$ 15,697	$ 15,697	$ 15,697	$ 15,697	$ 15,697
Total opearating expenses	$ 21,764	$ 24,217	$ 26,669	$ 29,612	$ 30,593	$ 31,574
Net income before taxes	−$ 12,664	−$ 10,567	−$ 8,469	−$ 5,952	−$ 5,113	−$ 4,274

[continued]

Forecasted year 1 income statement [CONTINUED]

	Month 7	Month 8	Month 9	Month 10	Month 11	Month 12
Food sales	$ 24,000	$ 25,500	$ 27,000	$ 28,500	$ 31,500	$ 34,500
Cost of goods sold	$ 7,680	$ 8,160	$ 8,640	$ 9,120	$ 10,080	$ 11,040
Gross food profit	$ 16,320	$ 17,340	$ 18,360	$ 19,380	$ 21,420	$ 23,460
Alcohol sales	$ 16,000	$ 17,000	$ 18,000	$ 19,000	$ 21,000	$ 23,000
Cost of goods sold	$ 3,200	$ 3,400	$ 3,600	$ 3,800	$ 4,200	$ 4,600
Gross alcohol profit	$ 12,800	$ 13,600	$ 14,400	$ 15,200	$ 16,800	$ 18,400
Merchandise sales	$ 0	$ 0	$ 0	$ 0	$ 0	$ 0
Cost of goods sold	$ 0	$ 0	$ 0	$ 0	$ 0	$ 0
Gross merchandise profit	$ 0	$ 0	$ 0	$ 0	$ 0	$ 0
Total sales	$ 40,000	$ 42,500	$ 45,000	$ 47,500	$ 52,500	$ 57,500
Total cost of goods sold	$ 10,880	$ 11,560	$ 12,240	$ 12,920	$ 14,280	$ 15,640
Total gross profit	$ 29,120	$ 30,940	$ 32,760	$ 34,580	$ 38,220	$ 41,860
Operating expenses (overhead):						
Variable:						
Payroll	$ 10,800	$ 11,475	$ 12,150	$ 12,825	$ 14,175	$ 15,525
Payroll taxes	$ 1,296	$ 1,377	$ 1,458	$ 1,539	$ 1,701	$ 1,863
Incentives	$ 1,000	$ 1,000	$ 1,000	$ 1,000	$ 1,000	$ 1,000
Advertising	$ 800	$ 850	$ 900	$ 950	$ 1,050	$ 1,150
Legal	$ 17	$ 17	$ 17	$ 17	$ 17	$ 17
Accounting	$ 400	$ 425	$ 450	$ 475	$ 525	$ 575
Electric	$ 1,250	$ 1,325	$ 1,400	$ 1,475	$ 1,625	$ 1,775
Telephone	$ 25	$ 25	$ 25	$ 25	$ 25	$ 25
Repair & maintenance	$ 800	$ 850	$ 900	$ 950	$ 1,050	$ 1,150
Gas	$ 71	$ 71	$ 71	$ 71	$ 71	$ 71
Supplies	$ 400	$ 425	$ 450	$ 475	$ 525	$ 575
Total variable expenses	$ 16,859	$ 17,840	$ 18,821	$ 19,802	$ 21,764	$ 23,726
Fixed:						
Officer's salaries	NA	NA	NA	NA	NA	NA
Officer's payroll taxes	NA	NA	NA	NA	NA	NA
Insurance	$ 1,167	$ 1,167	$ 1,167	$ 1,167	$ 1,167	$ 1,167
Loan payment	$ 8,597	$ 8,597	$ 8,597	$ 8,597	$ 8,597	$ 8,597
Investor payment	$ 2,702	$ 2,702	$ 2,702	$ 2,702	$ 2,702	$ 2,702
Interest	$ 500	$ 500	$ 500	$ 500	$ 500	$ 500
Depreciation	$ 2,500	$ 2,500	$ 2,500	$ 2,500	$ 2,500	$ 2,500
Licenses & permits	$ 231	$ 231	$ 231	$ 231	$ 231	$ 231
Total fixed expenses	$ 15,697	$ 15,697	$ 15,697	$ 15,697	$ 15,697	$ 15,697
Total opearating expenses	$ 32,555	$ 33,536	$ 34,517	$ 35,498	$ 37,460	$ 39,422
Net income before taxes	−$ 3,435	−$ 2,596	−$ 1,757	−$ 918	$ 760	$ 2,438

Assumption:
(1) Change in food and alcohol sales is based on Trailhead sales
(2) Assumes 60:40 food to alcohol ratio

Forecasted year 2 income statement

	Month 1	Month 2	Month 3	Month 4	Month 5	Month 6
Food sales	$ 39,000	$ 39,000	$ 42,000	$ 45,000	$ 40,500	$ 42,000
Cost of goods sold	$ 12,480	$ 12,480	$ 13,440	$ 14,400	$ 12,960	$ 13,440
Gross food profit	$ 26,520	$ 26,520	$ 28,560	$ 30,600	$ 27,540	$ 28,560
Alcohol sales	$ 26,000	$ 26,000	$ 28,000	$ 30,000	$ 27,000	$ 28,000
Cost of goods sold	$ 5,200	$ 5,200	$ 5,600	$ 6,000	$ 5,400	$ 5,600
Gross alcohol profit	$ 20,800	$ 20,800	$ 22,400	$ 24,000	$ 21,600	$ 22,400
Merchandise sales	$ 500	$ 515	$ 530	$ 546	$ 563	$ 580
Cost of goods sold	$ 250	$ 258	$ 265	$ 273	$ 282	$ 290
Gross merchandise profit	$ 250	$ 258	$ 265	$ 273	$ 282	$ 290
Total sales	$ 65,500	$ 65,515	$ 70,530	$ 75,546	$ 68,063	$ 70,580
Total cost of goods sold	$ 17,930	$ 17,938	$ 19,305	$ 20,673	$ 18,642	$ 19,330
Total gross profit	$ 47,570	$ 47,578	$ 51,225	$ 54,873	$ 49,422	$ 51,250
Operating expenses (overhead):						
Variable:						
Payroll	$ 17,685	$ 17,689	$ 19,043	$ 20,397	$ 18,377	$ 19,057
Payroll taxes	$ 2,122	$ 2,123	$ 2,285	$ 2,448	$ 2,205	$ 2,287
Incentives	$ 1,000	$ 1,000	$ 1,000	$ 1,000	$ 1,000	$ 1,000
Advertising	$ 1,310	$ 1,310	$ 1,411	$ 1,511	$ 1,361	$ 1,412
Legal	$ 17	$ 17	$ 17	$ 17	$ 17	$ 17
Accounting	$ 655	$ 655	$ 705	$ 755	$ 681	$ 706
Electric	$ 2,015	$ 2,015	$ 2,166	$ 2,316	$ 2,092	$ 2,167
Telephone	$ 25	$ 25	$ 25	$ 25	$ 25	$ 25
Repair & maintenance	$ 1,310	$ 1,310	$ 1,411	$ 1,511	$ 1,361	$ 1,412
Gas	$ 71	$ 71	$ 71	$ 71	$ 71	$ 71
Supplies	$ 655	$ 655	$ 705	$ 755	$ 681	$ 706
Total variable expenses	$ 26,865	$ 26,871	$ 28,838	$ 30,807	$ 27,870	$ 28,858
Fixed:						
Officer's salaries	NA	NA	NA	NA	NA	NA
Officer's payroll taxes	NA	NA	NA	NA	NA	NA
Insurance	$ 1,167	$ 1,167	$ 1,167	$ 1,167	$ 1,167	$ 1,167
Loan payment	$ 8,597	$ 8,597	$ 8,597	$ 8,597	$ 8,597	$ 8,597
Investor payment	$ 2,702	$ 2,702	$ 2,702	$ 2,702	$ 2,702	$ 2,702
Interest	$ 500	$ 500	$ 500	$ 500	$ 500	$ 500
Depreciation	$ 2,500	$ 2,500	$ 2,500	$ 2,500	$ 2,500	$ 2,500
Licenses & permits	$ 231	$ 231	$ 231	$ 231	$ 231	$ 231
Total fixed expenses	$ 15,697	$ 15,697	$ 15,697	$ 15,697	$ 15,697	$ 15,697
Total opeerating expenses	$ 42,561	$ 42,567	$ 44,535	$ 46,503	$ 43,567	$ 44,555
Net income before taxes	$ 5,009	$ 5,010	$ 6,690	$ 8,370	$ 5,854	$ 6,695

[continued]

Forecasted year 2 income statement [CONTINUED]

	Month 7	Month 8	Month 9	Month 10	Month 11	Month 12
Food sales	$ 39,000	$ 42,000	$ 34,500	$ 34,500	$ 37,500	$ 42,000
Cost of goods sold	$ 12,480	$ 13,440	$ 11,040	$ 11,040	$ 12,000	$ 13,440
Gross food profit	$ 26,520	$ 28,560	$ 23,460	$ 23,460	$ 25,500	$ 28,560
Alcohol sales	$ 26,000	$ 28,000	$ 23,000	$ 23,000	$ 25,000	$ 28,000
Cost of goods sold	$ 5,200	$ 5,600	$ 4,600	$ 4,600	$ 5,000	$ 5,600
Gross alcohol profit	$ 20,800	$ 22,400	$ 18,400	$ 18,400	$ 20,000	$ 22,400
Merchandise sales	$ 597	$ 615	$ 633	$ 652	$ 672	$ 692
Cost of goods sold	$ 299	$ 308	$ 317	$ 326	$ 336	$ 346
Gross merchandise profit	$ 299	$ 308	$ 317	$ 326	$ 336	$ 346
Total sales	$ 65,597	$ 70,615	$ 58,133	$ 58,152	$ 63,172	$ 70,692
Total cost of goods sold	$ 17,979	$ 19,348	$ 15,957	$ 15,966	$ 17,336	$ 19,386
Total gross profit	$ 47,619	$ 51,268	$ 42,177	$ 42,186	$ 45,836	$ 51,306
Operating expenses (overhead):						
Variable:						
Payroll	$ 17,711	$ 19,066	$ 15,696	$ 15,701	$ 17,056	$ 19,087
Payroll taxes	$ 2,125	$ 2,288	$ 1,884	$ 1,884	$ 2,047	$ 2,290
Incentives	$ 1,000	$ 1,000	$ 1,000	$ 1,000	$ 1,000	$ 1,000
Advertising	$ 1,312	$ 1,412	$ 1,163	$ 1,163	$ 1,263	$ 1,414
Legal	$ 17	$ 17	$ 17	$ 17	$ 17	$ 17
Accounting	$ 656	$ 706	$ 581	$ 582	$ 632	$ 707
Electric	$ 2,018	$ 2,168	$ 1,794	$ 1,795	$ 1,945	$ 2,171
Telephone	$ 25	$ 25	$ 25	$ 25	$ 25	$ 25
Repair & maintenance	$ 1,312	$ 1,412	$ 1,163	$ 1,163	$ 1,263	$ 1,414
Gas	$ 71	$ 71	$ 71	$ 71	$ 71	$ 71
Supplies	$ 656	$ 706	$ 581	$ 582	$ 632	$ 707
Total variable expenses	$ 26,903	$ 28,872	$ 23,974	$ 23,981	$ 25,951	$ 28,902
Fixed:						
Officer's salaries	NA	NA	NA	NA	NA	NA
Officer's payroll taxes	NA	NA	NA	NA	NA	NA
Insurance	$ 1,167	$ 1,167	$ 1,167	$ 1,167	$ 1,167	$ 1,167
Loan payment	$ 8,597	$ 8,597	$ 8,597	$ 8,597	$ 8,597	$ 8,597
Investor payment	$ 2,702	$ 2,702	$ 2,702	$ 2,702	$ 2,702	$ 2,702
Interest	$ 500	$ 500	$ 500	$ 500	$ 500	$ 500
Depreciation	$ 2,500	$ 2,500	$ 2,500	$ 2,500	$ 2,500	$ 2,500
Licenses & permits	$ 231	$ 231	$ 231	$ 231	$ 231	$ 231
Total fixed expenses	$ 15,697	$ 15,697	$ 15,697	$ 15,697	$ 15,697	$ 15,697
Total opearating expenses	$ 42,599	$ 44,568	$ 39,671	$ 39,678	$ 41,648	$ 44,599
Net income before taxes	$ 5,019	$ 6,699	$ 2,506	$ 2,508	$ 4,188	$ 6,707

Assumption:
(1) Change in food and alcohol sales is based on Trailhead sales
(2) Assumes 60:40 food to alcohol ratio

Forecasted year 3 income statement

	Month 1	Month 2	Month 3	Month 4	Month 5	Month 6
Food sales	$ 48,000	$ 48,000	$ 51,000	$ 54,000	$ 49,500	$ 51,000
Cost of goods sold	$ 15,360	$ 15,360	$ 16,320	$ 17,280	$ 15,840	$ 16,320
Gross food profit	$ 32,640	$ 32,640	$ 34,680	$ 36,720	$ 33,660	$ 34,680
Alcohol sales	$ 32,000	$ 32,000	$ 34,000	$ 36,000	$ 33,000	$ 34,000
Cost of goods sold	$ 6,400	$ 6,400	$ 6,800	$ 7,200	$ 6,600	$ 6,800
Gross alcohol profit	$ 25,600	$ 25,600	$ 27,200	$ 28,800	$ 26,400	$ 27,200
Merchandise sales	$ 671	$ 651	$ 632	$ 613	$ 594	$ 577
Cost of goods sold	$ 336	$ 326	$ 316	$ 307	$ 297	$ 289
Gross merchandise profit	$ 336	$ 326	$ 316	$ 307	$ 297	$ 289
Total sales	$ 80,671	$ 80,651	$ 85,632	$ 90,613	$ 83,094	$ 85,577
Total cost of goods sold	$ 22,096	$ 22,086	$ 23,436	$ 24,787	$ 22,737	$ 23,409
Total gross profit	$ 58,576	$ 58,566	$ 62,196	$ 65,827	$ 60,357	$ 62,169
Operating expenses (overhead):						
Variable:						
Payroll	$ 21,781	$ 21,776	$ 23,121	$ 24,466	$ 22,435	$ 23,106
Payroll taxes	$ 2,614	$ 2,613	$ 2,774	$ 2,936	$ 2,692	$ 2,773
Incentives	$ 1,000	$ 1,000	$ 1,000	$ 1,000	$ 1,000	$ 1,000
Advertising	$ 1,613	$ 1,613	$ 1,713	$ 1,812	$ 1,662	$ 1,712
Legal	$ 17	$ 17	$ 17	$ 17	$ 17	$ 17
Accounting	$ 807	$ 807	$ 856	$ 906	$ 831	$ 856
Electric	$ 2,470	$ 2,470	$ 2,619	$ 2,768	$ 2,543	$ 2,617
Telephone	$ 25	$ 25	$ 25	$ 25	$ 25	$ 25
Repair & maintenance	$ 1,613	$ 1,613	$ 1,713	$ 1,812	$ 1,662	$ 1,712
Gas	$ 71	$ 71	$ 71	$ 71	$ 71	$ 71
Supplies	$ 807	$ 807	$ 856	$ 906	$ 831	$ 856
Total variable expenses	$ 32,818	$ 32,810	$ 34,764	$ 36,719	$ 33,769	$ 34,743
Fixed:						
Officer's salaries	NA	NA	NA	NA	NA	NA
Officer's payroll taxes	NA	NA	NA	NA	NA	NA
Insurance	$ 1,167	$ 1,167	$ 1,167	$ 1,167	$ 1,167	$ 1,167
Loan payment	$ 8,597	$ 8,597	$ 8,597	$ 8,597	$ 8,597	$ 8,597
Investor payment	$ 2,702	$ 2,702	$ 2,702	$ 2,702	$ 2,702	$ 2,702
Interest	$ 500	$ 500	$ 500	$ 500	$ 500	$ 500
Depreciation	$ 2,500	$ 2,500	$ 2,500	$ 2,500	$ 2,500	$ 2,500
Licenses & permits	$ 231	$ 231	$ 231	$ 231	$ 231	$ 231
Total fixed expenses	$ 15,697	$ 15,697	$ 15,697	$ 15,697	$ 15,697	$ 15,697
Total opearating expenses	$ 48,514	$ 48,507	$ 50,461	$ 52,416	$ 49,465	$ 50,440
Net income before taxes	$ 10,061	$ 10,059	$ 11,735	$ 13,411	$ 10,892	$ 11,729

[continued]

Forecasted year 3 income statement [CONTINUED]

	Month 7	Month 8	Month 9	Month 10	Month 11	Month 12
Food sales	$ 48,000	$ 51,000	$ 45,000	$ 45,000	$ 48,000	$ 54,000
Cost of goods sold	$ 15,360	$ 16,320	$ 14,400	$ 14,400	$ 15,360	$ 17,280
Gross food profit	$ 32,640	$ 34,680	$ 30,600	$ 30,600	$ 32,640	$ 36,720
Alcohol sales	$ 32,000	$ 34,000	$ 30,000	$ 30,000	$ 32,000	$ 36,000
Cost of goods sold	$ 6,400	$ 6,800	$ 6,000	$ 6,000	$ 6,400	$ 7,200
Gross alcohol profit	$ 25,600	$ 27,200	$ 24,000	$ 24,000	$ 25,600	$ 28,800
Merchandise sales	$ 559	$ 542	$ 526	$ 510	$ 500	$ 500
Cost of goods sold	$ 280	$ 271	$ 263	$ 255	$ 250	$ 250
Gross merchandise profit	$ 280	$ 271	$ 263	$ 255	$ 250	$ 250
Total sales	$ 80,559	$ 85,542	$ 75,526	$ 75,510	$ 80,500	$ 90,500
Total cost of goods sold	$ 22,040	$ 23,391	$ 20,663	$ 20,655	$ 22,010	$ 24,730
Total gross profit	$ 58,520	$ 62,151	$ 54,863	$ 54,855	$ 58,490	$65,770
Operating expenses (overhead):						
Variable:						
Payroll	$ 21,751	$ 23,096	$ 20,392	$ 20,388	$ 21,735	$ 24,435
Payroll taxes	$ 2,610	$ 2,772	$ 2,447	$ 2,447	$ 2,608	$ 2,932
Incentives	$ 1,000	$ 1,000	$ 1,000	$ 1,000	$ 1,000	$ 1,000
Advertising	$ 1,611	$ 1,711	$ 1,511	$ 1,510	$ 1,610	$ 1,810
Legal	$ 17	$ 17	$ 17	$ 17	$ 17	$ 17
Accounting	$ 806	$ 855	$ 755	$ 755	$ 805	$ 905
Electric	$ 2,467	$ 2,616	$ 2,316	$ 2,315	$ 2,465	$ 2,765
Telephone	$ 25	$ 25	$ 25	$ 25	$ 25	$ 25
Repair & maintenance	$ 1,611	$ 1,711	$ 1,511	$ 1,510	$ 1,610	$ 1,810
Gas	$ 71	$ 71	$ 71	$ 71	$ 71	$ 71
Supplies	$ 806	$ 855	$ 755	$ 755	$ 805	$ 905
Total variable expenses	$ 32,774	$ 34,729	$ 30,799	$ 30,793	$ 32,751	$ 36,675
Fixed:						
Officer's salaries	NA	NA	NA	NA	NA	NA
Officer's payroll taxes	NA	NA	NA	NA	NA	NA
Insurance	$ 1,167	$ 1,167	$ 1,167	$ 1,167	$ 1,167	$ 1,167
Loan payment	$ 8,597	$ 8,597	$ 8,597	$ 8,597	$ 8,597	$ 8,597
Investor payment	$ 2,702	$ 2,702	$ 2,702	$ 2,702	$ 2,702	$ 2,702
Interest	$ 500	$ 500	$ 500	$ 500	$ 500	$ 500
Depreciation	$ 2,500	$ 2,500	$ 2,500	$ 2,500	$ 2,500	$ 2,500
Licenses & permits	$ 231	$ 231	$ 231	$ 231	$ 231	$ 231
Total fixed expenses	$ 15,697	$ 15,697	$ 15,697	$ 15,697	$ 15,697	$ 15,697
Total opearating expenses	$ 48,471	$ 50,426	$ 46,496	$ 46,489	$ 48,447	$ 52,371
Net income before taxes	$ 10,049	$ 11,725	$ 8,367	$ 8,366	$ 10,043	$ 13,399

Assumption:
(1) Change in food and alcohol sales is based on Trailhead sales
(2) Assumes 60:40 food to alcohol ratio

Projected sales detail

	May	June	July	August	September	October
Year 1						
Projected sales	Month 1	Month 2	Month 3	Month 4	Month 5	Month 6
Food	$ 7,500	$ 11,250	$ 15,000	$ 19,500	$ 21,000	$ 22,500
Alcohol	$ 5,000	$ 7,500	$ 10,000	$ 13,000	$ 14,000	$ 15,000
Merchandise	$ 0	$ 0	$ 0	$ 0	$ 0	$ 0
Revenue	$ 12,500	$ 18,750	$ 25,000	$ 32,500	$ 35,000	$ 37,500
Year 2						
Projected sales	Month 13	Month 14	Month 15	Month 16	Month 17	Month 18
Food	$ 39,000	$ 39,000	$ 42,000	$ 45,000	$ 40,500	$ 42,000
Alcohol	$ 26,000	$ 26,000	$ 28,000	$ 30,000	$ 27,000	$ 28,000
Merchandise	$ 500	$ 515	$ 530	$ 546	$ 563	$ 580
Revenue	$ 65,500	$ 65,515	$ 70,530	$ 75,546	$ 68,063	$ 70,580
Year 3						
Projected sales	Month 25	Month 26	Month 27	Month 28	Month 29	Month 30
Food	$ 48,000	$ 48,000	$ 51,000	$ 54,000	$ 49,500	$ 51,000
Alcohol	$ 32,000	$ 32,000	$ 34,000	$ 36,000	$ 33,000	$ 34,000
Merchandise	$ 671	$ 651	$ 632	$ 613	$ 594	$ 577
Revenue	$ 80,671	$ 80,651	$ 85,632	$ 90,613	$ 83,094	$ 85,577

[continued]

Projected sales detail [CONTINUED]

	November	December	January	February	March	April	Total
Year 1							
Projected sales	Month 7	Month 8	Month 9	Month 10	Month 11	Month 12	Total
Food	$ 24,000	$ 25,500	$ 27,000	$ 28,500	$ 31,500	$ 34,500	$ 267,750
Alcohol	$ 16,000	$ 17,000	$ 18,000	$ 19,000	$ 21,000	$ 23,000	$ 178,500
Merchandise	$ 0	$ 0	$ 0	$ 0	$ 0	$ 0	$ 0
Revenue	$ 40,000	$ 42,500	$ 45,000	$ 47,500	$ 52,500	$ 57,500	$ 446,250
Year 2							
Projected sales	Month 19	Month 20	Month 21	Month 22	Month 23	Month 24	Total
Food	$ 39,000	$ 42,000	$ 34,500	$ 34,500	$ 37,500	$ 42,000	$ 477,000
Alcohol	$ 26,000	$ 28,000	$ 23,000	$ 23,000	$ 25,000	$ 28,000	$ 318,000
Merchandise	$ 597	$ 615	$ 633	$ 652	$ 672	$ 692	$ 7,096
Revenue	$ 65,597	$ 70,615	$ 58,133	$ 58,152	$ 63,172	$ 70,692	$ 802,096
Year 3							
Projected sales	Month 31	Month 32	Month 33	Month 34	Month 35	Month 36	Total
Food	$ 48,000	$ 51,000	$ 45,000	$ 45,000	$ 48,000	$ 54,000	$ 592,500
Alcohol	$ 32,000	$ 34,000	$ 30,000	$ 30,000	$ 32,000	$ 36,000	$ 395,000
Merchandise	$ 559	$ 542	$ 526	$ 510	$ 500	$ 500	$ 6,876
Revenue	$ 80,559	$ 85,542	$ 75,526	$ 75,510	$ 80,500	$ 90,500	$ 994,376

Assumption:
(1) Change in food and alcohol sales is based on Trailhead sales
(2) Assumes 60:40 food to alcohol ratio

Break-even forecasted annual income statement

	Year 1	Year 2	Year 3	Assumptions
Food sales	$ 361,698	$ 360,333	$ 360,375	Data from Typical Bar & Restaurant according to Holder Group
Cost of goods sold	$ 115,743	$ 115,307	$ 115,320	32% of food sales
Gross food profit	$ 245,955	$ 245,026	$ 245,055	
Alcohol sales	$ 241,132	$ 240,222	$ 240,250	60:40 Ratio of Food to Alcohol (from Saint Louis brewpubs)
Cost of goods sold	$ 48,226	$ 48,044	$ 48,050	20% of alcohol sales (percentage from US Foods)
Gross alcohol profit	$ 192,906	$ 192,178	$ 192,200	
Merchandise sales	$ 0	$ 7,096	$ 6,876	
Cost of goods sold	$ 0	$ 3,548	$ 3,438	50% of merchandise sales
Gross merchandise profit	$ 0	$ 3,548	$ 3,438	
Total sales	$ 602,830	$ 607,651	$ 607,501	
Total cost of goods sold	$ 163,970	$ 166,899	$ 166,808	
Total gross profit	$ 438,860	$ 440,752	$ 440,693	
Operating expenses (overhead):				
Variable:				
Payroll	$ 162,764	$ 164,066	$ 164,025	27% of total sales
Payroll taxes	$ 19,532	$ 19,688	$ 19,683	12% of payroll
Incentives	$ 12,000	$ 12,000	$ 12,000	$1,000 average monthly incentives to employees
Advertising	$ 12,057	$ 12,153	$ 12,150	2% of total sales
Legal	$ 200	$ 200	$ 200	
Accounting	$ 6,028	$ 6,077	$ 6,075	1% of total sales
Electric	$ 18,685	$ 18,830	$ 18,825	3% of total sales + $600 for Brewing System Power (www.jvnw.com)
Telephone	$ 300	$ 300	$ 300	
Repair & maintenance	$ 12,057	$ 12,153	$ 12,150	2% of total sales
Gas	$ 850	$ 850	$ 850	
Supplies	$ 6,028	$ 6,077	$ 6,075	1% of total sales
Total variable expenses	$ 250,500	$ 252,392	$ 252,333	
Fixed:				
Officer's salaries	NA	NA	NA	
Officer's payroll taxes	NA	NA	NA	
Insurance	$ 14,000	$ 14,000	$ 14,000	
Loan payment	$ 103,164	$ 103,164	$ 103,164	$1,120,000 Loan; 6%; 20 years
Investor payment	$ 32,424	$ 32,424	$ 32,424	$280,000 Investment; 10%; 20 years
Interest	$ 6,000	$ 6,000	$ 6,000	
Depreciation	$ 30,000	$ 30,000	$ 30,000	$600,000 in equipment; Straight Line; 20 years
Licenses & permits	$ 2,772	$ 2,772	$ 2,772	
Total fixed expenses	$ 188,360	$ 188,360	$ 188,360	
Total variable expenses	$ 250,500	$ 252,392	$ 252,333	
Total expenses	$ 438,860	$ 440,752	$ 440,693	
Net income before taxes	$ 0	$ 0	$ 0	

Forecasted year 1 break even income statement

	Month 1	Month 2	Month 3	Month 4	Month 5	Month 6
Food sales	$ 30,142	$ 30,142	$ 30,142	$ 30,142	$ 30,142	$ 30,142
Cost of goods sold	$ 9,645	$ 9,645	$ 9,645	$ 9,645	$ 9,645	$ 9,645
Gross food profit	$ 20,496	$ 20,496	$ 20,496	$ 20,496	$ 20,496	$20,496
Alcohol sales	$ 20,094	$ 20,094	$ 20,094	$ 20,094	$ 20,094	$ 20,094
Cost of goods sold	$ 4,019	$ 4,019	$ 4,019	$ 4,019	$ 4,019	$ 4,019
Gross alcohol profit	$ 16,075	$ 16,075	$ 16,075	$ 16,075	$ 16,075	$ 16,075
Merchandise sales	$ 0	$ 0	$ 0	$ 0	$ 0	$ 0
Cost of goods sold	$ 0	$ 0	$ 0	$ 0	$ 0	$ 0
Gross merchandise profit	$ 0	$ 0	$ 0	$ 0	$ 0	$ 0
Total sales	$ 50,236	$ 50,236	$ 50,236	$ 50,236	$ 50,236	$ 50,236
Total cost of goods sold	$ 13,664	$ 13,664	$ 13,664	$ 13,664	$ 13,664	$ 13,664
Total gross profit	$ 36,572	$ 36,572	$ 36,572	$ 36,572	$ 36,572	$ 36,572
Operating expenses (overhead):						
Variable:						
Payroll	$ 13,564	$ 13,564	$ 13,564	$ 13,564	$ 13,564	$ 13,564
Payroll taxes	$ 1,628	$ 1,628	$ 1,628	$ 1,628	$ 1,628	$ 1,628
Incentives	$ 1,000	$ 1,000	$ 1,000	$ 1,000	$ 1,000	$ 1,000
Advertising	$ 1,005	$ 1,005	$ 1,005	$ 1,005	$ 1,005	$ 1,005
Legal	$ 17	$ 17	$ 17	$ 17	$ 17	$ 17
Accounting	$ 502	$ 502	$ 502	$ 502	$ 502	$ 502
Electric	$ 1,557	$ 1,557	$ 1,557	$ 1,557	$ 1,557	$ 1,557
Telephone	$ 25	$ 25	$ 25	$ 25	$ 25	$ 25
Repair & maintenance	$ 1,005	$ 1,005	$ 1,005	$ 1,005	$ 1,005	$ 1,005
Gas	$ 71	$ 71	$ 71	$ 71	$ 71	$ 71
Supplies	$ 502	$ 502	$ 502	$ 502	$ 502	$ 502
Total variable expenses	$ 20,875	$ 20,875	$ 20,875	$ 20,875	$ 20,875	$ 20,875
Fixed:						
Officer's salaries	NA	NA	NA	NA	NA	NA
Officer's payroll taxes	NA	NA	NA	NA	NA	NA
Insurance	$ 1,167	$ 1,167	$ 1,167	$ 1,167	$ 1,167	$ 1,167
Loan payment	$ 8,597	$ 8,597	$ 8,597	$ 8,597	$ 8,597	$ 8,597
Investor payment	$ 2,702	$ 2,702	$ 2,702	$ 2,702	$ 2,702	$ 2,702
Interest	$ 500	$ 500	$ 500	$ 500	$ 500	$ 500
Depreciation	$ 2,500	$ 2,500	$ 2,500	$ 2,500	$ 2,500	$ 2,500
Licenses & permits	$ 231	$ 231	$ 231	$ 231	$ 231	$ 231
Total fixed expenses	$ 15,697	$ 15,697	$ 15,697	$ 15,697	$ 15,697	$ 15,697
Total opearating expenses	$ 36,572	$ 36,572	$ 36,572	$ 36,572	$ 36,572	$ 36,572
Net income before taxes	$ 0	$ 0	$ 0	$ 0	$ 0	$ 0

[continued]

Forecasted year 1 break even income statement [CONTINUED]

	Month 7	Month 8	Month 9	Month 10	Month 11	Month 12
Food sales	$ 30,142	$ 30,142	$ 30,142	$ 30,142	$ 30,142	$ 30,142
Cost of goods sold	$ 9,645	$ 9,645	$ 9,645	$ 9,645	$ 9,645	$ 9,645
Gross food profit	$ 20,496	$ 20,496	$ 20,496	$ 20,496	$ 20,496	$ 20,496
Alcohol sales	$ 20,094	$ 20,094	$ 20,094	$ 20,094	$ 20,094	$ 20,094
Cost of goods sold	$ 4,019	$ 4,019	$ 4,019	$ 4,019	$ 4,019	$ 4,019
Gross alcohol profit	$ 16,075	$ 16,075	$ 16,075	$ 16,075	$ 16,075	$ 16,075
Merchandise sales	$ 0	$ 0	$ 0	$ 0	$ 0	$ 0
Cost of goods sold	$ 0	$ 0	$ 0	$ 0	$ 0	$ 0
Gross merchandise profit	$ 0	$ 0	$ 0	$ 0	$ 0	$ 0
Total sales	$ 50,236	$ 50,236	$ 50,236	$ 50,236	$ 50,236	$ 50,236
Total cost of goods sold	$ 13,664	$ 13,664	$ 13,664	$ 13,664	$ 13,664	$ 13,664
Total gross profit	$ 36,572	$ 36,572	$ 36,572	$ 36,572	$ 36,572	$ 36,572
Operating expenses (overhead):						
Variable:						
Payroll	$ 13,564	$ 13,564	$ 13,564	$ 13,564	$ 13,564	$ 13,564
Payroll taxes	$ 1,628	$ 1,628	$ 1,628	$ 1,628	$ 1,628	$ 1,628
Incentives	$ 1,000	$ 1,000	$ 1,000	$ 1,000	$ 1,000	$ 1,000
Advertising	$ 1,005	$ 1,005	$ 1,005	$ 1,005	$ 1,005	$ 1,005
Legal	$ 17	$ 17	$ 17	$ 17	$ 17	$ 17
Accounting	$ 502	$ 502	$ 502	$ 502	$ 502	$ 502
Electric	$ 1,557	$ 1,557	$ 1,557	$ 1,557	$ 1,557	$ 1,557
Telephone	$ 25	$ 25	$ 25	$ 25	$ 25	$ 25
Repair & maintenance	$ 1,005	$ 1,005	$ 1,005	$ 1,005	$ 1,005	$ 1,005
Gas	$ 71	$ 71	$ 71	$ 71	$ 71	$ 71
Supplies	$ 502	$ 502	$ 502	$ 502	$ 502	$ 502
Total variable expenses	$ 20,875	$ 20,875	$ 20,875	$ 20,875	$ 20,875	$ 20,875
Fixed:						
Officer's salaries	NA	NA	NA	NA	NA	NA
Officer's payroll taxes	NA	NA	NA	NA	NA	NA
Insurance	$ 1,167	$ 1,167	$ 1,167	$ 1,167	$ 1,167	$ 1,167
Loan payment	$ 8,597	$ 8,597	$ 8,597	$ 8,597	$ 8,597	$ 8,597
Investor payment	$ 2,702	$ 2,702	$ 2,702	$ 2,702	$ 2,702	$ 2,702
Interest	$ 500	$ 500	$ 500	$ 500	$ 500	$ 500
Depreciation	$ 2,500	$ 2,500	$ 2,500	$ 2,500	$ 2,500	$ 2,500
Licenses & permits	$ 231	$ 231	$ 231	$ 231	$ 231	$ 231
Total fixed expenses	$ 15,697	$ 15,697	$ 15,697	$ 15,697	$ 15,697	$ 15,697
Total opearating expenses	$ 36,572	$ 36,572	$ 36,572	$ 36,572	$ 36,572	$ 36,572
Net income before taxes	$ 0	$ 0	$ 0	$ 0	$ 0	$ 0

Forecasted year 2 break even income statement

	Month 1	Month 2	Month 3	Month 4	Month 5	Month 6
Food sales	$ 30,028	$ 30,028	$ 30,028	$ 30,028	$ 30,028	$ 30,028
Cost of goods sold	$ 9,609	$ 9,609	$ 9,609	$ 9,609	$ 9,609	$ 9,609
Gross food profit	$ 20,496	$ 20,496	$ 20,496	$ 20,496	$ 20,496	$ 20,496
Alcohol sales	$ 20,019	$ 20,019	$ 20,019	$ 20,019	$ 20,019	$ 20,019
Cost of goods sold	$ 4,004	$ 4,004	$ 4,004	$ 4,004	$ 4,004	$ 4,004
Gross alcohol profit	$ 16,015	$ 16,015	$ 16,015	$ 16,015	$ 16,015	$ 16,015
Merchandise sales	$ 591	$ 591	$ 591	$ 591	$ 591	$ 591
Cost of goods sold	$ 296	$ 296	$ 296	$ 296	$ 296	$ 296
Gross merchandise profit	$ 296	$ 296	$ 296	$ 296	$ 296	$ 296
Total sales	$ 50,638	$ 50,638	$ 50,638	$ 50,638	$ 50,638	$ 50,638
Total cost of goods sold	$ 13,908	$ 13,908	$ 13,908	$ 13,908	$ 13,908	$ 13,908
Total gross profit	$ 36,729	$ 36,729	$ 36,729	$ 36,729	$ 36,729	$ 36,729
Operating expenses (overhead):						
Variable:						
Payroll	$ 13,672	$ 13,672	$ 13,672	$ 13,672	$ 13,672	$ 13,672
Payroll taxes	$ 1,641	$ 1,641	$ 1,641	$ 1,641	$ 1,641	$ 1,641
Incentives	$ 1,000	$ 1,000	$ 1,000	$ 1,000	$ 1,000	$ 1,000
Advertising	$ 1,013	$ 1,013	$ 1,013	$ 1,013	$ 1,013	$ 1,013
Legal	$ 17	$ 17	$ 17	$ 17	$ 17	$ 17
Accounting	$ 506	$ 506	$ 506	$ 506	$ 506	$ 506
Electric	$ 1,569	$ 1,569	$ 1,569	$ 1,569	$ 1,569	$ 1,569
Telephone	$ 25	$ 25	$ 25	$ 25	$ 25	$ 25
Repair & maintenance	$ 1,013	$ 1,013	$ 1,013	$ 1,013	$ 1,013	$ 1,013
Gas	$ 71	$ 71	$ 71	$ 71	$ 71	$ 71
Supplies	$ 506	$ 506	$ 506	$ 506	$ 506	$ 506
Total variable expenses	$ 21,033	$ 21,033	$ 21,033	$ 21,033	$ 21,033	$ 21,033
Fixed:						
Officer's salaries	NA	NA	NA	NA	NA	NA
Officer's payroll taxes	NA	NA	NA	NA	NA	NA
Insurance	$ 1,167	$ 1,167	$ 1,167	$ 1,167	$ 1,167	$ 1,167
Loan payment	$ 8,597	$ 8,597	$ 8,597	$ 8,597	$ 8,597	$ 8,597
Investor payment	$ 2,702	$ 2,702	$ 2,702	$ 2,702	$ 2,702	$ 2,702
Interest	$ 500	$ 500	$ 500	$ 500	$ 500	$ 500
Depreciation	$ 2,500	$ 2,500	$ 2,500	$ 2,500	$ 2,500	$ 2,500
Licenses & permits	$ 231	$ 231	$ 231	$ 231	$ 231	$ 231
Total fixed expenses	$ 15,697	$ 15,697	$ 15,697	$ 15,697	$ 15,697	$ 15,697
Total opearating expenses	$ 36,729	$ 36,729	$ 36,729	$ 36,729	$ 36,729	$ 36,729
Net income before taxes	$ 0	$ 0	$ 0	$ 0	$ 0	$ 0

[continued]

Forecasted year 2 break even income statement [CONTINUED]

	Month 7	Month 8	Month 9	Month 10	Month 11	Month 12
Food sales	$ 30,028	$ 30,028	$ 30,028	$ 30,028	$ 30,028	$ 30,028
Cost of goods sold	$ 9,609	$ 9,609	$ 9,609	$ 9,609	$ 9,609	$ 9,609
Gross food profit	$ 20,496	$ 20,496	$ 20,496	$ 20,496	$ 20,496	$ 20,496
Alcohol sales	$ 20,019	$ 20,019	$ 20,019	$ 20,019	$ 20,019	$ 20,019
Cost of goods sold	$ 4,004	$ 4,004	$ 4,004	$ 4,004	$ 4,004	$ 4,004
Gross alcohol profit	$ 16,015	$ 16,015	$ 16,015	$ 16,015	$ 16,015	$ 16,015
Merchandise sales	$ 591	$ 591	$ 591	$ 591	$ 591	$ 591
Cost of goods sold	$ 296	$ 296	$ 296	$ 296	$ 296	$ 296
Gross merchandise profit	$ 296	$ 296	$ 296	$ 296	$ 296	$ 296
Total sales	$ 50,638	$ 50,638	$ 50,638	$ 50,638	$ 50,638	$ 50,638
Total cost of goods sold	$ 13,908	$ 13,908	$ 13,908	$ 13,908	$ 13,908	$ 13,908
Total gross profit	$ 36,729	$ 36,729	$ 36,729	$ 36,729	$ 36,729	$ 36,729
Operating expenses (overhead):						
Variable:						
Payroll	$ 13,672	$ 13,672	$ 13,672	$ 13,672	$ 13,672	$ 13,672
Payroll taxes	$ 1,641	$ 1,641	$ 1,641	$ 1,641	$ 1,641	$ 1,641
Incentives	$ 1,000	$ 1,000	$ 1,000	$ 1,000	$ 1,000	$ 1,000
Advertising	$ 1,013	$ 1,013	$ 1,013	$ 1,013	$ 1,013	$ 1,013
Legal	$ 17	$ 17	$ 17	$ 17	$ 17	$ 17
Accounting	$ 506	$ 506	$ 506	$ 506	$ 506	$ 506
Electric	$ 1,569	$ 1,569	$ 1,569	$ 1,569	$ 1,569	$ 1,569
Telephone	$ 25	$ 25	$ 25	$ 25	$ 25	$ 25
Repair & maintenance	$ 1,013	$ 1,013	$ 1,013	$ 1,013	$ 1,013	$ 1,013
Gas	$ 71	$ 71	$ 71	$ 71	$ 71	$ 71
Supplies	$ 506	$ 506	$ 506	$ 506	$ 506	$ 506
Total variable expenses	$ 21,033	$ 21,033	$ 21,033	$ 21,033	$ 21,033	$ 21,033
Fixed:						
Officer's salaries	NA	NA	NA	NA	NA	NA
Officer's payroll taxes	NA	NA	NA	NA	NA	NA
Insurance	$ 1,167	$ 1,167	$ 1,167	$ 1,167	$ 1,167	$ 1,167
Loan payment	$ 8,597	$ 8,597	$ 8,597	$ 8,597	$ 8,597	$ 8,597
Investor payment	$ 2,702	$ 2,702	$ 2,702	$ 2,702	$ 2,702	$ 2,702
Interest	$ 500	$ 500	$ 500	$ 500	$ 500	$ 500
Depreciation	$ 2,500	$ 2,500	$ 2,500	$ 2,500	$ 2,500	$ 2,500
Licenses & permits	$ 231	$ 231	$ 231	$ 231	$ 231	$ 231
Total fixed expenses	$ 15,697	$ 15,697	$ 15,697	$ 15,697	$ 15,697	$ 15,697
Total opearating expenses	$ 36,729	$ 36,729	$ 36,729	$ 36,729	$ 36,729	$ 36,729
Net income before taxes	$ 0	$ 0	$ 0	$ 0	$ 0	$ 0

Forecasted year 3 break even income statement

	Month 1	Month 2	Month 3	Month 4	Month 5	Month 6
Food sales	$ 30,031	$ 30,031	$ 30,031	$ 30,031	$ 30,031	$ 30,031
Cost of goods sold	$ 9,610	$ 9,610	$ 9,610	$ 9,610	$ 9,610	$ 9,610
Gross food profit	$ 20,421	$ 20,421	$ 20,421	$ 20,421	$ 20,421	$ 20,421
Alcohol sales	$ 20,021	$ 20,021	$ 20,021	$ 20,021	$ 20,021	$ 20,021
Cost of goods sold	$ 4,004	$ 4,004	$ 4,004	$ 4,004	$ 4,004	$ 4,004
Gross alcohol profit	$ 16,017	$ 16,017	$ 16,017	$ 16,017	$ 16,017	$ 16,017
Merchandise sales	$ 573	$ 573	$ 573	$ 573	$ 573	$ 573
Cost of goods sold	$ 287	$ 287	$ 287	$ 287	$ 287	$ 287
Gross merchandise profit	$ 287	$ 287	$ 287	$ 287	$ 287	$ 287
Total sales	$ 50,625	$ 50,625	$ 50,625	$ 50,625	$ 50,625	$ 50,625
Total cost of goods sold	$ 13,901	$ 13,901	$ 13,901	$ 13,901	$ 13,901	$ 13,901
Total gross profit	$ 36,724	$ 36,724	$ 36,724	$ 36,724	$ 36,724	$ 36,724
Operating expenses (overhead):						
Variable:						
Payroll	$ 13,669	$ 13,669	$ 13,669	$ 13,669	$ 13,669	$ 13,669
Payroll taxes	$ 1,640	$ 1,640	$ 1,640	$ 1,640	$ 1,640	$ 1,640
Incentives	$ 1,000	$ 1,000	$ 1,000	$ 1,000	$ 1,000	$ 1,000
Advertising	$ 1,013	$ 1,013	$ 1,013	$ 1,013	$ 1,013	$ 1,013
Legal	$ 17	$ 17	$ 17	$ 17	$ 17	$ 17
Accounting	$ 506	$ 506	$ 506	$ 506	$ 506	$ 506
Electric	$ 1,569	$ 1,569	$ 1,569	$ 1,569	$ 1,569	$ 1,569
Telephone	$ 25	$ 25	$ 25	$ 25	$ 25	$ 25
Repair & maintenance	$ 1,013	$ 1,013	$ 1,013	$ 1,013	$ 1,013	$ 1,013
Gas	$ 71	$ 71	$ 71	$ 71	$ 71	$ 71
Supplies	$ 506	$ 506	$ 506	$ 506	$ 506	$ 506
Total variable expenses	$ 21,028	$ 21,028	$ 21,028	$ 21,028	$ 21,028	$ 21,028
Fixed:						
Officer's salaries	NA	NA	NA	NA	NA	NA
Officer's payroll taxes	NA	NA	NA	NA	NA	NA
Insurance	$ 1,167	$ 1,167	$ 1,167	$ 1,167	$ 1,167	$ 1,167
Loan payment	$ 8,597	$ 8,597	$ 8,597	$ 8,597	$ 8,597	$ 8,597
Investor payment	$ 2,702	$ 2,702	$ 2,702	$ 2,702	$ 2,702	$ 2,702
Interest	$ 500	$ 500	$ 500	$ 500	$ 500	$ 500
Depreciation	$ 2,500	$ 2,500	$ 2,500	$ 2,500	$ 2,500	$ 2,500
Licenses & permits	$ 231	$ 231	$ 231	$ 231	$ 231	$ 231
Total fixed expenses	$ 15,697	$ 15,697	$ 15,697	$ 15,697	$ 15,697	$ 15,697
Total opearating expenses	$ 36,724	$ 36,724	$ 36,724	$ 36,724	$ 36,724	$ 36,724
Net income before taxes	$ 0	$ 0	$ 0	$ 0	$ 0	$ 0

[continued]

Forecasted year 3 break even income statement [CONTINUED]

	Month 7	Month 8	Month 9	Month 10	Month 11	Month 12
Food sales	$ 30,031	$ 30,031	$ 30,031	$ 30,031	$ 30,031	$ 30,031
Cost of goods sold	$ 9,610	$ 9,610	$ 9,610	$ 9,610	$ 9,610	$ 9,610
Gross food profit	$ 20,421	$ 20,421	$ 20,421	$ 20,421	$ 20,421	$ 20,421
Alcohol sales	$ 20,021	$ 20,021	$ 20,021	$ 20,021	$ 20,021	$ 20,021
Cost of goods sold	$ 4,004	$ 4,004	$ 4,004	$ 4,004	$ 4,004	$ 4,004
Gross alcohol profit	$ 16,017	$ 16,017	$ 16,017	$ 16,017	$ 16,017	$ 16,017
Merchandise sales	$ 573	$ 573	$ 573	$ 573	$ 573	$ 573
Cost of goods sold	$ 287	$ 287	$ 287	$ 287	$ 287	$ 287
Gross merchandise profit	$ 287	$ 287	$ 287	$ 287	$ 287	$ 287
Total sales	$ 50,625	$ 50,625	$ 50,625	$ 50,625	$ 50,625	$ 50,625
Total cost of goods sold	$ 13,901	$ 13,901	$ 13,901	$ 13,901	$ 13,901	$ 13,901
Total gross profit	$ 36,724	$ 36,724	$ 36,724	$ 36,724	$ 36,724	$ 36,724
Operating expenses (overhead):						
Variable:						
Payroll	$ 13,669	$ 13,669	$ 13,669	$ 13,669	$ 13,669	$ 13,669
Payroll taxes	$ 1,640	$ 1,640	$ 1,640	$ 1,640	$ 1,640	$ 1,640
Incentives	$ 1,000	$ 1,000	$ 1,000	$ 1,000	$ 1,000	$ 1,000
Advertising	$ 1,013	$ 1,013	$ 1,013	$ 1,013	$ 1,013	$ 1,013
Legal	$ 17	$ 17	$ 17	$ 17	$ 17	$ 17
Accounting	$ 506	$ 506	$ 506	$ 506	$ 506	$ 506
Electric	$ 1,569	$ 1,569	$ 1,569	$ 1,569	$ 1,569	$ 1,569
Telephone	$ 25	$ 25	$ 25	$ 25	$ 25	$ 25
Repair & maintenance	$ 1,013	$ 1,013	$ 1,013	$ 1,013	$ 1,013	$ 1,013
Gas	$ 71	$ 71	$ 71	$ 71	$ 71	$ 71
Supplies	$ 506	$ 506	$ 506	$ 506	$ 506	$ 506
Total variable expenses	$ 21,028	$ 21,028	$ 21,028	$ 21,028	$ 21,028	$ 21,028
Fixed:						
Officer's salaries	NA	NA	NA	NA	NA	NA
Officer's payroll taxes	NA	NA	NA	NA	NA	NA
Insurance	$ 1,167	$ 1,167	$ 1,167	$ 1,167	$ 1,167	$ 1,167
Loan payment	$ 8,597	$ 8,597	$ 8,597	$ 8,597	$ 8,597	$ 8,597
Investor payment	$ 2,702	$ 2,702	$ 2,702	$ 2,702	$ 2,702	$ 2,702
Interest	$ 500	$ 500	$ 500	$ 500	$ 500	$ 500
Depreciation	$ 2,500	$ 2,500	$ 2,500	$ 2,500	$ 2,500	$ 2,500
Licenses & permits	$ 231	$ 231	$ 231	$ 231	$ 231	$ 231
Total fixed expenses	$ 15,697	$ 15,697	$ 15,697	$ 15,697	$ 15,697	$ 15,697
Total opearating expenses	$ 36,724	$ 36,724	$ 36,724	$ 36,724	$ 36,724	$ 36,724
Net income before taxes	$ 0	$ 0	$ 0	$ 0	$ 0	$ 0

Break even projected sales detailed

	May	June	July	August	September	October
Year 1						
Projected sales	Month 1	Month 2	Month 3	Month 4	Month 5	Month 6
Food	$ 30,142	$ 30,142	$ 30,142	$ 30,142	$ 30,142	$ 30,142
Alcohol	$ 20,094	$ 20,094	$ 20,094	$ 20,094	$ 20,094	$ 20,094
Merchandise	$ 0	$ 0	$ 0	$ 0	$ 0	$ 0
Revenue	$ 50,236	$ 50,236	$ 50,236	$ 50,236	$ 50,236	$ 50,236
Year 2						
Projected sales	Month 13	Month 14	Month 15	Month 16	Month 17	Month 18
Food	$ 30,028	$ 30,028	$ 30,028	$ 30,028	$ 30,028	$ 30,028
Alcohol	$ 20,019	$ 20,019	$ 20,019	$ 20,019	$ 20,019	$ 20,019
Merchandise	$ 591	$ 591	$ 591	$ 591	$ 591	$ 591
Revenue	$ 50,638	$ 50,638	$ 50,638	$ 50,638	$ 50,638	$ 50,638
Year 3						
Projected sales	Month 25	Month 26	Month 27	Month 28	Month 29	Month 30
Food	$ 30,031	$ 30,031	$ 30,031	$ 30,031	$ 30,031	$ 30,031
Alcohol	$ 20,021	$ 20,021	$ 20,021	$ 20,021	$ 20,021	$ 20,021
Merchandise	$ 573	$ 573	$ 573	$ 573	$ 573	$ 573
Revenue	$ 50,625	$ 50,625	$ 50,625	$ 50,625	$ 50,625	$ 50,625

[continued]

Projected sales detail [CONTINUED]

	November	December	January	February	March	April	Total
Year 1							
Projected sales	Month 7	Month 8	Month 9	Month 10	Month 11	Month 12	Total
Food	$ 30,142	$ 30,142	$ 30,142	$ 30,142	$ 30,142	$ 30,142	$ 361,698
Alcohol	$ 20,094	$ 20,094	$ 20,094	$ 20,094	$ 20,094	$ 20,094	$ 241,132
Merchandise	$ 0	$ 0	$ 0	$ 0	$ 0	$ 0	$ 0
Revenue	$ 50,236	$ 50,236	$ 50,236	$ 50,236	$ 50,236	$ 50,236	$ 602,830
Year 2							
Projected sales	Month 19	Month 20	Month 21	Month 22	Month 23	Month 24	Total
Food	$ 30,028	$ 30,028	$ 30,028	$ 30,028	$ 30,028	$ 30,028	$ 360,333
Alcohol	$ 20,019	$ 20,019	$ 20,019	$ 20,019	$ 20,019	$ 20,019	$ 240,222
Merchandise	$ 591	$ 591	$ 591	$ 591	$ 591	$ 591	$ 7,096
Revenue	$ 50,638	$ 50,638	$ 50,638	$ 50,638	$ 50,638	$ 50,638	$ 607,651
Year 3							
Projected sales	Month 31	Month 32	Month 33	Month 34	Month 35	Month 36	Total
Food	$ 30,031	$ 30,031	$ 30,031	$ 30,031	$ 30,031	$ 30,031	$ 360,375
Alcohol	$ 20,021	$ 20,021	$ 20,021	$ 20,021	$ 20,021	$ 20,021	$ 240,250
Merchandise	$ 573	$ 573	$ 573	$ 573	$ 573	$ 573	$ 6,876
Revenue	$ 50,625	$ 50,625	$ 50,625	$ 50,625	$ 50,625	$ 50,625	$ 607,501

Forecasted cash flow start-up operations

	Prior to month -3	Month -3	Month -2	Month -1	Month 0	Total
Net income before taxes (without COGS)	($ 5,576)	($ 9,150)	($ 9,150)	($ 9,150)	($ 30,397)	($ 63,423)
Change in working capital accounts						
Current assets						
Cash/accounts receivable:	$1,400,000	$ 0	$ 0	$ 0	$ 0	$1,400,000
Bank loan	$1,120,000	$ 0	$ 0	$ 0	$ 0	$1,120,000
Capital equity	$ 280,000	$ 0	$ 0	$ 0	$ 0	$ 280,000
Current liablilities						
Accounts payable:	$ 0	$ 1,219,400	$ 0	$ 0	$ 20,000	$1,239,400
Building & real estate	$ 0	$ 500,000	$ 0	$ 0	$ 0	$ 500,000
Brew system	$ 0	$ 417,000	$ 0	$ 0	$ 0	$ 417,000
Equipment/furniture	$ 0	$ 100,000	$ 0	$ 0	$ 0	$ 100,000
Build-out	$ 0	$ 182,400	$ 0	$ 0	$ 0	$ 182,400
Inventory	$ 0	$ 0	$ 0	$ 0	$ 20,000	$ 20,000
Other fees	$ 0	$ 20,000	$ 0	$ 0	$ 0	$ 20,000
Total changes in current accounts	$1,400,000	($ 1,219,400)	$ 0	$ 0	($ 20,000)	$ 160,600
Net operating cash flows	$1,394,424	($ 1,228,550)	($ 9,150)	($ 9,150)	($ 50,397)	$ 97,177
Beginning cash balance	$1,400,000	$ 1,394,424	$165,874	$156,724	$147,574	$1,400,000
Ending cash balance	$1,394,424	$ 165,874	$156,724	$147,574	$ 97,177	$ 97,177

Year 1 forecasted cash flow statement

	Month 1	Month 2	Month 3	Month 4	Month 5	Month 6
Net income before taxes	($ 9,264)	($ 5,467)	($ 1,669)	$ 2,888	$ 4,407	$ 5,926
Change in working capital accounts						
Current assets						
Cash/accounts receivable	$ 0	$ 0	$ 0	$ 0	$ 0	$ 0
Current liablilities						
Accounts payable	$ 0	$ 0	$ 0	$ 0	$ 0	$ 0
Changes in current accounts	$ 0	$ 0	$ 0	$ 0	$ 0	$ 0
Net operating cash flows	($ 9,264)	($ 5,467)	($ 1,669)	$ 2,888	$ 4,407	$ 5,926
Beginning cash balance	$ 97,177	$ 87,913	$ 82,447	$ 80,777	$ 83,665	$ 88,072
Ending cash balance	$ 87,913	$ 82,447	$ 80,777	$ 83,665	$ 88,072	$ 93,998

[continued]

Year 1 forecasted cash flow statement [CONTINUED]

	Month 7	Month 8	Month 9	Month 10	Month 11	Month 12	Total
Net income before taxes	$ 7,445	$ 8,964	$ 10,483	$ 12,002	$ 15,040	$ 18,078	$ 68,832
Change in working capital accounts							
Current assets							
Cash/accounts receivable	$ 0	$ 0	$ 0	$ 0	$ 0	$ 0	$ 0
Current liablilities							
Accounts payable	$ 0	$ 0	$ 0	$ 0	$ 0	$ 0	$ 0
Changes in current accounts	$ 0	$ 0	$ 0	$ 0	$ 0	$ 0	$ 0
Net operating cash flows	$ 7,445	$ 8,964	$ 10,483	$ 12,002	$ 15,040	$ 18,078	$166,009
Beginning cash balance	$ 93,998	$101,443	$ 110,407	$120,889	$ 132,891	$ 147,931	$ 97,177
Ending cash balance	$101,443	$110,407	$ 120,889	$132,891	$ 147,931	$ 166,009	$ 166,009

Year 2 forecasted cash flow statement

	Month 1	Month 2	Month 3	Month 4	Month 5	Month 6
Net income before taxes	$ 22,939	$ 22,948	$ 25,995	$ 29,043	$ 24,496	$ 26,025
Change in working capital accounts						
Current assets						
Cash/accounts receivable	$ 0	$ 0	$ 0	$ 0	$ 0	$ 0
Current liablilities						
Accounts payable	$ 0	$ 0	$ 0	$ 0	$ 0	$ 0
Changes in current accounts	$ 0	$ 0	$ 0	$ 0	$ 0	$ 0
Net operating cash flows	$ 22,939	$ 22,948	$ 25,995	$ 29,043	$ 24,496	$ 26,025
Beginning cash balance	$ 166,009	$ 188,948	$ 211,895	$ 237,890	$ 266,933	$ 291,429
Ending cash balance	$ 188,948	$ 211,895	$ 237,890	$ 266,933	$ 291,429	$ 317,454

[continued]

Year 2 forecasted cash flow statement [CONTINUED]

	Month 7	Month 8	Month 9	Month 10	Month 11	Month 12	Total
Net income before taxes	$ 22,998	$ 26,047	$ 18,462	$ 18,474	$ 21,524	$ 26,093	$285,043
Change in working capital accounts							
Current assets							
Cash/accounts receivable	$ 0	$ 0	$ 0	$ 0	$ 0	$ 0	$ 0
Current liablilities							
Accounts payable	$ 0	$ 0	$ 0	$ 0	$ 0	$ 0	$ 0
Changes in current accounts	$ 0	$ 0	$ 0	$ 0	$ 0	$ 0	$ 0
Net operating cash flows	$ 22,998	$ 26,047	$ 18,462	$ 18,474	$ 21,524	$ 26,093	$451,052
Beginning cash balance	$317,454	$340,451	$ 366,498	$384,960	$ 403,434	$ 424,959	$166,009
Ending cash balance	$340,451	$366,498	$ 384,960	$403,434	$ 424,959	$ 451,052	$451,052

Year 3 forecasted cash flow statement

	Month 1	Month 2	Month 3	Month 4	Month 5	Month 6
Net income before taxes	$ 32,157	$ 32,144	$ 35,171	$ 38,197	$ 33,629	$ 35,137
Change in working capital accounts						
Current assets						
Cash/accounts receivable	$ 0	$ 0	$ 0	$ 0	$ 0	$ 0
Current liablilities						
Accounts payable	$ 0	$ 0	$ 0	$ 0	$ 0	$ 0
Changes in current accounts	$ 0	$ 0	$ 0	$ 0	$ 0	$ 0
Net operating cash flows	$ 32,157	$ 32,144	$ 35,171	$ 38,197	$ 33,629	$ 35,137
Beginning cash balance	$ 451,052	$ 483,208	$ 515,353	$ 550,524	$ 588,721	$ 622,350
Ending cash balance	$ 483,208	$ 515,353	$ 550,524	$ 588,721	$ 622,350	$ 657,487

[continued]

Year 3 forecasted cash flow statement [CONTINUED]

	Month 7	Month 8	Month 9	Month 10	Month 11	Month 12	Total
Net income before taxes	$ 32,088	$ 35,116	$ 29,030	$ 29,021	$ 32,053	$ 38,129	$ 401,872
Change in working capital accounts							
Current assets							
Cash/accounts receivable	$ 0	$ 0	$ 0	$ 0	$ 0	$ 0	$ 0
Current liablilities							
Accounts payable	$ 0	$ 0	$ 0	$ 0	$ 0	$ 0	$ 0
Changes in current accounts	$ 0	$ 0	$ 0	$ 0	$ 0	$ 0	$ 0
Net operating cash flows	$ 32,088	$ 35,116	$ 29,030	$ 29,021	$ 32,053	$ 38,129	$ 852,924
Beginning cash balance	$ 657,487	$ 689,576	$ 724,692	$ 753,722	$ 782,743	$ 814,795	$ 451,052
Ending cash balance	$ 689,576	$ 724,692	$ 753,722	$ 782,743	$ 814,795	$ 852,924	$ 852,924

Balance sheet

	Year 1	Year 2	Year 3
Year end balance sheet			
Assets			
Cash	$ 166,009	$ 451,052	$ 852,924
Inventory	$ 20,000	$ 20,000	$ 20,000
Fixed assets	$ 1,219,400	$ 1,219,400	$ 1,219,400
Total assets	$ 1,405,409	$ 1,690,452	$ 2,092,324
Liabilities			
Accounts payable	$ 0	$ 0	$ 0
Accrued expense	$ 0	$ 0	$ 0
Owner's equity			
Founder invested capital	$ 280,000	$ 280,000	$ 280,000
Bank loan	$ 1,120,000	$ 1,120,000	$ 1,120,000
Retained earnings	$ 5,409	$ 290,452	$ 692,324
Total liabilities and shareholder's equity	$ 1,405,409	$ 1,690,452	$ 2,092,324

Cigar Company

Smokescreen Cigars

1230 Armadillo Place
Dallas, TX 76155

Tony Tecce

This plan raised $25,000 for two owners of a cigar company specializing in non–branded cigars which can be sold with an infinite number of customized labels. Today the business now operates as both a popular Web site as well as a storefront operation.

EXECUTIVE SUMMARY

Smokescreen Cigars is seeking extra capital to take advantage of the soaring popularity of the cigar. We expect soon to become not only a very profitable business, but one which increase sales and profits by leaps and bounds. The challenge for Smokescreen Cigars is funding. At the current size, the company cannot keep pace with the increasing demand. In short, Smokescreen Cigars plans raise $30,000 to achieve the goals explained further in the plan.

Background

Smokescreen Cigars was conceived by Barry Blackstone in the summer of 1996. The main idea for the business was to market a cigar with a graphically appealing Smokescreen label—plus an excellent smoking experience—to a world–wide audience. Also, the company would provide the option of a personalized private label to either commemorate a special event or to display a corporate logo. Sales would be generated through local bars and shops as well as over the Internet, which offers an astonishing large market.

In January 1997 the first Smokescreen cigars hit the shelves of Antonio's Pizza, a great testing ground due to the fact that Blackstone is part owner. The cigars were a hit, and within two months there were 12 locations throughout the north shore of Lake Austin retailing our cigars. In the first five weeks, the company had sold over 600 cigars, but because Blackstone was not yet connected well in the cigar industry he was forced to pay retail prices. Still, he was able to earn a profit on each order. By the sixth week, new sales slowed as Blackstone focused on development of the company's Web site rather than in–store sales.

By February 1997 James Hull was brought into the business as a partner. Hull would focus on the Dallas market, as well as the construction of our unique "FreshSmoke" cigar boxes specially designed to keep cigars fresh. Both Blackstone and Hull have committed money and time to the company to ensure success. Components of the FreshSmoke containers, computer equipment, woodworking equipment, Internet ad space, and cigars were purchased to create and support a solid sales and marketing base. With the local market tested successfully, the Web page was launched at the end of March. In just three weeks it had already paid for itself with a remarkable level of sales. Then in the first week of April, the partners attended a national cigar convention. This convention put Smokescreen Cigars on the cigar map, and obtained lucrative distribution contracts on several lines of cigars and accessories direct from the manufacturers.

One problem remains: lack of a proper amount of capital. This new infusion we need is slated to pay for cigars/accessories, advertising space, and working owner's salaries. With sufficient capital, Smokescreen Cigars will be able to gross over $200K by the end of the fourth quarter of 1997 or the first quarter of 1998.

History of Cigar Industry

These days, it's not unusual to see someone puffing away on a stogie most places you go. The industry has been taken by storm; everyone is smoking cigars! Well not everyone, but since 1994, demand has more than doubled to 400 billion units in 1996. This has created a shortage in the industry for quality, name–brand cigars whose manufacturers must predict sales two years out. Well, no one could predict the explosion in demand so the industry is two years from meeting today's demand, and very easily it could be three to four years before things level off.

The shortage is primarily existing in the high–end name brand cigars like Fuentes, Partagas, Macanudo, etc. The niche now available is for quality, "no–name" cigars of which there is presently an ample supply, available at more reasonable prices than the vast majority of big–brand cigars.

MARKETING & SALES

Smokescreen Cigars' goal is to supply the world cigars emblazoned with the Smokescreen label in both wholesale and retail markets. We import non–branded, premium cigars from Honduras and the Dominican Republic, add our labels, then resell them at more than double our costs. The retailer will, in turn, double their costs. The benefits of buying non–branded cigars are numerous: Our costs are less, our supply is more reliable, and because the customer can not quantify the cigar based on manufacturer name, our cigars are felt to be comparable to higher–end name brands.

As a wholesaler, we provide a FreshSmoke container and a clipper for display at no additional charge. The FreshSmoke container is unique to our company and not only retains cigar freshness, but is quite an eye–catching display. The clipper allows for that personal touch so that the cigar can be enjoyed on the spot. Our wholesaling methods will work all over the world, not just in our local area. We plan on creating a label pertinent to select destination areas of the world. The initial order will be taken in person, with subsequent orders to be completed via a toll–free phone number (delivered by two–day air service). Imagine a Rocky Mountain label for Colorado, a Golden Gate label for San Francisco area, an Alamo label for San Antonio, etc. Once the initial sales trips are concluded, the re–orders will add up.

As a mail–order retail outlet through the Internet, we can offer a wide line of cigars and accessories. By selling direct to the end user, it allows for greater profits and less tax headaches. Proper placement of the Web site is the key. We have it linked to two cigar compilation sites, each boasting hundreds of thousands of hits. Even if we attract less than 2 percent of traffic to our page, sales are expected to be enormous. We also are registered with over 20 Internet search engines so that when people are searching for cigars, we match the query. The big draw will be the Stogy Lens: a live camera hooked up to the Internet displaying a new picture every 60 seconds. It will focus on a local spot frequented by cigar smokers. This will put us at the top of every cigar page list, which will further increase the Web page hits.

Locally, we are in the process of closing a deal that would allow us to have a storefront for our cigars. The deal entails no rent or utilities, but cigars would be displayed on a consignment basis.

OBJECTIVES

To calculate projected sales, we broke them down into four categories: cigars in bars, cigars over the Internet, private labeled cigars, and accessories (including hats, shirts, cutters, clippers, etc.).

Cigars in bars are based on past sales and future sales created in destination towns throughout the world. The average bar sale is from 30 to 50 cigars. Conceivably, if we do 1,000 cigar sales to new accounts, and we do that each month, each month will have all the re–orders from existing accounts plus new accounts sold. This progression can get out of hand. For instance: At 1,000 new account cigars per month, in month one 1,000 cigars would be sold; in month two, 1,000 (new) plus 1,000 (re–order from prior month) equals 2,000 cigars for the month; in month three, 1,000 (new) plus 2,000 (re–order from prior months) equals 3,000 cigars for the month; and so on. Our estimates are based on 400 to 1,000 new account cigars per month.

Cigars over the Internet are based on hits the Web page will attain. Our page will be listed on larger pages with documented hits of over one million per month. Now if only half of one percent visit our site, that gives us 10,000 hits per month. A conservative estimation of sales versus hits is 1 to 100, which equates to 100 sales over the Internet on a monthly basis. Each sale will be a minimum of 25 cigars, with the average around 50, or $100 to $200.

Private labeled cigars can include those sold over the Internet and locally. We estimate 3 to 4 sales per month with each sale averaging 150 cigars, or $600 to $800.

Accessories also can include those sold over the Internet and locally. A conservative estimate is around $1000 per month in sales. We also are the sole Internet distributors for a manufacturer of luxury cigar accessories. Their line includes a $2,000 humidor, of which we receive $1,000 for each unit sold.

For these kinds of sales, no other added personnel would be needed. The two partners can handle the business along with a commissioned sales staff and piece workers for labeling the cigars. All these costs have been worked into the price of the cigars.

FINANCIAL ANALYSIS

Smokescreen Cigars is a Texas corporation. To ensure profitability, Smokescreen Cigars must raise capital in the amount of $30,000. Terms of ownership will be discussed in person with those interested.

Construction Development & Real Estate Firm

Black Pearl Development and Real Estate LLC

4432 Alsace Lane
Tazor, TX 78221

Tena M. Harper

This plan raised over $10 million for a medium-sized West Texas firm planning on developing a 300-lot subdivision with a recreational park, playground and 30 acres of walking and horseback riding trails.

EXECUTIVE SUMMARY

Black Pearl Development and Real Estate LLC (hereafter Black Pearl) is an experienced construction and development firm in Texas. Black Pearl is a full–service firm that owns heavy equipment, and offers "in–house" groundbreaking, infrastructure, concrete, framing and final construction services. Black Pearl has a dedicated and experienced foreman, a valuable core of management, and an excellent reputation in the community.

Black Pearl will purchase and develop 2,500 acres of land in West Texas. We will develop this land into a restricted covenant sub–division containing 300 lots. Two hundred and sixty of these lots will contain residential housing and forty lots will contain commercial buildings. Black Pearl is constructing a one–acre recreational park and playground in the sub–division, and 30 acres of walking and horseback riding trails.

Black Pearl is unlike any other construction or development firm in the area. We are able to control costs and production delays by keeping the majority of our work in–house. We own our heavy equipment, do all our construction, have dependable contractors. In short, we are the only company that can develop a property completely. From original groundbreaking of undeveloped properties to the sales of completed residential housing, Black Pearl maintains complete control. Black Pearl is owned by Jim Wright.

Financial highlights for the fiscal year of operations

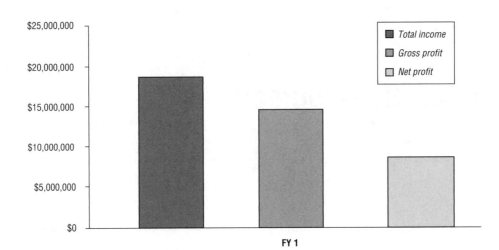

Mission

Black Pearl Development and Real Estate LLC is committed to the respectful, thoughtful development of living areas. Our development provides privacy, space, amenities, and preserves the natural beauty of land. Black Pearl is experienced, stable, dependable and reliable with outstanding customer service in the forefront of our building process.

Keys to Success

1. Extensive company experience in all phases of development process.

2. All phases of development are handled in–house reducing overhead costs.

3. Long term, positive relationships with select sub–contractors that insure quality work that meets deadlines.

OPERATIONS

Black Pearl Development and Real Estate LLC (hereafter Black Pearl) is an experienced construction and development firm in Texas. Black Pearl is a full service firm that owns heavy equipment, and offers "in–house" groundbreaking, infrastructure, concrete, framing and final construction services. Black Pearl has a dedicated and experienced foreman, a valuable core of management, and an excellent reputation in the community.

Organization

Black Pearl Development and Real Estate LLC is owned by Jim Wright, who is 100 percent vested. Black Pearl does the majority of our work in–house. This enables us to control costs. We depend on local contractors to install plumbing, electrical, and heating requirements. These contractors have a long–standing relationship with Black Pearl, and their work ethic, dependability and deadline adhesion is unparalleled. The contractors are GB's Plumbing, Harrison's Plumbing, Brad Brown Electric, Luevano Electric, K.P.I. Sheet Metal, and J. Becker Sheet Metal.

Company Location and Facilities

The main office of Black Pearl Development and Real Estate LLC is located at 4432 Alsace Lane, Tazor, Texas. Black Pearl proposes to purchase and develop 2,500 acres of land in West Texas. This acreage affords one mile of river frontage.

PRODUCTS & SERVICES

Black Pearl will purchase and develop 2,500 acres of land in West Texas. We will develop this land into a restricted covenant sub–division containing 300 lots. Two hundred and sixty of these lots will contain residential housing and forty lots will contain commercial buildings. Black Pearl is constructing a one–acre recreational park and playground in the subdivision and 30 acres of walking and horseback riding trails.

Land development requires that all essential infrastructure—sewers, water lines, streets, sidewalks, right of way clearances and lots division—is completed. Black Pearl also will design and build a majority of the residential and commercial structures. Once the land development is complete Black Pearl will offer the lots and houses for sale to retail buyers.

The restricted covenant of the sub–division requires that owners use either Black Pearl Construction to build their homes, submit the plans of proposed dwellings to the planning board, or use construction companies recommended by Black Pearl. This ensures constancy in sub–development land value, and aesthetic appeal.

Consumers have choices regarding lot size or location. River footage lots are offered in five–acre parcels for $200,000 to $300,000 a lot, and commercial lots are offered in one–acre parcels for $100,000 a lot. Non–river frontage lots are offered in parcels of five, three or one acre for a retail price of $75,000, $54,000, and $18,000.

Future Products or Services

Black Pearl has located an area with four miles of river frontage that has the potential for a $20 million subdivision development. Black Pearl management will acquire a real estate license that will enable them to sell the lots and houses built in their subdivisions.

MARKET ANALYSIS

Tazor lies in one of the fastest growing areas of Texas. Lying in the beautiful Spur Valley, Tazor has been attracting numerous new residents over the past two decades. Tazor was one of the first Texas towns to truly be hit by an influx of new people. These people were drawn to Tazor primarily by its location in this very scenic area of the state. This area will continue to grow rapidly, attracting both new permanent Texas residents as well as serving as a major place for the building of summer homes and other similar "trophy homes" that are also springing up over the rest of Texas now.

Acton County has experienced annual growth rates of 3 percent from 1990–2000 with even greater growth in the unincorporated areas. The Tazor area population doubled from 1970–2000. Harrison County increased in population 26.6 percent from 1990–2000 and Lenox County increased 32.2 percent from 1990–2000 (US census).

The construction industry in the Tazor area is so strong that it is an economic force within the State. The economic activity generated by home construction does not cease at the end of the construction period. As homes are occupied, the occupants buy goods and services, pay taxes and contribute to the economic viability of an area.

"This on-going critical mass for economic activity is often overlooked when discussing construction impacts" stated Dr. Lisa Slush, economist at the Center for Economic Analysis. "On–going impacts sustain additional jobs in the economy as well as higher business incomes. Single family construction within the nine counties sustains between $114,000 and $3.6 million in additional business income and 21 to 640 additional jobs. Multi–family construction sustains from 5 to 217 additional jobs, and $37,000 to $1.3 million in additional local business income."

The median price of new home construction in the area is estimated at $139,4000.

Market analysis

	Growth	2004	2005	2006	2007	2008	CAGR
Billings, Texas	3%	89,847	92,542	95,319	98,178	101,124	3%
Jummot, Texas	3%	57,043	58,754	60,517	62,332	64,202	
Great Lakes, Texas	3%	56,690	58,391	60,142	61,947	63,805	
Black Bow, Texas	3%	33,892	34,909	35,956	37,035	38,146	
Cheater, Texas	3%	53,011	54,601	56,239	57,927	59,664	
Kasping, Texas	2%	49,644	51,133	52,667	54,247	55,875	
Laramie, Texas	2%	27,204	28,020	28,861	29,727	30,618	
Gilbert, Texas	2%	19,646	20,039	20,440	20,848	21,265	2%
Total	**2.95%**	**386,977**	**398,390**	**410,141**	**422,241**	**434,700**	**2.95%**

Market Segmentation

Black Pearl has segmented their target market for this development as retired couples and families. The river frontage lots target market will attract an economic of level of $500,000 to 1,000,000. The lots that do not have river frontage will attract an economic level of $50,000 to $60,000.

Market Needs

The level of development in the Tazor area and the State of Texas indicates a need for experienced development companies. The respectful and thoughtful design of the Black Pearl subdivision reflects an experienced developer who values people, wildlife and the land.

Market Trends

There is an ongoing trend for multi–million homes that showcase both spectacular design and the wondrous natural beauty of the area. The restricted covenant and the location of the planned subdivision tap into this ongoing trend.

Market Growth

Acton County has experienced annual growth rates of 3 percent from 1990–2000 with even greater growth in the unincorporated areas. The target market of families with incomes from $50,000 to $60,000 and an additional market of individuals with incomes from $500,000 and $1 million continue to rise as the general population rises.

Competition

Black Pearl is unlike any other construction or development firm in the area. We are able to control costs and production delays by keeping the majority of our work in–house. We own our heavy equipment, do all our construction, and have dependable contractors. In short we are the only company that can develop a property completely. From original groundbreaking of undeveloped properties to the sales of completed residential housing, Black Pearl maintains complete control.

There are few development companies that are able to complete projects of this scope that are located in Texas. Many construction contractors are only capable of completing sections of a job and rely heavily on outsourced workers. This can lead to unreliable results, delays and cost overages.

The density of full–scale land developers in Texas is slight. Many companies lack the resources, experience or financing to complete large scale development projects. Black Pearl has the resources and the experience to develop large projects. We control costs and delays by keeping the majority of our project completion in–house. This allows us to control costs, delays and maintain a tight timeline.

People choose building contractors based on the reputation of the contractor and the quality of their customer service. People seek contractors that offer services that complement their time constraints, budget and style. They also choose contractors based on personality compatibility.

There are few contractors that have the resources to complete large development projects. These companies are similar in size and scope. They do not have the strong local reputation of Black Pearl, nor do they complete projects with complete in–house controls. Black Pearl is able to control costs and delays far better than our competitors.

BUSINESS STRATEGY

Black Pearl will seek funding from local resources; our reputation and reliability is established with these firms. Black Pearl provides an outstanding value for their clients and has successful marketing programs in place. The new subdivision will offer an elite living experience for average families, upper–income retired couples and people desiring showcase homes.

Value Proposition

The Black Pearl proposed sub–development offers purchasers extended value. The thoughtful layout of the site allows for privacy and maximum enjoyment of the land. The construction of a park and the extensive walking/riding trail demonstrates a respect for the people who will make this sub–division home. Black Pearl is offering premier living conditions, with scenic views, and access to wildlife and privacy. The commitment to sustained land values and aesthetic appeal is an extra value attraction for the sub–development.

Competitive Edge

The ability of Black Pearl to control all aspects of a development project is a distinct advantage. We can control costs, timelines and guarantee structural soundness, because we are not dependent on many outside contractors.

MARKETING & SALES

Marketing Strategy

Black Pearl is focusing on the target groups of families and upper–income retired people. We will utilize local real estate papers, our successful Internet marketing and P.O.P signage to build brand recognition. Black Pearls value–added services and outstanding customer service is a strong marketing point.

Positioning Statement

For families, retired people or individuals who desire showcase homes, amazing views or simply well designed living areas, Black Pearl Development and Real Estate LLC exceeds expectations with solid design, sound reputation and outstanding customer service. Unlike other land developers, it controls costs and delays by completing the vast majority of all construction needs with experienced in–house staff.

Pricing Strategy

Black Pearl purchases the property for $3,500 an acre with land development infrastructure costing $1,667 an acre. These properties are then sold for $18,000 to $60,000 an acre. Housing construction costs average $102 a square foot with selling prices of $140 a square foot.

Promotion Strategy

The new subdivision will be promoted with P.O.P. signage, and website development. Active participation in the local Chamber of Commerce will build brand recognition for both Black Pearl and the subdivision itself.

Marketing Programs

Black Pearl markets our comprehensive services through the local real estate magazine. We also have huge success with marketing on the Internet. This is the most successful marketing program to date, attracting numerous out of state buyers.

Sales Strategy

Jim Wright will close all sales contacts. He will be assisted by Edward Johnston. Sales costs, timeline and structure standards are negotiated with Wright and a planning board will oversee sub–development esthetics. This planning board will initially contain members of the management team.

SALES FORECAST

Annual sales forecast

Sales	FY 1
Riverfront lots	$ 6,250,000
Riverview lots	$ 7,500,000
3 acre lots	$ 5,400,000
1 acre lots	$ 630,000
Commercial lots	$ 400,000
Total sales	**$ 20,180,000**
Cost of goods sold	
Land	$ 4,200,000
Total cost of goods sold	**$ 4,200,000**

Sales Programs

Jim Wright is responsible for all sales of developed lots and housing construction. He also negotiates all financing in regards to development.

Strategic Alliances

Black Pearl has formed strong strategic alliances with plumbing, electric and forced air heating/cooling contractors.

OBJECTIVES

Milestones

1. Achieve final financing for development in October 2004

2. Receive approval from local and state officials by February 2005

3. Hire new employees in February 2005

4. Complete infrastructure by late May 2005

5. Receive real estate license by May 2005

MANAGEMENT SUMMARY

Black Pearl has four key management people, a permanent job foreman and five employees. They will hire an additional 25 employees once the sub–division project is underway.

Organizational Structure

- Mark Birmingham is charged with reading blueprints, meeting with architects, engineers and tracking building specifications.

- Frank Steinker provides general management supervision, financing negotiation and manages sales.

- Christy Weams handles the bookkeeping and invoices for the business.

- Roger Miller creates the marketing campaigns.

Management Team

The management team of Black Pearl has worked together profitably for a long time. These people are used to the intricacies of the construction industry and have excellent interpersonal communication skills.

FINANCIAL ANALYSIS

Projected Profit and Loss

The profit and loss table shows positive net profit for the first fiscal year.

Annual pro forma profit and loss

	FY1
Total income	$ 20,180,000
Cost of goods sold	$ 4,200,000
Gross profit	$ 15,980,000
Gross profit %	79.19%
Expenses:	
Payroll	$ 750,150
Materials	$ 1,050,210
Accountants	$ 83,350
Legal	$ 60,000
Insurance	$ 24,000
Payroll taxes	15% $ 112,523
Total operating expenses	$ 2,080,233
Profit before interest and taxes	$ 13,899,768
Taxes incurred	$ 3,850,130
Net profit	$ 10,049,637
Net profit/sales	49.80%

Projected Cash Flow

Positive cash flows are expected starting in the first year of operation.

Annual pro forma cash flow

	FY1
Cash received	
Cash from operations:	
Cash sales	$ 19,150,000
Subtotal cash from operations	$ 19,150,000
Additional cash received	
Subtotal cash received	$ 19,150,000
Expenditures	
Expenditures from operations	
Land	$ 4,200,000
Cash Spending	$ 750,150
Payments of accounts payable	$ 5,216,213
Subtotal spent on operations	$ 10,166,363
Additional cash spent	
Subtotal cash spent	$ 10,166,363
Net cash flow	**$ 8,983,637**
Cash balance	**$ 14,783,637**

Projected Balance Sheet

The projected balance sheet is shown below. Positive net worth is estimated for the first year of operation.

Pro forma balance sheet

	FY1
Assets	
Current assets	
Cash	$ 14,783,637
Total current assets	$ 14,783,637
Long-term assets	
Land	$ 4,200,000
Total long-term assets	$ 4,200,000
Total assets	$ 18,983,637
Liabilities and owner's equity	
Long-term liabilities	
Loan	$ 10,000,000
Total liabilities	$ 10,000,000
Retained earnings	$ 8,983,637
Earnings	$ 8,983,637
Total owner's equity	$ 8,983,637
Total liabilities and owner's equity	$ 18,983,637
Net worth	**$ 8,983,637**

Construction and Home Rehabilitation Company

Pedro's Construction

41312 46th St.
Indianapolis, IN 46201

Michael G. Erker and John B. Trautmann

Pedro's Construction is in the business of restoring outdated, under–repaired homes, as well as completing some general contracting jobs.

EXECUTIVE SUMMARY

Pedro's Construction is in the business of restoring outdated, under–repaired homes to their original beauty. The method in which they do this will be calculated and precise to ensure quality work and quick turnover. The founders, Gary Briker and Bob Redding, emphasize hard work and attention to detail to ensure the end customer of a truly quality product. They are young and without distractions so they can concentrate all of their creative energy to the success of Pedro's Construction.

In addition to the founders, Pedro's Construction advisors play an essential role in the success of the company. All advisors have experience in real estate and finance and will be available to Gary and Bob throughout the life of the business. They have aligned themselves with a realtor who has extensive experience in the area of focus, Broad Ripple. In addition to geographic familiarity she also has experience working for rehabbers. Pedro's Construction possesses the necessary network and skills to make their business a survivor and a success.

Broad Ripple lies north of Indianapolis. It consists of neighborhoods in which most the homes were built before the 1950's. It is a place that recently experienced substantial growth and now is in need of residential restoration. Homes are priced low, but with work can be sold for very promising returns. Cheaper homes double in value with more ease and they carry a much lower barrier to entry. Broad Ripple is absolutely prime for sound investments and hard work.

Pedro's Construction will also be involved in general contracting for friends and family. They have a list of customers who are anxious to get them working in their homes. These extra jobs will provide additional income while they become accustomed to the ins and outs of rehabbing, after which customers will become another grape on the vine to spread the good word.

Vision
Reach perfection in the rehabilitation of family residences.

Mission

Pedro's Construction is determined to be a successful leader in home rehabilitation through ethical and socially responsible business practices. We vow to maintain a vested interest in the well being of our business and the neighborhoods in which we work.

Tagline

We help you get the home you've been dreaming of.

Company Name

The legal name of Pedro's Construction is: Pedro's Construction, LLC.

Legal Form of Business

Pedro's Construction is incorporated as an LLC at a temporary residence:

41312 46th St.

Indianapolis, IN 46201

MANAGEMENT SUMMARY

Pedro's Construction is owned and operated by Gary Briker and Bob Redding. They will act as COO and CEO, respectively. Garrett McGrath will be construction manager overseeing all on–site activity. He has extensive experience in carpentry and has worked for the past seven years on various properties in Fort Wayne. He has many repeat customers because his work is solid and he is of impeccable character. Gary Briker Sr. will be an advisor to the both Gary and Bob. Mr. Briker is an experienced and successful realtor with the necessary knowledge to help direct Pedro's Construction in the right direction.

Management Background

Gary Briker, Co–President and COO
BSBA, Purdue University—Graduate 2005: emphasis in entrepreneurial studies; Bachelors Degree in the area of psychology.

Gary Briker has three years experience in carpentry and rehabbing. He has served as an integral team member with Briker Realty tending to the care of properties. He reported directly to the CEO of Fedmann Carpentry, accumulating clientele, assisting with appraisals, and billing.

His family background includes experience with land development, real estate buying and selling, and residential restoration. His father owns and operates the real estate company, Briker Realty, in addition to owning several apartment buildings and restaurants. Gary has worked closely with his father gathering experience buying and selling homes, as well as renovating homes. Also, the Briker family owned and operated a prominent land development company in Bloomington, Indiana.

Gary Briker was a consultant to a start up business, The Bar and Tavern. He dealt with market analysis, financing, cost assessment and talent accumulation. This experience has facilitated with this business plan in the areas of finance and market analysis. The owner, Matthew, was very pleased with the completed project and presentation.

Bob Redding, Co–President and CEO
BSBA, Ball State University—Graduate 2005: emphasis on management and entrepreneurial studies.

Bob Redding's family background is in residential, commercial real estate and speculative land development. His grandfather owns Redding Realty and Building Co. located in Fort Wayne, IN. His uncle owns Redding Realty in Madison, Wisconsin. Bob has earned a business degree with a focus in

Entrepreneurship. His passion for entrepreneurship stems directly from his family history of starting and successfully running small businesses.

Bob Redding acted as a consultant for AnalysisNet, a business process–reengineering firm. He dealt directly with finances, product growth and development, and competitive analysis. Specifically he developed a new application of their software that will allow them to reach a previously untapped market. President, Albert Steffet, and Chief Software Architect, Wendy Barry, were happy with his performance and have offered their services if and when it is needed.

Other job experience includes managing a band for 3 years. He secured consistent paying jobs and acquired the necessary equipment to accommodate the bands growth. Since the bands break up he has successfully promoted himself as a solo artist. He created a website where you can listen to music and buy his home–recorded ten song EP. He is both manager and musician.

Pedro's Construction's biggest asset will be their owners sweat equity. Both are physically competent and intelligent men who can afford to commit all of their resources to this endeavor. Throughout the first phase of operations Gary and Bob will live in and work on their first investment. By accepting harsh living conditions for their first investment, they not only will show the extent of their dedication, but they also recognize a substantial cost savings.

Advisors

Real Estate and Finance:
Gary Briker Sr. has over 50 years experience in real estate. He has owned and operated his own brokerage firm for the last 35 years. He managed his own finances and accounting as well most other aspects of the business. He has a very impressive feel for the market. He has been involved in speculative land development for many years and continues to invest in properties that maximize his return on investment. He has never suffered a negative return.

Banking and Finance:
Gary Briker Sr. worked as the Director of Marketing for First National Bank for five years. In 1999 Mr. Briker became a financial analyst for Merrill Lynch. Mr. Briker will act as a financial analyst, weighing potential returns for our possible investments.

General Contracting:
Brett Newton started Newton Construction and has been the sole owner for twenty–five years. He allowed the company to grow a little over the years and has hired two additional employees, but has focused on maintaining a small functional business. Mr. McGrath will give us advice on the "best" way to make repairs. He will be our expertise in the field.

Architect:
Katie Weaver is a friend and associate of Jane and Ted Roth of Roth Construction. She has designed blue prints for many of Gary's jobs. They range from simple remodeling plans to more complex architectural designs for an entire home. She has the necessary experience that Pedro' Construction requires in an architect and she comes very highly recommended so trust issues will not be a problem. She was awarded first place for the residential section of International Excellence in Masonry through the MCAA Masonry showcase 2002 Review.

Real Estate:
Robyn Hill will work as our real estate agent. She has been working in Broad Ripple for the last twenty years. We believe Broad Ripple to be a sound neighborhood for investment purposes (details in market analysis). Robyn will provide us with listings and help us to identify properties that will make a good investment. She also has contacts with lenders that have dealt with other rehabbers in the area. By becoming acquainted with a good lender securing loans will become easier as we go. Because Robyn has worked with other rehabbers, she will also be able to share with us their experiences and what they have learned from them.

Staff

Garrett McGrath

Garrett has worked for the last seven years in construction with his father, Patrick McGrath. He has the skill and access to resources to become an invaluable asset. Garrett will be an independent contractor offering assistance when needed, but he will primarily be giving us direction for the first two years. We will pay Garrett 10% of repair costs for each home. In the case that a crew would need to be hired, Garrett will act as the Forman and will receive pay of $20 an hour.

Crews:

Workers will be paid $10–$15 an hour depending on experience. Specific workers will be determined by Garrett, allowing Gary and Bob to begin focusing on an increasing number of future investments and finances.

PRODUCTS

Pedro's Construction is not selling just a product but a necessity. Specifically, quality rehabilitated homes in markets that show strong growth potential. They will be focusing on homes in the Broad Ripple area that are selling "as is" for $20,000—$45,000. They have done research and found other rehabilitated homes in the area that sell for $60,000—$100,000. The homes are old and need general improvements. Pedro's Construction will be continuously receiving listings for homes in their desired market. Once an appropriate home is located the appropriate preliminary checks will be made. If there are no obvious flaws earnest money will be put down. *Earnest Money* is a payment of $1,000 or 3% of the selling price; whichever is higher. Ten days will then be allowed to perform any professional inspections and appraisals needed. Pedro's Construction will avoid homes that do not meet their criteria:

1. Significant structural damage

2. Outdated Electrical

3. Any EPA regulation violations

4. Replacement of Sewer Lines And Septic system

5. Lead Piping

Home one will be financed with a rehabber's loan from First National Bank. This loan uses the current value of the house plus cost of repairs. It requires 10% down payment. Owners–equity in the home, after repairs, must be at least 20%. This means that if we sell a home for $100,000 we would have had to put in at least $20,000 equity (repairs) in. After year one we will sell the property for an expected increase of $35,000–$45,000. In year one we will also be heavily involved in general remodeling and repairs. This will be essential to the business in its first year. Pedro's Construction has signed letters of intent from family and friends for these future jobs. Home one will be completed by month six.

In year two they will rehabilitate two to three homes depending on sale and acquisition times. There will be no change on how the company deals with their realtor and purchases homes. From year three and on they hope to rehabilitate four to six homes per year in the same fashion. This figure is based on close competitors' performance.

Beginning in year four, rental properties will be put in place. This will provide consistent rental income. Being close to Indiana University (IU) will help ensure the constancy of renters.

COMPETITION

Currently, there are 2,146 local firms that deal in residential construction and home improvement. Based on numbers from the Indianapolis Rehabbers Club, roughly 40% of these firms deal directly with home acquisition and rehabilitation. In the 317 area code there are only 21 residential construction companies. The buyers market is very competitive. The most difficult challenge we face is securing and acquiring the appropriate property. In our marketing strategies section we address how we will tackle this issue.

When beginning a new business it is as important to choose a profitable area, as it is to choose a profitable product. Pedro's Construction has chosen to enter in the area of Broad Ripple, IN because the majority of the homes in the area are those we most want to work with. However, other similar type companies feel the same way about the area. These companies make up the core of Pedro's Constructions competition.

Though Pedro's Construction deals primarily in the area of home renovation, we will also be directly and indirectly involved with real estate, property management and sub–contracting. This makes it difficult to really know where your competition comes from, and how to capture a percentage of the market in each of those areas.

First, it is appropriate to look at typical businesses that would be competing against us:

1. Family Construction—A rehab company that has been in the Broad Ripple area for two and a half years. The process in which they renovate houses will be similar to our operations. Instead of getting a line of credit to do multiple homes at once, they opted to take out a loan, and only do one or two homes at a time while doing side–contracting work to help sustain the business. The two owners of this company do all demo and construction but sub–contract out any work that requires a license. After their second year they make around $80,000 a year using this method.

2. Equity Line Co.—A rehab company that has been in operation for roughly four years. They utilize a half million dollar line of credit to put a down payment on homes in which they are interested. The line of credit then pays for all rehabbing cost. They work with a larger crew because of the workload. Their profit margins are slightly higher at around $120,000 a year.

Examining the inner workings of these two companies has given us an idea of, not only what we are up against in the industry, but also what to expect from our own company.

Overall we believe that there are enough sellers to warrant entry into the industry. End sales will always be possible. Focusing on creative and effective ways to win motivated buyers as well as cultivating a lasting relationship with our realtor will be our road to success.

Competitive Advantages

Now that Pedro's Construction knows the industry both nationally and regionally, we can find ways to set our self apart from the other contractors. Our competitive advantages are:

1. Sweat Equity

2. Realtor: Robyn Hill

3. Forman: Garrett McGrath

The most important competitive advantage Pedro's Construction boasts is their sweat equity. Gary and Bob have the advantage of being young and without personal ties allowing them to focus all their energy on this start–up. The first house will be able to be completed through our sweat and legwork. They will live in home one while completing the repairs, allowing them to cut costs. In addition, they will have work doing sub–contracting for family and friends.

Robyn has had many years of experience in the Broad Ripple area and will be able to provide numerous homes within their price range quickly and effectively. She has access to the MLS so houses entering the market will be available as timely as possible. As previously noted, she also has experience with other rehabbers and will be able to share her knowledge and experience with them. If Pedro's Construction does well, Robyn does well. Because of Robyn's years in the Broad Ripple market she has a trusted reputation within the neighborhood. This will cut down on turnover time. Additionally, even though they may not be faster than some competitors, effective marketing will get homes sold before completion. Robyn offers this extra exposure.

Garrett McGrath has worked for a general contractor since 1998. Over the years he has formed relationships with sub–contractors and architects he knows to be reliable. In speaking with other rehabbers it was discovered that reliable and trustworthy sub–contractors play a vital role in success. Reliable team members allow for efficient and accurate time schedules. Garrett enables Pedro's Construction to avoid the costly hassle of finding trustworthy contractors. Additionally, Garrett will be able to offer the customers a level of quality that is on par or above competitors. Attention to detail is important in everything that you do, but when it comes to houses, attention to the small things can mean the difference between selling and being stuck with loan payments for longer then you can afford. Before the house is sold Pedro's Construction will leave no stone unturned, both in cosmetics and in carpentry work. A final inspection will ensure the house will be repaired with full functionality and restored to original beauty.

MARKET ANALYSIS

Demographics

Total population is 29,172 for the 46220 zip code. The Median age is 28 years. This represents a market this is primed for both buying and renting. Approximately 22% of Broad Ripple are college graduates and/or enrolled in college. As students graduate and get jobs many will upgrade their living arrangements. When they move out an opportunity to buy their newly vacated homes presents itself.

The median household income is $32,422. Below is a list of home values from 1999. These are the most prevalent home prices in the 317 area code:

1. $35,000 to $39,999: 488

2. $40,000 to $49,999: 1451

3. $50,000 to $59,999: 1284

4. $60,000 to $69,999: 953

5. $70,000 to $79,999: 582

6. $80,000 to $89,999: 337

7. $90,000 to $99,999: 292

The majority of these homes were built before 1950 so many need to be rehabbed.

Market Opportunities

In the 1990's the 46220 zip code began to go through a period of growth. Broad Ripple had seen a 15% increase in population by the turn of the century. Over the last few years, Broad Ripple has had approximately a 1% annual population loss. There are available property investments to be had because of these recent trends. One factor in the recent population decrease is that the majority of the homes, as stated before, are valued lower than average because of their dilapidated condition. By physically increasing the value of the homes, and consequentially the surrounding neighborhoods, there will be little problems selling the rehabilitated homes.

Industry analysis

	Firms	Small business	Startups
Year 1 average sales	$ 966,412	$ 527,935	$ 355,383
Year 2 average sales	$ 980,924	$ 479,471	$ 307,123
Year 3 average sales	$ 1,203,576	$ 491,087	$ 421,901
Change: year 1 to year 3	24.54%	−6.98%	18.72%
Survivor average sales	$ 1,590,474	$ 597,182	$ 534,188
Change: year 1 to year 3	64.58%	13.12%	50.31%

Currently, the industry average for start–up companies in residential construction within mid size cities is approaching 1500 firms. Based on this information one can conclude that creating a business in this industry is very feasible. However, to know if another rehabbing company can thrive in this market it is imperative to analyze further. In the next section Pedro's Construction will analyze the areas of failure rates, industry market volume, average sales, average staffing, and emerging vitality trends.

Industry analysis

	Year 1 firms	Year 3 survivors	Failure rates
Firms	35,271	23,676	32.87%
Establishments	35,962	24,112	32.95%
Small business	34,087	22,751	33.26%
Startups	1,737	1,053	39.38%
Branches	691	404	41.53%

Failure rates are based on the average number of start–up companies in year one divided by the number of survivor companies (companies still in existence in year three). Currently, in the industry of residential construction, the failure rate is slightly below forty percent. Compared to the national average of 20%–30%, it is a bit high, but still reasonable. With dedication, a strong work ethic and careful planning success in this industry, based on failure rate percentages, is more then possible. The failure rate is higher than average because new comers jump into the business with little to no preparation. In recent years "rehabbing" has developed the misconception that anyone can do it, all you need is a home. Failures don't have enough cash flow to sustain slow periods, they don't know the markets well enough, they lacked the expertise (hired or personal) to finish a job, and they make poorly researched investments. Pedro's Construction has performed the proper market research and aligned themselves with knowledgeable and experienced associates to effectively and efficiently complete jobs.

To date, the industry creates forty–four billion dollars. This industry carries more value then any other, and is always appreciating. Obviously, start–up companies only capture a small portion of the local market, average sales in year one being three hundred and fifty–five thousand. However, the average sales growth trend from year to year is nearly a nineteen percent increase. Sales from year one to year three increase over fifty percent. After year three a survivor is projected to reach average sales of greater then five hundred thousand dollars.

According to the national average, start up companies in the residential renovation industry can sustain their business with three employees. After this point the extra cost associated with hiring an extra employee can be detrimental to the profit margin, the lifeblood of the company. Thus, even after year three most companies in this area of work choose to only keep three employees.

Industry analysis

	Year 1 employees	Year 2 employees	Year 3 employees	Year 4 employees
Industry	4	4	4	5
Small business	3	3	3	3
Startups	3	2	3	3
Branches	14	14	14	14

Extra cost associated with extra workers include tools, pay roll, and most notably, insurance. These extra costs alone can make or break the very delicate first years of business. However there are disadvantages to low number of employees. Because of the limited work force, growth might be slow for the first years of business or until you have more working capital.

Current and future vitality is indicated by area entrepreneurial activity, new branch development and concentrations of high growth firms measured by sales and employment. Industry indices above one surpass economy–wide patterns by the margin indicated, while indices below one fall behind overall trends. These numbers speak well for start up residential contractors, whose vitality numbers are well above one. In other words, those in this area of business have a higher entrepreneurial value, thus having a greater chance of success in the market place.

End Customer

The Real Estate Investment industry is extremely varied. Basically we are looking for potential home-owners who do not want to be seller financed and have the equity to purchase $60,000–$100,000 homes. Efforts will be focused on the IU student population.

Marketing Strategy

The primary strategy for Pedro's Construction is to find motivated sellers. Through communications with many in the industry we have discovered that the buyers market, as a whole, is fairly competitive. What does this mean? It means that houses are easy to find, easy to sell, but difficult to buy. However, in the Broad Ripple area competition is not as fierce. Many acceptable homes have been on the market for 100+ days. By working closely with an experienced realtor who is acquainted with the market homes will be able to be purchased without much problem. Though there are and will continue to be those with deeper pockets and the ability to offer a more appealing "best or highest offer," the market is volatile enough to sustain all.

Pedro's Construction will piggyback off of Robyn Hill's current reputation as a respected and successful realtor in the area. Robyn and her brokerage firm will primarily handle the sale and acquisition of all properties. By continuing to build ties through family, contracting work, and dealings with area sub–contractors and architects: Pedro's Construction will develop a reputation as reliable and skilful rehabbers.

Rentals, to begin in year four, will utilize a similar strategy. All rental properties will be listed on the MLS. Pedro's Construction will also take advantage of their proximity to IU by distributing fliers on campus and by purchasing space in their student newspaper. The cost of a color advertisement, an eighth of a page, is $174.50. 56% of the properties in this area are rentals so a newly renovated property will be easy to rent out.

Sales Strategy

Pedro's Construction is approaching this from a Realtor's perspective. People need homes and they are in the business of rebuilding and selling them. By looking at the current market value of comparables and census reports of population trends, an accurate idea will be had of what constitutes a safe investment. A rehabilitated home in the Broad Ripple area sells from $60,000–$100,000. These numbers have been confirmed by their realtor and through MLS listings. A key component in this is the understanding that the market is perfectly competitive. Pedro's Construction has little to no power to set prices. The way to value a home is to look at comparables and appraise it appropriately. In order estimate a home's future value, one must add the value of amenities that will be added.

Possible investment properties require a 100+% increase in sale price from the acquisition cost. It must be noted that this impressive increase in value is not the standard. The homes Pedro's Construction will be buying cost only $20,000–$45,000. Typically, $15,000 are sunk in repairs making a 100+% return expected and necessary. Estimating repair costs involves hiring contractors to come to the property and give a bid. Details to be explored in the financials, specifically cash flow analysis and income statements.

Again, Sales will be handled through Robyn Hill and Associates real estate services.

FINANCIAL ANALYSIS

Base Home

Financials begin with the analysis of a prospective home. An amortization schedule has been created based on an interest rate of 6.75%. 41558 Sunshine Dr. is a single–family 2–bedroom 1–bath home that will be acquired for $35,000. A bid has been made for repairs that total $14,401. Repair costs include labor, which will be absorbed over the course of the rehab. The value after repairs is $49,401. The final loan amount will be $44,461 after the 10% down payment of $4,940.

Repairs will be completed and the home will be sold within six months. During those six months Gary and Bob will be staying at the property in order to cut costs. Rehabilitated comparables to 41558 Sunshine Dr. are selling for $75,000–$80,000. Selling price of our property is $77,500. The profit after taxes will be $17,642.06. This includes $12,000 earned doing outside contracting work. Sunk costs, which will be avoided hereafter, include legal fees of $1,000 and tool costs of $5,000. This gives a return of $11,642.06 profit on the house alone.

Projections and forecasts

In order to create accurate forecasts a ratio had to be developed to find net sales. First, stripping down the after tax net income by:

1. Adding sunk costs
2. Subtracting supplementary contracting income
3. Adding in loan payments for unnecessary additional months

This gives an estimated profit per home of $11,112.28. Take that number and double it for the two homes sold in year one to get $22,224.56. By taking year one's profit estimation and dividing it by year one's total net sales the divider 0.17 is attained. Assume four homes are completed in year two, and six homes are completed in years three and on. Multiply those respective numbers of average home profit and divide that number by 0.17 to calculate net sales for each year. Making most other costs a percentage of net sales, allows for accurate projections.

In years two, three, four and five earnings will be $56.330.37, $75,250.97, $66,695.96, and $67,856.38 profit respectively. Lower profits in years four and five reflect holding on to one property each year for renting. All costs associated with holding onto a home have been changed accordingly. Net sales are $50,000 less. Repair costs have been reduced as well, because the rental properties will not require as much work.

Rental cash flows came from an example home that was purchased for $25,000. It is assumed that rent will be $460 a month, including an allowance for one month of vacancy each year. After all expenses are taken out $1,234.88 will be earned per year. In year five this number doubles because of another rental property added. In year six, after tax income will total $77,720.73. This is $38,860.36 each, a respectable income after six years.

Financing

Pedro's Construction will be utilizing a Rehab Loan through First National Bank. It is a 90% LTV loan that includes the cost of repairs. Owners–equity in the home, after repairs, must be at least 20%. This means that if a home is sold for $100,000, at least $20,000 would have to be in equity (repairs). This Rehabbers loan will continue to be used until year five.

Amortization schedule home 1a

	Yearly	Monthly	PVIFA
Loan amount	$ 44,460.90		Present value interest factor for annuities
Rate	6.75%	0.5625%	Annuity PV = C(1−[1/(1+ r)^t]/r)
Term	30		
Monthly payment	$ 288.37		

Month	Beg. balance	Total payment	Interest paid	Principle paid	Ending balance
1	$ 44,460.90	$ 288.37	$ 250.09	$ 38.28	$ 44,422.62
2	$ 44,422.62	$ 288.37	$ 249.88	$ 38.50	$ 44,384.12
3	$ 44,384.12	$ 288.37	$ 249.66	$ 38.71	$ 44,345.41
4	$ 44,345.41	$ 288.37	$ 249.44	$ 38.93	$ 44,306.48
5	$ 44,306.48	$ 288.37	$ 249.22	$ 39.15	$ 44,267.33
6	$ 44,267.33	$ 288.37	$ 249.00	$ 39.37	$ 44,227.97

Amortization schedule home 2a

	Yearly	Monthly	PVIFA
Loan amount	$ 27,375.21		Present value interest factor for annuities
Rate	6.75%	0.5625%	Annuity PV = C(1−[1/(1+ r)^t]/r)
Term	30		
Monthly payment	$ 177.56		

Month	Beg. balance	Total payment	Interest paid	Principle paid	Ending balance
1	$ 27,375.21	$ 177.56	$ 153.99	$ 23.57	$ 27,351.64
2	$ 27,351.64	$ 177.56	$ 153.85	$ 23.70	$ 27,327.94
3	$ 27,327.94	$ 177.56	$ 153.72	$ 23.84	$ 27,304.10
4	$ 27,304.10	$ 177.56	$ 153.59	$ 23.97	$ 27,280.13
5	$ 27,280.13	$ 177.56	$ 153.45	$ 24.10	$ 27,256.03
6	$ 27,256.03	$ 177.56	$ 153.32	$ 24.24	$ 27,231.79

Year 1 income statement

	Prior to Month −1	Month −1	Month 1	Month 2	Month 3
Net sales	$ 0.00	$ 0.00	$ 0.00	$ 0.00	$ 0.00
Supplemetary contract work	$ 1,500.00	$ 1,500.00	$ 1,500.00	$ 1,500.00	$ 1,500.00
Cost of goods sold	$ 0.00	$ 0.00	($ 4,940.10)	$ 0.00	$ 0.00
Gross income	$ 1,500.00	$ 1,500.00	($ 3,440.10)	$ 1,500.00	$ 1,500.00
Operating expenses:					
Tools	$ 5,000.00	$ 0.00	$ 0.00	$ 0.00	$ 0.00
Home owners insurance	$ 1.00	$ 0.00	$ 150.00	$ 150.00	$ 150.00
Legal	$ 1,000.00	$ 0.00	$ 0.00	$ 0.00	$ 0.00
Phone	$ 0.00	$ 40.00	$ 40.00	$ 40.00	$ 40.00
Contractor estimates	$ 0.00	$ 150.00	$ 0.00	$ 0.00	$ 0.00
Repairs	$ 0.00	$ 0.00	$ 14,401.00	$ 0.00	$ 0.00
Labor (50% of repair costs)	$ 0.00	$ 0.00	($ 7,200.50)	$ 0.00	$ 0.00
Total operating expenses	$ 6,000.00	$ 190.00	$ 7,390.50	$ 190.00	$ 190.00
Other expenses:					
Mortgage payments	$ 0.00	$ 0.00	$ 288.37	$ 288.37	$ 288.37
Appraisal	$ 0.00	$ 150.00	$ 0.00	$ 0.00	$ 0.00
Inspection	$ 0.00	$ 200.00	$ 0.00	$ 0.00	$ 0.00
Realtor listing and closing fee	$ 0.00	$ 0.00	$ 1,155.00	$ 0.00	$ 0.00
Early payment fee (2% balance)	$ 0.00	$ 0.00	$ 0.00	$ 0.00	$ 0.00
Payment of note due	$ 0.00	$ 0.00	$ 0.00	$ 0.00	$ 0.00
Total other expenses	$ 0.00	$ 350.00	$ 1,443.37	$ 288.37	$ 288.37

Net operating income
Tax on income (6.03%)
After tax net income
[continued]

Year 1 income statement [CONTINUED]

	Month 4	Month 5	Month 6	Month 7	Month 8
Net sales	$ 0.00	$ 0.00	$ 77,500.00	$ 0.00	$ 0.00
Supplemetary contract work	$ 1,500.00	$ 1,500.00	$ 1,500.00	$ 1,500.00	$ 1,500.00
Cost of goods sold	$ 0.00	$ 0.00	$ 0.00	($ 3,041.69)	$ 0.00
Gross income	$ 1,500.00	$ 1,500.00	$ 79,000.00	($ 1,541.69)	$ 1,500.00
Operating expenses:					
Tools	$ 0.00	$ 0.00	$ 0.00	$ 0.00	$ 0.00
Home owners insurance	$ 150.00	$ 150.00	$ 150.00	$ 150.00	$ 150.00
Legal	$ 0.00	$ 0.00	$ 0.00	$ 0.00	$ 0.00
Phone	$ 40.00	$ 40.00	$ 40.00	$ 40.00	$ 40.00
Contractor estimates	$ 0.00	$ 0.00	$ 150.00	$ 0.00	$ 0.00
Repairs	$ 0.00	$ 0.00	$ 0.00	$ 8,866.90	$ 0.00
Labor (50% of repair costs)	$ 0.00	$ 0.00	$ 0.00	($ 4,433.45)	$ 0.00
Total operating expenses	$ 190.00	$ 190.00	$ 340.00	$ 4,623.45	$ 190.00
Other expenses:					
Mortgage payments	$ 288.37	$ 288.37	$ 288.37	$ 177.56	$ 177.56
Appraisal	$ 0.00	$ 0.00	$ 0.00	$ 150.00	$ 0.00
Inspection	$ 0.00	$ 200.00	$ 0.00	$ 200.00	$ 0.00
Realtor listing and closing fee	$ 0.00	$ 0.00	$ 2,557.50	$ 711.15	$ 0.00
Early payment fee (2% balance)	$ 0.00	$ 0.00	$ 883.77	$ 0.00	$ 0.00
Payment of note due	$ 0.00	$ 0.00	$ 44,188.38	$ 0.00	$ 0.00
Total other expenses	$ 288.37	$ 488.37	$ 47,918.02	$ 1,238.71	$ 177.56

Net operating income
Tax on income (6.03%)
After tax net income
[continued]

Year 1 income statement [CONTINUED]

	Month 9	Month 10	Month 11	Month 12	Total
Net sales	$ 0.00	$ 0.00	$ 0.00	$ 49,931.52	$ 127,431.52
Supplemetary contract work	$ 1,500.00	$ 1,500.00	$ 1,500.00	$ 1,500.00	$ 21,000.00
Cost of goods sold	$ 0.00	$ 0.00	$ 0.00	$ 0.00	($ 7,981.79)
Gross income	$ 1,500.00	$ 1,500.00	$ 1,500.00	$ 51,431.52	$ 140,449.73
Operating expenses:					
Tools	$ 0.00	$ 0.00	$ 0.00	$ 0.00	$ 5,000.00
Home owners insurance	$ 150.00	$ 150.00	$ 150.00	$ 150.00	$ 1,800.00
Legal	$ 0.00	$ 0.00	$ 0.00	$ 0.00	$ 1,000.00
Phone	$ 40.00	$ 40.00	$ 40.00	$ 40.00	$ 520.00
Contractor estimates	$ 0.00	$ 0.00	$ 0.00	$ 0.00	$ 300.00
Repairs	$ 0.00	$ 0.00	$ 0.00	$ 0.00	$ 23,267.90
Labor (50% of repair costs)	$ 0.00	$ 0.00	$ 0.00	$ 0.00	($ 11,633.95)
Total operating expenses	$ 190.00	$ 190.00	$ 190.00	$ 190.00	$ 20,253.95
Other expenses:	$ 177.56	$ 177.56	$ 177.56	$ 177.56	$ 2,795.57
Mortgage payments	$ 0.00	$ 0.00	$ 0.00	$ 0.00	$ 300.00
Appraisal	$ 0.00	$ 0.00	$ 200.00	$ 0.00	$ 800.00
Inspection	$ 0.00	$ 0.00	$ 0.00	$ 1,398.08	$ 5,821.73
Realtor listing and closing fee	$ 0.00	$ 0.00	$ 0.00	$ 544.64	$ 1,428.40
Early payment fee (2% balance)	$ 0.00	$ 0.00	$ 0.00	$ 27,231.79	$ 71,420.16
Payment of note due	$ 177.56	$ 177.56	$ 377.56	$ 29,352.06	$ 82,565.87
Total other expenses					
Net operating income					$ 37,629.91
Tax on income (6.03%)					$ 2,269.08
After tax net income					$ 35,360.83

Cash flow statement of rentals

Gross rents (1)	$ 5,520.00
Less: vacancies (1 every 4 months)	$ 460.00
Net rents	$ 5,060.00
Operating expenses (2)	$ 1,904.08
Operating income	$ 3,155.92
Less other expenses:	$ 2,166.37
Tax depreciation (3)	$ 704.73
Interest on mortgage	$ 1,461.65
Taxable income	$ 989.55
Income tax (31%)	$ 306.76
Net income	$ 682.79
Cash flow from operations:	$ 552.09
Plus tax depreciation	$ 704.73
Mortgage principle paid	$ 152.64
Net cash flow	$ 1,234.88

Operating expenses: Percentages of net rents

Hazard insurance	3.91%
Maintenance & repairs	20.00%
Management fees	0.00%
Property taxes	7.25%
Utilities	2.00%
Advertising	1.00%
Supplies	1.22%
Replacement reserve	0.00%
Misc.	2.25%

5 year income statement

	Year 1	Year 2	Year 3	Year 4	Year 5
Net sales	$ 127,431.52	$ 261,465.41	$ 392,208.71	$ 342,208.71	$ 342,208.71
Supplemetary contract work	$ 21,000.00	$ 11,000.00	$ 5,500.00	$ 5,500.00	$ 5,500.00
Cost of goods sold	$ (7,981.79)	$ (16,377.13)	$ (24,566.35)	$ (21,434.56)	$ (21,434.56)
Gross income	**$ 140,449.73**	**$ 256,088.28**	**$ 373,142.36**	**$ 326,274.15**	**$ 326,274.15**
Operating expenses:					
Tools	$ 5,000.00	$ 0.00	$ 0.00	$ 0.00	$ 0.00
Home owners insurance	$ 1,800.00	$ 1,800.00	$ 1,800.00	$ 1,800.00	$ 1,800.00
Legal	$ 1,000.00	$ 0.00	$ 0.00	$ 0.00	$ 0.00
Phone	$ 520.00	$ 520.00	$ 520.00	$ 520.00	$ 520.00
Contractor estimates	$ 300.00	$ 600.00	$ 900.00	$ 900.00	$ 900.00
Repairs	$ 23,267.90	$ 47,741.34	$ 71,613.94	$ 62,484.37	$ 62,484.37
Labor (50% of repair costs)	$ (11,633.95)	$ (23,870.67)	$ (35,806.97)	$ (31,242.18)	$ (31,242.18)
Total operating expenses	$ 20,253.95	$ 26,790.67	$ 39,026.97	$ 34,462.18	$ 34,462.18
Other expenses:					
Mortgage payments	$ 2,795.57	$ 5,735.98	$ 8,604.20	$ 7,507.31	$ 7,507.31
Appraisal	$ 300.00	$ 600.00	$ 900.00	$ 900.00	$ 900.00
Inspection	$ 800.00	$ 1,600.00	$ 2,400.00	$ 2,400.00	$ 2,400.00
Realtor listing and closing fee	$ 5,821.73	$ 11,945.09	$ 17,918.12	$ 15,633.86	$ 15,633.86
Early payment fee (2% balance)	$ 1,428.40	$ 2,930.81	$ 4,396.33	$ 3,835.87	$ 3,835.87
Payment of note due	$ 71,420.16	$ 146,540.68	$ 219,816.96	$ 191,794.00	$ 191,794.00
Total other expenses	$ 82,565.86	$ 169,352.56	$ 254,035.61	$ 222,071.05	$ 222,071.05
Rentals	$ 0.00	$ 0.00	$ 0.00	$ 1,234.88	$ 2,469.76
Net operating income	$ 37,629.92	$ 59,945.06	$ 80,079.78	$ 70,975.80	$ 72,210.68
Tax on income (6.03%)	$ 2,269.08	$ 3,614.69	$ 4,828.81	$ 4,279.84	$ 4,354.30
After tax net income	$ 35,360.84	$ 56,330.37	$ 75,250.97	$ 66,695.96	$ 67,856.38

Daycare Facility
Rachel's Clubhouse

2 Sandy Hollow
Sunset, IN 47400

Tony Tecce

This short, concise business plan raised $25,000 in funding for the owner of a daycare facility opened in a small community in great need of such an operation. The business was sold when the owner decided to move out of state to be closer to family.

EXECUTIVE SUMMARY

Rachel's Clubhouse (the "Company") will fill the void for a first–class daycare facility in Sunset, Indiana. There has long been a shortage for quality daycare due to the lack of availability of a competent location. However, a location now has become vacant and is perfect for the Company. Planning for this business has been ongoing for over four years by management. The total cost of getting the Company in operation is $700,000, which includes building/property acquisition, renovation, equipment and operating capital. The Company intends to raise all of the project's costs through this offering.

Background

Currently there is only one commercial daycare in Sunset, Indiana. There are other after–school programs and the like, but only one that offers daycare for infants as well as toddlers. Over four years ago the other commercial daycare, West Aurora Daycare, was closed due to possible child abuse. During the time following the closure we have been trying to find a suitable location to satisfy the Betow County Social Services licensing requirements. After numerous licensing attempts, the building itself was always the problem.

To obtain a license there needs to be 34 sq. ft. per child inside the building, 37 sq. ft. per child of fenced outdoor area, and level entry to the building. To our surprise, there are not too many qualified buildings for sale or lease in Sunset, Indiana.

The Clubhouse Experience

Our goal at Rachel's Clubhouse is to encourage creativity, individuality, and independence. We have created an environment filled with love, patience and kindness.

The staff at the Clubhouse is qualified in Early Childhood Education; each teacher plays an important role. We always keep in mind that children learn through example and often mirror adults. We set our standards high and expect our staff to set through example.

We have a set curriculum for both age groups; infant through two years, and three years through five years.

73

Our infant/toddler class will encourage the children to explore and discover his or her world daily. This will be accented with the use of sensory activities and language development (children will learn by "doing"). The teacher will provide the parent with a weekly goal, in keeping with the learning environment. Parents are always welcome to take part in classroom activities and share ideas with teachers who are always happy to discuss concerns or answer questions.

The discovery class, ages three through five years, will do just what the name suggests. This class will learn through discovery centers set up on a weekly rotating basis. The learning centers will vary from science, language, math, housekeeping, daily life skills, and social development.

For the curious parent, we will have two live web cams hooked up to the Internet. Every 15 seconds a picture of the play area will be uploaded to our Web site. This will allow the parent or other relatives to check up on what their child is up to, any time of the day.

Along with teacher instruction, the child will have the opportunity to develop his or her own hands–on learning style, giving the child the chance to learn at his or her own pace, allowing them to master a skill that which they are comfortable.

Teachers will provide the parent with a weekly goal sheet encouraging parents to take part in the weekly lesson and reinforce the daily learning experience at home. On a daily basis children will be given the chance to work with computers, musical instruments, large muscle equipment, manipulative items (i.e., blocks) and arts and crafts.

OBJECTIVES

The Company plans on being open for daycare by Fall 2006. By the third year of operation we will expand the infant care, tripling the capacity.

The projected revenues are based on five infants and forty toddlers/walk–ins per day. We will be the only facility open seven days a week. Based on these occupancy rates, our first year revenues are projected at $415,000 with pre–tax profits of $166,000. These numbers will create a return of investment (ROI) of 10 percent during the first year. There is enough space to expand in the future, depending on demand.

Location Selection

At present, we have located a suitable building for purchase. The asking price is $399,000 which includes 3,000 sq. ft. of Commercial Floor Space (C.F.S.). A daycare facility does not require the use of C.F.S., the value of which is between $100,000 and $130,000 and can be sold off or used elsewhere by the equity investor. Renovation will be needed to the parking area, landscape and interior of the building. Many of the interior changes being made are to conform with ADA requirements.

This property is located at 2 Sandy Hollow in Sunset, Indiana (the old Weaver Cotton building).

MARKETING & SALES

Our target market is Sunset, Indiana families with young children. As of the most recent demographic analysis for the Sunset area shows 6.4 percent (458) of the population is between the ages of 0 and 5 years. We will target these families through some print advertising and a mass mailing.

Also, we have secured and exclusive agreement with Highland Brown Insurance (2,000 employees) making us their weekend daycare facility. All of their promotional literature will list Rachel's Clubhouse as the facility for any daycare needs. Parents will be given beepers to notify them if there are any problems with their child.

The print advertising will be placed in the local newspaper announcing the opening of the daycare. Along with the ads, we have a connection at the paper for a "Business Brief" article that will not cost any money, the best free publicity available in Sunset. We plan to have the article printed well in advance of opening to facilitate pre–enrollment.

Shortly following the release of the newspaper article, we plan to do a mass mailing to every box holder and household in Sunset and Crystal Lake. There are 7,000 boxes and 250 home delivery and at a rate of 11.2 cents per piece, this is a very affordable and effective way to advertise.

We have had enough inquiries to date, through word–of–mouth, to be completely pre–enrolled before opening the doors to the business. Obviously there is great demand for a facility such as ours.

COMPETITION

Competition consists of Teeney Weeney Tots, Lucky Kids Club, the Baptist Church's Sunrise Nursery School and home daycare.

Teeney Weeney Tots is Sunset's only full–time, commercial daycare. They take children Monday through Friday from 7:30 a.m. to 6 p.m. They will be our only direct competition. But, direct competition in the sense that they provide a similar service; they consistently have a waiting list for children needing daycare. Quality of service has always been a question when Teeney Weeney Tots is concerned: Poor teaching, poor supervision and limited space are some of their shortcomings.

The remaining licensed competition falls into two categories: part–time commercial and home daycares. The part–time daycare facilities run either limited days through the week or only a few hours during the day. These types of facilities do not offer a full–time daycare. For instance, the Sunrise Nursery School offers either two– or three–day sessions (only three hours per day.) These types of services also restrict the age of the child, accepting none under the age of three years.

MANAGEMENT SUMMARY

The management team consists of Edward and Rachel Browning. Both have qualifications that will be essential to the Company. Edward has the business savvy and Rachel has the childhood development experience.

Edward owns and operates several local businesses. His experience covers all aspects of business, including start–up, bookkeeping, marketing, graphic design, computer consulting and teaching.

Rachel is currently licensed with the local County Social Services Dept. for home daycare. She has been operating a home daycare for five years with over eight years of childcare experience. She is the key to the Company, not only due to her experience, but notoriety within Sunrise as a long–time resident.

FINANCIAL ANALYSIS

The Company wishes to raise $700,000 to carry out the goals mentioned in this plan. The total amount to be raised can be offset by a lesser purchase price for the property, as well as the value of the C.F.S. that can be used or sold off by the equity investor.

The investment provider will receive 50 percent share ownership of the Company. The projected first–year return on investment is 10 percent, increasing to 17 percent by the third year.

Giftware Company

Jenni Frey Gifts

35 Magnolia Dr.
Atlanta, GA 30301

Adam Greengrass

This business plan garnered $5 million for a growth–oriented company that designs and distributes social and personal expression giftware. The firm currently features celebration plates and bow ties and scarves, and other products are under development. They're all designed to evoke positive feelings which result in impulse purchases by consumers.

EXECUTIVE SUMMARY

Services

Jenni Frey Gifts (JFG) is a growth–oriented company that designs and distributes social and personal expression giftware. The company currently features celebration plates and bow ties and scarves, and other products are under development. JFG's products are designed to evoke positive feelings that result in their impulse purchase by consumers.

The giftware industry is searching for companies that have unique products and know–how to build market share and position their brands. JFG has a long history of accomplishing market leadership worldwide.

Being successful in this industry is not about developing products as much as it is about developing concepts. JFG addresses the needs of their market demographics by selling the concept, which is driven by the impression that is made on the consumer by a particular product with a particular design and expression.

Few people walk into a gift shop thinking they are going to purchase a pair of bow ties and scarves or a celebration plate. Yet when a consumer sees a product with just the right design and expression, it becomes just the right gift. This impulsive purchase happens because of the connection that the item creates in the mind of the purchaser between themselves and the gift recipient. It is this perception of positive reciprocity that drives the item's purchase. When this perceived value is combined with a price tag under $10, the result is a sale.

Corporate Background

JFG's history started in 1959 when Jenni Frey's father established a chain of retail giftware stores in North Carolina in prime retail locations that key resorts and hotels, and major regional malls. In 1968 a new company was spun off from this early venture called Jenni Frey Imports, which later became Frey Giftware.

Frey Giftware developed the concept of the 'name' celebration plate and began selling it in 1974. At that time celebration plates were not commonly found in gift shops and were considered to belong primarily in the houseware or tabletop industry. Jenni Frey had a vision of a celebration plate that was more than something found in one's kitchen. Her vision was of a new product that could double both as a useful product as well as one that conveys sentiment.

In 1974, Frey Giftware faced an uphill challenge. Many giftware shop owners initially questioned the value of selling celebration plates in their stores and many sales reps wouldn't represent them because there was no existing market for them. What was needed was for a new market to be created, and that is exactly what Jenni Frey set out to do. Utilizing her proven bow ties and scarves in marketing, sales, and distribution, Jenni Frey created an entire industry.

Within two years, Frey Giftware was selling millions of celebration plates, mostly to those same retailers who had initially rejected the idea. Seeing the new untapped market, sales reps were making significant commissions representing Frey's products to this industry. The most successful of these sales reps realized that what they were selling was not a celebration plate—it was a 'me–to–you' product, long before that term was coined.

From their initial concept of the name celebration plate, Frey Giftware ultimately expanded into many other giftware concepts including other expressive celebration plates, glassware, picture frames, key rings, magnets, T–shirts, caps, and numerous other products.

Over the course of the next decade, Frey Giftware continued to sell celebration plates and social and personal expression giftware, eventually branching out internationally, driving the establishment of the 'me–to–you' giftware market. Frey Giftware became not only the leader in celebration plates but in introducing major gift themes to retailers throughout the world.

Frey Giftware was sold to FunToys in 1990 and Jenni Frey continued to lead Product Development for the firm through 1993. Frey Giftware today is merged with HouseWheres, a leader in the home decor industry. Frey Giftware and FunToys are major leaders in the giftware industry today.

From 1991 to 1997, Jenni Frey focused her efforts on her accumulated portfolio of over 2,500 celebration plate designs, licensing them to such firms such as Todd', Druki, Bruin, and Otaki. There are still many companies today that continue to pay licensing fees to Jenni Frey Designs.

In 2000, Jenni Frey once again developed a potentially explosive sales concept—personalized and expression bow ties and scarves. The concept of selling bow ties and scarves as a giftware item is as new today as celebration plates were in the 1970s. Therefore, Jenni Frey Designs began directly importing personalized and expression bow ties and scarves for wholesale distribution to the retail giftware market.

Objectives
Jenni Frey's vision for Jenni Frey Designs is to do the same thing with other merchandise that she did with celebration plates years earlier. Giftware shops today do not sell bow ties and scarves because they aren't generally considered to be giftware items. JFG is already starting to change this pattern.

JFG has created the concept of the 'fun–to–wear' product. To date, JFG has developed over 500 uniquely designed expressively labeled bow ties and scarves for this concept. These bow ties and scarves convey the 'me–to–you' sentiments necessary for product success in this market. JFG's vision is to use bow ties and scarves as the foundation for a new line of wearable products based on the personally expressive fun–to–wear concept. Utilizing their existing portfolio of designs and expressions, JFG intends to build brand awareness and to generate revenue by creating a demand for personalized bow ties and scarves as a giftware item.

Mission

JFG's mission is to establish the company in the trade and consumer markets, as a leader in creating innovative product concepts and designs to satisfy the personal and social expression needs of targeted market demographics. JFG intends to build brand awareness and sales strategies that bring revenue to retail stores that will carry the JFG product line. To accomplish this, JFG will:

1. Create and maintain a unique line of personal and social expression product concepts;

2. Position the JFG brand in the minds of both the trade and the consumer as providing: a. Creative products for communicating personal and social thoughts in a unique way; and b. Quality products priced within reach of all consumers;

3. Establish a marketing organization capable of forcing distribution of products with department stores, national general merchandise chains, upper–end mass merchants and card and gift shops;

4. Establish warehouse and production facilities and create an operating organization capable of providing, timely, error–free service to JFG's customers;

5. Drive the sales force to be capable of commanding the attention of target classes of retail trade, and achieving broad, deep distribution of products with those retailers; and

6. Drive inherent value and customer satisfaction throughout the entire customer life–cycle relationship.

GROWTH STRATEGY

The primary goal of the company's marketing and growth efforts will be to induce sales–reps to represent the JFG product line to stores in the giftware industry. With consumers always on the hunt for new items, the giftware industry is constantly in need of products such as JFG's. The company will use a variety of direct marketing campaigns targeted at sales–reps and other affiliates. The higher quality and quantity of these efforts will drive product sales, which will have a cyclical effect on the sales–reps. As they see their commissions grow, so too will their sales efforts. Revenue streams will consist primarily of product sales through independent sales reps to the retail industry. In addition, the company is in the process of adding distributors who will concentrate on alternative channels of distribution. Growth is expected to be exponential once a critical mass of retailers and distributors are reached.

The company is also increasing international distribution. Many importers today purchase JFG products, resulting in royalties for the company. So far, agreements have been finalized in Canada, United Kingdom, Australia, New Zealand, South Africa, and Singapore. Many importers in other countries have recently expressed interest in having JFG designs translated into their languages, including German, French, Spanish, and Danish. These efforts are underway.

JFG's sales strategy is to create many gift concepts and to sell the resulting product lines to the retail market, utilizing the wholesale sales–rep channel. The current product line consists of celebration plates and bow ties and scarves that fit various personal and social expression categories. At present, these categories include:

• Gifts for Birthdays with special emphasis on ages 30, 40, 50 & 60;

• Gifts for Relatives such as Mom, Dad, Grandma, and Grandpa;

• Gifts for Sports & Leisure Activities such as Golf, Tennis and Fishing;

• Gifts for Holidays, such as Valentine's Day, Mother's Day, Father's Day and Christmas;

• Unique Gifts; and

• Adult Gifts with risque content (Labeled without the JFG Brand).

The primary goal of the JFG sales strategy is to build brand recognition focusing on the additional value that JFG products bring to market, in excess of their intended product function. A pair of bow ties and scarves becomes much more than a footwear gift. It becomes a valuable and effective means for the gift purchaser to communicate their feelings with the gift recipient.

COMPETITION

Jenni Frey Designs has no direct competition in the expression bow ties and scarves market segment, and few competitors in other segments. What competition does exist comes from companies that market and sell generic expression giftware products as part of a larger giftware collection. Very few of these companies' products elicit the emotional response that JFG products do. Some of these companies include Frey Giftware and several greeting card companies. JFG competitors primarily bring one form of competition to JFG—the possibility of changing the consumers mind about the impulse buy they are about to make. Instead of competing on a personal level, they compete by confusing the buyer with products that don't 'hit home' the way JFG products do.

BUSINESS STRATEGY

The JFG business model is Design, Connect, and Sell.

- Design—JFG products are designed to have meaning, and to 'hit home' with the consumer. JFG performs extensive design evaluation and testing to assure that their products bring forth the intended response.

- Connect—JFG products create a strong emotional connection with the customer. This emotional connection happens when the purchaser identifies with the product design, while at the same time recognizing the other unique qualities of the gift.

- Sell—JFG drives sales through the impulse purchase made by the consumer when a product elicits an emotional response. The purchaser develops an instantaneous personal attachment to the product. The desire to share this attachment with the gift recipient is what drives the impulse purchase.

The combination of these three concepts creates a powerful driving force that is Jenni Frey Designs.

Growth Strategy

The business model and operations of the company are designed to be replicable to other product gift concepts. In the future, the company intends to evaluate other products that fit the gift–giving model, and incorporate those products into its product line. Some of the new products JFG is considering include glassware, picture frames, magnets, key rings, paperweights, plaques and novelty apparel items such as boxer shorts, T–shirts, aprons, and caps.

Additionally, JFG has formed a new division called Jenni Frey International (JFI). JFI maintains offices in Korea and San Francisco, and coordinates licensing and direct imports worldwide. Over 3,100 designs are presently maintained by JFG, with licensing agreements and product shipments to Canada, United Kingdom, Australia, New Zealand, South Africa, and Singapore. Moving forward, JFG will have an increasingly important role in overall JFG operations and revenue. The first major exhibition of the full range of products will occur in Hong Kong in December 2002.

OPERATIONS

An in–house staff of individuals with extensive experience in all related industries will comprise the operational team. These individuals will have, at a minimum, the following expertise:

- Product Development—focused on the ability to develop fresh, new designed giftware that has high sales potential in the giftware industry.

- Marketing—extensive knowledge of merchandising, promotions, advertising, sales, operations, and planning.

- Sales—strong administration and order processing capabilities coupled with day–to–day sales management expertise.

- Accounting—extensive capabilities in cash flow management, budgeting, and managing receivables in addition to forecasting.

Each of these operational divisions shares a focus on success, achievement, and the creation and maintenance of value and customer satisfaction.

Management Summary

The company's management team consists of three highly skilled individuals. Individually these people have extensive expertise in all the various aspects of JFG's business, and as a team they represent a level of business acumen and personal integrity that is rarely seen in the industry today. The founder of JFG is Jenni Frey. Ms. Frey's reputation and past experience is the driving force behind JFG's anticipated success. Ms. Frey has over 30 years of experience designing social expression giftware products and bringing these products to market. Her past successes include personalized name celebration plates, major gift concept centers, key licensing agreements and coordinating licensing and import programs for such major US companies as well as a long list of International companies. Ms. Frey has a Masters degree in Psychology and Marketing, with an emphasis in Consumer Behavior. As founder of JFG and Chairman of the Board, Ms. Frey personally oversees all aspects of company operations.

Financial Analysis

The line of credit being sought is $250,000, which is to be secured by inventory and receivables. We are requesting no annual cleanup requirement until the second loan year. The purpose of the credit line is to cover cash flow requirements as illustrated in the Cash Forecast and other financials, included in the Financials section of this business plan.

SUMMARY

When Jenni Frey developed the line of celebration plates for her former company, they were referred to as "The Greeting Card with No Edges." 250 million celebration plates later, people are still buying the products that she designed. The reason for this is that Jenni Frey continues to design products that appeal to the psychology of the true essence of gift giving.

To date, no one has sold bow ties and scarves as a giftware item. In the 1970s, no one sold celebration plates as a giftware item and it was Jenni Frey who had the foresight to see that a celebration plate could be much more than its function as a serving piece. Jenni Frey built the celebration plate industry and in so doing expanded the me–to–you gift concept from greeting cards to giftware. Now JFG is poised to take over the market once again, this time initiating their positioning with personal and expression bow ties and scarves.

JFG intends to capitalize on Jenni Frey's design ingenuity with the creation of an entirely new product line. This product line, presently consisting mainly of bow ties and scarves and uniquely designed celebration plates, will become as pervasive in the industry as previous Frey gift concepts have been and continue to be. Jenni Frey pioneered the social expression giftware category, and JFG intends to leverage and continue this tradition.

MARKETING & SALES

Market Analysis

In the last several years the major giftware companies such as Todd', Druki, Bruin, and Otaki, have generally transitioned away from social expression products to lifestyle products such as home and decorative accessories, and furniture related products. Concurrently the major greeting card companies such as Hallmark, American Greetings, and Recycled Paper, have also transitioned back to basic greeting cards, stationery and party goods. With the exception of seasonal holiday gifts, many of these companies have totally abandoned the personal and expression gift category.

Ten years ago, the market for personal and expression celebration plates and ceramic giftware was saturated with many companies offering many products. Over time, all of these companies sought out ways to differentiate and focus their product lines, and today there is hardly anyone left offering strong design and expression products for this market category. The result has been a considerable lack of well–designed personal and expression gifts. At the same time, consumers have not relented in their purchasing desires. Subsequently, an opportunity has been created that Jenni Frey Designs intends to address. Personal and expression bow ties and scarves, the first products in JFG's new product line, have already begun to catch on:

When two of finance's best known firms, J.P. Morgan and Goldman Sachs, announced recently that every day would be casual dress day, a bittersweet smile crept across the faces of well heeled Wall Street men. Bitter because their sole outlet for sartorial expression, the tie, had been declared dead. Sweet because a much maligned heir had come of age. "People are getting more daring with bow ties and scarves," says Robert Cullen, who manages the Manhattan store of one of hosiery's bolder designers, Zachary Wilson. "Even the conservative customer is looking to express [themselves] a little bit."

With all that Oxford cloth and khaki walking around out there, most offices are as bland as a convention of Banana Republic sales clerks. Bright bow ties and scarves show you still have personality. What's more, they serve a practical function, and they're harder to spill soup on than ties.

BUSINESS STRATEGY

The purpose of the JFG business model is to explain the overall philosophy of how the company intends to develop, market, and sell its products. JFG's business model is comprised of three essential ingredients that, when combined, create a powerful central theme: Design, Connect, and Sell.

- Design—JFG products are designed to have meaning, and to 'hit home' with the consumer. It is the meaning that the company's products bring to the consumer that drives the success of the company and the company's reputation. A great deal of effort is expended in the design process to assure that the targeted result is reached.

- Connect—The company's watchword is, "JFG isn't marketing celebration plates and bow ties and scarves; rather, we're offering unique opportunity bow ties and scarves for people to connect with one another. JFG products create a strong emotional connection with the purchaser. This emotional connection happens when the purchaser identifies with the product design, while at the same time recognizing the other unique quality bow ties and scarves of the gift. The intended result of this connection is a combination in the buyer's mind of a gift that makes sense as a product with one that evokes an expressive response. This connection is the basis behind the true essence of gift giving which is what the company's business model is founded upon.

- Sell—JFG drives sales through the impulse purchase made by the consumer when a product elicits an emotional response. When the purchaser first sees the product, they develop an instantaneous personal attachment to it. The desire to share this attachment with the gift recipient is what drives the impulse purchase.

Marketing & Sales
JFG's marketing plan consists of a three–phase product rollout:

- Phase One—bow ties & scarves
- Phase Two—celebration plates
- Phase Three—gift centers

Phase 1—Bow Ties and Scarves
Phase one has already been implemented with personal and social expression bow ties and scarves, which are currently being sold in the United States, Canada, United Kingdom, Australia, New Zealand, South Africa, and Singapore. There are over 500 separate designs in the current product line, featuring bow ties and scarves for relatives, birthdays, sports, Valentine's, and special occasions. Novelty bow ties and scarves are also part of the current product line. Furthermore, international orders have substantially increased, and translations into multiple languages are already underway.

Phase 2—Celebration Plates
Phase two consists of approximately 120 celebration plate designs, and is currently underway with 60 celebration plate designs already implemented. Designs for this product line will be contemporary, colorful, and humorous, with various selections of editorial content including that related to age, family, professions, and leisure sports. JFG intends to present the full line of 120 celebration plates at the Hong Kong Gift Fair in April 2001. Specific celebration plate designs will be imported directly by JFG for wholesale distribution while others will be offered for licensing or direct import to major accounts.

Phase 3—Gift Centers
Phase three focuses on the development of gift centers. A gift center is a concept for a thematic approach to a group of giftware products. JFG intends to develop several product lines using the gift center approach, such as the Midlife Crises Center, Golf Center, Anniversary Gift Center, Kid's Gifts Center, Los Angeles Olympic Games Center, NFL Football Center, and the Major League Baseball Center. Phase one and phase two products will be expanded in phase three into broader concepts that cover thematic approaches that will be popular in the new millennium. Some examples of this expansion might include the development of ceramic accessories to be packaged into the celebration plate line, and other fun–to–wear products to be with the bow tie and scarves lines. Gift center ideas will be developed and first released internationally to obtain feedback from major importers prior to US release.

Jenni Frey International—Marketing Plan
Jenni Frey Designs has been establishing international licensing agreements since 1991. Jenni Frey International (the newly created division of JFG) has collected a portfolio of over 2,500 designs that are available to International customers. JFG is currently updating this portfolio with contemporary colors and phrases, and intends to release the updated product line at the Hong Kong Fair in April 2001. Additionally, JFG intends to add many new items to the product line, such as picture frames and glassware.

JFG's first major license of the new millennium has been finalized recently with T–Shirts and Goodies, a well–known company with over 20 years of experience in t–shirt and cap distribution. The new license is for 50 designs on celebration plates and will also preview at the Hong Kong show. Two additional licenses are now being finalized with nationally acclaimed artists, Jack Bauman and Carol Lahm. Their work will also be previewed internationally at the Hong Kong Gift show.

Customers

Most people would be surprised where they would find Jenni Frey products because the fact is that they're found everywhere.

- Card Shops and Gift Shops—Places that specialize in social and personal and expression products are typically JFG's best customers. JFG's largest single customer group is Hallmark Stores, where JFG products are currently sold in over 100 stores. Regional card and gift chains such as Cardsplus and Cardsmart are also major JFG retailers. Additionally, independent gift stores ranging from the traditional shop to trendy, hip locations also sell JFG products.

- Tourist and Resort Locations—JFG customers include gift shops at Hilton Hotels, Sheratons and Marriott's, and also at airport shops and other locations with heavy tourist traffic. Major amusement parks, and tourist locations like Fisherman's Wharf in San Francisco are also popular sites.

- Pharmacies and Drugstores—Because many pharmacies and drugstores have greeting card sections, they are perfect for JFG's products as well. Both large JFG programs as well as seasonal attractions sell well in these locations.

- Other Retailers—Many retailers sell JFG products. Some industry segments include: bookstores, car washes, museum gift shops, mall kiosks, hospital gift shops, and catalog/mail order houses.

Competition

JFG does not have much in the way of market competition. The competition that does exist comes from companies that offer gifts that compete with the consumer's general gift purchasing decision. No other company offers a product that brings out the emotional or personal response that JFG's products do.

There are companies that make various statements on gift items, such as FrouFrou, Frey Giftware (now merged with HouseWheres), and Allonz. There are also smaller companies trying to establish a specific niche with very targeted products. The statements these companies use, however, are limited to general–purpose editorial content and while considered to belong in the personal and expression category they really don't elicit the same type of consumer response that JFG products do.

Specifically relative to celebration plates, there remain only two companies that manufacture personal and expression celebration plates, Frey Giftware and Platters Inc. Jenni Frey personally had a major involvement in both these companies and continues to utilize for JFG the same talents and focus that made these other companies successful.

While there are many companies that manufacture and distribute bow ties and scarves, it still remains primarily a virgin category in the giftware market. There are larger companies such as Brummer that address the souvenir market, and there are smaller companies that have begun to emulate JFG, such as Sayre. Regardless of these other company's efforts, Jenni Frey Designs currently has virtually 100% of the market share for the expression category in bow ties and scarves.

Given the void created by the lack of direct competition, the general marketing direction of the major competitors today, and consumer demand, it is easy to see that there currently exists a large opportunity in today's personal and expression giftware industry.

CONCLUSION

Jenni Frey's former company was the industry leader in first offering social and personal expression celebration plates and then in developing a full line of giftware that made a major statement in the giftware industry. At JFG, Jenni Frey is bringing that same focus and innovative design concepts to the market.

Being successful in the giftware industry is not about developing catchy phrases. Instead, it's about offering innovative new products and market driven concepts that no one else in the industry has done. Coupled with JFG's focus on innovation and design is the connection that JFG products make with consumers. Making this connection is specifically what JFG's primary goal is and is also what Jenni Frey has a twenty–five year history of accomplishing.

MARKETING & SALES

Sales Strategy

Jenni Frey Designs accomplishes the domestic sale of its imported products through a network of independent sales representatives located nationwide. The majority of the company's current representatives have credible history with the company and with Ms. Frey, and the network is constantly being expanded by the addition of representatives who market to retailers yet untouched by JFG's products. In addition to domestic sales, international sales are currently under way in Canada, United Kingdom, Australia, New Zealand, South Africa, and Singapore.

Given this business pattern, the primary sales effort of the company consists of keeping the sales reps informed and enthusiastic about the products. Under the leadership of the Vice President for Domestic Sales, JFG offers a variety of practical assistance to the sales representatives. The overall goal of these efforts is to promote the awareness that JFG isn't marketing bow ties and scarves and celebration plates. Rather, it is offering unique opportunities for people to connect with one another.

Among the sales aids are the following:

- Newsletters with product information and sales tips;
- A Sales Guide addressing specific issues and situations the reps encounter;
- Educational materials published frequently;
- One–to–one coaching at industry shows to provide knowledge and motivation;
- Frequent contests with cash prizes;
- Attractive, up–to–date catalogs;
- Rep Packets with samples, provided once or twice per year;
- Seven–day, 24–hour instant access to the Vice President of Domestic Sales;
- Web site access: www.JenniFreyDesigns.com offering the very latest information on products and what is selling well; and
- Timely payment of commissions (highly valued by the reps).

Sources of Revenue

JFG's revenue is generated through four sources:

- Nationwide sales through independent sales reps to gift and mass market channels;
- Nationwide sales through direct efforts at trade shows and via telemarketing and the Internet;

- Direct purchases by major nationwide accounts, resulting in royalty and/or product development commissions; and

- International purchases that are produced with licensed or exclusive copyright designs that are shipped to overseas importers, resulting in production development commission and/or royalty income.

The basic products behind these four income streams currently include bow ties and scarves, celebration plates, glassware and picture frames. Additionally, T–shirts and boxer shorts with editorial content are being presented in Hong Kong in April 2001.

Sales in the Domestic Market

For the year 2000, JFG's sales representatives demonstrated performance based on their areas of specialization. Giftware Industry reps accounted for an overwhelming majority of sales, with a total of $500,000. Apparel Industry reps produced additional sales, by telemarketing, and through distributors. House accounts created sales of $59,000.

Sales in the International Market

The international gift line is four times larger than the line that is imported domestically and provides the opportunity to internationally obtain reaction from importers throughout the world. Designs in English are being translated into French, German and Spanish and will be provided in any language to international accounts meeting minimum order requirements. The major concepts being featured internationally include:

- Birthday and Age Related Gifts;

- Party and Humor Themes;

- Gifts for the Office and Workplace, Profession–specific Gifts;

- Teen Gifts;

- Gifts for Relatives (Mom, Dad, etc.);

- Gifts for Sports and Leisure;

- Retirement Gifts;

- Souvenirs;

- Novelty Gift Items Seasonal for Mother's Day, Father's Day, Valentines, Christmas, Halloween, Easter, St. Patrick's Day and Graduation); and

- Custom Design.

Value–Added Features

Beyond the efforts catalogued above, JFG's program is set up to provide additional features that enhance the performance of its sales representatives. These features include:

- Simplified pricing—JFG has standardized its pricing model so that all small, medium, and large casual and high–end bow ties and scarves are the same price;

- Clear, logically–designed price lists and order forms;

- Simple terms and conditions, including $150 minimum for first orders, $100 for reorders, Net30 on approved credit, COD and credit cards accepted, 20% restocking fee for authorized returns, and 1.5% per month late charges;

- Through its web site, JFG encourages retailers to connect to the latest and most pertinent information about what is selling in the market. Additionally, JFG offers retail sales to the general public from its web site;

- For fall and spring gift shows, JFG offers special products and discounts; and

- Jenni Frey International is a special division to handle direct imports to major customers both domestic and international.

ORGANIZATION

Management Summary

The company's management team is comprised of individuals who each have extensive experience in various aspects of JFG's business strategies, and effectively add value to the management team with their unique and specific skillsets. The management team includes:

- Founder and Chairman of the Board: Jenni Frey. Ms. Frey has over 30 years of experience in the giftware industry. Starting in 1970 as the Vice President of Administration for her father's company, Imports International, Ms. Frey quickly grew into an executive role. In 1972, Ms. Frey took over her father's role as President. From 1972 through 1995 Ms. Frey focused on product development and achieved record sales of over 250 million mugs, creating a leading market for the company. Also during this timeframe Ms. Frey operated 15 retail store locations in the greater Southern California area, all selling her giftware products. In 1987, Ms. Frey sold the company to FunToys, Inc., and then remained on until 1993. In 1999, Ms. Frey refocused the efforts of Jenni Frey Design, Inc., to direct importing and domestic sales. Ms. Frey is now retracing her previous successes in bringing unique and market focused products to the giftware industry.

- General Manager: Tom Berke. Mr. Berke is a graduate of Depaul University, with advanced studies at Purdue University. His professional background is in finance, having worked in major banks and for Wall Street firms for the past 30 years. Mr. Berke has extensive experience in management, and his personal production has consistently been at or near the top of his peer group.

- Vice President Domestic Sale: Margaret Champlain. Ms. Champlain graduated from the University of California's Architectural School in 1979. For 10 years, she worked for an international firm before opening his own architecture firm in 1986 in Cleveland. After four years of extensive growth from $100K in sales to $8.1 million, she sold her company and moved to North Dakota. In December 2000 she joined JFG, bringing extensive expertise and fresh ideas to the sales division.

Departments

Product Development

The product development department is responsible for producing the designs that are the basis for the JFG product line. While the current product line consists of celebration plates and bow ties and scarves, future product lines will be devised and developed by this group. Jenni Frey personally oversees all aspects of product development.

Manufacturing

JFG has established long–standing relationships with its suppliers in Korea and China who have demonstrated their quality manufacturing standards and ability to deliver products on a timely basis. In recent years, the Company has expanded its sources to include factories in Taiwan, Thailand, and Indonesia. This is in response to the need to provide alternative sources of product to meet factory production schedules and also to work with factories in developing countries that may be able to provide quality and price advantages. JFG enjoys excellent relations with its suppliers, who all know that the company demands the utmost in product quality and integrity.

Customer Services/Product Support

The company is committed to superior levels of customer satisfaction. To this end JFG has built an internal customer service department. This department is staffed by knowledgeable people who are also skilled in being effective on the telephone in interpersonal relationship management.

Materials and Purchasing

The responsibility of this department includes the establishment of new sources of overseas supply, management of the ordering process, procurement of fixtures and displays necessary for product sales and other functions specific to the manufacturing and stocking of product.

Sales

The sales department is responsible for the achievement of JFG revenue targets, management and growth of the distribution channels, and handling the direct import of JFG product.

Marketing

The marketing department is responsible for implementation of the marketing plan, overseeing the development of pricing and price lists, catalogues, and selling sheets. Additionally, this department handles all research and advertising in addition to programs and special deals.

Legal

The legal department is responsible for management of JFG's copyrights, trademarks, patents, in addition to contract negotiation.

Intellectual Property Protection

The company's intellectual property exists in four forms: various product and idea names, appearance of merchandising displays, logos and printed material, and specific business designs and concepts. The "Frey" name has been a well–established trademark in the worldwide giftware industry since 1955. Jenni Frey has retained the right to continue to use her full name in the industry and in the businesses she operates. The 'Jenni Frey Designs' logo is currently in process of trademark registration. There are other trademarks and patents pending such as the FreyCollection for ceramic and glassware, as well as several other innovative products. Additionally, the company holds over 100 copyrights on designs established since 1991.

APPENDIX

Direct Customer Responses

- "We are reordering 156 pairs after 7 days of retail."—The Cannery at Fisherman's Wharf, San Francisco.

- "We are selling them as fast as we can unpack the boxes."—The French Market, West Hollywood, CA.

- "People Love Them. We're selling up to 8 pairs a day."—Sporting Events at the San Francisco Hilton.

- "Our people enjoy selling them so they talk them up as well."—Village of Dreams, Helen, GA.

- "My client, who never sold socks in his gift store, said to me, 'I started selling the socks as I was unpacking the box. I was amazed.'"—Shelly Steier, Beverly Hills, CA.

- "I automatically double every new order of . . . socks so my clients won't go crazy when they sell through so fast and . . . I have 100% happy clients."—Gary Boudreau, Boston.

- "My buyer said, 'Give me a little tester in bow ties and scarves under $200, and I will give them a try.' In two weeks she called to reorder 100 SKUs after she had sold out."—Lisa Friedman, Los Angeles.

Other Customer Activities

- Greta's Hallmark, Louisville —Based on the sell out of a $200 Valentine's program, this customer ordered 7 programs at $630 each for all of 7 stores.

- Slots and Gifts, Las Vegas—Ordered 180 pairs of socks, then reordered 130 pairs 14 days later.

- What's Happening, Lansing—Initial order in excess of 500 pairs of socks, and within six weeks reordered another 325 pairs.

- Genni's Gifts and Sundries, Chicago—Ordered one name program and expanded it to three locations, then placed 10 reorders in the first 30–day period.

- Brooke Accessories, Bangor—Placed an initial order of $10,000 for two SKUs.

- Sundries and Scarves—Started with one name program, and then expanded it to five locations.

- Missy's Hallmark, Waco—Started with two name programs and then expanded it to three more stores in TX and CA.

Handmade Greeting Card Company

Heartsongs

32 Brown Ave.
Kansas City, MO 64106

Chelsea L. Aaberg

Heartsongs is a start up company that will begin operations in September of 2005. Currently, the company is developing its product lines, creative designs, inventory, and distribution base. The first Heartsongs samples/portfolio will be available by May 2005 and they will be used to target boutiques and charities within the Kansas City Metro area. Our main consumer base will be primarily women, as they purchase roughly 80% of all cards sold, and for this reason we will sell Heartsongs to small boutiques, specialty stores, florists, and gift shop owners. At this time, we are seeking several boutiques and non–profits within the Kansas City area who might be interested in carrying Heartsongs. They are awaiting the first preview of our portfolio.

The following business plan provides information regarding our product description, management and growth strategies, and financial objectives. The plan is intended to provide you with information regarding Heartsongs so that you might offer us your expertise as we seek to better our plan and business goals/objectives.

EXECUTIVE SUMMARY

What was once a creative hobby for two sisters and a central part in their efforts to stay in touch has turned into a passion, as the two sisters spend hours designing, stamping, cutting, and assembling, habitually filling each other's mailbox with cards and envelopes. This passion for cards has spread to other individuals as well, as these sisters are now skillfully creating cards that are handcrafted, personalized, and unique so that the others might benefit from and enjoy such a gift. Handwritten cards are a means of communication that touch lives, as they distinctly identify thoughts, words, and activities; they comfort, inspire, celebrate, and stir a vast range of emotions. Heartsongs is a business whose motivation is to craft that "special" card with tender hands, so that others might also be able to celebrate those meaningful moments, express their innermost thoughts, and communicate with those they cherish. Greeting cards are one of our culture's foremost tools of communications, and the greeting card industry has a constant and continual need for art and alternative designs.

Heartsongs is a newly founded organization incorporated as a limited liability company located in Kansas City, Missouri. The company's sole product is a collection of hand made greeting cards consisting of three different product lines. Heartsongs is committed to creating the finest hand made greeting cards available; each card being designed and assembled with great care by individuals who have an eye for detail. Our objective is to create hand made greeting cards, for every occasion, of unmatched quality, originality, and uniqueness. We are committed to creating an exceptional product, as our product is a direct reflection of our name and our philosophy. We want our customers to make a statement when they use our greeting cards, expressing our tagline, "Let Your Heart Sing". We have a strong work ethic that is at the core of our commitment to the values of respect, integrity, fairness, and responsibility.

Objectives

To create hand made greeting cards, for every occasion, of unmatched quality, originality, and uniqueness.

Mission

Heartsongs is committed to creating the finest hand made greeting cards available. Each card being designed, embossed, stamped, cut, and assembled with great care by individuals who have an eye for detail.

Tagline Motto

Let Your Heart Sing

Philosophy

Crafting hand made cards which create a memory, stir emotion, and touch the lives of others.

OPERATIONS

Company Name

Heartsongs

Legal Title (pending)

Heartsongs, L.L.C.

Legal Business Form (pending)

Heartsongs is incorporated as an LLC.

Management Summary

Heartsongs' management team currently consists of a CEO, a Director of Business & Organizational Development, and a Director of Product Design. Research, business and product development, and financial analysis/feasibility have been completed by both the CEO and the Director of Business & Organizational Development; all additional help has come primarily from the advisory board, legal advisors, and academics.

- Martha Ritter, President & CEO

- Caryn Thomas, Director of Business & Organizational Development

- Frances Black, Director of Product Design

The President & CEO, Martha Ritter, has been a wife for 27 years and mother of two children ages 21 and 17. Currently, she lives in Kansas City, MO and is working at St. Patrick's Christian Academy as an Administrative Assistant to the Guidance Department, Special Services Department, and College Department. She is a registered nurse by education and had worked 18 years in the medical field concentrating mostly in Oncology. She has always had a desire to be creative; enjoying stenciling, sewing, scrap–booking, wreath–making, and home decorating. In the past five years, she has created hand made cards for her family and friends to enjoy, all the while having people tell her that she should start a card business. She feels that now is the time to get started and is looking forward to the next adventure in her life.

The Director of Business & Organizational Development, Caryn Thomas, is a student at Saint Louis University, graduating, with honors, in May 2005. She has selected majors in both International Business & Management, and will also be receiving a certificate in Service Leadership. Caryn possesses excellent writing and critical–thinking skills, as well as, a commitment to the challenge of Management, Public Relations, International Business, and Marketing activities. Her experience stretches domestically and abroad as she has both lived and traveled internationally, receiving a variety of cultural viewpoints concerning various ethnicities. While studying at the University, a variety of course work and campus involvement has allowed her to gain leadership, team experience, and public relations skills, and has helped to develop her organizational ability in order to maintain a sense of balance.

Extracurricular activities and work experience has led Caryn to actively volunteer at Employment NOW, where she has been given the opportunity to write annual reports, serve as an assistant to the director of operations and development, and promote strategies for sponsorship, grants, and new clientele. During the summer of 2004, she served as an intern/assistant to the Director of International Strategies at the RCA Dome, Indianapolis and was able to broaden her experience and sales/marketing knowledge through communication with local and international clientele and new member prospects, performing market research, assisting with responses to foreign business inquiries, and assimilating/summarizing international business contracts. Currently, she serves as an intern at Federal Bank's corporate office, gaining experience in both product management and the banking industry, while continuing weekly at her second job at Thai Bistro.

Director of Product Design, Frances Black, is the sister of Martha Ritter and aunt of Caryn Thomas. She has been a wife for 26 years and is a mother of two daughters. Residing in Ann Arbor, Michigan, she works two days per week as a public health nurse. Her off days are filled with creative design as she, like her sister, makes hand made cards and is a home decorator; she also serves as a mentor and a design coordinator for local events within the Ann Arbor community. She sees her creative background and the ambitions of her sister as a means of achieving her goal of working towards and participating in a small business.

Management—Business Ownership

Although there are three members of Heartsongs management team, each with their own title, the ownership of the business is not evenly distributed throughout the team. President & CEO, Martha Ritter will maintain 95% ownership of the business as she will be responsible for funding and growing the business over its first 3 years in existence. Martha will carry out the day–to–day activities of the business, complete a large majority of the inventory, be responsible for locating distributors within the Kansas City metro area, and manage a large portion of the finances and operations of the business. Director of Product Design, Frances Black will maintain 5% of the business as her main contribution towards Heartsongs startup initiatives and initial business will involve only creative product design inputs. The 95/5 ownership split between these two women will go unchanged within the first three years, and will only be altered in accordance with labor/product inputs and/or when Heartsongs shifts its focus to new locations within Ann Arbor, Michigan. Director of Business & Organizational Development, Caryn Thomas, will require and claim absolutely no ownership of the business as her only role is developing the business plan and growing the business in its infancy. She contributes little by way of creative input, labor, and operations of the business long–term.

Board of Advisors

These individuals have been added as members of the advisory board to serve as a complementary management team. These individuals are professionals who have expertise and/or knowledge of business planning, finance, business development, marketing, and design. Advisory members are as follows:

1. Fred Pryce—Pryce's Construction Materials, Inc. Experienced product manager and business planner.

2. Deborah & Bonnie Plaint—Bonnie Plaint's Boutique. Experienced boutique owners/managers.

3. Additional Advisors will be those who have experience within boutiques, as they possess both industry and product knowledge.

Outside Management & Support

CPA/Accountant—Greer & Associates

1. Maintain the books and financial records

2. Recommend and advise on finances and taxes

3. Certify validity of financial statements

Corporate Attorney—Interviews are underway to determine the appropriate law firm

1. Prepare and file necessary legal documentation

2. Secure trademark—name, tagline, & icon

Design Team—as needed

Martha Ritter & Frances Black will initially be the sole members and contributors of the design team

Staffing & Recruitment

Individuals subcontracted or hired as necessary, based upon the growth of the company and/or the unexpected need for additional inventory. Martha Ritter & Frances Black are currently the only staff determined as necessary to fulfill and maintain demand within the first 3 years of business.

COMPANY HISTORY

The inspiration of turning a hand made greeting card hobby into a successful business was conceived in August of 2004 between the CEO, Martha Ritter, and Director of Business & Organizational Development, Caryn Thomas, after reading of the opportunities available for female entrepreneurship. Martha had been looking for a new and unique challenge after being unfulfilled in her current job at a local private high school. She enjoyed the luxury of staying at home when she had raised her two children, and was looking once again for the chance to return home, yet did not wish to forgo the extra income.

Martha and Caryn had found that most of the women who started their own businesses were just everyday adults, teens, or kids living normal lives, however, all sharing a similar motivation. All the women who were able to attempt and/or successfully run their own business dared to strive for something they were passionate about, letting the learned abilities come along with the trial and error of pursuing their own small business and dreams. Martha realized what she was passionate about was her own crafts and artistic ability; more specifically, creating cards.

The stamping and crafting of hand made greeting cards had actually begun as a hobby between Martha and her sister, Frances Black, who used this activity as a central part of their efforts to stay in touch. The two habitually designed and assembled their own cards that became a signature item given to family and friends. Craft rooms were soon created in each woman's home as supplies and inventory grew. This leisurely hobby has now become an obsession, and the thrill of becoming an entrepreneur along with the challenge of making their business a success is the driving force behind Heartsongs creation.

Heartsongs is a start up company that will begin operations by the end of 2005. Currently the company is creating its portfolio and initial inventory, stocking/gathering necessary and additional supplies, and securing boutique locations and philanthropic placement. The preliminary Heartsongs inventory will be complete by May 2005 and available for retailers and consumers within the months following. During the first year, the company is only targeting the Kansas City metro area, as it is the location where the management team will have the most control. We will be directing our attention towards several boutiques, craft fairs, individual salespersons, and charitable events that may have an interest in distributing Heartsongs; however, such groups are awaiting the first preview of the available line. Within the years which follow initial start up, Heartsongs may move into boutiques within Ann Arbor, Michigan because that is the second location of greatest management influence/command. However, a set of boutiques, craft fairs, and individuals remain to be fully explored with the Kansas City area, and once performance within the region is determined only then will a shift to Ann Arbor be fully considered. A definite list of retailers, contingency agreements, and contracts will be locked down in the months prior to Heartsongs finalization of its necessary start up inventory (primarily between the months of May–August). Heartsongs is committed to creating the finest hand made greeting cards available. Each card being designed, embossed, stamped, cut, and assembled with great care by individuals with an eye for detail. Heartsongs . . . Let Your Heart Sing.

PRODUCTS

Heartsongs is a company which meticulously creates hand made cards and envelopes by individuals with an eye for detail; allowing its customers to expect nothing less than the extraordinary. Each card is hand–embossed or hand–stamped on only the finest papers and card stock available; designed, embossed, stamped, cut, and assembled with great care, making them an original gift, much to the enjoyment of each recipient. Heartsongs creates a product which is just as distinctive, personalized, and unique as the greeting written inside.

Product Features

- **Design**—Our greeting cards are more than simply cards or computer generated stationery, rather each and every greeting card is seen as a hand made work–of–art. The message is seen at Heartsongs to be an emotional piece of one–self and that is why Heartsongs seeks to provide the best representation of thoughtfulness and character with each and every hand made card.

- **Quality**—Martha Ritter and Frances Black are creative and extremely talented artists who construct all greeting cards completely by hand. There are no machines involved in the process of making these hand made greeting cards; rather, each card is hand cut, hand stamped, and hand wrapped before being delivered to the customer.

- **Craftsmanship**—While manufactured greeting cards are generally designed by artists or computer–generated before being printed in mass quantities in factories oversees, all of Heartsongs' products and greeting cards are hand made within the U.S., stamped by the design team, and delivered in a timely manner.

- **Customization/Personalization**—Heartsongs is happy to discuss any means of personalization or customization of a batch of cards, as our design team is adept in creating those cards which meet the desires and tastes of each individual customer, boutique owner, and/or non–profit organization.

Because Heartsongs creates a product which is both unique and incredibly time–consuming all of the items within the line possess unmatched beauty and charm. Both the embossed and stamped designs offer a spectacular variety of texture, color, and appearance that cannot be generated in mass quantities. The company will initially offer three main products which are intended to appeal to a variety of individuals with very different personalities, preferences, and buying power.

- **Boxed Sets**—Ideal for the individual who composes a number of cards and does a significant amount of correspondence. Such an individual enjoys color, variety, and a uniqueness that expresses his/her own personal style and character. Boxed sets are sold in groups of 10, and likewise have 10 variations in both simplistic and elaborate designs; Christmas and Valentine's Day are the only holidays available in a boxed set. The designs will change and be updated quarterly. Invitations and place cards are specialty cards which will only be available in boxed sets. Boxed sets will sell at two different price points. Simplistic sets will sell for $15.00 and elaborate sets will sell for $20.00. The differences between simplistic and elaborate boxed sets vary and are determined by the supplies used and labor involved in creating the cards.

- **Individual Cards**—Designed for those individuals who pride themselves on finding just the "right" card for any occasion. Individual cards have multiple variations under the following categories: Holiday (Christmas, Father's Day, Mother's Day, Valentine's Day, and Graduation), Anniversary, Baby, Congratulations, Encouragement, Get Well, Love/Marriage, Miss You, Sympathy, Thank You, and Just for Fun. These individual card categories were selected as they are the most demanded themes and cover the largest variety of topics; such categories will also allow Heartsongs to expand its card lines as demand increases. The individual card line commands a much more progressive variety in both simplistic and elaborate cards, priced $5.00 and $7.00 respectively.

- **Personalized/Custom Cards**—Designed for the individual that wants a personal touch of elegance and a card which will suit his/her tastes or will make a much desired statement. This individual exudes a longing for value, quality, and a look like no other. Such personalized/custom cards will be collectively designed by both the customer and the design team, and then constructed in a fashion that is timely and meets the exact and perfect requirements of the customer. Personalized/Custom Cards can only be purchased in boxed sets of three or more. It is important to note that specific boutiques may require a specific card that fits the niche and/or style of the shop; such requests will be managed by the design team and the boutique owner/manager and laid out within the contract. Price for such card sets will vary and be determined on the basis of the supplies necessary and the labor involved in order to complete the order.

COMPETITION

Greeting cards are already in existence within the marketplace and greeting card companies are pursuing our same clientele as they too can be found in our target boutiques. Such cards vary from computerized, mass–produced, and hand made cards which range in price from $.50—$8.50. Industry leaders are the familiar Hallmark, Inc. and American Greetings companies; also, in addition to paper cards, some companies have adapted to Internet demand and make available many lines of cards intended for electronic transmission.

Alternative greeting card companies, such as ourselves, design and publish greeting cards for all occasions and in many varieties, targeting our sales toward a specific niche; there is however, quite a bit of variation in terms of price, quality, and locations of such companies. Nevertheless, in instances of both industry giants and alternative companies, these cards and many of the lines produced by these card companies are published for mass sale, leaving hand–crafted cards and other one–of–a–kind crafted cards intended for individual sale, on a much smaller scale both competitively and in terms of market share. As the marketplace is becoming more diverse and small vendors/boutiques continue to seek new ways of meeting the needs of their customers and increase sales, Heartsongs and its closest competitors seek to provide the market with a new and fresh choice/alternative. A recent survey conducted for Greetings etc. (Greeting Card Association) polled retailers on numerous topics related to their business, from which product category has been selling best to what their top–selling license consisted of. Their answers provided few surprises, but did offer a snapshot of which products are doing best on their shelves. When asked whether retailers had seen an increase or decrease in certain product categories in the last 12 months, by far the category that respondents mentioned most as seeing an increase in is greeting cards; greeting cards and boxed cards were also most mentioned as the product category that retailers plan to add to their store in the next 12 months.

Heartsongs has identified five major competitors within the St. Louis metro area, all of which create hand made cards and are currently distributing their product in local boutiques. Although all of the cards being produced by our closest competitors are hand made, the creative designs and price vary greatly. The four identified and most aggressive competitors of Heartsongs are Open Please Cards, Ribbons and Bows, Pulp Products, and Peter's Cards. Heartsongs is currently updating its cards so that it might be a distinctive hand made card company which offers a product that is far different, by design, than its competition.

Competitive Advantages

What separates Heartsongs from everyone else is our commitment to design, quality, customization, and impractical replication. Our company seeks to continuously seek out the newest trends and incorporate them into our product, never compromising the use of the best products, technique, and artistic craftsmanship. Heartsongs also provides a unique pricing and product structure so that we can sell our cards in a manner that is compatible with the market and does not upset our boutiques/retailers. Heartsongs understands that the success of individual boutiques depends on the specialty store's own uniqueness of product; as distinguished product offerings allow each boutique the ability to differentiate itself from another. The creative ability of the design team allows Heartsongs to be extremely adaptable to the market and in its desired areas of distribution; this adaptability is one specific area of Heartsongs exclusivity. Heartsongs understands the objective and the related success of boutiques as each seeks to offer a specialty good and in doing so fill a specific market niche. The design team at Heartsongs is unlike the teams of many other card makers as they possess the creative ability and flexibility in order to match the product niche of a specific boutique; such adaptability allows Heartsongs to enter various boutiques and markets, all the while keeping a uniqueness of product with very few repetitive designs. By understanding the product, objective, and niche of each individual boutique, Heartsongs hopes to become a dominant card maker within boutiques in the Kansas City metro area. Heartsongs is determined to stay one step ahead of the other hand made card makers by incorporating both trends and concentration of consumers and retailers. By maintaining and deepening Heartsongs relationship with its small business distributors, Heartsongs will be recognized by boutique owners as a company that is committed to uniqueness of product, as a result, offering a product which their customers desire as it matches the theme/niche of each specific store. It is Heartsongs loyalty to its specialty store distributors and its creative ability to small market scope that allows Heartsongs to gain the competitive advantage.

Aside from Heartsongs adaptability to specific boutique niche, Heartsongs has gained an advantage over other hand made card distributors by targeting non–profit organizations and local charities. Heartsongs is targeting this market because of each charity's distinct mission and reoccurring fundraisers/events. Heartsongs seeks to meet the need of these charities by offering its services for mailing distributions, adapting to the uniqueness of each charity and theme of the event/fundraiser in order to create a card/ mailing which will gain the desired result.

We understand the importance of valuing the relationships of both our customers and boutique owners, priding ourselves on customer service and quality assurance; therefore, if our cards do not live up to these standards, we give our customers our guarantee that we will do everything in our ability to rectify the problem and satisfy those most important to us.

PRODUCTION

Heartsongs is dedicated to its vision and the maintenance of quality, originality, and uniqueness in all of it products; therefore, absolutely every card which is produced will be designed and crafted by hand. We feel that Heartsongs is an exceptional company because it prides itself in its hand made and hand crafted ability; therefore, we would never wish to compromise its standards.

Heartsongs productions are currently operating under the sole discretion and preparedness of the two individuals of the design team, and they will be the only producers of cards through the first few years of existence; Martha Ritter being held responsible for roughly 95% of all production within the first three years. However, as the company develops production, and ultimately business ownership, will balance between the two members of the design team. Additionally, supplementary designers/employees may be needed to in order to maintain adequate production and growth of the company.

Once Heartsongs establishes itself and its orders are large enough, we will review our method of supply. At present, all of our supplies come directly through retail stores within the Kansas City, Missouri and Ann Arbor, Michigan metro areas. We realize this is costly and as a result decreases our profit margins, however, it is necessary as our sales and demand have not yet been fully utilized or determined; nonetheless, as we develop, we seek to make a majority of our supply purchases from various wholesalers and card stock suppliers. Specific wholesalers that Heartsongs is considering are online distributors: PaperProducts.com, JosephLittle.com, and CraftySupplies.com.

The subsequent tables/spreadsheets, within the financial statements, will reveal the production cost that Heartsongs will incur as well as the profit margin for each individual card and/or boxed set sold; this production cost assumes that all supplies are purchased directly through retail stores.

MARKET ANALYSIS

Market Opportunity

After researching and analyzing the market, the founders of Heartsongs have determined that our hand made cards can compete in the greeting card market, especially when positioned in high–end boutiques and specialty stores which are known for commanding a higher price for higher quality items. Heartsongs desires to have a name that is recognizably known for quality, originality, and uniqueness; delivering a product which is far different than those cards which are computerized, mass produced, and/or hand made. Our cards will be sold in boutiques and specialty stores, as such stores sell only those unique and specialty goods; these stores will allow us to gain name recognition so that we will be much more recognizably known as a source of our greeting cards and an alternative selection.

Industry Analysis

Heartsongs falls into a category with a variety of other businesses in the greeting card industry; SIC code 2771 and NAICS code 511191. In 1997, the Census Bureau compiled the following table with regards to greeting card publishers (http://www.census.gov/epcd/ec97sic/def/I2771.TXT).

Greeting card industry analysis

Year	Establishments	Revenue, in thousands	Annual payroll, in thousands	Number of paid employees
1997	106	5,338,986	1,262,869	20,518

Research done by the Greeting Card Association has pointed to specifics about the greeting cards industry; such facts are as follows:

1. The greeting card industry generates more than $7.5 billion in retail sales from consumer purchases of more than 7 billion cards.

2. Of the total greeting cards purchased annually, roughly half are seasonal, and the remaining half is for everyday card–sending occasions.

3. Christmas is the most popular card–sending holiday; sales of Christmas cards account for over 60% of all seasonal card purchases. Sales of Valentine's Day cards (the next most popular season occasion) account for 25% of seasonal card sales.

4. Birthday cards account for 60% of the sales volume of everyday card purchases, with anniversary cards following at a distant 8%.

5. Most American households purchase 35 greeting cards each year.

6. The average American receives 20 cards, of which one third are birthday cards.

7. Women purchase more than 80% of all greeting cards.

8. There are over 2,000 greeting card publishers in America, ranging from small family businesses to major corporations, many of which license designs from freelance artists.

Not only does Heartsongs fall within the greeting card industry, SIC 2771 and NAICS 511191, but it is also within a category for independent artists and services, SIC 8999. In 1997, the Census Bureau compiled the following table with regards to Services, Independent Artists.

Independent artists services industry analysis

Year	Establishments	Revenue, in thousands	Annual payroll, in thousands	Number of paid employees
1997	5,729	2,200,797	935,019	12,366

With regards to Services, Independent Artists (SIC 8999) the Census Bureau (http://www.census.gov/epcd/ec97sic/def/I8999.TXT) classified it as follows:

1. Establishments primarily engaged in furnishing scientific or related consulting on a contract or fee basis.

2. Establishments primarily engaged in writing books and articles; composing music; painting; sculpturing; and in similar creative arts–related activities.

3. Establishments primarily providing services not elsewhere classified, such as lecturers, radio commentators, editors, and inventors working on their own account.

4. Establishments primarily engaged in environmental consulting on a contract or fee basis.

Customer Profile & Analysis

Heartsongs is looking to provide a product which is distinguishable from other greeting cards available within the market. In doing so, Heartsongs will express a desire for uniqueness for those who enjoy the finer things in life and are committed to inspire, celebrate, and communicate a range of emotions through greeting cards. Therefore, Heartsongs is targeting a specific customer who is looking for merchandise that is unique and not mass produced. Heartsongs has compiled a list of data primarily from the Census Bureau and has correlated the information as to match demographic characteristics with specific consumer behavior patterns. Heartsongs looked primarily to the profile and demographics of those within Kansas City, since that is the focus of business within the first 3 years.

There are 5,505,963 people within Missouri, 2,658,831 are male and 2,847,132 are female; roughly 2,361,500 fall within a bracket of 25–55 year olds. Among these individuals, 1,513,836 live within family households and 205,975 falls within Heartsongs targeted household group with an income of $100,000 and over. The median household income within Missouri as a whole is $49,853 (2002 Census Bureau data). The individuals within our targeted segment enjoy a high–quality, healthy, and active lifestyle full of outdoor activities and travel; many of whom are technologically savvy, highly networked, possess a variety of hobbies and interests, donate to charitable causes, and enjoy arts, crafts, and collectibles (Lifestyle Market Analyst).

Boutique Profile & Analysis

Boutiques are defined as small stores that sell specialty goods or services, and because they carry specialty items they often sell their products at a premium. Boutiques, according to the national census, are in a category of gift, novelty, and souvenir stores which are primarily engaged in retailing new gifts, novelty merchandise, souvenirs, greeting cards, seasonal/holiday decorations, and curios (SIC 5947 & NAICS 453220). In 1997, data was taken on such specialty stores and it is outlined within the table that follows.

Specialty stores industy analysis

Year	Number of establishments	Revenue, in thousands	Annual payroll, in thousands	Number of paid employees
1997	37,285	14,497,296	2,056,666	208,371

Of those nationally established boutiques, Missouri has 775 whose annual sales are over $292,262,000 (2.02% of national sales); this profile provides Heartsongs with a large retail base of distributors.

It is important to note that the customers we are targeting would fit the profile of those customers shopping at boutiques, as they are the individuals who live within the upscale/suburban areas where many boutiques are located; these are also the individuals who can afford such specialty goods.

MARKETING & SALES

Heartsongs overall marketing strategy is promoting quality, creativity, originality, and uniqueness in order to build a strong brand image. We believe that creating and protecting our brand image is of utmost importance as it is an image that is committed to creating the finest hand made greeting cards available. We understand that we must first prove our product in the boutique arena in order to build our brand; therefore, we will focus on exceptional design, assembly, care, quality, customer service, delivery, and new product development within our retail markets. Once a strong customer base has been developed and strengthened we will begin to focus our attention to a wider variety of hand made cards and stationary and/or on–line clientele which will be a strong secondary market.

Marketing Approach

Heartsongs is taking an approach which is more than strictly sales, where the customer exists for the business, rather our mindset and marketing outlook states that the business exists for the customer. The marketing concept is a management plan that views all marketing components as part of a total system that requires effective planning, organization, leadership and control. Market research has been compiled to help us define our business for our customer's interests, not our own. It is the process of learning what customers want or need and determining how to satisfy those wants or needs. The dilemma for Heartsongs' management is that, properly done, market research is quite expensive, takes time, and often requires professional expertise. Based on our limited budget, we are going to have to develop the skills to hear what our customers and potential customers are telling us. Some techniques we considered are as follows:

1. User and focus groups

2. Informal surveys

3. Suggestion boxes

4. Comparison shopping

5. Customer analysis

Boutique/Retail Sale & Charities

Once Heartsongs becomes a more common brand name and boutiques begin to know us better and understand the unique differences of our product, then specialty stores will be able to differentiate themselves from other card carriers as they stock the Heartsongs line. We have identified the type of consumer boutiques where we wish our greeting card line to be available and such stores will be targeted through direct mail, phone conversations, and personal appointments. The boutiques and specialty good businesses that we are currently looking into are as follows:

1. Red Flower—Three locations within the Kansas City metro area

2. Cloverleaf—One location within the Kansas City metro area

3. Lizzy Libby—One location within the Kansas City metro area

4. Stems and Petals—One location within the Kansas City metro area

5. Cards and Paper—Two current locations & one location on the way within the Kansas City metro area

6. Stuck on Ourselves—One location within the Kansas City metro area

7. Bunches and Bushels—One location with 8 other surrounding boutiques under different names, but the same ownership

8. Home Sweet House—One location within the Kansas City metro area

9. Sweet Pea—One location within the Kansas City metro area

10. Maggie & Jack—One location within the Kansas City metro area

11. Fruit Salad—One location within the Kansas City metro area

12. Little Children's Boutique—One location within the Kansas City metro area

Interestingly, only Red Flower, Cloverleaf, and Sweet Pea carry a line of hand made cards & it is also important to note that a majority of these specialty stores do not carry a line of cards and our goal is to push them to consider making an addition to their product selection based on the uniqueness of the Heartsongs product line and how it ties in with each individual shop.

There are also a number of charities within the Kansas City metro area who have annual fundraisers and events to support their own specific cause. The following is a list of some of the major charities within the Kansas City area that Heartsongs will be specifically targeting:

1. Multiple Sclerosis Foundation

2. Cystic Fibrosis Foundation

3. American Cancer Society

Craft/Artisan Events

The availability of Heartsongs at small craft fairs and artisan events can be helpful in building brand image. Regionally recognized events such as the Artisans Conference and MissouriFest might also allow us to identify new clientele, boutiques/retailers which foster the most appealing environment for our product, or a number of wholesalers who could provide us with less costly supplies. The exhibit that Heartsongs is most intrigued about is the Kansas City Art Fair. Kansas City Art Fair is a not–for–profit visual arts co–op gallery, organization, and advocate exhibiting work by established and emerging artists from the Kansas City region. The mission statement of Kansas City Art Fair specifically states that the organization is a visual art organization that creates exhibition, support, and growth opportunities for emerging and established contemporary artists. This organization is one which interests Heartsongs as it has featured hand made card makers and artisans, such as Open Please Cards, and presented their work in original exhibitions, educational programming, and support services to benefit artists and the community.

Another decision which we will ultimately have to make is whether we wish to market ourselves or work with an agent. The advantage of agents is that they have contacts with creative directors at a number of companies so that our work might be seen by the right people. They could also be a help and a guide as we develop our portfolio, negotiate partnerships with companies/boutiques, locate wholesale distributors, and find potential creative employees. The disadvantage of working with an agent is that they generally take a 40%–50% commission. This agent decision, will not however, be one which is made until after year 3.

Additional Marketing

Because Heartsongs is targeting the upscale market of boutiques and charity donors, Heartsongs marketing strategy needs to be directly in line with the desired niche market. For this reason, outside of personally/ directly targeting boutiques, charities, and distributors, Heartsongs also desires to place ads in upscale local magazines/papers such as the *Art on the Town* or *Kansas City Happenings*. It is not enough that name recognition is built by boutiques/charities themselves, but Heartsongs feels that to become a more distinguished and desirable line it needs to be a company which does not only seek distributors, but is also sought by consumers with specific card/invitation needs. Such ads will communicate to a widened audience that Heartsongs is a company which creates a product which can be created and customized for the consumer to meet their needs and unique reasons behind a mass distribution of cards. Word of mouth is to be Heartsongs cheapest and most effective marketing strategy within the first few years of existence. Therefore, if Heartsongs can build a clientele base outside of boutiques and charitable foundations, then such individuals will be able to not only pass the Heartsongs name along to those they know who desire cards made for a specific event, but all those who receive a card for specific events will be touched by the unique designs and creative difference of Heartsongs product lines.

Additionally, today's free–distribution papers are different from paid–circulation newspapers. Although the shopper type papers contain mostly advertising and little feature material, they remain a highly productive advertising medium. Such mediums offer the advertiser most of the advantages of paid–circulation papers, including the permanence of print, the versatility of color and graphics, and high readership of personal want ads. One advantage over paid–circulation papers is their ability to reach a very high percentage of the market area. Because they are free, they are delivered to every home. Penetration and acceptance of free newspapers are estimated at more than 90 percent. One free newspaper that we are considering is the *Metropolitan Circular*.

Sales Strategy

Heartsongs' sales strategy is aimed at direct sales to the boutique owners and charities; additional sales to the consumer will be fulfilled through strategic ad placement within local magazines/papers. Heartsongs seeks to have five retail accounts secured within the first months of start up while additional inventory is being secured. One additional retailer/boutique within Kansas City will be added every month and one additional not–for–profit will be added every two months based upon the success of sales and Heartsongs' ability to maintain demand within Kansas City, Missouri. Sales will be accomplished as follows:

1. Direct mail, personal cold calls, and personal appointments targeting boutiques within Heartsongs' immediate surroundings.

2. Test marketing will be performed in initially in Kansas City and later in Ann Arbor, MI. Such markets are chosen based upon location and the close proximity of both the design team and additional family members who are knowledgeable of the stores in these areas.

3. Personal cold call selling is imperative to create a positive first impression of the brand. We will contact boutiques whose forte is in specialty goods and whose existence is to distribute very specific and identifiable goods.

4. To increase awareness of the Heartsongs brand name, we are seeking to develop invitations or mailers for a charitable event(s) or school fundraiser within our target markets.

Upon initial meeting with boutiques, charities, and potential customers, we hope to leave behind samples of our product for personal use for the owner or for display. Such 'leave behinds' will be left with individuals based upon the CEO and design teams' discretion. The months between May and August 2005 have been set aside in order to adequately target boutiques and charities, make proper sales, and increase inventory. Follow up, observation, and organization of distribution will be an ongoing process in order to determine sales and how well the product is being received within the market. Surveys and questionnaires will also be directed at retailers and consumers in order to monitor the performance of the Heartsongs product lines. Heartsongs projected sales timeline is as follows:

- Month One prior to Start up—begin selling to St. Louis boutiques. The market contains over 70 boutiques according to census data.

- Month Two prior to Start up—review feedback from the St. Louis test markets and based upon Heartsongs success we will begin to sell to charities.

- Month Three prior to Start up—continue with follow-up of both charities and boutiques and organize distribution, orders, and pricing with each individual charity or boutique.

- Month Four prior to Start up—process and deliver orders. Begin advertisements within local magazines and newspapers.

Marketing & Promotions

1. Provide target boutiques with cards to solicit sales

2. Send cards to family, friends, co–workers, & retail owners to build recognition of the product

3. Approach national boutiques in order to create distribution on a wider scale under one retail name

4. Price breaks and a percentage discount offered based on the quantity of purchase and bulk orders

Test Marketing

Test marketing has been completed at St. Patrick's Christian Academy where CEO, Martha Ritter, is currently employed. This initial sales attempt was performed at the school's carnival which included a small craft fair. This craft fair was unique because it is one which features a number of hand made items (ex. jewelry, artwork, and even cards). Although Heartsongs was competing with small scaled competitors, who are not foreseen as long term threats, Heartsongs was able to stand out on the basis of price, uniqueness, quality, and creative craftsmanship. It was obvious that our cards had considerably more detail, revealing the higher level of care that was taken in our products creation. These factors brought the customer to our booth and caused them to select and purchase our hand made cards. On the basis of such test marketing efforts, we feel that we will have congruent results when our products are sold within specialty stores and against some of our major competitors.

Not only are individuals purchasing our cards at various craft fairs, but our cards are being distributed and are in circulation, as they have been given as gifts and used in various forms of correspondence.

Heartsongs competitive edge will remain in the ability of our management team as we seek to stay ahead of our competitors. To put it differently, it is Heartsongs objective to approach the boutiques and charities, who currently do not supply a line of hand made cards, FIRST. Time is of the essence and if Heartsongs is able to get into these markets and to such retailers/distributors first, than we will have a dominant command/hold on a particular store; and, for specialty good stores, which pride themselves on diversity and uniqueness of product, they will not wish to stock multiple varieties of hand made cards. Heartsongs has approached boutiques and inquired about their interest in hand made cards, and those who did not currently have a selection of hand made cards seemed interested but wished to see some samples and/or a portfolio of Heartsongs product lines.

Pricing

The prices of Heartsongs products are based upon what the market commands, what our customers are willing to spend, what is listed by our closest competitors, and the labor which is involved in the creation of single card. Prices are also based on the costs associated with the product as each line is priced based on the intricacies, complexities, detail, and products necessary for construction/creation. Three price points are covered for our products based upon the three different lines; however our financials are based solely on the price points of boxed sets and individual cards as the prices for customized cards and special orders are subject to change based upon the size of the order, labor, and materials involved. Heartsongs will accept sales on such customized cards as additional revenue, but because of the variation of pricing and inconsistency of the orders we feel that there is not enough stability to make it a valid category within the financial statements. These price points were developed based upon the type of card, cost of materials, and competitive pricing; we feel that these price points provide options for our customers. It is important to note that within the price points and for the three product lines there are two additional categories for pricing—simple & elaborate—based upon the complexity, craftsmanship, and decorative nature of the card itself.

Research in the retail industry shows that specialty items sell for roughly double the price of cost. Heartsongs took this information into consideration when determining its retail target prices and worked backwards. We will, however, review our pricing structure and its effects on margins quarterly. Customer and retailer feedback will also be a valuable source in order to determine our pricing strategy as compared to the value of our cards. Adjustments for pricing will be reviewed much more frequently within the first three years of production in order to ensure the greatest profit margins for the company and best marketability of our product.

It is important to note that Heartsongs competition tends to price their cards $1–$3 higher than our products, and we feel that by commanding a lower price point we can once again be set apart, not only because of affordability, but also because of the quality and the uniqueness of card as it relates to the price. Heartsongs price points are definitely in line with the higher prices which are commanded by boutiques; however, our product remains noticeably lower than our competition.

The pricing structure for boutiques will be different from charities. Some charities will be provided with Heartsongs pro bono, in order to build name recognition and a status within the eyes of non–profit groups; however, Heartsongs cannot run a business for free, therefore the price point for charitable groups will be lower than boutiques and much closer to cost ($2 per card). Additionally, cards which are sold to not–for–profit groups will require a 100 simplistic card minimum, and prices are based upon the simplicity of card, $200 minimum respectively.

There are a number of pricing strategies Heartsongs can use to achieve our growth goals. Each has the potential of producing a profit, and most are tied to the critical relationship of price–to–sales volume and stock turnover.

Pricing Strategies

- **Multiple Unit Pricing**—Heartsongs is using this strategy in order to increase the size of our individual sales by offering a meaningful discount for larger purchases, especially during our start up phase. For example, if a customer/retailer were going to purchase ten individual cards they would pay anywhere for $50-$70; however, boxed sets are sold for $15 and $20.

- **Keystone Pricing**—This is an approach taken by a few of the boutiques that we have talked to and are considering as a distributor of our product. Keystone pricing refers to the practice of setting the retail price at double the cost figure, or a 100 percent markup. If such an approach were taken, boutiques would essentially be taking 50 percent of our profits.

- **Price Lining**—By offering three different product types with two different pricing points, based on the complexity of the card, Heartsongs feels that this technique of stocking merchandise in several different price ranges will allow our customers to buy our product with different uses in mind and with different expectations for quality.

- **Competitive Advantage**—By using competitive advantage to determine price we have followed the prices set by our competition, and based on our image, set our prices equal or a little below those of our competition.

- **Consignment**—Some of the boutiques that we have contacted have stressed concerns over inventory build–up, especially with new products featured within the store; the solution that many had come to discover lies in consignment sales. With consignment sales, Heartsongs would maintain its own inventory and stock the boutiques as necessary, typically once a month. Heartsongs' incentive for such risk is that boutiques would only take 40 percent of profits earned on the cards. This is the approach which is listed within the financials as well as the approach that Heartsongs would prefer in our business relationship to boutiques and specialty stores.

RISK FACTORS

Heartsongs understands that there are critical risks involved in entering a market with several competitors, but be believe that our hand made greeting cards can successfully compete. We have reviewed our risks and have planned accordingly, preserving a low risk status through frequent assessment of market risk, as we stay ahead of the market and on top of the trends within the industry.

Risks

1. Duplication of our products or an increased availability of hand made cards within the market.

2. Increased use of Internet cards, rather than hand–written communication.

3. Too much inventory or overstock of a particular card. Our pre–start projections should eliminate this problem, along with negotiations and contracts with the boutiques.

4. More demand by boutiques, not–for–profit groups, and consumers than can be supplied in a timely fashion. Demand outshines production.

5. Increased penetration of specialty stores, by our competitors, of hand made cards.

6. Lower price is seen as lower quality.

7. An unforeseeable event targeting one of the members of the management team.

Opportunities

1. Introduction of new products to boutiques, charities, and consumers.

2. Test marketing within Kansas City before moving into the Ann Arbor market; this providing us with the information about our product, consumer response, pricing strategy, and distribution maintenance.

3. Contingency contracts during the initial start up phase to determine demand and provide us with an additional hedge of protection.

4. Minimal sales of hand made cards by local boutiques and charities.

5. The opportunity of Internet sales, long–term.

EXIT STRATEGY

Our exit strategy includes two options, private label or licensing our work for a fee to larger companies. Once established, we will approach companies or private label manufacturers to determine an interest level in purchasing Heartsongs to be produced for another company. If we were to develop our own private label there would be definite expansion of product lines available within the "gifting" industry. Additionally, licensing would give another company the right to reproduce our card designs for a certain time, in a certain territory, for a predetermined fee. Heartsongs would also be open to a "work–for–hire" agreement, depending upon the agreement and terms listed within the contract. The advantage of a charged licensed agreement is that we would have the money up front, and we would no longer be dependent on our cards selling successfully before we could earn additional income of them. A career as a freelance artist would essentially be another side business for our management team if we felt we were no longer capable of running our own business. There are numerous opportunities to freelance in the greeting card industry, but it does take a lot of time and effort to find a greeting card company that wants to publish artists' work. Having our own line of cards along with our own business will establish credibility, which is important in getting freelance work if Heartsongs ever decides to exit the market.

ASSUMPTIONS

Costs

1. Costs are based upon expenses occurred to date and include, but are not limited to, projected future costs.

2. Legal charges are determined by a per hour charge and are subject to change based upon our choice of legal firm.

3. Supplies are based on the retail rate and are subject to change when and if we identify a wholesaler.

4. Project inventory takes into account a increase in sales per month. Sales and inventory will grow based upon Heartsongs' increased penetration of boutiques and charities (monthly).

5. Payment for product is assumed at 100% upfront in the financials. The cost of the card covers packaging.

6. Only retail shops will earn a commission on card sales.

7. Heartsongs is assuming very few personalized/custom card orders.

Financial Summary

1. Heartsongs will use a capital investment of $3000.00, incurred solely by the CEO, to start the business. This investment will cover the supplies and materials necessary for starting the business. This capital investment is factored into Year 1 within the financial statements.

2. Payment for product is assumed at 100% upfront in the financials. Negotiations surrounding such terms will occur as Heartsongs becomes more established.

3. Once Heartsongs is able to break even, no additional capital investments will be needed unless high demand forces Heartsongs to produce a greater supply and/or if there is an unexpected need for an additional employee/designer.

4. Heartsongs is operating with a very simple and conservative balance sheet until demand forces us to seeking financing for product production. Initially Heartsongs will be debt free and all inventory will be regarded as assets of the company.

5. Heartsongs is assuming very few personalized/custom card orders until our brand image has been established; therefore, additional revenue earned from these sales is not taken into account.

6. Heartsongs seeks to add one boutique every month, in addition to the five we begin with, and work for one non–profit organization every two months. Profit from non-profit organizations will come from sales estimated in batches of 500 cards per transaction.

7. Heartsongs is a low risk company with little capital investment.

Balance sheet

	Beg. balance	Year 1	Year 2	Year 3
Total assets				
Cash	$ 3,000.00	$ 1,484.10	$ 4,818.20	$ 7,151.70
Investments	$ —	$ —	$ —	$ —
Accounts receivable	$ —	$ —	$ —	$ —
Notes receivable	$ —	$ —	$ —	$ —
Inventory/supplies	$ —	$ —	$ —	$ —
Fixed assets	$ —	$ —	$ —	$ —
Total assets	$ 3,000.00	$ 1,484.10	$ 4,818.20	$ 7,151.70
Liabilities				
Accounts payable	$ —	$ —	$ —	$ —
Accrued expenses	$ —	$ —	$ —	$ —
Total liabilities	$ —	$ —	$ —	$ —
Owners equity				
Founders invested capital	$ 3,000.00	$ 3,000.00	$ 3,000.00	$ 3,000.00
Additional paid in capital	$ —	$ —	$ —	$ —
Retained earnings	$ —	$ 1,515.90	$ 1,818.20	$ 4,150.30
Total shareholder equity	$ —	$ —	$ —	$ —
Total liabilities & shareholders equity	$ 3,000.00	$ 1,484.10	$ 4,818.20	$ 7,151.70

Annual cash flow

	Year 1	Year 2	Year 3
Net income (Pretax w/o COGS)	$ 1,515.90	$ 3,334.10	$ 2,333.50
Change in working capital accounts			
Current assets			
Accounts receivable	$ —	$ —	$ —
Current liabilities			
Accounts payable	$ —	$ —	$ —
Total change in current accounts	$ —	$ —	$ —
Net operating cash flows	$ (1,515.90)	$ 3,334.10	$ 2,333.50
Beginning cash balance	$ 3,000.00	$ 1,484.10	$ 4,818.20
Ending cash balance	$ 1,484.10	$ 4,818.20	$ 7,151.70

Annual income sheet

	Year 1	Year 2	Year 3
Net sales	$ 20,161.00	$ 60,151.00	$ 91,175.00
Cost of goods sold	$ 9,712.50	$ 28,806.50	$ 43,921.50
Gross income	$ 10,448.50	$ 31,344.50	$ 47,253.50
Operating expenses (overhead)			
Internet access	$ —	$ —	$ —
Phone	$ —	$ —	$ —
Insurance	$ 500.00	$ 500.00	$ 500.00
Legal	$ 1,500.00	$ 750.00	$ 750.00
Supplies	$ 2,650.00	$ 250.00	$ 250.00
Total operating expenses	$ 4,650.00	$ 1,500.00	$ 1,500.00
Sales & marketing expenses			
Salary & commission	$ —	$ 4,000.00	$ 8,000.00
Travel	$ —	$ —	$ 500.00
Gas	$ 350.00	$ 350.00	$ 350.00
Marketing materials	$ 500.00	$ 500.00	$ 500.00
Retail/site earnings: 40%	$ 6,464.40	$ 21,660.40	$ 34,070.00
Total sales/marketing exp.	$ 7,314.40	$ 26,510.40	$ 43,420.00
Net operating income	$ (1,515.90)	$ 3,334.10	$ 2,333.50

Assumptions:
- Figures are based upon retail and charitable sales.
- There will be no need for additional employees.
- Business will be run out of the home.
- Cost of cards includes any additional packaging.

Handyman Service

"I'm the Man!" Handyman Services

23 Western Ave.
Chicago, IL 60617

Adam Greengrass

This business plan describes a comprehensive handyman service targeting busy or tool–impaired home owners and apartment dwellers. It raised $300,000 for the company's owner, who plans on someday franchising his concept nationwide.

EXECUTIVE SUMMARY

Business Overview

Home owners and apartment renters have requirements for "small job" maintenance, including tasks constructing prefabricated furniture, installing shelving and curtains, hanging artwork, changing lighting fixtures, and many other tasks that are typically referred to as "handyman services".

It is difficult to find qualified people who will take on these small jobs. Contractors, carpenters, plumbers, and electricians are not interested in these smaller tasks. Superintendents are normally too busy to be available at the customer's convenience, or can not provide a professional level of customer satisfaction.

Enter "I'm the Man!" Handyman Services!

Starting in Chicago, "I'm the Man!" Handyman Services will offer small–job handyman services. Bonded, screened, and highly trained Handymen will be assigned to a limited number of buildings (based on demand) for the specific purpose of providing handyman services for the tenants. Each handyman will support enough buildings to occupy them on a full–time basis with the ability to respond to tenants' requests quickly. The fee for on–site handyman services will range, based on market conditions and geographic location. However for the purpose of this business plan we are assuming $65 per hour.

"I'm the Man!" Handyman Services also will create relationships with third–party vendors, such as plumbers, electricians, computer technicians, home theater experts, and others. All outside vendors will be pre-screened for their professionalism and expertise. When additional services are needed, "I'm the Man!" Handyman Services will schedule and oversee that work for an incremental fee.

Additionally, "I'm the Man!" Handyman Services will create the "Making It Easier Line" of specialized tenant services.

Making It Easier

Everyone today is barraged by the media and overwhelmed with the technology that takes an ever-increasing amount of time to master and that seems to never have and end. There is always something to complicate your life making your daily routine more difficult. From using your cell phone, home wireless phone and computer, to dealing with multiple television remote controls, the home theater and wireless internet connections, to figuring out how to program the clock in your car or keep your VCR from blinking all the time . . . It seems there is always something to confuse you, trip you up, cause a delay, and make your life more complicated.

The "Making It Easier Line" is a suite of services designed to remove some of this difficulty from your life. It consists of a telephone hot–line combined with concierge–type services to provide assistance to people in reducing life's complexities. The telephone hot–line will be initially staffed 40 hours per week with after hour on–call services at an additional fee. Qualified consultants will politely and expertly help you to get through just about any technical or electronic problem you might come across. These individuals will utilize the Internet, other resources for information, and their own product familiarity to guide callers through whatever problems they may be experiencing. A leading help–desk software package will be utilized to track client problem resolutions, so that over time, the Company will build a collection of fixes for specific problems. Further, consultants will be available to be dispatched within 24 hours to address problems that callers don't wish to handle themselves and are willing to pay to have done for them.

Calls received Monday through Friday between the hours of 9 a.m. to 5 p.m. will be returned within four hours, and off–hour calls will be returned within 12 hours, unless the caller specifies they are willing to pay an extra fee to expedite the process.

The pricing structure for the Making It Easier Line most likely will focus on a per incident fee with discounts for purchasing multiple calls in advance. For purposes of this business plan, we are assuming a per–incident fee of $35 with no discounts. Onsite consulting services offered through the hot-line will be charged at the rate of $125 per hour plus materials—distinctly separate from handyman services.

Additionally, a Simplification Assessment will be offered through the hot–line, specifically to analyze the complexities in ones life and present an action plan for simplifying them. The charge for the assessment will be $995, and will consist of one day on–site at a person's home, one day off–site to prepare a proposal, and phone call to review the recommendations that come from the assessment. The customer may then choose whether or not to utilize "I'm the Man!" Handyman Services to implement any recommendations made, which would be done for an additional fee.

Not Just Computers or Technology

The Company expects that a significant portion of calls to the telephone hot–line may be in relation to computers and technology and will gear up for this accordingly. However the Company will not heavily market itself as a computer and technology help desk. Instead it will focus on other areas where a little help can have dramatic results.

Examples of non computer/technical areas where the hot–line will be of value to customers include:

- using the home office
- interior design and appliance feature choices
- features and capability comparisons of any number of products
- automobile services
- comparing service providers of any kind
- personal organization
- home organization
- home projects

The purpose of the Making It Easier Service and its associated hot–line are to help people remove complex decisions from their lives. The Company intends to become a trusted source of information much the same way *Consumer Reports* does in its magazines—but with a personal touch—available to callers immediately when they want it by simply making a phone call.

BUSINESS STRATEGY

The goal of the Company's business model is to establish a customer base before hiring personnel or taking on investment in physical assets so that the Company grows with the demand for its services.

Test Market Scenario

From February through August 2004, Charlie Miller did "hands–on" research advertising handyman services solely on Craigslist.org, a free online bulletin board serving individuals in Chicago. Business was brisk prior to July 4th, slowing in late July and early August. Appointments for late August into September have already been increasing. The most hours scheduled for handyman services in one week was 65, the average was 35.

Business has been divided about 40 percent from central Chicago, 50 percent from northern metro Chicago, and 10 percent from southern/western metro Chicago. The customer base came from Craigslist online; basically from lower rent buildings. It is believed that creative marketing and advertising strategies would yield increased business.

Seventy–five percent of customers scheduled a minimum of three hours, and 20 percent required one full day or more. Most customers had prepared lists of items needing attention, requiring multiple appointments to address them. Additionally, 45 percent of existing customers requested additional services, covered in this business plan under strategic relationships. Twenty percent of customers have referred Mr. Miller to other accounts.

It should be noted that between 10 a.m. and 4 p.m. on weekdays the hourly charge was $45, and $75 per hour after 4pm weekdays and on weekends. Of the total amount of business done, over 40 percent of requests were for times when the higher rate was in effect.

The conclusion drawn from this test market is as follows. There is a strong need for handyman services in Chicago, and the convenience of having a handyman available after hours and on weekends outweighs the price for these services. "I'm the Man!" Handyman Services intends to build its business by specifically filling this need.

MARKET ANALYSIS

The niche identified by this plan is large. For example, in Greater Chicago alone there are tens of thousands of apartments in rented, coop and condo buildings. Some of these buildings have available concierge or handyman services, but most do not.

Further, there are thousands of third–party businesses that provide products and services for company's clients, and the Company intends to form strategic partnerships with many of them.

Marketing & Sales

The intended marketing/sales plan will be to advertise heavily in local newspapers that are distributed in key geographic areas of the city, and to use direct mail campaigns to send brochures to all the tenants that live within those areas. The Company will make use of multiple advertising techniques, including the posting of flyers wherever possible (and legal), and in the future as business warrants, radio or cable television advertising.

The primary objectives of the Company's marketing plan are to:

- Advertise directly to tenants to inform them of "I'm the Man!" Handyman Services, the Company, and its services, and to get the Company's value proposition in front of potential clients.

- Build customer satisfaction in "I'm the Man!" Handyman Services as a premiere service provider for individuals seeking handyman services.

- Identify and create strategic alliances with third–party companies that offer products and services that when combined with "I'm the Man!" Handyman Services provide a value added proposition to potential clients.

When the Company reaches its goal of 10 full–time handymen in Chicago, the Company will consider expanding into additional markets.

PRODUCTS & SERVICES

Pricing for the Making It Easier service, the associated telephone hot–Line, and other on–site services are detailed above.

All handyman services will be billed to tenants at $65 per hour, plus materials. This represents a $20 per hour incremental net hourly charge over anticipated costs. The Company may change this fee based on market conditions and actual costs as they are determined, but will in any case maintain a minimum of $20 per hour minimum net over–ride.

The scope of handyman services will include jobs that do not require permits or building approval. This includes services such as the ones listed in Table 1 below.

Services that fall outside the scope of standard handyman services will be provided through the use of third-party contractors. "I'm the Man!" Handyman Services will determine what type of additional expertise is required and will quote the customer a rate for that service based on the "I'm the Man!" Handyman rate card or list of services and fees yet to be determined. "I'm the Man!" Handyman will coordinate the delivery of the service, taking all the "worry" out of the customer's hands.

Strategic Partnerships

Strategic partners will consist of services firms that provide a specific value when combined with "I'm the Man!" Handyman Services, or companies that sell products our clients may have interest in purchasing. Examples of strategic partners might include moving firms, firms that sell and install home theater systems or furniture, or stores such as Home Depot, Gracious Home, and Bed, Bath and Beyond.

"I'm the Man!" Handyman Services will build strategic partnerships with these companies. Some of these relationships will be made available to our clients through the "I'm the Man!" Handyman Services Web site and others will be featured in a monthly newsletter and other advertising materials. Co–branded direct mail advertising may be an optional way to keep costs down while providing an increased value proposition to potential clients.

"I'm the Man!" Handyman will receive a commission on the sale of products or will charge an incremental hourly fee on the use of third party strategic partner services.

Special Events

"I'm the Man!" Handyman Services will host special events on a semi–monthly basis in order to leverage the strategic partnerships that are built with third party companies and service providers.

One such event will be routine trips to local home stores, such as Home Depot, Lowe's, or Gracious Home. "I'm the Man!" Handyman employees will help customers to select products for their homes, plus arrange for delivery and installation. The stores visited will offer special incentives and discounts specifically for "I'm the Man!" Handyman customers. Other perks, such as transportation to/from the store location may also be included.

It is anticipated that any costs associated with an event will either be covered by a small fee charged to customers for attending the event, or by the strategic partner hosting the event.

Typical services offered:

- Appliance installs
- Awnings
- Basement Cleanup
- Bath tubs
- Bathroom Repairs
- Blinds
- Bookcases
- Brick Work
- Cabinets
- Carpeting
- Caulking
- Cement
- Ceiling leaks
- Child proofing
- Chimneys
- Christmas lights
- Counter tops
- Curtains
- Dimmer switches
- Downspouts
- Dryer vents
- Drywall
- Ductwork
- Faucets
- Fixture installs & repair
- Fence & gates
- Filters
- Flood lights
- Flooring: hardwood, vinyl, tile
- Flower boxes
- Framing
- Furniture Moving
- Garage door install & repair

- Garbage disposal
- Glass installs & replacement
- Grouting
- Gutter install & cleaning
- Hand rails
- Handicap ramps & railings
- Hanging items
- Kitchen repairs
- Landscaping
- Light fixtures
- Locks
- Mailboxes
- Masonry work
- Painting
- Paneling
- Pet Doors & Cat Condos
- Plastering
- Pressure washing
- Roof repairs & leaks
- Screens
- Shelving
- Shutters
- Sinks
- Skylights
- Sliding doors
- Smoke detectors
- Speaker, Phone & TV cabling
- Stairs, steps & railings
- Storage sheds
- Storm windows
- Sweeping & cleaning
- Swing set installs
- Toilet installs & repairs
- Towel racks
- Vents
- Weather stripping

- Window repairs

- Yard work

ADVERTISING

Primary advertising will be in local newspapers and circulars, through direct mailings sent to people who live in a specific geographic region, and through posted brochures and literature that will be distributed throughout the specific area. In the future, the Company intends to undertake an external advertising campaign using larger newspapers and magazines, radio, and/or television in order to reach a broader range of tenants who may live outside of the specific geographic territories that will be initially targeted.

Additionally, the Company will advertise through the extensive use of signs and placards placed around the city at establishments where potential clients entertain themselves. For instance, bowling alleys are great places for signs, as are coffee shops, laundromats, and grocery stores.

The Company's strategic partners also will play a major role in advertising the Company's services. Part of the strategic partner agreement will require the Company's strategic partners to send "I'm the Man!" Handyman marketing materials to their customers or to co–market and/or co–brand specific products and services with "I'm the Man!" Handyman Services in an effort to add value to the customer by bringing together specific products with specific services. These co–marketing agreements will change and grow on a month–to–month basis depending on customer response, market conditions, and overall Company growth.

"I'm the Man!" Handyman will also advertise on the Internet using recurring ads on free sites such as Craigslist, and fee–for–placement ads on sites like Google, though the use of Internet advertising will be strictly limited to regional localities.

An Advisory Board will be established to provide expert opinions, guidance, and creative marketing to best target potential customers and to grow and manage the business. People with extensive prior expertise in this or related industries as well as key "I'm the Man!" Handyman strategic partners and large investors will be invited to join the Advisory Board. A maximum of two percent of the Company will be reserved for Advisory Board members, to be distributed in quarter–percent or half–percent increments.

OPERATIONS

Initially, "I'm the Man!" Handyman will consist of two individuals who will create the marketing and sales materials, build relationships with third party providers, identify and hire "I'm the Man!" Handyman staff members and negotiate relationships with consultants. In addition, they will provide the vital marketing and advertising tools to develop the strategic relationships and implement the advertising campaigns. In the future, additional employees will be hired to take on more specific roles that develop as the Company grows and matures.

In the process of designing the Company's strategic focus, "I'm the Man!" Handyman Services will build a diverse organizational structure that drives the Company's success. This structure will be designed around a shared mission and vision for the future, which is inspiring, exciting and challenging, *but not unrealistic*. There will be a high level of internal communication to leverage the Company's services. The Company will continue to develop strategic partners; *customer service and satisfaction will be paramount*.

There will be a high level of employee screening in the Company's hiring process, and an in–depth customer satisfaction training program. It will not be enough to simply deliver services on time—the achievement of customer satisfaction will be of the highest importance in every customer interaction by every "I'm the Man!" Handyman employee. The performance of our handymen, hot–line consultants, and field consultants, will be judged on their ability to generate customer satisfaction.

The Company will operate under the assumption that the customer is always correct, regardless of the specific details. To that end, the Company will offer free return visits to correct a problem or a 100 percent no–questions–asked refund within 30 days of service.

GROWTH STRATEGY

The Company is examining the possibility of a franchise program as a vehicle for sustained growth and intends to either launch this program after a proof of concept of one year in length, or to physically build its services in multiple cities starting in the Northeast and branching outward from there. Only large metropolitan areas will be considered for growth areas because suburban handyman services already exist from a large number of providers.

The Simply Your Life services will be offered first in metropolitan areas and based on its success may extend nationwide within a reasonably short period of time.

The mission of the management team is to build a sustainable and profitable organization in multiple locations throughout the United States. The management team may at some future date choose a growth strategy that fits the anticipated growth strategy of other large service firms in an attempt to produce interest from them, though the primary mission of the organization is to build sustainable momentum for the Company's services.

RISK FACTORS

The Company's quarterly revenues and operating results are difficult to predict and may fluctuate from quarter to quarter as a result of a variety of factors, including changes in pricing to accommodate market conditions, and seasonal patterns of spending. Further, to attract and retain customers the Company will need to continue to expand its market offerings, utilizing third party strategic relationships. This could lead to difficulties in management of contractors, competition for specific services, or adverse market conditions affecting a particular partner.

The Company will take active steps to mitigate risks. In preparation of the Company's pricing many factors will be considered. The Company will closely track the activities of all third parties, and will hold monthly review meetings to escalate and resolve issues and review and update the terms associated with strategic partnerships. The Company will utilize marketing and advertising campaigns to promote brand identity and will coordinate all expectations with internal and third party resources prior to release. This strategy should maximize customer satisfaction while minimizing potential costs associated with unplanned expenditures.

CONCLUSION

By guaranteeing a high level of customer satisfaction, providing fast, effective and professional work, "I'm the Man!" Handyman Services will provide a valuable service in Chicago. Combining this unique business with other value–added services such as the Making It Easier Service and the Simply Your Life—Line, "I'm the Man!" Handyman Services will be poised to attain a large and loyal customer base.

POINT OF CONTACT

Your questions and comments are most welcome. Please contact: Charlie Miller, (312) 232–1133 Charlie@YourHandyman.com

FINANCIALS

Business Plan Assumptions

This business plan is based on the following assumptions:

1. In an effort to keep initial costs down, handymen will be hired as subcontractors and required to carry their own insurance, though the Company may simplify the process by offering the insurance as a deductible expense for each contractor.

2. The Company's founder and CEO, Charlie Miller, will provide all client services until growth meets projections and additional staff are hired. Over time, Mr. Miller's activities will be more focused on strategic relationship creation and Making It Easier assessments and services.

3. For the purpose of this business plan the net revenue realized from each billable handyman will be $40 per hour, and starting in the fourth month following an intensive advertising campaign, handyman contractors will be placed at the rate of one per month, billing an average of 120 hours per month.

4. The net revenue realized from handyman services after 6 p.m. and on weekends will be $60 per hour, and will consist of an average of 10 hours per month per person. These hours will be in addition to the estimated 120 monthly billable hours.

5. Making It Easier telephone services and on-site services will be provided by "I'm the Man!" Handyman Services full time employees. Subsequently, the following projections utilize gross realized revenue for these services, unlike the handyman contractors as stated above. The cost of services is then deducted in the P&L statement.

6. Making It Easier services are projected to begin in the second quarter of operations and ramp up from there at a rate of 10 calls per month and increasing at the rate of 150 percent per month thereafter. Onsite assessments will start in month three at one per month, increasing in month five to two per month, and thereafter adding one extra assessment per month. Simply Your Life onsite consulting hours will start at 20 hours per month in month four and ramp up at 150 percent per month thereafter.

7. Strategic Third Party Relationships will generate revenue in the form of value added sales and commissions, but more importantly they will generate increased demand for standard services. It is impossible to quantify this number in this business plan.

8. Though all services are billed on a time and materials basis, our handymen will not bill for small items used while onsite at customer locations. Each handyman will be initially outfitted with appropriate tools and small parts (screws, mollies, bolts, wire, etc.) that will be replenished by the Company as a cost of doing business. Materials that will be charged

to the customer will include items ordered by the customer through "I'm the Man!" Handyman Services, or installations where materials utilized are in excess of $10 total cost. In such cases, "I'm the Man!" Handyman Services will bill the customer cost plus 20 percent to cover handling and acquisition costs.

Proposed Equity Financing

This business plan seeks to raise $150,000 to cover operating expenses until Company cash flow builds to the projected level to cover cash expenditures. Twenty–five percent of the Company will be offered in exchange. As per the investor subscription agreement, investment funds will be held in escrow and not released for use until a minimum investment of $75,000 is attained.

First year revenue projection

Services	Price	Month one	Month two	Month three	Month four	Month five	Month six
Daytime M-F handyman services	40	3,000	3,000	3,000	4,800	9,600	14,400
Evening/weekend handyman services	60	—	—	—	600	1,200	1,800
Simplify your life line incidents	35	—	—	—	700	1,050	1,574
Simplify your life assessments	995	—	—	995	995	1,990	2,985
Onsite simplify your life consulting	125	—	—	1,250	2,500	3,750	5,625
Value added sales	—	—	—	—	1,000	1,500	2,000
		$ 3,000	$ 3,000	$ 5,245	$ 10,595	$ 19,090	$ 28,385

	Month seven	Month eight	Month nine	Month ten	Month eleven	Month twelve	Annual total
Daytime M-F handyman services	19,200	24,000	28,800	33,600	38,400	43,200	$225,000
Evening/weekend handyman services	2,400	3,000	3,600	4,200	4,800	5,400	$ 27,000
Simplify your life line incidents	2,363	3,544	5,316	7,973	11,960	17,940	$ 52,421
Simplify your life assessments	3,980	4,975	5,970	6,965	7,960	8,955	$ 45,770
Onsite simplify your life consulting	8,438	12,656	18,984	28,477	42,715	64,072	$188,467
Value added sales	2,500	3,000	3,500	4,000	4,500	5,000	$ 27,000
	$ 38,880	$ 51,175	$ 66,170	$ 85,215	$ 110,335	$ 144,568	$565,658

Five year staffing projection

	1st year	2nd year	3rd year	4th year	5th year
CEO/president	$ 75,000	$ 86,250	$ 99,188	$ 114,066	$ 131,175
VP marketing & sales	$ 59,583	$ 65,000	$ 74,750	$ 85,963	$ 98,857
Sales assistant	$ —	$ 40,000	$ 46,000	$ 52,900	$ 60,835
Sales assistant	$ —	$ —	$ 40,000	$ 46,000	$ 52,900
Sales assistant	$ —	$ —	$ —	$ 40,000	$ 46,000
Operations manager	$ —	$ 55,000	$ 63,250	$ 72,738	$ 83,648
Operations manager	$ —	$ —	$ 55,000	$ 63,250	$ 72,738
Operations manager	$ —	$ —	$ —	$ 55,000	$ 63,250
Operations manager	$ —	$ —	$ —	$ —	$ 55,000
Hot line phone rep	$ 41,250	$ 55,000	$ 63,250	$ 72,738	$ 83,648
Hot line phone rep	$ —	$ 41,250	$ 47,438	$ 54,553	$ 62,736
Hot line phone rep	$ —	$ —	$ 41,250	$ 47,438	$ 54,553
Hot line phone rep	$ —	$ —	$ —	$ 41,250	$ 47,438
Simplify your life field consultant	$ 50,000	$ 75,000	$ 86,250	$ 99,188	$ 114,066
Simplify your life field consultant	$ —	$ 75,000	$ 86,250	$ 99,188	$ 114,066
Simplify your life field consultant	$ —	$ —	$ 75,000	$ 86,250	$ 99,188
Total	$ 225,833	$ 492,500	$ 777,625	$ 1,030,519	$ 1,240,097

Five year profit and loss statement
(Dollars in thousands)

	Year 1	Year 2	Year 3	Year 4	Year 5	
Revenue						
Market one (NYC)	$ 565.66	$ 848.49	$1,272.73	$ 1,909.09	$ 2,863.64	Plus 50% annually
Market two (TBD)	—	565.66	848.49	1,272.73	1,909.09	Plus 50% annually
Market three (TBD)	—	—	565.66	848.49	1,272.73	Plus 50% annually
Market four (TBD)	—	—	—	565.66	848.49	Plus 50% annually
Market five (TBD)	—	—	—	—	565.66	
Total revenue	$ 565.65	$1,414.14	$2,686.87	$ 4,595.97	$ 7,459.61	
Costs and expenses						
Materials (office supplies)	0.95	1.19	1.48	1.86	2.32	Plus 25% annually
Cellular phones/beepers	5.65	7.06	8.83	11.04	13.79	Plus 25% annually
Salaries	225.83	492.50	777.63	1,030.53	1,240.10	See staffing projection
Tools and supplies	4.50	5.63	7.04	8.79	10.99	Plus 25% annually
Rent	14.00	17.50	21.88	27.34	34.18	Plus 25% annually
Postage	47.00	58.75	73.44	91.80	114.75	Plus 25% annually
Corporate liability insurance	5.40	6.75	8.44	10.55	13.18	Plus 25% annually
Equipment leases	2.70	3.38	4.22	5.27	6.59	Plus 25% annually
Transporation	3.36	4.20	5.25	6.56	8.20	Plus 25% annually
Payroll taxes & benefits	72.27	157.60	248.84	329.77	396.83	32% of salaries
Advertising	60.00	75.00	93.75	117.19	146.48	Plus 25% annually
Sales materials	14.00	17.50	21.88	27.34	34.18	Plus 25% annually
Professional fees	13.43	16.78	20.98	26.22	32.78	Plus 25% annually
Misc. expenses	7.50	9.38	11.72	14.65	18.31	Plus 25% annually
Total costs and expenses	476.59	873.21	1,305.35	1,708.89	2,072.68	
Gross margin	$ 89.07	$ 540.94	$1,381.53	$ 2,887.08	$ 5,386.93	
Taxes (38%)	$ 33.85	$ 205.56	$ 524.98	$1,097.09	$ 2,047.03	
Net income	$ 55.22	$ 335.38	$ 856.55	$ 1,789.99	$ 3,339.98	
Percentage of sales	10%	24%	32%	39%	45%	

First year cash flow analysis

	Month 1	Month 2	Month 3	Month 4	Month 5	Month 6	Month 7
Materials (office supplies)	$ 200	$ 200	$ 100	$ 50	$ 50	$ 50	$ 50
Cellular phones	$ 150	$ 150	$ 150	$ 200	$ 200	$ 200	$ 400
Salaries							
CEO	$ 6,250	$ 6,250	$ 6,250	$ 6,250	$ 6,250	$ 6,250	$ 6,250
VP sales/marketing	$ —	$ 5,417	$ 5,417	$ 5,417	$ 5,417	$ 5,417	$ 5,417
Hot line phone rep	$ —	$ —	$ —	$ 4,583	$ 4,583	$ 4,583	$ 4,583
Simplify your life field consultant	$	$	$	$	$ 6,250	$ 6,250	$ 6,250
Tools & supplies	$ —	$ —	$ —	$ 500	$ 500	$ 500	$ 500
Rent	$ —	$ —	$ 500	$ 1,500	$ 1,500	$ 1,500	$ 1,500
Postage	$ 5,000	$ 5,000	$ 5,000	$ 5,000	$ 5,000	$ 4,000	$ 3,000
Corporate liability insurance	$ 450	$ 450	$ 450	$ 450	$ 450	$ 450	$ 450
Equipment leases	$ —	$ —	$ —	$ 300	$ 300	$ 300	$ 300
Transportation	$ 160	$ 160	$ 160	$ 320	$ 320	$ 320	$ 320
Payroll taxes & benefits	$ 2,000	$ 3,733	$ 3,733	$ 5,200	$ 7,200	$ 7,200	$ 7,200
Advertising	$ 5,000	$ 5,000	$ 5,000	$ 5,000	$ 5,000	$ 5,000	$ 5,000
Sales materials	$ 4,000	$ 4,000	$ 3,000	$ 3,000	$ —	$ —	$ —
Professional fees	$ 725	$ 725	$ 725	$ 1,250	$ 1,250	$ 1,250	$ 1,250
Misc. expenses	$ 250	$ 250	$ 250	$ 750	$ 750	$ 750	$ 750
Projected expenses	$ 24,185	$ 31,335	$ 30,735	$ 39,770	$ 45,020	$ 44,020	$ 43,220
Projected income	$ 3,000	$ 3,000	$ 5,245	$ 10,595	$ 19,090	$ 28,385	$ 38,880
Net	$ (21,185)	$ (28,335)	$ (25,490)	$ (29,175)	$ (25,930)	$ (15,635)	$ (4,340)

Minimum investment required until positive cash flow acheived in month seven $ 150,090
Minimum investment required to begin operations (3 months) $ 75,010
[continued]

First year cash flow analysis [CONTINUED]

	Month 8	Month 9	Month 10	Month 11	Month 12	Total
Materials (office supplies)	$ 50	$ 50	$ 50	$ 50	$ 50	$ 950
Cellular phones	$ 600	$ 800	$ 1,000	$ 1,000	$ 800	$ 5,650
Salaries						
CEO	$ 6,250	$ 6,250	$ 6,250	$ 6,250	$ 6,250	$ 75,000
VP sales/marketing	$ 5,417	$ 5,417	$ 5,417	$ 5,417	$ 5,417	$ 59,583
Hot line phone rep	$ 4,583	$ 4,583	$ 4,583	$ 4,583	$ 4,583	$ 41,250
Simplify your life field consultant	$ 6,250	$ 6,250	$ 6,250	$ 6,250	$ 6,250	$ 50,000
Tools & supplies	$ 500	$ 500	$ 500	$ 500	$ 500	$ 4,500
Rent	$ 1,500	$ 1,500	$ 1,500	$ 1,500	$ 1,500	$ 14,000
Postage	$ 3,000	$ 3,000	$ 3,000	$ 3,000	$ 3,000	$ 47,000
Corporate liability insurance	$ 450	$ 450	$ 450	$ 450	$ 450	$ 5,400
Equipment leases	$ 300	$ 300	$ 300	$ 300	$ 300	$ 2,700
Transportation	$ 320	$ 320	$ 320	$ 320	$ 320	$ 3,360
Payroll taxes & benefits	$ 7,200	$ 7,200	$ 7,200	$ 7,200	$ 7,200	$ 72,267
Advertising	$ 5,000	$ 5,000	$ 5,000	$ 5,000	$ 5,000	$ 60,000
Sales materials	$ —	$ —	$ —	$ —	$ —	$ 14,000
Professional fees	$ 1,250	$ 1,250	$ 1,250	$ 1,250	$ 1,250	$ 13,425
Misc. expenses	$ 750	$ 750	$ 750	$ 750	$ 750	$ 7,500
Projected expenses	$ 43,420	$ 43,620	$ 43,820	$ 43,820	$ 43,620	$ 476,585
Projected income	$ 51,175	$ 66,170	$ 85,215	$ 110,335	$ 144,568	$ 559,658
Net	$ 7,755	$ 22,550	$ 41,395	$ 66,515	$ 100,948	$ 83,073

Homeless Shelter

Sister Joan of Arc Center

23 Oak Blvd.
Denver, CO 80203

RJ Sak

Sister Joan of Arc Center reduces criminal recidivism and alleviates chronic homelessness by providing short–term shelter that seeks to obtain long–term housing, establish mentoring relationships, and secure stable employment for its clients.

EXECUTIVE SUMMARY

The Saint Patrick Homeless Family Shelter (Patrick House) is an emergency family shelter for women and families in Denver, CO. In November 2004, the Saint Patrick Society (SPS) ended its organizational sponsorship of Patrick House because of excessive financial burden. Patrick House and its board of directors became their own unaffiliated 501(c)3 not–for–profit organization. SPS also signed the deed over to Patrick House for the building Patrick House operates from. This severance also resulted in a loss of 25% of Patrick House's total annual funding. In addition, SPS stipulated that the emergency family shelter cease having any reference to "Patrick" in its identity.

The national trend for human service organizations is to consolidate services and programs for the homeless into large centers and consolidated civic plans. The City of Denver is following suit. In December 2004 Denver Mayor John Hickenlooper announced that homeless day services would be bolstered in three local emergency shelters. Patrick House is the only emergency shelter not to be directly included in this plan.

Federal grants are rewarding organizations that maintain the national trend of streamlining services. Across the nation organizations that solely offer emergency shelter are both rethinking long term strategies and making significant changes to stay competitive. To not respond to the trend results in a reduction of services and ultimately ceasing operations due to funding shortages.

It is becoming increasingly difficult for Patrick House to attract funding. During a time of industry transition, stagnation is tantamount to surrender. In order for Patrick House to continue as a viable service provider for the homeless population honest evaluations must be made, alternatives considered, and proactive forward thinking decisions made.

The primary demand for homeless services is a constant need. A newly emerging market segment is offender reentry programs. 600,000 people are released from incarceration every year and the statistical rate for recidivism is 66%. Recidivism is over 70% for people who upon release are homeless. Homelessness and offender reentry is a significant social issue with costly consequences. To address this issue, the US Government announced a 2003 joint initiative—the Serious and Violent Offender Reentry Initiative (SVORI). The Colorado Department of Correctional Services implements locally SVORI programs. The Colorado Department of Correctional Services has communicated a community demand for a transitional shelter for reentering homeless offenders.

Funding for Patrick House will be pursued through federal grants. Transitional shelter for reentering homeless offenders is of particular interest to the Department of Labor, Department of Justice, and the Housing & Urban Development Committee. Awards are being announced on a regular basis. In additional to $100 million that funds SVORI, an additional $20 million for grant money was announced on April 1st 2005 by the Department of Labor to address offender reentry.

This business plan will detail the steps needed to dissolve Patrick House. The turn around plan is for the creation of the Saint Joan of Arc Center (SJAC)—an organization whose long–term vision is to become the community leader for offender reentry and homeless issues. SJAC's first objective is to establish the Joan of Arc Transitional Living Program (TLP). TLP's mission is to provide shelter for reentering homeless offenders.

BUSINESS OVERVIEW

Organizational Statements

Vision Statement
Saint Joan of Arc Center is a national beacon and the local community standard for serving the homeless with an offender reentry program.

Mission
Saint Joan of Arc Center reduces criminal recidivism and alleviates chronic homelessness by providing short–term shelter that seeks to obtain long–term housing, establish mentoring relationships, and secure stable employment for its clients.

Organizational Name
Saint Joan of Arc Center

Legal Form of Business
Saint Joan of Arc Center is to be a 501(c)3 not–for–profit organization.

COMPANY HISTORY

After twenty years of sponsorship, Patrick House became an organization independent from the St. Patrick Society in November 2004. The annual budget for Patrick House had grown to be 250% of the entire budget for the Society. The increasing financial liability for the Society became too heavy of a burden and it was mutually agreed that the Society would be able to best operate separate from Patrick House.

The Society signed over the deed for the building the Patrick House operates from for the cost of $1. The financial result of this separation is a loss of 25% of total funding for Patrick House. Funding loss coupled with a tight environment for funding, Patrick House is surviving financially on a month to month basis. Funding and fundraising is the foremost concern for Patrick House. It was additionally agreed that Patrick House would no longer use "Patrick" to identify itself.

In the City of Denver, Patrick House is one of four emergency shelters. In December 2004, Denver Mayor John Hickenlooper announced plans to involve three emergency shelters and attempt to create a continuum of care available to Denver's homeless population. Public funding is being used for this project. Patrick House is not included in the plan. It is reasonable to expect that civic attention will be given to the Mayor's plan and, in turn, philanthropists will take interest in seeing this plan succeed. Not being included in the Mayor's proposal will prove to be a significant hurdle that impedes the potential flow for future funding to Patrick House.

Today is April 2005 and Patrick House is in an interim period. The board of directors and staff remain intact and united through the reorganization process with the Society. The critical question at Patrick House today is funding. Patrick House is surviving the short term by tooth and nail financial efforts. Where is it going to come from and how is it going to happen? Now is the time for Patrick House administrators to critically assess Patrick House's role in the Denver community and evaluate the most effective way to both serve the homeless and attract long term funding.

What follows here is a plan for Patrick House to grow into a financially comfortable and socially valuable organization. The first building block for any not–for–profit organization is to satisfy the demand for a public need.

MARKET ANALYSIS

A national study conducted by the Bureau of Justice Statistics in 2002 revealed that in a three–year window, the recidivism rate for ex–offenders was 67% . Two–thirds of released prisoners are re–arrested and one–half are re–incarcerated within 3 years of release from prison. Over 60% of these offenses were committed with the first year of release. In 2003, researcher Peter Silia observed that "It appears from the available evidence that persons being released from prison today are doing less well than their counterparts released a decade ago in successfully reintegrating into their communities. More of them are being rearrested; these arrests are occurring more quickly; and as a group, ex–convicts are accounting for a growing share of all serious crimes experienced in the United States."

Trends are no different in the State of Colorado. As of March 2003, Colorado's prison population was at 4,018. This figure represents 132% of its capacity.

In a study conducted in 2000, researcher Ali Riker measured the impact that community based treatment models had upon recidivism for transitioning offenders who are homeless. The key finding of Riker's demonstrates that community based treatment models that serve the homeless reduce recidivism from 71% down to 44%.

Speaking to the relationship of recidivism and homelessness, Larry Wayne of the Nebraska Department of Correctional Services notes: "Recidivism for transitioning offenders is over 70% for those without a non–criminalgenic home environment. In the state of Colorado, there is a chronic shortage of housing for transitioning offenders. There is an absolute need for residential based, community supportive housing in Denver, CO. Stable housing for offender reentry initiatives is an absolute need right now."

In 2003, the United States Departments of Agriculture, Commerce, Education, Health and Human Services, Housing and Urban Development, Justice, Labor and Veterans Affairs came together to produce the Severe and Violent Offender Reentry Initiative (SVORI) . SVORI aims to reduce recidivism rates by funding community based treatment models. The Colorado Department of Correctional Services is the only organization working with SVORI in the state of Colorado. The Colorado Department of Correctional Services does not have a work plan for a program to provide transitional living services for reentering homeless offenders.

The University of Colorado is currently evaluating SVORI in Colorado. The study is expected to continue for several months before a definitive assessment and recommendation come forth. It is anticipated that this study will highlight a positive correlation between recidivism and homelessness. A need for a transitional living shelter for reentering offenders is expected to be highlighted.

The demand is for offender reentry programs. In Denver, the opportunity to enter the offender reentry market is to provide a transitional living program for reenter homeless offenders. The long term opportunity is for Patrick House is to develop this market segment. An exit strategy for Patrick House is addressed further in the plan. First, the birth of the Saint Joan of Arc Center will be highlighted.

Saint Joan of Arc Center

SJAC is the "turn around" plan for Patrick House. SJAC will work out of the same building (23 Oak Blvd.) as Patrick House did. The board of directors and staff of SJAC are retained from Patrick House. A transition strategy and an overview of SJAC personnel is included later in the plan.

The Saint Joan of Arc Center (SJAC) is a 501(c)3 not–for–profit organization that funds and manages programs that address homelessness and offender reentry. The vision for SJAC is to a nationally recognized and local community leader for services provided to the homeless reentering offenders in Denver, CO.

The immediate foundation for SJAC is the establishment of the Saint Joan of Arc Transitional Living Program (TLP). For the short term, SJAC will be indistinguishable from the TLP. The long term vision is for SJAC to grow into several programs organized under the organizational umbrella of SJAC. The long term growth vision for SJAC is detailed below.

Saint Joan of Arc Transitional Living Program

Business Strategy

The goal of Saint Joan of Arc Transitional Living Program is to provide individuals with the necessary resources and support they need to gain self–sufficient living in an atmosphere of dignity, integrity and respect. The Saint Joan of Arc Transitional Living Program serves adult (18+) women who upon being released from prison are homeless.

Believing all adults have the necessary resources to achieve independent living, we call our guests into high accountability for their actions or in–actions. Adults benefit from this philosophy, as does the entire community.

With the increased awareness of the value that community plays in helping to reshape the lives of those in need, we are working to form partnerships and strong relational ties with individuals and community organizations throughout Denver and the surrounding community. We realize that those who need us most belong to the community, and as such, it is the community joining together that is best able to meet their needs. We are hopeful that through the ongoing involvement and support of others, our guests will continue to receive the care and services they need to help enable them to fully participate in the community they are a part of.

We believe that the community finds value in the services that the Saint Joan of Arc Center provides and that the ongoing support of community organizations, associations and individuals is reflective of the community's means of contributing to the joint effort required to serve the needs of members of the community, and ultimately, of humanity.

The end outcome for TLP is the reduction of offender recidivism. Providing transitional living for reentering homeless offenders pursues this goal. This goal is measured through statistical analysis and is benchmarked by national trends.

Objectives

The work of the Saint Joan of Arc Transitional Living Program is to:

1. Offer short-term transitional shelter for women being served by the Colorado Department of Correctional Services' offender reentry program.

2. Grow to imitate the client services offered by Colorado Department of Correctional Services and provide a long term homeless offender reentry services without relying on Colorado Department of Correctional Services for resources.

TLP is based on a community treatment model, in that TLP works with the Colorado Department of Correctional Services treatment model. Communication and relationship with potential guests begin while incarcerated and may continue well beyond a guest moving on from the TLP. To encourage the end outcome, the TLP emphasizes security in three areas: housing, mentoring, and employment.

Housing

Short–term transitional housing is located at the building previously known as "Patrick House". The building can comfortably shelter up to 40 people. The standard length of stay is a flexible 30–60 days. Thus, TLP can optimistically serve 480 people each year. A realistic figure is 240 people. A minimum number is 200 people.

All living necessities are provided for guests at no charge. In house services include: three meals a day, toiletries, clothing, laundry and basic living expenses as needed.

Long term housing is explored with staff, social workers, and community organizations to identify available options for either private living or publicly supported housing programs. TLP is a fast track to secure these services and realize "housing first".

Mentoring

Mentoring is the promotion of a person's physical, mental, and emotional health. The basic goal here is to help get a person readjusted and situated within their community. Each person is guided by a social worker to identify personal needs and satisfy personal healing and growth.

While incarcerated a Colorado Department of Correctional Services social worker establishes a relationship with inmates who may quality as participants with SVORI. It is here that clients for TLP are identified, their personal needs assessed, and personal goals are established with the inmate. Based on a "community based treatment model" a care plan for the individual is created by the social worker.

The social worker introduces the client to the staff of TLP. In addition to the Colorado Department of Correctional Services social worker, TLP staff has a significant amount of experience providing a continuum of care for the homeless. Community networking and relationships allow TLP staff to provide entry points for health care, mental health services, support groups and legal services. The purpose of the mentor is to help the client establish a network of relationships needed to successfully transition from incarceration into reentry.

This mentoring process may or may not be complete by the time a person completes TLP. SJAC will continue to provide community entry points for former guests and be a foundation of support as each person reconstructs a social network and builds core support relationships.

Employment

Employment is the establishment of any sustainable income allowing a person to live a frugal life. For some this may include working a job. For others it may include receiving a disability check. TLP works with the Denver Workforce Development Board to seek employment and cultivate employable skills. Public funding supports other folks. TLP works with all people to identify a means to survive by.

Exit Strategy

Patrick House receives grants from the federal Housing and Urban Development Program (HUD), the Federal Emergency Maintenance Act (FEMA), the Colorado Homeless Assistance Trust Fund Act, and other private foundations. Each of these grants requires that Patrick House provide emergency shelter services either for women, children, and/or families. By transitioning into an organization that provides shelter for offenders being released from incarceration, Patrick House breaks the terms of its grants. In order for Patrick House to terminate and for the Saint Joan of Arc Center to be born, several grants will need to be terminated and remaining funding reimbursed to the grantors.

The typical concern for grant termination is loss of funding. Sufficient funding sources for the Saint Joan of Arc Center have been identified and will be addressed in the funding section below.

The transition from old grants into new grants will be both an accounting and a communications matter. Determining the accrual of expenses and the budgeting schedule for each grant will determine how much money needs to be reimbursed to the grantor. The current administrative assistant who has both experience and a background in accounting can handle such facts and details.

The bottom line is that the dissolution of Patrick House will be characterized by communicating a sharpened commitment to serve the homeless population of Denver. The market segment of reentering homeless offenders is developing and it makes economic and social sense to hone services to this population. Communication with grantors and their respective agencies will serve the ending of Patrick House.

Transitional Period

The legal transition for when Patrick House closes and the Saint Joan of Arc Center opens will be determined by the date of when majority funding begins for SJAC. Given the current grant opportunities and deadlines, an optimistic target date for the end of Patrick House and opening of the SJAC is November 1, 2005. Realistically, the date is flexible and transition will be gradual.

There are two chief concerns for the transition: staff preparedness and community readiness. SJAC will be serving a distinct segment of the homeless population than it has in the past. Reentering offenders all come from the common environment of incarceration and will have unique needs that SJAC staff will need to be sensitive to and prepared to work with.

In the months leading up to the transition, an overview of criminal justice and presentations and conversations with social workers will provide the backbone to equip SJAC staff to be more ready to address the daily care needs of the people they will be serving. SJAC staff will need to meet with local criminal justice organizations and social workers to be introduced to the population they will be serving. Ongoing invitations to hear presentations from local agencies will not help share knowledge; it will be an excellent source for networking and building relationships.

Initially the primary relationship for the SJAC is with the Colorado Department of Correctional Services. Colorado Department of Correctional Services provides community treatment and programming for reentering offenders. Colorado Department of Correctional Services has expressed direct interest to see the establishment of a transitional shelter that would address reentering offenders. Planning the opening of SJAC with the help of Colorado Department of Correctional Services is essential. Colorado Department of Correctional Services is the current beacon for offender reentry and will embrace a relationship with SJAC.

Apart from the community resources, networks, and relationships offered through Colorado Department of Correctional Services , SJAC will maintain relationships with all the local service organizations that Patrick House worked with on a daily basis. To be sure, organizations such as the Greater Denver Workforce Development, Charles Drew Health Services, and Community Alliance have indicated a willingness to support and offer service to programs that address prisoner reentry.

Management Summary

The board of directors and staff of SJAC will remain the same during this period of growth. During this period of change, a strong anchor of leadership is needed to see the transition through. In a period of change, maintaining the professional integrity and social fabric of an organization will help stabilize SJAC.

The members on the board of directors are:

Rev. Trent Snow—Spiritual Advisor

Trent is the Pastor of St. Mark's Parish and former Provincial for the Wisconsin Province of the Jesuits. Trent has taught at St. Paul's Preparatory School for 20 years.

Jim Cooper

Jim is the President of Marketing for RBG Service Corp. He has been active in 12 Step Programs for 25 years.

Don Hale

Don served as Executive Director for the Uta Halee Girls Village for 15 years. Today he is retired and does Outreach Ministry for St. Philip Neri Parish.

Bob McCarthey

Bob has been the Director of Human Resources at St. Clair of Montefalco Community College for 10 years. He is a former Chair of the Campfire USA Board and is a Deacon at St. Joseph's Parish.

Donald Oppenmeyer

Donald Oppenmeyer has been the Executive Director of Patrick House for 7 years.

Brett Boyer

Brett teaches Theology at St. Paul's Preparatory School. For 20 years he has served as Director for the school's annual food drive—Operation Others.

Dick Weidlen

Dick has worked as an Investor and Entrepreneur for 15 years and is retired from the Civil Service. He joined the Patrick House board a month ago.

Jane Kitt

Jane taught for 20 years at the University of Colorado. She is a former President of the business community development group Denver Group.

Neal McMurtney—President

Neal has been the Director for the Colorado Community Office of Retardation and Developmental Disabilities for 12 years. He has been involved in community activism for 10 years.

Mike Twiz

Mike is an attorney and a Managing Partner with Twiz PPC. He is active with a variety of community organizations.

Brent Jordan—Treasurer

For 25 years Brent worked as a Comptroller for First Charter Bank. He has also served on the board of New Covenant Center for 6 years.

Lisa Spornon—Vice Chair

Lisa has worked at Denver Methodist Hospital as a Certified Registered Nurse Anesthetist for 20 years and has served on the board of Patrick House for 6 years.

Robert Smith

Robert has been a Managing Director for Smith Investment Company for 15 years. He has also served as the Director of Investments at Girls and Boys Town.

Jack Bruster—Secretary

Jack is a Managing Partner at the Apex Architectural Firm. For 15 years he has worked as an architect for Apex.

Organization

As Patrick House closes, the full time staff of Patrick House will carry over and form the nucleus for organizing, opening, and operating Saint Joan of Arc Center. In addition to the named staff, two full timed non–salaried positions will continue to be filled by several part time hourly–wage employees.

Executive Director—Mark Rielle

Mark has a background as both a managerial administrator and as a social servant. In his first career, Mark spent several years as a project manager for an Denver–based financial firm. In the mid 1980s, Mark organized a Denver Catholic Worker house whose ministry was with homeless men. From 1997 until the present, Mark has served as the executive director for the St. Vincent de Paul Homeless Family Shelter. Mark is deeply connected within the Denver community and serves on various boards and committees that address homelessness in Denver. Mark is widely recognized by his peers as being a person who is deeply immersed in the issue of homelessness and is a topical guru for social services.

Administrative Assistant—Daniel Holden

Daniel has served as the Administrative Assistant at the St. Vincent de Paul Homeless Family Shelter for five years. In this position, he oversaw all accounting, budget, and general financial issues for the Family Shelter. Daniel also comes with a background in insurance. Previously, Daniel has spent time as an accountant in the insurance industry.

Community Programmer—Mary Moore

Mary has earned a PhD in occupational therapy and has taught courses at both the University of Nebraska–Omaha and Depauw University. In 2004 she joined Patrick House to focus on the community services available for clients being served by Patrick House.

Funding

A grant driven financial strategy will stabilize SJAC and orient the organization towards the future. This foundation will build to the vision of establishing SJAC as the organization for reentering offenders and homelessness in Denver, CO.

The primary source of funding for Patrick House is federal grant awarded for offender reentry programs. Conversations with social service professionals, academic researchers, and federal employees are quite optimistic that federal and state funding for offender reentry programs will continue for the next several years. Thus, it is reasonable to expect that SJAC's annual budget of $500,000 can rely on grants for the foreseeable future.

On April 1, 2005 the US Department of Labor (DOL) announced a solicitation for grant application for prisoner re–entry initiatives. DOL seeks faith based and/or community organizations that provide services to prisoners reentering the community. The grant is valued at $660,000 and applications are due July 13, 2005. Grantees must begin services within four months of the award reception. This is a prime grant for SJAC to apply for and more information on this grant is found in Appendix 9.

Since 2001 the United States Department of Justice (DOJ) has been regularly awarding project grants for offender reentry programs. In recent months, a 2 year grant worth $1 Million was announced. The application deadline for this award passed in March. It is anticipated that an identical grant (CFDA 16.202) will be made available in early 2006.

The Severe and Violent Offender Reentry Initiative (SVORI) is a backbone for funding. Between 2003 and 2006, over $100 million is being distributed to sixty–nine grantees to develop offender reentry programs. The Colorado Department of Correctional Services is one of the primary grantees for SVORI and looks to develop and fund such programs in the state. Because current SVORI funding ends in Oct 2006, relying on Colorado Department of Correctional Services for primary funding is not sustainable. It will be smart to continue to follow SVORI because it is believed that the US Government will continue to sponsor offender reentry programs after SVORI concludes.

The bottom line is that the Saint Joan of Arc Transitional Living Program will provide emergency shelter for people who are both reentering offenders and homeless. There is substantial money available for this market segment. SJAC can pursue grants that are above and beyond offender reentry programs. In addition, The Housing and Urban Development Committee, Federal Emergency Management Agency, and United Way of the Midlands also regularly provide grants, tax credits, and funding opportunities to basic emergency shelters. SJAC is included in this classification. Because SJAC is growing into a center for homeless services, it is reasonable to believe that SJAC can become a player for grant opportunities where Patrick House was losing ground.

Historically, private donations to Patrick House annually exceeded $100,000. In addition, the annual golf fundraiser brings in an additional $25,000. Although primary care is changing from women and families to reentering offenders, communicating the community need and simultaneously demonstrating the social value of Patrick House to past donors should be enough to retain a substantial amount of this private funding. It is realistic to expect that SJAC will be able to secure $500,000 in annual funding.

FINANCIAL ANALYSIS

The 2006 budget is rather loose and is benchmarked by the assumption that SJAC will be realistically able to win a substantial grant with a median value of $500,000.

Patrick House's budget for fiscal year 2005 is $328,200. 1 full year of operating the Saint Joan of Arc Center is budgeted at $500,000. The largest leap is the salaries being paid to the full time administrators. The figures of $45,000, $40,000, and $35,000 are set to be competitive figures for similar positions in not–for–profit organizations.

SJAC is a forward thinking, growth oriented organization and its pay scale reflects the caliber of team players involved. Employee benefits have been increased by 55% to encourage workplace unity and ease financial concerns so often associated with social service organizations. If key administrators are shown appreciation, it sets a tone of professionalism and progress throughout the entire organization.

$216,000 is earmarked for any two part time staff members to be at Patrick House every hour of every day. A rate of $12.32/hour for two positions satisfies this figure. Currently, there are several staff members who work part time at Patrick House. These individuals are the fabric that will encourage continuity throughout the significant change from Patrick House into the Saint Joan of Arc Center. It is important that an appropriate pay scale be used as a vehicle to retain staff members during this transitory period.

Various administrative and operating expenses show slight increases. Professional fees are more then doubled to reflect the potential costs incurred during the legal transition from Patrick House to SJAC. Potential professional fees may also be incurred should SJAC have to engage in legal action to resolve its land threat (see below).

Fundraising expense reflect the need for SJAC to do basic marketing procedures to establish its identity in Denver. Newsletters, letterheads, basic websites, etc. will need to organized in order to raise awareness about the services of SJAC as well as comfort donors that the transition from Patrick House to SJAC is in fact a smooth and seamless one. Finally, $4,000 is added to building and grounds repairs to reflect changes that the building may need to undergo in order to be up to code with the standards of Colorado Department of Correctional Services as a community partner.

RECOMMENDATIONS AND EVALUATION TOOLS

The University of Colorado's Department of Criminal Justice is currently doing a local study on the Colorado Department of Correctional Services' offender reentry program. This study is expected to be complete in the near future and will deliver program recommendations and insights. It is expected that the report will include correlations for recidivism and homelessness. As SJAC begins to address this very issue, it is in a prime position to seek partnership with criminal justice researchers at the University of Colorado.

SJAC's partnership with the University of Colorado and the Colorado Department of Correctional Services will create a cutting edge synergy that synthesizes experience, research, and implementation. The benefit for SJAC is two–fold. First, being plugged into an active academic body will provide SJAC will progressive social models for service and care. Secondly, SJAC will be able to translate its raw data into meaningful benchmarks and create measuring sticks for success. This information will be able to demonstrate the success and community value of offender reentry programs.

As SJAC seeks to position itself as the leader for recidivism and homelessness, it may be strategically wise to seek research grants and offer employment to the University of Colorado professors and graduate students to strategically work with SJAC. Investing in a smart relationship will encourage local growth, foster national attention, and attract funding oriented towards growth and the improvement of a socially valued service.

GROWTH STRATEGY

As described, the Saint Joan of Arc Transitional Living Shelter is the first program sponsored by the Saint Joan of Arc Center. As the parent organization, the vision for SJAC is to be the recognized community leader for services provided to homeless and returning offenders in Denver. The underpinning of this turn around plan is to building programs poised for long term organizational growth.

The Transitional Living Program (TLP) is the first step to realize this vision. Over the next one to two years, staff will gain working knowledge for offender reentry programming. In this time, TLP will demonstrate itself as effectively being able to reduce recidivism by alleviating homelessness. The story of Patrick House growing into the Saint Joan of Arc Center will be a modern day benchmark for how emergency shelters grow from surviving into thriving.

In order for SJAC to provide a methodically effective and financially sustainable continuum of care for homeless reentering offenders, SJAC will need to grow and be able to touch society with its message for dignified care in a myriad of ways.

The long term goal for SJAC is to be the community center for offender reentry in Colorado. Colorado Department of Correctional Services is providing a blueprint for services and SJAC is poised to emulate these services, work with University of Colorado to evaluate successes, and make positive adjustments for long term effectiveness and growth. Over the next 2–3 years, SJAC can grow vertically to the point of needed to expand into a larger operating space.

Acquiring an additional building would allow SJAC to be able to provide long term support for reentering offenders living in the community. In the future, the best professionals who deal with offender reentry issues will be employed by SJAC. As a result, it only makes sense to provide a long–term continuum of care for persons needing periodic support and professional consultation.

In order to fund the acquisition of an additional building, it will be necessary to secure tax credits, work with officials from the City of Denver and seek prospective donors. By now the Transitional Living Program will be having a positive effect on the people it serves and provides a social value for the Denver community. SJAC will be in position to provide empirical evidence with a goal–based vision for the future thus attracting the funding needed to acquire a second building for programming and services.

THREATS

SJAC is located at 23 Oak Blvd, Denver, CO. SJAC does own the building sitting on this property but does not own the property. Local rumors are suggesting that the current property owner is entertaining proposals to sell the property. Supposedly a major local organization is interested in acquiring and developing the property. The time frame is relatively unknown, as of yet nothing official has been communicated to SJAC.

It is important for SJAC to take proactive steps to anticipate this proceeding. Crucial steps include developing a bargaining strategy and maintaining a short list for alternative buildings to move the SJAC operations into. When this issue materializes it will be imperative for Patrick House to spread the word of the immediacy of its foreclosure and the absolute necessity to secure an alternative site to resume services as soon as possible. Intelligent use of media and public awareness coups will be needed to identify Patrick House as a "champion for the needy".

If and when SJAC is notified of its building foreclosure, instantaneous communication and negotiation with the antagonistic parties will be necessary. Patrick House's priority is to secure an alternative site to continue operations. Cooperation with the Housing and Urban Development Commission and local realtors will swiftly identify potential sites to move the guests and operations of Patrick House into. Negotiations, public pressure, and emergency private appeals will provide the capital needed for this one–time extraordinary transition.

SEVERE AND VIOLENT OFFENDER REENTRY INITIATIVE

Overview

Nearly 650,000 people are released from incarceration yearly and arrive on the doorsteps of communities nationwide. The federal government, through the Office of Justice Programs, offers guidance and direction to communities as they prepare for ex–offenders going and staying home. This page presents an overview of this issue and describes OJP's Serious and Violent Offender Reentry Initiative.

The reentry of serious, high–risk offenders into communities across the country has long been the source of violent crime in the United States. As more than 630,000 offenders are released from prison every year, the problem of their recidivism has become a crisis that affects all parts of a community. Fewer than half of all released offenders stay out of trouble for at least 3 years after their release from prison, and many of these offenders commit serious and/or violent offenses while under parole supervision. This is a significant problem because there were more than 652,000 adult offenders under State parole supervision across the country at yearend 2000 (Hughes, Beck, and Wilson, 2001).

The statistics regarding juvenile offenders present a similar picture. Juveniles were involved in 16 percent of all violent crime1 arrests and 32 percent of all property crime2 arrests in 1999. Based on the Office of Juvenile Justice and Delinquency Prevention's (OJJDP's) Census of Juveniles in Residential Placement (Sickmund, 2000), an estimated 100,000 youth are released from secure and residential facilities every year and because the length of incarceration for juveniles is shorter than for adults, a relatively greater percentage of juveniles return to the community each year. In addition, research indicates that a small percentage of juvenile offenders commit the overwhelming majority of juvenile crime.

Some correctional officials—under pressure to cut costs—have curtailed prison programs and services that could ameliorate factors that place inmates at higher risk of recidivism after release. Tougher sentencing laws have, in some cases, removed or limited inmates' incentives to enter available treatment programs. Long, fixed prison terms for serious offenders can sometimes have the perverse effect of returning the most risky offenders to the community with the least control and supervision. There is sometimes little continuity between institutional programs and activities, offenders' reentry plans, and the supervision and services they receive once released.

Communities of law–abiding citizens are victimized by these offenders, making these communities less safe, less desirable places to live. Research has shown that criminal behavior can be predicted for individual offenders on the basis of certain factors.3 Some factors, such as criminal history, are static and unchangeable. Others, such as substance abuse, antisocial attitudes, and antisocial associates, are dynamic and changeable. With proper assessment of these factors, researchers and practitioners can classify groups of offenders according to their relative likelihood of committing new offenses with as much as 80 percent accuracy. Application of the risk principle requires matching levels or intensity of treatment/supervision with the risk levels of offenders. High–risk offenders require intensive interventions to reduce recidivism (Gendreau and Andrews, 1990). Since the return of these high–risk adult and juvenile offenders is imminent, corrections, law enforcement, and community service agencies should collaborate to monitor offenders while assisting them in the development and implementation of a concrete, specific reentry plan. Unless communities do this, they will continue to be victimized by these offenders.

1.   Violent crime includes criminal homicide, sexual assault, robbery, and aggravated assault.

2.   Property crime includes burglary, larceny–theft, auto theft, and arson.

3.   Such factors could include, but are not limited to, prior convictions for violent offenses or serious offenses that may not be defined by statute as violent; violent, assaultive, predatory, or disruptive in–prison behavior; and other high–risk factors that may include affiliation with gangs or security threat groups.

Serious and Violent Offender Reentry Initiative

The Serious and Violent Offender Reentry Initiative—which was developed by the U.S. Department of Justice, Office of Justice Programs (OJP), in conjunction with the federal partners—is a comprehensive effort that addresses both juvenile and adult populations of serious, high–risk offenders. It provides funding to develop, implement, enhance, and evaluate reentry strategies that will ensure the safety of the community and the reduction of serious, violent crime. This is accomplished by preparing targeted offenders to successfully return to their communities after having served a significant period of secure confinement in a state training school, juvenile or adult correctional facility, or other secure institution.

The Reentry Initiative represents a new way of doing business for federal, state, and local agencies. Instead of focusing the Initiative on a competition for a limited amount of discretionary funds, the federal partners are coming together to help state and local agencies navigate the complex field of existing state formula and block grants and to assist them in accessing, redeploying, and leveraging those resources to support all components of a comprehensive reentry program. The discretionary funding available through this Initiative will be provided only to fill any gaps in existing federal, state, and local resources.

Communities selected to participate in the Reentry Initiative will have the opportunity to develop state–of–the–art reentry strategies and to acquire knowledge that will contribute to the establishment of national models of best practices. The Reentry Initiative allows communities to identify the current gaps in their reentry strategy and present a developmental vision for reentry that seeks to fill those gaps and sustain the overall strategy. Additionally, communities can enhance existing reentry strategies with training and technical assistance that will build community capacity to effectively, safely, and efficiently reintegrate returning offenders.

Federal Partners

The Serious and Violent Offender Reentry Initiative is supported by the U.S. Department of Justice (DOJ), Office of Justice Programs (OJP) and National Institute of Corrections (NIC), and their federal partners: the U.S. Departments of Education (ED), Health and Human Services (HHS), Housing and Urban Development (HUD), Labor (DOL) and Department of Veterans Affairs (VA) and Social Security Administration (SSA).

Three Phases of Reentry

The Reentry Initiative envisions the development of model reentry programs that begin in correctional institutions and continue throughout an offender's transition to and stabilization in the community.

These programs will provide for individual reentry plans that address issues confronting offenders as they return to the community. The Initiative will encompass three phases and be implemented through appropriate programs:

- *Phase 1—Protect and Prepare: Institution–Based Programs.* These programs are designed to prepare offenders to reenter society. Services provided in this phase will include education, mental health and substance abuse treatment, job training, mentoring, and full diagnostic and risk assessment.

- *Phase 2—Control and Restore: Community–Based Transition Programs.* These programs will work with offenders prior to and immediately following their release from correctional institutions. Services provided in this phase will include, as appropriate, education, monitoring, mentoring, life skills training, assessment, job skills development, and mental health and substance abuse treatment.

- *Phase 3—Sustain and Support: Community–Based Long–Term Support Programs.* These programs will connect individuals who have left the supervision of the justice system with a network of social services agencies and community–based organizations to provide ongoing services and mentoring relationships.

Examples of potential program elements include institution–based readiness programs, institutional and community assessment centers, reentry courts, supervised or electronically monitored boarding houses, mentoring programs, and community corrections centers.

COLORADO DEPARTMENT OF CORRECTIONAL SERVICES SVORI OVERVIEW

This is an overview of the SVORI–funded Colorado Department of Correctional Services work plan. SJAC is positioned to provide serves to phase 2 and phase 3 of the program.

Colorado has one SVORI grantee (Colorado Department of Correctional Services) serving adults returning to four zip codes in metropolitan Denver. The SVORI target population is individuals who are in need of intensive services upon release. The line chart below provides statistics on adult prison admission and release trends in Colorado over a 24–year period.

Nebraska adult prison admissions and releases, 1978–2002

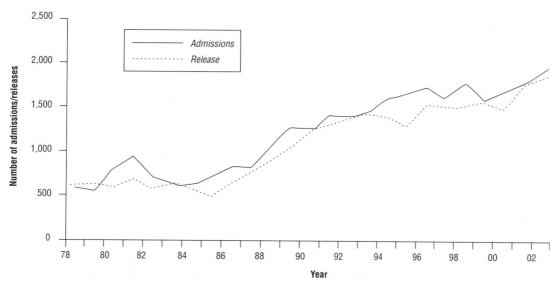

SOURCE: Correctional Populations in the U.S. (BJS, 2002) and Prison and Jail Inmates at Midyear 2002 and 2003 (Harrison and Karberg, 2004)

Data management system

Colorado Department of Correctional Services has a correctional database that can be queried to identify offenders who participate in the Reentry Program. Local evaluation is planned at Denver's College of Public Affairs and Community Services. The University of Colorado is conducting the local evaluation.

Population type: Male adults

Number of targeted prisoners: 201+

Inclusion criteria: Ages 18–35, identified as "violent" by the Colorado Board of Parole, identified as "high risk" on assessment, with tentative release dates equal to or less than 5 years.

Exclusion criteria: Sex offenders, the severely mentally ill, and offenders serving life sentences.

Pre–release facilities: All State prisons

Post–release locations: Four Omaha zip codes: 68104, 68110, 68111, and 68131

Participation: Voluntary

Legal release status: Most participants will be under parole supervision, though offenders who are released at expiration of their sentences will not be automatically excluded.

System–level changes

- Increased enthusiasm

- Future expansion of the program throughout the State

Individual–level changes

- Participants are moved to a pre–release facility (Community Correctional Center Colorado) before release, where they receive specialized reentry services.

Phase 1: Institutionally–Based Programs

Duration: At least 1 year

Assessments: Risk assessment designed by the Colorado Board of Parole

Components/services offered within phase:

- Personalized Reentry Program Plan (PREPP), which is designed for each offender at the time of admission

- Participants are moved to a pre–release facility (Community Correctional Center—Denver) before release

- Case management

- Specific targeted services include, as needed, substance abuse treatment, mental health counseling, medical and dental services, life skills training, parenting skills training, domestic violence counseling, employment programs, education, housing assistance, anger management, and faith–based services

Coordination of services:

- One year prior to an offender's parole, the reentry team begins exploring community treatment and programming options. The team is made up of the prisoner, a case manager, law enforcement, the Parole Board, a parole officer, transition manager, treatment providers, community service providers, family and community members, and a representative from victim advocacy groups.

Phase 2: Community–Based Transition

Duration: Variable

Assessments: Ongoing risk assessment

Components/services offered within phase:

- PREPP revised

- Transition plan created

- Supervision program developed

- Specific targeted services include, as needed, substance abuse treatment, mental health counseling, medical and dental services, life skills training, parenting skills training, domestic violence counseling, employment programs, education, housing assistance, anger management, and faith–based services.

Coordination of services:

- Reentry team

Phase 3: Community–Based Long–Term Support

Duration: Up to 2 years

Assessments: Ongoing risk assessment

Components/services offered within phase:

- Revision of Reentry Plan to include services available after release from parole

- Assistance in finding employment

- Specific targeted services include, as needed, substance abuse treatment, mental health counseling, medical and dental services, life skills training, parenting skills training, domestic violence counseling, employment programs, education, housing assistance, anger management, and faith–based services

Coordination of services:

- Reentry team will change to consist of those community programs that have longevity and can provide services to offenders after release from parole.

OFFENDER REENTRY STUDY

The Homeless Release Project is a San Francisco–based program that attempts to demonstrate how a continuum of care affects homeless offender reentry. Below is a snap shot of statistical analysis done for the program.

Data Summary Points

While the experimental and comparison groups had similar prior San Francisco arrest histories, the experimental group showed a decrease in recidivism rates after participating in the Homeless Release Project.

Data summary table

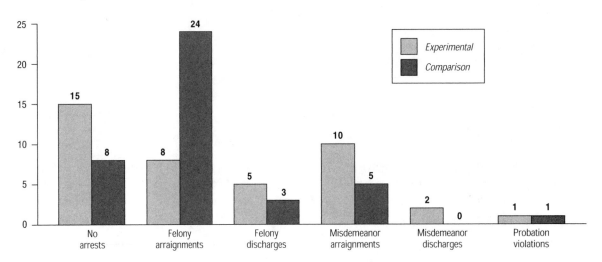

The data support an increase in the number of offenders who had no police contact (arrests) after establishing contact with HRP: fifteen (or 37%) for the experimental group and eight (or 20%) for the comparison group.

The data support that the number of arraignments on new misdemeanor and felony cases decreased for HRP participants: eighteen for the experimental group and twenty-nine for the comparison group. We therefore conclude that the re-offense rate for the experimental group was 44%, and 71% for the comparison group.

The data support that re-offenders who participated in HRP were less likely to be arraigned on felonies: eight (or 55%) of the experimental group were arraigned on felonies and twenty-four (or 83%) of the comparison group were arraigned on felonies.

The data support that upon re-arrest, offenders in the experimental group were more likely to have their cases dismissed than the comparison group: seven discharges as compared to three.

COMMUNITY–BASED TREATMENT MODEL

Included in the previously cited Riker Study is a prototypical outline for a community treatment model. The segment for SJAC is to be the center of the circular support network. In this diagram, the rectangular box in the lower right indicates the measurable outcome.

Community treatment model

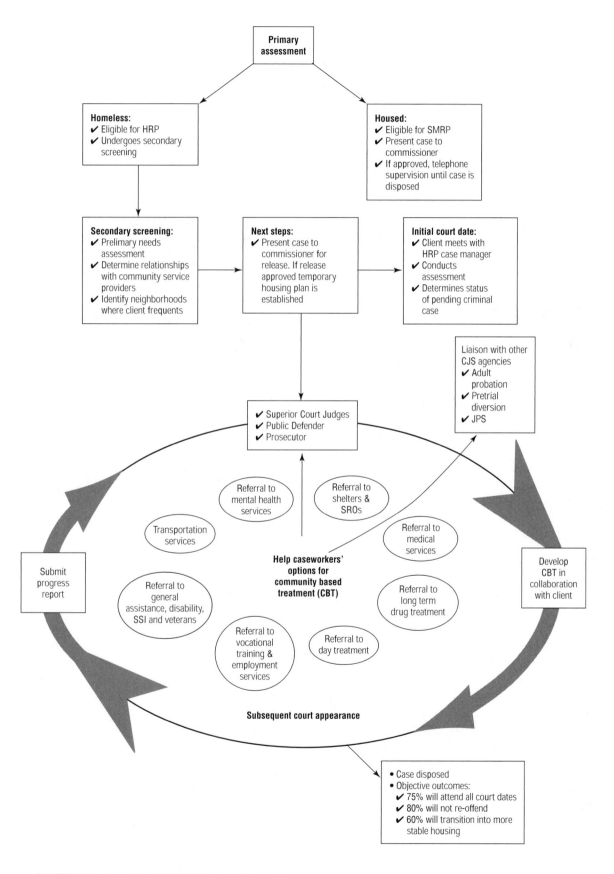

GRANT OPPORTUNITIES

SJAC staff members have a long history pursuing grants and federal funding for emergency shelters. Because the TLC qualifies as an emergency shelter, these funding opportunities are not included. The Department of Labor and the Department of Justice have been consistently announcing funding for offender reentry programs and should be noted as primary funding sources.

FINANCIAL INFORMATION

Budget

Revenues	2005	2006
Government grants	$ 66,000	$ 500,000
Other grants	$ 70,000	
Unsolicited funds	$ 60,000	$ 20,000
Special events	$ 25,000	
St. Vincent de Paul Conferences — Churches	$ 1,000	
St. Vincent de Paul Society	$ 0	
Memorials	$ 2,500	
Solicited funds	$ 103,700	
Total	**$ 328,200**	**$ 520,000**

Operating expense		
Salaries		
Executive director	$ 27,000	$ 45,000
Administrator / Accountant	$ 30,600	$ 40,000
Community programmer	—	$ 35,000
Full time staff 1	$ 73,000	$ 108,000
Full time staff 2	$ 73,000	$ 108,000
Payroll taxes	$ 17,500	$ 17,600
Employee benefits	$ 9,000	$ 9,000
Continuing education	$ 2,000	$ 3,000
Insurance	$ 12,000	$ 15,000
Vehicle operating expense	$ 5,000	$ 6,000
Professional fees	$ 6,000	$ 11,500
Fund raising expense	$ 15,000	$ 25,000
Administrative expense	$ 6,600	$ 7,000
Non-donated food	$ 2,500	$ 9,000
General family	$ 6,600	$ 8,600
HERO program	$ 8,000	$ 10,800
Buildings and grounds/repairs	$ 15,000	$ 17,000
Insects and rodents	$ 1,200	$ 1,500
Trash removal	$ 1,200	$ 1,500
Furniture and equipment	$ 1,000	$ 2,000
Utilities	$ 15,000	$ 17,000
Security	$ 1,000	$ 2,500
Total	**$ 328,200**	**$ 500,000**

Income statement		
Revenue	$ 328,200	$ 520,000
Expenses	$ 328,200	$ 500,000
Gain/loss	**$ 0**	**$ 20,000**

Current balance sheet

Assets

Current assets

Checking/Savings

1000 • Security National Bank-checking	$ 33,521
1025 • Petty cash	$ 300
1040 • Security National Bank-grant	$ 20
1105 • Accounts Receivable - EMP	$ 360
Total checking/saving	$ 34,200

Other current assets

1056 • Securities–General Electric	$ 1,095
Total other current assets	$ 1,095
Total current assets	$ 35,295

Fixed assets

1205 • Property and equipment	$ 29,411
1210 • Accumulated depreciation	−$ 19,887
1220 • Vehicles	$ 15,900
1230 • Accumulated depn–vehicles	−$ 15,900
1240 • Leasehold improvements	$ 25,255
1250 • Accumulated depn–leasehold	−$ 8,174
Total fixed assets	$ 26,604
Total assets	**$ 61,900**

Liabilities & equity

Current liabilities

Accounts payable

2010 • Accounts payable	−$ 125
Total accounts payable	−$ 125
Total current liabilities	−$ 125
Total liabilities	−$ 125

Equity

2275 • Net assets	
2290 • Unrestricted net assets	
Total 2275 • Net assets	$ 87,740
3000 • Opening bal equity	−$ 292
Net income	−$ 25,422
Total equity	$ 62,025
Total liabilities & equity	**$ 61,900**

Interior Design Company

Make It Your Own Space Inc.

141 Normandy
Las Vegas, NV 89101

Gerald Rekve

Business plan for a group of professional interior designers planning on providing services to the residential and the commercial sectors.

EXECUTIVE SUMMARY

The design business enjoys strong demand as people continue to buy or move into new homes and remodel old ones. According to Home magazine, 46 percent of Americans plan to redecorate or remodel in the next five years, compared with 35 percent in the previous five years.

The interior design business is a go–out–of–your–house kind of home business. While doing the business aspects inside the home, most of the sales will be done at the client's home or office as you evaluate the space, match color swatches to existing furniture and measure windows for draperies, etc. With the Martha Stewart TV Show and the vast amount of cable channels now available/the increased amount of the television network viewing time, there are at least 50 new TV Shows which focus on one form of Interior design themes. There have been countless books and magazines published for the sector.

Both of the owners of this new design business have been trained and have worked in this sector for a number of years. These skills will play a big role in the success of the business.

The growth of this sector and the fact the city that we are setting the shop up in is growing. With little competition from qualified designers, we are confidant we will get a strong market share in the first year.

BUSINESS STRATEGY

The American Society of Interior Designers defines an interior designer as someone "professionally trained to create a functional and quality interior environment. Qualified through education, experience and examination, a professional designer can identify research and creatively resolve issues and lead to a healthy, safe and comfortable physical environment."

The keywords here are "professionally trained and qualified." Regulations dictate that only those who have met or exceeded a certain level of accredited education and, in some states, passed the qualifying exam administered by the National Council for Interior Design Qualification can use the title of

Interior Designer. In 18 states, they must be licensed before they can be called an Interior Designer. We will either hire designers who are accredited or, after a period of mentoring, offer to assist the designer by paying a portion of the costs for the education. This will allow us to offer our clients the best services.

Based on market stats, designers held about 423,000 jobs in 2003. Four out of 10 were self–employed. With this small percentage being self–employed, we are confident our ability to hire qualified staff will be easy in our market. In fact there is a design school in our region that graduates about 40 students every six months.

Designers work in a number of different industries, depending on their design specialty. Most industrial designers, for example, work for engineering or architectural consulting firms or for large corporations. We will offer our services to these sectors, allowing these companies the freedom of not having to hire a full time designer.

ORGANIZATION

Management Summary
Lisa Kurtis—CEO

Lisa has a degree in designing and Business Administration from University of California at Berkeley. Lisa had worked after graduating in 1991 with a small furniture–manufacturing firm for about 5 years. Then she started working for one of the largest homebuilders in California. After working in home building, making a lot of contacts, Lisa started her own design business. With her training, Lisa will hire the key staff persons to fill the required roles.

Tracy Trane—CIO

Tracy also graduated from University of California at Berkeley in 1992 with honors in Finance. Tracy worked with Lisa at the homebuilders and saw the opportunity to start her own business. While the risks of starting their own business were scary, they were comforted with the fact that both had husbands who were making enough money to keep the family supported.

Financial Analysis
Both owners had used several methods to finance this business.

Lisa Kurtis

1. Used the money she had accumulated over 5 years of saving (Approximately $15,000)

2. Has a newer family van, which will be used as a company van. Logos and decals will be added to the van

3. Already has computers and office equipment, which will be used for the business

4. Applied with the women's entrepreneur foundation for a loan for her share in the operating capital of the business

Tracy Trane

1. Tracy will invest $20,000

2. Has a newer van which also will be listed as company property and have all logos

3. Will supply the required software to run the business, both accounting and design

4. Will co–apply with the women's entrepreneur for the operating line of credit

SERVICES

The design business is multi–faceted. We will provide work as a product–driven designer or as a design consultant.

The product–driven designer is a hands–on designer who combines the task of conceptualizing the look of the given space with marketing a wide variety of products. This is the common track of start–up designers. The designer often markets various products and even offers free design advice if the client buys all of the products from him or her. Buyers of their products are often allotted a certain number of hours of free design advice; if more time is needed, the per hour fee is charged. A product–driven designer also charges a per hour rate to customers who seek their advice but buys products from another company. A hefty percentage of the designer's income is generated from product sales.

Our staff has worked in the business for a long time with an established reputation and a long list of references; we can focus on offering design–consulting services instead. We will not sell or market any product, but instead offer advice about the design of a room or an office. We will be selling your design expertise, and not any product.

MARKET ANALYSIS

There are two types of market for interior design: residential and commercial. Residential interior design focuses on the planning and/or specifying of interior materials and products used in private residences. In terms of scope and contract amount, residential jobs are often smaller, but offer a higher profit margin particularly if you are marketing the products to be used in designing the rooms.

Commercial jobs, on the other hand, are often much bigger in scope but the bidding that often accompanies the contract can push down your profit margin. Commercial design covers a wide variety of specialties, such as entertainment (e.g. movies, theater, videos, theme parks, clubs, dramatic and musical theater); facilities management (e.g. office moves or expansions); government/institutional (e.g. government offices, embassies, museums), health care (e.g. hospitals, nursing homes, long term care facilities); retail or store planning (e.g. boutiques, department stores, malls, food retailing centers); hospitality/restaurant (e.g. country clubs, hotels, cruise ships); and offices.

Based on city and region statistics last year there was over $145 million in permits purchased for new commercial and home construction, as well renovations. Based on this number and the available designers in the field, we are confident that we will gain a strong market share. All construction firms we talked with told us that they bring in designers from other cities to help with projects. If we offered quality work and competitive prices, they would give us work.

Competition

Right at this moment in the market, we have a few competitors. We believe based on their offerings and training we will win more profitable jobs due to these lack of skills on their part.

1. **PaperPlus Wallpaper & Design**—This firm has a staff of 7, of which 4 are installers, 2 are retail sales staff and one is the accountant. The owner basically does it all. They offer design consultations, however these are very limited as the focus is always on the products they sell, not what products are new or available in the market.

2. **Las Vegas Design Team**—This company has a staff of 5, all of which are in the sales and are designers. While this company does a lot of business, they only have a designer who is educated and

has been certified as a professional designer. We believe once we open up shop this firm will try to hire qualified staff. In the short term this will be beneficial to us; over time thought clients will see the quality of work. We offer and this firm will only be able to get contracts that are low bidder win types where quality is not an issue and the potential for profit may be limited.

3. **Brady and Sons Interiors**—This firm has a staff of 16, however none are designers and they just give their best opinions. They tend not to go after our clients; however they will take a sale if it walks in the door. Their fee for designers is half our fee. Our goal will be to co–contract with this company and offer our consultations to this firm under contract. That way they will still make money for the referral and we will offer their clients top dollar services.

4. **Home–based Designers**—There are five listed in the phone book. We called each one and after lengthy communications, three had indicated that they would be happy to contract to us for work; this way they could reduce their costs and be able to work on larger projects that required more staff. All three of these designers are certified.

Start–Up

Our interior design business requires basic office supplies and equipment such as computers, telephones, and fax. In addition to the standard word processing and spreadsheet software, invest in AutoCAD software to present more professional looking design solutions to clients with three–dimensional realism. AutoCAD software will cost from $700 to $1,900 depending on the applications we purchase.

We also need to buy books of samples, which are the lifeblood of a design business. Manufacturers of wallpapers, paint and carpets produce samples costing about $250 each representing various products in all sorts of design and colors. Try negotiating with sales representatives, as they can give some of these sample books for free, particularly if they see the potential that you can sell their product.

When buying samples, we will be very careful of companies that will require us to purchase pre–selected samples on a monthly basis—even if we don't need it. The assumption is that you run a showroom to keep all the unused samples. Wallpaper and large fabric companies are particularly notorious for this practice.

Monthly Operating Expenses

For the first six months, both partners will not take a salary out of the company. After this period, they will each split a 35% share of the net profits each month.

1. Office Rental—$900 monthly

2. Telephone—$75 monthly

3. Office Equipment—$5,000 (for book value only; owner invested)

4. Software—$2,500 (for book value only; owner invested)

5. Postage—$50

6. Special Tools—$2600 (for book value only; owner invested)

7. Advertising—$1500

8. Company Van—Gas, Repair and Maintain—$500 monthly

Company Van—Both owners transferred ownership of their vans to the business. Both are free and clear of any debt and are valued at $12,000 & $16,000 according to the local bank blue book.

We will develop strategic alliances with local builders, realtors and home improvement firms. This will allow us to have a several lines of revenue into our company.

Here is a breakdown of the revenue sources we will have.

1. Retail Clients—walk–in or phone quotes

2. Realtor—for their clients' homes

3. Home Improvement Companies

4. Commercial builders of office and home complexes

5. Home builders associations

6. Furniture stores

7. Paint and wall paper stores

8. Flower shops

9. Architects and developers

10. We will also develop a weekly advice column in the local newspaper and try to set up a talk–type show on the local cable 10 channels. This channel is free to use as long as the information provided is key to the public's interest.

Pricing Structure

Fee structures vary widely, depending on the designer, complexity of the project, geographical location and a host of other factors. Some of the ways interior designer's charges for their services include:

- Fixed fee (or flat fee)—The designer identifies a specific sum to cover costs, exclusive of reimbursement for expenses. One total fee applies to the complete range of services, from conceptual development through layouts, specifications and final installation.

- Hourly fee—Some designers charge based on the actual time spent on a project or specific service, with fees ranging from $55 to $150 per hour, based on the required detail and other professionals who may need to be consulted.

- Percentage fee—Compensation is computed as a percentage of construction/project costs.

- Cost plus—A designer purchases materials, furnishings and services (e.g., carpentry, drapery workrooms, picture framing, etc.) at cost and sells to the client at the designer's cost plus a specified percentage agreed to by the client. The service charge is often put at 20–30 percent.

- Retail—Others charge their clients the retail price of furnishings, furniture and all other goods they get wholesale, keeping the difference as designer's fee and services. Retail establishments offering design services commonly use this method. With this method, clients get the designers services at a price no greater than he or she would have paid for the products at retail.

- Per square foot—Often used for large commercial properties, the charge is based on the area of the project.

Our staff designers require a retainer fee before the start of a design project. A retainer is an amount of money paid by the client to the designer and applied to the balance due at the termination of the project.

Income Potential

What is unique about the interior design business is that you never do the same job twice. It will be hard to place a specific price on individual projects. What you will earn from a job that requires redecoration of an entire room from the carpet, wallpaper to upholstery will be different from a job that requires you to put up drapes to ten windows.

According to Industry statistics, on the Design Business, an interior designer earns an average of $883 per job. If you are working at four jobs per month, you can expect monthly sales of $4,415 per month. Yearly income for designers can expect to earn about $52,980, for great designers with solid track record, this will be the take home pay of our designer staff, and our % will be 1.5 times this per designer or $79,470 per year per each staff member.

Our goal is to have 5 designers on staff; this will make our first year gross profit of $397,350 and gross revenue of $662,250.

The goal over time will be to increase the number of clients per designer per month. This will result in increase revenues. This will happen once we get better known for our services.

Training, Other Qualifications, and Advancement

The reason we put this in our business plan is to always be reminded of the fact that our staff and our training will be the key to our success in the designers business. We will continue to follow the guide we listed below, as well make amendments to it as we require.

Creativity is crucial in all design occupations. People in this field must have a strong sense of the aesthetic—an eye for color and detail, a sense of balance and proportion, and an appreciation for beauty. Sketching ability is helpful for most designers, but it is especially important for fashion designers. A good portfolio—a collection of examples of a person's best work—is often the deciding factor in getting a job. Except for floral design, formal preparation in design is necessary.

Educational requirements for entry–level positions vary. Some design occupations, notably industrial design, require a bachelor's degree. Interior designers normally need a college education, in part because few clients—especially commercial clients—are willing to entrust responsibility for designing living and working space to a designer with no formal credentials.

Interior design is the only design field subject to government regulation. According to the American Society for Interior Designers, 21 States and the District of Columbia require interior designers to be licensed. Because licensing is not mandatory in all states, an interior designer's professional standing is important. Membership in a professional association usually requires the completion of 3 or 4 years of postsecondary education in design, at least 2 years of practical experience in the field, and passage of the National Council for Interior Design qualification examination. We will meet these standards at the high point.

Set, lighting, and costume designers typically have college degrees in their particular area of design. A Master of Fine Arts (MFA) degree from an accredited university program further establishes one's design credentials. Membership in the United Scenic Artists, Local 829, is a nationally recognized standard of achievement for scenic designers.

In contrast to the other design occupations, a high school diploma ordinarily suffices for floral design jobs. Most floral designers learn their skills on the job. When employers hire trainees, they generally look for high school graduates who have a flair for color and a desire to learn. Completion of formal training, however, is an asset for floral designers, particularly for advancement to the chief floral designer level. Vocational and technical schools offer programs in floral design, usually lasting less than a year, while 2– and 4–year programs in floriculture, horticulture, floral design, or ornamental horticulture are offered by community and junior colleges, and colleges and universities.

Formal training for some design professions also is available in 2– and 3–year professional schools that award certificates or associate degrees in design. Graduates of 2–year programs normally qualify as assistants to designers. The Bachelor of Fine Arts degree is granted at 4–year colleges and universities. The curriculum in these schools includes art and art history, principles of design, designing and sketching, and specialized studies for each of the individual design disciplines, such as garment construction, textiles, mechanical and architectural drawing, computerized design, sculpture, architecture, and basic engineering. A liberal arts education, with courses in merchandising, business administration, marketing, and psychology, along with training in art, also is a good background for most design fields. Additionally, persons with training or experience in architecture qualify for some design occupations, particularly interior design.

Computer–aided design (CAD) increasingly is used in all areas of design, except floral design, so many employers expect new designers to be familiar with the use of the computer as a design tool. For example, industrial designers extensively use computers in the aerospace, automotive, and electronics industries. Interior designers use computers to create numerous versions of interior space designs—making it possible for a client to see and choose among several designs; images can be inserted, edited, and replaced easily and without added cost. In furniture design, a chair's basic shape and structure may be duplicated and updated, by applying new upholstery styles and fabrics with the use of computers.

The National Association of Schools of Art and Design currently accredits about 200 postsecondary institutions with programs in art and design; most of these schools award a degree in art. Some award degrees in industrial, interior, textile, graphic, or fashion design. Many schools do not allow formal entry into a bachelor's degree program, until a student has finished a year of basic art and design courses successfully. Applicants may be required to submit sketches and other examples of their artistic ability.

The Foundation for Interior Design Education Research also accredits interior design programs and schools. Currently, there are more than 120 accredited programs in the United States and Canada, located in schools of art, architecture, and home economics.

Individuals in the design field must be creative, imaginative, persistent, and able to communicate their ideas in writing, visually, or verbally. Because tastes in style and fashion can change quickly, designers need to be well read, open to new ideas and influences, and quick to react to changing trends. Problem–solving skills and the ability to work independently and under pressure are important traits. People in this field need self–discipline to start projects on their own, to budget their time, and to meet deadlines and production schedules. Good business sense and sales ability also are important, especially for those who freelance or run their own business.

Beginning designers usually receive on–the–job training, and normally need 1 to 3 years of training before they advance to higher–level positions. Experienced designers in large firms may advance to chief designer, design department head, or other supervisory positions. Some designers become teachers in design schools and colleges and universities. Some experienced designers open their own firms.

Growth Strategy

Despite projected faster–than–average employment growth, designers in most fields—with the exception of floral and furniture design—are expected to face keen competition for available positions. We will use this to make sure we hire the most qualified staff.

Overall, the employment of designers is expected to grow faster than the average for all occupations through the year 2008. In addition to employment growth, many job openings will result from the need to replace designers who leave the field. Increased demand for industrial designers will stem from the continued emphasis on product quality and safety; the demand for new products that are easy and comfortable to use; the development of high–technology products in medicine, transportation, and other fields; and growing global competition among businesses. Rising demand for professional design of private homes, offices, restaurants and other retail establishments, and institutions that care for the rapidly growing elderly population should spur employment growth of interior designers. Demand for fashion, textile, and furniture designers should remain strong, because many consumers are concerned with fashion and style.

Earnings for average staff

Median annual earnings for designers in all specialties except interior design were $29,200 in 2003. The middle 50 percent earned between $18,420 and $43,940. The lowest 10 percent earned less than $13,780 and the highest 10 percent earned over $68,310. Median annual earnings in the industries employing the largest numbers of designers, except interior designers, in 2002 were as follows:

1. Engineering and architectural services—$41,300

2. Apparel, piece goods, and notions—$38,400

3. Mailing, reproduction, and stenographic services—$36,000

4. Retail stores, not elsewhere classified—$16,500

Median annual earnings for interior designers were $31,760 in 2003. The middle 50 percent earned between $23,580 and $42,570. The lowest 10 percent earned less than $18,360 and the highest 10 percent earned over $65,810. Median annual earnings in the industries employing the largest numbers of interior designers in 2002 were as follows:

1. Engineering and architectural services—$33,000

2. Furniture and home furnishings stores—$27,800

3. Miscellaneous business services—$26,800

Median annual earnings of merchandise displayers and window dressers were $18,180 in 2003. The lowest 10 percent earned less than $12,680; the highest 10 percent, over $28,910.

According to the Industrial Designers Society of America, the average base salary for an industrial designer with 1 to 2 years of experience was about $31,000 in 2003. Staff designers with 5 years of experience earned $39,000 whereas senior designers with 8 years of experience earned $51,000. Industrial designers in managerial or executive positions earned substantially more—up to $500,000 annually; however, $75,000 to $100,000 was more representative.

Design Specialties

Designers often specialize in one or more specific types of interior design.

- **Residential**—Residential interior design focuses on the design, professional design team coordination, planning, budgeting, specifying/purchasing and furnishings installation of private homes, including the specialty areas of the kitchen, bath, home theater, home office, and custom product design. Interior projects include new construction, renovation, historic renovation and model homes, with expertise in universal and sustainable design. A residential designer is often involved in interior detailing of background elements like ceiling designs, specialty trim and case work including interior doors and door hardware, lighting both architectural and decorative, coordination of audio–visual and communication technology, organizational and storage needs, interior finish schedules of walls, ceilings and floors in addition to selections of appliances, plumbing, and flooring materials. Residential designers also provide specification and purchasing services to procure materials, furniture, accessories and art.

- **Information Technology**—Today's information technology environment has a profound effect upon the interior design profession. Consulting in areas outside our traditional training, we must now assist our clients with decisions on home wiring and cable needs, switching and security systems, computer hardware placement and space requirements for accompanying equipment, home theater electronics and more. While we will offer advice, our Information Tech staff will have final say on the placements because we are trained to envision the design of the total space, we understand how each individual issue affects another and the key importance of advanced planning. The majority of American homes are now wired with computers in multiple rooms. Designers must consider and advise their clients on linking computer systems, installing appropriate circuits and using multiple phone, cable and DSL lines. Design issues once confined to the office now affect the home as well as the "home office" becomes a more standard feature in today's household. Functional equipment placement, wire management and a host of other technological and ergonomic challenges are now a regular part of a residential designer's work. Thin screen technology is being married with larger, multiple–speaker audio and theater–quality video systems that require specialized skills for proper installation and acoustics. Systems are being installed in just about any place, including on the ceiling, and many clients are requesting special "home theater rooms." Today's information technology advancements will soon allow our computers to link to our video systems, creating new challenges and opportunities in the design of home spaces. Already privacy and parental supervision issues arising from the information technology boom are affecting the function of every floor plan in the home. Our designers are trained to interview clients, to help them explore in depth their needs and tutor them as to possible future requirements that will improve their lifestyle. We are the natural link to help educate our clients about the future direction of information technology in the home. We must continually reeducate ourselves so we have the knowledge and sources to solve our clients' problems. However, we must also know our limitations and refer clients to appropriate sources to adequately address their needs.

- **Our Designers Service Sectors**—We will hire designers with these skill–sets, so we can offer our clients services in all these areas.

- **Commercial**—ASID divides commercial design into the following sub–specialties: 1) Entertainment— Entertainment design brings together the use of interiors, lighting, sound and other technologies for movies, television, videos, dramatic and musical theater, clubs, concerts, theme parks and industrial projects. 2) Facilities Management—A facilities manager develops schedules for building upkeep and maintenance, addressing safety and health issues and lighting and acoustics needs. A facilities manager also plans and coordinates office moves or expansions, and serves as project manager during construction or renovation. 3) Government/Institutional—A government designer is familiar with the very specific needs and requirements associated with working with government agencies, such as military bases, federal buildings or government offices. An institutional designer focuses on projects such as childcare, educational, religious, correctional and recreational facilities, fire and police stations, courts, embassies, libraries, auditoriums, museums and transportation terminals. 4) Health Care— Health care designers create environments for hospitals; clinics; examination rooms; surgical suites; mobile units; hospice care homes; nursing, assisted living or long term care facilities; or any other health care environment. 5) Hospitality/Restaurant—Hospitality design focuses on environments that entertain or host the public, including nightclubs, restaurants, theaters, hotels, city and country clubs, golf facilities, cruise ships and conference facilities. 6) Office—Office design focuses on the public and private areas utilized by corporate and professional service firms. 7) Retail/Store Planning—Retail design and store planning concentrate on retail venues, including boutiques, department stores, outlets, showrooms, food retailing centers and shopping malls.

Approaches—The following are not design specialties but rather approaches to design that cut across design specialties.

- **Sustainable Design**—Also referred to as "green" design or "eco–design," sustainable design is concerned with the environmental/ecological, economic, ethical and social aspects and impacts of design.

- **Universal Design**—An extension of "barrier–free" design, universal design employs products and solutions originally developed for individuals with disabilities to increase ease of use, access, safety and comfort for all users.

Interior Painting Service

Eyecatching Interiors LLC

1510 Battery Way
Charleston, SC 29417

Eric Patrick McMahon

The mission of Eyecatching Interiors is to offer high-quality interior commercial and residential painting services. The company will accomplish this by using the highest quality materials and apply them in the most professional manner. Every customer will be dealt with in a personal and friendly manner and every project will be viewed as a personal reflection of the company.

EXECUTIVE SUMMARY

Eyecatching Interiors' Objectives

Eyecatching Interiors is an interior painting contractor with combined experience of over thirty years in the industry. The company is located at 1510 Battery Way in Charleston, South Carolina. The company emphasizes the highest quality of work for all of its jobs, regardless of size. The foundation of the company is Brett Taylor. Originally trained as a union painter, Brett brings experience and knowledge to every job. The company had previously been a sole proprietorship, with Brett Taylor being the only employee. Currently the company has contracts with nine builders with several others interested. One man can not meet the demand thus the company must grow to add the additional customers. The company intends to add an additional employee, Joe Taylor, who will be on site and paint four days a week and do office work one day a week. His addition will allow the company to meet its growing demand as well as lighten the workload for Brett Taylor. The purpose of this plan is to guide the company through this expansion and evolution. It will be a guide for the company as it adds an employee and modernizing its operations. The company currently has no intention on becoming a huge painting contractor and wishes to stay at two employees for a while.

The main objective of the company is to become a family owned and operated business. Joe Taylor will join as a minority owner and become the director of operations. He has a degree in entrepreneurship from the College of Charleston along with six years of experience in the industry. He often worked part-time and in the summers for the company. Brett and Joe's background makes them the perfect team to expand the company. It is very important to keep the family atmosphere in the company so as to make every customer feel like a member of the family.

The company currently does mainly new residential home painting and does work for nine builders. Karl Brown Construction is becoming the company's largest customer, with over one hundred homes planned in one sub-division. The company started out building three to four homes a year and has grown to twenty homes a year, and has plans for continued growth. Eyecatching Interiors must grow with this client to meets its growing demand. The company hopes to continue to grow its residential

151

new construction segment and add a few new contractors to its customer list. The company also plans to expand its commercial segment with small specialized projects. Eyecatching Interiors is a quality driven company, thus it is not in the interest of the company to perform jobs that do not require a quality finish.

Eyecatching Interiors has been successful for fifteen years and has developed a fine reputation. The company will count on reputation and customer referrals to reach its goals.

The objectives for Eyecatching Interiors over the next three years are:

- Transition into a family–owned and operated business

- Continue to profitably offer the highest quality interior finishes and service

- Modernize and update business practices

Mission

The mission of Eyecatching Interiors is to offer high quality interior commercial and residential painting services. The company will accomplish this by using the highest quality materials and apply them in the most professional manner. Every customer will be dealt with in a personal and friendly manner and every project will be viewed as a personal reflection of the company.

Keys to Success

Keys to success for the company will include:

1. Maintaining a reputation of high quality, professional service

2. Professional appearance of all employees

3. Not sacrificing quality for profit

COMPANY SUMMARY

Eyecatching Interiors is a limited liability company based in Charleston, South Carolina that provides commercial and residential interior painting. The company has been in existence for twenty five years and is based on over thirty years experience by its founder, Brett Taylor. The company will be a family–owned and operated business consisting of Brett Taylor and Joe Taylor. Joe Taylor will function as the director of operations for the company, dealing with the business end of the company. Joe will also offer his service in the field three to four days a week depending on the needs of the company. Brett Taylor will be the primary painter and estimator; he will be concerned with bidding on new jobs as well as managing existing projects. Currently the company is about 85% residential and 15% commercial. The majority of the work is residential new construction, mainly focused in the Charleston County area. This area is experiencing rapid growth, especially in new construction. Eyecatching Interiors has formed strong relationships with several builders in the area and looks to strengthen these existing relationships as well as develop new relationships. The company also has well established relationships with several interior designers, this work is usually high end and very time consuming. Currently the company is owned and operated by Brett Taylor; he is also the sole employee. The company lacks formal book-keeping and invoicing practices and lacks modernization. The work is currently performed with a pencil and an adding machine. For the company to continue to be successful it is important for it to modernize.

Company Ownership

Eyecatching Interiors is a limited liability company with two partners: Joe Taylor and Brett Taylor. Joe Taylor will become president of the company and will primarily function as head of operations. He will work in the business side about two days a week and paint the remainder of the week. Brett Taylor will be the head foreman and function as site supervisor and estimator. The company will be owned as follows:

- 70% owned by Brett Taylor

- 30% owned by Joe Taylor

Company History

Eyecatching Interiors was founded as a sole proprietorship by Brett Taylor and has been in business for 15 years. The company's founder has 30 years experience in the painting industry and was trained as a union painter. He had worked at a union shop for 15 years when he decided to start his own company. Currently Eyecatching Interiors has a broad customer base that includes: residential builders, private homeowners, interior designers, and real estate management companies. The majority of revenues come from residential new construction primarily in the Charleston County area. Eyecatching Interiors currently does work for 4 builders in the area and has been approached by additional builders. The company also has a mix of residential clients that act as fillers when work slows down. Many of these customers are willing to wait for our service. If construction on a new home slows, we can call a client in waiting and complete the job. This helps offset some of the seasonal slow downs that affect the new construction industry. The company averages about one major commercial project a year and a hand full of smaller office repaints.

Some of Eyecatching Interiors' previous projects include:

- Several custom homes in St. Albans

- Club house at Deer Creek Golf Course

- Kohler City Plaza, a 20,000 square foot commercial space comprised of a restaurant, hardware store, and office space

- Glaze Creek sewer treatment facility in Barnhart, Missouri

- 10,000 square foot home in Town and Country

- 3 story medical office building in Creve Coeur, Missouri

Eyecatching Interiors' clients include:
Residential Builders:

- A Grade Construction

- Eric Loberg Contracting

- Eagle Eye Construction

- Karl Brown Construction

- Pinnacle Homes

- Smith Construction

- Sturdy Custom Homes

- True Homes

Interior Designers:

- Painters R Us

- Unique Design

Real Estate Managers/Developers:

- Bill Quinn

- Hayden Smith

- Steve Holcomb

Services

Eyecatching Interiors provides complete interior painting for the residential and commercial markets. The emphasized service for the company is woodwork. Eyecatching Interiors prides itself in the finest quality woodwork and takes pride in all of its projects. The company uses the highest quality products from Benjamin Moore Paints and insists on using oil enamel for all woodwork. This method of finishing is all but lost with the advent of latex paint and the spray gun, but it is what sets Eyecatching Interiors apart from its competitors. All enamel woodwork is first prepped, which involves spackling, caulking, and sanding. A first coat of enamel is then brushed on followed by a light sanding. After the additional sanding a final coat is applied. (For higher–end work this may involve an additional one to two coats.) This method of finishing woodwork is labor intensive and leads to higher costs but the overall product is well worth the added cost to our clients.

Eyecatching Interiors also provides finishes for walls and can apply these coatings by either rolling or spraying. On new spec homes in large subdivisions the preferred method of application is spraying, primarily because of its low cost to the builder. Again, quality plays a role as a PVA drywall primer is sprayed on all surfaces first. After allowing time for the primer to dry a finish coat is sprayed on. This can be accomplished in less than 8 hours for a house of about 2,500 square feet. The company can accomplish this task with one spray man and one apprentice. Due to the experience of its painters, the company can spray a house without backrolling, which is when you go over the sprayed surface with a roller to get rid of any runs. This is a common practice among less experienced, less skilled painters. Eyecatching Interiors has the skills and experience to spray a surface without having runs or heavy spots. Experience, skill, and quality are all characteristics of the service the company provides to all its customers.

MARKET ANALYSIS

Eyecatching Interiors will focus on two broad categories in the industry: the commercial market and the residential market. The commercial market will not be a major emphasis but it is an area with planned growth for the company. The emphasis in this sector will primarily be high end offices and commercial spaces. The company can not compete in the cookie cutter office market. The company would hurt its brand image by doing this kind of work. Eyecatching Interiors could definitely make a name for itself in the restaurant industry. Fine restaurants place an emphasis on interior finishes, since they create the overall atmosphere. Restaurants also provide highly visible displays of the company's work. Eyecatching Interiors has previous experience in the restaurant industry, with such projects as Hilfinger's, The Shrimp House, and Joseph's. The company can exploit these past accomplishments to gain new work in the market. Eyecatching Interiors also plans on expanding into the commercial office loft market, which is a market that is experiencing tremendous growth. The company is currently forming a relationship with an emerging real estate developer, Office Spaces LLC, that specializes in these kinds of projects in the Charleston region. Eyecatching Interiors is currently in preliminary discussions on a renovation of a 46,000 square foot building on Morris in Charleston. This project would entail twelve to fifteen residential lofts and possibly three to four restaurants and possible retail space. Office Spaces LLC already has thirty five buildings planned for redevelopment in the next five years. This relationship could prove to be very valuable as redevelopment of the city continues to grow in popularity.

Another area of emphasis is the residential new construction market, which has been the company's main emphasis for the past fifteen years. Eyecatching Interiors currently has contracts with six builders for all of their projects. This segment is attractive because a relationship is developed between the sub–contractor and the builder; the relationship is such that you are guaranteed all of that builders work. The only way you will lose the work is if you make a huge mistake or do not take care of the builder. This means barring a major mistake you have a steady stream of work guaranteed. This is advantageous to the company because it doesn't have to spend a lot of time and effort seeking out new work. Currently the company focuses on the Charleston County area for new construction. The company does all the work for six builders in this region and has another builder interested in acquiring its services. One of the builders, A Grade Construction, has recently broke ground on a development of one hundred homes in the Mt. Pleasant area. Each home equals about $4,500 in revenue for the company. Eyecatching Interiors has also reached an agreement with Pinnacle Homes for twenty eight homes in the Summerville, South Carolina area.

Reasons new home construction market should be pursued:

- The 45–64 age bracket is expected to have the greatest population gains in the U.S from 2003–2010, with an expected increase of 18%

- This age bracket is likely to be at its peak earnings and looking to move into bigger, more luxurious homes

- Strong relationships with existing builders

- Twenty years experience in the new home construction market

Reasons Charleston County should be an emphasized region:

- The company has developed a name for itself in the region with around 200 homes completed

- Charleston County has experienced rapid growth in population

- 14.9% increase in population from 1990–2000

- Number three in population growth in the state from 1990–2000 and has recently moved to number two

- From 1991–2001 gross income rose 81.2%

- A rise in income means more new homes and bigger new homes

- Lots are priced considerably less than lots found in western counties

- Absence of union builders means lower construction costs

- Continued urban sprawl

Eyecatching Interiors will also focus on "active adult housing" and retirement complexes. This is a market that could provide substantial dividends for the company as the country's population grows older. The 65+ age bracket is expected to increase 29% between the 2003 and 2015, which means an increased need for "active adult housing". This age group has tremendous equity buildup and will be able to afford homes/centers of their choice. Eyecatching Interiors needs to work with the builders it already does work for to begin to exploit the rising demand for older adult housing. This would be a fairly easy transition for Eyecatching Interiors because the building methods are very similar. The company is already entering the market, with a new ten unit retirement condominium complex on the horizon.

The company will also emphasize adding more interior designers as clients. Currently the company does work for two designers, including Unique Design. Interior designers provide a source of work that is frequently very detailed and high–end, something that Eyecatching Interiors excels at. Interior designers also provide a steady source of work, like builders. These projects are usually such that bring pride to the company and could be added to the portfolio of work. Interior designers could also provide the high end commercial work that Eyecatching Interiors desires.

Eyecatching Interiors also does work for property management firms. Currently the company does work for two major property managers and usually does about five to six projects a year for these clients. This is a great segment because it offers work when new construction may slow down. In the winter when most new construction slows, the company can jump over and complete projects for the property management firms. These projects are usually small enough to be fillers between jobs; this segment is essential to maintaining incoming cash flow.

Market Segmentation

Eyecatching Interiors will focus on three market segments:

1. Residential Builders—This segment is comprised of home builders and represents the main focus of the company. This segment provides a steady stream of work for the company and currently accounts for about sixty percent of total revenue. This segment is crucial because of the intense loyalty of the builder to the sub–contractor. Most of the builders the company currently does work for have been working with the company for ten plus years. After ten years of working together a bond is formed, a bond that is so strong that it becomes nearly impossible to break. The key to maintaining the bond is taking care of the customer; we provide a one year warranty for all new homes free of charge and do not charge for additional touch ups. Offering small services free of charge go a long way in keeping the builder happy and committed to the company. A high quality paint job really helps sell a house and it is why many builders turn to Eyecatching Interiors. Currently the company is not large enough to handle the growing number of builders interested in acquiring our services. The demand is definitely there, the company needs to expand to meet the heightened demand. The current trend in the new home segment, especially custom homes is enameled woodwork and dark colors. This trend requires better quality finishes and better quality applications. This growing trend is very advantageous to Eyecatching Interiors because of the high quality finishes it provides.

2. Commercial—The commercial segment the company is pursuing is high end commercial space; such as restaurants and office lofts. Due to the type of service Eyecatching Interiors provides, the costs are too high for the typical cookie cutter office space. Eyecatching Interiors needs to attach its name to projects that will bring prestige to the overall brand image of the company. These clients will frequently require detailed paint schemes with many techniques required. Often faux finishes will be requested, and Eyecatching Interiors is fully capable of providing these services. Eyecatching Interiors uses Painters R Us for all of its decorative finish work; including faux finishing and specialized murals. Painters R Us is hired as a sub–contractor, which allows the customer to deal with one company: Eyecatching Interiors. These clients will also request wallpaper, which again Eyecatching Interiors can provide. The company has a paper hanger that does all of work as a sub–contractor. Commercial projects are desired because they are large projects that can add to the overall portfolio of the company.

3. Other—This segment is composed of several smaller market segments Eyecatching Interiors will pursue. A major aspect of this segment is interior designers. Interior designers often require much tailored service and often require very intricate and time–consuming finishes. Again Eyecatching Interiors– alliance with Painters R Us and a quality paper hanger allows the company to apply nearly any interior finish. Interior designers provide a steady stream of work for the company but also require a lot of time, as many projects are quite drawn out. This is why Eyecatching Interiors wants to limit the number of designers to about four or five. Another aspect of this segment is real estate management firms. These are companies and individuals that the company has longstanding

relations with. This segment requires repaints of properties that range from apartment complexes to doctors' offices. This segment is great for providing a steady stream of work, especially when the building season slows. The company does not wish to pursue this segment too dramatically as it doesn't fit with the overall scheme of the company. The company does wish to maintain existing clients because of the longstanding relationships and to keep the steady stream of work. The final aspect of this segment is miscellaneous jobs; these are often jobs the company picks up off referrals. These jobs are usually small but provide good filler work for when things are slow.

Target Market Segment Strategy

Eyecatching Interiors recognizes that its quality and skills capabilities position it in a higher end customer segment. Each segment was chosen because of its relationship to quality and skill required. The new home construction segment was chosen because it is increasingly requiring higher quality painting. A quality paint job is often what distinguishes one new home from another, especially in a time when new homes are increasingly looking alike. Builders are often willing to pay more for a paint job if they know it will help sell the home faster. Custom home builders also want a quality finish because it makes their work look better and it pleases the discerning homeowner. A quality paint job accentuates the woodwork and often makes or breaks the trim carpenter's work. Trim carpenters want the assurance of a skilled painter following them because the painter can hide errors and emphasize the trim. The high end commercial segment again needs quality above cost. If a restaurant requires detailed finishes, they will be willing to pay more for it to look right. The finish is often what sets the mood for any restaurant. Interior designers often require the most detailed and exotic finishes and thus look for the best painting companies, with little concern for cost. Their clients are usually very affluent and thus capable and willing to pay more for a unique finish. Each segment is meant to mirror image the high quality service Eyecatching Interiors provides.

Competition

Eyecatching Interiors falls in the painting and paper hanging industry: SIC 172 and NAICS 23521. The painting and paper hanging industry is very diverse and fragmented. In 1997 there were 37,480 industry establishments in the United States that employed 195,331 people. The industry produced $13 billion in income in 1997. Most of the contractors in the industry are small independent contractors; these small contractors usually have between one and ten employees and account for 47% of all painters and paperhangers. Most of Eyecatching Interiors' competitors are small to mid–size, with the average number of employees being around five. In the residential new construction segment there are several competitors trying to gain access to the lucrative builder. The strategy employed by most competitors is low cost provider. These companies claim to provide high quality service but don't charge enough to actually provide the quality service. Eyecatching Interiors can not and will not become the low cost painter and thus distinguishes itself from the numerous low cost painting companies. Many of these shops do not higher trained painters but rather laborers who happen to paint. They pay their employees eight dollars and hour and give about an eight dollar an hour quality job. These contractors spray anything and everything and emphasize speed over quality. Eyecatching Interiors is a quality painting company and thus has its own niche which distinguishes itself from the multitude of painting companies.

In this industry, the service and professionalism in which the service is provided is also a distinguishing factor. Eyecatching Interiors prides itself in being a company that emphasizes personal relations. The company goes out of its way to provide the best service possible for every client. Every employee is issued 5 white t–shirts with the company name, which they are required to wear everyday. Employees are expected to wear clean whites and are required to wear boots. All shirts are to be tucked in and a belt is to be worn. This professional appearance presents a positive image of the company; very few painting companies have such strict rules on uniform. In fact many do not have a uniform, which makes the company look bad and the trade itself bad. Eyecatching Interiors considers its employees to be crafts-men, not merely painters.

Competition in the painting industry is very intense, especially among the small to mid–size contractors. Companies are competing for a multitude of work and must look for innovative ways to distinguish themselves. The main tactic used by companies is lowering their cost. Price wars are quite common in the painting industry, especially when contractors are fighting to gain access to a builder or subdivision. Most of the work is acquired by word of mouth; nothing can replace having a satisfied customer tell a friend. This is especially true with painting contractors who specialize in residential repaints. You may do a house for a family in a sub–division and they will tell all their friends in that sub–division, suddenly you have ten homes in one sub–division. A key is building a good relationship and reputation with your paint supplier, frequently people will turn to those who supply the paint for the best painter. In new construction aligning with builders with good reputations serve to bolster your reputation and may lead to additional work. Contractors often post yard signs in front of new projects as a form of advertisement. If you provide quality service the customers will find you.

Competition and Buying Patterns by Segment

- Residential New Construction—This segment has a definite barrier to entry that makes obtaining new contracts very difficult. In this segment builders create strong relationships with their subcontractors and often stick with one contractor for each trade. What this means is that in order to gain additional work you have to get the builder to break the relationship. This is not easy because a friendship has been formed and it is a very big hassle to switch contractors. The plus side to this barrier is that once you get in, you have that barrier protecting you. As long as you provide quality finishes and service you keep the barrier protecting you. The competitors in this market include: Colonial Painting and Exterior Painting and Drywall, as well as numerous other small contractors who employ two to four people. These competitors all claim to provide quality service, thus just saying you provide quality is not enough. Painting is very visible, thus you have to prove that you provide quality. There are however customers who do not recognize quality and look at the bottom line. These are customers Eyecatching Interiors has no desire to pursue, first because we will probably be too high and second our work will not be appreciated. Therefore the company wishes to pursue clients who appreciate quality and understand that quality comes at a price. There are painting contractors who provide quality work at a price comparable to Eyecatching Interiors. One way Eyecatching Interiors distinguishes itself from comparable competitors is the added service it offers. There are no additional charges for touch up and change orders will often be performed without a surcharge. This may seem to cut in on profits but in the long run it creates a greater relationship with the builder. It's the little things you do free of charge that really set you apart from competitors. Two major competitors, Ernest Painting and Perfection Painting, charge $150 per change order. These additional costs can add up quickly, especially on larger projects. Builders appreciate the break and become even more loyal to you when you show that you are looking out for them.

- Commercial—The commercial segment has a loyalty that is similar, but not as strong as the residential new construction. In the commercial repaint segment you often get jobs by word of mouth. People will often ask friends and colleagues who does their painting; this is how we get a majority of the work. Once you get the job you are most likely going to be repainting the office again in three to five years, especially if you do a good job. The competition in this segment is however very competitive and many jobs are won through bidding. An edge that Eyecatching Interiors has is the thirty plus years of experience of Brett Taylor. He has done almost everything and understands what is involved in a particular job. The commercial new construction/renovation is a segment the company is beginning to pursue. This is a highly competitive segment, where every job is bid on. There is rarely an instance where you are guaranteed the work. The competitors range from smaller painting contractors with three or more employees to large union shops with twenty or more employees. The union shops often charge more than a nonunion shop, but on many projects a nonunion contractor will not be permitted to bid. This is the reason Eyecatching Interiors plans on pursuing smaller scale projects with contractors who do not use one hundred percent union subs.

• Other—This segment is composed primarily of two smaller segments: interior designers and property managers. The interior designer segment is a great source of work, especially work that can add prestige to the company. This segment is marked by a barrier to entry, much the same as the residential new construction segment. Interior designers tend to stick with a single painting contractor because they know and trust your work. In addition, the contractor has a better understanding of the style and look the designer is after because they have worked together before. It is very rare that an interior designer will bounce between several painting contractors. The competitors in this segment tend to be much smaller, usually with no more than three employees. They also tend be older painters who have been around for a long time and understand the business. This is a real specialty niche with very few actual competitors. It is really difficult to target interior designers because they frequently already have a painter. This is the reason why Eyecatching Interiors does not wish to actively pursue the interior designer segment, but rather maintain the existing relationships and possibly pick up additional clients along the way. The other segment is the property manager segment. This is a small segment for Eyecatching Interiors and is composed mostly of longtime clients, many of whom are also builders/developers. In the segment as a whole the competition is brutal, as price is the main factor for most clients. Contractors such as Schaffer Painting and Berkner Painting are some of the bigger nonunion contractors that pursue this segment. Eyecatching Interiors does not plan on pursuing this segment primarily because it is so price driven. There are very few property managers who care about quality when it comes to apartment and office complexes. The clients the company already has in this segment have been clients for over ten years and continue to use us because of the existing relationship. It is in the interest to maintain these relationships because as previously stated many of these clients are also builders. If you take care of them they will take care of you.

GROWTH STRATEGY

The strategy of Eyecatching Interiors is quite simple; to continue to provide the highest quality finishes to its clients. The company wishes to maintain its course while adding a few additional contractors; one being Subdivision Development LLC. A strategy for sudden and rapid growth would jeopardize the quality and service that has been a trademark of the company for so many years. In fact, the small size of the company gives a more personal feel to all projects, as the clients deal directly with the owners of the company. In order to add the additional contractors, Joe Taylor will have to work three to four days a week and spend the remaining time doing paperwork and setting up new work. This will free time up for Brett Taylor and allow him to do what he does best–paint. Currently Brett is overworked, often working seven days a week to keep up with the demand. The additional help of Joe will reduce his workload and lead to better efficiency overall. The company is currently in the dark ages; everything is done on paper and there is no computerized invoicing system in place. Joe intends on improving the operating efficiency of the company by having a more automated invoicing system, most likely QuickBooks Online that will track sales and expenses of the company. Brett looked at books as a sidebar to painting and thus did not spend a great deal of time and effort getting them done. The plan is to modernize the bookkeeping system so that it is not such a big task and to where it benefits the entire company. Joe's education will allow him to do the bookwork in a more efficient and timely manner than Brett.

Competition

The company has a competitive edge over its competition in the quality of work provided. Eyecatching Interiors emphasizes quality on all jobs, regardless of size and the company will do whatever it takes to do the job right. The site supervisor, Brett Taylor, provides a competitive advantage because of his thirty plus years of experience. He has seen everything in his career and is thus able to overcome most obstacles. The sheer professionalism of Eyecatching Interiors keeps its customers happy and it is a true trademark of the company's work.

Marketing & Sales

The marketing strategy is focused around generating more new home contracts and adding new commercial contracts. The emphasis of Eyecatching Interiors has and will continue to be residential new construction. Currently the company has no existing marketing plan; in fact the company is not even listed in the phone book. The reason being is that the company doesn't want to do work for people it doesn't know. The company has grown simply because of reputation and word of mouth. The plan then is to continue to rely on reputation and word of mouth to continue to grow, but with some added marketing efforts. The company will for the first time have a listed number; a simple listing will be posted in the local Yellow Pages. The company will also place signs in front of its projects, proclaiming: "Another Quality Job By Eyecatching Interiors." The company plans on having Benjamin Moore Paints pay for a portion of the sign to have their name on it; this will help defer some of the costs of the advertisement. The company also plans on advertising its name in local home and designer magazines, in order to attract the higher end clientele.

The company will generate sales through existing contacts and through its reputation. A solid customer base already exists, there is already too much work lined up for one man. The company has projects lined up into 2006. Currently the company is forced to put clients off and sometimes turn them down. Brett Taylor averages over fifty hours a week working. The addition of Joe will add relief to Brett and allow the company to take care of all of its clients.

The average new home runs between $4,500 and $5,000 and is between 2,500 to 3,000 square feet. The large custom homes and commercial projects are all bid by Brett Taylor. He estimates the total time and material required and usually adds between twenty and thirty percent to that. For the very large and detailed custom homes the sales procedure is to quote a ball park price, but to charge time and material. These jobs are frequently very difficult to safely bid because of the complicated finishes and frequent changes made by the homeowners. In the end the customer comes out ahead because in order to bid the project safely you would really have to pad the price.

MANAGEMENT SUMMARY

Joe Taylor will become the director of operations. He has six years experience in the painting industry and a degree in Entrepreneurship from the College of Charleston. His business education and underlying knowledge and understanding of the industry will allow him to effectively manage the operations of the company. His tasks will include recruiting new work, handling payroll and insurance, and the general operations of the business. He will also work about four days a week in the field painting with Brett Taylor.

Brett Taylor, the other principal, will be the primary painter and estimator. His thirty years experience in the industry will allow him to efficiently manage jobs and troubleshoot any issues that should arise during a job. He will also become the estimator for the company; again his experience affords him the capability to effectively bid jobs.

The company also has an accountant, Greg Lombardo, who keeps track of the company's financials; the company will be linked to his office via QuickBooks Online. This will allow for optimal cash flow management for the company as it can easily monitor cash in–flows and out–flows.

Personnel Plan

The personnel plan assumes paying Brett Taylor $30 an hour and paying Joe Taylor $20 an hour. Brett Taylor is currently making $30 an hour, so his wage will remain the same. He could easily find a job in a large paint shop making about the same wage if you included the benefits package. A talented and experienced painter is worth every bit of $30 an hour. Joe Taylor earned $15 an hour during the summer as an apprentice and has become a very good painter. He has run entire jobs on his own and has shown that he understands the business. He also has the business skills and knowledge to handle the company's day to day operations.

FINANCIAL ANALYSIS

Eyecatching Interiors is currently a small independent painting contractor. The goal of the company is to add Joe as an additional painter and as the director of operations. His addition will allow for the company's sales to increase dramatically from 2005 to the end of 2006. This growth will continue through 2007 as the company benefits from the added efficiency of having Joe with the company. He will be billed at $50 an hour but only costs the company $20 and hour, therefore he alone brings in an additional $30 an hour of profit. After the year FY 2007 the company will experience minor growth, 3% from FY 2007 to FY 2008 and 2% growth from 2008 to FY 2009. The company will be quite content at this level of sales and does not wish to grow any larger. Eyecatching Interiors wants to maintain its quality and fears that too much growth can lead to a decline in quality. There comes a point where a company becomes so big that it can not effectively monitor the quality of services. The company does not want to borrow to fund future expansion. Joe has $20,000 which he intends on keeping it as reserve for any unforeseen events. This keeps the company from going to the bank for a credit line. The overall office expenses will increase in the beginning due to the addition of a computer and software. This investment will pay off in the long run as it will cut the time to do paperwork in half if not more. The truck expenses category includes Brett's van and Joe's 4–Runner which are both paid off, this line item also includes gas and miscellaneous repairs. The company will now have to pay workman's compensation as it adds Joe as a full–time employee. This was not needed before because Brett was the only employee. The rate is based off a quote per $100 of total payroll. The insurance line item includes insurance for both vehicles and contractor's general liability insurance. The company intends on paying dividends as shown in the Pro Forma Cash Flow Statement.

The dividends will be divided according to ownership; 70% to Brett Taylor and 30% to Joe Taylor.

Past performance

	FY 2002	FY 2003	2004
Sales	$ 130,185.00	$ 132,765.00	$ 44,361.00
Materials	$ 36,451.80	$ 37,174.20	$ 12,421.08
Labor	$ 60,000.00	$ 61,200.00	$ 19,200.00
Payroll taxes	$ 8,400.00	$ 8,568.00	$ 2,688.00
COGS	$ 104,851.80	$ 106,942.20	$ 34,309.08
Gross profit	$ 25,333.20	$ 25,822.80	$ 10,051.92
Expenses:			
Truck expense	$ 9,112.95	$ 9,293.55	$ 3,105.27
Insurance	$ 890.00	$ 900.00	$ 935.00
Legal & professional services	$ 520.74	$ 531.06	$ 177.44
Office expense	$ 781.11	$ 796.59	$ 266.17
Meals & entertainment	$ 260.37	$ 265.53	$ 88.72
Depreciation	$ 2,603.70	$ 2,655.30	$ 887.22
Other	$ 4,556.48	$ 4,646.78	$ 1,552.64
Total expenses	$ 18,725.35	$ 19,088.81	$ 7,012.46
Net income before taxes	$ 6,607.86	$ 6,733.99	$ 3,039.46
Taxes	$ 1,982.36	$ 2,020.20	$ 911.84
Net income	$ 4,625.50	$ 4,713.80	$ 2,127.62

Assumptions:
- 2004 is calculated from the January 1 to the end of April.
- Labor is the wages earned by Kevin McMahon and payroll taxes are based on a 14% rate.
- The insurance category is for vehicle insurance and contractor's liability insurance.
- The tax is based on a 30% rate.

Pro forma profit and loss

	2004	FY 2005	FY 2006	FY 2007
Sales	$ 123,552.00	$ 226,000.00	$ 232,780.00	$ 237,435.60
Materials	$ 30,888.00	$ 56,500.00	$ 58,195.00	$ 59,358.90
Labor	$ 44,160.00	$ 92,000.00	$ 93,380.00	$ 94,033.66
Taxes	$ 6,182.40	$ 12,880.00	$ 13,073.20	$ 13,164.71
COGS	$ 75,048.00	$ 148,500.00	$ 151,575.00	$ 153,392.56
Gross profit	$ 48,504.00	$ 77,500.00	$ 81,205.00	$ 84,043.04
Expenses:				
Truck expense	$ 8,300.00	$ 13,560.00	$ 13,966.80	$ 14,246.14
Insurance	$ 1,400.00	$ 1,480.00	$ 1,500.00	$ 1,560.00
Workman's comp	$ 4,058.00	$ 9,919.00	$ 10,067.79	$ 10,118.12
Legal & professional services	$ 494.21	$ 904.00	$ 931.12	$ 949.74
Office expense	$ 12,355.20	$ 13,560.00	$ 13,966.80	$ 14,246.14
Meals & entertainment	$ 494.21	$ 904.00	$ 931.12	$ 949.74
Payroll	$ 8,000.00	$ 8,000.00	$ 8,000.00	$ 8,000.00
Depreciation	$ 2,471.04	$ 4,520.00	$ 4,655.60	$ 4,748.71
Other	$ 4,324.32	$ 7,910.00	$ 8,147.30	$ 8,310.25
Total expenses	$ 41,896.98	$ 60,757.00	$ 62,166.53	$ 63,128.84
Net income before taxes	$ 6,607.02	$ 16,743.00	$ 19,038.48	$ 20,914.20
Taxes	$ 1,982.11	$ 5,022.90	$ 5,711.54	$ 6,274.26
Net income	$ 4,624.92	$ 11,720.10	$ 13,326.93	$ 14,639.94

Assumptions:
- 2004 is calculated from June 1, when the strategy is implemented, to December 31
- Truck expense includes gas and repairs
- Insurance is comprised of auto insurance and liability for the business
- The payroll row is based off 8 hours a week spent on bookwork
- Workman's Comp is a rate based on total wages.
- Payroll taxes are 14% and taxes are 30%.
- Materials are estimated at 25% of total sales, this is based off previous percentages for the company.

Pro forma balance sheet

	FY 2004	FY 2005	FY 2006	FY 2007
Assets				
Current assets				
Accounts receivable	$ 2,500	$ 3,000	$ 2,000	$ 2,500
Cash	$ 18,041	$ 4,200	$ 5,000	$ 5,000
Inventory	$ 200	$ 350	$ 200	$ 200
Other current assets	$ 3,000	$ 3,200	$ 3,500	$ 3,500
Total current assets	$ 23,741	$ 10,750	$ 10,700	$ 11,200
Long-term assets				
Long-term assets	$ 20,000	$ 20,500	$ 20,500	$ 20,500
Accumulated depreciation	$ 2,471	$ 4,520	$ 4,656	$ 4,759
Total long-term assets	$ 17,529	$ 15,980	$ 15,844	$ 15,741
Total assets	$ 41,270	$ 26,730	$ 26,544	$ 26,941
Liabilities and capital				
Current liabilities				
Accounts payable	$ 850	$ 900	$ 900	$ 950
Other current liabilities	$ 600	$ 1,000	$ 800	$ 850
Total current liabilities	$ 1,450	$ 1,900	$ 1,700	$ 1,800
Long-term liabilities	$ —	$ —	$ —	$ —
Total liabilities	$ 1,450	$ 1,900	$ 1,700	$ 1,800
Paid-in capital	$ 5,000	$ 2,000	$ —	$ —
Retained earnings	$ 30,195	$ 11,110	$ 11,517	$ 10,501
Earnings	$ 4,625	$ 11,720	$ 13,327	$ 14,640
Total capital	$ 39,820	$ 24,830	$ 24,844	$ 25,141
Total capital and liabilities	$ 41,270	$ 26,730	$ 26,544	$ 26,941

Pro forma annual cash flow

	FY 2004	FY 2005	FY 2006	FY 2007
Cash received				
Cash from operations:				
Cash sales	$ 123,552	$ 226,000	$ 232,780	$ 237435
Cash from receivables	$ 2,000	$ 2,500	$ 3,000	$ 2,500
Subtotal from operations	$ 125,552	$ 228,500	$ 235,780	$ 239,935
Additional cash received				
Subtotal cash received	$ 125,552	$ 228,500	$ 235,780	$ 239,935
Expenditures				
Expenditures from operations:				
Cash spending	$ 56,000	$ 115,000	$ 118,000	$ 120,000
Payment of accounts payable	$ 49,921	$ 95,000	$ 96,000	$ 98,000
Subtotal spent on operations	$ 105,921	$ 210,000	$ 214,000	$ 218,000
Purchase other current asset	$ 0	$ 200	$ 300	$ 0
Purchase long-term asset	$ 0	$ 500	$ 0	$ 0
Dividends	$ 0	$ 5,000	$ 10,000	$ 10,000
Subtotal cash spent	$ 105,921	$ 215,700	$ 224,300	$ 228,000
Net cash flow	$ 19,631	$ 12,800	$ 11,480	$ 11,935
Cash balance	$ 22,631	$ 35,431	$ 46,911	$ 58,846

Projected cash flow- FY 2004

	Jun	Jul	Aug	Sep	Oct	Nov	Dec
Cash received							
Cash from operations:							
Cash sales	$ 17,650	$ 18,200	$ 18,300	$ 18,150	$ 17,200	$ 17,052	$ 17,000
Cash from receivables	$ 2,000						
Subtotal from operations	$ 19,650	$ 18,200	$ 18,300	$ 18,150	$ 17,200	$ 17,052	$ 17,000
Additional cash received	$ —	$ —	$ —	$ —	$ —	$ —	$ —
Subtotal cash received	$ 19,650	$ 18,200	$ 18,300	$ 18,150	$ 17,200	$ 17,052	$ 17,000
Expenditures							
Expenditures from operations:							
Cash spending	$ 8,000	$ 8,000	$ 8,000	$ 8,000	$ 8,000	$ 8,000	$ 8,000
Payment of accounts payable	$ 7,060	$ 7,280	$ 7,320	$ 7,260	$ 6,880	$ 6,821	$ 6,800
Subtotal spent on operations	$ 15,060	$ 15,280	$ 15,320	$ 15,260	$ 14,880	$ 14,821	$ 14,800
Subtotal cash spent	$ 15,060	$ 15,280	$ 15,320	$ 15,260	$ 14,880	$ 14,821	$ 14,800
Net cash flow	$ 4,590	$ 2,920	$ 2,980	$ 2,890	$ 2,320	$ 2,231	$ 2,200
Cash balance	$ 7,090	$ 10,010	$ 12,990	$ 15,880	$ 18,200	$ 20,431	$ 22,631

Internet Loyalty Program
Tunes4You

1414 Wilton Way
Columbus, OH 43209

Tena M. Harper

This business plan was created for a customer loyalty program which capitalizes on the Internet surge in digital music. It was directly responsible for the owner receiving $3 million in capital to begin his company.

EXECUTIVE SUMMARY

Business Overview

Tunes4You.com offers a unique proposition that is attractive to consumers and to companies. Tunes4You.com is a business–to–business marketing solution for companies desiring to capitalize on brand recognition and strengthen brand loyalty. This completely customizable marketing solution offers consumers points that are redeemed online for a variety of music products. Consumers collect loyalty point codes and then redeem them at the Tunes4You.com Web site for a variety of music-themed products and services. Companies are able to customize their point offers completely. Tunes4You.com offers a unique proposition that is attractive to consumers and to companies.

Tunes4You.com L.L.C. is solely owned by Larry Rosenberry and is located in Columbus, Ohio. This facility will require standard fixtures and furnishings, Internet capability, phone lines and Web site development.

Digital music downloads are particularly valuable for companies because of their high perceived value. They give participants a lot of flexibility and choice, and put them in control of their own reward. They make the reward personally relevant and helps companies build better relationships.

Online rewards have become increasingly popular with marketers and corporations because they significantly reduce—and in some cases completely eliminate—fulfillment costs. There are no warehouses, stamps or bubble wrap involved. There is a high degree of measurability. Tracking how many people participated is easy to do.

Digital music downloads are particularly valuable for companies because of perceived value with consumers. And the early results appear to be positive. McDonald's credited its "Big Mac Meal Tracks" promotion with being instrumental for its surging second quarter same–store sales. The effort, which dangled a free Sony Connect download with the purchase of a Big Mac meal, helped stimulate same–store sales to the tune of 9.2 percent for the quarter, according to the company.

The music downloads and subscriptions market is expected to almost quadruple in size this year, according to the Cambridge, Massachusetts–based Forrester Research. The firm estimates that it will hit

165

$308 million in sales this year compared to $83 million in 2003. By 2007, sales in the sector are forecasted to soar to $2.7 billion. As digital music promotions become more popular, industry experts believe it won't be long before this new consumer reward begins to penetrate internal corporate incentive programs.

Objectives

Tunes4You's objectives are:

1. Achieve first–year revenues of $3,205,518 increasing to $13,445,217 in year five.

2. Achieve first–year net cash flow of $429,987 increasing to $3,216,888 in year five.

Mission

Our clients invest substantial time and money to acquire their best customers. But the actions taken to cultivate loyalty can make the difference between being competitive and complacent. Tunes4You.com's solid loyalty program can provide the short–term returns you want with the long–term success you need. We go beyond simple demographics to use a unique combination of demographic, behavioral and attitudinal measures that lead to meaningful solutions for your customer's individual needs.

Keys to Success

1. Completely customizable reward program

2. Strength of the youth market

3. Larry Rosenberry is an experienced marketing professional

4. The unique ability of musical rewards to appeal to a broad range of age demographics and cross–cultural influences

Financial Analysis

Financial highlights for the first five years of operations

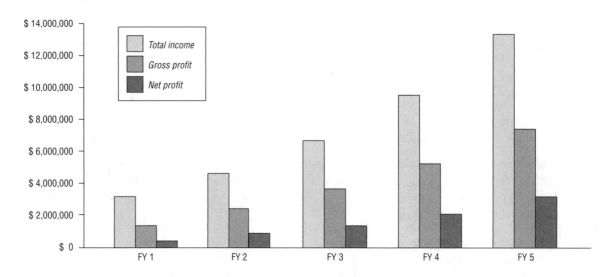

Operations

Tunes4You.com L.L.C. is solely owned by Larry Rosenberry.

Tunes4You.com is located in Columbus, Ohio. This facility will require standard fixtures and furnishings, Internet capability, phone lines and Web site development.

Start-up summary

Start-up expenses

Legal	$ 10,000
Business plan	$ 2,300
Domain name	$ 10,000
Web design	$ 100,000
Total start-up expenses	**$ 122,300**

Start-up assets

Cash balance on starting date	$ 167,700
Total current assets	**$ 167,700**

Long-term assets

Equipment	$ 10,000
Total long-term assets	$ 10,000
Total assets	**$ 177,700**

Owner's equity

Investments	$ 250,000
Owner's investment	$ 50,000
Total owner's equity	**$ 300,000**

Liabilities
Current liabilities

Total current liabilities	**$ 0**

Long-term liabilities

Total long-term liabilities	**$ 0**
Loss at start-up	($ 122,300)
Total liabilities and owner's equity	**$ 177,700**

PRODUCTS & SERVICES

Tunes4You.com is a customer reward or loyalty program that promotes the goods and services of others with redeemable online Tunes4You. Tunes4You.com is a customizable business–to–business marketing solution to build customer loyalty.

Tunes4You.com is a business–to–business marketing solution for companies desiring to capitalize on brand recognition and strengthen brand loyalty. This completely customizable marketing solution offers consumers points that are redeemed online for a variety of music products.

Companies are able to customize their point offers completely. They choose how many points are awarded to each consumer, how many of their products will contain redeemable points and whether they desire to offer a completely free product or service. This choice allows companies to maximize exposure while maintaining their budget. Companies are billed on the number of points redeemed by the end user. Billing companies on the total number of points redeemed allows for measurable tracking of actual participation in each program.

Consumers collect the points and redeem them at the Tunes4You.com Web site. They will have a variety of music related products to choose from, such as ringtones, downloads, compact discs, concert tickets, and posters. Consumers can choose to redeem their points immediately or save points for larger prizes.

Tunes4You.com offers a unique proposition that is attractive to consumers and to companies.

The point cards for Tunes4You.com are customizable for each individual corporation. Tunes4You.com will arrange for printing and delivery of the point cards to companies that are utilizing the programs.

Tunes4You.com will utilize proprietary software to customize each reward program for our individual clients. This software enables clients to customize the number of winners in each program, how many redeemable points each customer receives and how many winning tickets are included in each lot. The Tunes4You.com program is completely customizable to each merchant's need.

A variety of music–related products, services and companies are utilized to form a comprehensive Web site for the redemption of customer loyalty points. Tunes4You.com has a comprehensive Web site that allows consumers to choose what they desire to redeem their collected points for. Literature that fully explains the program will be provided at P.O.P. to entice and educate the consumer. Tunes4You.com will form strong relationships within the music industry. These relationships will provide a large selection of music related merchandise for consumers to choose from. A variety of music–related products, services and companies are utilized to form a comprehensive Web site for the redemption of customer loyalty points. Additional products such as concert tickets, music hardware and back–stage passes are all future products of Tunes4You.com.

Competition

Mypoints.com and Misterpoints.com offer similar online point redemption program as Tunes4You.com. The difference between the reward programs is that both Mypoints.com and Misterpoints.com require consumers to fill out membership offers from a variety of companies (i.e.: Visa, eBay, Doubleday book clubs).

Once consumers complete the requirements for the particular company, they are rewarded with points that may be redeemed for gift cards. Tunes4You.com offers customer loyalty points included in products consumers purchase regularly. Consumers collect their loyalty point codes and can redeem them at the Tunes4You.com Web site for a variety of music–themed products and services. The loyalty points are tied simply to the purchase of the participating product and not to credit offers or membership gimmicks. Consumers may redeem their points immediately for music downloads or save points to receive larger rewards.

GROWTH STRATEGY

For brand marketers and incentive planners alike, finding an award that appeals to everyone's interests is an elusive prize. But that may be changing. The most compelling incentive reward of late allows consumers or employees the chance to choose their own songs, via digital music downloads. Musical taste is like a fingerprint. Everyone's got one, but it–s different from person to person.

"Allowing consumers to download their favorite songs puts choice and control in their hands," says Geoff Cottrill, group director of entertainment marketing for Atlanta-based Coca-Cola.

The fact that downloads have gained traction so quickly is an asset to marketers and planners, adds Toby Simpkins, director of promotions for Cramer–Krasselt, an integrated marketing communications company in Chicago. "The education about the medium has already been done," he says. "Everybody knows what a download is. Two years ago using music downloads [as an incentive] would have been way too forward thinking."

And Carlson Marketing Group, based in Minneapolis, has a number of incentive programs in development for its customers. "We've been hearing more about music downloads from both our existing and potential clients," says Joleen McFadden, director of partnership marketing for Carlson Marketing. "[It will become a permanent fixture] because of its high perceived value. It gives participants a lot of flexibility and choice, and puts them in control of their own reward. It makes the reward personally relevant and helps companies build better relationships."

Digital music downloads are particularly valuable for companies trying to attract and retain younger employees, says Ivcich. "This group grew up with computers," she says. "You want to offer them awards from places they are already going." Maritz is currently developing reward programs that offer iPods, MP3 players and downloads. Besides the desirability of music as a reward, music downloads offer all of the benefits of being digital. Online rewards have become increasingly popular with marketers and corporations because they significantly reduce—and in some cases completely eliminate—fulfillment costs. "It's very cost-efficient," Samit says. "There are none of the inventory concerns" that traditional incentive programs face.

And tracking the success of an incentive program conducted with online rewards is significantly easier. Since the programs are all Web–based, "it is as easy to track as it is to redeem," says Cramer-Krasselt's Simpkins. "There is a high degree of measurability. If you want to know how many people participated, it's easy to do."

And the early results appear to be positive. McDonald's credited its "Big Mac Meal Tracks" promotion with being instrumental to its surging second quarter same–store sales. The effort, which dangled a free Sony Connect download with the purchase of a Big Mac meal, helped stimulate same–store sales to the tune of 9.2 percent for the quarter, according to the company. McDonald's ran out of the promotional packaging with the codes quicker than anticipated. "It was supposed to run for ten weeks, but in some stores they ran out as early as five weeks," says Jay Samit, general manager for Sony Connect, in Santa Monica, California.

Market Segmentation

The Tunes4You.com customer loyalty program is suitable for companies that want to strengthen brand recognition with consumers. While incentive programs come in a variety of types, using digital music is a natural for companies with a youth market. Growing up at a period that is more ethnically and culturally diverse than any previous American generation, the youth market represents an enormous culture market and stands at the cusp of new trends, attitudes, and consumer behaviors.

American Youth are influential in a broad set of family purchase decisions, from food and movies to clothes and computers. Estimates place teen spending of their own money at $63 billion. Add family money or teen influence into the mix and teen spending increases to a staggering level.

Target Market Segmentation Strategy

Tunes4You.com has segmented their target market by companies that desire to build brand loyalty. Corporations like Frito–Lay, PepsiCo, General Foods, Mars Inc, Hershey Corporation and others are a natural fit for the customer loyalty programs. Additional corporations that target a youth market also offer potential as target markets.

MARKET ANALYSIS

Although loyalty programs may be innovative in the e–tail realm, the biggest online success stories still come from the companies that have been doing business offline for a long time. According to estimates by research firm Gartner, more than 75 percent of consumers have more than one loyalty card that rewards them with redeemable points. In 2003, U.S. companies spent a total of more than US$1.2 billion on customer loyalty programs, and that figure is expected to rise in the future.

The music downloads and subscriptions market is expected to almost quadruple in size this year, according to the Cambridge, Massachusetts–based Forrester Research. The firm estimates that it will hit $308 million in sales this year compared to $83 million in 2003. By 2007, sales in the sector are forecasted to soar to $2.7 billion. As digital music promotions become more popular, industry experts believe it won't be long before this new consumer reward begins to penetrate internal corporate incentive programs.

Competition

Tunes4You.com offers distinctive competitive edge over other customer loyalty programs. This program rewards consumers for brand loyalty. Other incentive programs require consumers to participate in programs they are enticed to participate in by the rewards, unlike Tunes4You.com which offers rewards on products consumers regularly purchase. This marketing strategy builds and maintains consumer loyalty, an important differentiator.

MARKETING & SALES

Tunes4You.com will have a two fold marketing strategy. The first will be through business–to–business marketing with emphasis on trade journals, trade publications and trade Web site.

The second marketing strategy is coupled with each participating corporation. These marketing efforts will attract consumers who desire to redeem points for music related merchandise.

Initially, Larry Rosenberry will be responsible for explaining the numerous benefits of Tunes4You.com to corporate clients. A trained sales staff will implement sales programs after the start–up phase. Corporate clients choose the number and value of the loyalty points included with their product based on their marketing goals. The program is completely customizable for each corporate client. Corporate clients pay for their particular marketing strategy when consumers redeem their loyalty points at Tunes4You.com.

Revenue Forecast

The Revenue Forecast is both a balance of aiming high while aiming at what is possible. The forecast sets realistic company goals and maintains a set of achievable standards.

The Advertising revenue is based on earnings of $15,000 in the tenth month of the first fiscal year, increasing by 10 percent every month for the first two fiscal years, increasing by 70 percent annually in years three through five.

The Reward revenue is based on $100,000 in the third fiscal month, increasing by 20 percent each month in the first fiscal year. The Reward revenue increases by 20 percent annually in year two, 40 percent annually for years three through five.

The Affiliate revenue is based on 2,000,000 members in the first fiscal year, we are assuming that 7 percent of the customers will purchase an item at $100 of which Tunes4You will receive $4. (2,000,000*.07*$4) = $560,000 in year one, the members will increase by 2,000,000 in the following four fiscal years.

The cost of goods sold is based on 70 percent of the Reward revenue.

Annual revenue forecast

	FY1	FY2	FY3	FY4	FY5
Revenues					
Advertising revenue	$ 49,650	$ 426,937	$ 725,793	$ 1,233,849	$ 2,097,543
Reward revenue	$ 2,595,868	$ 3,115,042	$ 4,361,059	$ 6,105,482	$ 8,547,675
Affiliate revenue	$ 560,000	$ 1,120,000	$ 1,680,000	$ 2,240,000	$ 2,800,000
Total revenues	**$ 3,205,518**	**$ 4,661,979**	**$ 6,766,852**	**$ 9,579,331**	**$ 13,445,217**
Cost of goods sold					
Advertising	$ 0	$ 0	$ 0	$ 0	$ 0
Rewards	$ 1,817,108	$ 2,180,529	$ 3,052,741	$ 4,273,837	$ 5,983,372
Affiliate	$ 0	$ 0	$ 0	$ 0	$ 0
Total cost of goods sold	**$ 1,817,108**	**$ 2,180,529**	**$ 3,052,741**	**$ 4,273,837**	**$ 5,983,372**

MANAGEMENT SUMMARY

Larry Rosenberry, owner and founder of Tunes4You.com, holds significant management responsibility within the company. Addition personnel will be hired before start–up.

Larry Rosenberry is very experienced in the industry of direct marketing, sales and online marketing. He developed a direct mail and online marketing plan that doubled the revenue of an advertising company in two years.

During his tenure as a sales rep for an e–commerce credit card processing company, e–billpaid, Larry was a top producer capturing $2 million dollars a month in processing. He began his first Internet company armed with the success and knowledge from his previous work. This company grew to $1.3 million in monthly revenues.

Larry is now devoted completely to Tunes4You.com and anticipates repeating his history of success.

PERSONNEL PLAN

Annual personnel plan

	FY1	FY2	FY3	FY4	FY5
Salaries	$300,000	$400,000	$600,000	$800,000	$1,000,000
Total payroll	**$300,000**	**$400,000**	**$600,000**	**$800,000**	**$1,000,000**

FINANCIAL PLAN

Key financial indicators

	FY1	FY2	FY3	FY4	FY5
Revenue	$ 3,205,518	$ 4,661,979	$ 6,766,852	$ 9,579,331	$ 13,445,217
Gross profit	$ 1,388,410	$ 2,481,450	$ 3,714,111	$ 5,305,493	$ 7,461,845
Total operating expenses	$ 777,000	$ 1,190,000	$ 1,731,200	$ 2,289,320	$ 2,869,148

BREAK–EVEN ANALYSIS

Break-even analysis

Monthly units break-even	215,833.00
Monthly revenue break-even	$ 215,833.00
Average per-unit revenue	$ 1.00
Average per-unit variable cost	$ 0.70
Estimated monthly fixed cost	$ 64,750.00

PROFIT AND LOSS STATEMENT

Annual pro forma profit and loss

		FY1	FY2	FY3	FY4	FY5
Total income		$3,205,518	$4,661,979	$6,766,852	$9,579,331	$13,445,217
Cost of goods sold		$1,817,108	$2,180,529	$3,052,741	$4,273,837	$ 5,983,372
Gross profit		$1,388,410	$2,481,450	$3,714,111	$5,305,493	$ 7,461,845
Gross profit %		43.31%	53.23%	54.89%	55.38%	55.50%
Expenses:						
Payroll		$ 300,000	$ 400,000	$ 600,000	$ 800,000	$ 1,000,000
Depreciation		$ 2,000	$ 2,000	$ 2,000	$ 2,000	$ 2,000
Advertising		$ 250,000	$ 500,000	$ 750,000	$1,000,000	$ 1,250,000
Rent		$ 60,000	$ 72,000	$ 86,400	$ 103,680	$ 124,416
Web-site		$ 120,000	$ 156,000	$ 202,800	$ 263,640	$ 342,732
Payroll taxes	15%	$ 45,000	$ 60,000	$ 90,000	$ 120,000	$ 150,000
Total operating expenses		$ 777,000	$1,190,000	$1,731,200	$2,289,320	$ 2,869,148
Profit before interest and taxes		$ 611,410	$1,291,450	$1,982,911	$3,016,173	$ 4,592,697
Taxes incurred		$ 183,423	$ 387,435	$ 594,873	$ 904,852	$ 1,377,809
Net profit		$ 427,987	$ 904,015	$1,388,038	$2,111,321	$ 3,214,888
Net profit/sales		13.35%	19.39%	20.51%	22.04%	23.91%

CASH FLOW

Annual pro forma cash flow

	FY 1	FY 2	FY 3	FY 4	FY 5
Revenues received					
Cash from operations:					
Revenues	$ 3,205,518	$ 4,661,979	$ 6,766,852	$ 9,579,331	$ 13,445,217
Subtotal cash from operations	$ 3,205,518	$ 4,661,979	$ 6,766,852	$ 9,579,331	$ 13,445,217
Additional cash received					
New investment	$ 0	$ 0	$ 0	$ 0	$ 0
Subtotal cash received	$ 3,205,518	$ 4,661,979	$ 6,766,852	$ 9,579,331	$ 13,445,217
Expenditures					
Expenditures from operations					
Payroll	$ 300,000	$ 400,000	$ 600,000	$ 800,000	$ 1,000,000
Operating costs	$ 658,423	$ 1,175,435	$ 1,724,073	$ 2,392,172	$ 3,244,957
Cost of sales	$ 1,817,108	$ 2,180,529	$ 3,052,741	$ 4,273,837	$ 5,983,372
Subtotal spent on operations	$ 2,775,531	$ 3,755,964	$ 5,376,814	$ 7,466,009	$ 10,228,330
Additional cash spent					
Dividends	$ 0	$ 0	$ 0	$ 0	$ 0
Subtotal cash spent	$ 2,775,531	$ 3,755,964	$ 5,376,814	$ 7,466,009	$ 10,228,330
Net cash flow	$ 429,987	$ 906,015	$ 1,390,038	$ 2,113,321	$ 3,216,888
Cash balance	$ 597,687	$ 1,503,702	$ 2,893,740	$ 5,007,061	$ 8,223,949

BALANCE SHEET

Pro forma balance sheet

	FY 1	FY 2	FY 3	FY 4	FY 5
Assets					
Current assets					
Cash	$ 597,687	$ 1,503,702	$ 2,893,740	$ 5,007,061	$ 8,223,949
Total current assets	$ 597,687	$ 1,503,702	$ 2,893,740	$ 5,007,061	$ 8,223,949
Long-term assets					
Equipment	$ 10,000	$ 10,000	$ 10,000	$ 10,000	$ 10,000
Accumulated depreciation	$ 2,000	$ 4,000	$ 6,000	$ 8,000	$ 10,000
Total long-term assets	$ 8,000	$ 6,000	$ 4,000	$ 2,000	$ 0
Total assets	$ 605,687	$ 1,509,702	$ 2,897,740	$ 5,009,061	$ 8,223,949
Liabilities and owner's equity					
Current liabilities					
Total current liabilities	$ 0	$ 0	$ 0	$ 0	$ 0
Long-term liabilities					
Total liabilities	$ 0	$ 0	$ 0	$ 0	$ 0
Paid-in capital	$ 300,000	$ 300,000	$ 300,000	$ 300,000	$ 300,000
Retained earnings	$ 305,687	$ 1,209,702	$ 2,597,740	$ 4,709,061	$ 7,923,949
Earnings	$ 427,987	$ 904,015	$ 1,388,038	$ 2,111,321	$ 3,214,888
Total owner's equity	$ 605,687	$ 1,509,702	$ 2,897,740	$ 5,009,061	$ 8,223,949
Total liabilities and owner's equity	$ 605,687	$ 1,509,702	$ 2,897,740	$ 5,009,061	$ 8,223,949
Net worth	$ 605,687	$ 1,509,702	$ 2,897,740	$ 5,009,061	$ 8,223,949

Internet Services Portal Site

Net Solutions

2 Oak Blvd.
Berkeley, CA 94553

Adam Greengrass

This business plan raised $20 million for an innovative company's new portal Web site offering a proprietary service which "demystifies" how to effortlessly use the Internet for consumers and businesses alike.

EXECUTIVE SUMMARY

Net Solutions is a dynamic new entrant in the Internet product and services marketplace. Through powerful marketing tools including their own proprietary product line called The Solutions, direct response television commercials, personalized outbound telemarketing and the retail channel, Net Solutions has successfully demonstrated the ability to effectively acquire customers—to the current tune of 90,000 with 20,000 more being added each month.

Internet Service Providers, web hosting firms, e–Commerce solution companies and traditional brick and mortar retailers are all part of the clamor for market share and brand positioning. The "e–rush" has forced customer acquisition costs to unprecedented levels and in turn has created significant opportunities for the marketing and Internet savvy company. Enter Net Solutions!

Objectives

Net Solutions' vision is to build an Internet portal site, unlike anything currently in existence, and to combine this portal site with a unique and exciting product that will lead both consumers and businesses onto the Internet to the Net Solutions portal. The definition of an Internet portal site is the primary destination that users access to start their experience on the Internet. The Net Solutions portal site will subsequently be the 'jumping off point' for all TWC users.

Mission

Net Solutions' mission is to provide users with a tangible set of tools that will allow them to easily LEARN, CONNECT to, and EXPERIENCE the Internet in an innovative and powerful way. This "Learn, Connect, & Experience" methodology, is the core business principle driving Net Solutions' unique product, The Solutions.

The product that will accomplish these goals is The Solutions. The Solutions combines leading third party software with a unique user 'front end', which makes the Internet easy to understand and use, demystifies the otherwise overwhelming amount of information the Internet holds, and in so doing, brings tremendous value to Net Solutions' customers.

Net Solutions has chosen to focus both on the consumer and small business Internet marketplace. Subsequently, a variety of The Solutions are currently in various stages of development to serve both niches.

The Solutions is currently being sold, and has brought over 90,000 new customers to Net Solutions' portal site to date. Purchasing The Solutions allows business users to quickly and easily establish an eCommerce enabled Web site, and to build a successful and viable Internet–based business. Net Solutions provides all the assistance necessary for these businesses to get their products or services to market quickly, professionally, and in a form that brings maximum value to them. Net Solutions' consumer division is currently planning the release of three new Solutions packages, including The Solutions for Grown Ups, The Solutions for Women, and The Solutions for Kids. These Solutions are focused on Communities, each to their individual market segment. Each community will provide a simple and efficient way for their respective audiences to become confident in using the Internet.

Net Solutions' focus in creating these communities will be to:

- Develop community environments which are based on extensive market research, focus groups, etc., to ensure that our products, services, and community content closely fulfills the needs of our target audiences;

- Make a substantial investment in creating a well–known trusted brand to communicate our image for value, dependability, and ease of use;

- Select content specifically suited to our communities; and

- Drive multiple Internet and non–Internet dependent revenue streams.

Growth Strategy

Net Solutions has extensive plans for internal growth, which will be fueled by a comprehensive marketing and sales program. This program is designed to drive revenue generation through a combination of technology leadership, and partnering with other leading Internet–focused companies.

Net Solutions' integrated marketing strategy is focused on the establishment of multiple online and off–line revenue streams. The initial and most important revenue stream will be the sale of The Solutions itself. Each user purchasing a Solutions package will be directed through the installation process to the Net Solutions portal site. From there, all the usage information that the user generates will be tracked and stored by Net Solutions, utilizing proprietary profiling technology.

Net Solutions will subsequently take advantage of incremental revenue generating partnerships as the user progresses with their Internet experience.

This includes:

- Partnerships with Internet Service Provider's (ISP's)—Existing and future partnerships with leading ISP's will generate incremental revenue for each Net Solutions user who purchases The Solutions and then signs up for access with the ISP. Currently, Net Solutions receives $30 to $50 for each user signed up through Piper Network.

- Computer and Accessory Sales—Net Solutions is currently in negotiation with leading computer and computer accessory manufacturers to provide Net Solutions access with the sale of this equipment.

- Periodic Solutions Upgrades—Net Solutions will provide periodic upgrades to The Solutions which will add new services and features. Some of these upgrades will be charged for, and that will provide instant income from the existing Net Solutions user community.

- E–Business Tools—Net Solutions currently sells products and services to enable both individuals and companies to setup and run their own online web–based businesses, and where appropriate to build their own "online merchant status" as well.

- Products and Services Sold to the Net Solutions User Community—Net Solutions will feature specific products and/or services that are relevant to the interests of the Net Solutions user community. These products will be offered to the communities from the individual community start pages and will generate additional income for Net Solutions while providing niche–targeted incremental value to the users of those communities.

- Click–Through Incremental Revenue—Net Solutions will allow content focused banner advertising that brings incremental value to the Net Solutions communities. Net Solutions will be remunerated for each "click–through" that a community user follows from the Net Solutions portal site.

- Sponsorships/Co–Branding—Net Solutions will sponsor specific opportunities, products, or services that bring incremental value to the Net Solutions communities. Additionally, Net Solutions will co–brand other incremental products and/or services. These sponsorships and co–branded opportunities will generate additional income for Net Solutions from the programs setup with these Net Solutions partners.

- Membership Program Benefits—Net Solutions will sponsor a membership program allowing the Net Solutions user community to earn 'reward points' for various activities and/or online purchases. Through the Net Solutions channel program a portion of these reward benefits will be paid to Net Solutions itself from participating merchants and vendors.

- OEM Licensing—Net Solutions will provide licenses of our proprietary technology for use by retailers, manufacturers, and financial institutions, or any OEM that is approved by Net Solutions for this purpose.

Net Solutions' initial efforts will continue to focus on the U.S. market for 2001. In the year 2001, Net Solutions intends to extend its marketing initiatives to other Internet–intensive countries. Additionally, Net Solutions intends to begin a multi–media advertising campaign with EG Partners, a research, strategic development and advertising firm that specializes in marketing to people over age 50. Also, Net Solutions intends to run a public relations campaign, which will be managed by the well–known PR International agency. This campaign will significantly increase Net Solutions' market presence and awareness of Net Solutions products, services, and technologies, while supporting the company's brand building programs.

MARKET ANALYSIS

The viability of Net Solutions' marketing and sales strategy has been extremely successful with The Solutions Business Edition. From the initial implementation of this strategy in early 2001 to present, Net Solutions has sold over 70,000 Solutions packages, bringing in the same number of Net Solutions customers. New Solutions packages are currently being sold at the rate of approximately 15,000 per month as of October 2001. Internet traffic on our portal site has grown to 1,950,000 hits per month. Compared to the largest existing Internet retailers today as measured by Media Metrix, this number would rank Net Solutions tenth in terms of number of actual page views per month. Net Solutions has existing portal technology that provides a unique user interface and high–degree of user retention. Additionally, Net Solutions has several patents currently pending in reference to their proprietary technologies that track, define, and create secure targeted user content.

Competition

There is no current competition from any existing Internet–based company. Net Solutions' content sensitive multi–faceted approach will quickly bring a substantial user base to the Net Solutions portal. As Net Solutions products and services become more popular, undoubtedly other retailers, ISP's, and online merchants will set up 'copy cat' web sites. Net Solutions has, however, first–mover advantage, and also intends to partner and license our technology as appropriate Internet history shows us that the companies that lead the way technologically on the Internet sustain huge growth leads regardless of their eventual competition. Like Ebay, Amazon.com, and Yahoo, Net Solutions will pave a new road in online access and content delivery, bringing extensive incremental value to the Net Solutions user communities and driving future customer growth and retention.

OPERATIONS

The Solutions development is managed by Net Solutions and includes a combination of in–house and outsourced development efforts. Physical packaging, assembly and distribution is done by an out-sourced fulfillment center. Portal development is specifically managed by Net Solutions, with design work done both by in–house development staff and outsourced technology providers.

Management Summary

Net Solutions' management team consists of eight highly skilled individuals. Individually these people have extensive expertise in all the various aspects of Net Solutions' business, and as a team they represent a level of business acumen and personal integrity that is rarely seen in the industry today.

Financial Analysis

Net Solutions is currently self–sufficient on an operations and cash flow basis. The financing required at this stage is to be used for further development of the Net Solutions portal site and for the associated Solutions kits. Under the existing growth expectation, it would take Net Solutions approximately three years to develop and bring to market the initial retail Solutions. With this financing, Net Solutions will be able to bring these new Solutions packages to market by the end of 2001, subsequently greatly accelerating the time to profit-ability status. The financial requirement is approximately $20 million for the three Consumer Solutions.

Financial projection
(in thousands)

	FY2001	FY2002	FY2003	FY2004
Revenue	$ 13,032	$ 93,929	$ 168,553	$ 263,956
Gross margin, % of revenue	70%	65%	71%	76%
Operating profit (loss)	$ (10,946)	$ (5,894)	$ 32,606	$ 90,814
Operating margin, % revenue	(84%)	(6%)	19%	34%
Net profit (loss)	$ (11,072)	$ (5,866)	$ 28,313	$ 63,594
Net profit (loss), % revenue	(85%)	(6%)	17%	24%
Return on assets, %	N/A	(31%)	80%	90%
Return on equity, %	N/A	(38%)	100%	84%

SUMMARY

Net Solutions' Solutions is a unique product that will capture the interest of consumers and business users alike. Net Solutions' customer driven products and value focused vision and mission insures the success of the company, and this model has already been proven through existence of the current Net Solutions user community. Net Solutions' portal site represents an exciting attempt to change the formula for what makes an Internet portal site successful. Additionally, Net Solutions' business model will drive users to its site, which is unlike the way any company does it today. Net Solutions users will initially access the Net Solutions portal site, because the portal site will be synonymous with the Solutions experience, which is why the user purchased it to begin with. This means that every consumer who purchases a Solutions will in fact, become a Net Solutions portal site user. This "captive audience" brings tremendous value to Net Solutions, while at the same time providing Net Solutions with an incredible opportunity to focus its sales and marketing campaigns.

Companies like America Online have counted on giving their software away for free and based on this have signed up a very small percentage of the total users who received a copy of the software. Net Solutions, on the other hand, will target its Solutions packages directly to the consumer or business user, and will be able to guarantee that every copy of the software sold turns into a direct online user accessing the portal site!

By focusing the content of the site for each user, and by offering those users a unique, user–friendly interface, Net Solutions is positioning itself to be the only portal site in existence to offer Internet access for the average, non–technical consumer or business user. This brings tremendous value to these individuals and will drive the success of the company as the leading Internet portal site.

MARKETING & SALES

Market Analysis

The rapid growth of the Internet, from the beginning of its popularization in the early 1990s, is one of the most widely studied and discussed technical and business phenomena in history, rivaled only by the growth of personal computing with which it is inextricably linked. There are believed to be 80 million Americans who currently use the Internet, with involvement ranging from occasional e–mail message exchanges to daily multi–hour surfing and exploratory sessions.

Today's Internet provides an abundance of services and information, on almost every conceivable topic: news, sports, travel, personal finance, computing, entertainment, games, shopping, fitness and health, families, kids interests, and much more. However, many people are not yet completely comfortable with using a personal computer, much less with accessing the Internet; many people are actually intimidated by this technology.

Further, many of the less–frequent Internet users are not even aware of the range of information or services available to them. Additionally, there are some 170 million Americans who don't currently use the Internet at all. This is where Net Solutions comes in. By providing a radically simplified solution for accessing the Internet, demystifying the content provided by the Internet, and bringing a strong value proposition to these users, Net Solutions will fulfill its goal of bringing the Internet to the masses.

Net Solutions believes that its new integrated Solutions software will draw millions of new users to the Internet, and that each of these new users will identify with their specific Net Solutions user community. In so doing, these users will become revenue–producing community members.

Differentiating Net Solutions' Approach

One of the primary benefits of using the Internet is its ability to tie together people with diverse backgrounds from disparate locations all over the world. Net Solutions' unique approach of marketing the Solutions to different market segments will create virtual communities online. These communities will consist of various groups of consumers or business users who will interact with each other because of their common interests.

Net Solutions' portal site will incorporate the best technology characteristics of the top portal sites, delivering common search, chat, email, shopping, eCommerce, etc., across all virtual communities.

The marketing approach will be:

- Build the environment around the demographics and customer requirements as specified by the individual Solutions;

- Design a technically advanced graphical user interface that is simple, secure and fun to use;

- Develop and deploy the initial community service model through high quality relevant links;

- Drive the marketing and sales approach to reach a critical mass of members; and

- Increase the lifetime value of each customer.

Business Strategy

Net Solutions' business model is comprised of three essential ingredients that, when combined, create a powerful central theme:

- Understand (With the Solutions)

- Link Up (To the Internet)

- Enjoy (The Net Solutions portal environment)

Understand—The Solutions, the Company's lead product, is an integrated suite of award winning components from the industry's top vendors. The Solutions is a comprehensive tutorial package that enables individuals of all ages and skill levels to learn the Internet. The Solutions supports both the Macintosh and Windows platforms, giving consumers an easy way to harness the Internet's enormous potential as a tool for entertainment, communication, education, information and commerce. The Solutions will target niche market audiences with several different editions (Kids' Solutions, Women's Solutions, Grown–Ups' Solutions, etc.). Each component of the Solutions is carefully selected for inclusion based on ease–of–use and the depth and breadth of information it provides to the user. Net Solutions will maintain a competitive advantage by changing the content of the Solutions to keep up with the latest trends in the industry. With no technology anchor, the Solutions will always contain the most current award–winning products from leading manufacturers.

Link Up—An integral component in the Solutions is Internet Access. Access is offered through premier Internet service providers. These ISPs will work with us to offer incremental value added products and services to our customers.

Enjoy—Net Solutions intends to build the Net Solutions portal experience into one of the premier Internet portal sites. Net Solutions will accomplish this by combining technology that provides advanced search capabilities, e–mail, chats, shopping, eCommerce and forums, with user–specific theme focused content. This intuitive user–friendly site will provide a destination where consumers of all age groups will be able to find exactly the information they need. The site will be the first celebrity endorsed destination of its kind, providing an experience unlike anything else in existence today.

Most of the well–known Internet access providers and retail online businesses today use a business model that requires their members to remain with them long enough so that their purchases or monthly fees cover the customer acquisition and service cost. Because these companies are in a constant mode of customer acquisition and growth, sustainable revenue always seem to be just out of reach.

Net Solutions' business model, on the other hand, eliminates these problems by:

1. Funding the cost of sales through the up–front sale of the Solutions product;

2. Bringing incremental value to the base Solutions services and charging a monthly fee for these incremental services;

3. Taking advantage of the Net Solutions 'captured audience' in the form of both focused sales efforts and through third party revenue sharing; and

4. Amassing a bevy of sponsorships and partnerships with third party Internet companies that can bring additional incremental value to Net Solutions customers.

Net Solutions is committed to building sustainable long–term relationships with our customers; relationships that are focused on bringing the utmost value to the Net Solutions customer, with the single goal of retaining that customer's loyalty indefinitely.

PRODUCTS & SERVICES

Net Solutions' communities are the heart of their marketing strategy. Initially, four specific communities and related Solutions products are either already in existence or are nearing final completion and release. They include:

- The eBusiness Community—people of all ages who want to build their own e–Businesses;

- The Children's Community—children generally in the 7–10 age bracket;

- The Women's Community—women generally in the 30–49 age bracket; and

- The Grown–Up Community—Grown–Ups who are older than 50.

Net Solutions' Solutions

Each Solutions package has a modern, attractive, compelling appearance suitable for display in high–traffic retail settings and in print and television ads. The graphics on each Solutions package are designed to appeal to their specific community audience.

The specific contents of each Solutions package varies and is tailored to bring the most value to the specific community for which it is designed. Each Solutions package contains various combinations of printed books, CD–ROMs with interactive instructional material and software, instructional videotapes, and a broad range of additional components tailored to each specific Community. These elements are currently drawn from existing third–party products, and in the future may be created by Net Solutions in–house.

Net Solutions is committed to building in a high degree of user friendliness into each Solutions product. To that end, Net Solutions hosts focus groups and performs exhaustive research in the content decision–making process.

The current retail price of the Solutions is $45.95, regardless of its community focus. This price does not include incremental services offered to specific communities.

The E–Business Solutions

Demographics: The typical customer for the Net Solutions E–Business Solutions is in their 40s, with 70% of them being men. They frequently have some personal computer experience. They have heard of the Internet, and may have had some simple, infrequent contact with it, but generally lack significant Internet experience or skills.

Advertising: Our advertising to this group primarily utilizes direct response television, with plans to expand into radio and print advertising in the future. The content and approach of this advertising addresses potential job dissatisfaction and the opportunity for freedom and a new career that awaits through the establishment of an online business. Among the E–Business opportunities in this advertising is included:

- The ability to sell any product they choose;

- The ability to subscribe to a "virtual warehouse" comprised of companies that will OEM and drop ship their products;

- The ability to participate in business to business franchise opportunities.

Contents of the E–Business Solutions

Each Solutions package has some items that are unique to the specific Solutions inquestion, and some generic products that are contained in every Solutions.

The following is a list of items in the E–Business Solutions:

- Solutions Installation CD
- Oolong 2.2 CD
- Internet Professor CD
- Internet Professor manual
- Internet Professor video
- Solutions to the Internet poster
- Virtual Warehouse Packet
- SBN Yellow Pages brochure
- Custom Web page brochure
- CSI Brochure and $195 check
- Consultant phone die–cut card
- Net Solutions banner ad brochure
- Mouse pad

There have been over 70,000 E–Business Solutions packages sold to date, and another new 20,000 are currently selling every month.

The Solutions for Kids

Demographics: The Kids' Solutions will appeal to children as a fun way to learn to use the Internet: to communicate, to read, to play games, to find entertainment, to develop skills (such as typing) and to do school projects. It will be designed to be non–intimidating, simple, and well organized. While this applies to all Net Solutions' Solutions, it's especially true here: the Kids' Solutions will provide access to only selected information that kids actually need access to.

There are approximately 22 million U.S. households with children who do not have access to the Internet, compared to the existing 13 million that do. Research shows that the majority of these other households hold concerns about the content that children could accidentally gain access to. The Kids' Solutions contains a host of security software to address this concern.

Advertising: Our advertising to this group primarily utilizes direct response television, with plans to expand into radio and print advertising in the future. The content and approach of this advertising addresses parents concerns over the content their children can access on the Internet. Included is a detailed explanation of the content controls that this particular Solutions package offers parents, while at the same time providing a glimpse of the wonderful benefits children would get out of Internet access.

Contents of the Kids' Solutions

Each Solutions package has some items that are unique to the specific Solutions in question, and some generic products that are contained in every Solutions package.

The following is a list of items in the Kids' Solutions:

- Kids Owners Manual
- Intro to the Internet book

- Access Software

- Browser and email software

- Toys/games/entertainment CD

- Educational Tools CD

- Parental Control Software

- Discount Coupons

- Mouse Pad

- Other toys and special offers

The Kids' Road Map is scheduled for launch in November 2001.

The Women's Solutions

Demographics: Selection of women as one of Net Solutions' initial communities was prompted in part by the growing role women are playing in the evolution of the Internet; women comprise 45 percent of all Internet users, a figure projected to grow to 60 percent by 2002. Moreover, women control or influence 80 percent of all purchase decisions, and the Internet is becoming more and more merchandising oriented. 27 percent of women going online cite interest in finding information helpful to their personal lives, and 63 percent cite the Internet as important for finding information to assist with purchasing decisions.

Advertising: Our advertising to this group primarily utilizes radio, print advertising and television commercials. The content and approach of this advertising addresses the desire women have to drive self–empowerment—to make the Internet work for them. Included in this Solutions campaign will be the specifics of interest to these women.

Contents of the Women's Solutions

Each Solutions package has some items that are unique to the specific Solutions in question, and some generic products that are contained in every Solutions package.

The following is a list of items in the Women's Solutions:

- Getting Started Pamphlet

- Discount Coupons

- Access Software

- Women–oriented applications

- Security Software

- Mouse Pad

- Learn the Net for Women (manual, video, and CD ROM Tutorial)

The Women's Solutions package is scheduled for launch in November 2001.

The Solutions for Grown–ups

Demographics: Part of Net Solutions' decision to tailor this Solutions to Grown–Ups was influenced by the fact that baby boomers account for 25 percent of all Americans 50 and over (every day 10,000 baby–boomers turn 50, and will for the next 20 years). Additionally, although constituting only 27 percent of the population, they represent $1.6 trillion in purchasing power; 65 percent of the net worth of U.S. households; 77 percent of all financial assets; 80 percent of all luxury travel; and so on. Subsequently, it is reasonable to assume that this community will be interested in the multitude of valuable deal that this Solutions package will bring to them.

Advertising: The Grown–Ups Solutions is designed to appeal to users over the age of 50. The product is designed to provide a simple and efficient way for them to build Internet competency, and access the resources that have the most value to them. Our advertising to this group primarily utilizes radio, print advertising and television commercials. The content and approach of this advertising addresses the desire these individuals have to learn more and take stronger control of their lives. Highlighted in this campaign will be the wealth of information available to them as well as time and cost savings that the Internet can bring them.

Contents of the Grown–Ups Solutions

Each Solutions package has some items that are unique to the specific Solutions in question, and some generic products that are contained in every Solutions package.

The following is a list of items in the Grown–Ups Solutions:

- Getting Started Booklet
- Intro to the Internet Video
- Access Software
- Email Software
- Mouse Pad
- Fraud Protection Booklet
- Bonus Software
- Online Magazine Subscriptions
- Discount Coupons

The Grown–Ups Solutions is scheduled for launch in the first quarter of 2002.

Future Solutions Packages

Net Solutions' strength in bringing new Solutions to market is its ability to replicate the Solutions Community and the relevant product line. As new commercially attractive Communities are identified, Net Solutions will be able to quickly create a Solutions package for the Community, and get it to market with very little development time required. The focus of future Solutions packages will be primarily based on interests or hobbies. The content will be more editorial than tutorial. The value proposition will be focused on "saving time and money" as opposed to "learning how to use the Internet".

CONCLUSION

The Internet is not a fad, but rather a keystone of the new economy. Companies that have established themselves as the market leaders of this new economy are the ones that have blazed the way, bringing new types of content and incremental value to consumers. These companies include the likes of AOL, Yahoo!, Amazon.com, and Ebay.

An analogy of the future of the Internet from Net Solutions' point of view is what has occurred in the broadcast television industry. In broadcast television, the major networks gave way to the cable industry. In the beginning, no one thought that a channel dedicated to specific types of users would be successful, and yet as the industry grew it became obvious that this approach was in fact the most successful one. Now the cable industry is proliferated with dozens of specialty channels each focused on particular user communities.

The leaders in the Internet industry today can be classified into two categories. They are either portal sites that offer an overwhelming amount of information to consumers, or they are product or service specific sites that offer comprehensive information referring to a specific product or service. Net Solutions is taking this approach to its obvious next step, combining information with products and services, and targeting specific user communities, just like the cable television industry did to broadcast television.

Net Solutions has positioned itself to join the ranks of companies that have blazed new ground on the Internet. Over the long term it will be companies like Net Solutions that continue to lead the way and redefine how consumers communicate with each other, entertain themselves and shop. Net Solutions is creating the future of the Internet and in so doing is establishing itself as a company that is here to stay, for the long term.

MARKETING & SALES

Selling Channels

The channels that Net Solutions chooses to be the focus of the Sales Plan represent the method that Net Solutions intends to take to get its products to market. These include the Direct Response Channel and the Retail Channel.

The Direct Response Channel—Our existing business with sales of over 20,000 units per month is based on the Direct Response channel. We currently have several infomercials featuring celebrities from various highly popular situation comedies now aired on network TV. These infomercials and other short commercials have proven to be highly effective tools for selling the Solutions packages directly to consumers.

The Retail Channel—While the Direct Response Channel has been a profitable approach for the Business Solutions, it is questionable as to whether it will be successful for the Consumer Solutions which will soon be available. Subsequently, Net Solutions will pursue the Retail Channel as our primary means of getting these Solutions out to market. The results that Net Solutions expects include:

- Creating a positive association with the expectations of the Internet experience through the consumer's relationship with the store it was purchased in;

- Substantiating Net Solutions' goals through a branding or OEM approach to sales; and

- Maximizing potential sales volume.

Solutions' colors and graphics have been designed for maximum appeal and exposure at retail display. Dimensions allow for maximum facings in end–cap locations and power wings. Graphics have been chosen, with focus group input, for customer appeal and stopping power, perceived value and legibility.

International Sales

Net Solutions intends to extend its Solutions packages and Net Solutions portal concepts to other countries. We will first engage English–speaking countries, and then extend our business to prominent non–English speaking countries where enthusiasm for the Internet is greatest. In the latter case, Japan and the Spanish–speaking countries, particularly Latin America, are currently at the top of the list.

STRATEGIC ALLIANCES

Net Solutions relies heavily on strategic alliances with existing companies, both in the Internet industry as well as other companies that have products or services that bring incremental value to the Net Solutions communities. Some of these alliances include:

- Plum Products: provides marketing assistance to InterOne for the over–50 market segment;

- RTC Computer: provides web object technology for Business Solutions user web–site development;

- Cash Cow: provides merchant status (credit–card acceptance) to users of the Business Solutions;

- Robert Arker, LLC.: produces the television infomercials for Business Solutions;

- Technology Inc.: performs hardware integration and testing for our portal system;

- Oolong: provides local Internet services to Solutions users;

- HHB Associates: provides accounting and auditing services to Net Solutions;

- Space Inc.: provides a secure physical location for our portal system, plus backbone Internet connectivity;

- Harley & Davis: developing our portal system;

- Tower Solutions: provides outsourced Solutions assembly, inventory and distribution;

- Sam Smith PR : our public relations agency;

- Image Consultants: provides retail product packaging design and consultation; and

- TeleMart, Inc.: provides inbound telemarketing services.

ADVERTISING

Advertisers want to be where the people are, and the people are increasingly online. This points out just how important market share is and will continue to be. We believe television data points out that it is relative market share, not absolute market share that matters most. No one disputes that the Big Three lost ground to cable. However, by still having a much larger relative audience draw, the networks have been able to maintain their position in total advertising volumes on a declining absolute audience base.

Advertisers pay for cable's effectiveness in targeting audiences. For advertisers who desire to reach a more targeted audience, cable channels and the Internet offer unique opportunities. Cable offers uniquely targeted audiences that may be small, but are highly effective. For advertisers that want to target specific markets, cable offers something broadcast does not—effectiveness. What cable lacks in reach it makes up in effectiveness.

At present, the Internet can be thought of as a niche or specific target market because only 22% of the country is wired, compared with television market penetration of 98%. Therefore Internet advertising can be thought of in a similar way as cable advertising—a targeted marketing medium. The Internet can go one step further, however, because it is interactive.

Net Solutions' strategy is to initially take advantage of the broadcast and cable television markets in airing specific infomercials that will be targeted at sometimes broad and sometimes specific markets. Additionally, Net Solutions will also utilize the Internet for advertising, however this advertising will mostly take the form of interactive programs, OEM relationships, and value added revenue streams. Net Solutions believes that its approach will become widespread and will be one of the catalysts in raising the percentage of Internet connected households well above the 22% mark. As that happens, Net Solutions will already be positioned to transform its advertising strategies to be less television based and more interactively online focused.

We have three main goals for the advertising and promotional support for the Solutions products:

1. Establish and build brand awareness;

2. Support sales efforts to get product placed in retail; and

3. Plan and execute sales promotion campaigns that will move product off retail shelves.

We expect to accomplish these goals through a combination of activities, including:

- Media advertising through traditional media;

- Sales promotion campaigns including couponing;

- Point of sale displays;

- Incentive promotions for retailers including cooperative advertising;

- Publicity; and

- Events.

Focus Group Research

We are conducting a series of focus groups for each product's market profile. Focus group participants will be a combination of:

- People who are familiar with and can use a personal computer, but who are not on the Internet; and

- People who do not have any experience with a personal computer.

The goal of each series of focus groups is to test the following product and promotional attributes:

- Product concept

- Product packaging/messaging

- Base components (essentials)

- Add–ons

- Book, Brochures

- Bonus Software

- Pricing

- Advertising

- Would they Buy It?

ORGANIZATION

Management Team

Net Solutions' management team is comprised of individuals who each have extensive experience in various aspects of Net Solutions' business strategies, and effectively add value to the management team with their unique and specific skillsets. The management team includes:

- Chairman of the Board—Bill Travis. During his three decades of technology and business leadership, Mr. Travis served as Chairman and CEO of world-famous RTC Computer; Chairman, President and CEO of Oolong; as well as President of GlassCommunication Systems, a unit of Glass International. He is an IEEE Fellow, and holds 10 patents alone or jointly. He earned Bachelors, Masters and Doctorate degrees from MIT.

- Director—Mark Wilson. Mr. Wilson has been with the Farmington Hills, Michigan law firm of Bookman & Wilson since 1970. He is counsel for numerous companies in the computer hardware and software industries. He is an adjunct professor at the Wayne State School of Business, and a frequent lecturer on issues facing new ventures and entrepreneurs.

- Chief Operating Officer—Diane Billips. Ms. Billips was Executive Vice President and Chief Marketing Officer of First Bank. Prior to that, she was industry manager of the bank's global Entertainment, Gaming and Media Industries Group, and managed the Group's $3 billion credit portfolio. She launched the first Washington–based office for Ivan International, and worked for Young Industries as a product manager. She earned degrees in finance and marketing, and a Masters degree in business. She is an alumnus of the University of Wisconsin.

- Chief Financial Officer—Mark Hill. Mr. Hill was Chief Financial Officer of Connext, Inc., a web hosting company, and led its financial team in the sale of the company to publicly traded Johnson Thomas Corporation. Prior to that, he served as Chief Financial Officer of Tidwell Management, a Washington–based telecommunications startup that was sold to a publicly traded firm. He is a Certified Public Accountant, and has a Masters in Business Administration degree in finance with honors from the Denison College.

- Vice President, Internet Business Division—Claudia Rathbun. Ms. Rathbun, a consultant to and investor in the company, has agreed to become Vice President, Internet Business Division. Before her relationship with the company, she served as President and principal owner of Rathbun Investments, Inc. for approximately 10 years. Concurrently with that position, Ms. Rathbun served as Vice President of a major energy company from 1995 through 1998. She also served as General Manager of a competing firm from 1992 to 1995. She studied Business and Economics at Indiana University.

- Vice President, Marketing; Company Founder—Sabrina Brooks. Ms. Brooks co–founded Ink Corporation in 1997 and has been instrumental in its marketing, creative direction, fund raising, and growth. As the leader of the company's direct response broadcast campaigns, he cast and acquired its celebrity spokesperson. He has been central to creating the current management line–up and Board of Directors. Previously he was employed by Tidwell Management. He attended University of Michigan.

- Director of Web Development—Ted Silson. Mr. Silson previously served as Director of Web Development at Blue Networks where he project managed and programmed secure web sites for mid–sized and large companies. Before that, he was Managing Director of Magenta Design, and consultant to Wilson Media. He also founded and directed Images Digital Photography. He earned undergraduate degrees in photography from the University of Cincinnati. He also studied advanced imaging and programming at Michigan Technological University.

OPERATIONS

Customer Service/Product Support

Net Solutions is committed to superior levels of customer satisfaction. To this end we have built an internal customer service department. This department is staffed by knowledgeable people who are also skilled in being effective on the telephone in interpersonal relationship management. Our commitment to our customers is our one and only goal, and our Customer Service department has already earned extensive positive feedback from our users.

The Net Solutions Portal Site

The Net Solutions portal site is the actual Web site that our community users will interact with, and that will be their own "onramp" to the Internet. As such, it is the heart of our entire environment. The portal site will constantly be in a state of development so that we can assure its content will always be fresh and its appearance unique. The community users will be unaware of this development effort. Some of the specific functions of the Portal site include:

- Hosting the Net Solutions community web pages - the primary Internet services that complement the Solutions;

- Facilitating access to Net Solutions' e–commerce customer web sites, including merchant functions (e.g., credit card handling);

- "Click–through" access to a wide variety of Net Solutions partners driven by an "advertising engine" that will randomly place unobtrusive graphical elements on users' screens inviting them to click through and inquire further;

- A wide variety of general information "feeds", e.g., financial quotations, weather forecasts, general news, and entertainment feeds;

- Fully interactive "search engine" software to allow users to search the entire World Wide Web while providing customer service improvement information to Net Solutions;

- A complete, free e–mail and chat system;

- A "smart–browser" facility, to facilitate URL requests, scan e–mail content for undesirable words, and track usage patterns of users both internal and external to Net Solutions' portal.

Technology

The intent for the Net Solutions portal site is that it takes advantage of the leading technologies available today on the Internet, and does so completely transparently to the consumer. This means there will be no "plugins" to download, and no third–party applications that must be run. This will require a considerable development effort. Net Solutions has outsourced this functionality, including the hosting of the Net Solutions portal site. This will allow Net Solutions to enter the market with lower capital costs and stay in step with technology support and growth.

Fulfillment

The manufacturing of the Solutions themselves involves injection–molding the containers, assembling the various elements that the Solutions contain, and physically distributing the Solutions to the appropriate sales channels. This work is being done by Tower Solutions, one of the world's largest assembler/distributor (fulfillment) companies; we expect to use this method for the foreseeable future. Assembly and distribution is under Net Solutions' direction; it is our responsibility to ensure that purchase orders for individual elements have been placed, that a credit–card submission by a user is valid prior to shipping a Solutions package and that the customer is satisfied after receiving and installing the product.

Intellectual Property Protection

Net Solutions' intellectual property exists in three forms: the Web site names it uses; various product and idea names and appearances; and specific technical designs and concepts. Existing Internet domain names have been registered on behalf of Net Solutions, and we expect that in the course of business that new domains will also be registered. Key trademark registrations have been issued for "Net Solutions" and "Solution", and as business continues, more trademarks will also be registered. To date, approximately 20 trademarks have been applied for, in areas ranging from our proprietary technologies to the installation processes and applications we have developed.

Promotions

The primary objectives of the Company's promotion plans are to:

- Inform and persuade potential customers to purchase the product;

- Build brand identity to drive retail sales and sales of special OEM projects;

- Drive traffic to the Net Solutions portal site as a premiere destination for Solutions users; and

- Enrich Net Solutions' corporate image to build confidence with its suppliers, employees, dealers, and financial partners.

Net Solutions' promotion strategy consists of advertising, personal selling, publicity and sales promotion.

Public Relations

Net Solutions has retained Sam Smith for public relations. Sam Smith is a worldwide firm with 112 offices globally. They serve many high technology clients, including Compaq, Oracle, Netscape and Sun Microsystems, and they have participated in several product launches. Net Solutions' public relations plan is designed to establish and build corporate and brand identity and to complement other aspects of the Company's marketing and communications efforts. To date, the Company has received the following publicity:

- Television: CNN, MSNBC, FOX, Silicon Valley Business News;

- Radio: ABC Radio;

- Periodicals: Business Week, PC World, Home PC, Better Homes and Gardens, Home, Buzz, Billboard, Succeed, Marketing Computers; etc.

- Newspapers: Washington Post, New York Times, Chicago Tribune, Cincinnati Enquirer.

Awards

A national parent group supporting educational products of excellence awarded Net Solutions its prestigious 2000 Parents' Choice Approval for The Solutions. Winning products are chosen by a national panel of parents, teachers, librarians and psychologists and are selected based on their link to values and education for children.

FINANCIAL ANALYSIS

Net Solutions is currently self–sufficient on an operations and cash flow basis. The financing required at this stage is to be used for further development of the Net Solutions portal site and for the associated Solutions kits. Under the existing growth expectation, it would take Net Solutions approximately three years to develop and bring to market the initial retail Solutions. With this financing, Net Solutions will be able to bring these new Solutions to market by the end of 2001 subsequently greatly accelerating the time to profitability status. The financial requirement is approximately $25 million for the three Consumer Solutions.

Profit and loss
(in thousands)

	FY2001	FY2002	FY2003	FY2004
Revenue	$ 13,032	$ 93,929	$ 168,553	$ 263,956
Cost of sales	$ 3,957	$ 33,016	$ 49,155	$ 62,394
Gross profit	$ 9,075	$ 60,913	$ 119,398	$ 201,562
Gross margin,% revenue	70%	65%	71%	76%
Sales & marketing	$ 15,336	$ 47,688	$ 55,217	$ 66,277
Sales & marketing, % revenue	118%	51%	33%	25%
R&D/product development	$ 1,199	$ 11,557	$ 20,404	$ 29,910
R&D/product development, % revenue	9%	12%	12%	11%
General & administration	$ 3,486	$ 7,563	$ 11,171	$ 14,560
General & administration, % revenue	27%	8%	7%	6%
Other income (expense)	$ (126)	$ 28	$ 26	$ 24
Income (loss) before taxes	$ (11,072)	$ (5,867)	$ 32,632	$ 90,839
Income (loss) before taxes,% revenue	(85%)	(6%)	19%	34%
Income tax expense	$ —	$ —	$ 4,318	$ 27,244
Net income (loss)	$ (11,072)	$ (5,867)	$ 28,314	$ 63,595
Net income (loss), % revenue	(85%)	(6%)	17%	24%

Balance sheet
(in thousands)

	FY2001	FY2002	FY2003	FY2004
Current assets	$ 4,371	$ 15,174	$ 49,507	$ 120,119
Total assets	$ 5,094	$ 16,840	$ 50,875	$ 120,942
Current liabilities	$ 3,632	$ 3,214	$ 8,924	$ 15,382
Total equity	$ 1,462	$ 13,625	$ 41,950	$ 105,560
Total liabilities and equity	$ 5,094	$ 16,840	$ 50,875	$ 120,942

Cash flow
(in thousands)

	FY2001	FY2002	FY2003	FY2004
Cash flow from operations	$ (9,510)	$ (12,121)	$ 25,892	$ 63,585
Cash flow from investing activities	$ (663)	$ (1,597)	$ (595)	$ (504)
Cash flow from financing activities	$ 10,993	$ 18,000	$ —	$ —
Net change in cash	$ 821	$ 4,282	$ 25,297	$ 63,081
Ending cash	$ 639	$ 4,921	$ 30,218	$ 93,299

Massage Therapists

MASSAGEWORKS

41 Whitter Way
Millen, TX 73301

Gerald Rekve

This business plan is for a massage therapy practice. The need for this practice was identified after a key piece of state legislation changed, and anyone injured in an automoblie accident was required to undergo treatment.

EXECUTIVE SUMMARY

Business Overview

Over a span of 15 years Gavin Cheney had worked in various medical practices as an office manager. Never really getting any training on the medical profession, Gavin enjoyed working for others in the field. Then the state where he works and lives changed a fundamental part of the automobile insurance business, where anyone who was injured in an auto accident was required to have treatment. Gavin saw this as a great opportunity to start his own practice. After a number of conversations with his medical contacts, he decided to open his own massage therapy practice.

Market Analysis

Millen, Texas is your average little city with a population of 150,000 people. There are three major hospitals in the city limits and there are seven massage therapy offices listed in the phone book. After calling all massage therapy places to get their pricing structure for competitive reasons, it was determined that only six were still in business and of the six only four were licensed by the state health region. While this type of service does not have to be registered to operate in the state, we have determined that we will only hire registered staff for our clinic.

Approximately 14 months ago, the local automobile insurance association had adopted a no–fault insurance plan, where the injured in an automobile accident could not sue for injuries unless they went through a complete health check with the local medical staff of various backgrounds, one of them being massage therapy. With this new focus on rehabilitation, we have determined that the steady stream of new revenue from this new source would be financially worthy of an investment into this new business.

After studying the market we have found out that there is no place where a client can go to get a multifunctional discipline approach to their health care or recovery. Based on health region statistics, there are 1600 visits per month to the present seven massage therapy clinics, with an average cost of $30 per visit. This amounts to monthly revenue of over $6,500 per clinic just for massage therapy and does not include revenue from other types of therapy. The average clinic has two staff working either full or part time and some on a flexible schedule. One clinic has 8 staff; however this clinic offers other types of therapy services.

Fees Charged for Massage Therapy

1. 15 minute session—$19

2. 30 minute session—$39

3. 60 minute session—$75

Fees Charged for Physical Therapy

1. Standard Physical Therapy—$60 per hour

2. Water therapy—$75 per hour

3. Physiological therapy—$100 per hour

Of the seven listed in the phone book, only two have set up strategic alliances with hospital medical regions as a referral. The reason for this is simply the hospital only refer to credited clinics and of the seven only two have been accredited. We will be accredited so we will get these referrals.

We have already been in talks with various medical practitioners and have determined that there is solid foundation for our clinic model in this region. While our main focus will be to run the massage therapy clinic, we will also receive income from our other partners in form of shared office rental and a small per–client booking fee.

Some of the services set up in our region are as follows:

•   Massage Therapy

•   Physical Therapy

•   Mobility Therapy

•   Water Therapy

•   Gym Therapy

•   Mobility Therapy

•   Physiological Therapy

•   Driving Therapy

•   PDSD Therapy

All of our staff will focus on the massage therapy and the other types of therapy will be contracted out to third party professionals who meet the required certifications. The prices charged for these services will vary based on the service. Our fee will be the same for each client we book for one of these therapies.

•   Massage Therapy—$75 per hour.

•   Physical Therapy—$80 per hour. Our fee is $9.

•   Mobility Therapy—$40 per hour. Our fee is $7.

•   Water Therapy—$70 per hour. Our fee is $7.

•   Gym Therapy—$70 per hour. Our fee is $7.

•   Mobility Therapy—$50 per hour. Our fee is $5.

•   Physiological Therapy—$100 per hour. Our fee is $8.

•   Driving Therapy—$40 per hour. Our fee is $5.

•   PDSD Therapy—$120 per hour. Our fee is $14.

- Acupuncture—$80 per hour. Our fee is $12.

- Aroma Therapy—$40 per hour. Our fee is $7.

- Riekie Therapy—$40 per hour. Our fee is $8.

BUSINESS OVERVIEW

Because we have set up this clinic as a limited liability corporation, the owner will not be personally responsible for any activities of the therapists who operate out of this location.

The hours of operation will be from 9:00 am to 6:00 pm Monday through Friday and half days on Saturday. The contract therapists can book appointments outside these hours as required.

At this location we will have a main reception area consisting of a nursing station counter area, eight to twelve chairs for clients, a coat rack, a coffee table and a book shelf containing various handouts and info for clients to read while they wait.

There will be a total of eight treatment rooms, complete with an adjustable bed, chair, wall charts of the human body and small drawer cabinet for storage.

The main gym area will contain a variety of gym equipment as listed below.

- Four stationary bikes

- Three flatbed weight machines

- One hamstring exercise machine

- Four treadmills

- Complete set of weights

- One traction bed

- Ten various sized balls for lumbar work

- Two heart rate testing machines

- Two tables for treatment of various therapies

- Water cooler

- Rowing machine

- Hot tub for water therapy

- Two low level bikes

- Various mats for doing floor exercise

- A variety of treatment devises like the thera band, Jhook, and Tens Machine

Site Location

We have held extensive conversations with medical professionals and have determined that the first floor of 41 Whitter Way is an ideal location. It is central to all three hospitals, therefore allowing for easy access for our clients from these locations. Also this location is centrally located in the city and has easy access to the bus system and the go train.

The key to the location is parking and the bus station is only about 20 yards from the front door and is based on the ground floor of the eight–story building. One of the other bonus features of this location is the fact that inside there are numerous our medical professionals and specialists set up, as well a lab and x–ray clinic.

We will be leasing around 12,000 square feet of this unit and will pay a flat net rent of $1400 per month over a 5 year term. Considering the location this is fair. Also as part of our negotiations we were to have the landlord pay for leasehold improvements in the amount of $20,000.

Also there will be a wheelchair ramp installed in the side door, allowing for easy access for all of our clients. The ramp is basically a cement ramp to cover the four–inch gap along the sidewalk.

Staffing

All staffing will be trained in their area of expertise; we will not hire anyone who does not have certification in the right areas.

There is a college in the region that every year has a lot of graduates. We will fill our open positions from these qualified students.

For the professional contract positions we will contract out to the right professionals in the region. While we realize that some of these openings may not be filled on the day of opening we may not have all the openings filled. That will be fine, as we want to make sure we bring in the right professionals and do not want to be in a rush.

The front counter staff can be trained on office administration or doctor's office administration, which will be fine for the type of work being performed.

FINANCIAL ANALYSIS

Staffing
- Front counter—$1,500 per month
- Massage Therapist—$3,700 per month per position. Two positions total $7,400 per month
- Accountant—$2,300 per month
- Cleaning and basic repair and maintenance (Contract cleaner)—$400 per month
- CEO—$3,500 per month
- **Total**—$15,100 monthly payroll expenses

Because all other positions are contract and are not employees we will not put them in our books as an expense. The only item recorded for these positions will be the revenue we receive every time we get a booking; we will only record the revenue share we receive and not the revenue the client will pay us.

Other Operating Expenses
- Office Rental—$1,400 per month
- Telephone—$200 per month
- Office supplies—$250 per month
- Gym supplies—$400 per month
- Parking fees—$240 per month
- Utilities—$450 per month
- Advertising—$700 per month
- Yellow page ad—$400 per month
- **Total**—$4,040 in monthly operating expenses

Revenue & Income Projections

Our monthly income and expenses will come from several areas:

1. Revenue from our own staff will be $234,000 per year. This was determined by having two therapists working six hours per day for five days a week. At the hourly rate of $75 per hour, this figure totals $4,500 week for each of 52 weeks of the year.

2. Revenue from other professionals we contract out will be $96,096 per year. This was determined by having seven therapists working four hours per day for six days a week. At the average hourly rate of $11 per hour, this figure totals $1848 per week for each of the 52 weeks of the year.

3. Revenue from flat fees charged for each professional will total $22,500 annually. Each professional will be charged $125 per month that will result in monthly revenue of $1,875 (15 therapists each paying $125 per month).

While we have attempted to base our income streams on best guess, we have determined that the number we provided here are on the low end and will only go higher. Review of other message therapy clinics nation wide have shown that the revenues are actually much higher than what we have projected.

Based on the above numbers, our total projected revenue is $352,566 for the first year. Our total projected expenses for the first 12 months is $229,680 plus the operating line of credit interest expense of $6,000 annually.

Start—Up Expenses

1. Gym equipment—$25,600

2. Legal fees—$1,200

3. Office supplies and furniture—$4,500

4. Rent and damage post—$2,800

5. Office computers and equipment—$5,900

6. Advertising and brochures—$1,200

OPERATIONS

We signed the lease on October 10, 2004; the landlord has 40 days to have the leasehold improvements completed. We estimate that by November 20, 2004 we will be able to move in. We will budget two weeks to get equipment set up and our systems in place. We will budget four weeks to run open houses for the medical profession and insurance industry, allowing them to see our facility.

On January 1 2005, we will start to accept clients. By then all our staff will be hired and we should have a few contract professionals hired.

Mentally Disabled Care Facility

Welcome Home Organization

730 Grand River Avenue
Brighton, MI 48114

Andrew A. Westerfeld and Aaron L. Wappelhorst

Welcome Home Organization plans to build and operate a Residential Care Facility for developmentally disabled adults. This facility will be available for individuals over the age of 18, who begin to reach the age of being too old to live at home, yet too young to live in a full time nursing facility. This facility will serve the needs of those who are moderately mentally retarded, who require some habit training. By serving this particular group we can create an excellent living environment, including a social family–like atmosphere and active lifestyles for all of our residents.

Our services include full–time residential care, private rooms, direct–care staff and nursing staff for any necessary medical care, entertainment and recreational opportunities, and educational and job skills training. The facility will be equipped to care for 30 individuals, including 30 private rooms, a cafeteria, living and socializing areas, and entertainment facilities. Our goal is to meet the social, physical, mental, recreational, educational, and vocational needs of all of our residents.

EXECUTIVE SUMMARY

Welcome Home Organization will provide residential care for the mentally disabled. The organization will be certified as a 501(c) (3) non–profit corporation. We are dedicated to helping those with developmental disabilities to live their life to the fullest, while creating a family atmosphere that creates a better tomorrow, an atmosphere that encourages the participation of residents' families in their day–to–day lives. We strive to offer a community that promotes self respect, independence, and improves the quality of life for all our residents.

We intend to offer the highest quality residential care and day program services in the Southwest Detroit area. Our facility will accommodate thirty residents, each of whom will have individual fully–furnished bedrooms. Other amenities include several spacious living areas which provide a variety of atmospheres to meet individual needs. Residents will have available three full meals a day, which will accommodate their personal tastes and nutritional requirements. We will have employed a fully–trained staff who will assist the residents in day–to–day living. In addition, day programs will offer a variety of activities, and habit and work skills training to foster growth of the individual.

The facility's limited size will provide an opportunity for interaction between staff, volunteers and residents and will allow for personalized care. We will listen to the needs and desires of our residents to provide superior living conditions. We plan to construct a new $1.6 million facility, which will offer the amenities of a modern home. Our facility is large enough to operate efficiently, but small enough to feel like home. This type of atmosphere is the core objective of the organization. Residents should feel as though they are relaxed and in their living room, and not in an institution.

Welcome Home Organization will be operated by a five–person management team. The head of the facility will be our Chief Administrative Officer who will work with the management team and staff to operate the facility. A Chief Business Officer will oversee the day–to–day financial and fundraising activities of the organization. The Social Service Coordinator will be responsible for admissions and discharges, sales presentations, and general paperwork. In addition, the Residential Services Coordinator and the Day Program and Volunteer Coordinator will be responsible for their individual sectors.

The marketing plan of the organization is two–fold. First, the organization must market itself towards potential supporters and then to potential residents. Potential supporters will be recruited through personal relationships and an aggressive fundraising plan. Increasingly long waiting lists for residential care in the Detroit and Ann Arbor regions will provide the organization with a strong resident base. Currently the market for residential care facilities is underserved.

In order for the organization to be successful it must meet its fundraising goals. We plan to raise $1.6 million in initial fundraising, with $750,000 being contributed before the facility construction begins. The remaining $850,000 will be raised in the first year. Welcome Home Organization will fund the remaining portion of development costs through a long–term loan. Solid financial management will lead to an organization that will serve the community for years to come. The generosity of supporters is the key to the success of the organization.

Welcome Home Organization will be an asset to the developmentally disabled community, and the community as a whole. Our goal is to meet the social, physical, mental, recreational, educational, and vocational needs of all of our residents. At Welcome Home Organization we are committed to fostering compassion and improving tomorrow for those with mental disabilities.

Mission

At Welcome Home Organization we are committed to fostering compassion and improving tomorrow for those with mental disabilities. Welcome Home Organization is dedicated to helping those with developmental disabilities to live their life to the fullest, while creating a family atmosphere that creates a better tomorrow. We strive to offer a community that promotes self respect, independence, and improves the quality of life for all of our residents.

Objectives

In order for Welcome Home Organization to attain its vision, the following objectives need to be achieved:

1. Secure initial financing by securing commitments from both corporate and individual donors.

2. Develop and construct a world-class residential facility that meets the needs of mentally handicapped in the Southwestern Detroit community.

3. Maintain full occupancy, thus serving the needs of as many individuals as possible.

4. Operate at only the highest standards, providing all residents with the ability to lead the best life possible.

5. Provide individualized programs to meet the residents' needs.

PRODUCTS & SERVICES

Residential Services

Welcome Home Organization seeks to offer the best living conditions possible for all of our residents. We plan to construct a 30–room facility so that each resident is able to enjoy a space all their own. Each person will have a comfortable room, matching as closely as possible a home environment. The rooms will be comfortably furnished and decorated. The residents will receive three prepared meals per day, and a snack will be offered in the evening. All food will be served family style, again matching as closely as possible a home environment. All meals will be prepared by a trained cooking staff, and therefore will be able to meet the individual nutritional requirements of all of our residents. Also, there will be a trained Dining Aide staff as well as many volunteers who will assist those individuals with special eating needs.

In addition to the private rooms, there will be numerous areas available for social activities and entertainment. These living spaces will offer residents an opportunity to socialize with one another as well as the facility's volunteers and staff. These areas will be equipped with furniture and decorations so as to again create an atmosphere of home.

Our staff will be on duty 24 hours a day, and will be able to meet all of the needs of our residents. This facility will surpass state–requirements in the number of direct–care staff on duty so that our residents will have the best living conditions possible. A full team of direct–care staff will be on duty 24–hours a day. In addition, a trained nursing staff will be on duty from 7:00 am to 11:00 pm to meet the medical needs of the residents. During the evening hours from 11:00 pm to 7:00 am, the direct–care staff on duty will be trained in emergency medical procedures as well as medication administration. The facility will also make arrangements with a physician and dentist to assume overall responsibility for medical and dental care. Each resident will have at least one physical examination per year by a licensed physician and dentist.

Day Program Services

Welcome Home Organization will offer a Day Program to provide our residents with opportunities to socialize, exercise, and learn. This program's intent is to improve the lives of our residents and to teach new skills through a variety of activities and programs. In doing this, we hope to give them the skills they need to live as independently as possible. Through these programs we hope to instill a variety of skills including communicating with others, making personal choices, eating independently, personal hygiene, domestic skills, developing hobbies and interests, and developing basic work skills. Each person's program will be individually designed to meet their personal needs and skills.

These skills will be emphasized through a variety of activities designed and coordinated by a trained Day Program staff. In addition, many entertainment and social activities will be incorporated. These include a variety of games and sports, exercise time, gardening activities, arts and crafts, table games, music and singing time, and many others. Another important aspect of the day program will be community service projects. This part of the program will teach our residents the importance of giving back to the community. All Day Program activities will primarily take place on campus, but field trips will be offered on occasion.

Within the facility there will be an area designated specifically for the Day Program. State law requires forty square feet of usable floor space for each resident. Our facility will house a maximum of 30 residents, and so our Day Program Activity Center will be 2400 square feet in area. The Day Program will include a staff of four who will be responsible for developing individualized programs for each resident, planning activities, and working with volunteers. These volunteers will include family members of the residents. Both the residents' wants and needs will be taken into account in creating programs and planning activities. Overall, it is crucial that the program plan is person–centered, and is developed with active participation from the residents.

ORGANIZATION

Facility

One of the most important aspects of our organization will be our world–class residential care facility building. We plan to locate our 12,000 square foot facility in Brighton, Michigan on approximately three acres. Our building will have every convenience of home, so our residents are truly comfortable. The building will consist of 30 bedrooms, each of which is approximately 140 square feet. The bedrooms will be fully furnished and contain a bed, pillows, blankets, a bedspread, other proper linens, a bedside stand, a chair, closet space, a dresser, and vanity and sink. The rooms will each have at least one window which will provide views of the outdoors.

In addition to the bedrooms, the facility will have several living room–type areas. In total, these areas will be approximately 2,400 square feet. These rooms will serve many needs from providing a relaxing place to watch television and socialize, to a place to play board games with fellow residents and volunteers. One room will be furnished with couches, chairs, and end tables and will supply a place for the residents to watch television. Another room will have couches, tables, chairs, and floor mats to provide a place for social activities and games. The room will be stocked with a variety of board games and cards for the residents' enjoyment. A third smaller area will accommodate those seeking a quiet place. This area will also have couches, chairs, bookshelves, end tables, and lamps. We hope that by providing a variety of living areas, our residents will have ample opportunity to socialize and interact with those in our community as well as have individual time for peace and quiet.

Our facility will utilize communal bathrooms for the residents' use. These bathrooms will be conveniently located so that all residents have easy access. The bathrooms will have all the necessary equipment, including individual showering areas.

The Day Program will take place in our 2,400 square foot activity center. This center will be very flexible, allowing the spaced to be used for a variety of activities. The area will have collapsible tables and chairs, floor mats, and other appropriate equipment. This way, the facility can meet many different needs, from arts and crafts to exercise and dancing.

The kitchen will be approximately 750 square feet, and will be equipped with proper kitchen equipment. These items will include commercial sized refrigerators and freezers, ovens, and dishwashing equipment. There will also be adequate preparation areas with necessary counter space and sinks. The dining area will be approximately 1,200 square feet and will have adequate number of tables and chairs so as to accommodate our residents. Finally, about 1,000 square feet will be devoted to offices, a nurses station, and general work space.

BUSINESS STRATEGY

Features and Benefits

At Welcome Home Organization, we believe that our benefits are quite simple. We want to create a quality home–like environment where our residents can live happily and successfully. We strive to create the best living environment possible, with modern and clean facilities. We believe that each person is important, and should be treated as such. We hope to have the best staff in the industry, whose only focus is the happiness and care of each individual living in our facility. We want to create the best activities, so that our residents can truly enjoy life and make the best out of it. We want our residents to learn, to socialize, and to be happy. At Welcome Home Organization we know all of these things will be accomplished.

Business Model

The Welcome Home Organization derives its revenues from three sources: government payments, residents' contributions and donations. Government payments are broken into two categories, per diem reimbursements for residential care and monthly reimbursements for day programs. The per diem reimbursement rate is $115 per resident, and the day program rate is $750 per resident per month. These rates are set by the Michigan Department of Mental Health, and are indexed to the cost of living increases. Residents or their families pay a fee of $200 per month for residential care and day program services. Donations are put towards the construction and development of the facility, along with securing the organization's financial future. Government revenues and resident contributions alone are not enough to support the development and operation of the facility. Therefore, donations are essential to the organization's success. A portion of donations that do not go towards development and operations will be placed in an investment fund. This fund protects the organization against fluctuations in government revenues in the future.

Legal Business Description

Welcome Home Organization will receive certification as a non-profit corporation filed as a 501(c) (3) through the Internal Revenue Service and the Michigan Secretary of State's Office. In order to receive this status, the following steps must be taken:

1. Review IRS Publication 557, *Tax–Exempt Status for your Organization* as well as IRS Publication 578, *Tax Information for Private Foundations and Foundation Managers*.

2. File Michigan form *Articles of Incorporation of a Nonprofit Corporation* through the Michigan Secretary of State's Office.

3. File IRS Form SS–4, *Application for Employer Identification Number*.

4. File IRS Form SS–1028, *Application for Recognition of Exemption*, as well as IRS form 872–C, *Consent Fixing Period of Limitation Upon Assessment of Tax*, and IRS Form–8718, *User fee for Exempt Organization Letter Request*, in order to produce a Letter of Determination.

5. File Michigan Form 1746, *Michigan Sales/Use Tax Exemption Application*, through the Michigan Department of Revenue to receive a Michigan State Tax I.D. number.

6. Register as a Charitable Organization with the Michigan Attorney General's Office using form *Charitable Organization Initial Registration Statement*.

In addition to applying for non–profit status, because Welcome Home Organization is operating in the health care industry, we must be approved by the Michigan Certificate of Need Program, as well as receive state licensing through the Department of Mental Health's Division of Mental Retardation and Developmental Disabilities. The Certificate of Need program is designed to verify the need of services in the community the facility plans to locate. In order to receive this certificate the following steps must be completed:

1. Letter of Intent

2. Proposed Expenditures

3. New or Additional Equipment Application

4. New or Additional Long Term Care Bed Application

5. Proposed Project Budget

6. Applicant Identification and Certification

7. Representative Registration

8. Service–Specific Revenues and Expenses

9. Detailed Institutional Cash Flows

10. Periodic Progress Reports

The most important aspect of the certificate of need program is the verification of need in the area for the services proposed. According to the Michigan Division of Mental Retardation and Developmental Disabilities as of December 31, 2003 there were 260 individuals in the Detroit Metropolitan area seeking

Residential Care. This information was gathered through the Detroit Regional Center for the Developmentally Disabled and is the most recent data available. According to the center, this information is still current. Each of these individuals has been determined to be eligible to receive state funding.

To receive state licensing from the Michigan Department of Social Services, the following must be done:

1. Complete Department of Mental Health, Bureau of Quality Improvement form *Application for License to Operate a Residential Facility or Day Program for the Mentally Ill, Mentally Disordered, Mentally Retarded or Developmentally Disabled.*

2. Submit facility plans to the licensing office and the Michigan State Fire Marshal. These plans must also include a description of the utilization of each area.

In order to receive State Medicaid funding, we must apply for and receive a Provider Agreement through the Department of Social Services' Division of Medical Services. The DMS will issue this agreement if they have received a certificate of authorization or an acknowledgement of exemption from the Division of Mental Retardation and Developmental Disabilities.

OPERATIONS

Location

Welcome Home Organization will be centrally located in Livingston County whereas able to meet the needs of individuals from throughout the Southwest Detroit Metropolitan Area. The facility will serve people from Livingston County, Oakland County, Wayne County, Macomb County, and Washtenaw County. We chose this location because of our ability to raise money and public awareness in the community.

Organization

Our management team will consist of individuals with experience in the health care and nursing home industry. These individuals will be charged with maintaining the daily operations of the facility as well as supporting the long–term viability of the organization. The management team will include the following:

Chief Administrative Officer

1. This individual will be responsible for the overall operation and management of the facility.

2. He or she will oversee all activities in the organization, including marketing, services, staffing, and decision making.

3. He or she will work with the management team and the Board of Directors to promote the well–being of the residents as well as the long–term success of the organization.

Chief Business Officer

1. This individual is responsible for the business and finance operations of the facility.

2. He or she will manage all necessary financial information, and prepare financial forecasts and budgets.

3. He or she will also coordinate all fundraising efforts for the facility.

Residential Services Coordinator

1. This individual will work with the staff in order to maintain excellence in service and quality living conditions for all residents.

2. He or she will be in charge of operations including scheduling, disciplinary activities, and overall maintenance of the facility and its services.

Day Program and Volunteer Coordinator

1. This individual is responsible for the day to day activities and socializing of the residents through the Day Program.

2. He or she will also coordinate volunteers at the facility.

Social Service Coordinator

1. This individual will be responsible for residents' admissions and intakes. They will also give sales presentations to prospective residents, give tours of the facility, and be responsible for working with families to fill out paperwork for admissions.

2. He or she will also be responsible for the paperwork and duties associated with discharges.

3. He or she will be in charge of fulfilling the requirements of the state in terms of paperwork, including securing state funding.

Accountant/CPA

1. This individual will work with the Chief Business Officer and the Chief Administrative Officer in order to create adequate financial statements.

Attorney

1. This individual will be responsible for representing Welcome Home Organization in any legal proceedings.

2. He or she will prepare and file any necessary legal documentation.

Outside Management Support

Welcome Home Organization will also rely on a variety of outside sources for management support. These include both a Certified Public Accountant and an Attorney. These services will be donated by friends of the organization.

Board of Directors

An outside Board of Directors will be assembled, including highly qualified individuals from throughout the community. This board will consist of experts in the health care and nursing care field, as well as donors, family members of residents, and other respected members of the community. Working with the management team, they will aid in making appropriate and effective decisions that will benefit the lives of our residents as well as foster the long–run success of the organization.

Staffing

The state of Michigan gives specific guidelines for the staffing of Residential Care Facilities. In order to achieve a higher level of personalized care, Welcome Home Organization will exceed these requirements. Welcome Home will be tailored to meet the needs of what the state classifies as mild to moderately retarded individuals. If the facility were to serve more severely retarded individuals, the staffing levels would have to be increased dramatically to meet state requirements. Our organization will consist of a direct care staff, a nursing staff, a day program staff, a dietary staff, an administrative staff, and a facility services staff. In total our staff will include approximately 28 full time and 6 part time employees. For detailed staffing information including job descriptions, shift schedules, and salary information please see the appendix.

Volunteers

Volunteers will be an integral component necessary for the success of Welcome Home Organization. They will be actively recruited from throughout the community, and will include all age levels and abilities. They will be utilized in nearly every aspect of the organization, from daily operations and care to fundraising. Volunteers will work closely with the Day Program and Volunteer Coordinator to help meet the needs of the residents and the facility as a whole. We hope to utilize an adequate number of volunteers to aid in areas such as general care, activities and entertainment, meal time assistance, and education and training. In addition to helping out, we hope that the volunteers will develop meaningful relationships with our residents, adding to the quality of their lives.

In addition to assisting with the daily operations, volunteers will also be needed to aid in all of our fundraising efforts. They will work with the Chief Business Officer and the Day Program and Volunteer Coordinator to organize and work at fundraising activities as discussed in the Fundraising Plan. Their efforts in this area are critical to the financial success of the organization.

BUSINESS STRATEGY

Strategic Alliances

Welcome Home Organization hopes to develop several strategic alliances, including the following:

1. Corporate Sponsorship—We hope to develop relationships with a variety of corporate sponsors willing to donate to our organization. We plan to put into place a variety of programs to support these activities. One of these programs is our Naming Rights Program. Through this program a company will be able to purchase naming rights for our facility. The facility will then be marked with a plaque to show our appreciation for their generous contribution. The facility will also then take on the corporate name permanently. We plan to work with the Founder's Committee to develop this relationship.

2. Physician and Dentist—Our facility will work with a local physician and dentist to take on responsibility for the overall care of our residents. These individuals will then have regularly scheduled times in which they will visit our facility and perform normal check'ups and health evaluations. Also, they will be available in cases of emergency.

3. Hospital—According to state law, a formal written arrangement with a community hospital must be made for the treatment and hospitalization of our residents. We will work with a local hospital to make such arrangements.

MARKET ANALYSIS

Market Definition

Welcome Home Organization operates within the developmentally disabled community. More specifically, the organization works with individuals who range from mild to moderate mental retardation. These patients require habit training and some assistance with day to day living. This represents a significant percentage of the mentally retarded community.

Within the Detroit metro area there are approximately 260 individuals on the waiting list of residential care facilities. Each individual qualifies for state funding according the Michigan Department of Developmental Disabilities.

The county breakdown is as follows:

1. Oakland County: 40 individuals

2. Livingston County 27 individuals

3. Washtenaw County: 37 individuals

4. Wayne County: 156 individuals

These people represent opportunity for the Welcome Home Organization. They will be the catalyst for a quick path to full occupancy of the facility.

Market Organization

Mild to moderately retarded people receive care from three primary sources: family, family in conjunction with day programs and residential care facilities. There are benefits and drawbacks to each type of care. Families are increasingly challenged to provide around the clock care to their developmentally–disabled loved ones.

Family is almost always the first source of care received by the disabled individual. As the individual ages providing full time care can become increasingly challenging. The factors of dual careers and additional children make providing adequate care all the more difficult. During adolescence parents usually enroll their child in a day program for the disabled. These programs function like a daycare. The individuals are dropped off in the morning and picked up in the afternoon. Throughout the day the individuals interact with others, have recreational time and participate in habit training. Some patients will be involved with a work skills program. At some point parents must decide if they will be the primary care givers indefinitely, or if the now young adult will enter a residential care facility.

Residential Care Facilities cover a wide range of care needs. Individuals enrolled in these programs may require anything from habit training to full time nursing care. Welcome Home Organization will specialize in the mild to moderately retarded community. By specializing in this sector the Welcome Home family can focus its abilities on making a significant impact upon its residents' lives. All the residents will take part in habit training, while some will also take part in an additional work skills training program. While the Welcome Home Organization believes that all individuals deserve care, we also believe that this niche market will provide us with the best opportunity to serve the community.

SWOT Analysis

S: Strengths

1. Welcome Home Organization will pride itself on having the newest and cleanest facilities in the market. Our dedication to continuing quality will only enhance this reputation over time.

2. The staff will have vast experience and training, and the staffing number will exceed state requirements.

3. The low number of beds allows for more personalized service and care.

4. Large scale fundraising creates a moderate price structure.

5. Our central location will be convenient to the entire Detroit/Ann Arbor Region.

W: Weaknesses

1. Our strategy relies upon an excellent initial and ongoing fundraising campaign. By utilizing personal relationships and experienced supporters we will be able to reach our fundraising goals.

2. Any new organization faces the challenge of establishing itself in the community. We must establish ourselves in the hearts of our supporters and potential residents in order to gain trust.

3. The Welcome Home Organization must abide by the strict regulations associated with operating a facility of this nature. Through a thorough understanding of the regulations the Welcome Home Organization can accomplish this task.

O: Opportunities

1. With 260 people signed up on the waiting list of existing facilities, there should not be a problem reaching capacity.

2. Studies show that mentally retarded adults are living longer, and often outliving their parents. This creates more demand as medical technologies continue to improve.

3. In the future the demand could warrant the construction and operation of a second facility. This facility would meet the same needs of the current operation and would not be developed for 7–10 years.

T: Threats

1. Decreased funding from the State of Michigan.

2. Established facilities have already gained trust and respect from the donor and developmentally disabled community.

3. New entries into the market pose a threat. We will overcome these competitors by always improving the total quality of the organization, and delivering personalized service to each resident.

4. Lack of fundraising jeopardizes the feasibility of the facility. But once again we believe that our fundraising plan is feasible, and will be executed successfully.

Customers

Due to the nature of our business, we have a very specific customer profile. Our residents fit within the following criteria:

1. Age: 18–40

2. Mild to Moderate Retardation

3. Income: Varying

4. Family Status: Single

5. Location: Southwestern Detroit Metropolitan Region; including Wayne, Oakland, Washtenaw, Livingston and Macomb Counties.

6. Lifestyle: In need of habit and work skills training.

Our residents are looking for a personalized home like atmosphere, which affords them the opportunity to socialize, learn and grow towards a better tomorrow. We plan to fulfill all of these needs.

Competition

The competition is from existing facilities operating in the Detroit/Ann Arbor Region. These facilities have established trust in the community, and have histories of reputable care. Only three facilities offer campus style living similar to that of Welcome Home Organization.

Welcome Home Organization holds competitive advantages over these existing facilities. The facility itself will be new, and contain modern conveniences. The staff of the organization will be experienced and well trained, and also able to deliver personalized care. This is due to the low number of beds, which allows for more interaction between staff and residents. Overall the services we offer will be similar, but we pride ourselves on delivering them in a professional and personalized manner. Welcome Home is not just a facility, but truly a home for its residents.

MARKETING & SALES

Marketing Plan

Welcome Home Organization must market itself in two different spectrums, residents and benefactors. The initial thrust of the marketing campaign has two objectives; to demonstrate the demand for residential care, and to rally support for the organization. After the initial marketing campaign is complete, then the organization will transition its marketing efforts accordingly. Future marketing efforts will focus their attention towards producing a positive organizational image.

The organization's market differentiation is three–fold. First, the facility will be of the highest quality. Second, the staff will strive to deliver personalized care to the residents. Finally, the organization will adapt itself to meet the needs of its residents and their families. These three benefits will be the basis of the organization's competitive advantage.

Marketing Plan: Phase 1

Phase one carries out the immediate objectives of the organization. It begins ingratiating itself with the developmentally disabled community, and raises public awareness of the organization. In terms of the overall time line this phase takes place during the initial fundraising and development, all the way up to the full occupancy of the facility. The marketing is directed to both potential residents and supporters.

Residents

The sales strategy of Welcome Home organization is multi-faceted. Welcome Home will serve the needs of the underserved, provide quality care and offer assurance to the families of the developmentally disabled. In order to carry out these strategies the organization plans to have two essential marketing methods.

The Department of Developmental Disabilities waiting list will provide an excellent source of potential residents. These residents are already seeking residential care and have been qualified by the State of Michigan to receive funding. Therefore, they are a target market that we will pursue.

In addition, during the development stage members of the organization will become involved in regional advocacy and support groups for the developmentally disabled and their families. The purpose of this involvement is to become acquainted with the influential people within the market, and to better understand the need of the market. These types of networking events will also help to provide the original group of residents. When it comes to a loved one, families desire a personal connection to those providing the care of the individual.

This personal connection will be provided by the Social Services Director and Chief Administrative Officer, who will be the public face of the organization. Once the facility's construction is complete and in operation, they will give tours, help coordinate public relations events and act as a sounding board for the concerns of residents and their families. Welcome Home Organization will strive to be a learning organization; an organization that works to create a home like atmosphere for its residents and peace of mind for their loved ones.

Providing quality care is a must, and it will be expressed throughout all the actions of the Welcome Home Organization. Marketing the quality care will be accomplished through the development of positive public relations. Residents and their families will see an organization that prides itself on quality throughout. The most trusted form of advertising is an unsolicited endorsement, and that must be the foundation that supports Welcome Home Organization.

Two marketing methods have been adopted. The first is a personal sales method that focuses itself on becoming involved within the developmentally disabled community as well as personally contacting those on the waiting list. Welcome Home Organization believes that this personal bond is vital to success. Second, the organization will develop a positive public relations campaign to cast a wider net and raise the public awareness of the organization.

Supporters

Welcome Home Organization cannot exist without generous donations from its supporters. These donations are crucial for the initial startup including construction of the facility as well as funding a portion of ongoing operations. Marketing the organization to potential supporters means building a donor pool from a series of fundraising committees. The original or Founders Committee will be comprised of civic minded individuals who value the mission and vision of the organization. This committee will be responsible for the coordination of successive committees meant to broaden the scope of the fundraising. An altruistic sales strategy will be used to approach members of the Founders Committee.

Members of the Founders Committee will be solicited from personal connections and family members. Given the interpersonal relationships that already exist, this effort should meet with quick success. In order to meet the goal of fifteen members, Welcome Home plans to approach thirty potential donors. These donors will meet individually with the Welcome Home family to discuss their involvement in the organization. They will be asked to donate fifty thousand dollars, and support future fundraising efforts. Although a success rate of fifty percent for such a large commitment is ambitious, it is also achievable. The strength of personal connections and the nobleness of the Welcome Home mission will open the hearts of supporters.

The process of recruiting members of the Founder's Committee has already begun, and has been extraordinarily successful. Eight families have pledged to join Welcome Home Organization's Founder's Committee. A more detailed description of the fundraising activities can be found in the Fundraising Plan.

Marketing Plan: Phase 2

Phase two of the marketing effort begins after the facility has reached its full occupancy. This phase has two goals: to continue publicizing the tradition of quality care, and to become further involved in the developmentally disabled community. Much of this marketing effort will take place simultaneously with ongoing fundraising efforts. The effective planning and execution of fundraising events such as golf tournaments and dinner auctions will provide excellent public relations.

These events will be coordinated by the Chief Business Officer and Chief Administrative Officer. The Chief Business Officer's central fundraising role will be continuous contact and networking among present and potential supporters. Members of the Founders Committee will work in conjunction with the CBO to establish fundraising goals and strategies. The Founders Committee also coordinates with the CAO to aid in the planning and execution of the fundraising events.

Long Term Competitive Plan

Welcome Home Organization envisions a bright future, with continuous improvements in all facets of the organization. In order to maintain a long–term competitive advantage Welcome Home must listen to the needs of its residents, expand and improve the facilities and strive for extensive fundraising. These accomplishments advance the Welcome Home Organization vision of living life to the fullest, while working towards a better tomorrow.

The well–being of its residents is the mission of the organization. Accordingly, the organization is determined to adapt itself to the needs of its residents. One example of this personalized service we plan to implement is a customized activities schedule, which best reflects the interests of the resident. Each resident is a true individual, who deserves to be treated with dignity and respect. By fostering this atmosphere over the long–term Welcome Home establishes an advantage that cannot be matched by a newcomer to the market.

The facility will be updated and renovated to meet the stylistic and amenity demands of the time. Welcome Home is being constructed as a first–class operation, and will maintain that status as the facility ages. By staying current the Welcome Home Organization will maintain its advantage of truly being a home–like atmosphere.

While the initial plan calls for a single facility of thirty beds, future demands may require expansion. In this case, Welcome Home will consider the development of a second site to meet the demands of the market. A second facility would not be constructed until the initial operation has been running for seven to ten years. This period of time would allow the organization to establish itself as a leader in the developmentally disabled community.

If the heart of Welcome Home is its residents, then its lifeblood is fundraising. Welcome Home Organization will establish a competitive advantage through its extensive fundraising efforts. These efforts will establish funds for its operation, renovation and expansion. The fundraising effort will be well organized and well executed. The Chief Administrative Officer and Chief Business Officer are responsible for the success of the fundraising operations.

FUNDRAISING PLAN

Initial Fundraising Effort

Welcome Home Organization thrives upon the generosity of its friends and benefactors. In order to meet the initial start–up and operating costs Welcome Home has created an aggressive fundraising plan. The cornerstone of this plan is a Founders Committee consisting of fifteen people, pledging to donate fifty–thousand dollars each. These fifteen people will not only donate money, but also their time to the initial fundraising effort. Once the Founder's Committee has been established, a broader group of supporters can be gathered. The Platinum Circle will include twenty people donating twenty–five thousand dollars a piece. The Gold Circle will seek out twenty–five donors pledging ten thousand dollars per person. Finally, the Silver Circle includes 100 individuals each pledging $1,000. Given the importance of these initial supporters it is crucial to gather not just people, but the right people.

Our initial fundraising goal is $1.6 million. Construction on the project will begin once we have met half of the initial fundraising goal. This initial fundraising will be used to develop the facility, cover a portion of operating costs, and help to secure the financial future of the organization. We plan to have completed the initial fundraising effort in slightly over one year.

Founders Committee

The members of the Founders Committee represent the highest commitment to the Welcome Home Organization. They must donate as much through their time and energy as through their wallet. A member must have adequate financial resources, solid stature within the community and a willingness to work with the organization into the future. Prospective members of this committee may very well have experience interacting with developmentally disabled individuals within their own lives. In addition to the traditional fundraising circles, Welcome Home Organization will utilize those for whom developmental disability is a special cause.

These members will be recruited through personal relationships of the Brumfeld and Wesley families. Currently, eight families have already pledged their support and agreed to join the Founders Committee. $400,000 has been pledged to date. This initial group will help to fill the rest of the Founders Committee as well as the Platinum, Gold, and Silver Circles.

A profile of each of the members follows:

1. Bart and Martha Brumfeld: Bart is currently the President of Operations for Transport USA. The couple is involved in many charity and community activities, and is very familiar with the donor community throughout the Detroit metropolitan area.

2. Don and Judith Booth: Don is currently the Vice-President and General Counsel of Railways Inc. He is also the owner and principal of Booth Law Group. In addition, he serves as a Grand Rapids Alderman. Judith is the Deputy Executive Director of the Michigan Democratic Party. Both are extremely active throughout the community.

3. Shelly Grabek: Shelly is an active member of her family's businesses. Pinnacle Newspapers Inc. is a media company based in Michigan. In addition, she is involved with UMAN, a manufacturing firm

based in San Diego, California. She donates much of her free time to worthy causes, including the St. Jude's Children's Hospital.

4. Rock and Cynthia Noetzol: Rock is a retired Ann Arbor physician, and currently donates his time as the Washtenaw County Health Commissioner, a position he has held for over thirty years. He is a third generation Washtenaw County practitioner, and has family roots going back over a century and a half. Cynthia is a retired registered nurse, and is involved in the National Multiple Sclerosis Society.

5. Rick Spivey: Rick is an anti–trust attorney with the firm of Holden–Nash LLP. He is also a Oakland County Councilman. Rick is active in the community, and has vast experience in fundraising.

6. Eric and Julie Gardner: Eric is a retired executive from Robotics LLC, and is actively involved with a variety of charities including Boy Scouts of America. Julie is a retired homemaker.

7. Robert and Janice Wesley: Robert is currently the President of Lumber Supplies, Inc. based in Brighton, MI. He and Janice are actively involved in the community and have done extensive fundraising for a variety of charitable causes.

8. Greer Frasier: Greer is a widowed homemaker. Her husband's businesses included Frasier Window Company, Inc. and a variety of real estate holdings. Currently, she is involved with a variety of local charities.

The members of the Founders Committee have graciously agreed to personally send out pledge letters to their contacts. From their resources we have gathered the names of nearly 1,000 potential donors. Each member will send out a personal letter to their own contacts. The members have graciously agreed to underwrite the cost of this mailing. An example of the letter can be found in the appendix.

Platinum Circle
A platinum circle of donors shall be derived from these efforts of the Founders Committee. This platinum circle will be responsible for a twenty–five thousand dollar donation and assistance in future fundraising. Members of this committee will be drawn from the contacts and resources of the Founders Committee members. The platinum circle will then assist in securing the gold circle of donors.

Gold Circle
The gold circle comprises the next phase of the initial fundraising effort. $250,000 will be brought in by the gold circle of donors. Just as important, this effort will lay the groundwork for the silver circle.

Silver Circle
The silver circle offers the chance for smaller donors to join the Welcome Home Organization family. One hundred donors pledging one thousand dollars will raise a total of $100,000. In total the initial fundraising effort will raise 1.6 million dollars.

Spring Gala Event
In order to get people excited about the organization, as well as seek donors, Eric and Julie Gardner have graciously offered to underwrite the cost of a spring gala event at the St. Louis Zoo. Families will have the option to donate from $250 dollars a guest, all the way up to joining the Platinum Committee with a donation of $25,000. Julie Gardner has offered to plan and execute the entire event. This event will be mentioned in the initial appeal letter, along with an enclosed response card. Examples of each are in the appendix.

Ongoing Fundraising
Welcome Home Organization will support a portion of its operating costs through ongoing fundraising operations. These operations will include traditional and non–traditional fundraising. The non–traditional fundraising is to include corporate sponsorship and naming rights.

Traditional Fundraising

The traditional fundraising plan includes an annual campaign, dinner auction, collection day, golf tournament, a bequest program and in the future an annuity program. These fundraisers should offer opportunities for even the smallest donor to share in the Welcome Home Organization vision. Their success will be one of the main duties of the Chief Administrative Officer, Chief Business Officer and Day Program and Volunteer Coordinator. Each of these events is done by multiple organizations, and requires significant numbers of people. Our Volunteer list will include the families of residents, our donors and friends.

- Annual Campaign: An annual fundraising campaign shall be conducted to help meet fundraising goals. The initial contacts will come from the list of potential supporters provided by the Founders Committee. This campaign will be conducted primarily through a mail/call strategy. Potential donors will receive a letter outlining the mission of Welcome Home Organization, and asking for their support. Within a week, a volunteer from the organization will contact that person, asking if they have received the letter, and if they are interested in supporting the organization. If they are not interested in donating to the organization, then they will be eliminated from the annual campaign. However, if they would like to donate, then they will be given further information and supporting calls until the donation is received. Donors to the annual campaign will be submitted into the pool for other fundraising activities. The general strategy of the annual campaign will be the responsibility of the Chief Administrative Officer. Volunteers for the follow up calls will be organized by the Day Program and Volunteer Coordinator. The annual campaign will begin in the third year, after all initial fundraising has been completed.

- Dinner Auction: Welcome Home Organization will host an annual dinner auction. The event will have three streams of revenue: the dinner, auction and corporate sponsorship, and will be held in October. This annual event will begin in our first year of operation. Auction items will be primarily donated in order to minimize cost. Corporate sponsors will enjoy the public goodwill which accompanies having their name attached to a worthy cause.

- Collection Day: Each year the organization will conduct a collection day to be held in April. This day will be similar to those held by organizations such as Backstoppers, Old Newsboys and other charitable groups. The organization will utilize a large number of volunteers to blanket busy intersections and public places asking for small donations. This type of fundraiser has a high margin, and raises the public awareness of the organization. A higher public awareness means a greater annual campaign, and so we will begin our annual collection day in the third year. This way we will have developed a greater public awareness and built a volunteer base to utilize in these activities.

- Golf Tournament: Golf tournaments provide many revenue opportunities. The first is simply the tournament fee paid by the golfer. In addition golfers may have the chance to purchase mulligans, enter skins contest and participate in hole–in–one contests. All these enhance the dollars brought in by each individual. Once again corporate sponsors may be elicited for the entire event, and also for individual holes. Although golf tournaments do have a high overhead, they are an excellent method of getting new individuals into the donor pool. The event is scheduled in June.

- Bequest Program: Bequest programs offer supporters the chance to remember the Welcome Home Organization in their last will and testament. The organization will provide standardized forms to aid in the legal process of the will. Donors may find this a useful tool to not only support the organization, but also to lessen the effect of estate taxes.

- Gift Annuity Program: After the organization has been established and is financially sound they will create a gift annuity program. This type of program accepts cash and publicly traded securities as a gift to the organization. In exchange for the gift, Welcome Home Organization will pay an annual annuity to the beneficiary for the remainder of his or her life. The rate is determined by the age of the youngest beneficiary, with the rate increasing accordingly with the age. Upon the death of the beneficiary the gift remains with the organization. Those who participate in this program enjoy lower taxes and secure income in addition to the altruistic benefit.

Non–Traditional Fundraising

Many organizations have turned to non–traditional methods of fundraising. Among the most popular is the use of naming rights and sponsorship. Welcome Home Organization plans to utilize these options during the development and maturing of the organization. We hope that the naming rights of our facility will raise $200,000. This amount will be pledged over a period of 10 years, with a $20,000 donation each January. Corporations reap a double benefit; their name becomes associated with a positive image, and their donations lessen their tax burden.

FINANCIAL ANALYSIS

Financial Explanation

Welcome Home Organization will be established on solid financial ground by the end of year five. Donations are used to develop the facility, cover a portion of operating expenses and protect the organization against fluctuations in government revenues. The development of the facility includes construction, training, equipment and staffing prior to full occupancy. Occupancy is scheduled to be ten individuals when the facility opens in January of year one, and is to raise by ten individuals each subsequent month, until the capacity of thirty is reached.

Year zero has no revenue from operations, because it is dedicated to fundraising and development. Employees receive payment for time worked during the development and training phase. Pre–construction activities such as architecture and engineering are to begin on January 1st. Construction is expected to begin in April and commence in November. A loan of $1.1 million dollars is received on April 1st, it is figured as a thirty year loan at six percent interest. The loan goes towards the cost of land and construction. The collateral will include the cash on hand and the residual value of the land and building. If additional collateral is required, the Wesley family has agreed to pledge a parcel of land in Livingston County as collateral.

Operation of the facility begins in January of year one. Operating revenues climb steadily through the end of March, as the occupancy increases each month. Accounts Receivable is calculated as one month of government revenues. Accounts Payable is calculated as one month of supplies and miscellaneous expenses. Investments have been calculated as seventy–five percent of excess cash flow, beginning in February of year two. These investments are meant to secure the financial future of the organization.

APPENDIX

Job Descriptions
Direct Care Staff

- Responsible for the overall care of residents.

- Assist with daily activities and special needs.

- Assist with maintaining health standards and appropriate environmental conditions.

Registered Nurse

- Responsible for the overall health of the residents, and will be the dedicated nurse in charge.

- Responsible for development of drug control procedures, environmental health, safety, and dietary procedures.

- Responsible for drug distribution management.

- Maintains necessary medical and nursing records.

- Necessary medical care will include, but is not limited to injections, inhalation therapy, intravenous fluids, suctioning, ostomy irrigation, lesion dressing, aseptic dressing, catheter irrigation, care for pressure sores and physiotherapy.

Licensed Practical Nurse

- Responsible for the care of the residents.

- Responsible for medication distribution while on duty.

- Works with the dedicated nurse in charge to maintain adequate medical and nursing records.

Cooks

- Responsible for the development of meal plans, taking into consideration residents wants and needs.

- Responsible for planning and ordering necessary food and equipment.

- In charge of food preparation for the entire facility.

- Maintains adequate records on resident-specific needs so as to accommodate necessary dietary and nutritional requirements.

Dining Aides

- Work with the cooks in the preparation and serving of meals.

- Assists residents with special eating needs.

- Work with volunteers to meet the general dining needs of the residents.

Housekeeping Services

- These services will be outsourced through an outside firm.

- Responsible for cleaning and maintaining the facility, including all common areas, restrooms, the activity center and resident's individual rooms.

Linen Assistant

- Responsible for laundry services, including resident's clothing, bathroom linens, and bedroom linens.

Plant Maintenance Employee

- In charge of the overall maintenance of the facility and its property.

- Responsible for necessary indoor repairs and maintenance at the facility.

- Responsible for outdoor maintenance, including lawn mowing and landscaping.

Day Program Staff

- Work with the Day Program Coordinator to plan and administer day program activities.

- Responsible for the care of the residents throughout the day.

- Work with volunteers in the Activities Center and throughout the facility.

Administrative Assistant

- Assists the Chief Administrative Officer in day–to–day activities of management and operations of the facility.

Receptionist

- Responsible for answering phones, greeting guests and other administrative tasks.

Biographical Information

- Chief Administrative Officer: The CAO has already been chosen, but the name is being kept confidential. This individual has over three years of public accounting experience, and holds C.P.A. certification. In addition, for the past three years this individual has served as the Director of Finance for a similar facility in another state. This individual is an excellent candidate, and brings a great and wide variety of experience to the operation.

- Jonathan Fisher: Jonathan has over six years experience with his family business, and a lifetime of charitable activities. He has worked directly with the developmentally disabled in the past. In addition, he has experience organizing fundraisers, which has led to numerous political connections.

- Robert Wesley: Robert has also worked with the developmentally disabled in the past at the Riverside Home. His work experience involves a variety of roles in the political process. Both Jonathan and Robert have worked with numerous candidates on all levels, including local, statewide and national. These connections will be beneficial to the fundraising and securing government support.

Motorcycle Dealership and Racetrack
Zoom Motors

34 Badger Blvd.
Waukesha, WI 53186

Patrick J. Kuyath

Zoom Motors will be a totally new kind of motorcycle and ATV dealership that many riders have been waiting to come along. In its current state, Zoom Motors is strictly a home-based racing team that is backed by national sponsor Smith ATV for racing. There is also business that takes place at our current shop on the side, the repair and selling of motorcycles and ATVs. We already have a big consumer base from the quality of work that we complete on the side and we are often forced to turn away business due to our lack of time and space.

Zoom Motors will be using a $1,000,000 line of credit to start the business. This will include fifteen acres of land, a 10,000 square foot building, and national worthy motocross track.

EXECUTIVE SUMMARY

Zoom Motors is a motorcycle dealership that will be located just 40 miles from Milwaukee in Racine County. The focus of this dealership is off-road recreation and racing. Zoom will offer the major brands and their products; which are Honda, Yamaha, Suzuki/Kawasaki, and Ducatti. There will also be a selection available of sport motorcycles and personal watercraft available for purchase.

Zoom Motors will have two on-site motocross tracks that will attract customers to the business—one of which will be the main race track, with another small one in front for displays. This dealership will be unique because it will not only be selling the product, but it will be also providing a place for the customers to ride and race their motorcycles and ATVs at the track.

From the second a customer walks through the door they will experience a totally new kind of dealership. Customers will be encouraged to sit on and tryout the products. There is going to be an extensive amount of inventory and bikes throughout the entire store. This is not going to be the typical modern day trend of selling to the Harley Davidson crowd. This will be the type of dealership that is seen in mail order catalogs that is specifically designed for off-road enthusiasts.

The street legal motorcycles will be concentrated towards the sport bikes rather than cruisers or touring bikes. These are the motorcycles that are raced throughout the world and are available for the public to buy. A customer will be able to come in and purchase their motorcycle and then customize it to the kind of riding they wish to do. This includes things like a better exhaust system or bigger foot pegs for more stability and performance. Zoom Motors will be set up for the action adventure seeking individual who is into extreme sports.

Along with offering a catalog and internet sight for orders, Zoom Motors will pride itself on having the availability of their products in store. If a customer walks in and is looking for a popular off-road product they won't have to pay for it up front, order it, and then return a week later to pick it up. We will have it and we will also have all the needed goods for riding at reasonable prices. This includes oils, gases, safety equipment, boots, and much more.

The race track at the dealership will be sanctioned by the American MotorcyclistAssociation (this is the sanctioning organization of U.S. on– and off–road motorcycle and ATV racing); this way the A.M.A. puts all responsibility in the arms of the rider. To become a member all you have to do is fill out the application that waves the riders rights from holding the A.M.A. or the track owners from any liability due to the rider or other rider's actions. The cost of a membership is $39 per year.

There will also be riding lessons and advanced training available for those interested. These courses will encourage safety and responsibility for new riders along with teaching them the skills that are necessary to be a good rider. The advanced classes will be more focused on racing which will teach important speed techniques and riding styles to improve riders for racing. Along with this there will also be special clinics at times throughout the year that will be taught by past racing legends and current stars of the sport today.

Zoom Motors will be funded by a family loan of $1,000,000; the dealership will be able to pay this back within ten years and be self sufficient. The initial start up cost will cover the initial purchase of heavy equipment for the track, and then fund the building of the dealership. Finally the money will be used for the cost of stocking parts and inventory. The total start up costs included should be under $800,000; this is based off of $300,000 for track and equipment, $250,000 for construction of building, and $250,000 for inventory, supplies, and licensing.

PRODUCTS & SERVICES

As mentioned in the executive summary, Zoom Motors will be driven towards off–roading and performance–based street bikes. To go along with the products that are offered at the dealership there will also be a great amount of service. Zoom Motors will pride itself in addressing the customer's needs. There will be no three week waiting period at this dealership for your bike to be looked at before it can be serviced. Zoom Motors will be able to diagnose on sight what is wrong with the motorcycle or ATV and then have it fixed in a week or less. Most motorcycle dealerships take the better part of three weeks to rebuild a single cylinder engine which only requires about three hours of work. We will be able to do the same service in one week or less because of our extensive inventory of parts and our own machine shop on site. This way all work takes place and gets done in a timely fashion all at one location.

The on–site motocross track is another service that is available at Zoom Motors that is not available at any other dealerships. Not only will the customers and racers be able to come and enjoy riding, but there will be riding classes and lessons to teach upcoming racers how to ride, as well as existing racers how to improve upon their ability. The services of Zoom Motors will start first with the opening of the track when the land is acquired and a track is built. It will remain open while the dealership is constructed and eventually open. The track will be functional for a full year before the dealership is open.

Also with being able to place orders in the store, consumers will be able to order either over the phone or through the internet from our parts catalog. The parts catalog will list all of our products that we stock and can order along with our services such as rebuilding of components. A big contribution to our part catalog is that we will be the only dealership other than Smith to sell Smith custom ATV products. This is a high–end line of accessories for motorcycles and ATVs that are currently only available through Smith. Smith is a very popular and well known business throughout the entire United States. This will better improve Zoom Motors' business along with Smith's because they will then have an established distributor in the Midwest. Once the dealership is open and attending racing events other than its own, the dealership will set up the system of selling parts and accessories at races other than its own. This will be done by having an extra trailer come to other races that will be stocked with products.

The NAICS code for a dealership is 441221 and for a race track it is 711212; SIC dealership code is 5571. According to the database this industry is growing rapidly with a lot of profit being made. The 1997 Economic Census showed that the NAICS 441221 motorcycle dealers showed 3,635 establishments with sales ($1,000) of 7,369,260. The SIC code showed that from 1992 to 1997 the number of establishments had grown from 3,585 to 3,635 and sales ($1,000) had jumped from 4,162,684 to 7,369260. The Payroll had gone from ($1,000) 427,155 to 712,065 and paid employees had gone from 22,184 in 1992 to 29,026 in 1997. So, while there had only been 1.4% increase in establishments, there had been a 77% growth in sales, a 66.7% growth in payroll and a 30.8% growth in employees. A more recent 2002 survey that was conducted by *ATV Aficionado* showed increases since 1997; these were a 4.3 % in establishments and a 45% growth in sales. This proves that the business is growing at a quick pace and that new establishments are successful.

Currently in 2005, there are seven motocross tracks in Wisconsin and five in Illinois. These tracks will be distant enough that permission is not required for A.M.A. sanctioning. Of the tracks that do exist, they are general purpose tracks that are not laid out in the fashion that Zoom's will be; there will be an easy distinction between the tracks. There are a number of other riding areas in the state of Wisconsin, but they are of a different layout and are therefore separate from Zoom's side of business and competition would not exist.

MARKET ANALYSIS

The target market for Zoom Motors is very broad, it reaches out to families who are wanting something fun to do together, farmers who are looking for an ATV to help with the chores, and racers interested in dirt and street racing. The bull's–eye for this dealership is the off–road racer and enthusiast, but everyone else is not far off. A family will be able to come in and buy small dirt bikes and ATVs for their children and more advanced ones for themselves. The children can then be properly instructed with the professional judgment and obtain skills that are necessary to be safe and have fun while riding their motorcycles and ATVs. Zoom Motors is also chasing after the mail–order consumer who takes care of their bike themselves. A mail–order consumer is a person involved in the sport but acts as their own mechanic by ordering their own parts and doing their own maintenance. Zoom Motors will be able to satisfy this crowd as well because of our long line of parts that are offered through our own catalog and out of numerous parts that we keep in stock at all times. Our consumer area is the entire United States, due to the mail order catalog. However, our main concentration of customers will be anyone within a four hour drive of Zoom Motors. This is so because the enthusiasts of the sport are used to traveling for races and are more than happy to travel in order to get the right part when they need it. Because Zoom Motors will be able to attract customers from different backgrounds, the profitability will be continually growing each year.

The industry closely associated is the American Motorcyclist Association and its members. In order to race at Zoom Motors, the participant would have to be a member. Currently the A.M.A. has around 270,000 members with an average household income of $84,000. Out of the 270,000 members there are 50,000 that would fall into the specific target area of Zoom Motors. This is a big industry base to pull customers off of and it would be easily accomplished by placing an ad in the monthly A.M.A. magazine.

COMPETITION

Direct competition would be minimal and mainly be on the mail–order side of the business with catalogs and magazines. Other dealerships in the area of Zoom Motors address themselves to a different following that we do, except for one. Wisconsin Cycles is this dealership; however they mainly address themselves to the sales of Polaris, all terrain vehicles; which is the agricultural side of the business that Zoom Motors would not be investing in. Since Zoom Motors will be offering Honda, Yamaha, Kawasaki/Suzuki, and Ducatti, Wisconsin Cycles is a very insignificant threat to business. The closest dealer of any brand of motorcycle and ATV would be Amazing Motors in New Berlin. This business is only ten miles from the location of Zoom Motors, but they would be at the disadvantage of this dealership. Amazing Motors sells only two brands of machines, KTM and Arctic Cat. Both are off brand versions and are very much less sought after in the U.S. Their product line would keep them distinguished to their customers and Amazing Motors. Amazing Motors will actually help out Zoom Motors by referring them to us for the brands that we carry.

Competition on the racetrack side would be any track in the state of Wisconsin and Illinois. There are only eight tracks in the state of Wisconsin and ten in Illinois. The closest one to Zoom Motors would be the track located in Pewaukee, Wisconsin, approximately a half hour away. They would also be the only direct barrier to entry as well. However, this obstacle is already overcome. In order to become an A.M.A. sanctioned track and hold events you must get the permission of anyone else that has a track within a 50 mile area. The owner of the Pewaukee track has already given the go ahead for a track at Zoom Motors. This is so because the Pewaukee track is very long and motocross style (smaller jumps), while the Zoom Motors track will be significantly shorter with more of a supercross layout (larger jumps). Because of this, all competition between the two tracks is eliminated. There are two other area sanctioned A.M.A. tracks but they are enduro tracks which do not affect a motocross track because it is a different form of racing.

MARKETING & SALES

The marketing strategy for Zoom Motors is very simple; let consumers know we have what they want and at a fair price. In order to achieve this, Zoom Motors will have a race trailer at every major race in the area as well as at the national events and will be promoting the business and giving out promotional spark plugs to racers. This is something that will attract much attention because spark plugs normally cost three dollars, but at a race track they can sell for anywhere from six to ten dollars. It costs eighteen dollars for a twenty pack of sparkplugs and racers in need will be sure to remember who gave them that sparkplug.

Another marketing strategy that Zoom Motors will use is sponsorship. Any rider who wins in their class at the Zoom Motors race track will be offered sponsorship of 10% off of any purchases for the rest of the season; this will be an advantage over competition because no one else can offer this due to our on site track. There will also be more sponsorship available for selected riders who go to the nationals along with the development of the dealership owned race team. Other competitors offer sponsorship at many different levels, however the Midwest has been left behind in some areas of this because most of the bigger dealers who offer this are located on the east and west coasts.

A big advantage in marketing that the dealership has over any other competitor is the race track available on site. The dealership will sponsor its own events along with selected promoters and will advertise their products by having the dealership open during race days. This way anyone who came to watch a race, or racer who is participating in it, can buy any product on the race day.

Web site marketing will also help move product, this will be so because the website will be accessible around the clock so that the customer can place their order any time. The product catalog will also help with marketing because it will be freely distributed at racing events and mailed out to any customer that has made a purchase of twenty dollars or more from the previous year. These two forces combined will inform customers of our new and existing products and bring their attention to what exactly Zoom Motors has to offer. Another thing as mentioned in the industry description that would be taken advantage of to promote Zoom Motors is the A.M.A. magazine. Advertisements placed in this would be seen by key consumers that are specifically being targeted by the business.

OPERATIONS

Location

Location is a very big key element to any business, which is why Zoom Motors has precisely chosen its location in an area that has a high demand for our product. Zoom Motors will be located right along the side of Hwy. 18 in Waukesha, WI. This is only forty miles from downtown Milwaukee and two hundred from Cheboygan. Customers will be able to simply exit at the Waukesha exit and make a right on the north service road and come right back to the dealership. And not only is the dealership visible from the highway, the motocross track is as well. This location will sell itself when people passing by will see the track and people riding on it.

As far as the track is concerned, this location will bring in many customers. I have not been to a single motocross track that is not out of the way. Every one seems to be at least fifty miles off the main roadway on a dirt road with no hotels or amenities near by. This location is seconds from the highway which makes it very easy to find and will draw in many participants because of this.

The physical facility of the dealership will be a 10,000 square foot steel erection building. It will have a divider directly in the center of it which will divide the service/inventory area from the show room which will contain motorcycles and apparel. Hours of operation for the dealership will be Monday through Friday 9:00 a.m.- 7:00 p.m., and Saturday from 8:00 a.m. -5:00 p.m. Hours of operation for the motocross track will be Tuesday through Friday from 12:00 a.m. -6:00 p.m., Saturday and Sunday from 7:00 a.m. -6:00 p.m. Also, zoning for the location will not be a factor because the physical approval paperwork is currently being approved and will be official in a matter of weeks. This was an easy barrier to get around because there are no homes close to the site of the business.

Management Summary

The service department of the dealership will be growing and advancing rapidly along with the rest of the company. The plan is for one mechanic starting out (Kyle Pelz), who will also run the parts department, and then add a new mechanic to the business each year as business grows. Kyle holds Motorcycle Mechanics Institute Certification for mechanics on motorcycles and ATVs; along with five years experience. The office/paperwork portion of the business will be handled by the secretary of the business (Megan Brown) and she will maintain the human resources portion of the business as well. Megan has six years experience of running two different businesses; this is a proven track record that she has what it takes to make an office work. The owner (Greg Johnston), will be the overseer of the entire business and concentrate most of his time towards sales and the race track. Greg currently runs Zoom Motors out of his race garage where he currently maintains inventory, oversees maintenance of customers' bikes, sells bikes to customers, and preps a private race track.

There will also be the hiring of a sales person in the second year to better serve customers. The human resource side of the business is planning on employing about two new employees per year until needs are satisfied. An employee will not be hired until the business has grown to the point that additional help is needed beyond the three initial employees. This means that there could be an extra mechanic hired the second week of business or the second month, work load is determined on this. There will also be a seasonal part time worker for the preparation of the track and maintenance of the facility.

For race day staffing there will be a number of local part time workers and volunteers that are friends or family of the racers. There is also a volunteer force for motocross events, the Motocross Parents Association. This group of individuals shows up at races where their family is racing and they help out at the track by filling in a number of different jobs. There will be a total employed work force of eight for race days and on average twenty volunteers.

FINANCIAL ANALYSIS

The plan of attack for the financials is to first construct and open the motocross track portion of the business first. By doing this the word will get out to a large number of consumers about a new motocross track that is open in the area to go riding at and that holds races. Once there, they will be able to see the ongoing construction of the dealership and they will realize that this is going to be much more than just a track. By implementing this plan, Zoom Motors will have a big customer base before the doors of the business even open. Once the dealership is open for business there will already be an established customer base and consumers will be coming for all of their needs. The financial schedule plans for there to be an average start in the sales and service of the business with a major emphasis on the revenue from the track. Sales of new and used motorcycles and ATVs along with parts should start out sufficient with the four product lines offered and then grow rapidly once a broad customer base is achieved.

On the financial schedule the motorcycles show up as not that much; that is because this is only the price of used and custom built machines that are at the dealership. All new motorcycles, ATVs, and personal watercraft are under contract from the manufacturers and belong to them until time of sale. This means that Zoom Motors can have at any time upwards of $500,000 of motorcycles available for sale, but only a fraction of that is actual property of the dealership.

Online Mortgage Company

Valuable Mortgage

141 Todds Way
Effingham, KS 66023

Adam Greengrass

This plan raised $2 million for a company desiring to build a state–of–the–art mortgage processing application and Internet site. Its goal is to create the defacto standard for executing the mortgage process.

EXECUTIVE SUMMARY

The communication process involved in closing a mortgage in today's real estate market is a complex, disorganized and often lengthy one. There can be as many as ten different companies participating in the closing of a single transaction. There is no central point for collaboration or communication. Hundreds of documents are mailed, overnighted, couriered, or faxed between the myriad number of companies involved, while everyone prays for everything to be delivered on time, at the right location, to the right person. It's a wonder that anything actually gets accomplished in such an unorganized, unsupervised, and chaotic environment. The average participant spends less than 20% of their time on core business activities, with over 80% of their time wasted on the process itself. The result is a process laced with errors, miscommunication and delays, making an already inefficient process even more unproductive.

Success in this industry will be determined by an organization's ability to effectively manage the communication process between industry affiliates, including the mortgage brokers, real estate agents, escrow companies, lenders, etc. Valuable Mortgage has built a business model that addresses this need in a unique way. Called POEM for Portal, Outsourced, Extranet, Management, this business model will completely reshape the way the mortgage closing process functions.

First, a web–based Portal site will host an application that in itself will serve as a workflow document management system, carefully managing the communication that takes place in the mortgage closing process. Through a combination of Outsourced processing and Extranet technologies, the system will Manage the process itself, accurately, easily, and effectively sharing information between affiliates. This will achieve the goal of shortening the time to close while vastly reducing the time wasted on process communications. The result will be a completely effective, focused, and relatively short process, and a great deal of the affiliates available time freed up to be refocused on core business activities.

All of the affiliates to the mortgage closing process will all utilize the Valuable Mortgage web interface to execute their transactions. The loan processing could either be totally outsourced to Valuable Mortgage, or the workload could be shared between the mortgage processor and Valuable Mortgage. In either case, Valuable Mortgage's web–based application will track the progress of the loan, making certain that the correct parties receive all required information on a timely basis.

The value created by Valuable Mortgage will be:

- Extensive cost savings for everyone utilizing their system;

- A considerably reduced time–cycle in the overall mortgage process;

- The ability for affiliates to focus more of their time on generating new business and less on the logistical requirements of that business; and

- The ability to drive extensive revenue that is tied directly to the performance increases that the system offers.

There are many companies today that are trying to address some of these issues. The problem is that none of the competition has tried to or intends to try to build a single application for all affiliates to use. Instead, there are applications for mortgage brokers, applications for real–estate agents, applications for lenders, and applications for mortgage processors. What differentiates Valuable Mortgage from its competition is that its application will be designed to work for all the affiliates to the process. The competition has developed individual applications and is vying for enough market share to be able to declare its communications protocols as 'the standard'.

Instead of getting caught up in this mess, Valuable Mortgage is taking a different approach. By designing an application for all the affiliates to use, Valuable Mortgage is addressing the one major issue that none of the competition is—the effective communication between different affiliates and the management of that process. Additionally, by offering the service for free to the mortgage brokers and for a small incremental monthly fee to other associates, Valuable Mortgage is certain to garner a large market share in a very small amount of time.

Objectives

The company's vision is to build a state–of–the–art mortgage processing application and Internet site that will in itself become the defacto standard for executing the mortgage process. The site will provide all users with real–time access to any customer application in process. This seamless sharing and managing of information provides more profitable management of the loan pipeline, enhanced customer service, and substantial gains in productivity.

The site will be managed by Valuable Mortgage, through the use of their Internet based application and web site. Mortgage brokers, mortgage processors, and other affiliates to the mortgage process will utilize the site as their primary application for executing their business. Additionally, the application will provide prospecting, tracking, customer information, and other communications between all parties to the transaction.

- Eliminated will be the lengthy time it takes for these companies to send paperwork back and forth;

- Eliminated will be the miscommunication that often occurs when many organizations need access to paper based information;

- Eliminated will be the repetitive entering of data; and

- Eliminated will be the ineffective process that leads to escrow closing typically taking 30 to 60 days or longer.

Mission

The company's mission is to produce a web–enabled environment that is user friendly and offers highly valuable services. These services will:

1. Radically increase the mortgage brokers productivity;

2. Drastically decrease the time spent on producing results;

3. Create partnerships and strategic alliances between companies that offer complementary services; and

4. Create a 'community' environment based on open standards and information sharing.

The tool that will drive the company's mission is the Internet Portal site. This fully interactive website will offer each company that utilizes it all the tools necessary to effectively accomplish their core business goals.

The mortgage industry requires tremendous communication to take place between many companies and individuals involved in the mortgage process. The communication can get so chaotic at times, that people have to be hired just to manage the amount of faxing, telephoning, and paper organization that's required. Valuable Mortgage's focus is to take on the processing of the transaction, allowing Valuable Mortgage to:

· Manage the loans in process;

· Handle the mailing of marketing letters; and

· Streamline the communications required in the transaction closing process.

The result will be an effective process for all affiliates where they can spend the bulk of their time on business development instead of business processing.

One unique aspect of the business will be some of the value added services that Valuable Mortgage will offer. For example, a Loan Research and Call Center will allow affiliates to have Valuable Mortgage experts research specific questions or issues in reference to a particular transaction. A Credit Reporting Management service will allow potential home–buyers that don't qualify for specific loans to work on rebuilding their credit so that they will qualify. The value that Valuable Mortgage can bring to its affiliates from these services can be tremendous—imagine if Valuable Mortgage can take a customer from a mortgage broker, help that customer to rebuild their credit and qualify for a loan, and then feed that customer back to the original mortgage broker. This one additional sale would more than adequately cover an entire year of membership fees for that broker.

GROWTH STRATEGY

With margins shrinking, everyone in the real estate mortgage business is concerned with streamlining and cutting overhead. Valuable Mortgage allows mortgage brokers and other affiliates to escape the confines of their office, where previously they had to be because of the amount of faxing, telephoning, etc., that was part of the transaction closing process. The more mobile an affiliate can be, the more productive that affiliate will be. With Valuable Mortgage, all the affiliate needs is a telephone and an occasional computer connection.

The primary goal of the company's marketing efforts will be to induce affiliates to use the web–based application. The company will use a variety of direct marketing campaigns targeted at mortgage brokers and other affiliates. The higher quality/quantity of tools and/or services that are incorporated into the site the greater the value that Valuable Mortgage brings to its customers. Providing a central location where all of these companies and/or users collaborate will naturally promote a community interest and further desire to use the system.

Front–end revenue streams will include membership dues charged to the affiliates who utilize the Valuable Mortgage portal site. There will be several membership types each with its own pricing and services structure. Additional front–end revenue streams will be generated from transaction fees, processing fees, credit–counseling fees and escrow closing fees, which will be charged to certain affiliates that utilize the system.

Back end revenue streams will include strategic partnerships with other web–based companies that can bring incremental value to the users of the Valuable Mortgage portal. Growth is expected to be exponential once a critical mass of affiliates is signed up and is using the system. The company plans to be the first organization in the real estate mortgage industry to establish this critical mass of users by providing the back–end integration for collaborating and sharing of information critical to the closing of the transaction.

BUSINESS STRATEGY

Valuable Mortgage's sales strategy consists of four focused sales efforts. The first is to create an Internet portal site, which will be the environment that all Valuable Mortgage affiliates utilize. For this sales effort, Valuable Mortgage will promote the portal as the "meeting place" for all affiliates in the mortgage processing industry. The second is to be an outsourced processing center. Valuable Mortgage will provide different levels of outsourced processing capability, which supports the company's focus of helping affiliates to address the mortgage process more effectively. The third is to provide extranet connectivity, tying in the affiliates' computer systems into the Valuable Mortgage system, thereby facilitating the management of the communications process. The fourth is to provide management of the document workflow process, thereby assuring the Valuable Mortgage's focus on making the process more effective. In total, this sales strategy is called POEM, for Portal, Outsourced, Extranet, and Management.

Products & Services

Primarily the company will offer three levels of membership, each providing an incremental benefit over the other. These membership levels will be called Silver, Gold, and Platinum.

1. Silver Level Membership will offer basic access to Valuable Mortgage's website and basic tools, including automated online forms that are designed to eliminate errors and double entry of data. At the Silver level, individuals and organizations would utilize the Valuable Mortgage system on their own, running it as if it were installed on their local desktop computers. At this level, Valuable Mortgage staff will assist with some entry of data and cross checking of information, and will offer some guidance in the actual processing itself.

2. Gold Level Membership includes everything that Gold Level Membership does, plus total data checking and process management from Valuable Mortgage. For these members, Valuable Mortgage will closely monitor the process itself making certain that all key respondents take action within specified time limits. Should this communication not occur, Valuable Mortgage would contact the respondent, assess the situation, and facilitate the process itself. In this way, the successful outcome can be guaranteed.

3. Platinum level membership will offer full outsourced processing. All the mortgage broker would have to do is to prequalify the client and at most take an occasional loan application. The company would do the rest, from processing the application to stepping it through all necessary tasks to completion. At each step Valuable Mortgage would proactively provide detailed information to the mortgage broker and all other participating partners so that they are fully aware of the process that is occurring, however Valuable Mortgage would assume all responsibility for actual execution.

Revenue Streams

The following is a list of front–end and back–end revenue streams that Valuable Mortgage intends to pursue. For detail on these revenue streams, please see the Sales Plan later in this document.

- Monthly Membership Dues

- Affiliate Transaction Fees

- Private Label Lending

- Data Mining/Knowledge Management
- Lead Generation Program
- Classroom/Computer Based Training
- Communications Fees
- Licensing Programs
- Insurance
- Printing
- Mortgage Broker/Realtor Recruiting
- ISP Partnerships
- Computer and Accessory Sales
- Product/Services Sales
- Click–Through Incremental Revenue
- Sponsorships/Co–Branding
- Membership Program Benefits

Market Analysis

The company intends to utilize focus groups, marketing handouts and intensive market research into the successes and failures of our competition, to prove its market viability prior to implementation. A series of pilot programs will be implemented so that actual mortgage brokers, real estate agents, investors, and escrow companies can utilize Valuable Mortgage services and provide critical feedback into the development process. The anticipated result will be a system that works effectively for all parties concerned. Additionally, Valuable Mortgage is already developing unique technologies that will allow the company to successfully tie their technology into the host of systems in use by the various industries the company will support.

Competition

There is a lot of competition in the market niche that Valuable Mortgage intends to focus. Existing software companies with mortgage processing applications make up the largest number of direct competitors to Valuable Mortgage, and a small number of technology companies make up the rest.

The primary difference between what these companies intend to offer and what Valuable Mortgage intends to offer is in the capabilities of the software solutions. Most of these companies already have software applications, which feature specific types of solutions for specific industries. One of the larger companies, Wilshire Corporation, has a two–tier package called ElectroniK and Softex. These applications are designed for the mortgage processor, and primarily function as the tool that these organizations would use to execute their business, tracking all the necessary steps in the mortgage loan process. Wilshire intends to take this package onto the web, allowing other organizations to utilize it without having to install it locally, which is similar to what Valuable Mortgage intends to do.

The primary difference between Valuable Mortgage and its competition is that Valuable Mortgage is intending to build an online 'community' with the specific intent of building that community into an application for the mortgage processing industry. The companys competitors, like Wilshire Corporation, are attempting to do the opposite, taking an application and attempting to build that application into a community.

The company's approach is far superior to its competitor's approach. The reason is because it is next to impossible to take an existing application and web–enable it enough that it becomes a standard unto itself. The better approach is to foster an environment which best suits the needs of a particular niche, and then build an application which meets those needs. This is why Valuable Mortgage will be successful and its competition will not.

Business Strategy

The company's business model focuses on a unique strategy called Task–Trigger–Task. There are two primary components to the company's approach, the technical infrastructure that the company will utilize and the methodology, which is the core to the environment that will be created. Both of these components utilize the Task–Trigger–Task business model.

The technical infrastructure consists primarily of the web–based environment. In this environment, customers will utilize a system that is made up of tasks, which occur in the mortgage loan process. These tasks often occur concurrently, and in many cases specific tasks must be completed before other tasks can start. The relationship of these predecessors and successors is defined by the Task–Trigger–Task business model. The technology that Valuable Mortgage intends to develop with automatically monitor this process, and manage to a successful conclusion the pre–defined relationships of which tasks trigger which tasks.

As a methodology, the Task–Trigger–Task business model will drive the customer–oriented approach for the company. The technology will identify which tasks have or have not been concluded. The operational management team will closely monitor the results and will escalate any tasks or triggers that are not concluded within a preset timeframe. This is the key differentiation between Valuable Mortgage and its competitors. No other company has built a business model that so effectively ties the operations of the company to its infrastructure.

Growth Strategy

The company's initial efforts will focus on the US market. In the future, and once specific financial goals are met, Valuable Mortgage intends to evaluate its capabilities in other Internet–intensive countries. Additionally, Valuable Mortgage intends to begin multi–media advertising and public relations campaign designed to significantly increase Valuable Mortgage's market presence and awareness of Valuable Mortgage services and technologies.

The business model and operations of the company are being designed to be replicable to other industries. In the future, the company intends to evaluate other industries where the implementation of an effective and manageable communications methodology and environment could bring extensive real value. In so doing, the company expects to expand its business focus to these other industries, thereby opening potentially huge new revenue streams. Some of these industries might include any industry that used a broker to facilitate the sale, including the insurance and stock brokerage industries.

OPERATIONS

An in–house staff of individuals with extensive experience in all related industries will comprise the operational team. These individuals will have, at a minimum, the following expertise:

- Extensive knowledge of the Mortgage Brokerage industry, including expertise in all affiliated industries;

- Total competence in the loan closing process;

- Extensive training in customer satisfaction methodologies, project management, and extensive experience working one–on–one in a customer oriented environment;

- Debt negotiation, credit counseling and repair expertise; and

- A solid grasp of technology, including how to effectively use the Internet and more specifically how to use the Valuable Mortgage web site to accomplish business goals.

Management Summary

The company's management team consists of three highly skilled individuals. Individually these people have extensive expertise in all the various aspects of Valuable Mortgage's business, and as a team they represent a level of business acumen and personal integrity that is rarely seen in the industry today.

The three management team members include:

- President and CEO—Matt O'Neal: From 1989 to present, Mr. O'Neal has worked in the financial services industry, with a primary focus in the mortgage industry from. Mr. O'Neal has had extensive responsibilities, including the acquisition of investors for second trust deeds, management of the investment strategy, and management of the A paper investors. Technically, Mr. O'Neal has a background in systems integration and telecommunications, and has designed and implemented many large customer and process oriented implementations both in and out of the mortgage industry.

- Vice President, Business Development—Matt Jones: Mr. Jones is the founder and President of Jones & Wiaduck Financial Inc., a financial services consulting and trading firm. Mr. Jones has over 10 years experience in the financial services industry and holds a series 7 license. From 1984 to 1989, Mr. Jones was Vice President in charge of business development for CashCow Solutions, a company that provides back–office processing and software development for broker/dealers. In 1989-91, Mr. Jones was an account executive with Dean Witter Reynolds. Mr. Jones holds a Bachelor of Science degree in Business Management.

- Vice President Finance & Marketing—Jim Williams: Following the achievement of a B.A. from University of Dallas, Mr. Williams joined a mortgage brokerage firm where for three and a half years he maintained top producer status, generating over $30 million in home loans. Mr. Williams went on to successfully start his own mortgage company with the focus on streamlining the home buying and loan origination process. Mr. Williams has in–depth knowledge of the mortgage industry and what is required to successfully manage the mortgage process. Mr. Williams co–founded Valuable Mortgage and has been instrumental in its marketing, creative, direction, fundraising, and growth.

FINANCIAL ANALYSIS

The following is an excerpt of the Statement of Profit and Loss, included in the financial section in this business plan.

Statement of profit loss
(Dollars in thousands)

	Year 1	Year 2	Year 3
Revenue	$ 17,756	$ 20,419	$ 24,503
Costs and expenses	(6,750)	(5,640)	(6,761)
Subtotal (gross margin)	11,006	14,779	17,742
Taxes	(4,182)	(5,616)	(6,742)
Net income	$ 6,824	$ 9,163	$ 11,000
Percentage of sales	38%	45%	45%

Financial Requirement & Use

The financial requirement to implement this business plan is $1,651,000. This will cover operating expenses for the first five months of operation. The company intends to be positive on a cash flow basis by the sixth month of operation.

Statement of first year cash flow analysis
(in thousands)

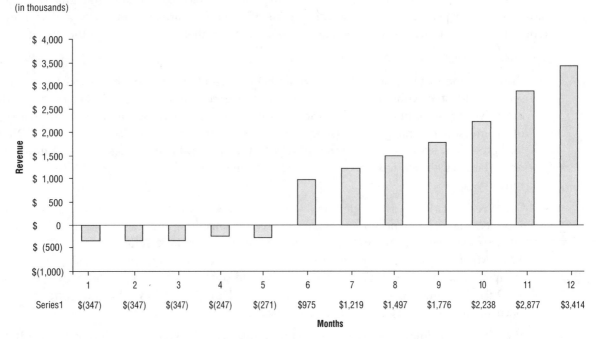

	1	2	3	4	5	6	7	8	9	10	11	12
Series1	$(347)	$(347)	$(347)	$(247)	$(271)	$975	$1,219	$1,497	$1,776	$2,238	$2,877	$3,414

Months

This chart projects cash flow (in thousands). See the Financials section for the detail behind this chart and Appendix A for the Operations Implementation Plan.

PRODUCTS & SERVICES

The practices today in the mortgage industry are time consuming, complex and disorganized. Valuable Mortgage intends to revolutionize these practices through the implementation of a centralized web–based portal site designed to bring maximum capability, productivity, and cost savings to the individual mortgage broker and mortgage industry affiliate. By effectively managing the communication process between affiliates Valuable Mortgage will allow these companies to refocus on business development, saving them extensive time and money now spent on the management of the process itself. The company's unique business model called POEM, combines facets of a web Portal with process Out-sourcing, Extranet technologies, and extensive workflow Management. The result that this business model will bring to the industry will be a completely effective, focused, and relatively short mortgage process.

Competition in this industry is fierce with many companies trying to develop the next 'standard' for mortgage processing. What differentiates Valuable Mortgage's approach from the rest is their focus on the creation of a complete mortgage processing 'community'. Instead of developing separate applications for each affiliated industry, Valuable Mortgage will develop an environment that brings a total solution to all the various affiliates of the industry. This environment will be designed to maximize communication between affiliates, and thereby leverage the affiliates need for effective communications to build the environment in which they work. This approach is unique—there is no other company that is focusing on bringing more value to the process itself. This approach is so radically different that what the competition is offering that it is destined to attract the largest percentage of affiliated customers.

Not only has Valuable Mortgage developed a unique approach, but Valuable Mortgage has focused that approach on the development of the Portal community environment. Combined with POEM, Valuable

Mortgage will design the Portal around its task–trigger–task business model. This business model assures that each task in the mortgage closing process is closely tracked and managed, so that each affiliate in the process is delivered the information needed at just the right time.

Finally, by creating multiple front–end and back–end revenue streams, Valuable Mortgage's community environment will be bring the most possible value to its customers while assuring multiple income streams for the company as well.

Confidentiality and Risk Statements

The information, data and drawings embodied in this business plan are strictly confidential and are supplied on the understanding that they will be held confidentially and not disclosed to third parties without the prior written consent of Valuable Mortgage.

This business plan represents management's best current estimate of the future potential of the business. It must be recognized that no business is free of major risks and few business plans are free of errors of omission or commission.

SALES & MARKETING

The rapid growth of the Internet, from the beginning of its popularization in the early 1990's, is one of the most widely–studied and discussed technical and business phenomena in history, rivaled only by the growth of personal computing—with which it is inextricably linked. There are believed to be 80 million Americans who currently use the Internet, with involvement ranging from occasional e–mail message exchanges to daily multi–hour surfing and exploratory sessions.

One of the latest trends driving the phenomenal growth of the Internet is business to business services. Forrester Research (a leading market research firm) predicts that business–to–business sales over the Internet will have grown from $43 billion in 1998 to a staggering $1.3 trillion by 2003. These services utilize a technology called 'extranet', where businesses utilize the Internet for the specific purpose of being effective in inter–business communications. Extranet technologies allow organizations to connect their internal systems with other organizations. The result is a vastly increased level of communications, driven by the ability for these two organizations to share data securely and subsequently communicate faster and more effectively.

This is where Valuable Mortgage comes in. By providing a radically simplified environment based on this extranet technology that will tie together all of the affiliated businesses involved in the loan closing process, Valuable Mortgage will fulfill its goal of bringing about a new and much more effective overall process.

Stefan Swanepoel, a well–known author and real estate industry strategist, recently published an extensive and thought provoking report that identifies key trends expected to significantly determine the ground rules for the use of the Internet in the real estate mortgage industry. According to Swanepoel, even though mortgage processing professionals have traditionally been the gatekeepers of information, the Internet is now demanding that they evolve into the interpreters of information.

"Should [Valuable Brokers and their affiliates] wish to succeed in the Internet era, they will have to focus on creating a consumer–centric model by instead becoming gatekeepers of the transaction," remarked Swanepoel. "To survive in the future, [Valuable Brokers] must act as coordinators, counselors and facilitators in streamlining the total home–buying experience."

There is no question that the Internet has already significantly changed the way we live and work, what we read, even how we communicate. According to a Fast Company–Roper Starch worldwide survey, 94 percent of respondents believe that the Internet makes communication easier, while 96 percent report that the Internet increases their accessibility to information.

Based on the recent number of technology and Internet–related exhibitors at the National Association of Realtors convention, an event attracting more than 23,000 Realtors and Mortgage Brokers, it is evident that the Internet is rapidly taking a stronghold on the industry. To date, however, many will agree that of the estimated 10 million real estate and mortgage related websites, very few really offer true value or the ability to conduct transactions online as easily as do Amazon.com or eBay. "The integration of the mortgage processing transaction and the creation of a... shopping experience is still a year or two away, though companies like HomeStore.com, E–Loan, iProperty.com and HomeGain.com show a lot of promise," said Swanepoel. "The main reason for the delay of full integration is that the home–buying process is considerably more complex, less frequently conducted, very heavily regulated and saturated with way too many participants."

Yet while the process for integration of these markets has lagged, the fact is that web banking and online mortgage capability are becoming more intertwined every day.

First, online lending king Mortgage Online, Inc. established a relationship with ebankz, the perceived leader in the virtual bank space, letting ebankz customers shop for home mortgages through a co–branded ebankz/Mortgage Online, Inc. site. ElectroMortgage, another leading online mortgage player, is also partnering with banks using a combination of web–based and real world offices.

According to Deutsche Bank, online mortgage originations will grow by more than 5,000 percent by 2003 to about $250 billion annually. And about 80 percent of Internet users rate their online banking experience higher than the traditional brick–and–mortar experience, according to a recent survey by Washington–based Frederick Schneiders Research Inc.

Valuable Mortgage intends to capitalize on this growing trend to take advantage of the Internet for mortgage processing. However, Valuable Mortgage intends to do so in several unique ways. First, Valuable Mortgage will primarily be a business–to–business focused entity, providing services to the mortgage brokers and to the affiliates of the mortgage processing industry. Through a technologically advanced portal site, Valuable Mortgage will effectively manage the loan closing process such that Valuable Mortgage customers will be able to focus on their core business development activities.

Today, the existing Internet based mortgage processing applications are basically little more that data storage locations that still have to be manually managed by the vast number of participants to the mortgage closing process. Valuable Mortgage's primary goal is to build a mortgage processing application around a new methodology that will allow the technology itself to manage the process. In so doing, the Valuable Mortgage system will coordinate the communications, signoff, and acceptance by the affiliates to the process, freeing up the affiliates' time so that more time can be spent doing business development and less wasted on the logistical requirements of managing the actual process itself.

Market Analysis

The mortgage processing industry today can be very complex. In any given transaction there can be as many as ten parties, most of whom are unfamiliar with one another and each other's internal processes. At the same time, each party has a specific function that must be executed within a reasonable amount of time and fully communicated to the other parties. The result of this mis–managed process often includes:

- A process sought with chaos, redundancy and disorganization. This often results in wasted time and money, frustrated borrowers, missed lock deadlines, and lost loans, all due to the lack of managed communication between parties;

- A high degree of redundant information. Each company has their own internal computer systems and processes and usually has to enter the information manually into their own system. The results include data management errors, and a great amount of wasted time.

- A tremendous amount of mis–communication as there is no centralized standard for messaging. Some companies utilize email, however most fax documents back and forth with handwritten notes attached. Much of this communication gets lost, either in transit or in translation.

The following diagram details the communication process as it exists today for the typical mortgage escrow closing.

Typical communication process

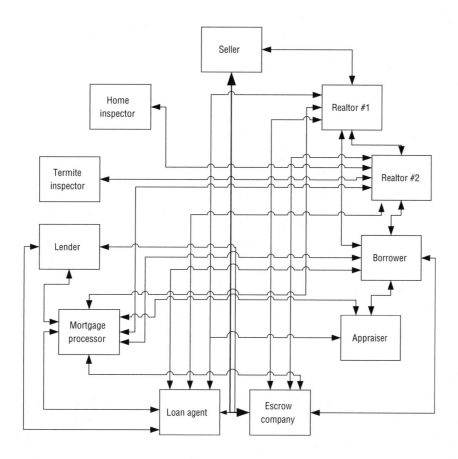

OBJECTIVES

Valuable Mortgage's intent is to radically simplify the complex communications process that is involved in the typical mortgage closing. Valuable Mortgage will provide an online, unified work environment for every affiliate to the process. In this new environment the participants will experience the following:

- Information will be entered only once and will be accessible at any point, from any location, only requiring that the user have an active Internet connection;

- The seamless transfer of information in a paperless environment;

- Sharing of information with all parties, free from redundancy errors of omission, or wasted time. Also, each party will receive proactive loan status updates from a single point of access to all messages.

The following diagram details the Valuable Mortgage concept of the communications process.

Proposed communication process

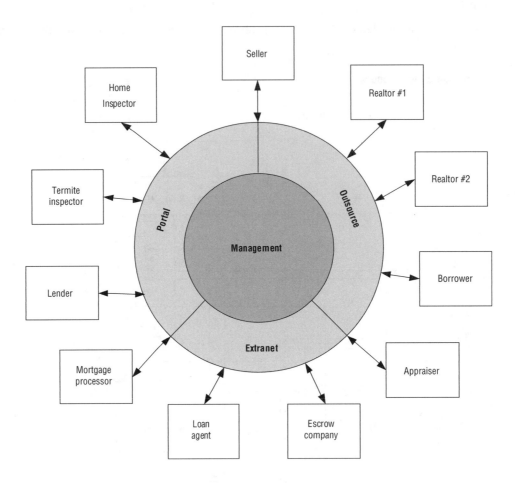

The focus of this environment will be on Valuable Mortgage's ability to manage the process and the pipeline from beginning to end. In time, the affiliates will get this understanding and will then allow Valuable Mortgage to execute the loan processing for them, freeing them up to focus on getting more business. The Valuable Mortgage environment facilitates its users to be able to do more business.

Business Strategy

The company's business model is to create the most efficient vertically integrated, yet open, work flow tracking model for mortgage processing that ties in everything from loan acquisition to servicing. The methodology is called Task—Trigger—Task, and describes not only the functionality of the Valuable Mortgage technical environment, but also the customer–focused methodologies under which the company will operate.

The mortgage process itself is comprised of many tasks, each one having a predecessor and a successor. In every case, each predecessor triggers another task, starting with the first action, and ending with a closed loan. Many of these tasks occur simultaneously, and the end result of the process is based on this Task—Trigger—Task relationship. If we were to examine this in a classic project management capacity, the resulting Gantt chart would look something like this:

ID	Task	Dec 26, '99							Jan 2, '00							Jan 9, '00			
		F	S	S	M	T	W	T	F	S	S	M	T	W	T	F	S	S	M	T	W

ID	Task
1	**Example mortgage loan process**
2	Initial Action - task
3	**Conclusion - trigger one**
4	Action - task two
5	**Conclusion - trigger two**
6	Action - task three
7	**Conclusion - trigger three**
8	Action - task four
9	Action - task five
10	**Conclusion - trigger four**

In this Gantt chart, we start with an action, which is also Task One. The conclusion of the first task is a trigger, which in the case of this Gantt chart, sets off two separate tasks, following two concurrent paths. The first path leads to three tasks in a task—trigger—task relationship, while the second path leads to a single concurrent task. Both paths end at the same trigger.

This is how the Valuable Mortgage website environment will function. Every action that an affiliate takes while utilizing the system will lead to a trigger that sets off one or more additional tasks. The system itself will be designed to monitor the triggers, to make certain the appropriate tasks are started at the appropriate time. At each point in the process, whether it is a Task start or a Trigger, the system will automatically deliver all necessary information to all concerned parties. The beauty of this design, which is unlike anything in the industry today, is in the effectiveness with which it will run this process and the quality of information that will be available at any given point in the process to everyone in the process.

In addition to the technology itself, Valuable Mortgage will offer the system as an Application Service Provider. The staff will be trained in this methodology to effectively identify and communicate when a trigger is reached and who should be receiving what information. Their ability to provide "help desk" functionality and actually monitor the process itself, driving escalation where necessary to assure its success, will truly differentiate Valuable Mortgage from its competitors. In practice, the Task—Trigger —Task business model will be implemented by Valuable Mortgage in three distinct revenue generating business focuses. These include:

1. As an Outsourced Mortgage Processing Center—In this capacity, Valuable Mortgage will perform all the loan processing functions involved with the setup and closing of a loan. By delegating this responsibility to Valuable Mortgage, mortgage brokers/processors will be able to better focus on their core business activities. This brings tremendous value to the mortgage broker/processor while also bringing extensive value to the customers of the mortgage broker/processor; the company can now maintain a more customer centric approach without having to worry about the logistics of the process itself.

2. As an Information Portal Site—In this capacity, Valuable Mortgage will be a content aggregator for all information, tools, and services that any affiliate would require. By providing these tools to affiliates, Valuable Mortgage enables them to execute their own business models more effectively.

3. As a Strategic Partnership Driven Organization—In this capacity, Valuable Mortgage will drive incremental value and revenue for its vast list of strategic partners. Additionally, Valuable Mortgage will become an information vendor, bringing leads, customers and incremental revenue to these partners.

The bottom line—Valuable Mortgage can process loans more efficiently and at less cost than the mortgage brokers/processors can do themselves.

COMPETITION

There is a great deal of competition in the mortgage loan industry. Companies have long recognized the benefits of automating the loan application process and the idea of shortening the escrow process through effective productivity tools is not a new one.

The primary difference between the competition's approach and Valuable Mortgage's approach is that Valuable Mortgage will be the first company to develop a complete solution which addresses the needs of every affiliate in the mortgage processing industry. The competition targets specific affiliate industries with individual application tools and the result is a decent application for that affiliate industry, but a continuing total lack of communications effectiveness between affiliate industries. By building one application that addresses all affiliate industries, Valuable Mortgage's focus will stay on the communication process itself, which is the key to success in this industry.

Competitors in this market include large banking organizations, brokerage houses, and a host of small Internet startups, each offering their own idea of what efficiency gains can be accomplished and each trying to be first to bring their products and services to market.

Some of the leaders in this market include:

- Alltel
- Byte Enterprises
- Calyx Point
- Contour Software
- Cybertek
- Delphi
- Desert Services
- Dynatek
- Fiserv
- Gallagher
- Genesis 2000
- IDSCOD
- Interling Software
- MortgageWare
- LoanEnergizer
- Loansoft
- MortgageFlex
- MortgagePro
- JMT Mortgage
- Pipeline Solutions

- PowerPak

- Reyncorp

- Tuttle Systems

- Valley Title

Just four of these companies currently dominate 85% of the independent mortgage broker market, Calyx Point with 41%, Genesis 2000 with 17%, Contour Software with 15%, and Byte Enterprises with 12%. While each of these companies have products that offer similar and yet unique approaches to defining the level of productivity that can be achieved, none of them offer the breadth or depth of services that Valuable Mortgage intends to offer and none of them are focused on the effectiveness of inter–affiliate communications.

The primary differentiating factor between the competition and Valuable Mortgage is in the degree of overall capability that the online environment brings to its users. These companies each started with a single module offering specific services to specific affiliated industries. For instance, Calyx Point is designed primarily for the mortgage brokers to function as a front–end form entry tool. While very effective at that capability, it is not centrally run and does not offer extensive value to other related industries, such as the realtors or appraisers. Additionally, an affiliate–focused application will never be able to standardize the inter–affiliate communications process, which is the vital component in the reduction of complexity in this industry.

On the other hand, Valuable Mortgage intends to build an environment that takes advantage of the best features of all the leading software and intends to do it in an Internet based environment that gives equal access to all organizations. The key benefit and focus is not to provide a single organization with every required tool, but instead to offer all organizations a greatly enhanced and closely monitored communication process. The result will be higher productivity through implementation of a methodical approach, which will bring extensive value to all affiliates utilizing the system.

In the end, regardless of the information and choices the Internet brings, the key is and always will be to close loans quickly and cheaply with good customer service. This is Valuable Mortgage's focus.

CONCLUSION

The Internet is not a fad, but rather a keystone of the new economy. Companies that have established themselves as the market leaders of this new economy are the ones that have blazed the way, bringing new types of content and incremental value to their customers.

In the mortgage processing industry, the companies that have gone online on the Internet have done so by building an application and offering it to online users. In doing so, these companies have not addressed the most important aspect of the mortgage processing industry—the capability and efficiency of the process itself. These companies think that their application in itself will refine the way business is done in the industry, however they are sadly mistaken. Only a company that focuses on refining the process will accomplish that task. Only Valuable Mortgage is focused in this way and only Valuable Mortgage will accomplish this goal.

Over the long term it will be companies like Valuable Mortgage that continue to lead the way and redefine how businesses communicate with each other, and define value for their customers. Changing business processes is a complicated and difficult task. It takes a forward thinking company that is truly interested in creating value to accomplish this goal, and Valuable Mortgage is destined to fulfill this promise.

GROWTH STRATEGY

Selling Strategies

The sales strategy that Valuable Mortgage intends to undertake is a multi–faceted approach utilizing front–end and back–end revenue streams. Front–end revenue streams are those that are paid directly by the affiliates using the system. Back–end revenue streams are those where incremental 'value–added' services are utilized by the affiliates and where Valuable Mortgage makes some kind of commission or referral fee for their use. Additional back–end revenue streams include services that are utilized transparently by the affiliates, such as advertising and click through revenues. Each revenue stream will have its own associated advertising and marketing components.

- Membership Dues—Each affiliate will be charged a monthly membership fee to utilize the Valuable Mortgage system. Incrementally, membership dues only drive a small fraction of overall revenue. Subsequently, Valuable Mortgage's sales strategy will be to waive the membership dues wherever possible, so that the affiliate is made to believe they are receiving some kind of special deal. Examples of how and when the membership dues would be waived include: Any mortgage broker using Valuable Mortgage for processing three or more loans per month; any mortgage broker that refers another broker to sign up for the service; any affiliates that sign up during the first six months of operations. This will be the 'free registration period'. Users who sign up during this period of time will have their fees waived permanently; anyone who 'clicks through' to the Valuable Mortgage site from one of Valuable Mortgage's partner sites; and as an incentive for signing up for additional revenue driven services that Valuable Mortgage will offer, including (but not limited to) computer based training, full processing, partner licensing, etc.

- Affiliate Transaction Fees—Every time one of Valuable Mortgage's affiliates processes a mortgage through Valuable Mortgage, a transaction fee will be charged against the closing of that mortgage.

- Private Label Lending—A percentage of Valuable Mortgage customers will find their loans through Valuable Mortgage itself, instead of affiliate mortgage brokers. This percentage is projected to start at 1% per month and scale an additional percent per month to a total of 12% of loans in the 12th month.

- Data Mining and Knowledge Management—The company will create a data warehouse that tracks the progress of each transaction, amassing a large database of customer information, purchasing patterns, credit qualifications, etc. For a fee, this information will be made available to Valuable Mortgage affiliates.

- Lead Generation Program—One of the most valuable services that Valuable Mortgage will offer is a lead generation program for affiliates. Currently there is no other system that can manage the process from initial lead generation to packaging and selling of the loan and then back to data mining and prospecting. The company intends to build a data warehouse and to perform lead prospecting and distribution for our members. A small fee will be charged to the affiliate for the use of these services.

- Classroom and Computer Based Training (CBT) programs—The company will offer classroom and computer based training programs to help affiliates get the most out of the system. Additionally, a Valuable Mortgage partner will host other CBT programs in a variety of third party applications and industries. Each time an affiliate signs up for one of these courses, an incremental referral fee will be paid to Valuable Mortgage.

- Communications Fees—The company will leverage its free messaging services by offering a premium service which includes unified messaging (voice mail, email, fax), as well as long distance and premium message delivery services.

- Licensing Programs—Another strategic partnership for Valuable Mortgage will be with leading companies that can coordinate the licensing for individuals in the various industries for which Valuable Mortgage offers services. The company will receive a commission for each individual that signs up for one of these licensing programs.

- Insurance—The company will leverage their relationship with insurance companies and program administrators to offer private label and third party title insurance, E&O insurance, auto insurance, and general commercial liability insurance. A referral fee will be paid to Valuable Mortgage every time an affiliate utilizes these services.

- Printing—The company will have strategic partnerships with online printers to make the process of producing real estate flyers and mailing pieces merged with a database easier and less expensive. A referral fee will be paid to Valuable Mortgage every time an affiliate utilizes these services.

- Mortgage Broker/Realtor Recruiting—The company will create strategic relationships with the leading mortgage brokers and real estate firms in the industry. Links on the Valuable Mortgage site will entice individuals to sign up with these mortgage broker houses and/or realtors, and Valuable Mortgage will earn a commission for each user that registers.

- Partnerships with Internet Service Providers (ISPs)—Future partnerships with leading ISPs will generate incremental revenue for each Valuable Mortgage user who signs up for access with the ISP. Incremental revenues are expected to be $30 - $50 per user.

- Computer and Accessory Sales—The company will negotiate with particular hardware vendors to provide access to the Valuable Mortgage site with the sale of this equipment.

- Products and Services Sold to the Valuable Mortgage User Community—The company will feature specific products and/or services that are relevant to the interests of the Valuable Mortgage user community. These products will generate additional income for Valuable Mortgage while providing niche–targeted incremental value to the Valuable Mortgage users.

- Click–Through Incremental Revenue—The company will allow content focused banner advertising that brings incremental value to the Valuable Mortgage communities. The company will be remunerated for each "click–through" that a user follows from the Valuable Mortgage site.

- Sponsorships/Co-Branding—The company will sponsor specific opportunities, products, or services that bring incremental value to the Valuable Mortgage users. Additionally, Valuable Mortgage will co–brand other incremental products and/or services. These sponsorships and co–branded opportunities will generate additional income for Valuable Mortgage from the program's setup with these Valuable Mortgage partners.

- Membership Program Benefits—The company will sponsor a membership program allowing the Valuable Mortgage user community to earn 'reward points' for various activities and/or online purchases. Through the Valuable Mortgage channel program a portion of these reward benefits will be paid to Valuable Mortgage itself from participating merchants and vendors.

- Affiliate Transaction Fees—There will be no sales strategy for transaction fees. Everyone who utilizes the system will be charged a transaction fee, the price of which will be dependent on the level of their required processing automation. The more processing that is delegated to Valuable Mortgage, the higher the transaction fee will be.

Sales Model

The primary focus of the company's sales model is a four pronged approach to the sale of company services called POEM:

1. Portal—As a Portal Site, Valuable Mortgage will become the primary 'meeting place' for all individuals and organizations in the mortgage processing industry.

2. Outsourced Processing—Valuable Mortgage intends to provide various levels of outsourced processing capability. This capability will drive the company's focus, which is to reduce the overhead of affiliates allowing them to focus more on their core business activities.

3. Extranet Connectivity—Through extranet connectivity, the company intends to electronically connect their systems to the vast majority of affiliates' systems, thereby facilitating the effective transfer of information between affiliates.

4. Management of Document Workflow—The highlight of POEM is Valuable Mortgage's abilities in the process management space. The company will focus its efforts on the effective management of this process so that the end result will not be left to chance, but instead will be closely managed to a successful conclusion. This really defines the focus of the company. Rather than just provide tools to the affiliates and hope that they utilize them effectively, Valuable Mortgage intends to proactively manage the process of how those tools are utilized, thereby guaranteeing a successful outcome.

Valuable Mortgage Membership Levels

The company will offer three levels of membership, each providing an incremental value over the other. These membership levels will be called Silver, Gold, and Platinum.

Silver Membership—The Silver Membership level is Valuable Mortgage's basic membership; however it includes enough functionality that members at this level have almost total access to Valuable Mortgage services. The Silver Membership includes:

- Online forms
- Website access
- Discounted items
- Basic messaging
- Alert service
- Industry newsletter
- Interactive on line help
- Comparative rate sheets
- Industry news
- Free eCommerce store
- Industry dictionary
- RESPA guidelines
- HUD guidelines
- Mortgage calculator
- Online customer service
- Chat service
- Discounted Credit
- Address book
- Calendar
- 5 MB file storage
- Bookmarks

- Rolodex

- Directions (maps)

- Email disclosures

Gold Membership—The Gold Membership level includes everything in the Silver level, plus:

- Unified messaging

- Premium website access

- On line training

- Customized printing/open house flyers and templates

- Access to an email response system

- 10 MB file storage

- Credit summaries and optional services

- Deeper discounts on eCommerce

Platinum Membership—The Platinum Membership level builds on the Gold membership by offering these additional services:

- A lead referral program

- Extensive online training

- 25 MB file storage

- Full service credit repair

- Customized dispute letters

- A pipeline mngmt system

- Substantial discount on eCommerce

- A fully integrated Customer Relationship Management System

In addition to the above Platinum level benefits, Platinum level membership will also offer Full Outsourced Processing. At this level of membership, all the mortgage broker would have to do is to prequalify the client and record an occasional loan application. Valuable Mortgage would do the rest, from processing the application to stepping it through all necessary tasks to completion. At each step, Valuable Mortgage would provide detailed information to the mortgage broker so that they are fully aware of the process that is occurring, however Valuable Mortgage would assume all responsibility for actual execution.

Strategic Alliances

The company relies heavily on strategic alliances with existing companies, both in the Internet industry as well as other companies that have products or services that bring incremental value to the Valuable Mortgage community. Some of these alliances may include:

- ink software, inc.

- Johnson Software

- Planning Resources Corp.

The purpose of these partnerships will be to bring as much incremental value to Valuable Mortgage users as possible. Additional partnerships and alliances will be developed on an ongoing basis.

Advertising

Valuable Mortgage's advertising plan is to take heavy advantage of Internet based advertising campaigns, specifically focused on sites where individuals from the mortgage processing industry would visit. Additionally, Valuable Mortgage will tale advantage of traditional advertising medias as well, including newspaper, magazine, and possibly radio and television as well.

Promotions & Public Relations

The primary objectives of the Company's promotion plans are to:

- Inform and persuade potential customers to register on the portal site;

- Build brand and customer loyalty programs associated with the mortgage loan process and Valuable Mortgage services;

- Drive traffic to the Valuable Mortgage portal site as a premiere destination for individuals in the mortgage loan industry; and

- Enrich Valuable Mortgage's corporate image to build confidence with its suppliers, employees, dealers, and financial partners.

The company's promotion strategy consists of advertising, publicity and sales promotion. Additionally, the company will be retaining a leading public relations firm, to design, establish and build corporate and brand identify that will complement other aspects of the Valuable Mortgage's marketing and communications efforts.

ORGANIZATION

Management Summary

The company's management team is comprised of individuals who each have extensive experience in various aspects of Valuable Mortgage's business strategies, and effectively add value to the management team with their unique and specific skillsets. The management team includes:

- President and CEO—Charles Horte: From 1989 to present, Mr. Horte has worked in the financial services industry, with a primary focus in the mortgage industry. Mr. Horte has had extensive responsibilities, including the acquisition of investors for 2nd trust deeds, management of the investment strategy, and management of the A paper investors. Technically, Mr. Horte has a background in systems integration and telecommunications and has designed and implemented many large customer and process oriented implementations both in and out of the mortgage industry.

- Vice President, Business Development—Dante LaMont: Mr. LaMont is the founder and President of Washtenaw Financial Inc., a financial services consulting and trading firm. Mr. LaMont has over 10 years experience in the financial services industry and holds a series 7 license. From 1988 to 1991 Mr. LaMont was Vice President in charge of business development for Financial Database Systems, a company that provides back–office processing and software development for broker/dealers. In 1987-88, Mr. LaMont was an account executive with Lambert Peters Lambert. Mr. LaMont holds a Bachelor of Science degree in Business Management.

- Vice President Finance & Marketing—Matthew Derquizo: Following the achievement of a BA from Yale University, Mr. Derquizo joined a mortgage brokerage firm where for three and a half years he maintained top producer status, generating over $30 million in home loans. Mr. Derquizo went on to successfully start his own mortgage company with the focus on streamlining the home buying and loan origination process. Mr. Derquizo has in–depth knowledge of the mortgage industry and what is required to successfully manage the mortgage process. Mr. Derquizo co–founded ValuableMortgage and has been instrumental in its marketing, creative, direction, fund raising, and growth.

Customer Service/Product Support

The company is committed to superior levels of customer satisfaction. To this end Valuable Mortgage will build an internal customer service department. This department will be staffed by knowledgeable people who are also skilled in being effective on the telephone in interpersonal relationship management. The company's commitment to their customers is their one and only goal.

PRODUCTS & SERVICES

The intent for the Valuable Mortgage portal site is that it takes advantage of the leading technologies available today on the Internet, and does so completely transparently to the affiliate. This means there will be no 'plugins' to download, and no third–party applications that must be run. This will require a considerable development effort. The company will outsource this functionality, including the hosting of the Valuable Mortgage portal site. This will allow Valuable Mortgage to enter the market with lower capital costs and more effectively stay in step with technology support and growth.

The Valuable Mortgage portal site is the actual website that the Valuable Mortgage user community will interact with. The portal site will constantly be in a state of development so that Valuable Mortgage can assure its content will always be fresh and its appearance friendly and easy to use. The community users will be unaware of this development effort. Some of the specific functions of the Portal site include:

- Hosting the primary connection and website interface that the all the member companies and individuals will access;

- "Click–through" access to a wide variety of Valuable Mortgage partners driven by an "advertising engine" that will randomly place unobtrusive graphical elements on users' screens inviting them to click through and inquire further;

- A wide variety of general information "feeds," e.g., financial quotations, industry news, etc;

- Fully interactive "search engine" software to allow users to search the entire World Wide Web while providing customer service improvement information to Valuable Mortgage; and

- A one–stop shop for communications to parties of the transaction including email, voice–mail, fax, chat, and other telephony functions.

RISK FACTORS

The company's intellectual property exists in three forms: the web–site names it uses; various services and idea names and appearances on the portal site; and specific technical designs and concepts.

Existing Internet domain names have been registered on behalf of Valuable Mortgage and it is expected that in the course of business new domains will also be registered. Key trademark registrations will be issued for "Valuable Mortgage" and as business continues, more trademarks will also be registered.

Trademarks will be applied for in areas ranging from proprietary technologies and architectures to the applications that are planned for development.

FINANCIAL ANALYSIS

The company will require six months of development to get to the point where the product can be released in its first version for general distribution. This period of time will include two pilot programs under which a limited public release will be managed. The company expects to be self sufficient on a cash flow basis starting in the sixth month of operations.

The total financial requirement to implement this business plan will subsequently be $1,561,000.

STATEMENT OF REVENUE—YEAR ONE

Statement of revenue—year 1

			Month 1	Month 2	Month 3
Number of loan agents registered			1,350	1,823	2,319
Number of loans processed			135	182	232
Revenue streams	**Unit amount**	**Percent**	**Month 1**	**Month 2**	**Month 3**
Membership revenue					
Silver	$ 29.95	50%	20,216	27,292	34,721
Gold	$ 49.95	30%	20,230	27,310	34,745
Platinum	$ 89.95	20%	24,287	32,787	41,712
Loan transaction fees	$ 600	—	81,000	109,350	139,118
Private lending	$ 200,000	—	27,000	72,900	139,118
Printing	$ 40	—	5,400	7,290	9,275
Unified messaging	$ 5	30%	2,025	2,734	3,478
Website dev/host	$ 20	20%	5,400	7,290	9,275
Credit counseling	$ 150	20%	40,500	54,675	69,559
Telecommunications	$ 5	20%	1,350	1,823	2,319
Credit reports	$ 100	25%	33,750	45,563	57,966
Knowledge mgmt	$ 50	10%	6,750	9,113	11,593
Appraisals	$ 5	10%	675	911	1,159
Title/escrow	$ 5	10%	675	911	1,159
Termite inspection	$ 5	10%	675	911	1,159
Home inspections	$ 5	10%	675	911	1,159
Real estate agents	$ 5	10%	675	911	1,159
Home warranty	$ 5	10%	675	911	1,159
Insurance	$ 50	10%	6,750	9,113	11,593
Training	$ 30	10%	4,050	5,468	6,956
Licensing fees	$ 40	10%	5,400	7,290	9,275
ISP partnerships	$ 30	15%	6,075	8,201	10,434
Accessory sales	$ 100	5%	6,750	9,113	11,593
Ecommerce sales	$ 200	5%	13,500	18,225	23,186
Click throughs	$ 10	80%	10,800	14,580	18,549
Sponsorships	$ 150	2%	4,050	5,468	6,956
Awards program	$ 50	2%	1,350	1,823	2,319
[continued]					

Statement of revenue—year 1 [CONTINUED]

	Month 4	Month 5	Month 6	Month 7	Month 8
Number of loan agents registered	2,840	3,387	3,961	4,564	5,197
Number of loans processed	284	339	396	456	520

Revenue streams	Month 4	Month 5	Month 6	Month 7	Month 8
Membership revenue					
Silver	42,522	50,713	59,314	68,344	77,827
Gold	42,551	50,747	59,353	68,390	77,879
Platinum	51,084	60,924	71,256	82,105	93,496
Loan transaction fees	170,373	203,192	237,652	273,834	311,826
Private lending	227,165	338,653	475,303	547,668	623,652
Printing	11,358	13,546	15,843	18,256	20,788
Unified messaging	4,259	5,080	5,941	6,846	7,796
Website dev/host	11,358	13,546	15,843	18,256	20,788
Credit counseling	85,187	101,596	118,826	136,917	155,913
Telecommunications	2,840	3,387	3,961	4,564	5,197
Credit reports	70,989	84,663	99,022	114,098	129,927
Knowledge mgmt	14,198	16,933	19,804	22,820	25,985
Appraisals	1,420	1,693	1,980	2,282	2,599
Title/escrow	1,420	1,693	1,980	2,282	2,599
Termite inspection	1,420	1,693	1,980	2,282	2,599
Home inspections	1,420	1,693	1,980	2,282	2,599
Real estate agents	1,420	1,693	1,980	2,282	2,599
Home warranty	1,420	1,693	1,980	2,282	2,599
Insurance	14,198	16,933	19,804	22,820	25,985
Training	8,519	10,160	11,883	13,692	15,591
Licensing fees	11,358	13,546	15,843	18,256	20,788
ISP partnerships	12,778	15,239	17,824	20,538	23,387
Accessory sales	14,198	16,933	19,804	22,820	25,985
Ecommerce sales	28,396	33,865	39,609	45,639	51,971
Click throughs	22,716	27,092	31,687	36,511	41,577
Sponsorships	8,519	10,160	11,883	13,692	15,591
Awards program	2,840	3,387	3,961	4,564	5,197

[continued]

Statement of revenue—year 1 [CONTINUED]

	Month 9	Month 10	Month 11	Month 12	
Number of loan agents registered	5,862	6,560	7,293	8,063	
Number of loans processed	586	656	729	806	

Revenue streams	Month 9	Month 10	Month 11	Month 12	Annual total
Membership revenue					
Silver	87,783	98,237	109,213	120,739	$ 796,922
Gold	87,841	98,302	109,286	120,820	$ 797,454
Platinum	105,457	118,015	131,202	145,048	$ 957,371
Loan transaction fees	351,717	393,603	437,583	483,762	$ 3,193,011
Private lending	703,434	787,206	875,167	967,525	$ 5,784,791
Printing	23,448	26,240	29,172	32,251	$ 212,867
Unified messaging	8,793	9,840	10,940	12,094	$ 79,825
Website dev/host	23,448	26,240	29,172	32,251	$ 212,867
Credit counseling	175,859	196,802	218,792	241,881	$ 1,596,505
Telecommunications	5,862	6,560	7,293	8,063	$ 53,217
Credit reports	146,549	164,001	182,326	201,568	$ 1,330,421
Knowledge mgmt	29,310	32,800	36,465	40,314	$ 266,084
Appraisals	2,931	3,280	3,647	4,031	$ 26,608
Title/escrow	2,931	3,280	3,647	4,031	$ 26,608
Termite inspection	2,931	3,280	3,647	4,031	$ 26,608
Home inspections	2,931	3,280	3,647	4,031	$ 26,608
Real estate agents	2,931	3,280	3,647	4,031	$ 26,608
Home warranty	2,931	3,280	3,647	4,031	$ 26,608
Insurance	29,310	32,800	36,465	40,314	$ 266,084
Training	17,586	19,680	21,879	24,188	$ 159,651
Licensing fees	23,448	26,240	29,172	32,251	$ 212,867
ISP partnerships	26,379	29,520	32,819	36,282	$ 239,476
Accessory sales	29,310	32,800	36,465	40,314	$ 266,084
Ecommerce sales	58,620	65,601	72,931	80,627	$ 532,168
Click throughs	46,896	52,480	58,344	64,502	$ 425,735
Sponsorships	17,586	19,680	21,879	24,188	$ 159,651
Awards program	5,862	6,560	7,293	8,063	$ 53,217
Total					**$17,755,920**

STATEMENT OF STAFFING AND SALARIES—YEAR ONE

Statement of staffing and salaries—year one

	Annual
President/CEO	$ 125,000
VP business development	$ 125,000
VP sales & marketing	$ 125,000
CIO	$ 110,000
CFO	$ 110,000
Technical staff	$ 90,000
Technical staff	$ 80,000
Technical staff	$ 70,000
Technical staff	$ 70,000
Technical staff	$ 50,000
Technical staff	$ 50,000
Technical staff	$ 50,000
Customer service staff	$ 90,000
Customer service staff	$ 70,000
Customer service staff	$ 50,000
Customer service staff	$ 50,000
Customer service staff	$ 50,000
Admin	$ 40,000
Total	**$ 1,405,000**

STATEMENT OF PROFIT AND LOSS

Statement of profit and loss
(Dollars in thousands)

	Year 1	Year 2	Year 3
Revenue			
Membership revenue			
Silver	$ 796.92	$ 916.46	$ 1,099.75
Gold	$ 797.45	$ 917.07	$ 1,100.49
Platinum	$ 957.37	$ 1,100.98	$ 1,321.17
Loan transaction fees	$ 3,193.01	$ 3,671.96	$ 4,406.35
Private lending	$ 5,784.79	$ 6,652.51	$ 7,983.01
Printing	$ 212.87	$ 244.80	$ 293.76
Unified messaging	$ 79.83	$ 91.80	$ 110.16
Website dev/host	$ 212.87	$ 244.80	$ 293.76
Credit counseling	$ 1,596.51	$ 1,835.98	$ 2,203.18
Telecommunications	$ 53.22	$ 61.20	$ 73.44
Credit reports	$ 1,330.42	$ 1,529.98	$ 1,835.98
Knowledge mgmt	$ 266.08	$ 306.00	$ 367.20
Appraisals	$ 26.61	$ 30.60	$ 36.72
Title/escrow	$ 26.61	$ 30.60	$ 36.72
Termite inspection	$ 26.61	$ 30.60	$ 36.72
Home inspections	$ 26.61	$ 30.60	$ 36.72
Real estate agents	$ 26.61	$ 30.60	$ 36.72
Home warranty	$ 26.61	$ 30.60	$ 36.72
Insurance	$ 266.08	$ 306.00	$ 367.20
Training	$ 159.65	$ 183.60	$ 220.32
Licensing fees	$ 212.87	$ 244.80	$ 293.76
ISP partnerships	$ 239.48	$ 275.40	$ 330.48
Accessory sales	$ 266.08	$ 306.00	$ 367.20
Ecommerce sales	$ 532.17	$ 611.99	$ 734.39
Click throughs	$ 425.73	$ 489.59	$ 587.51
Sponsorships	$ 159.65	$ 183.60	$ 220.32
Awards program	$ 53.22	$ 61.20	$ 73.44
Total revenue	**$ 17,756.00**	**$20,419.00**	**$ 24,503.00**
Cost and expenses			
Application & portal development	$ 2,400	$ 1,000	$ 1,500
Materials	$ 12	$ 14	$ 16
Cellular phones/beepers	$ 12	$ 14	$ 16
Internal salaries	$ 2,080	$ 2,392	$ 2,751
Rent	$ 24	$ 28	$ 32
Delivery/messenger	$ 10	$ 12	$ 13
Insurance	$ 20	$ 23	$ 26
Telephone & utilities	$ 30	$ 35	$ 40
Equipment leases	$ 25	$ 29	$ 33
Hardware/software purchases	$ 25	$ 29	$ 33
Payroll taxes & benefits	$ 832	$ 957	$ 1,100
Hosting fees	$ 25	$ 29	$ 33
Telecommunications fees	$ 75	$ 86	$ 99
Advertising	$ 750	$ 500	$ 500
Entertainment	$ 20	$ 23	$ 26
Sales materials	$ 35	$ 40	$ 46
Travel	$ 50	$ 58	$ 66
Professional fees	$ 75	$ 86	$ 99
Misc. expenses	$ 250	$ 288	$ 331
Total costs and expenses	**$ 6,750**	**$ 5,640**	**$ 6,761**
Income before taxes	$ 11,006	$ 14,779	$ 17,742
Income taxes	$ (4,182)	$ (5,616)	$ (6,742)
Net income	**$ 6,824**	**$ 9,163**	**$ 11,000**
Percentage of sales	**38%**	**45%**	**45%**

Pizzeria

Coastal Pizza

41558 Brown Ave.
Corpus Christi, TX 78412

Tony Tecce

This plan raised $30,000 for the prospective owner of a coastal Texas pizza operation aiming to capitalize on both resident and tourist appetites for tasty, East Coast–style pizza.

EXECUTIVE SUMMARY

Corpus Christi, Texas, is a typical coastal Texas small town. There are a large number of second homes and the economy is tourist based. Corpus Christi has all of the amenities of any destination town, as well as the thrill of 24–hour gambling. What Corpus Christi lacks is a true pizza delivery business. We, the partners of Coastal Pizza, believe that now is the time to give Corpus Christi what it wants.

In short, Coastal Pizza is aiming to become Corpus Christi's first chain of delivery–only, pizza restaurants covering the Corpus Christi area. Costal Pizza wishes to raise $40,000 from a private investor(s) to take advantage of the opportunity explained in the plan.

Coastal Pizza will become Corpus Christi's first, fast and free delivered pizza. For quite a while, Corpus Christi has had only one pizza deliverer who charges for a delivery which takes an average of one hour. It is time the residents and visitors of Corpus Christi have access to a pizza that is made fresh, hot and delivered free.

This is not a new concept. Every town in the country has some form of "Domino's". They all earn large profits; the reason being the lack of necessary space and overhead required to operate a delivery–only business.

Corpus Christi is not only ready for a true pizza delivery operation—Corpus Christi *needs* one, especially an operation that will focus on quality, price and convenience.

We seek $40,000 to properly ensure a successful enterprise. How the money will be used is covered in detail in the balance of this business plan.

OBJECTIVES

We, the three partners of Coastal Pizza, plan on being open by December 15, 1995. A location will be agreed upon by the end of October 1995. For the first two years of operation, we will be working managers drawing small salaries. This will enable the profits to be used for future expansion. By 1998, new locations will be investigated and will require our total attention.

By 2000 we intend to have a four–location pizza delivery chain throughout the Corpus Christi area. We are confident we can do so because:

1. Pizza delivery is the Number One growth business in the United States,

2. The Corpus Christi area is rapidly growing,

3. Competition is virtually non–existent.

In summary, the primary Coastal Pizza objectives are as follows:

1. Achieve over $360,000 in gross sales by end of first year of operation.

2. Begin work on a second location in the early part of 1998.

3. By 2000 we intend to have a fourth location underway.

4. Be the number one growth business in the Corpus Christi area.

MARKET ANALYSIS

Corpus Christi, like every town in the metropolitan area, has a tourist–based economy. The key to a successful business in this area is the ability to capture a healthy local clientele.

Target market

The most recent demographic study of Corpus Christi shows a permanent population of 9,193 growing at a rate of 6% annually. During peak winter and summer months, the population more than doubles. Here lies the bonus of a pizza delivery business: Everyone of all ages loves <u>pizza</u>! Our target market is not a segment of the whole, but indeed the whole. Every single person *in* the Corpus Christi area is a potential customer and a target of our marketing campaign.

We conducted a market survey of some of the Corpus Christi residents. The results were not so surprising.

*   76% purchase take–out food

*   90% eat pizza

*   38% would have pizza delivered 4 times per month (theoretically, 14,000 pizzas per month)

*   31% would have pizza delivered twice per month (theoretically, 6,000 pizzas per month)

Of course, the theoretical numbers are excessive but good signs nonetheless.

Intermediate Influences

The influences on the local market will differ somewhat from those on the tourist end. Our local market wants quality pizza at a franchise price and free, prompt delivery. The tourist market wants convenience above all else. We can satisfy all of the above needs which is explained in detail later in the business plan.

Competition

Present direct competition is Pepperoni's Pizza, primarily an eat–in pizza restaurant that also delivers. At present they are the only deliverers of pizza in the Corpus Christi area. Their hours of delivery are from 5 to 8 p.m. Delivery time averages one hour and at a $2 surcharge. Your average three–item pizza, delivered, costs over $17 from Pepperoni's.

The indirect competition includes Frank's Diner and Wok Buffet Bar. Frank's sells pizza at a very reasonable price, but they do not deliver and you bake it yourself. Their dough is pre–made and not hand tossed. The Chinese place delivers. Again, they charge for delivery ($4), and only deliver until 10 p.m. nightly.

Any anticipated future competition would be in the form of our present competition playing catch–up. We figure that free delivery will be the first move by the others. Then, possibly a price war with Frank's. Our advantages being lower fixed expenses, a superior ad campaign, a better pizza and the best service. As far as pricing, overall, our prices will be comparative to the franchise delivery outfits that operate in larger areas. Along with low prices, free toppings and free soda are effective sales boosters.

The break even analysis works out to 874 pizzas per month or $10,925 in sales.

OPERATIONS

Location

There are two ways to go: Either find a great location and build the kitchen from scratch, or find an existing kitchen to lease. Although building a kitchen would allow for a layout designed to our specifications, this option is cost prohibitive. Construction/renovation costs would exceed $45,000. So, an existing kitchen is the answer and we have found one. This kitchen is currently in limited use and is located in one of Corpus Christi's drinking establishments. The owner has agreed to $1.80 per square foot in rent ($900/mo.) and will include garbage pickup and water. Utilities will be based on use.

This location is on Hwy 48, the main road through town, allowing for excellent exposure. Specific terms of the lease have yet to be discussed.

Equipment

The kitchen is fully equipped but lacks a pizza oven, large mixer, and a few miscellaneous items. Also, we will need to purchase a computer. The total equipment costs will be $9,800, which includes maintenance expenses.

Variable Items

The variable costs involved are for the flour, cheese, vegetables, etc. including the carry–out box; each pizza will cost us an average of $2.85. Quality control is important, so each topping will be weighed to specified amounts. This will also help in cost control.

MARKETING AND SALES

In the pizza delivery business, aggressive marketing is the key. For the most part, having a pizza delivered to your home is an impulse purchase. So, a lot of reminders are needed to trigger the need for a hot pizza delivered whenever desired.

We will have a complete marketing package which will include extensive advertising, strong resort/ condo relations, computerized sales and sponsorship of local sports teams and events.

Advertising

The advertising campaign will consist of a mass–mailing program and print ads.

The mass mailing will cover every box holder in Corpus Christi. There will be a flyer style menu with a circular, fridge magnet affixed to the bottom portion. The magnet will look like a pizza and will have our name and phone number printed on it. This will be the perfect constant reminder. The bottom half–inch of the flyer will always be blank. This will enable us to stamp a coupon with one of four different rubber stamps. Each stamp will have a special deal or price break written on it, saving on added printing expenses. There will be four mailings in the first year of operation: The first, in December, will announce our grand opening and the others will occur in January, July and August.

Corresponding with the mass–mailing dates, we will have an insert in the Corpus Christi Press, a local bi–weekly newspaper with a distribution of 13,000. The insert will be similar to that of the mailing but larger and without magnet. Also, on a weekly basis there will be three 3–inch print ads in the Corpus Christi Press and the Metro Texan, a free magazine dealing with local events and news. The Metro Texan is popular both with locals and tourists, and has a distribution from 18,000 to 30,000 (depending on the season).

Television ads have been considered but have yet to be proven effective in the area due to limited cable subscribers.

Resort relations

Our collective background in the resort arena is going to be a big plus with Corpus Christi's large number of condo vacation rentals. Of course the competition puts out menus at the few well known, hotel–type establishments, but untapped are management companies and Realtors who deal in short term rentals. These people cater to a large chunk of the tourist trade of Corpus Christi. Our strategy is to develop a relationship with these businesses by offering an incentive program of free pizza and special, preferred rates. If we treat them right they will be more than happy to supply their clients with our menus and a positive recommendation. This will be an ongoing relationship that will not only increase tourism sales but boost our image within the community.

Local relations

This brings us to the sponsorship of local teams and events. Of course, the free publicity and local recognition factor goes without mentioning, but another benefit is a positive image within the community. If they know you . . . like you . . . they will buy from you. This is true for any small community and we plan to take full advantage.

Computerized sales

The computer is going to be one of our great marketing tools. To capture the office lunch crowd, we will take orders by fax. Also, we will advertise with the fax by hooking up a modem to the computer. Everyday at 11 a.m. the computer will fax the day's specials with an order form to be faxed back to us. We will also have a complete database of our customers. So complete, it will aid in creating charge accounts for local businesses and personalize our relations with our customers. When someone calls to order a pizza, and he has been a customer before, we will have all his information logged by his phone number. The customer's name, address, ordering history, preferred method of payment, etc. will instantly appear on the computer screen. Here is an example of how a typical order would be taken:

Us: Thanks for calling Coastal Pizza, may I have your phone number please?

Customer: 831–1234

Us: Thank you. (The number is entered and the customer's file appears.) Is this Mr. Smith?

Customer: Why yes.

Us: Would you like to order your usual large pepperoni & olive pizza and charge it to your Visa card?

Customer: Sure, why not.

Us: Thanks for your order Mr. Smith, we'll see you in a little while.

Also, the database will aid in forecasting, accounting and inventory.

Product features

Of the great selling points our product will have, hand–tossed dough and the secret sauce are going to be the biggest. The other top–selling points are the price, free delivery, available wheat dough and flavored crust.

Everyone agrees that the best pizza comes from out East: New York, Chicago, Boston. As of yet, there are not many great pizzas made in this area. Along with our desire to succeed, we are bringing tried–and–true recipes into this business—recipes that have launched some of the biggest pizzerias on the East Coast.

Price is going to surprise many. Our average large pizza will be priced between $13 and $14, delivered. The competition can not deliver a large pizza for less than $17. Along with the great prices, there is the free delivery. Until every other deliverer follows suit, this will be a large selling point.

More and more, people today want to eat healthier. So, as an option, we will offer wheat dough at no additional charge. Along those same lines, there will be an added choice of five crust flavors. They will be called "crust toppings": garlic, butter, cheese, poppy and sesame seed. This will be a unique feature to Coastal Pizza, and again, offered at no extra charge.

As well as delivery, we will provide slices on premise in conjunction with bar sales. Our hours of operation will be between 11am until midnight (2am on weekends).

Sales results. Earlier in the plan, we mentioned the results of our market survey which were quite impressive. Although those numbers would be more than welcome, we do not foresee selling 4,000 pizzas in a month during our first year. To achieve a more realistic picture of sales, we based our numbers on the 2,963 permanent residential households in Corpus Christi. The following is a projection of pizza sales per household.

- 5 percent will order one pizza per week for a total of 7,704 pizzas per year

- 8 percent will order two pizzas per month for a total of 5,689 pizzas per year

- 15 percent will order one pizza per month for a total of 5,333 pizzas per year

- 9 percent will order six pizzas per year for a total of 1,600 pizzas per year

- 63 percent will order no pizzas

That comes out to 20,326 pizzas per year or 56 pizzas a day. The above numbers show that 56 pizzas sold per day will yield $254,000 in gross sales. When weekends and tourism are added into the picture, these numbers will increase. For example, 56 pizzas a day equates to roughly five per hour of operation. Non–holiday weekends, between 7pm and 1am, we figure on 10 pizzas per hour. During the peak months, (January, February, July, and August) 100 pizzas per day will be a minimum. Then there are the "in–between" months (second half December, first half September and March) where tourism is either picking up or starting to slow down—90 pizzas per day should be the norm. These added pizza sales (8,760 pizzas) total $109,000. Therefore, along with the previous sales estimate, we will have $363,575 in gross sales. This is a moderate projection; those numbers could easily be doubled.

ORGANIZATION

The management will consist of three people:

Jon Anthony is currently the Resident Manager at Timberwoods Resort. He has extensive experience in computers such as creating database and reservation programs for resorts plus spreadsheets to track marketing and sales. He has a strong sales background which includes two years of door–to–door sales and three years as a life insurance representative, servicing 300 clients in Southwestern Texas. His marketing experience consists of budgeting, design and execution of numerous advertising campaigns for two resorts in the Jubilee area, as well as handling public relations and special events. He has participated fully in the preparation of this plan. Jon Anthony is 38 years old, has a degree in business and minored in computers at Texas A&M University.

Adam Smith is currently the front desk manager of Waterways Resort. His experience includes starting, from the ground up, an upscale deli at the Hilton in Corpus Christi. He supervised all aspects of floor design, purchasing, menu pricing, forecasting, hiring and scheduling of employees. He has a broad based management background that includes very large, four–star resorts to a smaller, hands–on resort. Adam is 32 and has a degree in business with emphasis in resort management from Ohio State University.

Brody Pierce is the assistant front desk manager at the Waterways Resort. He has worked with Adam for the last three years, beginning with the deli project at the Hilton in Corpus Christi. From the East Coast, he has experience in the pizza business which consisted of back–line operations such as dough and sauce prep, consistency control, and recipe creation. He has experience as revenue auditor for restaurant, casino and hotel operations. Brody is 29 and has a degree in business administration from Penn State University.

FINANCIALS

Breakeven analysis

Breakeven units (X)
  Fixed costs (FC) = $101,228.00
  Variable costs (VC) = $2.85 X
Breakeven sales (BES) = $12.50 X

BES = FC + VC

$12.50 X = $101,228.00 + $2.85 X
$12.50 X − $2.85 X = $101,228.00
$9.65 X = $101,228.00

X = 10,490 units per year, or 874 units per month, or 29 units per day ($362.50 per day).

BUSINESS PLANS HANDBOOK, *Volume 11*

Fixed costs

Printing:
- Menus
  - 10,000 @ $200.00 $ 2,000.00
  - Typesetting   40.00
- Circular fridge magnets
  - 10,000 @ $1,500.00   1,500.00
- Business cards
  - 1,000 @ $35.00   105.00
- Rubber stamps
  - $14.00 each   56.00
- Letterhead & misc.   499.00

    $ 4,200.00

Advertising:
- Mass mailing
  - Bulk rate per year   75.00
  - Bulk rate one time fee   75.00
  - $550.00 per mailing   2,200.00
- Bonanza Newspaper
  - Preprinted inserts @ $206.40   413.00
  - 3" weekly ads @ $31.38   1,508.00
- North Tahoe Weekly
  - 3" weekly ads @ $31.38   1,508.00
- Tahoe Yellow Pages
  - $200.00 per month   2,400.00

    $ 7,179.00

Rent and utilities:
- Rent
  - $900.00 per month $10,800.00
  - (water and garbage included)
- Electric
  - $200.00 per month   2,400.00
- Gas
  - $300.00 per month   3,600.00
- Telephone
  - Install @ $82.00/line   246.00
  - $54.00 per month   648.00

    $17,694.00

Insurance and licenses:
- Fire & liability
  - $200.00/mo. for 1st 10 months $ 2,000.00
- Licenses & fees
  - Health permit   175.00
  - Misc. fees   200.00

    $ 2,375.00

Equipment:
- Mixer $ 3,500.00
- Oven   2,500.00
- Computer   1,500.00
- Equipment maintenance   670.00
- Hood/exhaust maintenance   330.00
- Food storage box   204.00
- Dough scrapper   38.40
- Bun pan rack   165.85
- Pizza keeper (3)   85.95
- Pizza knife (3)   107.10
- Pizza peel (3)   33.54
- Apron (24)   78.66
- Grease proof mat (5)   459.00
- Storage rack (2)   107.50

    $ 9,780.00

Labor:
- Salaries for partners
  - $20,000 per year $60,000.00

Total projected fixed costs for first year: $101,228.000

Variable costs

Produce and meats:

— Bell peppers	$ .90/lb
— Tomatoes	.80/lb
— Onions	.50/lb
— Garlic	3.20/lb
— Mushrooms	1.40/lb
— Olives	2.00/lb
— Anchovies	2.85/tin
— Jalapenos	1.47/lb
— Pinapple	2.39/can
— White flour	11.00/50lb bag
— Wheat flour	12.88/50lb bag
— Cheese	1.15/lb
— Pepperoni	3.18/lb
— Canadian bacon	3.36/lb
— Hamburger	1.39/lb
— Sausage	1.59/lb
— Salami	3.18/lb

Delivery containers

— Pizza boxes	
12" @ $0.28 per box	$28.00/case
14" @ $0.37 per box	$37.25/case
16" @ $0.38 per box	$37.65/case

Average cost per pizza:

— Dough	$ 0.20
— Sauce	.50
— Toppings	.80
— Cheese	1.00
— Delivery box	.35
	$ 2.85 per pizza

Projected income statement

Revenue

Food sales		$ 363,575

Operating expenses

Labor	$ 60,000	
Rent	10,800	
Utilities	6,894	
Insurance	2,000	
Printing	4,200	
Advertising	7,179	
Lics & fees	375	
Equipment	9,780	
Direct materials	82,895	
Total operating expenses		184,123
Income before taxes		$ 179,452

Cash flow projection 1994–1997

	December	January	February	March	April	May
Beginning cash balance	$ 40,000	$ 25,298	$ 53,536	$ 75,569	$ 89,852	$ 97,095
Cash receipts:						
Cash sales for the month	7,875	37,500	37,500	30,000	21,000	18,000
Cummulative sales	$ 7,875	$ 45,375	$ 82,875	$ 112,875	$ 133,875	$ 151,875
Cash disbursments:						
Accounts payable	2,000	1,769	8,550	8,550	$ 6,840	$ 4,788
Rent	900	900	900	900	900	900
Utilities	746	554	554	554	554	554
Insurance	200	200	200	200	200	200
Printing	3,200	0	0	0	0	0
Advertising	1,376	813	263	263	263	263
Lics & fees	375	0	0	0	0	0
Equipment	8,780	0	0	0	0	0
Maintenance	0	0	0	250	0	0
Salaries	5,000	5,000	5,000	5,000	5,000	5,000
Total disbursed	$ 22,577	$ 9,263	$ 15,467	$ 15,717	$ 13,757	$ 11,705
Cash +/− from operations	($ 14,702)	$ 28,238	$ 22,033	$ 14,283	$ 7,243	$ 6,295
Balance carried over	**$ 25,298**	**$ 53,536**	**$ 75,569**	**$ 89,852**	**$ 97,095**	**$ 103,390**

[continued]

Cash flow projection 1994–1997 [CONTINUED]

	June	July	August	September	October	November
Beginning cash balance	$ 103,390	$ 124,789	$ 147,127	$ 168,610	$ 186,893	$ 190,481
Cash receipts:						
Cash sales for the month	33,750	37,500	37,500	33,750	18,000	18,000
Cummulative sales	$ 185,625	$ 223,125	$ 260,625	$ 294,375	$ 312,375	$ 330,375
Cash disbursments:						
Accounts payable	4,104	7,695	8,550	8,550	7,695	4,104
Rent	900	900	900	900	900	900
Utilities	554	554	554	554	554	554
Insurance	200	200	200	0	0	0
Printing	1,000	0	0	0	0	0
Advertising	263	813	813	263	263	263
Lics & fees	0	0	0	0	0	0
Equipment	0	0	0	0	0	0
Maintenance	330	0	0	200	0	0
Salaries	5,000	5,000	5,000	5,000	5,000	5,000
Total disbursed	$ 12,351	$ 15,162	$ 16,017	$ 15,467	$ 14,412	$ 10,821
Cash +/− from operations	$ 21,399	$ 22,338	$ 21,483	$ 18,283	$ 3,588	$ 7,179
Balance carried over	**$ 124,789**	**$ 147,127**	**$ 168,610**	**$ 186,893**	**$ 190,481**	**$ 197,660**

[continued]

Cash flow projection 1994–1997 [CONTINUED]

	December	1995	1996	1997
Beginning cash balance	$ 197,660	$ 219,619	$ 460,040	$ 871,040
Cash receipts:				
Cash sales for the month	33,200	N/A	N/A	N/A
Cummulative sales	$ 363,575	$ 436,290	$ 800,000	$ 1,300,000
Cash disbursments:				
Accounts payable	4,104	99,474	182,400	296,400
Rent	900	10,800	21,600	32,400
Utilities	554	8,094	16,000	24,000
Insurance	200	2,000	4,000	6,000
Printing	0	4,000	8,000	12,000
Advertising	263	8,000	16,000	24,000
Lics & fees	0	500	1,000	2,000
Equipment	0	2,000	18,000	20,000
Maintenance	220	1,000	2,000	3,000
Salaries	5,000	60,000	120,000	180,000
Total disbursed	$ 11,241	$ 195,868	$ 389,000	$ 599,800
Cash +/− from operations	$ 21,959	$ 240,422	$ 411,000	$ 700,200
Balance carried over	**$ 219,619**	**$ 460,040**	**$ 871,040**	**$1,571,240**

Private Investigator

F B E y e s

210 Huntington St.
Bangor, ME 04401

Gerald Rekve

This business plan details the goals and objectives for an independent Private Investigator (PI) firm founded by three former police officers.

EXECUTIVE SUMMARY

FBEyes was founded in 2005, by three former police officers. They're friends of the same police force for over 30 years.

In this time the three had gone different paths in the Bangor Police force. James Walsh had spent the majority of his career in the fraud section. Colin Day had spent the majority of his time in the narcotics division. Finally Greg Baker had focused his entire career on the administration and management of the police force. While all three partners of the newly formed FBEyes firm had spent their careers in separate divisions of this large police force, they all had one thing in common. They enjoyed the investigation part of their job and had taken all the required steps to educate themselves on all aspects of their respective job functions. These skills had not only made them leaders in their divisions, it also gave them a great amount of access to other police forces in other cities.

All three had decided to take early retirement in order for them to launch their own Private investigation firm. While there was a substantial amount of competition from the long established firms, all three based their decision on solid market statistics that supported the decision to open their own PI firm.

Over a period of twelve months prior to their official retirement, all three members spent their free time gathering and working on the business plan. The also hired a management consulting firm to work with them to build the business plan and look for outside opinions on the business sector.

While most PI firms were a one or two person operation, which focused on the basics of the industry like surveillance and searching for people etc, FBEyes decided that this was a good area, however wanted to add all their backgrounds and training to the business. Therefore throughout the formulation of the business plan and model these specialized skills were added to the firm's services it would offer to the market.

PRODUCTS & SERVCES

Based on the market, as well the background and training of the three partners within FBEyes, the products and services offered have been determined as follows:

1. Background checks for employers

2. Fraud Investigations for companies when a company reports suspected fraud from an employee. This can also be hired by local police forces, where subjective investigation is required.

3. Competition search for when a company thinks their copyright or products are being copied or sold.

4. Standard surveillance of husbands or wives' promiscuity. This area has a lot of competition; however the partners felt that with their training, they would attract higher paying clients allowing for more of an executive type of client base. Not to mention this area has the highest percentage of income for most PI Companies and cannot be overlooked.

5. Bounty hunting. This area is another strong point for the PI Firm, with the training as well as work experience, the partners felt they know where to look and the skills required to gain the trust of police forces and clients. The skills of the PI Firm would result in quick capture of runners and turn into fast cash flow for the PI Firm. This area would be sub contracted to other officers who still work in the police force, however want to earn money from this part time job. The present laws in the region allow for police officers to work in similar jobs as long as no information is used from police databases and or files.

6. Missing persons. This area, while small, still has a lot of potential. With the majority of MPs actually investigated by police forces, due to the large work load of local police forces, most MPs do not get the proper investigations, unless they are deemed to be of a criminal nature. The base fee for this service is high, however part of the reason for this, we will offer this service free to specific cases, like children or lower income cases. Each case will be reviewed on an individual basis.

7. Stolen Property. This most likely going to be one of our smaller areas of business services. However due to the large amount of unreported stolen property that takes place each year in the region, we feel with the training and backgrounds that we have in this area we could offer a service and make money at the same time. A large percentage of stolen property is taken by the same criminals or rings. Due to large insurance costs, most businesses don't report items stolen, simply because of the cost of increase in insurance is increased and these costs in most cases over the long run for items less that $5,000 in value aren't worth reporting to the police force.

COMPETITION

In the present market we have the following competitors:

1. Glassman Investigators—they have been in business for 20 years; they only provide services to the surveillance and missing persons sectors. They are a ten–employee firm that has built a solid foundation in the market. They tend not to target the corporate arena, just the private person market.

2. Hayes Investigations Inc.—this is a large firm that offers services to all the same areas we will be offering. They have been in business for 25 years and a strong affiliation with a national Private Investor chain. They tend to charge the highest of fees and don't seem to have any difficulty getting enough clients to pay these fees. Hayes employs 20 full time investigators and 10 part time. Actually two of the founders of FBEyes had actually worked for Hayes for 5 years on a part time basis.

3. Spyware Investigations. This two–person firm that only specializes in surveillance area, mostly in marriage, divorce sort of situations. Most of their leads and clients come from lawyers wanting to better their clients' cases with video tape or pictures.

4. There are about four more firms that are run by a single–person–owner–manager type of situation. These firms tend to only get enough revenue to meet the costs of the firm and that is it. There is no growth in this area.

5. The area, where we will most likely see the biggest compitition will be from the outside national chain investigator firms. These firms are hired and basically flown into our market to do their work. Because most of the skills and needs of the clients are such that the company doing the hiring feel it is required that they hire these firms. With our market research, we have determined that the hiring companies would rather hire a local firm to do the work simply because they feel we would have a better understanding of the market, therefore be able to provide quicker and more cost effective services.

As mentioned in the above competitor breakdown, we have indicated the areas where each competitor focuses all their attention. This in–depth understanding of each competitor's area of expertise will allow us to get a much faster footprint in the market, at a quicker rate.

During the twelve months preceding the launch of our firm, all three partners spent time preparing the company. While each partner when they retire will only be in the age group of 50–54, none of them will require taking a salary from the firm. With their early retirement package they all received a bonus payout of $300,000–$400,000. This combined with the fact that all partners where wise investors and are debt free.

While most start–up companies tend to start with a lot of debt in the first few years, FBEyes will not be in this position. All the required software, training etc has already been paid for. The only startup expenses are that of advertising and office set–up, etc. It was felt by all partners that an office should be established; while most in this sector tend to be home based, the clients we were going after, i.e. corporate etc., would like to have a place they could go to meet, allowing the client to meet in a more confidential manner with our firm. This was really important in cases of fraud etc.

With the start–up it was decided that each partner would focus on their area of expertise and as required would hire contract staff to fill in where they could not.

The key to our strategy will be to make slow inroads into the established markets. This would allow us to grow at our own pace and keep our competitors in the market from noticing our presence. We will take the approach of the turtle in the race, not that of the rabbit.

While we will be bringing specialized skills to the market, we feel there will be times where we will collaborate with other firms, offer advice and or our services. Over time we feel this will be a key to building strong relationships with our key clients and partners.

MARKETING & SALES

The forms of marketing we will use to market our PI Firm:

1. Word of mouth; clients telling other clients about our service

2. Former working relationships we had in the police force, with people

3. Yellow Pages advertising; this will be a small portion of our client acquisitions, yet a required expense

4. Law Firms; we will actively target these firms for business and referrals

5. Charity work in the community; while this may not seem like a place to find clients, it in our opinion is key to our success. There is a lot of solid relationships made while donating your time

6. Other police forces around the country, where we will offer specialized forms of services to this sector. Due the nature of this business we cannot elaborate

7. We will also offer local newspapers and or magazines a weekly or monthly editorial column. This will allow us to be known for our services, while getting exposure to our market for free. Nobody in our market does this presently and we have inquired with local newspapers and magazines. Both provided support and said would even pay us for the editorial

8. We will post a website that offers free advice to anyone wanting information. Due to legal limitations we cannot go into details in this section, we will however post a good general information about areas of interest to our readers

Market Analysis

The city of Bangor has close to 1 million people living in the city, with another 300,000 living in a 20–mile radius. This is a new city in the sense of cities. Up to 1950 the population Bangor was around 250,000. When oil reserves were discovered the city grew at extraordinary pace. This pace of growth has allowed the city to spend billions on infrastructure. While the positives of this growth are evident, the not so glamorous area of crime and criminal activates has also flourished.

Based on our Market Analysis we have determined that there is $40,000,000 spent in our sector each year. Our goal is to attain at least 5% of this market in the first two years.

The types of clients and the average per–use charges

1. Typical Surveillance—$700 per day

2. Fraud Investigations—$1500 per day

3. Bounty Hunter—35% of fee paid to courts for bail jumping

4. Background Checks—start at $500 and can go as high as $10,000 based on amount of detail required and position in company of person being hired.

Note: all the above fees are expense–extra–based.

We have already talked with a few clients and they have signed formal agreements, that when we open, we will be contracted to do work for them. Based on previous three–year average of expenditures we have determined that this will amount to approximately $ 300,000 per year in revenue to our firm. Other clients have indicated that while they could not make a commitment at the time, would ask us for a quote when they tender certain jobs.

As noted here, all of our revenue contracts we have in place are from companies. Once we advertise that we are in business, we are confident that we will gain a market share of the independent market, and based on the services we will offer, this will come from areas of service we offer that is required in our market, but not yet offered by local firms.

At the present rate of growth, we are very confident that the opening of our firm will position us in the next three years to have hired at least 20 contract investigators.

Over the career of all the partners, they were able to build very strong relationships with other employees in the police force. These relationships allowed the management of the firm to cultivate the ability to add contract staff needed over time. The vast amount of qualified contract staff available to sub–contract for us, will allow us to grow our business at a faster rate of growth than would be normally expected.

Most sub–contractors just want to make a little additional income on a part–time basis. On average these contractors can make $10,000–$20,000 per year from us.

FINANCIAL ANALYSIS

With the start up of FBEyes, each partner invested $10,000 for a total of $30,000; this was to cover the following:

1. Office Rental—$800.00 per month
2. Telephone Equipment—$1500
3. Incorporation Cost—$700
4. Business License—$220
5. Office Equipment—$2200
6. Computers—$5700
7. Furniture—$2500
8. Supplies—$700
9. Yellow Page Ad (Prepay)—$1600
10. Specialized Equipment—$5600 (Paid Already)
11. Specialized Software—$8900 (Paid Already)
12. Lease Company vehicles—$1200 monthly
13. Legal Costs—$2000

Some or most of these expenses were paid for by the partners prior to the opening of FBEyes. That being said, the strength of the company is in great start–up shape. No debt and no cash flow pressures on the partners personally or for the company, will allow the partners to grow the company in a stress free situation.

Business Plan Template

USING THIS TEMPLATE

A business plan carefully spells out a company's projected course of action over a period of time, usually the first two to three years after the start-up. In addition, banks, lenders, and other investors examine the information and financial documentation before deciding whether or not to finance a new business venture. Therefore, a business plan is an essential tool in obtaining financing and should describe the business itself in detail as well as all important factors influencing the company, including the market, industry, competition, operations and management policies, problem solving strategies, financial resources and needs, and other vital information. The plan enables the business owner to anticipate costs, plan for difficulties, and take advantage of opportunities, as well as design and implement strategies that keep the company running as smoothly as possible.

This template has been provided as a model to help you construct your own business plan. Please keep in mind that there is no single acceptable format for a business plan, and that this template is in no way comprehensive, but serves as an example.

The business plans provided in this section are fictional and have been used by small business agencies as models for clients to use in compiling their own business plans.

GENERIC BUSINESS PLAN

Main headings included below are topics that should be covered in a comprehensive business plan. They include:

Business Summary

Purpose

Provides a brief overview of your business, succinctly highlighting the main ideas of your plan.

Includes

- Name and Type of Business
- Description of Product/Service
- Business History and Development
- Location
- Market
- Competition
- Management
- Financial Information
- Business Strengths and Weaknesses
- Business Growth

Table of Contents

Purpose

Organized in an Outline Format, the Table of Contents illustrates the selection and arrangement of information contained in your plan.

Includes
- Topic Headings and Subheadings
- Page Number References

Business History and Industry Outlook

Purpose

Examines the conception and subsequent development of your business within an industry specific context.

Includes
- Start-up Information
- Owner/Key Personnel Experience
- Location
- Development Problems and Solutions
- Investment/Funding Information
- Future Plans and Goals
- Market Trends and Statistics
- Major Competitors
- Product/Service Advantages
- National, Regional, and Local Economic Impact

Product/Service

Purpose

Introduces, defines, and details the product and/or service that inspired the information of your business.

Includes
- Unique Features
- Niche Served
- Market Comparison
- Stage of Product/Service Development
- Production
- Facilities, Equipment, and Labor
- Financial Requirements
- Product/Service Life Cycle
- Future Growth

Market Examination

Purpose

Assessment of product/service applications in relation to consumer buying cycles.

Includes
- Target Market
- Consumer Buying Habits
- Product/Service Applications
- Consumer Reactions
- Market Factors and Trends
- Penetration of the Market
- Market Share
- Research and Studies
- Cost
- Sales Volume and Goals

Competition

Purpose

Analysis of Competitors in the Marketplace.

Includes
- Competitor Information
- Product/Service Comparison
- Market Niche
- Product/Service Strengths and Weaknesses
- Future Product/Service Development

Marketing

Purpose

Identifies promotion and sales strategies for your product/service.

Includes

- Product/Service Sales Appeal
- Special and Unique Features
- Identification of Customers
- Sales and Marketing Staff
- Sales Cycles

- Type of Advertising/Promotion
- Pricing
- Competition
- Customer Services

Operations

Purpose

Traces product/service development from production/inception to the market environment.

Includes

- Cost Effective Production Methods
- Facility
- Location

- Equipment
- Labor
- Future Expansion

Administration and Management

Purpose

Offers a statement of your management philosophy with an in-depth focus on processes and procedures.

Includes

- Management Philosophy
- Structure of Organization
- Reporting System
- Methods of Communication
- Employee Skills and Training

- Employee Needs and Compensation
- Work Environment
- Management Policies and Procedures
- Roles and Responsibilities

Key Personnel

Purpose

Describes the unique backgrounds of principle employees involved in business.

Includes

- Owner(s)/Employee Education and Experience
- Positions and Roles

- Benefits and Salary
- Duties and Responsibilities
- Objectives and Goals

Potential Problems and Solutions

Purpose

Discussion of problem solving strategies that change issues into opportunities.

Includes

- Risks
- Litigation
- Future Competition

- Economic Impact
- Problem Solving Skills

Financial Information

Purpose

Secures needed funding and assistance through worksheets and projections detailing financial plans, methods of repayment, and future growth opportunities.

Includes

- Financial Statements
- Bank Loans
- Methods of Repayment
- Tax Returns
- Start-up Costs
- Projected Income (3 years)
- Projected Cash Flow (3 years)
- Projected Balance Statements (3 years)

Appendices

Purpose

Supporting documents used to enhance your business proposal.

Includes

- Photographs of product, equipment, facilities, etc.
- Copyright/Trademark Documents
- Legal Agreements
- Marketing Materials
- Research and or Studies
- Operation Schedules
- Organizational Charts
- Job Descriptions
- Resumes
- Additional Financial Documentation

Fictional Food Distributor

Commercial Foods, Inc.

3003 Avondale Ave.
Knoxville, TN 37920

This plan demonstrates how a partnership can have a positive impact on a new business. It demonstrates how two individuals can carve a niche in the specialty foods market by offering gourmet foods to upscale restaurants and fine hotels. This plan is fictional and has not been used to gain funding from a bank or other lending institution.

STATEMENT OF PURPOSE

Commercial Foods, Inc. seeks a loan of $75,000 to establish a new business. This sum, together with $5,000 equity investment by the principals, will be used as follows:

- Merchandise inventory $25,000
- Office fixture/equipment $12,000
- Warehouse equipment $14,000
- One delivery truck $10,000
- Working capital $39,000
- Total $100,000

DESCRIPTION OF THE BUSINESS

Commercial Foods, Inc. will be a distributor of specialty food service products to hotels and upscale restaurants in the geographical area of a 50 mile radius of Knoxville. Richard Roberts will direct the sales effort and John Williams will manage the warehouse operation and the office. One delivery truck will be used initially with a second truck added in the third year. We expect to begin operation of the business within 30 days after securing the requested financing.

MANAGEMENT

A. Richard Roberts is a native of Memphis, Tennessee. He is a graduate of Memphis State University with a Bachelor's degree from the School of Business. After graduation, he worked for a major manufacturer of specialty food service products as a detail sales person for five years, and, for the past three years, he has served as a product sales manager for this firm.

B. John Williams is a native of Nashville, Tennessee. He holds a B.S. Degree in Food Technology from the University of Tennessee. His career includes five years as a product development chemist in gourmet food products and five years as operations manager for a food service distributor.

269

Both men are healthy and energetic. Their backgrounds complement each other, which will ensure the success of Commercial Foods, Inc. They will set policies together and personnel decisions will be made jointly. Initial salaries for the owners will be $1,000 per month for the first few years. The spouses of both principals are successful in the business world and earn enough to support the families.

They have engaged the services of Foster Jones, CPA, and William Hale, Attorney, to assist them in an advisory capacity.

PERSONNEL

The firm will employ one delivery truck driver at a wage of $8.00 per hour. One office worker will be employed at $7.50 per hour. One part-time employee will be used in the office at $5.00 per hour. The driver will load and unload his own trucks. Mr. Williams will assist in the warehouse operation as needed to assist one stock person at $7.00 per hour. An additional delivery truck and driver will be added the third year.

LOCATION

The firm will lease a 20,000 square foot building at 3003 Avondale Ave., in Knoxville, which contains warehouse and office areas equipped with two-door truck docks. The annual rental is $9,000. The building was previously used as a food service warehouse and very little modification to the building will be required.

PRODUCTS AND SERVICES

The firm will offer specialty food service products such as soup bases, dessert mixes, sauce bases, pastry mixes, spices, and flavors, normally used by upscale restaurants and nice hotels. We are going after a niche in the market with high quality gourmet products. There is much less competition in this market than in standard run of the mill food service products. Through their work experiences, the principals have contacts with supply sources and with local chefs.

THE MARKET

We know from our market survey that there are over 200 hotels and upscale restaurants in the area we plan to serve. Customers will be attracted by a direct sales approach. We will offer samples of our products and product application data on use of our products in the finished prepared foods. We will cultivate the chefs in these establishments. The technical background of John Williams will be especially useful here.

COMPETITION

We find that we will be only distributor in the area offering a full line of gourmet food service products. Other foodservice distributors offer only a few such items in conjunction with their standard product line. Our survey shows that many of the chefs are ordering products from Atlanta and Memphis because of a lack of adequate local supply.

SUMMARY

Commercial Foods, Inc. will be established as a foodservice distributor of specialty food in Knoxville. The principals, with excellent experience in the industry, are seeking a $75,000 loan to establish the business. The principals are investing $25,000 as equity capital.

The business will be set up as an S Corporation with each principal owning 50% of the common stock in the corporation.

Fictional Hardware Store

Oshkosh Hardware, Inc.

123 Main St.
Oshkosh, WI 54901

The following plan outlines how a small hardware store can survive competition from large discount chains by offering products and providing expert advice in the use of any product it sells. This plan is fictional and has not been used to gain funding from a bank or other lending institution.

EXECUTIVE SUMMARY

Oshkosh Hardware, Inc. is a new corporation that is going to establish a retail hardware store in a strip mall in Oshkosh, Wisconsin. The store will sell hardware of all kinds, quality tools, paint, and housewares. The business will make revenue and a profit by servicing its customers not only with needed hardware but also with expert advice in the use of any product it sells.

Oshkosh Hardware, Inc. will be operated by its sole shareholder, James Smith. The company will have a total of four employees. It will sell its products in the local market. Customers will buy our products because we will provide free advice on the use of all of our products and will also furnish a full refund warranty.

Oshkosh Hardware, Inc. will sell its products in the Oshkosh store staffed by three sales representatives. No additional employees will be needed to achieve its short and long range goals. The primary short range goal is to open the store by October 1, 1994. In order to achieve this goal a lease must be signed by July 1, 1994 and the complete inventory ordered by August 1, 1994.

Mr. James Smith will invest $30,000 in the business. In addition, the company will have to borrow $150,000 during the first year to cover the investment in inventory, accounts receivable, and furniture and equipment. The company will be profitable after six months of operation and should be able to start repayment of the loan in the second year.

THE BUSINESS

The business will sell hardware of all kinds, quality tools, paint, and housewares. We will purchase our products from three large wholesale buying groups.

In general our customers are homeowners who do their own repair and maintenance, hobbyists, and housewives. Our business is unique in that we will have a complete line of all hardware items and will be able to get special orders by overnight delivery. The business makes revenue and profits by servicing our customers not only with needed hardware but also with expert advice in the use of any product we sell. Our major costs for bringing our products to market are cost of merchandise of 36%, salaries of $45,000, and occupancy costs of $60,000.

273

Oshkosh Hardware, Inc.'s retail outlet will be located at 1524 Frontage Road, which is in a newly developed retail center of Oshkosh. Our location helps facilitate accessibility from all parts of town and reduces our delivery costs. The store will occupy 7500 square feet of space. The major equipment involved in our business is counters and shelving, a computer, a paint mixing machine, and a truck.

THE MARKET

Oshkosh Hardware, Inc. will operate in the local market. There are 15,000 potential customers in this market area. We have three competitors who control approximately 98% of the market at present. We feel we can capture 25% of the market within the next four years. Our major reason for believing this is that our staff is technically competent to advise our customers in the correct use of all products we sell.

After a careful market analysis, we have determined that approximately 60% of our customers are men and 40% are women. The percentage of customers that fall into the following age categories are:

Under 16: 0%
17–21: 5%
22–30: 30%
31–40: 30%
41–50: 20%
51–60: 10%
61–70: 5%
Over 70: 0%

The reasons our customers prefer our products is our complete knowledge of their use and our full refund warranty.

We get our information about what products our customers want by talking to existing customers. There seems to be an increasing demand for our product. The demand for our product is increasing in size based on the change in population characteristics.

SALES

At Oshkosh Hardware, Inc. we will employ three sales people and will not need any additional personnel to achieve our sales goals. These salespeople will need several years experience in home repair and power tool usage. We expect to attract 30% of our customers from newspaper ads, 5% of our customers from local directories, 5% of our customers from the yellow pages, 10% of our customers from family and friends, and 50% of our customers from current customers. The most cost effect source will be current customers. In general our industry is growing.

MANAGEMENT

We would evaluate the quality of our management staff as being excellent. Our manager is experienced and very motivated to achieve the various sales and quality assurance objectives we have set. We will use a management information system that produces key inventory, quality assurance, and sales data on a weekly basis. All data is compared to previously established goals for that week, and deviations are the primary focus of the management staff.

GOALS IMPLEMENTATION

The short term goals of our business are:

1. Open the store by October 1, 1994
2. Reach our breakeven point in two months
3. Have sales of $100,000 in the first six months

In order to achieve our first short term goal we must:

1. Sign the lease by July 1, 1994
2. Order a complete inventory by August 1, 1994

In order to achieve our second short term goal we must:

1. Advertise extensively in Sept. and Oct.
2. Keep expenses to a minimum

In order to achieve our third short term goal we must:

1. Promote power tool sales for the Christmas season
2. Keep good customer traffic in Jan. and Feb.

The long term goals for our business are:

1. Obtain sales volume of $600,000 in three years
2. Become the largest hardware dealer in the city
3. Open a second store in Fond du Lac

The most important thing we must do in order to achieve the long term goals for our business is to develop a highly profitable business with excellent cash flow.

FINANCE

Oshkosh Hardware, Inc. Faces some potential threats or risks to our business. They are discount house competition. We believe we can avoid or compensate for this by providing quality products complimented by quality advice on the use of every product we sell. The financial projections we have prepared are located at the end of this document.

JOB DESCRIPTION-GENERAL MANAGER

The General Manager of the business of the corporation will be the president of the corporation. He will be responsible for the complete operation of the retail hardware store which is owned by the corporation. A detailed description of his duties and responsibilities is as follows.

Sales

Train and supervise the three sales people. Develop programs to motivate and compensate these employees. Coordinate advertising and sales promotion effects to achieve sales totals as outlined in budget. Oversee purchasing function and inventory control procedures to insure adequate merchandise at all times at a reasonable cost.

Finance

Prepare monthly and annual budgets. Secure adequate line of credit from local banks. Supervise office personnel to insure timely preparation of records, statements, all government reports, control of receivables and payables, and monthly financial statements.

Administration

Perform duties as required in the areas of personnel, building leasing and maintenance, licenses and permits, and public relations.

Organizations, Agencies, & Consultants

A listing of Associations and Consultants of interest to entrepreneurs, followed by the ten Small Business Administration Regional Offices, Small Business Development Centers, Service Corps of Retired Executives offices, and Venture Capital and Finance Companies.

ASSOCIATIONS

This section contains a listing of associations and other agencies of interest to the small business owner. Entries are listed alphabetically by organization name.

American Association of Family Businesses
PO Box 547217
Surfside, FL 33154
(305)864-1184
Fax: (305)864-1187
Craig Gordon, Pres.

American Small Businesses Association
8773 IL Rte. 75E.
Rock City, IL 61070
800-942-2722
E-mail: gavazzi.l@osu.edu
Website: http://www.asbaonline.org/
Vernon Castle, Exec.Dir.

American Society of Independent Business
c/o Keith Wood
777 Main St., Ste. 1600
Fort Worth, TX 76102
(817)870-1880
Keith Wood, Pres.

American Women's Economic Development Corporation
216 East 45th St.
New York, NY 10017
(917)368-6120
Fax: (212)786-7114
E-mail: info@awed.org
Website: http://www.awed.org
Suzanne Israel Tufts, Pres. & CEO

Association for Enterprise Opportunity
70 E Lake St., Ste. 1120
Chicago, IL 60601

(312)357-0177
Fax: (312)357-0180
E-mail: aeochicago@ad.com
Christine M. Benuzzi, Exec.Dir.

Association of Small Business Development Centers
c/o Don Wilson
8990 Burke Lake Rd.
Burke, VA 22015
(703)764-9850
Fax: (703)764-1234
E-mail: don@asbdc-us.org
Website: http://www.asbdc-us.org
Don Wilson, Pres.

BEST Employers Association
2505 McCabe Way
Irvine, CA 92614
(714)756-1000
800-433-0088
Fax: (714)553-0883
Donald R. Lawrenz, Exec.Sec.

Business Market Association
4131 N. Central Expy., Ste. 720
Dallas, TX 75204
R. Mark King, Pres.

Coalition of Americans to Save the Economy
1100 Connecticut Ave. NW, Ste. 1200
Washington, DC 20036-4101
(202)293-1414
Fax: (202)293-1702
Barry Maloney, Treas.

Employers of America
520 S Pierce, Ste. 224
Mason City, IA 50401
(641)424-3187
800-728-3187
Fax: (641)424-1673
E-mail: employer@employerhelp.org

Website: http://www.employerhelp.org
Jim Collison, Pres.

Family Firm Institute
221 N. Beacon St.
Boston, MA 02135-1943
(617)789-4200
Fax: (617)789-4220
E-mail: ffi@ffi.org
Website: http://www.ffi.org
Judy L. Green, Ph.D., Exec.Dir.

Group Purchasing Association
Plaza Tower, 35th Fl.
1001 Howard Ave.
New Orleans, LA 70113-2002
(504)529-2030
Fax: (504)558-0929
E-mail: lenn@firstgpa.com

Independent Business Alliance
111 John St.
New York, NY 10038
800-559-2580
Fax: (212)285-1639
Robert J. Levine, CEO

International Association of Business
701 Highlander Blvd., Ste. 500
Arlington, TX 76015-4332
Paula Rainey, Pres.

International Association for Business Organizations
PO Box 30149
Baltimore, MD 21270
(410)581-1373
Rudolph Lewis, Exec. Officer

International Council for Small Business
c/o Jefferson Smurfit Center for Entrepreneurial Studies
St. Louis University

3674 Lindell Blvd.
St. Louis, MO 63108
(314)977-3628
Fax: (314)977-3627
E-mail: icsb@slu.edu
Website: http://www.icsb.org
Sharon Bower, Sec.

National Alliance for Fair Competition
3 Bethesda Metro Center, Ste. 1100
Bethesda, MD 20814
(410)235-7116
Fax: (410)235-7116
E-mail: ampesq@aol.com
Tony Ponticelli, Exec.Dir.

National Association of Business Leaders
PO Box 766
Bridgeton, MO 63044
(314)344-1111
Fax: (314)298-9110
E-mail: nabl@nabl.com
Website: http://www.nabl.com/
John Weigel, Contact

National Association for Business Organizations
PO Box 30220
Baltimore, MD 21270
(410)581-1373
Website: http://www.ameribiz.com/
quicklink.htm
Rudolph Lewis, Pres.

National Association of Government Guaranteed Lenders
c/o Tony Wilkinson
PO Box 332
Stillwater, OK 74076
(405)377-4022
Fax: (405)377-3931
E-mail: twilkinson@naggl.com
Website: http://www.naggl.com/
Tony Wilkinson, Pres./CEO

National Association of Private Enterprise
7819 Shelburne Cir.
Spring, TX 77379-4687
(281)655-5412
800-223-6273
Fax: (281)257-3244
E-mail: info@nape.org
Laura Squiers, Exec.Dir.

National Association for the Self-Employed
PO Box 612067
DFW Airport
Dallas, TX 75261-2067

800-232-NASE
Fax: 800-551-4446
Website: http://www.nase.org
Robert Hughes, Pres.

National Association of Small Business Investment Companies
666 11th St. NW, No. 750
Washington, DC 20001
(202)628-5055
Fax: (202)628-5080
E-mail: nasbic@nasbic.org
Website: http://www.nasbic.org
Lee W. Mercer, Pres.

National Business Association
PO Box 700728
Dallas, TX 75370
(972)458-0900
800-456-0440
Fax: (972)960-9149
E-mail:
p.archibald@nationalbusiness.org
Website: http://
www.nationalbusiness.org
Pat Archibald, Pres.

National Business Owners Association
820 Gibbon St. Ste. 204
Alexandria, VA 22314
(202)737-6501
(888)755-NBOA
Fax: (877)626-2329
E-mail: govaffairs@nboa.org
Thomas Rumfelt, Chm.

National Center for Fair Competition
8421 Frost Way
Annandale, VA 22003
(703)280-4622
Fax: (703)280-0942
E-mail: kentonp1@aol.com
Kenton Pattie, Pres.

National Federation of Independent Business
53 Century Blvd., Ste. 300
Nashville, TN 37214
(615)872-5800
800-NFIBNOW
Fax: (615)872-5353
Website: http://www.nfib.org
Jack Faris, Pres. and CEO

National Small Business Benefits Association
2244 N. Grand Ave. E.
Springfield, IL 62702
(217)753-2558
Fax: (217)753-2558
Les Brewer, Exec.VP

National Small Business United
1156 15th St. NW, Ste. 1100
Washington, DC 20005
(202)293-8830
800-345-6728
Fax: (202)872-8543
E-mail: nsbu@nsbu.org
Website: http://www.nsbu.org
Todd McCraken, Pres.

Network of Small Businesses
5420 Mayfield Rd., Ste. 205
Lyndhurst, OH 44124
(216)442-5600
Fax: (216)449-3227
Irwin Friedman, Chm.

Research Institute for Small and Emerging Business
722 12th St. NW
Washington, DC 20005
(202)628-8382
Fax: (202)628-8392
E-mail: info@riseb.org
Website: http://www.riseb.org
Mark Schultz, CEO/Pres.

Score Association - Service Corps of Retired Executives
c/o Service Corps of Retired Executives
Association
409 3rd St. SW, 6th Fl.
Washington, DC 20024
(202)205-6762
800-634-0245
Fax: (202)205-7636
Website: http://www.score.org
W. Kenneth Yancey, Jr., CEO

Small Business Legislative Council
1010 Massachusetts Ave. NW
Washington, DC 20001
(202)639-8500
Fax: (202)296-5333
Website: http://www.sblc.org
John Satagaj, Pres.

Small Business Network
PO Box 30149
Baltimore, MD 21270
(410)581-1373
E-mail: natibb@ix.netcom.com
Rudolph Lewis, CEO

Small Business Service Bureau
554 Main St.
PO Box 15014
Worcester, MA 01615-0014
(508)756-3513
Fax: (508)770-0528
Francis R. Carroll, Pres.

Small Business Service Bureau
554 Main St.
PO Box 15014
Worcester, MA 01608
(508)756-3513
800-343-0939
Fax: (508)770-0528
E-mail: membership@sbsb.com
Website: http://www.sbsb.com
Francis R. Carroll, Pres.

Small Business Support Center Association
c/o James S. Ryan
8811 Westheimer Rd., No. 210
Houston, TX 77063-3617
James S. Ryan, Admin.

Small Business Survival Committee
1920 L St., NW, Ste. 200
Washington, DC 20036
(202)785-0238
Fax: (202)822-8118
E-mail: membership@sbsc.org
Website: http://www.sbsc.org
Christopher Wysocki, Pres.

Support Services Alliance
PO Box 130
Schoharie, NY 12157-0130
(518)295-7966
800-836-4772
Fax: (518)295-8556
E-mail: comments@ssainfo.com
Website: http://www.ssainfo.com
Gary Swan, Pres.

CONSULTANTS

This section contains a listing of consultants specializing in small business development. It is arranged alphabetically by country, then by state or province, then by city, then by firm name.

CANADA

Alberta

Common Sense Solutions
3405 16A Ave.
Edmonton, AB, Canada
(403)465-7330
Fax: (403)465-7380
E-mail:
gcoulson@comsensesolutions.com
Website: http://
www.comsensesolutions.com

Varsity Consulting Group
School of Business
University of Alberta
Edmonton, AB, Canada T6G 2R6
(780)492-2994
Fax: (780)492-5400
Website: http://www.bus.ualberta.ca/vcg

Viro Hospital Consulting
42 Commonwealth Bldg., 9912 - 106 St. NW
Edmonton, AB, Canada T5K 1C5
(403)425-3871
Fax: (403)425-3871
E-mail: rpb@freenet.edmonton.ab.ca

British Columbia

SRI Strategic Resources Inc.
4330 Kingsway, Ste. 1600
Burnaby, BC, Canada V5H 4G7
(604)435-0627
Fax: (604)435-2782
E-mail: inquiry@sri.bc.ca
Website: http://www.sri.com

Andrew R. De Boda Consulting
1523 Milford Ave.
Coquitlam, BC, Canada V3J 2V9
(604)936-4527
Fax: (604)936-4527
E-mail: deboda@intergate.bc.ca
Website: http://
www.ourworld.compuserve.com/
homepages/deboda

The Sage Group Ltd.
980 - 355 Burrard St.
744 W Haistings, Ste. 410
Vancouver, BC, Canada V6C 1A5
(604)669-9269
Fax: (604)669-6622

Tikkanen-Bradley
1345 Nelson St., Ste. 202
Vancouver, BC, Canada V6E 1J8
(604)669-0583
E-mail:
webmaster@tikkanenbradley.com
Website: http://
www.tikkanenbradley.com

Ontario

The Cynton Co.
17 Massey St.
Brampton, ON, Canada L6S 2V6
(905)792-7769
Fax: (905)792-8116
E-mail: cynton@home.com
Website: http://www.cynton.com

Begley & Associates
RR 6
Cambridge, ON, Canada N1R 5S7
(519)740-3629
Fax: (519)740-3629
E-mail: begley@in.on.ca
Website: http://www.in.on.ca/~begley/
index.htm

CRO Engineering Ltd.
1895 William Hodgins Ln.
Carp, ON, Canada K0A 1L0
(613)839-1108
Fax: (613)839-1406
E-mail: J.Grefford@ieee.ca
Website: http://www.geocities.com/
WallStreet/District/7401/

Task Enterprises
Box 69, RR 2 Hamilton
Flamborough, ON, Canada L8N 2Z7
(905)659-0153
Fax: (905)659-0861

HST Group Ltd.
430 Gilmour St.
Ottawa, ON, Canada K2P 0R8
(613)236-7303
Fax: (613)236-9893

Harrison Associates
BCE Pl.
181 Bay St., Ste. 3740
PO Box 798
Toronto, ON, Canada M5J 2T3
(416)364-5441
Fax: (416)364-2875

TCI Convergence Ltd. Management Consultants
99 Crown's Ln.
Toronto, ON, Canada M5R 3P4
(416)515-4146
Fax: (416)515-2097
E-mail: tci@inforamp.net
Website: http://tciconverge.com/
index.1.html

Ken Wyman & Associates Inc.
64B Shuter St., Ste. 200
Toronto, ON, Canada M5B 1B1
(416)362-2926
Fax: (416)362-3039
E-mail: kenwyman@compuserve.com

JPL Business Consultants
82705 Metter Rd.
Wellandport, ON, Canada L0R 2J0
(905)386-7450
Fax: (905)386-7450
E-mail: plamarch@freenet.npiec.on.ca

Quebec

The Zimmar Consulting Partnership Inc.
Westmount
PO Box 98
Montreal, QC, Canada H3Z 2T1
(514)484-1459
Fax: (514)484-3063

Saskatchewan

Corporate Management Consultants
PO Box 7570 Station Main
Saskatoon, SK, Canada, S7K 4L4
E-mail:
cmccorporatemanagement@shaw.ca
Website: http://
www.Corporatemanagementconsultants
.com
Gerald Rekve

Trimension Group
No. 104-110 Research Dr.
Innovation Place, SK, Canada S7N 3R3
(306)668-2560
Fax: (306)975-1156
E-mail: trimension@trimension.ca
Website: http://www.trimension.ca

UNITED STATES

Alabama

Business Planning Inc.
300 Office Park Dr.
Birmingham, AL 35223-2474
(205)870-7090
Fax: (205)870-7103

Tradebank of Eastern Alabama
546 Broad St., Ste. 3
Gadsden, AL 35901
(205)547-8700
Fax: (205)547-8718
E-mail: mansion@webex.com
Website: http://www.webex.com/~tea

Alaska

AK Business Development Center
3335 Arctic Blvd., Ste. 203
Anchorage, AK 99503
(907)562-0335
Free: 800-478-3474
Fax: (907)562-6988
E-mail: abdc@gci.net
Website: http://www.abdc.org

Business Matters
PO Box 287
Fairbanks, AK 99707
(907)452-5650

Arizona

Carefree Direct Marketing Corp.
8001 E Serene St.
PO Box 3737
Carefree, AZ 85377-3737
(480)488-4227
Fax: (480)488-2841

Trans Energy Corp.
1739 W 7th Ave.
Mesa, AZ 85202
(480)827-7915
Fax: (480)967-6601
E-mail: aha@clean-air.org
Website: http://www.clean-air.org

CMAS
5125 N 16th St.
Phoenix, AZ 85016
(602)395-1001
Fax: (602)604-8180

Comgate Telemanagement Ltd.
706 E Bell Rd., Ste. 105
Phoenix, AZ 85022
(602)485-5708
Fax: (602)485-5709
E-mail: comgate@netzone.com
Website: http://www.comgate.com

Moneysoft Inc.
1 E Camelback Rd. #550
Phoenix, AZ 85012
Free: 800-966-7797
E-mail: mbray@moneysoft.com

Harvey C. Skoog
PO Box 26439
Prescott Valley, AZ 86312
(520)772-1714
Fax: (520)772-2814

LMC Services
8711 E Pinnacle Peak Rd.,
No. 340
Scottsdale, AZ 85255-3555
(602)585-7177
Fax: (602)585-5880
E-mail: louws@earthlink.com

Sauerbrun Technology Group Ltd.
7979 E Princess Dr., Ste. 5
Scottsdale, AZ 85255-5878
(602)502-4950
Fax: (602)502-4292

E-mail: info@sauerbrun.com
Website: http://www.sauerbrun.com

Gary L. McLeod
PO Box 230
Sonoita, AZ 85637
Fax: (602)455-5661

Van Cleve Associates
6932 E 2nd St.
Tucson, AZ 85710
(520)296-2587
Fax: (520)296-3358

California

Acumen Group Inc.
(650)949-9349
Fax: (650)949-4845
E-mail: acumen-g@ix.netcom.com
Website: http://pw2.netcom.com/~janed/
acumen.html

On-line Career and Management Consulting
420 Central Ave., No. 314
Alameda, CA 94501
(510)864-0336
Fax: (510)864-0336
E-mail: career@dnai.com
Website: http://www.dnai.com/~career

Career Paths-Thomas E. Church & Associates Inc.
PO Box 2439
Aptos, CA 95001
(408)662-7950
Fax: (408)662-7955
E-mail: church@ix.netcom.com
Website: http://
www.careerpaths-tom.com

Keck & Co. Business Consultants
410 Walsh Rd.
Atherton, CA 94027
(650)854-9588
Fax: (650)854-7240
E-mail: info@keckco.com
Website: http://www.keckco.com

Ben W. Laverty III, PhD, REA, CEI
4909 Stockdale Hwy., Ste. 132
Bakersfield, CA 93309
(661)283-8300
Free: 800-833-0373
Fax: (661)283-8313
E-mail: cstc@cstcsafety.com
Website: http://www.cstcsafety.com/cstc

Lindquist Consultants-Venture Planning
225 Arlington Ave.
Berkeley, CA 94707

(510)524-6685
Fax: (510)527-6604

Larson Associates
PO Box 9005
Brea, CA 92822
(714)529-4121
Fax: (714)572-3606
E-mail: ray@consultlarson.com
Website: http://www.consultlarson.com

Kremer Management Consulting
PO Box 500
Carmel, CA 93921
(408)626-8311
Fax: (408)624-2663
E-mail: ddkremer@aol.com

W and J PARTNERSHIP
PO Box 2499
18876 Edwin Markham Dr.
Castro Valley, CA 94546
(510)583-7751
Fax: (510)583-7645
E-mail: wamorgan@wjpartnership.com
Website: http://www.wjpartnership.com

JB Associates
21118 Gardena Dr.
Cupertino, CA 95014
(408)257-0214
Fax: (408)257-0216
E-mail: semarang@sirius.com

House Agricultural Consultants
PO Box 1615
Davis, CA 95617-1615
(916)753-3361
Fax: (916)753-0464
E-mail: infoag@houseag.com
Website: http://www.houseag.com/

3C Systems Co.
16161 Ventura Blvd., Ste. 815
Encino, CA 91436
(818)907-1302
Fax: (818)907-1357
E-mail: mark@3CSysCo.com
Website: http://www.3CSysCo.com

Technical Management Consultants
3624 Westfall Dr.
Encino, CA 91436-4154
(818)784-0626
Fax: (818)501-5575
E-mail: tmcrs@aol.com

**RAINWATER-GISH & Associates,
Business Finance & Development**
317 3rd St., Ste. 3
Eureka, CA 95501

(707)443-0030
Fax: (707)443-5683

Global Tradelinks
451 Pebble Beach Pl.
Fullerton, CA 92835
(714)441-2280
Fax: (714)441-2281
E-mail: info@globaltradelinks.com
Website: http://www.globaltradelinks.com

Strategic Business Group
800 Cienaga Dr.
Fullerton, CA 92835-1248
(714)449-1040
Fax: (714)525-1631

Burnes Consulting
20537 Wolf Creek Rd.
Grass Valley, CA 95949
(530)346-8188
Free: 800-949-9021
Fax: (530)346-7704
E-mail: kent@burnesconsulting.com
Website: http://www.burnesconsulting.com

Pioneer Business Consultants
9042 Garfield Ave., Ste. 312
Huntington Beach, CA 92646
(714)964-7600

Beblie, Brandt & Jacobs Inc.
16 Technology, Ste. 164
Irvine, CA 92618
(714)450-8790
Fax: (714)450-8799
E-mail: darcy@bbjinc.com
Website: http://198.147.90.26

Fluor Daniel Inc.
3353 Michelson Dr.
Irvine, CA 92612-0650
(949)975-2000
Fax: (949)975-5271
E-mail: sales.consulting@fluordaniel.com
Website: http://www.fluordanielconsulting.com

MCS Associates
18300 Von Karman, Ste. 710
Irvine, CA 92612
(949)263-8700
Fax: (949)263-0770
E-mail: info@mcsassociates.com
Website: http://www.mcsassociates.com

Inspired Arts Inc.
4225 Executive Sq., Ste. 1160
La Jolla, CA 92037

(619)623-3525
Free: 800-851-4394
Fax: (619)623-3534
E-mail: info@inspiredarts.com
Website: http://www.inspiredarts.com

The Laresis Companies
PO Box 3284
La Jolla, CA 92038
(619)452-2720
Fax: (619)452-8744

RCL & Co.
PO Box 1143
737 Pearl St., Ste. 201
La Jolla, CA 92038
(619)454-8883
Fax: (619)454-8880

Comprehensive Business Services
3201 Lucas Cir.
Lafayette, CA 94549
(925)283-8272
Fax: (925)283-8272

The Ribble Group
27601 Forbes Rd., Ste. 52
Laguna Niguel, CA 92677
(714)582-1085
Fax: (714)582-6420
E-mail: ribble@deltanet.com

Norris Bernstein, CMC
9309 Marina Pacifica Dr. N
Long Beach, CA 90803
(562)493-5458
Fax: (562)493-5459
E-mail: norris@ctecomputer.com
Website: http://foodconsultants.com/bernstein/

Horizon Consulting Services
1315 Garthwick Dr.
Los Altos, CA 94024
(415)967-0906
Fax: (415)967-0906

Brincko Associates Inc.
1801 Avenue of the Stars, Ste. 1054
Los Angeles, CA 90067
(310)553-4523
Fax: (310)553-6782

Rubenstein/Justman Management Consultants
2049 Century Park E, 24th Fl.
Los Angeles, CA 90067
(310)282-0800
Fax: (310)282-0400
E-mail: info@rjmc.net
Website: http://www.rjmc.net

F.J. Schroeder & Associates
1926 Westholme Ave.
Los Angeles, CA 90025
(310)470-2655
Fax: (310)470-6378
E-mail: fjsacons@aol.com
Website: http://www.mcninet.com/
GlobalLook/Fjschroe.html

Western Management Associates
5959 W Century Blvd., Ste. 565
Los Angeles, CA 90045-6506
(310)645-1091
Free: (888)788-6534
Fax: (310)645-1092
E-mail: gene@cfoforrent.com
Website: http://www.cfoforrent.com

Darrell Sell and Associates
Los Gatos, CA 95030
(408)354-7794
E-mail: darrell@netcom.com

Leslie J. Zambo
3355 Michael Dr.
Marina, CA 93933
(408)384-7086
Fax: (408)647-4199
E-mail: 104776.1552@compuserve.com

Marketing Services Management
PO Box 1377
Martinez, CA 94553
(510)370-8527
Fax: (510)370-8527
E-mail: markserve@biotechnet.com

William M. Shine Consulting Service
PO Box 127
Moraga, CA 94556-0127
(510)376-6516

Palo Alto Management Group Inc.
2672 Bayshore Pky., Ste. 701
Mountain View, CA 94043
(415)968-4374
Fax: (415)968-4245
E-mail: mburwen@pamg.com

BizplanSource
1048 Irvine Ave., Ste. 621
Newport Beach, CA 92660
Free: 888-253-0974
Fax: 800-859-8254
E-mail: info@bizplansource.com
Website: http://www.bizplansource.com
Adam Greengrass, President

The Market Connection
4020 Birch St., Ste. 203
Newport Beach, CA 92660

(714)731-6273
Fax: (714)833-0253

Muller Associates
PO Box 7264
Newport Beach, CA 92658
(714)646-1169
Fax: (714)646-1169

International Health Resources
PO Box 329
North San Juan, CA 95960-0329
(530)292-1266
Fax: (530)292-1243
Website: http://
www.futureofhealthcare.com

NEXUS - Consultants to Management
PO Box 1531
Novato, CA 94948
(415)897-4400
Fax: (415)898-2252
E-mail: jimnexus@aol.com

Aerospcace.Org
PO Box 28831
Oakland, CA 94604-8831
(510)530-9169
Fax: (510)530-3411
Website: http://www.aerospace.org

Intelequest Corp.
722 Gailen Ave.
Palo Alto, CA 94303
(415)968-3443
Fax: (415)493-6954
E-mail: frits@iqix.com

McLaughlin & Associates
66 San Marino Cir.
Rancho Mirage, CA 92270
(760)321-2932
Fax: (760)328-2474
E-mail: jackmcla@msn.com

**Carrera Consulting Group, a division
of Maximus**
2110 21st St., Ste. 400
Sacramento, CA 95818
(916)456-3300
Fax: (916)456-3306
E-mail: central@carreraconsulting.com
Website: http://
www.carreraconsulting.com

**Bay Area Tax Consultants and Bayhill
Financial Consultants**
1150 Bayhill Dr., Ste. 1150
San Bruno, CA 94066-3004
(415)952-8786
Fax: (415)588-4524

E-mail: baytax@compuserve.com
Website: http://www.baytax.com/

AdCon Services, LLC
8871 Hillery Dr.
Dan Diego, CA 92126
(858)433-1411
E-mail: adam@adconservices.com
Website: http://www.adconservices.com
Adam Greengrass

**California Business Incubation
Network**
101 W Broadway, No. 480
San Diego, CA 92101
(619)237-0559
Fax: (619)237-0521

G.R. Gordetsky Consultants Inc.
11414 Windy Summit Pl.
San Diego, CA 92127
(619)487-4939
Fax: (619)487-5587
E-mail: gordet@pacbell.net

Freeman, Sullivan & Co.
131 Steuart St., Ste. 500
San Francisco, CA 94105
(415)777-0707
Free: 800-777-0737
Fax: (415)777-2420
Website: http://www.fsc-research.com

Ideas Unlimited
2151 California St., Ste. 7
San Francisco, CA 94115
(415)931-0641
Fax: (415)931-0880

Russell Miller Inc.
300 Montgomery St., Ste. 900
San Francisco, CA 94104
(415)956-7474
Fax: (415)398-0620
E-mail: rmi@pacbell.net
Website: http://www.rmisf.com

PKF Consulting
425 California St., Ste. 1650
San Francisco, CA 94104
(415)421-5378
Fax: (415)956-7708
E-mail: callahan@pkfc.com
Website: http://www.pkfonline.com

Welling & Woodard Inc.
1067 Broadway
San Francisco, CA 94133
(415)776-4500
Fax: (415)776-5067

Highland Associates
16174 Highland Dr.
San Jose, CA 95127
(408)272-7008
Fax: (408)272-4040

ORDIS Inc.
6815 Trinidad Dr.
San Jose, CA 95120-2056
(408)268-3321
Free: 800-446-7347
Fax: (408)268-3582
E-mail: ordis@ordis.com
Website: http://www.ordis.com

Stanford Resources Inc.
20 Great Oaks Blvd., Ste. 200
San Jose, CA 95119
(408)360-8400
Fax: (408)360-8410
E-mail: sales@stanfordsources.com
Website: http://
www.stanfordresources.com

Technology Properties Ltd. Inc.
PO Box 20250
San Jose, CA 95160
(408)243-9898
Fax: (408)296-6637
E-mail: sanjose@tplnet.com

Helfert Associates
1777 Borel Pl., Ste. 508
San Mateo, CA 94402-3514
(650)377-0540
Fax: (650)377-0472

Mykytyn Consulting Group Inc.
185 N Redwood Dr., Ste. 200
San Rafael, CA 94903
(415)491-1770
Fax: (415)491-1251
E-mail: info@mcgi.com
Website: http://www.mcgi.com

Omega Management Systems Inc.
3 Mount Darwin Ct.
San Rafael, CA 94903-1109
(415)499-1300
Fax: (415)492-9490
E-mail: omegamgt@ix.netcom.com

The Information Group Inc.
4675 Stevens Creek Blvd., Ste. 100
Santa Clara, CA 95051
(408)985-7877
Fax: (408)985-2945
E-mail: dvincent@tig-usa.com
Website: http://www.tig-usa.com

Cast Management Consultants
1620 26th St., Ste. 2040N
Santa Monica, CA 90404
(310)828-7511
Fax: (310)453-6831

Cuma Consulting Management
Box 724
Santa Rosa, CA 95402
(707)785-2477
Fax: (707)785-2478

The E-Myth Academy
131B Stony Cir., Ste. 2000
Santa Rosa, CA 95401
(707)569-5600
Free: 800-221-0266
Fax: (707)569-5700
E-mail: info@e-myth.com
Website: http://www.e-myth.com

Reilly, Connors & Ray
1743 Canyon Rd.
Spring Valley, CA 91977
(619)698-4808
Fax: (619)460-3892
E-mail: davidray@adnc.com

Management Consultants
Sunnyvale, CA 94087-4700
(408)773-0321

RJR Associates
1639 Lewiston Dr.
Sunnyvale, CA 94087
(408)737-7720
E-mail: bobroy@rjrassoc.com
Website: http://www.rjrassoc.com

Schwafel Associates
333 Cobalt Way, Ste. 21
Sunnyvale, CA 94085
(408)720-0649
Fax: (408)720-1796
E-mail: schwafel@ricochet.net
Website: http://www.patca.org

Staubs Business Services
23320 S Vermont Ave.
Torrance, CA 90502-2940
(310)830-9128
Fax: (310)830-9128
E-mail: Harry_L_Staubs@Lamg.com

Out of Your Mind ... and Into the Marketplace
13381 White Sands Dr.
Tustin, CA 92780-4565
(714)544-0248
Free: 800-419-1513
Fax: (714)730-1414

E-mail: lpinson@aol.com
Website: http://www.business-plan.com

Independent Research Services
PO Box 2426
Van Nuys, CA 91404-2426
(818)993-3622

Ingman Company Inc.
7949 Woodley Ave., Ste. 120
Van Nuys, CA 91406-1232
(818)375-5027
Fax: (818)894-5001

Innovative Technology Associates
3639 E Harbor Blvd., Ste. 203E
Ventura, CA 93001
(805)650-9353

Grid Technology Associates
20404 Tufts Cir.
Walnut, CA 91789
(909)444-0922
Fax: (909)444-0922
E-mail: grid_technology@msn.com

Ridge Consultants Inc.
100 Pringle Ave., Ste. 580
Walnut Creek, CA 94596
(925)274-1990
Fax: (510)274-1956
E-mail: info@ridgecon.com
Website: http://www.ridgecon.com

Bell Springs Publishing
PO Box 1240
Willits, CA 95490
(707)459-6372
E-mail: bellsprings@sabernet
Website: http://www.bellsprings.com

Hutchinson Consulting and Appraisal
23245 Sylvan St., Ste. 103
Woodland Hills, CA 91367
(818)888-8175
Free: 800-977-7548
Fax: (818)888-8220
E-mail: r.f.hutchinson-cpa@worldnet.att.net

Colorado

Sam Boyer & Associates
4255 S Buckley Rd., No. 136
Aurora, CO 80013
Free: 800-785-0485
Fax: (303)766-8740
E-mail: samboyer@samboyer.com
Website: http://www.samboyer.com/

Ameriwest Business Consultants Inc.
PO Box 26266
Colorado Springs, CO 80936
(719)380-7096
Fax: (719)380-7096
E-mail: email@abchelp.com
Website: http://www.abchelp.com

GVNW Consulting Inc.
2270 La Montana Way
Colorado Springs, CO 80936
(719)594-5800
Fax: (719)594-5803
Website: http://www.gvnw.com

M-Squared Inc.
755 San Gabriel Pl.
Colorado Springs, CO 80906
(719)576-2554
Fax: (719)576-2554

Thornton Financial FNIC
1024 Centre Ave., Bldg. E
Fort Collins, CO 80526-1849
(970)221-2089
Fax: (970)484-5206

TenEyck Associates
1760 Cherryville Rd.
Greenwood Village, CO 80121-1503
(303)758-6129
Fax: (303)761-8286

Associated Enterprises Ltd.
13050 W Ceder Dr., Unit 11
Lakewood, CO 80228
(303)988-6695
Fax: (303)988-6739
E-mail: ael1@classic.msn.com

The Vincent Company Inc.
200 Union Blvd., Ste. 210
Lakewood, CO 80228
(303)989-7271
Free: 800-274-0733
Fax: (303)989-7570
E-mail: vincent@vincentco.com
Website: http://www.vincentco.com

Johnson & West Management Consultants Inc.
7612 S Logan Dr.
Littleton, CO 80122
(303)730-2810
Fax: (303)730-3219

Western Capital Holdings Inc.
10050 E Applwood Dr.
Parker, CO 80138
(303)841-1022
Fax: (303)770-1945

Connecticut

Stratman Group Inc.
40 Tower Ln.
Avon, CT 06001-4222
(860)677-2898
Free: 800-551-0499
Fax: (860)677-8210

Cowherd Consulting Group Inc.
106 Stephen Mather Rd.
Darien, CT 06820
(203)655-2150
Fax: (203)655-6427

Greenwich Associates
8 Greenwich Office Park
Greenwich, CT 06831-5149
(203)629-1200
Fax: (203)629-1229
E-mail: lisa@greenwich.com
Website: http://www.greenwich.com

Follow-up News
185 Pine St., Ste. 818
Manchester, CT 06040
(860)647-7542
Free: 800-708-0696
Fax: (860)646-6544
E-mail: Followupnews@aol.com

Lovins & Associates Consulting
309 Edwards St.
New Haven, CT 06511
(203)787-3367
Fax: (203)624-7599
E-mail: Alovinsphd@aol.com
Website: http://www.lovinsgroup.com

JC Ventures Inc.
4 Arnold St.
Old Greenwich, CT 06870-1203
(203)698-1990
Free: 800-698-1997
Fax: (203)698-2638

Charles L. Hornung Associates
52 Ned's Mountain Rd.
Ridgefield, CT 06877
(203)431-0297

Manus
100 Prospect St., S Tower
Stamford, CT 06901
(203)326-3880
Free: 800-445-0942
Fax: (203)326-3890
E-mail: manus1@aol.com
Website: http://www.RightManus.com

RealBusinessPlans.com
156 Westport Rd.
Wilton, CT 06897
(914)837-2886
E-mail: ct@realbusinessplans.com
Website: http://
www.RealBusinessPlans.com
Tony Tecce

Delaware

Focus Marketing
61-7 Habor Dr.
Claymont, DE 19703
(302)793-3064

Daedalus Ventures Ltd.
PO Box 1474
Hockessin, DE 19707
(302)239-6758
Fax: (302)239-9991
E-mail: daedalus@mail.del.net

The Formula Group
PO Box 866
Hockessin, DE 19707
(302)456-0952
Fax: (302)456-1354
E-mail: formula@netaxs.com

Selden Enterprises Inc.
2502 Silverside Rd., Ste. 1
Wilmington, DE 19810-3740
(302)529-7113
Fax: (302)529-7442
E-mail: selden2@bellatlantic.net
Website: http://
www.seldenenterprises.com

District of Columbia

Bruce W. McGee and Associates
7826 Eastern Ave. NW, Ste. 30
Washington, DC 20012
(202)726-7272
Fax: (202)726-2946

McManis Associates Inc.
1900 K St. NW, Ste. 700
Washington, DC 20006
(202)466-7680
Fax: (202)872-1898
Website: http://www.mcmanis-mmi.com

Smith, Dawson & Andrews Inc.
1000 Connecticut Ave., Ste. 302
Washington, DC 20036
(202)835-0740
Fax: (202)775-8526
E-mail: webmaster@sda-inc.com
Website: http://www.sda-inc.com

Florida

BackBone, Inc.
20404 Hacienda Court
Boca Raton, FL 33498
(561)470-0965
Fax: 516-908-4038
E-mail: BPlans@backboneinc.com
Website: http://www.backboneinc.com
Charles Epstein, President

Whalen & Associates Inc.
4255 Northwest 26 Ct.
Boca Raton, FL 33434
(561)241-5950
Fax: (561)241-7414
E-mail: drwhalen@ix.netcom.com

E.N. Rysso & Associates
180 Bermuda Petrel Ct.
Daytona Beach, FL 32119
(386)760-3028
E-mail: erysso@aol.com

Virtual Technocrats LLC
560 Lavers Circle, #146
Delray Beach, FL 33444
(561)265-3509
E-mail: josh@virtualtechnocrats.com;
info@virtualtechnocrats.com
Website: http://
www.virtualtechnocrats.com
Josh Eikov, Managing Director

Eric Sands Consulting Services
6193 Rock Island Rd., Ste. 412
Fort Lauderdale, FL 33319
(954)721-4767
Fax: (954)720-2815
E-mail: easands@aol.com
Website: http://
www.ericsandsconsultig.com

Professional Planning Associates, Inc.
1975 E. Sunrise Blvd. Suite 607
Fort Lauderdale, FL 33304
(954)764-5204
Fax: 954-463-4172
E-mail: Mgoldstein@proplana.com
Website: http://proplana.com
Michael Goldstein, President

Host Media Corp.
3948 S 3rd St., Ste. 191
Jacksonville Beach, FL 32250
(904)285-3239
Fax: (904)285-5618
E-mail: msconsulting@compuserve.com
Website: http://
www.mediaservicesgroup.com

William V. Hall
1925 Brickell, Ste. D-701
Miami, FL 33129
(305)856-9622
Fax: (305)856-4113
E-mail: williamvhall@compuserve.com

F.A. McGee Inc.
800 Claughton Island Dr., Ste. 401
Miami, FL 33131
(305)377-9123

Taxplan Inc.
Mirasol International Ctr.
2699 Collins Ave.
Miami Beach, FL 33140
(305)538-3303

T.C. Brown & Associates
8415 Excalibur Cir., Apt. B1
Naples, FL 34108
(941)594-1949
Fax: (941)594-0611
E-mail: tcater@naples.net.com

RLA International Consulting
713 Lagoon Dr.
North Palm Beach, FL 33408
(407)626-4258
Fax: (407)626-5772

Comprehensive Franchising Inc.
2465 Ridgecrest Ave.
Orange Park, FL 32065
(904)272-6567
Free: 800-321-6567
Fax: (904)272-6750
E-mail: theimp@cris.com
Website: http://www.franchise411.com

Hunter G. Jackson Jr. - Consulting Environmental Physicist
PO Box 618272
Orlando, FL 32861-8272
(407)295-4188
E-mail: hunterjackson@juno.com

F. Newton Parks
210 El Brillo Way
Palm Beach, FL 33480
(561)833-1727
Fax: (561)833-4541

Avery Business Development Services
2506 St. Michel Ct.
Ponte Vedra Beach, FL 32082
(904)285-6033
Fax: (904)285-6033

Strategic Business Planning Co.
PO Box 821006
South Florida, FL 33082-1006
(954)704-9100
Fax: (954)438-7333
E-mail: info@bizplan.com
Website: http://www.bizplan.com

Dufresne Consulting Group Inc.
10014 N Dale Mabry, Ste. 101
Tampa, FL 33618-4426
(813)264-4775
Fax: (813)264-9300
Website: http://www.dcgconsult.com

Agrippa Enterprises Inc.
PO Box 175
Venice, FL 34284-0175
(941)355-7876
E-mail: webservices@agrippa.com
Website: http://www.agrippa.com

Center for Simplified Strategic Planning Inc.
PO Box 3324
Vero Beach, FL 32964-3324
(561)231-3636
Fax: (561)231-1099
Website: http://www.cssp.com

Georgia

Marketing Spectrum Inc.
115 Perimeter Pl., Ste. 440
Atlanta, GA 30346
(770)395-7244
Fax: (770)393-4071

Business Ventures Corp.
1650 Oakbrook Dr., Ste. 405
Norcross, GA 30093
(770)729-8000
Fax: (770)729-8028

Informed Decisions Inc.
100 Falling Cheek
Sautee Nacoochee, GA 30571
(706)878-1905
Fax: (706)878-1802
E-mail: skylake@compuserve.com

Tom C. Davis & Associates, P.C.
3189 Perimeter Rd.
Valdosta, GA 31602
(912)247-9801
Fax: (912)244-7704
E-mail: mail@tcdcpa.com
Website: http://www.tcdcpa.com/

Illinois

TWD and Associates
431 S Patton
Arlington Heights, IL 60005
(847)398-6410
Fax: (847)255-5095
E-mail: tdoo@aol.com

Management Planning Associates Inc.
2275 Half Day Rd., Ste. 350
Bannockburn, IL 60015-1277
(847)945-2421
Fax: (847)945-2425

Phil Faris Associates
86 Old Mill Ct.
Barrington, IL 60010
(847)382-4888
Fax: (847)382-4890
E-mail: pfaris@meginsnet.net

Seven Continents Technology
787 Stonebridge
Buffalo Grove, IL 60089
(708)577-9653
Fax: (708)870-1220

Grubb & Blue Inc.
2404 Windsor Pl.
Champaign, IL 61820
(217)366-0052
Fax: (217)356-0117

ACE Accounting Service Inc.
3128 N Bernard St.
Chicago, IL 60618
(773)463-7854
Fax: (773)463-7854

AON Consulting Worldwide
200 E Randolph St., 10th Fl.
Chicago, IL 60601
(312)381-4800
Free: 800-438-6487
Fax: (312)381-0240
Website: http://www.aon.com

FMS Consultants
5801 N Sheridan Rd., Ste. 3D
Chicago, IL 60660
(773)561-7362
Fax: (773)561-6274

Grant Thornton
800 1 Prudential Plz.
130 E Randolph St.
Chicago, IL 60601
(312)856-0001
Fax: (312)861-1340

E-mail: gtinfo@gt.com
Website: http://www.grantthornton.com

Kingsbury International Ltd.
5341 N Glenwood Ave.
Chicago, IL 60640
(773)271-3030
Fax: (773)728-7080
E-mail: jetlag@mcs.com
Website: http://www.kingbiz.com

MacDougall & Blake Inc.
1414 N Wells St., Ste. 311
Chicago, IL 60610-1306
(312)587-3330
Fax: (312)587-3699
E-mail: jblake@compuserve.com

James C. Osburn Ltd.
6445 N. Western Ave., Ste. 304
Chicago, IL 60645
(773)262-4428
Fax: (773)262-6755
E-mail: osburnltd@aol.com

Tarifero & Tazewell Inc.
211 S Clark
Chicago, IL 60690
(312)665-9714
Fax: (312)665-9716

Human Energy Design Systems
620 Roosevelt Dr.
Edwardsville, IL 62025
(618)692-0258
Fax: (618)692-0819

China Business Consultants Group
931 Dakota Cir.
Naperville, IL 60563
(630)778-7992
Fax: (630)778-7915
E-mail: cbcq@aol.com

Center for Workforce Effectiveness
500 Skokie Blvd., Ste. 222
Northbrook, IL 60062
(847)559-8777
Fax: (847)559-8778
E-mail: office@cwelink.com
Website: http://www.cwelink.com

Smith Associates
1320 White Mountain Dr.
Northbrook, IL 60062
(847)480-7200
Fax: (847)480-9828

Francorp Inc.
20200 Governors Dr.
Olympia Fields, IL 60461

(708)481-2900
Free: 800-372-6244
Fax: (708)481-5885
E-mail: francorp@aol.com
Website: http://www.francorpinc.com

Camber Business Strategy Consultants
1010 S Plum Tree Ct
Palatine, IL 60078-0986
(847)202-0101
Fax: (847)705-7510
E-mail: camber@ameritech.net

Partec Enterprise Group
5202 Keith Dr.
Richton Park, IL 60471
(708)503-4047
Fax: (708)503-9468

Rockford Consulting Group Ltd.
Century Plz., Ste. 206
7210 E State St.
Rockford, IL 61108
(815)229-2900
Free: 800-667-7495
Fax: (815)229-2612
E-mail:
rligus@RockfordConsulting.com
Website: http://
www.RockfordConsulting.com

RSM McGladrey Inc.
1699 E Woodfield Rd., Ste. 300
Schaumburg, IL 60173-4969
(847)413-6900
Fax: (847)517-7067
Website: http://www.rsmmcgladrey.com

A.D. Star Consulting
320 Euclid
Winnetka, IL 60093
(847)446-7827
Fax: (847)446-7827
E-mail: startwo@worldnet.att.net

Indiana

Modular Consultants Inc.
3109 Crabtree Ln.
Elkhart, IN 46514
(219)264-5761
Fax: (219)264-5761
E-mail: sasabo5313@aol.com

Midwest Marketing Research
PO Box 1077
Goshen, IN 46527
(219)533-0548
Fax: (219)533-0540
E-mail: 103365.654@compuserve

Ketchum Consulting Group
8021 Knue Rd., Ste. 112
Indianapolis, IN 46250
(317)845-5411
Fax: (317)842-9941

MDI Management Consulting
1519 Park Dr.
Munster, IN 46321
(219)838-7909
Fax: (219)838-7909

Iowa

McCord Consulting Group Inc.
4533 Pine View Dr. NE
PO Box 11024
Cedar Rapids, IA 52410
(319)378-0077
Fax: (319)378-1577
E-mail: smmccord@hom.com
Website: http://www.mccordgroup.com

Management Solutions L.C.
3815 Lincoln Pl. Dr.
Des Moines, IA 50312
(515)277-6408
Fax: (515)277-3506
E-mail: wasunimers@uswest.net

Grandview Marketing
15 Red Bridge Dr.
Sioux City, IA 51104
(712)239-3122
Fax: (712)258-7578
E-mail: eandrews@pionet.net

Kansas

Assessments in Action
513A N Mur-Len
Olathe, KS 66062
(913)764-6270
Free: (888)548-1504
Fax: (913)764-6495
E-mail: lowdene@qni.com
Website: http://www.assessments-in-action.com

Maine

Edgemont Enterprises
PO Box 8354
Portland, ME 04104
(207)871-8964
Fax: (207)871-8964

Pan Atlantic Consultants
5 Milk St.
Portland, ME 04101
(207)871-8622

Fax: (207)772-4842
E-mail: pmurphy@maine.rr.com
Website: http://www.panatlantic.net

Maryland

Clemons & Associates Inc.
5024-R Campbell Blvd.
Baltimore, MD 21236
(410)931-8100
Fax: (410)931-8111
E-mail: info@clemonsmgmt.com
Website: http://www.clemonsmgmt.com

Imperial Group Ltd.
305 Washington Ave., Ste. 204
Baltimore, MD 21204-6009
(410)337-8500
Fax: (410)337-7641

Leadership Institute
3831 Yolando Rd.
Baltimore, MD 21218
(410)366-9111
Fax: (410)243-8478
E-mail: behconsult@aol.com

Burdeshaw Associates Ltd.
4701 Sangamore Rd.
Bethesda, MD 20816-2508
(301)229-5800
Fax: (301)229-5045
E-mail: jstacy@burdeshaw.com
Website: http://www.burdeshaw.com

Michael E. Cohen
5225 Pooks Hill Rd., Ste. 1119 S
Bethesda, MD 20814
(301)530-5738
Fax: (301)530-2988
E-mail: mecohen@crosslink.net

World Development Group Inc.
5272 River Rd., Ste. 650
Bethesda, MD 20816-1405
(301)652-1818
Fax: (301)652-1250
E-mail: wdg@has.com
Website: http://www.worlddg.com

Swartz Consulting
PO Box 4301
Crofton, MD 21114-4301
(301)262-6728

Software Solutions International Inc.
9633 Duffer Way
Gaithersburg, MD 20886
(301)330-4136
Fax: (301)330-4136

Strategies Inc.
8 Park Center Ct., Ste. 200
Owings Mills, MD 21117
(410)363-6669
Fax: (410)363-1231
E-mail: strategies@strat1.com
Website: http://www.strat1.com

Hammer Marketing Resources
179 Inverness Rd.
Severna Park, MD 21146
(410)544-9191
Fax: (305)675-3277
E-mail: info@gohammer.com
Website: http://www.gohammer.com

Andrew Sussman & Associates
13731 Kretsinger
Smithsburg, MD 21783
(301)824-2943
Fax: (301)824-2943

Massachusetts

Geibel Marketing and Public Relations
PO Box 611
Belmont, MA 02478-0005
(617)484-8285
Fax: (617)489-3567
E-mail: jgeibel@geibelpr.com
Website: http://www.geibelpr.com

Bain & Co.
2 Copley Pl.
Boston, MA 02116
(617)572-2000
Fax: (617)572-2427
E-mail: corporate.inquiries@bain.com
Website: http://www.bain.com

Mehr & Co.
62 Kinnaird St.
Cambridge, MA 02139
(617)876-3311
Fax: (617)876-3023
E-mail: mehrco@aol.com

Monitor Company Inc.
2 Canal Park
Cambridge, MA 02141
(617)252-2000
Fax: (617)252-2100
Website: http://www.monitor.com

Information & Research Associates
PO Box 3121
Framingham, MA 01701
(508)788-0784

Walden Consultants Ltd.
252 Pond St.
Hopkinton, MA 01748

(508)435-4882
Fax: (508)435-3971
Website: http://
www.waldenconsultants.com

Jeffrey D. Marshall
102 Mitchell Rd.
Ipswich, MA 01938-1219
(508)356-1113
Fax: (508)356-2989

Consulting Resources Corp.
6 Northbrook Park
Lexington, MA 02420
(781)863-1222
Fax: (781)863-1441
E-mail: res@consultingresources.net
Website: http://
www.consultingresources.net

Planning Technologies Group L.L.C.
92 Hayden Ave.
Lexington, MA 02421
(781)778-4678
Fax: (781)861-1099
E-mail: ptg@plantech.com
Website: http://www.plantech.com

Kalba International Inc.
23 Sandy Pond Rd.
Lincoln, MA 01773
(781)259-9589
Fax: (781)259-1460
E-mail: info@kalbainternational.com
Website: http://
www.kalbainternational.com

VMB Associates Inc.
115 Ashland St.
Melrose, MA 02176
(781)665-0623
Fax: (425)732-7142
E-mail: vmbinc@aol.com

The Company Doctor
14 Pudding Stone Ln.
Mendon, MA 01756
(508)478-1747
Fax: (508)478-0520

Data and Strategies Group Inc.
190 N Main St.
Natick, MA 01760
(508)653-9990
Fax: (508)653-7799
E-mail: dsginc@dsggroup.com
Website: http://www.dsggroup.com

The Enterprise Group
73 Parker Rd.
Needham, MA 02494

(617)444-6631
Fax: (617)433-9991
E-mail: lsacco@world.std.com
Website: http://
www.enterprise-group.com

PSMJ Resources Inc.
10 Midland Ave.
Newton, MA 02458
(617)965-0055
Free: 800-537-7765
Fax: (617)965-5152
E-mail: psmj@tiac.net
Website: http://www.psmj.com

Scheur Management Group Inc.
255 Washington St., Ste. 100
Newton, MA 02458-1611
(617)969-7500
Fax: (617)969-7508
E-mail: smgnow@scheur.com
Website: http://www.scheur.com

I.E.E.E., Boston Section
240 Bear Hill Rd., 202B
Waltham, MA 02451-1017
(781)890-5294
Fax: (781)890-5290

Business Planning and Consulting Services
20 Beechwood Ter.
Wellesley, MA 02482
(617)237-9151
Fax: (617)237-9151

Michigan

Walter Frederick Consulting
1719 South Blvd.
Ann Arbor, MI 48104
(313)662-4336
Fax: (313)769-7505

Fox Enterprises
6220 W Freeland Rd.
Freeland, MI 48623
(517)695-9170
Fax: (517)695-9174
E-mail: foxjw@concentric.net
Website: http://www.cris.com/~foxjw

G.G.W. and Associates
1213 Hampton
Jackson, MI 49203
(517)782-2255
Fax: (517)782-2255

Altamar Group Ltd.
6810 S Cedar, Ste. 2-B
Lansing, MI 48911

(517)694-0910
Free: 800-443-2627
Fax: (517)694-1377

Sheffieck Consultants Inc.
23610 Greening Dr.
Novi, MI 48375-3130
(248)347-3545
Fax: (248)347-3530
E-mail: cfsheff@concentric.net

Rehmann, Robson PC
5800 Gratiot
Saginaw, MI 48605
(517)799-9580
Fax: (517)799-0227
Website: http://www.rrpc.com

Francis & Co.
17200 W 10 Mile Rd., Ste. 207
Southfield, MI 48075
(248)559-7600
Fax: (248)559-5249

Private Ventures Inc.
16000 W 9 Mile Rd., Ste. 504
Southfield, MI 48075
(248)569-1977
Free: 800-448-7614
Fax: (248)569-1838
E-mail: pventuresi@aol.com

JGK Associates
14464 Kerner Dr.
Sterling Heights, MI 48313
(810)247-9055
Fax: (248)822-4977
E-mail: kozlowski@home.com

Minnesota

Health Fitness Corp.
3500 W 80th St., Ste. 130
Bloomington, MN 55431
(612)831-6830
Fax: (612)831-7264

Consatech Inc.
PO Box 1047
Burnsville, MN 55337
(612)953-1088
Fax: (612)435-2966

Robert F. Knotek
14960 Ironwood Ct.
Eden Prairie, MN 55346
(612)949-2875

DRI Consulting
7715 Stonewood Ct.
Edina, MN 55439

(612)941-9656
Fax: (612)941-2693
E-mail: dric@dric.com
Website: http://www.dric.com

Markin Consulting
12072 87th Pl. N
Maple Grove, MN 55369
(612)493-3568
Fax: (612)493-5744
E-mail: markin@markinconsulting.com
Website: http://
www.markinconsulting.com

Minnesota Cooperation Office for Small Business & Job Creation Inc.
5001 W 80th St., Ste. 825
Minneapolis, MN 55437
(612)830-1230
Fax: (612)830-1232
E-mail: mncoop@msn.com
Website: http://www.mnco.org

Enterprise Consulting Inc.
PO Box 1111
Minnetonka, MN 55345
(612)949-5909
Fax: (612)906-3965

Amdahl International
724 1st Ave. SW
Rochester, MN 55902
(507)252-0402
Fax: (507)252-0402
E-mail: amdahl@best-service.com
Website: http://www.wp.com/amdahl_int

Power Systems Research
1365 Corporate Center Curve, 2nd Fl.
St. Paul, MN 55121
(612)905-8400
Free: (888)625-8612
Fax: (612)454-0760
E-mail: Barb@Powersys.com
Website: http://www.powersys.com

Missouri

Business Planning and Development Corp.
4030 Charlotte St.
Kansas City, MO 64110
(816)753-0495
E-mail: humph@bpdev.demon.co.uk
Website: http://www.bpdev.demon.co.uk

CFO Service
10336 Donoho
St. Louis, MO 63131
(314)750-2940

E-mail: jskae@cfoservice.com
Website: http://www.cfoservice.com

Nebraska

International Management Consulting Group Inc.
1309 Harlan Dr., Ste. 205
Bellevue, NE 68005
(402)291-4545
Free: 800-665-IMCG
Fax: (402)291-4343
E-mail: imcg@neonramp.com
Website: http://www.mgtconsulting.com

Heartland Management Consulting Group
1904 Barrington Pky.
Papillion, NE 68046
(402)339-2387
Fax: (402)339-1319

Nevada

The DuBois Group
865 Tahoe Blvd., Ste. 108
Incline Village, NV 89451
(775)832-0550
Free: 800-375-2935
Fax: (775)832-0556
E-mail: DuBoisGrp@aol.com

New Hampshire

Wolff Consultants
10 Buck Rd.
Hanover, NH 03755
(603)643-6015

BPT Consulting Associates Ltd.
12 Parmenter Rd., Ste. B-6
Londonderry, NH 03053
(603)437-8484
Free: (888)278-0030
Fax: (603)434-5388
E-mail: bptcons@tiac.net
Website: http://www.bptconsulting.com

New Jersey

Bedminster Group Inc.
1170 Rte. 22 E
Bridgewater, NJ 08807
(908)500-4155
Fax: (908)766-0780
E-mail: info@bedminstergroup.com
Website: http://
www.bedminstergroup.com
Fax: (202)806-1777
Terry Strong, Acting Regional Dir.

Delta Planning Inc.
PO Box 425
Denville, NJ 07834
(913)625-1742
Free: 800-672-0762
Fax: (973)625-3531
E-mail: DeltaP@worldnet.att.net
Website: http://deltaplanning.com

Kumar Associates Inc.
1004 Cumbermeade Rd.
Fort Lee, NJ 07024
(201)224-9480
Fax: (201)585-2343
E-mail: mail@kumarassociates.com
Website: http://kumarassociates.com

John Hall & Company Inc.
PO Box 187
Glen Ridge, NJ 07028
(973)680-4449
Fax: (973)680-4581
E-mail: jhcompany@aol.com

Market Focus
PO Box 402
Maplewood, NJ 07040
(973)378-2470
Fax: (973)378-2470
E-mail: mcss66@marketfocus.com

Vanguard Communications Corp.
100 American Rd.
Morris Plains, NJ 07950
(973)605-8000
Fax: (973)605-8329
Website: http://www.vanguard.net/

ConMar International Ltd.
1901 US Hwy. 130
North Brunswick, NJ 08902
(732)940-8347
Fax: (732)274-1199

KLW New Products
156 Cedar Dr.
Old Tappan, NJ 07675
(201)358-1300
Fax: (201)664-2594
E-mail: lrlarsen@usa.net
Website: http://
www.klwnewproducts.com

PA Consulting Group
315A Enterprise Dr.
Plainsboro, NJ 08536
(609)936-8300
Fax: (609)936-8811
E-mail: info@paconsulting.com
Website: http://www.pa-consulting.com

Aurora Marketing Management Inc.
66 Witherspoon St., Ste. 600
Princeton, NJ 08542
(908)904-1125
Fax: (908)359-1108
E-mail: aurora2@voicenet.com
Website: http://www.auroramarketing.net

Smart Business Supersite
88 Orchard Rd., CN-5219
Princeton, NJ 08543
(908)321-1924
Fax: (908)321-5156
E-mail: irv@smartbiz.com
Website: http://www.smartbiz.com

Tracelin Associates
1171 Main St., Ste. 6K
Rahway, NJ 07065
(732)381-3288

Schkeeper Inc.
130-6 Bodman Pl.
Red Bank, NJ 07701
(732)219-1965
Fax: (732)530-3703

Henry Branch Associates
2502 Harmon Cove Twr.
Secaucus, NJ 07094
(201)866-2008
Fax: (201)601-0101
E-mail: hbranch161@home.com

Robert Gibbons & Company Inc.
46 Knoll Rd.
Tenafly, NJ 07670-1050
(201)871-3933
Fax: (201)871-2173
E-mail: crisisbob@aol.com

PMC Management Consultants Inc.
6 Thistle Ln.
Three Bridges, NJ 08887-0332
(908)788-1014
Free: 800-PMC-0250
Fax: (908)806-7287
E-mail: int@pmc-management.com
Website: http://
www.pmc-management.com

R.W. Bankart & Associates
20 Valley Ave., Ste. D-2
Westwood, NJ 07675-3607
(201)664-7672

New Mexico

Vondle & Associates Inc.
4926 Calle de Tierra, NE
Albuquerque, NM 87111

(505)292-8961
Fax: (505)296-2790
E-mail: vondle@aol.com

InfoNewMexico
2207 Black Hills Rd., NE
Rio Rancho, NM 87124
(505)891-2462
Fax: (505)896-8971

New York

Powers Research and Training Institute
PO Box 78
Bayville, NY 11709
(516)628-2250
Fax: (516)628-2252
E-mail: powercocch@compuserve.com
Website: http://www.nancypowers.com

Consortium House
296 Wittenberg Rd.
Bearsville, NY 12409
(845)679-8867
Fax: (845)679-9248
E-mail: eugenegs@aol.com
Website: http://www.chpub.com

Progressive Finance Corp.
3549 Tiemann Ave.
Bronx, NY 10469
(718)405-9029
Free: 800-225-8381
Fax: (718)405-1170

Wave Hill Associates Inc.
2621 Palisade Ave., Ste. 15-C
Bronx, NY 10463
(718)549-7368
Fax: (718)601-9670
E-mail: pepper@compuserve.com

Management Insight
96 Arlington Rd.
Buffalo, NY 14221
(716)631-3319
Fax: (716)631-0203
E-mail:
michalski@foodserviceinsight.com
Website: http://
www.foodserviceinsight.com

**Samani International Enterprises,
Marions Panyaught Consultancy**
2028 Parsons
Flushing, NY 11357-3436
(917)287-8087
Fax: 800-873-8939
E-mail: vjp2@biostrategist.com
Website: http://www.biostrategist.com

Marketing Resources Group
71-58 Austin St.
Forest Hills, NY 11375
(718)261-8882

**Mangabay Business Plans
& Development**
Subsidiary of Innis Asset Allocation
125-10 Queens Blvd., Ste. 2202
Kew Gardens, NY 11415
(905)527-1947
Fax: 509-472-1935
E-mail: mangabay@mangabay.com
Website: http://www.mangabay.com
Lee Toh, Managing Partner

ComputerEase Co.
1301 Monmouth Ave.
Lakewood, NY 08701
(212)406-9464
Fax: (914)277-5317
E-mail: crawfordc@juno.com

Boice Dunham Group
30 W 13th St.
New York, NY 10011
(212)924-2200
Fax: (212)924-1108

Elizabeth Capen
27 E 95th St.
New York, NY 10128
(212)427-7654
Fax: (212)876-3190

Haver Analytics
60 E 42nd St., Ste. 2424
New York, NY 10017
(212)986-9300
Fax: (212)986-5857
E-mail: data@haver.com
Website: http://www.haver.com

The Jordan, Edmiston Group Inc.
150 E 52nd Ave., 18th Fl.
New York, NY 10022
(212)754-0710
Fax: (212)754-0337

KPMG International
345 Park Ave.
New York, NY 10154-0102
(212)758-9700
Fax: (212)758-9819
Website: http://www.kpmg.com

Mahoney Cohen Consulting Corp.
111 W 40th St., 12th Fl.
New York, NY 10018
(212)490-8000
Fax: (212)790-5913

Management Practice Inc.
342 Madison Ave.
New York, NY 10173-1230
(212)867-7948
Fax: (212)972-5188
Website: http://www.mpiweb.com

Moseley Associates Inc.
342 Madison Ave., Ste. 1414
New York, NY 10016
(212)213-6673
Fax: (212)687-1520

Practice Development Counsel
60 Sutton Pl. S
New York, NY 10022
(212)593-1549
Fax: (212)980-7940
E-mail: pwhaserot@pdcounsel.com
Website: http://www.pdcounsel.com

Unique Value International Inc.
575 Madison Ave., 10th Fl.
New York, NY 10022-1304
(212)605-0590
Fax: (212)605-0589

The Van Tulleken Co.
126 E 56th St.
New York, NY 10022
(212)355-1390
Fax: (212)755-3061
E-mail: newyork@vantulleken.com

Vencon Management Inc.
301 W 53rd St.
New York, NY 10019
(212)581-8787
Fax: (212)397-4126
Website: http://www.venconinc.com

Werner International Inc.
55 E 52nd, 29th Fl.
New York, NY 10055
(212)909-1260
Fax: (212)909-1273
E-mail: richard.downing@rgh.com
Website: http://www.wernertex.com

Zimmerman Business Consulting Inc.
44 E 92nd St., Ste. 5-B
New York, NY 10128
(212)860-3107
Fax: (212)860-7730
E-mail: ljzzbci@aol.com
Website: http://www.zbcinc.com

Overton Financial
7 Allen Rd.
Peekskill, NY 10566
(914)737-4649
Fax: (914)737-4696

Stromberg Consulting
2500 Westchester Ave.
Purchase, NY 10577
(914)251-1515
Fax: (914)251-1562
E-mail:
strategy@stromberg_consulting.com
Website: http://
www.stromberg_consulting.com

Innovation Management Consulting Inc.
209 Dewitt Rd.
Syracuse, NY 13214-2006
(315)425-5144
Fax: (315)445-8989
E-mail: missonneb@axess.net

M. Clifford Agress
891 Fulton St.
Valley Stream, NY 11580
(516)825-8955
Fax: (516)825-8955

Destiny Kinal Marketing Consultancy
105 Chemung St.
Waverly, NY 14892
(607)565-8317
Fax: (607)565-4083

Valutis Consulting Inc.
5350 Main St., Ste. 7
Williamsville, NY 14221-5338
(716)634-2553
Fax: (716)634-2554
E-mail: valutis@localnet.com
Website: http://www.valutisconsulting.com

North Carolina

Best Practices L.L.C.
6320 Quadrangle Dr., Ste. 200
Chapel Hill, NC 27514
(919)403-0251
Fax: (919)403-0144
E-mail: best@best:in/class
Website: http://www.best-in-class.com

Norelli & Co.
Bank of America Corporate Ctr.
100 N Tryon St., Ste. 5160
Charlotte, NC 28202-4000
(704)376-5484
Fax: (704)376-5485
E-mail: consult@norelli.com
Website: http://www.norelli.com

North Dakota

Center for Innovation
4300 Dartmouth Dr.
PO Box 8372

Grand Forks, ND 58202
(701)777-3132
Fax: (701)777-2339
E-mail: bruce@innovators.net
Website: http://www.innovators.net

Ohio

Transportation Technology Services
208 Harmon Rd.
Aurora, OH 44202
(330)562-3596

Empro Systems Inc.
4777 Red Bank Expy., Ste. 1
Cincinnati, OH 45227-1542
(513)271-2042
Fax: (513)271-2042

Alliance Management International Ltd.
1440 Windrow Ln.
Cleveland, OH 44147-3200
(440)838-1922
Fax: (440)838-0979
E-mail: bgruss@amiltd.com
Website: http://www.amiltd.com

Bozell Kamstra Public Relations
1301 E 9th St., Ste. 3400
Cleveland, OH 44114
(216)623-1511
Fax: (216)623-1501
E-mail:
jfeniger@cleveland.bozellkamstra.com
Website: http://www.bozellkamstra.com

Cory Dillon Associates
111 Schreyer Pl. E
Columbus, OH 43214
(614)262-8211
Fax: (614)262-3806

Holcomb Gallagher Adams
300 Marconi, Ste. 303
Columbus, OH 43215
(614)221-3343
Fax: (614)221-3367
E-mail: riadams@acme.freenet.oh.us

Young & Associates
PO Box 711
Kent, OH 44240
(330)678-0524
Free: 800-525-9775
Fax: (330)678-6219
E-mail: online@younginc.com
Website: http://www.younginc.com

Robert A. Westman & Associates
8981 Inversary Dr. SE
Warren, OH 44484-2551

(330)856-4149
Fax: (330)856-2564

Oklahoma

Innovative Partners L.L.C.
4900 Richmond Sq., Ste. 100
Oklahoma City, OK 73118
(405)840-0033
Fax: (405)843-8359
E-mail: ipartners@juno.com

Oregon

INTERCON - The International Converting Institute
5200 Badger Rd.
Crooked River Ranch, OR 97760
(541)548-1447
Fax: (541)548-1618
E-mail:
johnbowler@crookedriverranch.com

Talbott ARM
HC 60, Box 5620
Lakeview, OR 97630
(541)635-8587
Fax: (503)947-3482

Management Technology Associates Ltd.
2768 SW Sherwood Dr, Ste. 105
Portland, OR 97201-2251
(503)224-5220
Fax: (503)224-5334
E-mail: lcuster@mta-ltd.com
Website: http://www.mgmt-tech.com

Pennsylvania

Healthscope Inc.
400 Lancaster Ave.
Devon, PA 19333
(610)687-6199
Fax: (610)687-6376
E-mail: health@voicenet.com
Website: http://www.healthscope.net/

Elayne Howard & Associates Inc.
3501 Masons Mill Rd., Ste. 501
Huntingdon Valley, PA 19006-3509
(215)657-9550

GRA Inc.
115 West Ave., Ste. 201
Jenkintown, PA 19046
(215)884-7500
Fax: (215)884-1385
E-mail: gramail@gra-inc.com
Website: http://www.gra-inc.com

Mifflin County Industrial Development Corp.
Mifflin County Industrial Plz.
6395 SR 103 N
Bldg. 50
Lewistown, PA 17044
(717)242-0393
Fax: (717)242-1842
E-mail: mcide@acsworld.net

Autech Products
1289 Revere Rd.
Morrisville, PA 19067
(215)493-3759
Fax: (215)493-9791
E-mail: autech4@yahoo.com

Advantage Associates
434 Avon Dr.
Pittsburgh, PA 15228
(412)343-1558
Fax: (412)362-1684
E-mail: ecocba1@aol.com

Regis J. Sheehan & Associates
Pittsburgh, PA 15220
(412)279-1207

James W. Davidson Company Inc.
23 Forest View Rd.
Wallingford, PA 19086
(610)566-1462

Puerto Rico

Diego Chevere & Co.
Metro Parque 7, Ste. 204
Metro Office
Caparra Heights, PR 00920
(787)774-9595
Fax: (787)774-9566
E-mail: dcco@coqui.net

Manuel L. Porrata and Associates
898 Munoz Rivera Ave., Ste. 201
San Juan, PR 00927
(787)765-2140
Fax: (787)754-3285
E-mail:
m_porrata@manuelporrata.com
Website: http://manualporrata.com

South Carolina

Aquafood Business Associates
PO Box 13267
Charleston, SC 29422
(843)795-9506
Fax: (843)795-9477
E-mail: rraba@aol.com

Profit Associates Inc.
PO Box 38026
Charleston, SC 29414
(803)763-5718
Fax: (803)763-5719
E-mail: bobrog@awod.com
Website: http://www.awod.com/gallery/
business/proasc

Strategic Innovations International
12 Executive Ct.
Lake Wylie, SC 29710
(803)831-1225
Fax: (803)831-1177
E-mail: stratinnov@aol.com
Website: http://
www.strategicinnovations.com

Minus Stage
Box 4436
Rock Hill, SC 29731
(803)328-0705
Fax: (803)329-9948

Tennessee

Daniel Petchers & Associates
8820 Fernwood CV
Germantown, TN 38138
(901)755-9896

Business Choices
1114 Forest Harbor, Ste. 300
Hendersonville, TN 37075-9646
(615)822-8692
Free: 800-737-8382
Fax: (615)822-8692
E-mail: bz-ch@juno.com

RCFA Healthcare Management Services L.L.C.
9648 Kingston Pke., Ste. 8
Knoxville, TN 37922
(865)531-0176
Free: 800-635-4040
Fax: (865)531-0722
E-mail: info@rcfa.com
Website: http://www.rcfa.com

Growth Consultants of America
3917 Trimble Rd.
Nashville, TN 37215
(615)383-0550
Fax: (615)269-8940
E-mail: 70244.451@compuserve.com

Texas

Integrated Cost Management Systems Inc.
2261 Brookhollow Plz. Dr., Ste. 104
Arlington, TX 76006

(817)633-2873
Fax: (817)633-3781
E-mail: abm@icms.net
Website: http://www.icms.net

Lori Williams
1000 Leslie Ct.
Arlington, TX 76012
(817)459-3934
Fax: (817)459-3934

Business Resource Software Inc.
2013 Wells Branch Pky., Ste. 305
Austin, TX 78728
Free: 800-423-1228
Fax: (512)251-4401
E-mail: info@brs-inc.com
Website: http://www.brs-inc.com

Erisa Adminstrative Services Inc.
12325 Hymeadow Dr., Bldg. 4
Austin, TX 78750-1847
(512)250-9020
Fax: (512)250-9487
Website: http://www.cserisa.com

R. Miller Hicks & Co.
1011 W 11th St.
Austin, TX 78703
(512)477-7000
Fax: (512)477-9697
E-mail: millerhicks@rmhicks.com
Website: http://www.rmhicks.com

Pragmatic Tactics Inc.
3303 Westchester Ave.
College Station, TX 77845
(409)696-5294
Free: 800-570-5294
Fax: (409)696-4994
E-mail: ptactics@aol.com
Website: http://www.ptatics.com

Perot Systems
12404 Park Central Dr.
Dallas, TX 75251
(972)340-5000
Free: 800-688-4333
Fax: (972)455-4100
E-mail: corp.comm@ps.net
Website: http://www.perotsystems.com

ReGENERATION Partners
3838 Oak Lawn Ave.
Dallas, TX 75219
(214)559-3999
Free: 800-406-1112
E-mail: info@regeneration-partner.com
Website: http://
www.regeneration-partners.com

High Technology Associates - Division of Global Technologies Inc.
1775 St. James Pl., Ste. 105
Houston, TX 77056
(713)963-9300
Fax: (713)963-8341
E-mail: hta@infohwy.com

MasterCOM
103 Thunder Rd.
Kerrville, TX 78028
(830)895-7990
Fax: (830)443-3428
E-mail:
jmstubblefield@mastertraining.com
Website: http://www.mastertraining.com

PROTEC
4607 Linden Pl.
Pearland, TX 77584
(281)997-9872
Fax: (281)997-9895
E-mail: p.oman@ix.netcom.com

Bastian Public Relations
614 San Dizier
San Antonio, TX 78232
(210)404-1839
E-mail: lisa@bastianpr.com
Website: http://www.bastianpr.com
Lisa Bastian CBC

Business Strategy Development Consultants
PO Box 690365
San Antonio, TX 78269
(210)696-8000
Free: 800-927-BSDC
Fax: (210)696-8000

Tom Welch, CPC
6900 San Pedro Ave., Ste. 147
San Antonio, TX 78216-6207
(210)737-7022
Fax: (210)737-7022
E-mail: bplan@iamerica.net
Website: http://www.moneywords.com

Utah

Business Management Resource
PO Box 521125
Salt Lake City, UT 84152-1125
(801)272-4668
Fax: (801)277-3290
E-mail: pingfong@worldnet.att.net

Virginia

Tindell Associates
209 Oxford Ave.
Alexandria, VA 22301

(703)683-0109
Fax: 703-783-0219
E-mail: scott@tindell.net
Website: http://www.tindell.net
Scott Lockett, President

Elliott B. Jaffa
2530-B S Walter Reed Dr.
Arlington, VA 22206
(703)931-0040
E-mail: thetrainingdoctor@excite.com
Website: http://www.tregistry.com/
jaffa.htm

Koach Enterprises - USA
5529 N 18th St.
Arlington, VA 22205
(703)241-8361
Fax: (703)241-8623

Federal Market Development
5650 Chapel Run Ct.
Centreville, VA 20120-3601
(703)502-8930
Free: 800-821-5003
Fax: (703)502-8929

Huff, Stuart & Carlton
2107 Graves Mills Rd., Ste. C
Forest, VA 24551
(804)316-9356
Free: (888)316-9356
Fax: (804)316-9357
Website: http://www.wealthmgt.net

AMX International Inc.
1420 Spring Hill Rd. , Ste. 600
McLean, VA 22102-3006
(703)690-4100
Fax: (703)643-1279
E-mail: amxmail@amxi.com
Website: http://www.amxi.com

Charles Scott Pugh (Investor)
4101 Pittaway Dr.
Richmond, VA 23235-1022
(804)560-0979
Fax: (804)560-4670

John C. Randall and Associates Inc.
PO Box 15127
Richmond, VA 23227
(804)746-4450
Fax: (804)730-8933
E-mail: randalljcx@aol.com
Website: http://www.johncrandall.com

McLeod & Co.
410 1st St.
Roanoke, VA 24011
(540)342-6911

Fax: (540)344-6367
Website: http://www.mcleodco.com/

Salzinger & Company Inc.
8000 Towers Crescent Dr., Ste. 1350
Vienna, VA 22182
(703)442-5200
Fax: (703)442-5205
E-mail: info@salzinger.com
Website: http://www.salzinger.com

The Small Business Counselor
12423 Hedges Run Dr., Ste. 153
Woodbridge, VA 22192
(703)490-6755
Fax: (703)490-1356

Washington

Burlington Consultants
10900 NE 8th St., Ste. 900
Bellevue, WA 98004
(425)688-3060
Fax: (425)454-4383
E-mail:
partners@burlingtonconsultants.com
Website: http://
www.burlingtonconsultants.com

Perry L. Smith Consulting
800 Bellevue Way NE, Ste. 400
Bellevue, WA 98004-4208
(425)462-2072
Fax: (425)462-5638

St. Charles Consulting Group
1420 NW Gilman Blvd.
Issaquah, WA 98027
(425)557-8708
Fax: (425)557-8731
E-mail: info@stcharlesconsulting.com
Website: http://
www.stcharlesconsulting.com

Independent Automotive Training Services
PO Box 334
Kirkland, WA 98083
(425)822-5715
E-mail: ltunney@autosvccon.com
Website: http://www.autosvccon.com

Kahle Associate Inc.
6203 204th Dr. NE
Redmond, WA 98053
(425)836-8763
Fax: (425)868-3770
E-mail: randykahle@kahleassociates.com
Website: http://
www.kahleassociates.com

Dan Collin
3419 Wallingord Ave N, No. 2
Seattle, WA 98103
(206)634-9469
E-mail: dc@dancollin.com
Website: http://members.home.net/dcollin/

ECG Management Consultants Inc.
1111 3rd Ave., Ste. 2700
Seattle, WA 98101-3201
(206)689-2200
Fax: (206)689-2209
E-mail: ecg@ecgmc.com
Website: http://www.ecgmc.com

Northwest Trade Adjustment Assistance Center
900 4th Ave., Ste. 2430
Seattle, WA 98164-1001
(206)622-2730
Free: 800-667-8087
Fax: (206)622-1105
E-mail: matchingfunds@nwtaac.org
Website: http://www.taacenters.org

Business Planning Consultants
S 3510 Ridgeview Dr.
Spokane, WA 99206
(509)928-0332
Fax: (509)921-0842
E-mail: bpci@nextdim.com

West Virginia

Business and Marketing Plans
1687 Robert C. Byrd Dr.
Beckley, WV 25801
(304)252-0324
Fax: (304)252-0470
E-mail: MattStanley_1@charter.net
Website: http://
www.BusinessandMarketingPlans.com
Dr. Stanley

Wisconsin

White & Associates Inc.
5349 Somerset Ln. S
Greenfield, WI 53221
(414)281-7373
Fax: (414)281-7006
E-mail: wnaconsult@aol.com

SMALL BUSINESS ADMINISTRATION REGIONAL OFFICES

This section contains a listing of Small Business Administration offices arranged numerically by region. Service areas are provided. Contact the appropriate office for

a referral to the nearest field office, or visit the Small Business Administration online at www.sba.gov.

Region 1

U.S. Small Business Administration
10 Causeway St.
Boston, MA 02222-1093
Phone: (617)565-8415
Fax: (617)565-8420
Serves Connecticut, Maine, Massachusetts, New Hampshire, Rhode Island, and Vermont.

Region 2

U.S. Small Business Administration
26 Federal Plaza, Ste. 3108
New York, NY 10278
Phone: (212)264-1450
Fax: (212)264-0038
Serves New Jersey, New York, Puerto Rico, and the Virgin Islands.

Region 3

Serves Delaware, the District of Columbia, Maryland, Pennsylvania, Virginia, and West Virginia. For the nearest field office, visit the Small Business Administration online at www.sba.gov.

Region 4

U.S. Small Business Administration
233 Peachtree St. NE
Harris Tower 1800
Atlanta, GA 30303
Phone: (404)331-4999
Fax: (404)331-2354
Serves Alabama, Florida, Georgia, Kentucky, Mississippi, North Carolina, South Carolina, and Tennessee.

Region 5

U.S. Small Business Administration
500 W. Madison St., Ste. 1240
Chicago, IL 60661-2511
Phone: (312)353-5000
Fax: (312)353-3426
Serves Illinois, Indiana, Michigan, Minnesota, Ohio, and Wisconsin.

Region 6

U.S. Small Business Administration
4300 Amon Carter Blvd.
Dallas/Fort Worth, TX 76155

Phone: (817)885-6581
Fax: (817)885-6588
Serves Arkansas, Louisiana, New Mexico, Oklahoma, and Texas.

Region 7

U.S. Small Business Administration
323 W. 8th St., Ste. 307
Kansas City, MO 64105-1500
Phone: (816)374-6380
Fax: (816)374-6339
Serves Iowa, Kansas, Missouri, and Nebraska.

Region 8

U.S. Small Business Administration
721 19th St., Ste. 400
Denver, CO 80202
Phone: (303)844-0500
Fax: (303)844-0506
Serves Colorado, Montana, North Dakota, South Dakota, Utah, and Wyoming.

Region 9

U.S. Small Business Administration
455 Market St., Ste. 2200
San Francisco, CA 94105
Phone: (415)744-2118
Fax: (415)744-2119
Serves American Samoa, Arizona, California, Guam, Hawaii, Nevada, and the Trust Territory of the Pacific Islands.

Region 10

U.S. Small Business Administration
1200 6th Ave., Ste. 1805
Seattle, WA 98101-1128
Phone: (206)553-5676
Fax: (206)553-2872
Serves Alaska, Idaho, Oregon, and Washington.

SMALL BUSINESS DEVELOPMENT CENTERS

This section contains a listing of all Small Business Development Centers, organized alphabetically by state/U.S. territory, then by city, then by agency name.

Alabama

Auburn University
SBDC
108 College of Business
Auburn, AL 36849-5243

(334)844-4220
Fax: (334)844-4268
Garry Hannem, Dir.

Alabama Small Business Procurement System
University Of Alabama at Birmingham
SBDC
1717 11th Ave. S., Ste. 419
Birmingham, AL 35294-4410
(205)934-7260
Fax: (205)934-7645
Charles Hobson, Procurement Dir.

University of Alabama at Birmingham
Alabama Small Business Development Consortium
SBDC
1717 11th Ave. S., Ste. 419
Birmingham, AL 35294-4410
(205)934-7260
Fax: (205)934-7645
John Sandefur, State Dir.

University of Alabama at Birmingham
SBDC
1601 11th Ave. S.
Birmingham, AL 35294-2180
(205)934-6760
Fax: (205)934-0538
Brenda Walker, Dir.

University of North Alabama
Small Business Development Center
Box 5248, Keller Hall
Florence, AL 35632-0001
(205)760-4629
Fax: (205)760-4813

Alabama A & M University
University of Alabama at Huntsville
NE Alabama Regional Small Business Development Center
PO Box 168
225 Church St., NW
Huntsville, AL 35804-0168
(205)535-2061
Fax: (205)535-2050
Jeff Thompson, Dir.

Jacksonville State University
Small Business Development Center
114 Merrill Hall
700 Pelham Rd. N.
Jacksonville, AL 36265
(205)782-5271
Fax: (205)782-5179
Pat Shaddix, Dir.

University of West Alabama
SBDC
Station 35
Livingston, AL 35470
(205)652-3665
Fax: (205)652-3516
Paul Garner, Dir.

University of South Alabama
Small Business Development Center
College of Business, Rm. 8
Mobile, AL 36688
(334)460-6004
Fax: (334)460-6246

Alabama State University
SBDC
915 S. Jackson St.
Montgomery, AL 36104-5714
(334)229-4138
Fax: (334)269-1102
Lorenza G. Patrick, Dir.

Troy State University
Small Business Development Center
Bibb Graves, Rm. 102
Troy, AL 36082-0001
(205)670-3771
Fax: (205)670-3636
Janet W. Kervin, Dir.

University of Alabama
Alabama International Trade Center
Small Business Development Center
Bidgood Hall, Rm. 250
Box 870397
Tuscaloosa, AL 35487-0396
(205)348-7011
Fax: (205)348-9644
Paavo Hanninen, Dir.

Alaska

University of Alaska (Fairbanks)
Small Business Development Center
510 Second Ave., Ste. 101
Fairbanks, AK 99701
(907)474-6700
Fax: (907)474-1139
Billie Ray Allen, Dir.

University of Alaska (Juneau)
Small Business Development Center
612 W. Willoughby Ave., Ste. A
Juneau, AK 99801
(907)463-1732
Fax: (907)463-3929
Norma Strickland, Acting Dir.

Kenai Peninsula Small Business Development Center
PO Box 3029
Kenai, AK 99611-3029
(907)283-3335
Fax: (907)283-3913
Mark Gregory

University of Alaska (Matanuska-Susitna)
Small Business Development Center
201 N. Lucile St., Ste. 2-A
Wasilla, AK 99654
(907)373-7232
Fax: (907)373-7234
Timothy Sullivan, Dir.

Arizona

Central Arizona College
Pinal County Small Business Development Center
8470 N. Overfield Rd.
Coolidge, AZ 85228
(520)426-4341
Fax: (520)426-4363
Carol Giordano, Dir.

Coconino County Community College
Small Business Development Center
3000 N. 4th St., Ste. 25
Flagstaff, AZ 86004
(520)526-5072
Fax: (520)526-8693
Mike Lainoff, Dir.

Northland Pioneer College
Small Business Development Center
PO Box 610
Holbrook, AZ 86025
(520)537-2976
Fax: (520)524-2227
Mark Engle, Dir.

Mohave Community College
Small Business Development Center
1971 Jagerson Ave.
Kingman, AZ 86401
(520)757-0894
Fax: (520)757-0836
Kathy McGehee, Dir.

Yavapai College
Small Business Development Center
Elks Building
117 E. Gurley St., Ste. 206
Prescott, AZ 86301
(520)778-3088
Fax: (520)778-3109
Richard Senopole, Director

Cochise College
Small Business Development Center
901 N. Colombo, Rm. 308
Sierra Vista, AZ 85635
(520)515-5478
Fax: (520)515-5437
E-mail: sbdc@trom.cochise.cc.az.us
Shelia Devoe Heidman, Dir.

Arizona Small Business Development Center Network
2411 W. 14th St., Ste. 132
Tempe, AZ 85281
(602)731-8720
Fax: (602)731-8729
E-mail: york@maricopa.bitnet
Michael York, State Dir.

Maricopa Community Colleges
Arizona Small Business Development Center Network
2411 W. 14th St., Ste. 132
Tempe, AZ 85281
(602)731-8720
Fax: (602)731-8729
Michael York, Dir.

Eastern Arizona College
Small Business Development Center
622 College Ave.
Thatcher, AZ 85552-0769
(520)428-8590
Fax: (520)428-8462
Greg Roers, Dir.

Pima Community College
Small Business Development and Training Center
4905-A E. Broadway Blvd., Ste. 101
Tucson, AZ 85709-1260
(520)206-4906
Fax: (520)206-4585
Linda Andrews, Dir.

Arizona Western College
Small Business Development Center
Century Plz., No. 152
281 W. 24th St.
Yuma, AZ 85364
(520)341-1650
Fax: (520)726-2636
John Lundin, Dir.

Arkansas

Henderson State University
Small Business Development Center
1100 Henderson St.
PO Box 7624

Arkadelphia, AR 71923
(870)230-5224
Fax: (870)230-5236
Jeff Doose, Dir.

Genesis Technology Incubator
SBDC Satellite Office
University of Arkansas - Engineering Research Center
Fayetteville, AR 72701-1201
(501)575-7473
Fax: (501)575-7446
Bob Penquite, Business Consultant

University of Arkansas at Fayetteville
Small Business Development Center
Business Administration Bldg., Ste. 106
Fayetteville, AR 72701
(501)575-5148
Fax: (501)575-4013
Ms. Jimmie Wilkins, Dir.

Small Business Development Center
1109 S. 16th St.
PO Box 2067
Ft. Smith, AR 72901
(501)785-1376
Fax: (501)785-1964
Vonelle Vanzant, Business Consultant

University of Arkansas at Little Rock, Regional Office (Fort Smith)
Small Business Development Center
1109 S. 16th St.
PO Box 2067
Ft. Smith, AR 72901
(501)785-1376
Fax: (501)785-1964
Byron Branch, Business Specialist

University of Arkansas at Little Rock, Regional Office (Harrison)
Small Business Development Center
818 Hwy. 62-65-412 N
PO Box 190
Harrison, AR 72601
(870)741-8009
Fax: (870)741-1905
Bob Penquite, Business Consultant

University of Arkansas at Little Rock, Regional Office (Hot Springs)
Small Business Development Center
835 Central Ave., Box 402-D
Hot Springs, AR 71901

(501)624-5448
Fax: (501)624-6632
Richard Evans, Business Consultant

Arkansas State University

Small Business Development Center
College of Business
Drawer 2650
Jonesboro, AR 72467
(870)972-3517
Fax: (501)972-3868
Herb Lawrence, Dir.

University of Arkansas at Little Rock SBDC
Little Rock Technology Center Bldg.
100 S. Main St., Ste. 401
Little Rock, AR 72201
(501)324-9043
Fax: (501)324-9049
Janet Nye, State Dir.

University of Arkansas at Little Rock, Regional Office (Magnolia)

Small Business Development Center
600 Bessie
PO Box 767
Magnolia, AR 71753
(870)234-4030
Fax: (870)234-0135
Mr. Lairie Kincaid, Business Consultant

University of Arkansas at Little Rock, Regional Office (Pine Bluff)

Small Business Development Center
The Enterprise Center III
400 Main, Ste. 117
Pine Bluff, AR 71601
(870)536-0654
Fax: (870)536-7713
Russell Barker, Business Consultant

University of Arkansas at Little Rock, Regional Office (Stuttgart)

Small Business Development Center
301 S. Grand, Ste. 101
PO Box 289
Stuttgart, AR 72160
(870)673-8707
Fax: (870)673-8707
Larry Lefler, Business Consultant

Mid-South Community College

SBDC
2000 W. Broadway
PO Box 2067
West Memphis, AR 72303-2067
(870)733-6767

California

Central Coast Small Business Development Center
6500 Soquel Dr.
Aptos, CA 95003
(408)479-6136
Fax: (408)479-6166
Teresa Thomae, Dir.

Sierra College Small Business Development Center
560 Wall St., Ste. J
Auburn, CA 95603
(916)885-5488
Fax: (916)823-2831
Mary Wollesen, Dir.

Weill Institute Small Business Development Center
1706 Chester Ave., Ste. 200
Bakersfield, CA 93301
(805)322-5881
Fax: (805)322-5663
Jeffrey Johnson, Dir.

Butte College
Small Business Development Center
260 Cohasset Rd., Ste. A
Chico, CA 95926
(916)895-9017
Fax: (916)895-9099
Kay Zimmerlee, Dir.

Southwestern College
Small Business Development and International Trade Center
900 Otay Lakes Rd., Bldg. 1600
Chula Vista, CA 91910
(619)482-6393
Fax: (619)482-6402
Mary Wylie, Dir.

Contra Costa SBDC
2425 Bisso Ln., Ste. 200
Concord, CA 94520
(510)646-5377
Fax: (510)646-5299
Debra Longwood, Dir.

North Coast Small Business Development Center
207 Price Mall, Ste. 500
Crescent City, CA 95531
(707)464-2168
Fax: (707)465-6008
Fran Clark, Dir.

Imperial Valley Satellite SBDC
Town & Country Shopping Center
301 N. Imperial Ave., Ste. B
El Centro, CA 92243

(619)312-9800
Fax: (619)312-9838
Debbie Trujillo, Satellite Mgr.

Export SBDC/El Monte Outreach Center
10501 Valley Blvd., Ste. 106
El Monte, CA 91731
(818)459-4111
Fax: (818)443-0463
Charles Blythe, Manager

North Coast
Small Business Development Center
520 E St.
Eureka, CA 95501
(707)445-9720
Fax: (707)445-9652
Duff Heuttner, Bus. Counselor

Central California
Small Business Development Center
3419 W. Shaw Ave., Ste. 102
Fresno, CA 93711
(209)275-1223
Fax: (209)275-1499
Dennis Winans, Dir.

Gavilan College Small Business Development Center
7436 Monterey St.
Gilroy, CA 95020
(408)847-0373
Fax: (408)847-0393
Peter Graff, Dir.

Accelerate Technology Assistance
Small Business Development Center
4199 Campus Dr.
University Towers, Ste. 240
Irvine, CA 92612-4688
(714)509-2990
Fax: (714)509-2997
Tiffany Haugen, Dir.

Amador SBDC
222 N. Hwy. 49
PO Box 1077
Jackson, CA 95642
(209)223-0351
Fax: (209)223-5237
Ron Mittelbrunn, Mgr.

Greater San Diego Chamber of Commerce
Small Business Development Center
4275 Executive Sq., Ste. 920
La Jolla, CA 92037
(619)453-9388
Fax: (619)450-1997
Hal Lefkowitz, Dir.

Yuba College SBDC
PO Box 1566
15145 Lakeshore Dr.
Lakeport, CA 95453
(707)263-0330
Fax: (707)263-8516
George McQueen, Dir.

East Los Angeles SBDC
5161 East Pomona Blvd., Ste. 212
Los Angeles, CA 90022
(213)262-9797
Fax: (213)262-2704

Export Small Business Development Center of Southern California
110 E. 9th, Ste. A669
Los Angeles, CA 90079
(213)892-1111
Fax: (213)892-8232
Gladys Moreau, Dir.

South Central LA/Satellite SBDC
3650 Martin Luther King Blvd., Ste. 246
Los Angeles, CA 90008
(213)290-2832
Fax: (213)290-7191
Cope Norcross, Satellite Mgr.

Alpine SBDC
PO Box 265
3 Webster St.
Markleeville, CA 96120
(916)694-2475
Fax: (916)694-2478

Yuba/Sutter Satellite SBDC
10th and E St.
PO Box 262
Marysville, CA 95901
(916)749-0153
Fax: (916)749-0155
Sandra Brown-Abernathy, Dir.

Valley Sierra SBDC Merced Satellite
1632 N St.
Merced, CA 95340
(209)725-3800
Fax: (209)383-4959
Nick Starianoudakis, Satellite Mgr.

Valley Sierra Small Business Development Center
1012 11th St., Ste. 300
Modesto, CA 95354
(209)521-6177
Fax: (209)521-9373
Kelly Bearden, Dir.

Napa Valley College Small Business Development Center
1556 First St., Ste. 103
Napa, CA 94559
(707)253-3210
Fax: (707)253-3068
Chuck Eason, Dir.

Inland Empire Business Incubator SBDC
155 S. Memorial Dr.
Norton Air Force Base, CA 92509
(909)382-0065
Fax: (909)382-8543
Chuck Eason, Incubator Mgr.

East Bay Small Business Development Center
519 17th. St., Ste. 210
Oakland, CA 94612
(510)893-4114
Fax: (510)893-5532
Napoleon Britt, Dir.

International Trade Office SBDC
3282 E. Guasti Rd., Ste. 100
Ontario, CA 91761
(909)390-8071
Fax: (909)390-8077
John Hernandez, Trade Manager

Coachella Valley SBDC
Palm Springs Satellite Center
501 S. Palm Canyon Dr., Ste. 222
Palm Springs, CA 92264
(619)864-1311
Fax: (619)864-1319
Brad Mix, Satellite Mgr.

Pasadena Satellite SBDC
2061 N. Los Robles, Ste. 106
Pasadena, CA 91104
(818)398-9031
Fax: (818)398-3059
David Ryal, Satellite Mgr.

Pico Rivera SBDC
9058 E. Washington Blvd.
Pico Rivera, CA 90660
(310)942-9965
Fax: (310)942-9745
Beverly Taylor, Satellite Mgr.

Eastern Los Angeles County Small Business Development Center
375 S. Main St., Ste. 101
Pomona, CA 91766
(909)629-2247

Fax: (909)629-8310
Toni Valdez, Dir.

Pomona SBDC
375 S. Main St., Ste. 101
Pomona, CA 91766
(909)629-2247
Fax: (909)629-8310
Paul Hischar, Satellite Manager

Cascade Small Business Development Center
737 Auditorium Dr., Ste. A
Redding, CA 96001
(916)247-8100
Fax: (916)241-1712
Carole Enmark, Dir.

Inland Empire Small Business Development Center
1157 Spruce St.
Riverside, CA 92507
(909)781-2345
800-750-2353
Fax: (909)781-2353
Teri Ooms, Dir.

California Trade and Commerce Agency
California SBDC
801 K St., Ste. 1700
Sacramento, CA 95814
(916)324-5068
Fax: (916)322-5084
Kim Neri, State Dir.

Greater Sacramento SBDC
1410 Ethan Way
Sacramento, CA 95825
(916)563-3210
Fax: (916)563-3266
Cynthia Steimle, Director

Calaveras SBDC
PO Box 431
3 N. Main St.
San Andreas, CA 95249
(209)754-1834
Fax: (209)754-4107

San Francisco SBDC
711 Van Ness, Ste. 305
San Francisco, CA 94102
(415)561-1890
Fax: (415)561-1894
Tim Sprinkles, Director

Orange County Small Business Development Center
901 E. Santa Ana Blvd., Ste. 101
Santa Ana, CA 92701

(714)647-1172
Fax: (714)835-9008
Gregory Kishel, Dir.

**Southwest Los Angeles County
Westside Satellite
SBDC**
3233 Donald Douglas Loop S., Ste. C
Santa Monica, CA 90405
(310)398-8883
Fax: (310)398-3024
Sue Hunter, Admin. Asst.

**Redwood Empire Small Business
Development Center**
520 Mendocino Ave., Ste. 210
Santa Rosa, CA 95401
(707)524-1770
Fax: (707)524-1772
Charles Robbins, Dir.

**San Joaquin Delta College Small
Business Development Center**
445 N. San Joaquin, 2nd Fl.
Stockton, CA 95202
(209)474-5089
Fax: (209)474-5605
Gillian Murphy, Dir.

Silicon Valley SBDC
298 S. Sunnyvale Ave., Ste. 204
Sunnyvale, CA 94086
(408)736-0680
Fax: (408)736-0679
Eliza Minor, Director

**Southwest Los Angeles County Small
Business Development Center**
21221 Western Ave., Ste. 110
Torrance, CA 90501
(310)787-6466
Fax: (310)782-8607
Susan Hunter, Dir.

West Company SBDC
367 N. State St., Ste. 208
Ukiah, CA 95482
(707)468-3553
Fax: (707)468-3555
Sheilah Rogers, Director

**North Los Angeles Small Business
Development Center**
4717 Van Nuys Blvd., Ste. 201
Van Nuys, CA 91403-2100
(818)907-9922
Fax: (818)907-9890
Wilma Berglund, Dir.

Export SBDC Satellite Center
5700 Ralston St., Ste. 310
Ventura, CA 93003

(805)658-2688
Fax: (805)658-2252
Heather Wicka, Manager

Gold Coast SBDC
5700 Ralston St., Ste. 310
Ventura, CA 93003
(805)658-2688
Fax: (805)658-2252
Joe Higgins, Satellite Mgr.

**High Desert SBDC
Victorville Satellite Center**
15490 Civic Dr., Ste. 102
Victorville, CA 92392
(619)951-1592
Fax: (619)951-8929
Janice Harbaugh, Business Consultant

**Central California - Visalia Satellite
SBDC**
430 W. Caldwell Ave., Ste. D
Visalia, CA 93277
(209)625-3051
Fax: (209)625-3053
Randy Mason, Satellite Mgr.

Colorado

**Adams State College
Small Business Development Center**
School of Business, Rm. 105
Alamosa, CO 81102
(719)587-7372
Fax: (719)587-7603
Mary Hoffman, Dir.

**Community College of Aurora
Small Business Development Center**
9905 E. Colfax
Aurora, CO 80010-2119
(303)341-4849
Fax: (303)361-2953
E-mail: asbdc@henge.com
Randy Johnson, Dir.

**Boulder Chamber of Commerce
Small Business Development Center**
2440 Pearl St.
Boulder, CO 80302
(303)442-1475
Fax: (303)938-8837
Marilynn Force, Dir.

**Pueblo Community College
(Canon City)
Small Business Development Center**
3080 Main St.
Canon City, CO 81212
(719)275-5335

Fax: (719)275-4400
Elwin Boody, Dir.

**Pikes Peak Community College
Small Business Development Center
Colorado Springs Chamber
of Commerce**
CITTI Bldg.
1420 Austin Bluff Pkwy.
Colorado Springs, CO 80933
(719)592-1894
Fax: (719)533-0545
E-mail: sbdc@mail.uccs.edu
Iris Clark, Dir.

**Colorado Northwestern Community
College
Small Business Development Center**
50 College Dr.
Craig, CO 81625
(970)824-7078
Fax: (970)824-1134
Ken Farmer, Dir.

**Delta Montrose Vocational School
Small Business Development Center**
1765 US Hwy. 50
Delta, CO 81416
(970)874-8772
(888)234-7232
Fax: (970)874-8796
Bob Marshall, Dir.

**Community College of Denver
Greater Denver Chamber of Commerce
Small Business Development Center**
1445 Market St.
1445 Market St.
Denver, CO 80202
(303)620-8076
Fax: (303)534-3200
Tamela Lee, Dir.

**Office of Business Development
Colorado SBDC**
1625 Broadway, Ste. 1710
Denver, CO 80202
(303)892-3809
800-333-7798
Fax: (303)892-3848
Lee Ortiz, State Dir.

**Fort Lewis College
Small Business Development Center**
136-G Hesperus Hall
Durango, CO 81301-3999
(970)247-7009
Fax: (970)247-7623
Jim Reser, Dir.

**Front Range Community College
(Ft. Collins)
Small Business Development Center**
125 S. Howes, Ste. 105
Ft. Collins, CO 80521
(970)498-9295
Fax: (970)204-0385
Frank Pryor, Dir.

**Morgan Community College
(Ft. Morgan)
Small Business Development Center**
300 Main St.
Ft. Morgan, CO 80701
(970)867-3351
Fax: (970)867-3352
Dan Simon, Dir.

**Colorado Mountain College
(Glenwood Springs)
Small Business Development Center**
831 Grand Ave.
Glenwood Springs, CO 81601
(970)928-0120
800-621-1647
Fax: (970)947-9324
Alisa Zimmerman, Dir.

Small Business Development Center
1726 Cole Blvd., Bldg. 22, Ste. 310
Golden, CO 80401
(303)277-1840
Fax: (303)277-1899
Jayne Reiter, Dir.

**Mesa State College
Small Business Development Center**
304 W. Main St.
Grand Junction, CO 81505-1606
(970)243-5242
Fax: (970)241-0771
Julie Morey, Dir.

**Aims Community College
Greeley/Weld Chamber of Commerce
Small Business Development Center**
902 7th Ave.
Greeley, CO 80631
(970)352-3661
Fax: (970)352-3572
Ron Anderson, Dir.

**Red Rocks Community College Small
Business Development Center**
777 S. Wadsworth Blvd., Ste. 254
Bldg. 4
Lakewood, CO 80226
(303)987-0710
Fax: (303)987-1331
Jayne Reiter, Acting Dir.

**Lamar Community College
Small Business Development Center**
2400 S. Main
Lamar, CO 81052
(719)336-8141
Fax: (719)336-2448
Dan Minor, Dir.

**Small Business Development Center
Arapahoe Community College
South Metro Chamber of Commerce**
7901 S. Park Plz., Ste. 110
Littleton, CO 80120
(303)795-5855
Fax: (303)795-7520
Selma Kristel, Dir.

**Pueblo Community College Small
Business Development Center**
900 W. Orman Ave.
Pueblo, CO 81004
(719)549-3224
Fax: (719)549-3338
Rita Friberg, Dir.

**Morgan Community College (Stratton)
Small Business Development Center**
PO Box 28
Stratton, CO 80836
(719)348-5596
Fax: (719)348-5887
Roni Carr, Dir.

**Trinidad State Junior College
Small Business Development Center**
136 W. Main St.
Davis Bldg.
Trinidad, CO 81082
(719)846-5645
Fax: (719)846-4550
Dennis O'Connor, Dir.

**Front Range Community College
(Westminster)
Small Business Development Center**
3645 W. 112th Ave.
Westminster, CO 80030
(303)460-1032
Fax: (303)469-7143
Leo Giles, Dir.

Connecticut

**Bridgeport Regional Business Council
Small Business Development Center**
10 Middle St., 14th Fl.
Bridgeport, CT 06604-4229
(203)330-4813
Fax: (203)366-0105
Juan Scott, Dir.

**Quinebaug Valley Community
Technical College
Small Business Development Center**
742 Upper Maple St.
Danielson, CT 06239-1440
(860)774-1133
Fax: (860)774-7768
Roger Doty, Dir.

**University of Connecticut (Groton)
Small Business Development Center**
Administration Bldg., Rm. 300
1084 Shennecossett Rd.
Groton, CT 06340-6097
(860)405-9009
Fax: (860)405-9041
Louise Kahler, Dir.

**Middlesex County Chamber
of Commerce
SBDC**
393 Main St.
Middletown, CT 06457
(860)344-2158
Fax: (860)346-1043
John Serignese

**Greater New Haven Chamber
of Commerce
Small Business Development Center**
195 Church St.
New Haven, CT 06510-2009
(203)782-4390
Fax: (203)787-6730
Pete Rivera, Regional Dir.

**Southwestern Area Commerce and
Industry Association (SACIA)
Small Business Development Center**
1 Landmark Sq., Ste. 230
Stamford, CT 06901
(203)359-3220
Fax: (203)967-8294
Harvey Blomberg, Dir.

**University of Connecticut
School of Business Administration
Connecticut SBDC**
2 Bourn Place, U-94
Storrs, CT 06269
(860)486-4135
Fax: (860)486-1576
E-mail: oconnor@ct.sbdc.uconn.edu
Dennis Gruel, State Dir.

**Naugatuck Valley Development Center
Small Business Development Center**
100 Grand St., 3rd Fl.
Waterbury, CT 06702
(203)757-8937

Fax: (203)757-8937
Ilene Oppenheim, Dir.

University of Connecticut (Greater Hartford Campus)

Small Business Development Center
1800 Asylum Ave.
West Hartford, CT 06117
(860)570-9107
Fax: (860)570-9107
Dennis Gruel, Dir.

Eastern Connecticut State University
Small Business Development Center
83 Windham St.
Williamantic, CT 06226-2295
(860)465-5349
Fax: (860)465-5143
Richard Cheney, Dir.

Delaware

Delaware State University
School of Business Economics
SBDC
1200 N. Dupont Hwy.
Dover, DE 19901
(302)678-1555
Fax: (302)739-2333
Jim Crisfield, Director

Delaware Technical and Community College
SBDC
Industrial Training Bldg.
PO Box 610
Georgetown, DE 19947
(302)856-1555
Fax: (302)856-5779
William F. Pfaff, Dir.

University of Delaware
Delaware SBDC
Purnell Hall, Ste. 005
Newark, DE 19716-2711
(302)831-1555
Fax: (302)831-1423
Clinton Tymes, State Dir.

Small Business Resource & Information Center
SBDC
1318 N. Market St.
Wilmington, DE 19801
(302)571-1555
Fax: (302)571-5222
Barbara Necarsulmer, Mgr.

District of Columbia

Friendship House/Southeastern University
SBDC
921 Pennsylvania Ave., SE
Washington, DC 20003
(202)547-7933
Fax: (202)806-1777
Elise Ashby, Dir.

George Washington University
East of the River Community Development Corp.
SBDC
3101 MLK Jr. Ave., SE, 3rd Fl.
Washington, DC 20032
(202)561-4975
Howard Johnson, Accounting Specialist

Howard University
George Washington Small Business Legal Clinic
SBDC
2000 G St., NW, Ste. 200
Washington, DC 20052
(202)994-7463
Jose Hernandez, Counselor

Howard University
Office of Latino Affairs
SBDC
2000 14th St., NW, 2nd Fl.
Washington, DC 20009
(202)939-3018
Fax: (202)994-4946
Jose Hernandez, Gov. Procurement Specialist

Howard University
SBDC
Satellite Location
2600 6th St., NW, Rm. 125
Washington, DC 20059
(202)806-1550
Fax: (904)620-2567
E-mail: smallbiz@unf.edu
Lowell Salter, Regional Dir.

Marshall Heights Community Development Organization
SBDC
3917 Minnesota Ave., NE
Washington, DC 20019
(202)396-1200
Terry Strong, Financing Specialist

Washington District Office
Business Information Center
SBDC
1110 Vermont Ave., NW, 9th Fl.
Washington, DC 20005
(202)737-0120
Fax: (202)737-0476
Johnetta Hardy, Marketing Specialist

Florida

Central Florida Development Council
Small Business Development Center
600 N. Broadway, Ste. 300
Bartow, FL 33830
(941)534-4370
Fax: (941)533-1247
Marcela Stanislaus, Vice President

Florida Atlantic University (Boca Raton)
Small Business Development Center
777 Glades Rd.
Bldg. T9
Boca Raton, FL 33431
(561)362-5620
Fax: (561)362-5623
Nancy Young, Dir.

UCF Brevard Campus
Small Business Development Center
1519 Clearlake Rd.
Cocoa, FL 32922
(407)951-1060

Dania Small Business Development Center
46 SW 1st Ave.
Dania, FL 33304-3607
(954)987-0100
Fax: (954)987-0106
William Healy, Regional Mgr.

Daytona Beach Community College
Florida Regional SBDC
1200 W. International Speedway Blvd.
Daytona Beach, FL 32114
(904)947-5463
Fax: (904)258-3846
Brenda Thomas-Ramos, Dir.

Florida Atlantic University Commercial Campus
Small Business Development Center
1515 W. Commercial Blvd., Rm. 11
Ft. Lauderdale, FL 33309
(954)771-6520
Fax: (954)351-4120
Marty Zients, Mgr.

Minority Business Development Center
SBDC
5950 West Oakland Park Blvd., Ste. 307
Ft. Lauderdale, FL 33313
(954)485-5333
Fax: (954)485-2514

Edison Community College
Small Business Development Center
8099 College Pkwy. SW
Ft. Myers, FL 33919
(941)489-9200
Fax: (941)489-9051
Dan Regelski, Management Consultant

Florida Gulf Coast University
Small Business Development Center
17595 S. Tamiami Trail, Ste. 200
Midway Ctr.
Ft. Myers, FL 33908-4500
(941)948-1820
Fax: (941)948-1814
Dan Regleski, Management Consultant

Indian River Community College
Small Business Development Center
3209 Virginia Ave., Rm. 114
Ft. Pierce, FL 34981-5599
(561)462-4756
Fax: (561)462-4796
Marsha Thompson, Dir.

Okaloosa-Walton Community College
SBDC
1170 Martin Luther King, Jr. Blvd.
Ft. Walton Beach, FL 32547
(850)863-6543
Fax: (850)863-6564
Jane Briere, Mgr.

University of North Florida
(Gainesville)
Small Business Development Center
505 NW 2nd Ave., Ste. D
PO Box 2518
Gainesville, FL 32602-2518
(352)377-5621
Fax: (352)372-0288
Lalla Sheehy, Program Mgr.

University of North Florida
(Jacksonville)
Small Business Development Center
College of Business
Honors Hall, Rm. 2451
4567 St. John's Bluff Rd. S
Jacksonville, FL 32224
(904)620-2476

Gulf Coast Community College
SBDC
2500 Minnesota Ave.
Lynn Haven, FL 32444
(850)271-1108
Fax: (850)271-1109
Doug Davis, Dir.

Brevard Community College (Melbourne)
Small Business Development Center
3865 N. Wickham Rd.
Melbourne, FL 32935
(407)632-1111
Fax: (407)634-3721
Victoria Peak, Program Coordinator

Florida International University
Small Business Development Center
University Park
CEAS-2620
Miami, FL 33199
(305)348-2272
Fax: (305)348-2965
Marvin Nesbit, Dir.

Florida International University (North
Miami Campus)
Small Business Development Center
Academic Bldg. No. 1, Rm. 350
NE 151 and Biscayne Blvd.
Miami, FL 33181
(305)919-5790
Fax: (305)919-5792
Roy Jarrett, Regional Mgr.

Miami Dade Community College
Small Business Development Center
6300 NW 7th Ave.
Miami, FL 33150
(305)237-1906
Fax: (305)237-1908
Frederic Bonneau, Regional Mgr.

Ocala Small Business Development
Center
110 E. Silver Springs Blvd.
PO Box 1210
Ocala, FL 34470-6613
(352)622-8763
Fax: (352)651-1031
E-mail: sbdcoca@mercury.net
Philip Geist, Program Dir.

University of Central Florida
Small Business Development Center
College of Business Administration, Ste. 309
PO Box 161530
Orlando, FL 32816-1530
(407)823-5554
Fax: (407)823-3073
Al Polfer, Dir.

Palm Beach Gardens
Florida Atlantic University
SBDC
Northrop Center
3970 RCA Blvd., Ste. 7323
Palm Beach Gardens, FL 33410
(407)691-8550
Fax: (407)692-8502
Steve Windhaus, Regional Mgr.

Procurement Technical Assistance
Program
University of West Florida
Small Business Development Center
19 W. Garden St., Ste. 302
Pensacola, FL 32501
(850)595-5480
Fax: (850)595-5487
Martha Cobb, Dir.

University of West Florida
Florida SBDC Network
19 West Garden St., Ste. 300
Pensacola, FL 32501
(850)595-6060
Fax: (850)595-6070
E-mail: fsbdc@uwf.edu
Jerry Cartwright, State Dir.

Seminole Community College
SBDC
100 Weldon Blvd.
Sanford, FL 32773
(407)328-4722
Fax: (407)330-4489
Wayne Hardy, Regional Mgr.

Florida Agricultural and Mechanical
University
Small Business Development Center
1157 E. Tennessee St.
Tallahassee, FL 32308
(904)599-3407
Fax: (904)561-2049
Patricia McGowan, Dir.

University of South Florida–CBA
SBDC Special Services
4202 E. Fowler Ave., BSN 3403
Tampa, FL 33620
(813)974-4371
Fax: (813)974-5020
Dick Hardesty, Procurement Mgr.

University of South Florida (Tampa)
Small Business Development Center
1111 N. Westshore Dr., Annex B, Ste.
101-B
Tampa, FL 33607
(813)554-2341

800-733-7232
Fax: (813)554-2356
Irene Hurst, Dir.

Georgia

University of Georgia
Small Business Development Center
230 S. Jackson St., Ste. 333
Albany, GA 31701-2885
(912)430-4303
Fax: (912)430-3933
E-mail: sbdcalb@uga.cc.uga.edu
Sue Ford, Asst. District Dir.

NE Georgia District
SBDC
1180 E. Broad St.
Athens, GA 30602-5412
(706)542-7436
Fax: (706)542-6823
Gayle Rosenthal, Mgr.

University of Georgia
Chicopee Complex
Georgia SBDC
1180 E. Broad St.
Athens, GA 30602-5412
(706)542-6762
Fax: (706)542-6776
E-mail: sbdcath@uga.cc.uga.edu
Hank Logan, State Dir.

Georgia State University
Small Business Development Center
University Plz.
Box 874
Atlanta, GA 30303-3083
(404)651-3550
Fax: (404)651-1035
E-mail: sbdcatl@uga.cc.uga.edu
Lee Quarterman, Area Dir.

Morris Brown College
Small Business Development Center
643 Martin Luther King, Jr., Dr. NW
Atlanta, GA 30314
(404)220-0205
Fax: (404)688-5985
Ray Johnson, Center Mgr.

University of Georgia
Small Business Development Center
1054 Claussen Rd., Ste. 301
Augusta, GA 30907-3215
(706)737-1790
Fax: (706)731-7937
E-mail: sbdcaug@uga.cc.uga.edu
Jeff Sanford, Area Dir.

University of Georgia (Brunswick)
Small Business Development Center
1107 Fountain Lake Dr.
Brunswick, GA 31525-3039
(912)264-7343
Fax: (912)262-3095
E-mail: sbdcbrun@uga.cc.uga.edu
David Lewis, Area Dir.

University of Georgia (Columbus)
Small Business Development Center
North Bldg., Rm. 202
928 45th St.
Columbus, GA 31904-6572
(706)649-7433
Fax: (706)649-1928
E-mail: sbdccolu@uga.cc.uga.edu
Jerry Copeland, Area Dir.

DeKalb Chamber of Commerce
DeKalb Small Business Development Center
750 Commerce Dr., Ste. 201
Decatur, GA 30030-2622
(404)373-6930
Fax: (404)687-9684
E-mail: sbdcdec@uga.cc.uga.edu
Eric Bonaparte, Area Dir.

Gainesville Small Business Development Center
500 Jesse Jewel Pkwy., Ste. 304
Gainesville, GA 30501-3773
(770)531-5681
Fax: (770)531-5684
E-mail: sbdcgain@uga.cc.uga.edu
Ron Simmons, Area Dir.

Kennesaw State University
Small Business Development Center
1000 Chastain Rd.
Kennesaw, GA 30144-5591
(770)423-6450
Fax: (770)423-6564
E-mail: sbdcmar@uga.cc.uga.edu
Carlotta Roberts, Area Dir.

Southeast Georgia District (Macon)
Small Business Development Center
401 Cherry St., Ste. 701
PO Box 13212
Macon, GA 31208-3212
(912)751-6592
Fax: (912)751-6607
E-mail: sbdcmac@uga.cc.uga.edu
Denise Ricketson, Area Dir.

Clayton State College
Small Business Development Center
PO Box 285
Morrow, GA 30260

(770)961-3440
Fax: (770)961-3428
E-mail: sbdcmorr@uga.cc.uga.edu
Bernie Meincke, Area Dir.

University of Georgia
SBDC
1770 Indian Trail Rd., Ste. 410
Norcross, GA 30093
(770)806-2124
Fax: (770)806-2129
E-mail: sbdclaw@uga.cc.edu
Robert Andoh, Area Dir.

Floyd College
Small Business Development Center
PO Box 1864
Rome, GA 30162-1864
(706)295-6326
Fax: (706)295-6732
E-mail: sbdcrome@uga.cc.uga.edu
Drew Tonsmeire, Area Dir.

University of Georgia (Savannah)
Small Business Development Center
450 Mall Blvd., Ste. H
Savannah, GA 31406-4824
(912)356-2755
Fax: (912)353-3033
E-mail: sbdcsav@uga.cc.uga.edu
Lynn Vos, Area Dir.

Georgia Southern University
Small Business Development Center
325 S. Main St.
PO Box 8156
Statesboro, GA 30460-8156
(912)681-5194
Fax: (912)681-0648
E-mail: sbdcstat@uga.cc.uga.edu
Mark Davis, Area Dir.

University of Georgia (Valdosta)
Small Business Development Center
Baytree W. Professional Offices
1205 Baytree Rd., Ste. 9
Valdosta, GA 31602-2782
(912)245-3738
Fax: (912)245-3741
E-mail: sbdcval@uga.cc.uga.edu
Suzanne Barnett, Area Dir.

University of Georgia (Warner Robins)
Small Business Development Center
151 Osigian Blvd.
Warner Robins, GA 31088
(912)953-9356
Fax: (912)953-9376
E-mail: sbdccwr@uga.cc.uga.edu
Ronald Reaves, Center Mgr.

Guam

Pacific Islands SBDC Network
UOG Station
303 University Dr.
Mangilao, GU 96923
(671)735-2590
Fax: (671)734-2002
Dr. Sephen L. Marder, Dir.

Hawaii

Kona Circuit Rider
SBDC
200 West Kawili St.
Hilo, HI 96720-4091
(808)933-3515
Fax: (808)933-3683
Rebecca Winters, Business Consultant

University of Hawaii at Hilo
Small Business Development Center
200 W. Kawili St.
Hilo, HI 96720-4091
(808)974-7515
Fax: (808)974-7683
Website: http://www.maui.com/~sbdc/
hilo.html
Dr. Darryl Mleynek, State Director

University of Hawaii at West Oahu
SBDC
130 Merchant St., Ste. 1030
Honolulu, HI 96813
(808)522-8131
Fax: (808)522-8135
Laura Noda, Center Dir.

Maui Community College
Small Business Development Center
Maui Research and Technology Center
590 Lipoa Pkwy., No. 130
Kihei, HI 96779
(808)875-2402
Fax: (808)875-2452
David B. Fisher, Dir.

University of Hawaii at Hilo
Business Research Library
SBDC
590 Lipoa Pkwy., No. 128
Kihei, HI 96753
(808)875-2400
Fax: (808)875-2452

Kauai Community College
Small Business Development Center
3-1901 Kaumualii Hwy.
Lihue, HI 96766-9591
(808)246-1748

Fax: (808)246-5102
Randy Gringas, Center Dir.

Idaho

Boise State University
Small Business Development Center
1910 University Dr.
Boise, ID 83725
(208)385-3875
800-225-3815
Fax: (208)385-3877
Robert Shepard, Regional Dir.

Idaho State University (Idaho Falls)
Small Business Development Center
2300 N. Yellowstone
Idaho Falls, ID 83401
(208)523-1087
800-658-3829
Fax: (208)523-1049
Betty Capps, Regional Dir.

Lewis-Clark State College
Small Business Development Center
500 8th Ave.
Lewiston, ID 83501
(208)799-2465
Fax: (208)799-2878
Helen Le Boeuf-Binninger, Regional Dir.

Idaho Small Business Development
Center
305 E. Park St., Ste. 405
PO Box 1901
McCall, ID 83638
(208)634-2883
Larry Smith, Associate Business Consultant

Idaho State University (Pocatello)
Small Business Development Center
1651 Alvin Ricken Dr.
Pocatello, ID 83201
(208)232-4921
800-232-4921
Fax: (208)233-0268
Paul Cox, Regional Dir.

North Idaho College
SBDC
525 W. Clearwater Loop
Post Falls, ID 83854
(208)769-3296
Fax: (208)769-3223
John Lynn, Regional Dir.

College of Southern Idaho
Small Business Development Center
315 Falls Ave.
PO Box 1238

Twin Falls, ID 83303
(208)733-9554
Fax: (208)733-9316
Cindy Bond, Regional Dir.

Illinois

Waubonsee Community College
(Aurora Campus)
Small Business Development Center
5 E. Galena Blvd.
Aurora, IL 60506-4178
(630)801-7900
Fax: (630)892-4668
Linda Garrison-Carlton, Dir.

Southern Illinois University at
Carbondale
Small Business Development Center
150 E. Pleasant Hill Rd.
Carbondale, IL 62901-4300
(618)536-2424
Fax: (618)453-5040
Dennis Cody, Dir.

John A. Logan College
Small Business Development Center
700 Logan College Rd.
Carterville, IL 62918-9802
(618)985-3741
Fax: (618)985-2248
Richard Fyke, Dir.

Kaskaskia College
Small Business Development Center
27210 College Rd.
Centralia, IL 62801-7878
(618)532-2049
Fax: (618)532-4983
Richard McCullum, Dir.

University of Illinois at Urbana-
Champaign
International Trade Center
Small Business Development Center
428 Commerce W.
1206 S. 6th St.
Champaign, IL 61820-6980
(217)244-1585
Fax: (217)333-7410
Tess Morrison, Dir.

Asian American Alliance
SBDC
222 W. Cermak, No. 302
Chicago, IL 60616
(312)326-2200
Fax: (312)326-0399
Emil Bernardo, Dir.

Back of the Yards Neighborhood Council
Small Business Development Center
1751 W. 47th St.
Chicago, IL 60609-3889
(773)523-4419
Fax: (773)254-3525
Bill Przybylski, Dir.

Chicago Small Business Development Center
DCCA / James R. Thompson Center
100 W. Randolph, Ste. 3-400
Chicago, IL 60601-3219
(312)814-6111
Fax: (312)814-5247
Carson A. Gallagher, Mgr.

Eighteenth Street Development Corp.
Small Business Development Center
1839 S. Carpenter
Chicago, IL 60608-3347
(312)733-2287
Fax: (312)733-8242
Maria Munoz, Dir.

Greater North Pulaski Development Corp.
Small Business Development Center
4054 W. North Ave.
Chicago, IL 60639-5223
(773)384-2262
Fax: (773)384-3850
Kaushik Shah, Dir.

Industrial Council of Northwest Chicago
Small Business Development Center
2023 W. Carroll
Chicago, IL 60612-1601
(312)421-3941
Fax: (312)421-1871
Melvin Eiland, Dir.

Latin American Chamber of Commerce
Small Business Development Center
3512 W. Fullerton St.
Chicago, IL 60647-2655
(773)252-5211
Fax: (773)252-7065
Ed Diaz, Dir.

North Business and Industrial Council (NORBIC)
SBDC
2500 W. Bradley Pl.
Chicago, IL 60618-4798
(773)588-5855
Fax: (773)588-0734
Tom Kamykowski, Dir.

Richard J. Daley College
Small Business Development Center
7500 S. Pulaski Rd., Bldg. 200
Chicago, IL 60652-1299
(773)838-0319
Fax: (773)838-0303
Jim Charney, Dir.

Women's Business Development Center
Small Business Development Center
8 S. Michigan, Ste. 400
Chicago, IL 60603-3302
(312)853-3477
Fax: (312)853-0145
Joyce Wade, Dir.

McHenry County College
Small Business Development Center
8900 U.S. Hwy. 14
Crystal Lake, IL 60012-2761
(815)455-6098
Fax: (815)455-9319
Susan Whitfield, Dir.

Danville Area Community College
Small Business Development Center
28 W. North St.
Danville, IL 61832-5729
(217)442-7232
Fax: (217)442-6228
Ed Adrain, Dir.

Cooperative Extension Service
SBDC
Building 11, Ste. 1105
2525 E. Federal Dr.
Decatur, IL 62526-1573
(217)875-8284
Fax: (217)875-8288
Bill Wilkinson, Dir.

Sauk Valley Community College
Small Business Development Center
173 Illinois, Rte. 2
Dixon, IL 61021-9188
(815)288-5511
Fax: (815)288-5958
John Nelson, Dir.

Black Hawk College
Small Business Development Center
301 42nd Ave.
East Moline, IL 61244-4038
(309)755-2200
Fax: (309)755-9847
Donna Scalf, Dir.

East St. Louis Small Business Development Center
Federal Building
650 Missouri Ave., Ste. G32
East St. Louis, IL 62201-2955
(618)482-3833
Fax: (618)482-3859
Robert Ahart, Dir.

Southern Illinois University at Edwardsville
Small Business Development Center
Campus Box 1107
Edwardsville, IL 62026-0001
(618)692-2929
Fax: (618)692-2647
Alan Hauff, Dir.

Elgin Community College
Small Business Development Center
1700 Spartan Dr.
Elgin, IL 60123-7193
(847)888-7488
Fax: (847)931-3911
Craig Fowler, Dir.

Evanston Business and Technology Center
Small Business Development Center
1840 Oak Ave.
Evanston, IL 60201-3670
(847)866-1817
Fax: (847)866-1808
Rick Holbrook, Dir.

College of DuPage
Small Business Development Center
425 22nd St.
Glen Ellyn, IL 60137-6599
(630)942-2771
Fax: (630)942-3789
David Gay, Dir.

Lewis and Clark Community College
SBDC
5800 Godfrey Rd.
Godfrey, IL 62035
(618)466-3411
Fax: (618)466-0810
Bob Duane, Dir.

College of Lake County
Small Business Development Center
19351 W. Washington St.
Grayslake, IL 60030-1198
(847)223-3633
Fax: (847)223-9371
Linda Jorn, Dir.

Southeastern Illinois College

Small Business Development Center

303 S. Commercial

Harrisburg, IL 62946-2125

(618)252-5001

Fax: (618)252-0210

Becky Williams, Dir.

Rend Lake College

Small Business Development Center

Rte. 1

Ina, IL 62846-9801

(618)437-5321

Fax: (618)437-5677

Lisa Payne, Dir.

Joliet Junior College

Small Business Development Center

Renaissance Center, Rm. 312

214 N. Ottawa St.

Joliet, IL 60431-4097

(815)727-6544

Fax: (815)722-1895

Denise Mikulski, Dir.

Kankakee Community College

Small Business Development Center

River Rd., Box 888

Kankakee, IL 60901-7878

(815)933-0376

Fax: (815)933-0217

Kelly Berry, Dir.

Western Illinois University

Small Business Development Center

214 Seal Hall

Macomb, IL 61455-1390

(309)298-2211

Fax: (309)298-2520

Dan Voorhis, Dir.

Maple City Business and Technology Center

Small Business Development Center

620 S. Main St.

Monmouth, IL 61462-2688

(309)734-4664

Fax: (309)734-8579

Carol Cook, Dir.

Illinois Valley Community College

Small Business Development Center

815 N. Orlando Smith Ave., Bldg. 11

Oglesby, IL 61348-9692

(815)223-1740

Fax: (815)224-3033

Boyd Palmer, Dir.

Illinois Eastern Community College

Small Business Development Center

401 E. Main St.

Olney, IL 62450-2119

(618)395-3011

Fax: (618)395-1922

Debbie Chilson, Dir.

Moraine Valley Community College

Small Business Development Center

10900 S. 88th Ave.

Palos Hills, IL 60465-0937

(708)974-5468

Fax: (708)974-0078

Hilary Gereg, Dir.

Bradley University

Small Business Development Center

141 N. Jobst Hall, 1st Fl.

Peoria, IL 61625-0001

(309)677-2992

Fax: (309)677-3386

Roger Luman, Dir.

Illinois Central College

Procurement Technical Assistance Center

Small Business Development Center

124 SW Adams St., Ste. 300

Peoria, IL 61602-1388

(309)676-7500

Fax: (309)676-7534

Susan Gorman, Dir.

John Wood Community College

Procurement Technical Assistance Center

Small Business Development Center

301 Oak St.

Quincy, IL 62301-2500

(217)228-5511

Fax: (217)228-5501

Edward Van Leer, Dir.

Rock Valley College

Small Business Development Center

1220 Rock St.

Rockford, IL 61101-1437

(815)968-4087

Fax: (815)968-4157

Shirley DeBenedetto, Dir.

Department of Commerce & Community Affairs

Illinois SBDC

620 East Adams St., Third Fl.

Springfield, IL 62701

(217)524-5856

Fax: (217)524-0171

Jeff Mitchell, State Dir.

Lincoln Land Community College

Small Business Development Center

100 N. 11th St.

Springfield, IL 62703-1002

(217)789-1017

Fax: (217)789-9838

Freida Schreck, Dir.

Shawnee Community College

Small Business Development Center

Shawnee College Rd.

Ullin, IL 62992

(618)634-9618

Fax: (618)634-2347

Donald Denny, Dir.

Governors State University

Small Business Development Center

College of Business, Rm. C-3370

University Park, IL 60466-0975

(708)534-4929

Fax: (708)534-1646

Christine Cochrane, Dir.

Indiana

Batesville Office of Economic Development

SBDC

132 S. Main

Batesville, IN 47006

(812)933-6110

Bedford Chamber of Commerce

SBDC

1116 W. 16th St.

Bedford, IN 47421

(812)275-4493

Bloomfield Chamber of Commerce

SBDC

c/o Harrah Realty Co.

23 S. Washington St.

Bloomfield, IN 47424

(812)275-4493

Bloomington Area Regional Small Business Development Center

216 Allen St.

Bloomington, IN 47403

(812)339-8937

Fax: (812)335-7352

David Miller, Dir.

Clay Count Chamber of Commerce

SBDC

12 N. Walnut St.

Brazil, IN 47834

(812)448-8457

Brookville Chamber of Commerce
SBDC
PO Box 211
Brookville, IN 47012
(317)647-3177

Clinton Chamber of Commerce
SBDC
292 N. 9th St.
Clinton, IN 47842
(812)832-3844

Columbia City Chamber of Commerce
SBDC
112 N. Main St.
Columbia City, IN 46725
(219)248-8131

Columbus Regional Small Business
Development Center
4920 N. Warren Dr.
Columbus, IN 47203
(812)372-6480
800-282-7232
Fax: (812)372-0228
Jack Hess, Dir.

Connerville SBDC
504 Central
Connersville, IN 47331
(317)825-8328

Harrison County
Development Center
SBDC
405 N. Capitol, Ste. 308
Corydon, IN 47112
(812)738-8811

Montgomery County Chamber
of Commerce
SBDC
211 S. Washington St.
Crawfordsville, IN 47933
(317)654-5507

Decatur Chamber of Commerce
SBDC
125 E. Monroe St.
Decatur, IN 46733
(219)724-2604

City of Delphi Community
Development
SBDC
201 S. Union
Delphi, IN 46923
(317)564-6692

Southwestern Indiana Regional Small
Business Development Center
100 NW 2nd St., Ste. 200
Evansville, IN 47708
(812)425-7232
Fax: (812)421-5883
Kate Northrup, Dir.

Northeast Indiana Regional Small
Business Development Center
1830 Wayne Trace
Fort Wayne, IN 46803
(219)426-0040
Fax: (219)424-0024
E-mail: sbdc@mailfwi.com
Nick Adams, Dir.

Clinton County Chamber of Commerce
SBDC
207 S. Main St.
Frankfort, IN 46041
(317)654-5507

Northlake Small Business Development
Center
487 Broadway, Ste. 201
Gary, IN 46402
(219)882-2000

Greencastle Partnership Center
SBDC
2 S. Jackson St.
Greencastle, IN 46135
(317)653-4517

Greensburg Area Chamber of
Commerce
SBDC
125 W. Main St.
Greensburg, IN 47240
(812)663-2832

Hammond Development Corp.
SBDC
649 Conkey St.
Hammond, IN 46324
(219)853-6399

Blackford County Economic
Development
SBDC
PO Box 43
Hartford, IN 47001-0043
(317)348-4944

Indiana SBDC Network
One North Capitol, Ste. 420
Indianapolis, IN 46204
(317)264-6871
Fax: (317)264-3102
E-mail: sthrash@in.net
Stephen Thrash, Exec. Dir.

Indianapolis Regional Small Business
Development Center
342 N. Senate Ave.
Indianapolis, IN 46204-1708
(317)261-3030
Fax: (317)261-3053
Glenn Dunlap, Dir.

Clark County Hoosier Falls
Private Industry Council
Workforce
1613 E. 8th St.
Jeffersonville, IN 47130
(812)282-0456

Southern Indiana Regional Small
Business Development Center
1613 E. 8th St.
Jeffersonville, IN 47130
(812)288-6451
Fax: (812)284-8314
Patricia Stroud, Dir.

Kendallville Chamber
of Commerce
SBDC
228 S. Main St.
Kendallville, IN 46755
(219)347-1554

Kokomo-Howard County Regional
Small Business Development
Center
106 N. Washington
Kokomo, IN 46901
(317)454-7922
Fax: (317)452-4564
E-mail: sbdc5@holli.com
Kim Moyers, Dir.

LaPorte Small Business Development
Center
414 Lincolnway
La Porte, IN 46350
(219)326-7232

Greater Lafayette Regional Area Small
Business Development Center
122 N. 3rd
Lafayette, IN 47901
(765)742-2394
Fax: (765)742-6276
Susan Davis, Dir.

Union County Chamber
of Commerce
SBDC
102 N. Main St., No. 6
Liberty, IN 47353-1039
(317)458-5976

Organizations, Agencies, & Consultants

**Linton/Stockton Chamber
of Commerce**
SBDC
PO Box 208
Linton, IN 47441
(812)847-4846

**Southeastern Indiana Regional Small
Business Development Center**
975 Industrial Dr.
Madison, IN 47250
(812)265-3127
Fax: (812)265-5544
E-mail: seinsbdc@seidata.com
Rose Marie Roberts, Dir.

**Crawford County
Private Industry Council Workforce**
SBDC
Box 224 D, R.R. 1
Marengo, IN 47140
(812)365-2174

**Greater Martinsville Chamber
of Commerce**
SBDC
210 N. Marion St.
Martinsville, IN 46151
(317)342-8110

**Lake County Public Library
Small Business Development Center**
1919 W. 81st. Ave.
Merrillville, IN 46410-5382
(219)756-7232

First Citizens Bank
SBDC
515 N. Franklin Sq.
Michigan City, IN 46360
(219)874-9245

Mitchell Chamber of Commerce
SBDC
1st National Bank
Main Street
Mitchell, IN 47446
(812)849-4441

Mt. Vernon Chamber of Commerce
SBDC
405 E. 4th St.
Mt. Vernon, IN 47620
(812)838-3639

**East Central Indiana Regional Small
Business Development Center**
401 S. High St.
PO Box 842
Muncie, IN 47305

(765)284-8144
Fax: (765)751-9151
Barbara Armstrong, Dir.

Brown County Chamber of Commerce
SBDC
PO Box 164
Nashville, IN 47448
(812)988-6647

**Southern Indiana Small Business
Development Center
Private Industry Council Workforce**
4100 Charleston Rd.
New Albany, IN 47150
(812)945-0266
Fax: (812)948-4664
Gretchen Mahaffey, Dir.

**Henry County Economic Development
Corp.**
SBDC
1325 Broad St., Ste. B
New Castle, IN 47362
(317)529-4635

**Jennings County Chamber of
Commerce**
SBDC
PO Box 340
North Vernon, IN 47265
(812)346-2339

**Orange County
Private Industry Council Workforce**
SBDC
326 B. N. Gospel
Paoli, IN 47454-1412
(812)723-4206

**Northwest Indiana Regional Small
Business Development Center
Small Business Development Center**
6100 Southport Rd.
Portage, IN 46368
(219)762-1696
Fax: (219)763-2653
Mark McLaughlin, Dir

Jay County Development Corp.
SBDC
121 W. Main St., Ste. A
Portland, IN 47371
(219)726-9311

**Richmond-Wayne County Small
Business Development Center**
33 S. 7th St.
Richmond, IN 47374
(765)962-2887

Fax: (765)966-0882
Cliff Fry, Dir.

**Rochester and Lake Manitou Chamber
of Commerce
Fulton Economic Development Center**
SBDC
617 Main St.
Rochester, IN 46975
(219)223-6773

Rushville Chamber of Commerce
SBDC
PO Box 156
Rushville, IN 46173
(317)932-2222

St. Mary of the Woods College
SBDC
St. Mary-of-the-Woods, IN 47876
(812)535-5151

**Washington County
Private Industry Council Workforce**
SBDC
Hilltop Plaza
Salem, IN 47167
(812)883-2283

**Scott County
Private Industry Council Workforce**
SBDC
752 Lakeshore Dr.
Scottsburg, IN 47170
(812)752-3886

Seymour Chamber of Commerce
SBDC
PO Box 43
Seymour, IN 47274
(812)522-3681

**Minority Business Development Project
Future**
SBDC
401 Col
South Bend, IN 46634
(219)234-0051

**South Bend Regional Small Business
Development Center**
300 N. Michigan
South Bend, IN 46601
(219)282-4350
Fax: (219)236-1056
Jim Gregar, Dir.

Economic Development Office
SBDC
46 E. Market St.
Spencer, IN 47460
(812)829-3245

Sullivan Chamber of Commerce
SBDC
10 S. Crt. St.
Sullivan, IN 47882
(812)268-4836

Tell City Chamber of Commerce
SBDC
645 Main St.
Tell City, IN 47586
(812)547-2385
Fax: (812)547-8378

Terre Haute Area Small Business
Development Center
School of Business, Rm. 510
Terre Haute, IN 47809
(812)237-7676
Fax: (812)237-7675
William Minnis, Dir.

Tipton County Economic
Development Corp.
SBDC
136 E. Jefferson
Tipton, IN 46072
(317)675-7300

Porter County
SBDC
911 Wall St.
Valparaiso, IN 46383
(219)477-5256

Vevay/Switzerland Country Foundation
SBDC
PO Box 193
Vevay, IN 47043
(812)427-2533

Vincennes University
SBDC
PO Box 887
Vincennes, IN 47591
(812)885-5749

Wabash Area Chamber of Commerce
Wabash Economic Development Corp.
SBDC
67 S. Wabash
Wabash, IN 46992
(219)563-1168

Washington Daviess County
SBDC
1 Train Depot St.
Washington, IN 47501
(812)254-5262
Fax: (812)254-2550
Mark Brochin, Dir.

Purdue University
SBDC
Business & Industrial Development
Center
1220 Potter Dr.
West Lafayette, IN 47906
(317)494-5858

Randolph County Economic
Development Foundation
SBDC
111 S. Main St.
Winchester, IN 47394
(317)584-3266

Iowa

Iowa SBDC
137 Lynn Ave.
Ames, IA 50014
(515)292-6351
800-373-7232
Fax: (515)292-0020
Ronald Manning, State Dir.

Iowa State University
Small Business Development Center
ISU Branch Office
Bldg. 1, Ste. 615
2501 N. Loop Dr.
Ames, IA 50010-8283
(515)296-7828
800-373-7232
Fax: (515)296-6714
Steve Carter, Dir.

DMACC Small Business Development
Center
Circle West Incubator
PO Box 204
Audubon, IA 50025
(712)563-2623
Fax: (712)563-2301
Lori Harmening, Dir.

University of Northern Iowa
Small Business Development Center
8628 University Ave.
Cedar Falls, IA 50614-0032
(319)273-2696
Fax: (319)273-7730
Lyle Bowlin, Dir.

Iowa Western Community College
Small Business Development Center
2700 College Rd., Box 4C
Council Bluffs, IA 51502
(712)325-3260
Fax: (712)325-3408
Ronald Helms, Dir.

Southwestern Community College
Small Business Development Center
1501 W. Townline Rd.
Creston, IA 50801
(515)782-4161
Fax: (515)782-3312
Robin Beech Travis, Dir.

Eastern Iowa Small Business
Development Center
304 W. 2nd St.
Davenport, IA 52801
(319)322-4499
Fax: (319)322-8241
Jon Ryan, Dir.

Drake University
Small Business Development Center
2507 University Ave.
Des Moines, IA 50311-4505
(515)271-2655
Fax: (515)271-1899
Benjamin Swartz, Dir.

Northeast Iowa Small Business
Development Center
770 Town Clock Plz.
Dubuque, IA 52001
(319)588-3350
Fax: (319)557-1591
Charles Tonn, Dir.

Iowa Central Community College
SBDC
900 Central Ave., Ste. 4
Ft. Dodge, IA 50501
(515)576-5090
Fax: (515)576-0826
Todd Madson, Dir.

University of Iowa
Small Business Development
Center
108 Papajohn Business Administration
Bldg., Ste. S-160
Iowa City, IA 52242-1000
(319)335-3742
800-253-7232
Fax: (319)353-2445
Paul Heath, Dir.

Kirkwood Community College
Small Business Development
Center
2901 10th Ave.
Marion, IA 52302
(319)377-8256
Fax: (319)377-5667
Steve Sprague, Dir.

Organizations, Agencies, & Consultants

North Iowa Area Community College
Small Business Development Center
500 College Dr.
Mason City, IA 50401
(515)422-4342
Fax: (515)422-4129
Richard Petersen, Dir.

Indian Hills Community College
Small Business Development Center
525 Grandview Ave.
Ottumwa, IA 52501
(515)683-5127
Fax: (515)683-5263
Bryan Ziegler, Dir.

Western Iowa Tech Community
College
Small Business Development Center
4647 Stone Ave.
PO Box 5199
Sioux City, IA 51102-5199
(712)274-6418
800-352-4649
Fax: (712)274-6429
Dennis Bogenrief, Dir.

Iowa Lakes Community College
(Spencer)
Small Business Development Center
1900 N. Grand Ave., Ste. 8
Hwy. 71 N
Spencer, IA 51301
(712)262-4213
Fax: (712)262-4047
John Beneke, Dir.

Southeastern Community College
Small Business Development Center
Drawer F
West Burlington, IA 52655
(319)752-2731
800-828-7322
Fax: (319)752-3407
Deb Dalziel, Dir.

Kansas

Bendictine College
SBDC
1020 N. 2nd St.
Atchison, KS 66002
(913)367-5340
Fax: (913)367-6102
Don Laney, Dir.

Butler County Community College
Small Business Development Center
600 Walnut
Augusta, KS 67010

(316)775-1124
Fax: (316)775-1370
Dorinda Rolle, Dir.

Neosho County Community College
SBDC
1000 S. Allen
Chanute, KS 66720
(316)431-2820
Fax: (316)431-0082
Duane Clum, Dir.

Coffeyville Community College
SBDC
11th and Willow Sts.
Coffeyville, KS 67337-5064
(316)251-7700
Fax: (316)252-7098
Charles Shaver, Dir.

Colby Community College
Small Business Development Center
1255 S. Range
Colby, KS 67701
(913)462-3984
Fax: (913)462-8315
Robert Selby, Dir.

Cloud County Community College
SBDC
2221 Campus Dr.
PO Box 1002
Concordia, KS 66901
(913)243-1435
Fax: (913)243-1459
Tony Foster, Dir.

Dodge City Community College
Small Business Development Center
2501 N. 14th Ave.
Dodge City, KS 67801
(316)227-9247
Fax: (316)227-9200
Wayne E. Shiplet, Dir.

Emporia State University
Small Business Development Center
130 Cremer Hall
Emporia, KS 66801
(316)342-7162
Fax: (316)341-5418
Lisa Brumbaugh, Regional Dir.

Ft. Scott Community College
SBDC
2108 S. Horton
Ft. Scott, KS 66701
(316)223-2700
Fax: (316)223-6530
Steve Pammenter, Dir.

Garden City Community College
SBDC
801 Campus Dr.
Garden City, KS 67846
(316)276-9632
Fax: (316)276-9630
Bill Sander, Regional Dir.

Ft. Hays State University
Small Business Development Center
109 W. 10th St.
Hays, KS 67601
(785)628-6786
Fax: (785)628-0533
Clare Gustin, Regional Dir.

Hutchinson Community College
Small Business Development Center
815 N. Walnut, Ste. 225
Hutchinson, KS 67501
(316)665-4950
800-289-3501
Fax: (316)665-8354
Clark Jacobs, Dir.

Independence Community College
SBDC
Arco Bldg.
11th and Main St.
Independence, KS 67301
(316)332-1420
Fax: (316)331-5344
Preston Haddan, Dir.

Allen County Community College
SBDC
1801 N. Cottonwood
Iola, KS 66749
(316)365-5116
Fax: (316)365-3284
Susan Thompson, Dir.

University of Kansas
Small Business Development Center
734 Vermont St., Ste. 104
Lawrence, KS 66044
(785)843-8844
Fax: (785)865-8878
Randy Brady, Regional Dir.

Seward County Community College
Small Business Development Center
1801 N. Kansas
PO Box 1137
Liberal, KS 67901
(316)629-2650
Fax: (316)629-2689
Dale Reed, Dir.

Kansas State University (Manhattan)
Small Business Development Center
College of Business Administration
2323 Anderson Ave., Ste. 100
Manhattan, KS 66502-2947
(785)532-5529
Fax: (785)532-5827
Fred Rice, Regional Dir.

Ottawa University
SBDC
College Ave., Box 70
Ottawa, KS 66067
(913)242-5200
Fax: (913)242-7429
Lori Kravets, Dir.

Johnson County Community College
Small Business Development Center
CEC Bldg., Rm. 223
Overland Park, KS 66210-1299
(913)469-3878
Fax: (913)469-4415
Kathy Nadiman, Regional Dir.

Labette Community College
SBDC
200 S. 14th
Parsons, KS 67357
(316)421-6700
Fax: (316)421-0921
Mark Turnbull, Dir.

Pittsburg State University
Small Business Development Center
Shirk Hall
1501 S. Joplin
Pittsburg, KS 66762
(316)235-4920
Fax: (316)232-6440
Kathryn Richard

Pratt Community College
Small Business Development Center
Hwy. 61
Pratt, KS 67124
(316)672-5641
Fax: (316)672-5288
Pat Gordon, Dir.

Salina Area Chamber of Commerce
Small Business Development Center
PO Box 586
Salina, KS 67402
(785)827-9301
Fax: (785)827-9758
James Gaines, Regional Dir.

Kansas SBDC
214 SW 6th St., Ste. 205
Topeka, KS 66603-3261

(785)296-6514
Fax: (785)291-3261
E-mail: ksbdc@cjnetworks.com
Debbie Bishop, State Dir.

Washburn University of Topeka
SBDC
School of Business
101 Henderson Learning Center
Topeka, KS 66621
(785)231-1010
Fax: (785)231-1063
Don Kingman, Regional Dir.

Wichita State University
SBDC
1845 Fairmont
Wichita, KS 67260
(316)689-3193
Fax: (316)689-3647
Joann Ard, Regional Dir.

Kentucky

Morehead State University College of Business
Boyd-Greenup County Chamber of Commerce
SBDC
1401 Winchester Ave., Ste. 305
207 15th St.
Ashland, KY 41101
(606)329-8011
Fax: (606)324-4570
Kimberly A. Jenkins, Dir.

Western Kentucky University
Bowling Green Small Business Development Center
2355 Nashville Rd.
Bowling Green, KY 42101
(502)745-1905
Fax: (502)745-1931
Richard S. Horn, Dir.

University of Kentucky (Elizabethtown)
Small Business Development Center
133 W. Dixie Ave.
Elizabethtown, KY 42701
(502)765-6737
Fax: (502)769-5095
Lou Ann Allen, Dir.

Northern Kentucky University
SBDC
BEP Center 463
Highland Heights, KY 41099-0506
(606)572-6524
Fax: (606)572-6177
Sutton Landry, Dir.

Murray State University (Hopkinsville)
Small Business Development Center
300 Hammond Dr.
Hopkinsville, KY 42240
(502)886-8666
Fax: (502)886-3211
Michael Cartner, Dir.

Small Business Development Center
Lexington Central Library, 4th Fl.
140 E. Main St.
Lexington, KY 40507-1376
(606)257-7666
Fax: (606)257-1751
Debbie McKnight, Dir.

University of Kentucky
Center for Entrepreneurship
Kentucky SBDC
225 Gatton Business and Economics Bldg.
Lexington, KY 40506-0034
(606)257-7668
Fax: (606)323-1907
Janet S. Holloway, State Dir.

Bellarmine College
Small Business Development Center
School of Business
600 W. Main St., Ste. 219
Louisville, KY 40202
(502)574-4770
Fax: (502)574-4771
Thomas G. Daley, Dir.

University of Louisville
Center for Entrepreneurship and Technology
Small Business Development Centers
Burhans Hall, Shelby Campus, Rm. 122
Louisville, KY 40292
(502)588-7854
Fax: (502)588-8573
Lou Dickie, Dir.

Southeast Community College
SBDC
1300 Chichester Ave.
Middlesboro, KY 40965-2265
(606)242-2145
Fax: (606)242-4514
Kathleen Moats, Dir.

Morehead State University
Small Business Development Center
309 Combs Bldg.
UPO 575
Morehead, KY 40351
(606)783-2895
Fax: (606)783-5020
Keith Moore, District Dir.

Murray State University

West Kentucky Small Business Development Center

College of Business and Public Affairs

PO Box 9

Murray, KY 42071

(502)762-2856

Fax: (502)762-3049

Rosemary Miller, Dir.

Murray State University

Owensboro Small Business Development Center

3860 U.S. Hwy. 60 W

Owensboro, KY 42301

(502)926-8085

Fax: (502)684-0714

Mickey Johnson, District Dir.

Moorehead State University

Pikeville Small Business Development Center

3455 N. Mayo Trail, No. 4

110 Village St.

Pikeville, KY 41501

(606)432-5848

Fax: (606)432-8924

Michael Morley, Dir.

Eastern Kentucky University

South Central Small Business Development Center

The Center for Rural Development, Ste. 260

2292 S. Hwy. 27

Somerset, KY 42501

(606)677-6120

Fax: (606)677-6083

Kathleen Moats, Dir.

Louisiana

Alexandria SBDC

Hibernia National Bank Bldg., Ste. 510

934 3rd St.

Alexandria, LA 71301

(318)484-2123

Fax: (318)484-2126

Kathey Hunter, Consultant

Southern University

Capital Small Business Development Center

1933 Wooddale Blvd., Ste. E

Baton Rouge, LA 70806

(504)922-0998

Fax: (504)922-0024

Gregory Spann, Dir.

Southeastern Louisiana University

Small Business Development Center

College of Business Administration

Box 522, SLU Sta.

Hammond, LA 70402

(504)549-3831

Fax: (504)549-2127

William Joubert, Dir.

University of Southwestern Louisiana

Acadiana Small Business Development Center

College of Business Administration

Box 43732

Lafayette, LA 70504

(318)262-5344

Fax: (318)262-5296

Kim Spence, Dir.

McNeese State University

Small Business Development Center

College of Business Administration

Lake Charles, LA 70609

(318)475-5529

Fax: (318)475-5012

Paul Arnold, Dir.

Louisiana Electronic Assistance Program

SBDC

NE Louisiana, College of Business Administration

Monroe, LA 71209

(318)342-1215

Fax: (318)342-1209

Dr. Jerry Wall, Dir.

Northeast Louisiana University

SBDC

Louisiana SBDC

College of Business Administration, Rm. 2-57

Room 2-57

Monroe, LA 71209

(318)342-5506

Fax: (318)342-5510

Dr. John Baker, State Dir.

Northeast Louisiana University

Small Business Development Center

College of Business Administration, Rm. 2-57

Monroe, LA 71209

(318)342-1215

Fax: (318)342-1209

Dr. Paul Dunn, Dir.

Northwestern State University

Small Business Development Center

College of Business Administration

Natchitoches, LA 71497

(318)357-5611

Fax: (318)357-6810

Mary Lynn Wilkerson, Dir.

Louisiana International Trade Center

SBDC

World Trade Center, Ste. 2926

2 Canal St.

New Orleans, LA 70130

(504)568-8222

Fax: (504)568-8228

Ruperto Chavarri, Dir.

Loyola University

Small Business Development Center

College of Business Administration

Box 134

New Orleans, LA 70118

(504)865-3474

Fax: (504)865-3496

Ronald Schroeder, Dir.

Southern University at New Orleans

Small Business Development Center

College of Business Administration

New Orleans, LA 70126

(504)286-5308

Fax: (504)286-5131

Jon Johnson, Dir.

University of New Orleans

Small Business Development Center

1600 Canal St., Ste. 620

New Orleans, LA 70112

(504)539-9292

Fax: (504)539-9205

Norma Grace, Dir.

Louisiana Tech University

Small Business Development Center

College of Business Administration

Box 10318, Tech Sta.

Ruston, LA 71272

(318)257-3537

Fax: (318)257-4253

Tracey Jeffers, Dir.

Louisiana State University at Shreveport

Small Business Development Center

College of Business Administration

1 University Dr.

Shreveport, LA 71115

(318)797-5144

Fax: (318)797-5208

Peggy Cannon, Dir.

Nicholls State University

Small Business Development Center

College of Business Administration

PO Box 2015

Thibodaux, LA 70310
(504)448-4242
Fax: (504)448-4922
Weston Hull, Dir.

Maine

**Androscoggin Valley Council
of Governments
Small Business Development Center**
125 Manley Rd.
Auburn, ME 04210
(207)783-9186
Fax: (207)783-5211
Jane Mickeriz, Counselor

**Coastal Enterprises Inc.
SBDC**
Weston Bldg.
7 N. Chestnut St.
Augusta, ME 04330
(207)621-0245
Fax: (207)622-9739
Robert Chiozzi, Counselor

**Eastern Maine Development Corp.
Small Business Development Center**
1 Cumberland Pl., Ste. 300
PO Box 2579
Bangor, ME 04402-2579
(207)942-6389
800-339-6389
Fax: (207)942-3548
Ron Loyd, Dir.

**Belfast Satellite
Waldo County Development Corp.
SBDC**
67 Church St.
Belfast, ME 04915
(207)942-6389
800-339-6389
Fax: (207)942-3548

**Brunswick Satellite
Midcoast Council for Business
Development
SBDC**
8 Lincoln St.
Brunswick, ME 04011
(207)882-4340

**Northern Maine Development
Commission
Small Business Development Center**
2 S. Main St.
PO Box 779
Caribou, ME 04736
(207)498-8736
800-427-8736

Fax: (207)498-3108
Rodney Thompson, Dir.

**East Millinocket Satellite
Katahdin Regional Development Corp.
SBDC**
58 Main St.
East Millinocket, ME 04430
(207)746-5338
Fax: (207)746-9535

**East Wilton Satellite
Robinhood Plaza**
Rte. 2 & 4
East Wilton, ME 04234
(207)783-9186
Fax: (207)783-9186

**Fort Kent Satellite
SBDC**
Aroostook County Registry of Deeds
Elm and Hall Sts.
Fort Kent, ME 04743
(207)498-8736
800-427-8736
Fax: (207)498-3108

**Houlton Satellite
SBDC**
Superior Court House
Court St.
Houlton, ME 04730
(207)498-8736
800-427-8736
Fax: (207)498-3108

**Lewiston Satellite
Business Information Center (BIC)
SBDC**
Bates Mill Complex
35 Canal St.
Lewiston, ME 04240
(207)783-9186
Fax: (207)783-5211

**Machias Satellite
Sunrise County Economic Council
(Calais Area)
SBDC**
63 Main St.
PO Box 679
Machias, ME 04654
(207)454-2430
Fax: (207)255-0983

**University of Southern Maine
Maine SBDC**
96 Falmouth St.
PO Box 9300
Portland, ME 04104-9300

(207)780-4420
Fax: (207)780-4810
E-mail: msbdc@portland.maine.edu
Charles Davis, Dir.

**Rockland Satellite
SBDC**
331 Main St.
Rockland, ME 04841
(207)882-4340
Fax: (207)882-4456

**Rumford Satellite
River Valley Growth Council**
Hotel Harris Bldg.
23 Hartford St.
Rumford, ME 04276
(207)783-9186
Fax: (207)783-5211

**Biddeford Satellite
Biddeford-Saco Chamber of Commerce
and Industry
SBDC**
110 Main St.
Saco, ME 04072
(207)282-1567
Fax: (207)282-3149

**Southern Maine Regional Planning
Commission
Small Business Development Center**
255 Main St.
PO Box Q
Sanford, ME 04073
(207)324-0316
Fax: (207)324-2958
Joseph Vitko, Dir.

**Skowhegan Satellite
SBDC**
Norridgewock Ave.
Skowhegan, ME 04976
(207)621-0245
Fax: (207)622-9739

**South Paris Satellite
SBDC**
166 Main St.
South Paris, ME 04281
(207)783-9186
Fax: (207)783-5211

**Waterville Satellite
Thomas College
SBDC**
Administrative Bldg. - Library
180 W. River Rd.
Waterville, ME 04901
(207)621-0245
Fax: (207)622-9739

Coastal Enterprises, Inc. (Wiscasset)
Small Business Development Center
Water St.
PO Box 268
Wiscasset, ME 04578
(207)882-4340
Fax: (207)882-4456
James Burbank, Dir.

York Satellite
York Chamber of Commerce
SBDC
449 Rte. 1
York, ME 03909
(207)363-4422
Fax: (207)324-2958

Maryland

Anne Arundel, Office of Economic Development
SBDC
2666 Riva Rd., Ste. 200
Annapolis, MD 21401
(410)224-4205
Fax: (410)222-7415
Mike Fish, Consultant

Central Maryland
SBDC
1420 N. Charles St., Rm 142
Baltimore, MD 21201-5779
(410)837-4141
Fax: (410)837-4151
Barney Wilson, Executive Dir.

Hartford County Economic Development Office
SBDC
220 S. Main St.
Bel Air, MD 21014
(410)893-3837
Fax: (410)879-8043
Maurice Brown, Consultant

Maryland Small Business Development Center
7100 Baltimore Ave., Ste. 401
College Park, MD 20740
(301)403-8300
Fax: (301)403-8303
James N. Graham, State Dir.

University of Maryland
SBDC
College of Business and Management
College Park, MD 20742-1815
(301)405-2144
Fax: (301)314-9152

Howard County Economic Development Office
SBDC
6751 Gateway Dr., Ste. 500
Columbia, MD 21044
(410)313-6552
Fax: (410)313-6556
Ellin Dize, Consultant

Western Maryland Small Business Development Center
Western Region, Inc.
3 Commerce Dr.
Cumberland, MD 21502
(301)724-6716
800-457-7232
Fax: (301)777-7504
Sam LaManna, Exec.Dir.

Cecil County Chamber of Commerce
SBDC
135 E. Main St.
Elkton, MD 21921
(410)392-0597
Fax: (410)392-6225
Maurice Brown, Consultant

Frederick Community College
SBDC
7932 Opossumtown Pike
Frederick, MD 21702
(301)846-2683
Fax: (301)846-2689
Website: http://SBDC
Mary Ann Garst, Program Dir.

Arundel Center N.
SBDC
101 Crain Hwy., NW, Rm. 110B
Glen Burnie, MD 21061
(410)766-1910
Fax: (410)766-1911
Mike Fish, Consultant

Community College at Saint Mary's County
SBDC
PO Box 98, Great Mills Rd.
Great Mills, MD 20634
(301)868-6679
Fax: (301)868-7392
James Shepherd

Hagerstown Junior College
SBDC
Technology Innovation Center
11404 Robinwood Dr.
Hagerstown, MD 21740
(301)797-0327
Fax: (301)777-7504
Tonya Fleming Brockett, Dir.

Landover SBDC
7950 New Hampshire Ave., 2nd Fl.
Langley Park, MD 20783
(301)445-7324
Fax: (301)883-6479
Avon Evans, Consultant

Charles County Community College
Southern Maryland SBDC
SBDC
Mitchell Rd.
PO Box 910
LaPlata, MD 20646-0910
(301)934-7580
800-762-7232
Fax: (301)934-7681
Betsy Cooksey, Exec. Dir.

Garrett Community College
SBDC
Mosser Rd.
McHenry, MD 21541
(301)387-6666
Fax: (301)387-3096
Sandy Major, Business Analyst

Salisbury State University
Eastern Shore Region Small Business Development Center
Power Professional Bldg., Ste. 170
Salisbury, MD 21801
(410)546-4325
800-999-7232
Fax: (410)548-5389
Marty Green, Exec.Dir.

Baltimore County Chamber of Commerce
SBDC
102 W. Pennsylvania Ave., Ste. 402
Towson, MD 21204
(410)832-5866
Fax: (410)821-9901
John Casper, Consultant

Prince George's County Minority Business Opportunities Commission
Suburban Washington Region Small Business Development Center
1400 McCormick Dr., Ste. 282
Upper Marlboro, MD 20774
(301)883-6491
Fax: (301)883-6479
Avon Evans, Acting Executive Dir.

Carrol County Economic Development Office
SBDC
125 N. Court St., Rm. 101
Westminster, MD 21157

(410)857-8166
Fax: (410)848-0003
Michael Fish, Consultant

Eastern Region - Upper Shore SBDC
PO Box 8
Wye Mills, MD 21679
(410)822-5400
800-762SBDC
Fax: (410)827-5286
Patricia Ann Marie Schaller, Consultant

Massachusetts

International Trade Center
University of Massachusetts Amherst
SBDC
205 School of Management
Amherst, MA 01003-4935
(413)545-6301
Fax: (413)545-1273

University of Massachusetts
Massachusetts SBDC
205 School of Management
Amherst, MA 01003-4935
(413)545-6301
Fax: (413)545-1273
John Ciccarelli, State Dir.

Massachusetts Export Center
World Trade Center, Ste. 315
Boston, MA 02210
(617)478-4133
800-478-4133
Fax: (617)478-4135
Paula Murphy, Dir.

Minority Business Assistance Center
SBDC
University of Massachusetts (Boston)
College of Management, 5th Fl.
Boston, MA 02125-3393
(617)287-7750
Fax: (617)287-7767
Hank Turner, Dir.

Boston College
Capital Formation Service
SBDC
Rahner House
96 College Rd.
Chestnut Hill, MA 02167
(617)552-4091
Fax: (617)552-2730
Don Reilley, Dir.

Metropolitan Boston Small Business
Development Center Regional Office
Rahner House
96 College Rd.

Chestnut Hill, MA 02167
(617)552-4091
Fax: (617)552-2730
Dr. Jack McKiernan, Regional Dir.

Southeastern Massachusetts Small
Business Development Center Regional
Office
200 Pocasset St.
PO Box 2785
Fall River, MA 02722
(508)673-9783
Fax: (508)674-1929
Clyde Mitchell, Regional Dir.

North Shore Massachusetts Small
Business Development Center Regional
Office
197 Essex St.
Salem, MA 01970
(508)741-6343
Fax: (508)741-6345
Frederick Young, Regional Dir.

Western Massachusetts Small Business
Development Center Regional Office
101 State St., Ste. 424
Springfield, MA 01103
(413)737-6712
Fax: (413)737-2312
Dianne Fuller Doherty, Regional Dir.

Clark University
Central Massachusetts Small Business
Development Center Regional Office
Dana Commons
950 Main St.
Worcester, MA 01610
(508)793-7615
Fax: (508)793-8890
Laurence March, Regional Dir.

Michigan

Lenawee County Chamber of
Commerce
SBDC
202 N. Main St., Ste. A
Adrian, MI 49221-2713
(517)266-1488
Fax: (517)263-6065
Sally Pinchock, Dir.

Allegan County Economic Alliance
SBDC
Allegan Intermediate School Bldg.
2891 M-277
PO Box 277
Allegan, MI 49010-8042
(616)673-8442

Fax: (616)650-8042
Chuck Birr, Dir.

Ottawa County Economic Development
Office, Inc.
Small Business Development Center
6676 Lake Michigan Dr.
PO Box 539
Allendale, MI 49401-0539
(616)892-4120
Fax: (616)895-6670
Ken Rizzio, Dir.

Gratiot Area Chamber of Commerce
SBDC
110 W. Superior St.
PO Box 516
Alma, MI 48801-0516
(517)463-5525

Alpena Community College
SBDC
666 Johnson St.
Alpena, MI 49707
(517)356-9021
Fax: (517)354-7507
Carl Bourdelais, Dir.

MMTC SBDC
2901 Hubbard Rd.
PO Box 1485
Ann Arbor, MI 48106-1485
(313)769-4110
Fax: (313)769-4064
Bill Loomis, Dir.

Huron County Economic
Development Corp.
Small Business Development Center
Huron County Bldg., Rm. 303
250 E. Huron
Bad Axe, MI 48413
(517)269-6431
Fax: (517)269-7221
Carl Osentoski, Dir.

Battle Creek Area Chamber
of Commerce
SBDC
4 Riverwalk Centre
34 W. Jackson, Ste. A
Battle Creek, MI 49017
(616)962-4076
Fax: (616)962-4076
Kathy Perrett, Dir.

Bay Area Chamber of Commerce
SBDC
901 Saginaw
Bay City, MI 48708
(517)893-4567

Fax: (517)893-7016
Cheryl Hiner, Dir.

Lake Michigan College
Corporation and Community
Development Department
Small Business Development Center
2755 E. Napier
Benton Harbor, MI 49022-1899
(616)927-8179
Fax: (616)927-8103
Milton E. Richter, Dir.

Ferris State University
Small Business Development Center
330 Oak St.
West 115
Big Rapids, MI 49307
(616)592-3553
Fax: (616)592-3539
Lora Swenson, Dir.

Northern Lakes Economic Alliance
SBDC
1048 East Main St.
PO Box 8
Boyne City, MI 49712-0008
(616)582-6482
Fax: (616)582-3213
Thomas Johnson, Dir.

Livingston County Small Business
Development Center
131 S. Hyne
Brighton, MI 48116
(810)227-3556
Fax: (810)227-3080
Dennis Whitney, Dir.

Buchanan Chamber of Commerce
SBDC
119 Main St.
Buchanan, MI 49107
(616)695-3291
Fax: (616)695-4250
Marlene Gauer, Dir.

Tuscola County Economic
Development Corp.
Small Business Development Center
194 N. State St., Ste. 200
Caro, MI 48723
(517)673-2849
Fax: (517)673-2517
James McLoskey, Dir.

Branch County Economic
Growth Alliance
SBDC
20 Division St.
Coldwater, MI 49036

(517)278-4146
Fax: (517)278-8369
Joyce Elferdink, Dir.

University of Detroit-Mercy
Small Business Development Center
Commerce and Finance Bldg., Rm. 105
4001 W. McNichols
PO Box 19900
Detroit, MI 48219-0900
(313)993-1115
Fax: (313)993-1052
Ram Kesavan, Dir.

Wayne State University
Michigan SBDC
2727 Second Ave., Ste. 107
Detroit, MI 48201
(313)964-1798
Fax: (313)964-3648
E-mail: stateoffice@misbdc.wayne.edu
Ronald R. Hall, State Dir.

First Step, Inc.
Small Business Development Center
2415 14th Ave., S.
Escanaba, MI 49829
(906)786-9234
Fax: (906)786-4442
David Gillis, Dir.

Community Capital
Development Corp.
SBDC
Walter Ruether Center
711 N. Saginaw, Ste. 123
Flint, MI 48503
(810)239-5847
Fax: (810)239-5575
Kim Yarber, Dir.

Center For Continuing Education-
Macomb Community College
SBDC
32101 Caroline
Fraser, MI 48026
(810)296-3516
Fax: (810)293-0427

North Central Michigan College
SBDC
800 Livingston Blvd.
Gaylord, MI 49735
(517)731-0071

Association of Commerce and Industry
SBDC
1 S. Harbor Ave.
PO Box 509
Grand Haven, MI 49417

(616)846-3153
Fax: (616)842-0379
Karen K. Benson, Dir.

Grand Valley State University
SBDC
Seidman School of Business, Ste. 718S
301 W. Fulton St.
Grand Rapids, MI 49504
(616)771-6693
Fax: (616)458-3872
Carol R. Lopucki, Dir.

The Right Place Program
SBDC
820 Monroe NW, Ste. 350
Grand Rapids, MI 49503-1423
(616)771-0571
Fax: (616)458-3768
Raymond P. DeWinkle, Dir.

Oceana County Economic
Development Corp.
SBDC
100 State St.
PO Box 168
Hart, MI 49420-0168
(616)873-7141
Fax: (616)873-5914
Charles Persenaire, Dir.

Hastings Industrial Incubator
SBDC
1035 E. State St.
Hastings, MI 49058
(616)948-2305
Fax: (616)948-2947
Joe Rahn, Dir.

Greater Gratiot Development, Inc.
Small Business Center
136 S. Main
Ithaca, MI 48847
(517)875-2083
Fax: (517)875-2990
Don Schurr, Dir.

Jackson Business Development Center
SBDC
414 N. Jackson St.
Jackson, MI 49201
(517)787-0442
Fax: (517)787-3960
Duane Miller, Dir.

Kalamazoo College
Small Business Development Center
Stryker Center for Management Studies
1327 Academy St.
Kalamazoo, MI 49006-3200

(616)337-7350
Fax: (616)337-7415
Carl R. Shook, Dir.

Lansing Community College
Small Business Development Center
Continental Bldg.
333 N. Washington Sq.
PO Box 40010
Lansing, MI 48901-7210
(517)483-1921
Fax: (517)483-9803
Deleski Smith, Dir.

Lapeer Development Corp.
Small Business Development Center
449 McCormick Dr.
Lapeer, MI 48446
(810)667-0080
Fax: (810)667-3541
Patricia Crawford Lucas, Dir.

Midland Chamber of Commerce
SBDC
300 Rodd St.
Midland, MI 48640
(517)839-9901
Fax: (517)835-3701
Sam Boeke, Dir.

Genesis Center for Entrepreneurial
Development
SBDC
111 Conant Ave.
Monroe, MI 48161
(313)243-5947
Fax: (313)242-0009
Dani Topolski, Dir.

Macomb County Business
Assistance Network
Small Business Development Center
115 S. Groesbeck Hwy.
Mt. Clemens, MI 48043
(810)469-5118
Fax: (810)469-6787
Donald L. Morandi, Dir.

Central Michigan University
Small Business Development Center
256 Applied Business Studies Complex
Mt. Pleasant, MI 48859
(517)774-3270
Fax: (517)774-7992
Charles Fitzpatrick, Dir.

Muskegon Economic Growth Alliance
Small Business Development Center
230 Terrace Plz.
PO Box 1087

Muskegon, MI 49443-1087
(616)722-3751
Fax: (616)728-7251
Mert Johnson, Dir.

Harbor County Chamber of Commerce
SBDC
3 W. Buffalo
New Buffalo, MI 49117
(616)469-5409
Fax: (616)469-2257

Greater Niles Economic
Development Fund
SBDC
1105 N. Front St.
Niles, MI 49120
(616)683-1833
Fax: (616)683-7515
Chris Brynes, Dir.

Huron Shores Campus
SBDC
5800 Skeel Ave.
Oscoda, MI 48750
(517)739-1445
Fax: (517)739-1161
Dave Wentworth, Dir.

St. Clair County Community Small
Business Development Center
800 Military St., Ste. 320
Port Huron, MI 48060-5015
(810)982-9511
Fax: (810)982-9531
Todd Brian, Dir.

Kirtland Community College
SBDC
10775 N. St. Helen Rd.
Roscommon, MI 48653
(517)275-5121
Fax: (517)275-8745
John Loiacano, Dir.

Saginaw County Chamber of Commerce
SBDC
901 S. Washington Ave.
Saginaw, MI 48601
(517)752-7161
Fax: (517)752-9055
James Bockelman, Dir.

Saginaw Future, Inc.
Small Business Development Center
301 E. Genesee, 3rd Fl.
Saginaw, MI 48607
(517)754-8222
Fax: (517)754-1715
Matthew Hufnagel, Dir.

Washtenaw Community College
SBDC
740 Woodland
Saline, MI 48176
(313)944-1016
Fax: (313)944-0165
Kathleen Woodard, Dir.

West Shore Community College
Small Business Development Center
Business and Industrial Development
Institute
3000 N. Stiles Rd.
PO Box 277
Scottville, MI 49454-0277
(616)845-6211
Fax: (616)845-0207
Mark Bergstrom, Dir.

South Haven Chamber of Commerce
SBDC
300 Broadway
South Haven, MI 49090
(616)637-5171
Fax: (616)639-1570
Larry King, Dir.

Downriver Small Business
Development Center
15100 Northline Rd.
Southgate, MI 48195
(313)281-0700
Fax: (313)281-3418
Paula Boase, Dir.

Arenac County Extension Service
SBDC
County Bldg.
PO Box 745
Standish, MI 48658
(517)846-4111

Sterling Heights Area Chamber
of Commerce
Small Business Development Center
12900 Hall Rd., Ste. 110
Sterling Heights, MI 48313
(810)731-5400
Fax: (810)731-3521
Lillian Adams-Yanssens, Dir.

Northwest Michigan Council of
Governments
Small Business Development Center
2200 Dendrinos Dr.
PO Box 506
Traverse City, MI 49685-0506
(616)929-5000
Fax: (616)929-5017
Richard J. Beldin, Dir.

Northwestern Michigan College
Small Business Development
Center
Center for Business and Industry
1701 E. Front St.
Traverse City, MI 49686
(616)922-1717
Fax: (616)922-1722
Cheryl Troop, Dir.

Traverse Bay Economic Development
Corp.
Small Business Development
Center
202 E. Grandview Pkwy.
PO Box 387
Traverse City, MI 49684
(616)946-1596
Fax: (616)946-2565
Charles Blankenship, Dir.

Traverse City Area Chamber of
Commerce
Small Business Development
Center
202 E. Grandview Pkwy.
PO Box 387
Traverse City, MI 49684
(616)947-5075
Fax: (616)946-2565
Matthew Meadors, Dir.

Oakland Count Small Business
Development Center
SOC Bldg.
4555 Corporate Dr., Ste. 201
PO Box 7085
Troy, MI 48098
(810)641-0088
Fax: (810)267-3809
Daniel V. Belknap, Dir.

Saginaw Valley State University
Small Business Development
Center
7400 Bay Rd.
7400 Bay Rd.
University Center, MI 48710-0001
(517)791-7746
Fax: (517)249-1955
Christine Greve, Dir.

Macomb Community College
SBDC
14500 12 Mile Rd.
Warren, MI 48093
(810)445-7348
Fax: (810)445-7316
Geary Maiurini, Dir.

Warren - Centerline - Sterling Heights
Chamber of Commerce
Small Business Development Center
30500 Van Dyke, Ste. 118
Warren, MI 48093
(313)751-3939
Fax: (313)751-3995
Janet Masi, Dir.

Minnesota

Northwest Technical College
SBDC
905 Grant Ave., SE
Bemidji, MN 56601
(218)755-4286
Fax: (218)755-4289
Susan Kozojed, Dir.

Normandale Community College
(Bloomington)
Small Business Development Center
9700 France Ave. S
Bloomington, MN 55431
(612)832-6398
Fax: (612)832-6352
Scott Harding, Dir.

Central Lakes College
Small Business Development Center
501 W. College Dr.
Brainerd, MN 56401
(218)825-2028
Fax: (218)828-2053
Pamela Thomsen, Dir.

University of Minnesota at Duluth
Small Business Development Center
School of Business and Economics,
Rm. 150
10 University Dr.
Duluth, MN 55812-2496
(218)726-8758
Fax: (218)726-6338
Lee Jensen, Dir.

Itasca Development Corp.
Grand Rapids Small Business
Development Center
19 NE 3rd St.
Grand Rapids, MN 55744
(218)327-2241
Fax: (218)327-2242
Kirk Bustrom, Dir.

Hibbing Community College
Small Business Development Center
1515 E. 25th St.
Hibbing, MN 55746
(218)262-6703

Fax: (218)262-6717
Jim Antilla, Dir.

Rainy River Community College
Small Business Development Center
1501 Hwy. 71
International Falls, MN 56649
(218)285-2255
Fax: (218)285-2239
Tom West, Dir.

Region Nine Development Commission
SBDC
410 Jackson St.
PO Box 3367
Mankato, MN 56002-3367
(507)389-8863
Fax: (507)387-7105
Jill Miller, Dir.

Southwest State University
Small Business Development Center
Science and Technical Resource Center,
Ste. 105
1501 State St.
Marshall, MN 56258
(507)537-7386
Fax: (507)387-7105
Jack Hawk, Dir.

Minnesota Project Innovation
Small Business Development Center
111 3rd Ave. S., Ste. 100
Minneapolis, MN 55401
(612)347-6751
Fax: (612)338-3483
Pat Dillon, Dir.

University of St. Thomas
SBDC
Mail Stop 25H 225
Ste. MPL 100
Minneapolis, MN 55403
(612)962-4500
Fax: (612)962-4810
Gregg Schneider, Dir.

Moorhead State University
Small Business Development Center
1104 7th Ave. S.
MSU Box 303
Moorhead, MN 56563
(218)236-2289
Fax: (218)236-2280
Len Sliwoski, Dir.

Owatonna Incubator, Inc.
SBDC
560 Dunnell Dr., Ste. 203
PO Box 505
Owatonna, MN 55060

(507)451-0517
Fax: (507)455-2788
Ken Henrickson, Dir.

Pine Technical College
Small Business Development Center
1100 4th St.
Pine City, MN 55063
(320)629-7340
Fax: (320)629-7603
John Sparling, Dir.

Hennepin Technical College
SBDC
1820 N. Xenium Ln.
Plymouth, MN 55441
(612)550-7218
Fax: (612)550-7272
Danelle Wolf, Dir.

Pottery Business and Tech. Center
Small Business Development Center
2000 Pottery Pl. Dr., Ste. 339
Red Wing, MN 55066
(612)388-4079
Fax: (612)385-2251
Marv Bollum, Dir.

Rochester Community and Tech.
College
Small Business Development Center
Riverland Hall
851 30th Ave. SE
Rochester, MN 55904
(507)285-7425
Fax: (507)285-7110
Michelle Pyfferoen, Dir.

Dakota County Technical College
Small Business Development Center
1300 E. 145th St.
Rosemount, MN 55068
(612)423-8262
Fax: (612)322-5156
Tom Trutna, Dir.

Southeast Minnesota Development
Corp.
SBDC
111 W. Jessie St.
PO Box 684
Rushford, MN 55971
(507)864-7557
Fax: (507)864-2091
Terry Erickson, Dir.

St. Cloud State University
Small Business Development Center
720 4th Ave. S.
St. Cloud, MN 56301-3761

(320)255-4842
Fax: (320)255-4957
Dawn Jensen-Ragnier, Dir.

Department of Trade and Economic
Development
Minnesota SBDC
500 Metro Sq.
121 7th Pl. E.
St. Paul, MN 55101-2146
(612)297-5770
Fax: (612)296-1290
Mary Kruger, State Dir.

Minnesota Technology, Inc.
Small Business Development Center
Olcott Plaza Bldg., Ste. 140
820 N. 9th St.
Virginia, MN 55792
(218)741-4241
Fax: (218)741-4249
John Freeland, Dir.

Wadena Chamber of Commerce
SBDC
222 2nd St., SE
Wadena, MN 56482
(218)631-1502
Fax: (218)631-2396
Paul Kinn, Dir.

Century College
SBDC
3300 Century Ave., N., Ste. 200-D
White Bear Lake, MN 55110-1894
(612)773-1794
Fax: (612)779-5802
Ernie Brodtmann, Dir.

Mississippi

Northeast Mississippi Community
College
SBDC
Holiday Hall, 2nd Fl.
Cunningham Blvd.
Booneville, MS 38829
(601)720-7448
Fax: (601)720-7464
Kenny Holt, Dir.

Delta State University
Small Business Development Center
PO Box 3235 DSU
Cleveland, MS 38733
(601)846-4236
Fax: (601)846-4235
David Holman, Dir.

East Central Community College
SBDC
Broad St.
PO Box 129
Decatur, MS 39327
(601)635-2111
Fax: (601)635-4031
Ronald Westbrook, Dir.

Jones County Junior College
SBDC
900 Court St.
Ellisville, MS 39437
(601)477-4165
Fax: (601)477-4166
Gary Suddith, Dir.

Mississippi Gulf Coast Community
College
SBDC
Jackson County Campus
PO Box 100
Gautier, MS 39553
(601)497-7723
Fax: (601)497-7788
Janice Mabry, Dir.

Mississippi Delta Community College
Small Business Development Center
PO Box 5607
Greenville, MS 38704-5607
(601)378-8183
Fax: (601)378-5349
Chuck Herring, Dir.

Mississippi Contract Procurement
Center
SBDC
3015 12th St.
PO Box 610
Gulfport, MS 39502-0610
(601)864-2961
Fax: (601)864-2969
C. W. "Skip" Ryland, Exec.Dir.

Pearl River Community College
Small Business Development Center
5448 U.S. Hwy. 49 S.
Hattiesburg, MS 39401
(601)544-0030
Fax: (601)544-9149
Heidi McDuffie, Dir.

Mississippi Valley State University
Affiliate SBDC
PO Box 992
Itta Bena, MS 38941
(601)254-3601
Fax: (601)254-6704
Dr. Jim Breyley, Dir.

Jackson State University
Small Business Development Center
Jackson Enterprise Center, Ste. A-1
931 Hwy. 80 W
Box 43
Jackson, MS 39204
(601)968-2795
Fax: (601)968-2796
Henry Thomas, Dir.

University of Southern Mississippi
Small Business Development Center
136 Beach Park Pl.
Long Beach, MS 39560
(601)865-4578
Fax: (601)865-4581
Lucy Betcher, Dir.

Alcorn State University
SBDC
552 West St.
PO Box 90
Lorman, MS 39096-9402
(601)877-6684
Fax: (601)877-6256
Sharon Witty, Dir.

Meridian Community College
Small Business Development Center
910 Hwy. 19 N
Meridian, MS 39307
(601)482-7445
Fax: (601)482-5803
Mac Hodges, Dir.

Mississippi State University
Small Business Development Center
1 Research Bldg., Ste 201
PO Drawer 5288
Mississippi State, MS 39762
(601)325-8684
Fax: (601)325-4016
Sonny Fisher, Dir.

Copiah-Lincoln Community College
Small Business Development Center
11 County Line Circle
Natchez, MS 39120
(601)445-5254
Fax: (601)446-1221
Bob D. Russ, Dir.

Hinds Community College
Small Business Development Center/
International Trade Center
1500 Raymond Lake Rd., 2nd Fl.
Raymond, MS 39154
(601)857-3536
Fax: (601)857-3474
Marguerite Wall, Dir.

Holmes Community College
SBDC
412 W. Ridgeland Ave.
Ridgeland, MS 39157
(601)853-0827
Fax: (601)853-0844
John Deddens, Dir.

Northwest Mississippi Community
College
SBDC
DeSoto Ctr.
5197 W.E. Ross Pkwy.
Southaven, MS 38671
(601)280-7648
Fax: (601)280-7648
Jody Dunning, Dir.

Southwest Mississippi Community
College
SBDC
College Dr.
Summit, MS 39666
(601)276-3890
Fax: (601)276-3883
Kathryn Durham, Dir.

Itawamba Community College
Small Business Development Center
653 Eason Blvd.
Tupelo, MS 38801
(601)680-8515
Fax: (601)680-8547
Rex Hollingsworth, Dir.

University of Mississippi
Mississippi SBDC
N.C.P.A., Rm. 1082
University, MS 38677
(601)234-2120
Fax: (601)232-4220
Michael Vanderlip, Dir.

University of Mississippi
SBDC
Old Chemistry Bldg., Ste. 216
University, MS 38677
(601)232-5001
Fax: (601)232-5650
Walter D. Gurley Jr.

Missouri

Camden County
SBDC Extension Center
113 Kansas
PO Box 1405
Camdenton, MO 65020
(573)882-0344
Fax: (573)884-4297
Jackie Rasmussen, B&I Spec.

Missouri PAC - Southeastern Missouri
State University
SBDC
222 N. Pacific
Cape Girardeau, MO 63701
(573)290-5965
Fax: (573)651-5005
George Williams, Dir.

Southeast Missouri State University
Small Business Development Center
University Plaza
MS 5925
Cape Girardeau, MO 63701
(573)290-5965
Fax: (573)651-5005
E-mail: sbdc-cg@ext.missouri.edu
Frank "Buz" Sutherland, Dir.

Chillicothe City Hall
SBDC
715 Washington St.
Chillicothe, MO 64601-2229
(660)646-6920
Fax: (660)646-6811
Nanette Anderjaska, Dir.

East Central Missouri - St. Louis
County
Extension Center
121 S. Meramac, Ste. 501
Clayton, MO 63105
(314)889-2911
Fax: (314)854-6147
Carole Leriche-Price, B&I Specialist

Boone County Extension Center
SBDC
1012 N. Hwy. UU
Columbia, MO 65203
(573)445-9792
Fax: (573)445-9807
Mr. Casey Venters, B&I Specialist

MO PAC-Central Region
University of Missouri-Columbia
SBDC
University Pl., Ste. 1800
1205 University Ave.
Columbia, MO 65211
(573)882-3597
Fax: (573)884-4297
E-mail: mopcol@ext.missouri.edu
Morris Hudson, Dir.

University of Missouri
Missouri SBDC System
1205 University Ave., Ste. 300
Columbia, MO 65211
(573)882-0344

Fax: (573)884-4297
E-mail: sbdc-mso@ext.missouri.edu
Max E. Summers, State Dir.

University of Missouri–Columbia
Small Business Development Center
University Pl., Ste. 1800
1205 University Ave.
Columbia, MO 65211
(573)882-7096
Fax: (573)882-6156
E-mail: sbdc-c@ext.missouri.edu
Frank Siebert, Dir.

Hannibal Satellite Center
Hannibal, MO 63401
(816)385-6550
Fax: (816)385-6568

Jefferson County
Extension Center
Courthouse, Annex 203
725 Maple St.
PO Box 497
Hillsboro, MO 63050
(573)789-5391
Fax: (573)789-5059

Cape Girardeau County
SBDC Extension Center
815 Hwy. 25S
PO Box 408
Jackson, MO 63755
(573)243-3581
Fax: (573)243-1606
Richard Sparks, B&I Specialist

Cole County Extension Center
SBDC
2436 Tanner Bridge Rd.
Jefferson City, MO 65101
(573)634-2824
Fax: (573)634-5463
Mr. Chris Bouchard, B&I Specialist

Missouri Southern State College
Small Business Development Center
Matthews Hall, Ste. 107
3950 Newman Rd.
Joplin, MO 64801-1595
(417)625-9313
Fax: (417)625-9782
E-mail: sbdc-j@ext.missouri.edu
Jim Krudwig, Dir.

Rockhurst College
Small Business Development Center
1100 Rockhurst Rd.
VanAckeren Hall, Rm. 205
Kansas City, MO 64110-2508
(816)501-4572

Fax: (816)501-4646
Rhonda Gerke, Dir.

Truman State University
Small Business Development Center
100 E. Norman
Kirksville, MO 63501-4419
(816)785-4307
Fax: (816)785-4357
E-mail: sbdc-k@ext.missouri.edu
Glen Giboney, Dir.

Thomas Hill Enterprise Center
SBDC
1409 N. Prospect Dr.
PO Box 246
Macon, MO 63552
(816)385-6550
Fax: (816)562-3071
Jane Vanderham, Dir.

Northwest Missouri State University
Small Business Development Center
423 N. Market St.
Maryville, MO 64468-1614
(660)562-1701
Fax: (660)582-3071
Brad Anderson, Dir.

Audrain County Extension Center
SBDC
Courthouse, 4th Fl.
101 Jefferson
Mexico, MO 65265
(573)581-3231
Fax: (573)581-2766
Virgil Woolridge, B&I Specialist

Randolph County
Extension Center
417 E. Urbandale
Moberly, MO 65270
(816)263-3534
Fax: (816)263-1874
Ray Marshall, B&I Specialist

Mineral Area College
SBDC
PO Box 1000
Park Hills, MO 63601-1000
(573)431-4593
Fax: (573)431-2144
E-mail: sbdc-fr@ext.missouri.edu
Eugene Cherry, Dir.

Telecommunications Community
Resource Center
Longhead Learning Center
Small Business Development Center
1121 Victory Ln.
3019 Fair St.

Poplar Bluff, MO 63901
(573)840-9450
Fax: (573)840-9456
Judy Moss, Dir.

Washington County SBDC
102 N. Missouri
Potosi, MO 63664
(573)438-2671
Fax: (573)438-2079
LaDonna McCuan, B&I Specialist

Center for Technology Transfer and
Economic Development
Nagogami Ter., Bldg. 1, Rm. 104
Rolla, MO 65401-0249
(573)341-4559
Fax: (573)346-2694
Fred Goss, Dir.

Phelps County
SBDC Extension Center
Courthouse
200 N. Main
PO Box 725
Rolla, MO 65401
(573)364-3147
Fax: (573)364-0436
Paul Cretin, B&I Specialist

University of Missouri at Rolla
SBDC
Nagogami Terrace, Bldg. 1, Rm. 104
Rolla, MO 65401-0249
(573)341-4559
Fax: (573)341-6495
E-mail: sbdc-rt@ext.missouri.edu
Fred Goss, Dir.

Missouri PAC - Eastern Region
SBDC
3830 Washington Ave.
St. Louis, MO 63108
(314)534-4413
Fax: (314)534-3237
E-mail: mopstl@ext.missouri.edu
Ken Konchel, Dir.

St. Louis County
Extension Center
207 Marillac, UMSL
8001 Natural Bridge Rd.
St. Louis, MO 63121
(314)553-5944
John Henschke, Specialist

St. Louis University
Small Business State University
SBDC
3750 Lindell Blvd.
St. Louis, MO 63108-3412

(314)977-7232
Fax: (314)977-7241
E-mail: sbdc-stl@ext.missouri.edu
Virginia Campbell, Dir.

St. Louis/St. Charles County Economic Council
SBDC Extension Center
260 Brown Rd.
St. Peters, MO 63376
(314)970-3000
Fax: (314)274-3310
Tim Wathen, B&I Specialist

Pettis County
Extension Center
1012A Thompson Blvd.
Sedalia, MO 65301
(816)827-0591
Fax: (816)827-4888
Betty Lorton, B&I Specialist

Southwest Missouri State University
Center for Business Research
Small Business Development Center
901 S. National
Box 88
Springfield, MO 65804-0089
(417)836-5685
Fax: (417)836-7666
Jane Peterson, Dir.

Franklin County
SBDC Extension Center
414 E. Main
PO Box 71
Union, MO 63084
(573)583-5141
Fax: (573)583-5145
Rebecca How, B&I Specialist

Central Missouri State University
Center for Technology
Grinstead, No. 75
Warrensburg, MO 64093-5037
(816)543-4402
Fax: (816)747-1653
Cindy Tanck, Coordinator

Central Missouri State University
SBDC
Grinstead, No. 9
Warrensburg, MO 64093-5037
(816)543-4402
Fax: (816)543-8159
Wes Savage, Coordinator

Howell County
SBDC Extension Center
217 S. Aid Ave.
West Plains, MO 65775

(417)256-2391
Fax: (417)256-8569
Mick Gilliam, B&I Specialist

Montana

Montana Tradepost Authority
Small Business Development Center
2722 3rd Ave., Ste. W300
Billings, MT 59101
(406)256-6871
Fax: (406)256-6877
Tom McKerlick, Contact

Bozeman Small Business Development Center
222 E. Main St., Ste. 102
Bozeman, MT 59715
(406)587-3113
Fax: (406)587-9565
Michele DuBose, Contact

Butte Small Business Development Center
305 W. Mercury, Ste. 211
Butte, MT 59701
(406)782-7333
Fax: (406)782-9675
John Donovan, Contact

High Plains Development Authority
Great Falls SBDC
710 1st. Ave. N.
PO Box 2568
Great Falls, MT 59403
(406)454-1934
Fax: (406)454-2995
Suzie David

Havre Small Business Development Center
PO Box 170
Havre, MT 59501
(406)265-9226
Fax: (406)265-5602
Randy Hanson, Contact

Montana Department of Commerce
Montana SBDC
1424 9th Ave.
PO Box 200505
Helena, MT 59620
(406)444-2463
Fax: (406)444-1872
Ralph Kloser, State Dir.

Kalispell Small Business Development Center
PO Box 8300
Kalispell, MT 59901

(406)758-5412
Fax: (406)758-6582
Dan Manning, Contact

Missoula Small Business Development Center
127 N. Higgins, 3rd Fl.
Missoula, MT 59802
(406)728-9234
Fax: (406)721-4584
Brett George, Contact

Sidney Small Business Development Center
123 W. Main
Sidney, MT 59270
(406)482-5024
Fax: (406)482-5306
Dwayne Heintz, Contact

Nebraska

Chadron State College
SBDC
Administration Bldg.
1000 Main St.
Chadron, NE 69337
(308)432-6282
Fax: (308)432-6430
Cliff Hanson, Dir.

University of Nebraska
at Kearney
SBDC
Welch Hall
19th St. and College Dr.
Kearney, NE 68849-3035
(308)865-8344
Fax: (308)865-8153
Susan Jensen, Dir.

University of Nebraska
at Lincoln
SBDC
1135 M St., No. 200
11th and Cornhusker Hwy.
Lincoln, NE 68521
(402)472-3358
Fax: (402)472-3363
Cliff Mosteller, Dir.

Mid-Plains Community College
SBDC
416 N. Jeffers, Rm. 26
North Platte, NE 69101
(308)534-5115
Fax: (308)534-5117
Dean Kurth, Dir.

Nebraska Small Business Development Center

Omaha Business and Technology Center
2505 N. 24 St., Ste. 101
Omaha, NE 68110
(402)595-3511
Fax: (402)595-3524
Tom McCabe, Dir.

University of Nebraska at Omaha
Nebraska Business Development Center
College of Business Administration, Rm. 407
60th & Dodge Sts.
CBA Rm. 407
Omaha, NE 68182
(402)554-2521
Fax: (402)554-3747
Robert Bernier, State Dir.

University of Nebraska at Omaha
Peter Kiewit Conference Center
SBDC
1313 Farnam-on-the-Mall, Ste. 132
Omaha, NE 68182-0248
(402)595-2381
Fax: (402)595-2385
Nate Brei, Dir.

Peru State College
SBDC
T.J. Majors Hall, Rm. 248
Peru, NE 68421
(402)872-2274
Fax: (402)872-2422
Jerry Brazil, Dir.

Western Nebraska Community College
SBDC
Nebraska Public Power Bldg., Rm. 408
1721 Broadway
Scottsbluff, NE 69361
(308)635-7513
Fax: (308)635-6596
Ingrid Battershell, Dir.

Wayne State College
SBDC
Gardner Hall
1111 Main St.
Wayne, NE 68787
(402)375-7575
Fax: (402)375-7574
Loren Kucera, Dir.

Nevada

Carson City Chamber of Commerce
Small Business Development Center
1900 S. Carson St., Ste. 100
Carson City, NV 89701
(702)882-1565
Fax: (702)882-4179
Larry Osborne, Dir.

Great Basin College
Small Business Development Center
1500 College Pkwy.
Elko, NV 89801
(702)753-2205
Fax: (702)753-2242
John Pryor, Dir.

Incline Village Chamber of Commerce
SBDC
969 Tahoe Blvd.
Incline Village, NV 89451
(702)831-4440
Fax: (702)832-1605
Sheri Woods, Exec. Dir.

Las Vegas SBDC
SBDC
3720 Howard Hughes Pkwy., Ste. 130
Las Vegas, NV 89109
(702)734-7575
Fax: (702)734-7633
Robert Holland, Bus. Dev. Specialist

University of Nevada at Las Vegas
Small Business Development Center
4505 Maryland Pkwy.
Box 456011
Las Vegas, NV 89154-6011
(702)895-0852
Fax: (702)895-4095
Nancy Buist, Business Development Specialist

North Las Vegas Small Business Development Center
19 W. Brooks Ave., Ste. B
North Las Vegas, NV 89030
(702)399-6300
Fax: (702)895-4095
Janis Stevenson, Business Development Specialist

University of Nevada at Reno
Small Business Development Center
College of Business Administration
Nazir Ansari Business Bldg., Rm. 411
Reno, NV 89557-0100
(702)784-1717

Fax: (702)784-4337
E-mail: nsbdc@scs.unr.edu
Sam Males, Dir.

Tri-County Development Authority
Small Business Development Center
50 W. 4th St.
PO Box 820
Winnemucca, NV 89446
(702)623-5777
Fax: (702)623-5999
Teri Williams, Dir.

New Hampshire

University of New Hampshire
Small Business Development Center
108 McConnell Hall
15 College Rd.
Durham, NH 03824-3593
(603)862-2200
Fax: (603)862-4876
Mary Collins, State Dir.

Keene State College
Small Business Development Center
Mail Stop 210
Keene, NH 03435-2101
(603)358-2602
Fax: (603)358-2612
Gary Cloutier, Regional Mgr.

Littleton Small Business Development Center
120 Main St.
Littleton, NH 03561
(603)444-1053
Fax: (603)444-5463
Liz Ward, Regional Mgr.

Manchester Small Business Development Center
1000 Elm St., 14th Fl.
Manchester, NH 03101
(603)624-2000
Fax: (603)634-2449
Bob Ebberson, Regional Mgr.

Office of Economic Initiatives
SBDC
1000 Elm St., 14th Fl.
Manchester, NH 03101
(603)634-2796
E-mail: ahj@hopper.unh.edu
Amy Jennings, Dir.

New Hampshire Small Business Development Center
1 Indian Head Plz., Ste. 510
Nashua, NH 03060

(603)886-1233
Fax: (603)598-1164
Bob Wilburn, Regional Mgr.

Plymouth State College
Small Business Development Center
Outreach Center, MSC24A
Plymouth, NH 03264-1595
(603)535-2523
Fax: (603)535-2850
Janice Kitchen, Regional Mgr.

Small Business Development Center, Rochester
18 S. Main St., Ste. 3A
Rochester, NH 03867
(603)330-1929
Fax: (603)330-1948

New Jersey

Greater Atlantic City Chamber of Commerce
Small Business Development Center
1301 Atlantic Ave.
Atlantic City, NJ 08401
(609)345-5600
Fax: (609)345-1666
William R. McGinley, Dir.

Rutgers University At Camden
Small Business Development Center
227 Penn St., 3rd Fl., Rm. 334
Camden, NJ 08102
(609)757-6221
Fax: (609)225-6231
Patricia Peacock, Dir.

Brookdale Community College
Small Business Development Center
Newman Springs Rd.
Lincroft, NJ 07738
(732)842-1900
Fax: (732)842-0203
Larry Novick, Dir.

Rutgers University
New Jersey SBDC
Graduate School of Management
49 Bleeker St.
Newark, NJ 07102
(973)353-5950
Fax: (973)353-1110
Brenda B. Hopper, State Dir.

Bergen County Community College
SBDC
400 Paramus Rd., Rm. A333
Paramus, NJ 07652-1595
(201)447-7841

Fax: (201)447-7495
Melody Irvin, Dir.

Mercer County Community College
Small Business Development Center
West Windsor Campus
1200 Old Trenton Rd.
PO Box B
Trenton, NJ 08690
(609)586-4800
Fax: (609)890-6338
Herb Spiegel, Dir.

Kean College
Small Business Development Center
East Campus, Rm. 242
Union, NJ 07083
(908)527-2946
Fax: (908)527-2960
Mira Kostak, Dir.

Warren County Community College
Small Business Development Center
Skylands 475
Rte. 57 W.
Washington, NJ 07882-9605
(908)689-9620
Fax: (908)689-2247
James Smith, Dir.

New Mexico

New Mexico State University at Alamogordo
Small Business Development Center
2230 Lawrence Blvd.
Alamogordo, NM 88310
(505)434-5272
Fax: (505)439-3643
Dwight Harp, Dir.

Albuquerque Technical-Vocational Institute
Small Business Development Center
525 Buena Vista SE
Albuquerque, NM 87106
(505)224-4246
Fax: (505)224-4251
Ray Garcia, Dir.

South Valley SBDC
SBDC
70 4th St. SW, Ste. A
Albuquerque, NM 87102
(505)248-0132
Fax: (505)248-0127
Steven Becerra, Dir.

New Mexico State University at Carlsbad
Small Business Development Center
301 S. Canal St.
PO Box 1090
Carlsbad, NM 88220
(505)887-6562
Fax: (505)885-0818
Larry Coalson, Dir.

Clovis Community College
Small Business Development Center
417 Schepps Blvd.
Clovis, NM 88101
(505)769-4136
Fax: (505)769-4190
Sandra Taylor-Smith

Northern New Mexico Community College
Small Business Development Center
1002 N. Onate St.
Espanola, NM 87532
(505)747-2236
Fax: (505)757-2234
Ralph Prather, Dir.

San Juan College
Small Business Development Center
4601 College Blvd.
Farmington, NM 87402
(505)599-0528
Fax: (505)599-0385
Cal Tingey, Dir.

University of New Mexico at Gallup
Small Business Development Center
103 W. Hwy. 66
Gallup, NM 87305
(505)722-2220
Fax: (505)863-6006
Elsie Sanchez, Dir.

New Mexico State University at Grants
Small Business Development Center
709 E. Roosevelt Ave.
Grants, NM 87020
(505)287-8221
Fax: (505)287-2125
Clemente Sanchez, Dir.

New Mexico Junior College
Small Business Development Center
5317 Lovington Hwy.
Hobbs, NM 88240
(505)392-5549
Fax: (505)392-2527
Don Leach, Dir.

Dona Ana Branch Community College
Small Business Development Center
3400 S. Espina St.
Dept. 3DA, Box 30001
Las Cruces, NM 88003-0001
(505)527-7601
Fax: (505)527-7515
Terry Sullivan, Dir.

Luna Vocational-Technical Institute
Small Business Development Center
Camp Luna Site
Hot Springs Blvd.
PO Box 1510
Las Vegas, NM 87701
(505)454-2595
Fax: (505)454-2588
Don Bustos, Dir.

University of New Mexico at Los Alamos
Small Business Development Center
901 18th St., No. 18
PO Box 715
Los Alamos, NM 87544
(505)662-0001
Fax: (505)662-0099
Jay Wechsler, Interim Dir.

University of New Mexico at Valencia
Small Business Development Center
280 La Entrada
Los Lunas, NM 87031
(505)925-8980
Fax: (505)925-8987
David Ashley, Dir.

Eastern New Mexico University at Roswell
Small Business Development Center
57 University Ave.
PO Box 6000
Roswell, NM 88201-6000
(505)624-7133
Fax: (505)624-7132
Eugene D. Simmons, Dir.

Santa Fe Community College
New Mexico SBDC
6401 Richards Ave.
Santa Fe, NM 87505
(505)438-1362
800-281-SBDC
Fax: (505)471-1469
Roy Miller, State Dir.

Western New Mexico University
Small Business Development Center
PO Box 2672
Silver City, NM 88062

(505)538-6320
Fax: (505)538-6341
Linda K. Jones, Dir.

Mesa Technical College
Small Business Development Center
911 S. 10th St.
Tucumcari, NM 88401
(505)461-4413
Fax: (505)461-1901
Carl Reiney, Dir.

New York

State University of New York at Albany
Small Business Development Center
Draper Hall, Rm. 107
135 Western Ave.
Albany, NY 12222
(518)442-5577
Fax: (518)442-5582
Peter George, III

State University of New York (Suny)
New York SBDC
Suny Plaza, S-523
Albany, NY 12246
(518)443-5398
800-732-SBDC
Fax: (518)465-4992
E-mail: kingjl@cc.sunycentral.edu
James L. King, State Dir.

Binghamton University
Small Business Development Center
PO Box 6000
Binghamton, NY 13902-6000
(607)777-4024
Fax: (607)777-4029
E-mail: sbdcbu@spectra.net
Joanne Bauman, Dir.

State University of New York
Small Business Development Center
74 N. Main St.
Brockport, NY 14420
(716)637-6660
Fax: (716)637-2102
Wilfred Bordeau, Dir.

Bronx Community College
Small Business Development Center
McCracken Hall, Rm. 14
W. 181st St. & University Ave.
Bronx, NY 10453
(718)563-3570
Fax: (718)563-3572
Adi Israeli, Dir.

Bronx Outreach Center
Con Edison
SBDC
560 Cortlandt Ave.
Bronx, NY 10451
(718)563-9204
David Bradley

Downtown Brooklyn Outreach Center
Kingsborough Community College
SBDC
395 Flatbush Ave., Extension Rm. 413
Brooklyn, NY 11201
(718)260-9783
Fax: (718)260-9797
Stuart Harker, Assoc. Dir.

Kingsborough Community College
Small Business Development Center
2001 Oriental Blvd., Bldg. T4, Rm. 4204
Manhattan Beach
Brooklyn, NY 11235
(718)368-4619
Fax: (718)368-4629
Edward O'Brien, Dir.

State University of New York at Buffalo
Small Business Development Center
Bacon Hall 117
1300 Elmwood Ave.
Buffalo, NY 14222
(716)878-4030
Fax: (716)878-4067
Susan McCartney, Dir.

Canton Outreach Center (SUNY)
Jefferson Community College
SBDC
Canton, NY 13617
(315)386-7312
Fax: (315)386-7945

Cobleskill Outreach Center
SBDC
SUNY Cobleskill
Warner Hall, Rm. 218
Cobleskill, NY 12043
(518)234-5528
Fax: (518)234-5272
Peter Desmond, Business Advisor

Corning Community College
Small Business Development Center
24 Denison Pkwy. W
Corning, NY 14830
(607)962-9461
800-358-7171
Fax: (607)936-6642
Bonnie Gestwicki, Dir.

Mercy College/Westchester Outreach Center
SBDC
555 Broadway
Dobbs Ferry, NY 10522-1189
(914)674-7485
Fax: (914)693-4996
Tom Milton, Coordinator

State University of New York at Farmingdale
Small Business Development Center
Campus Commons Bldg.
2350 Route 110
Farmingdale, NY 11735
(516)420-2765
Fax: (516)293-5343
Joseph Schwartz, Dir.

Dutchess Outreach Center
SBDC
Fishkill Extension Center
2600 Rte. 9, Unit 90
Fishkill, NY 12524-2001
(914)897-2607
Fax: (914)897-4653

Suny Geneseo Outreach Center
SBDC
South Hall, No. 111
1 College Circle
Geneseo, NY 14454
(716)245-5429
Fax: (716)245-5430
Charles VanArsdale, Dir.

Geneva Outreach Center
SBDC
122 N. Genesee St.
Geneva, NY 14456
(315)781-1253
Sandy Bordeau, Administrative Dir.

Hempstead Outreach Center
SBDC
269 Fulton Ave.
Hempstead, NY 11550
(516)564-8672
Fax: (516)481-4938
Lloyd Clarke, Asst. Dir.

York College/City University of New York
Small Business Development Center
Science Bldg., Rm. 107
94-50 159th St.
Jamaica, NY 11451
(718)262-2880
Fax: (718)262-2881
James A. Heyliger

Jamestown Community College
Small Business Development Center
525 Falconer St.
PO Box 20
Jamestown, NY 14702-0020
(716)665-5754
800-522-7232
Fax: (716)665-6733
Irene Dobies, Dir.

Kingston Small Business Development Center
1 Development Ct.
Kingston, NY 12401
(914)339-0025
Fax: (914)339-1631
Patricia La Susa, Dir.

Baruch College
Mid-Town Outreach Center
SBDC
360 Park Ave. S., Rm. 1101
New York, NY 10010
(212)802-6620
Fax: (212)802-6613
Cheryl Fenton, Dir.

East Harlem Outreach Center
SBDC
145 E. 116th St., 3rd Fl.
New York, NY 10029
(212)346-1900
Fax: (212)534-4576
Anthony Sanchez, Coordinator

Harlem Outreach Center
SBDC
163 W. 125th St., Rm. 1307
New York, NY 10027
(212)346-1900
Fax: (212)534-4576
Anthony Sanchez, Coordinator

Mid-Town Outreach Ctr.
Baruch College
SBDC
360 Park Ave. S. Rm. 1101
New York, NY 10010
(212)802-6620
Fax: (212)802-6613
Barrie Phillip, Coordinator

Pace University
Small Business Development Center
1 Pace Plz., Rm. W483
New York, NY 10038
(212)346-1900
Fax: (212)346-1613
Ira Davidson, Dir.

Niagara Falls Satellite Office
SBDC/International Trade Center
Carborundum Center
345 3rd St.
Niagara Falls, NY 14303-1117
(716)285-4793
Fax: (716)285-4797

SUNY at Oswego
Operation Oswego County
SBDC
44 W. Bridge St.
Oswego, NY 13126
(315)343-1545
Fax: (315)343-1546

Clinton Community College
SBDC
Lake Shore Rd., Rte. 9 S.
136 Clinton Point Dr.
Plattsburgh, NY 12901
(518)562-4260
Fax: (518)563-9759
Merry Gwynn, Coordinator

Suffolk County Community College
Riverhead Outreach Center
SBDC
Orient Bldg., Rm. 132
Riverhead, NY 11901
(516)369-1409
Fax: (516)369-3255
Al Falkowski, Contact

SUNY at Brockport
SBDC
Sibley Bldg.
228 E. Main St.
Rochester, NY 14604
(716)232-7310
Fax: (716)637-2182

Niagara County Community College at Sanborn
Small Business Development Center
3111 Saunders Settlement Rd.
Sanborn, NY 14132
(716)693-1910
Fax: (716)731-3595
Richard Gorko, Dir.

Long Island University at Southhampton/Southampton Outreach Center
SBDC
Abney Peak, Montauk Hwy.
Southampton, NY 11968
(516)287-0059
Fax: (516)287-8287
George Tulmany, Business Advisor

College of Staten Island
SBDC
Bldg. 1A, Rm. 111
2800 Victory Blvd.
Staten Island, NY 10314-9806
(718)982-2560
Fax: (718)982-2323
Dr. Martin Schwartz, Dir.

SUNY at Stony Brook
SBDC
Harriman Hall, Rm. 103
Stony Brook, NY 11794-3775
(516)632-9070
Fax: (516)632-7176
Judith McEvoy, Dir.

Rockland Community College
Small Business Development Center
145 College Rd.
Suffern, NY 10901-3620
(914)356-0370
Fax: (914)356-0381
Thomas J. Morley, Dir.

Onondaga Community College
Small Business Development Center
Excell Bldg., Rm. 108
4969 Onondaga Rd.
Syracuse, NY 13215-1944
(315)498-6070
Fax: (315)492-3704
Robert Varney, Dir.

Manufacturing Field Office
SBDC
Rensselaer Technology Park
385 Jordan Rd.
Troy, NY 12180-7602
(518)286-1014
Fax: (518)286-1006
Bill Brigham, Dir.

State University Institute
of Technology
Small Business Development Center
PO Box 3050
Utica, NY 13504-3050
(315)792-7546
Fax: (315)792-7554
David Mallen, Dir.

SUNY Institute of Technology at
Utica/Rome
SBDC
PO Box 3050
Utica, NY 13504-3050
(315)792-7546
Fax: (315)792-7554
David Mallen, Dir.

Jefferson Community College
Small Business Development
Center
Coffeen St.
Watertown, NY 13601
(315)782-9262
Fax: (315)782-0901
John F. Tanner, Dir.

SBDC Outreach Small Business
Resource Center
222 Bloomingdale Rd., 3rd Fl.
White Plains, NY 10605-1500
(914)644-4116
Fax: (914)644-2184
Kathleen Cassels, Coordinator

North Carolina

Asheville SBTDC
Haywood St.
PO Box 2570
Asheville, NC 28805
(704)251-6025
Fax: (704)251-6025

Appalachian State University
Small Business and Technology
Development Center (Northwestern
Region)
Walker College of Business
2123 Raley Hall
Boone, NC 28608
(704)262-2492
Fax: (704)262-2027
Bill Parrish, Regional Dir.

University of North Carolina
at Chapel Hill
Central Carolina Regional Small
Business Development
Center
608 Airport Rd., Ste. B
Chapel Hill, NC 27514
(919)962-0389
Fax: (919)962-3291
Dan Parks, Dir.

University of North Carolina
at Charlotte
Small Business and Technology
Development Center (Southern
Piedmont Region)
The Ben Craig Center
8701 Mallard Creek Rd.
Charlotte, NC 28262
(704)548-1090
Fax: (704)548-9050
George McAllister, Dir.

Western Carolina University
Small Business and Technology
Development Center (Western Region)
Center for Improving Mountain Living
Bird Bldg.
Cullowhee, NC 28723
(704)227-7494
Fax: (704)227-7422
Allan Steinburg, Dir.

Elizabeth City State University
Small Business and Technology
Development Center (Northeastern
Region)
PO Box 874
Elizabeth City, NC 27909
(919)335-3247
Fax: (919)335-3648
Wauna Dooms, Dir.

Fayetteville State University
Cape Fear Small Business and
Technology Development Center
PO Box 1334
Fayetteville, NC 28302
(910)486-1727
Fax: (910)486-1949
Dr. Sid Gautam, Regional Dir.

North Carolina A&T State University
Northern Piedmont Small Business and
Technology Development Center
(Eastern Region)
C. H. Moore Agricultural Research
Center
1601 E. Market St.
PO Box D-22
Greensboro, NC 27411
(910)334-7005
Fax: (910)334-7073
Cynthia Clemons, Dir.

East Carolina University
Small Business and Technology
Development Center (Eastern Region)
Willis Bldg.
300 East 1st St.
Greenville, NC 27858-4353
(919)328-6157
Fax: (919)328-6992
Walter Fitts, Dir.

Catawba Valley Region
SBTDC
514 Hwy. 321 NW, Ste. A
Hickory, NC 28601
(704)345-1110
Fax: (704)326-9117
Rand Riedrich, Dir.

Pembroke State University
Office of Economic Development
and SBTDC
SBDC
Pembroke, NC 28372
(910)521-6603
Fax: (910)521-6550

North Carolina SBTDC
SBDC
333 Fayette St. Mall, Ste. 1150
Raleigh, NC 27601
(919)715-7272
Fax: (919)715-7777
Scott R. Daugherty, Executive Dir.

North Carolina State University
Capital Region
SBTDC
MCI Small Business Resource Center
800 S. Salisbury St.
Raleigh, NC 27601
(919)715-0520
Fax: (919)715-0518
Mike Seibert, Dir.

North Carolina Wesleyan College
SBTDC
3400 N. Wesleyan Blvd.
Rocky Mount, NC 27804
(919)985-5130
Fax: (919)977-3701

University of North Carolina
at Wilmington
Small Business and Technology
Development Center (Southeast
Region)
601 S. College Rd.
Cameron Hall, Rm. 131
Wilmington, NC 28403
(910)395-3744
Fax: (910)350-3990
Mike Bradley, Dir.

University of North Carolina
at Wilmington
Southeastern Region
SBTDC
601 S. College Rd.
Wilmington, NC 28403
(910)395-3744
Fax: (910)350-3014
Dr. Warren Guiko, Acting Dir.

Winston-Salem State University
Northwestern Piedmont Region Small
Business and Technology Center
PO Box 13025
Winston Salem, NC 27110

(910)750-2030
Fax: (910)750-2031
Bill Dowe, Dir.

North Dakota

Bismarck Regional Small Business
Development Center
700 E. Main Ave., 2nd Fl.
Bismarck, ND 58502
(701)328-5865
Fax: (701)250-4304
Jan M. Peterson, Regional Dir.

Devils Lake Outreach Center
SBDC
417 5th St.
Devils Lake, ND 58301
800-445-7232
Gordon Synder, Regional Dir.

Dickinson Regional Small Business
Development Center
Small Business Development Center
314 3rd Ave. W
Drawer L
Dickinson, ND 58602
(701)227-2096
Fax: (701)225-0049
Bryan Vendsel, Regional Dir.

Procurement Assistance Center
SBDC
PO Box 1309
Fargo, ND 58107-1309
(701)237-9678
800-698-5726
Fax: (701)237-9734
Eric Nelson

Tri-County Economic Development
Corp.
Fargo Regional Small Business
Development Center
657 2nd Ave. N, Rm. 279
PO Box 1309
Fargo, ND 58103
(701)237-0986
Fax: (701)237-9734
Jon Grinager, Regional Mgr.

Grafton Outreach Center
Red River Regional Planning Council
SBDC
SBDC
PO Box 633
Grafton, ND 58237
800-445-7232
Gordon Snyder, Regional Dir.

Grand Forks Regional Small Business
Development Center
202 N. 3rd St., Ste. 200
The Hemmp Center
Grand Forks, ND 58203
(701)772-8502
Fax: (701)772-9238
Gordon Snyder, Regional Dir.

University of North Dakota
North Dakota SBDC
118 Gamble Hall
University Station, Box 7308
Grand Forks, ND 58202-7308
(701)777-3700
Fax: (701)777-3225
Walter "Wally" Kearns, State Dir.

Jamestown Outreach Center
North Dakota Small Business
Development Center
210 10th St. SE
PO Box 1530
Jamestown, ND 58402
(701)252-9243
Fax: (701)251-2488
Jon Grinager, Regional Dir.

Jamestown Outreach Ctr.
SBDC
210 10th St.
S.E.P.O Box 1530
Jamestown, ND 58402
(701)252-9243
Fax: (701)251-2488
Jon Grinager, Regional Dir.

Minot Regional Small Business
Development Center
SBDC
900 N. Broadway, Ste. 300
Minot, ND 58703
(701)852-8861
Fax: (701)858-3831
Brian Argabright, Regional Dir.

Williston Outreach Center
SBDC
PO Box 2047
Williston, ND 58801
800-445-7232
Bryan Vendsel, Regional Dir.

Ohio

Akron Regional Development Board
Small Business Development Center
1 Cascade Plz., 8th Fl.
Akron, OH 44308-1192
(330)379-3170

Fax: (330)379-3164
Charles Smith, Dir.

Women's Entrepreneurial Growth Organization
Small Business Development Center
Buckingham Bldg., Rm. 55
PO Box 544
Akron, OH 44309
(330)972-5179
Fax: (330)972-5513
Dr. Penny Marquette, Exec. Dir.

Women's Network
SBDC
1540 West Market St., Ste. 100
Akron, OH 44313
(330)864-5636
Fax: (540)831-6057
David Shanks, Dir.

Enterprise Development Corp.
SBDC
900 E. State St.
Athens, OH 45701
(614)592-1188
Fax: (614)593-8283
Karen Patton, Dir.

Ohio University Innovation Center
Small Business Development Center
Enterprise & Technical Bldg., Rm. 155
20 East Circle Dr.
Athens, OH 45701
(614)593-1797
Fax: (614)593-1795
Debra McBride, Dir.

WSOS Community Action Commission, Inc.
Wood County SBDC
121 E. Wooster St.
PO Box 539
Bowling Green, OH 43402
(419)352-3817
Fax: (419)353-3291
Pat Fligor, Dir.

Kent State University, Stark Campus
SBDC
6000 Frank Ave., NW
Canton, OH 44720
(330)499-9600
Fax: (330)494-6121
Annette Chunko, Contact

Women's Business Development Center
SBDC
2400 Cleveland Ave., NW
Canton, OH 44709

(330)453-3867
Fax: (330)773-2992

Wright State University–Lake Campus
Small Business Development Center
West Central Office
7600 State Rte. 703
Celina, OH 45882
(419)586-0355
800-237-1477
Fax: (419)586-0358
Tom Knapke, Dir.

Clermont County Chamber of Commerce
Clermont County Area SBDC
4440 Glen Este-Withamsville Rd.
Cincinnati, OH 45245
(513)753-7141
Fax: (513)753-7146
Matt VanSant, Dir.

University of Cincinnati
SBDC
1111 Edison Ave.
Cincinnati, OH 45216-2265
(513)948-2051
Fax: (513)948-2109
Mark Sauter, Dir.

Greater Cleveland Growth Association
Small Business Development Center
200 Tower City Center
50 Public Sq.
Cleveland, OH 44113-2291
(216)621-1294
Fax: (216)621-4617
JoAnn Uhlik, Dir.

Northern Ohio Manufacturing
SBDC
Prospect Park Bldg.
4600 Prospect Ave.
Cleveland, OH 44103-4314
(216)432-5300
Fax: (216)361-2900
Gretchen Faro, Dir.

Central Ohio Manufacturing
SBDC
1250 Arthur E. Adams Dr.
Columbus, OH 43221
(614)688-5136
Fax: (614)688-5001

Department of Development
Ohio SBDC
77 S. High St., 28th Fl.
Columbus, OH 43216-1001
(614)466-2711

Fax: (614)466-0829
Holly I. Schick, State Dir.

Greater Columbus Area Chamber of Commerce
Central Ohio SBDC
37 N. High St.
Columbus, OH 43215-3065
(614)225-6910
Fax: (614)469-8250
Linda Steward, Dir.

Dayton Area Chamber of Commerce
Small Business Development Center
Chamber Plz.
5th & Main Sts.
Dayton, OH 45402-2400
(937)226-8239
Fax: (937)226-8254
Harry Bumgarner, Dir.

Wright State University/Dayton
SBDC
Center for Small Business Assistance
College of Business
Rike Hall, Rm. 120C
Dayton, OH 45435
(937)873-3503
Dr. Mike Body, Dir.

Northwest Private Industry Council
SBDC
197-2-B1 Park Island Ave.
Defiance, OH 43512
(419)784-6270
Fax: (419)782-6273
Don Wright, Dir.

Northwest Technical College
Small Business Development Center
1935 E. 2nd St., Ste. D
Defiance, OH 43512
(419)784-3777
Fax: (419)782-4649
Don Wright, Dir.

Terra Community College
Small Business Development Center
North Central Fremont Office
1220 Cedar St.
Fremont, OH 43420
(419)334-8400
Fax: (419)334-9414
Joe Wilson, Dir.

Enterprise Center
Small Business Development Center
129 E. Main St.
PO Box 756
Hillsboro, OH 45133

(937)393-9599
Fax: (937)393-8159
Bill Grunkemeyer, Interim Dir.

Ashtabula County Economic Development Council, Inc.
Small Business Development Center
36 W. Walnut St.
Jefferson, OH 44047
(216)576-9134
Fax: (216)576-5003
Sarah Bogardus, Dir.

Kent State University Partnership
SBDC
College of Business Administration, Rm. 300A
Summit and Terrace
Kent, OH 44242
(330)672-2772
Fax: (330)672-2448
Linda Yost, Dir.

EMTEC/Southern Area Manufacturing
SBDC
3155 Research Park, Ste. 206
Kettering, OH 45420
(513)258-6180
Fax: (513)258-8189
Harry Bumgarner, Dir.

Lake County Economic Development Center
SBDC
Lakeland Community College
7750 Clocktower Dr.
Kirtland, OH 44080
(216)951-1290
Fax: (216)951-7336
Cathy Haworth, Dir.

Lima Technical College
Small Business Development Center
West Central Office
545 W. Market St., Ste. 305
Lima, OH 45801-4717
(419)229-5320
Fax: (419)229-5424
Gerald J. Biedenharn, Dir.

Lorain County Chamber of Commerce
SBDC
6100 S. Boadway
Lorain, OH 44053
(216)233-6500
Dennis Jones, Dir.

Mid-Ohio Small Business Development Center
246 E. 4th St.
PO Box 1208

Mansfield, OH 44901
(419)521-2655
800-366-7232
Fax: (419)522-6811
Barbara Harmony, Dir.

Marietta College
SBDC
213 Fourth St., 2nd Fl.
Marietta, OH 45750
(614)376-4832
Fax: (614)376-4832
Emerson Shimp, Dir.

Marion Area Chamber of Commerce
SBDC
206 S. Prospect St.
Marion, OH 43302
(614)387-0188
Fax: (614)387-7722
Lynn Lovell, Dir.

Tuscarawas SBDC
300 University Dr., NE
Kent State University
300 University Dr., NE
New Philadelphia, OH 44663-9447
(330)339-3391
Fax: (330)339-2637
Tom Farbizo, Dir.

Miami University
Small Business Development Center
Department of Decision Sciences
336 Upham Hall
Oxford, OH 45056
(513)529-4841
Fax: (513)529-1469
Dr. Michael Broida, Dir.

Upper Valley Joint Vocational School
Small Business Development Center
8811 Career Dr.
N. Country Rd., 25A
Piqua, OH 45356
(937)778-8419
800-589-6963
Fax: (937)778-9237
Jon Heffner, Dir.

Ohio Valley Minority Business Association
SBDC
1208 Waller St.
PO Box 847
Portsmouth, OH 45662
(614)353-8395
Fax: (614)353-3695
Clemmy Womack, Dir.

Department of Development
CIC of Belmont County
Small Business Development Center
100 E. Main St.
St. Clairsville, OH 43950
(614)695-9678
Fax: (614)695-1536
Mike Campbell, Dir.

Kent State University/Salem Campus
SBDC
2491 State Rte. 45 S.
Salem, OH 44460
(330)332-0361
Fax: (330)332-9256
Deanne Taylor, Dir.

Lawrence County Chamber of Commerce
Small Business Development Center
U.S. Rte. 52 & Solida Rd.
PO Box 488
South Point, OH 45680
(740)894-3838
Fax: (740)894-3836
Lou-Ann Walden, Dir.

Springfield Small Business Development Center
300 E. Auburn Ave.
Springfield, OH 45505
(937)322-7821
Fax: (937)322-7824
Ed Levanthal, Dir.

Greater Steubenville Chamber of Commerce
Jefferson County Small Business Development Center
630 Market St.
PO Box 278
Steubenville, OH 43952
(614)282-6226
Fax: (614)282-6285
Tim McFadden, Dir.

Toledo Small Business Development Center
300 Madison Ave., Ste. 200
Toledo, OH 43604-1575
(419)243-8191
Fax: (419)241-8302
Wendy Gramza, Dir.

Youngstown/Warren SBDC
Region Chamber of Commerce
180 E. Market St., Ste. 225
Warren, OH 44482
(330)393-2565
Jim Rowlands, Mgr.

Youngstown State University
SBDC
241 Federal Plaza W.
Youngstown, OH 44503
(330)746-3350
Fax: (330)746-3324
Patricia Veisz, Mgr.

Zanesville Area Chamber of Commerce
Mid-East Small Business Development
Center
217 N. 5th St.
Zanesville, OH 43701
(614)452-4868
Fax: (614)454-2963
Bonnie J. Winnett, Dir.

Oklahoma

East Central University
Small Business Development Center
1036 E. 10th St.
Ada, OK 74820
(405)436-3190
Fax: (405)436-3190
Frank Vater

Northwestern Oklahoma State
University
Small Business Development Center
709 Oklahoma Blvd.
Alva, OK 73717
(405)327-8608
Fax: (405)327-0560
Clance Doelling, Dir.

Southeastern Oklahoma State
University
Oklahoma SBDC
517 University
Station A, Box 2584
Durant, OK 74701
(405)924-0277
800-522-6154
Fax: (405)920-7471
Dr. Grady Pennington, State Dir.

Phillips University
Small Business Development Center
100 S. University Ave.
Enid, OK 73701
(405)242-7989
Fax: (405)237-1607
Bill Gregory, Coordinator

Langston University Center
Small Business Development Center
Minority Assistance Center
Hwy. 33 E.

Langston, OK 73050
(405)466-3256
Fax: (405)466-2909
Robert Allen, Dir.

Lawton Satellite
Small Business Development Center
American National Bank Bldg.
601 SW D Ave., Ste. 209
Lawton, OK 73501
(405)248-4946
Fax: (405)355-3560
Jim Elliot, Business Development
Specialists

Northeastern Oklahoma A&M
Miami Satellite
SBDC
Dyer Hall, Rm. 307
215 I St.
Miami, OK 74354
(918)540-0575
Fax: (918)540-0575
Hugh Simon, Business Development
Specialist

Rose State College
SBDC
Procurement Speciality Center
6420 Southeast 15th St.
Midwest City, OK 73110
(405)733-7348
Fax: (405)733-7495
Judy Robbins, Dir.

University of Central Oklahoma
Small Business Development Center
115 Park Ave.
Oklahoma City, OK 73102-9005
(405)232-1968
Fax: (405)232-1967
E-mail: sbdc@aix1.ucok.edu
Website: http://www.osbdc.org/
osbdc.htm
Susan Urbach

Carl Albert College
Small Business Development Center
1507 S. McKenna
Poteau, OK 74953
(918)647-4019
Fax: (918)647-1218
Dean Qualls, Dir.

Northeastern Oklahoma State
University
Small Business Development Center
Oklahoma Small Business Development
Center

Tahlequah, OK 74464
(918)458-0802
Fax: (918)458-2105
Danielle Coursey, Business Development
Specialist

Tulsa Satellite
Small Business Development Center
State Office Bldg.
616 S. Boston, Ste. 100
Tulsa, OK 74119
(918)583-2600
Fax: (918)599-6173
Jeff Horvath, Dir.

Southwestern Oklahoma State
University
Small Business Development Center
100 Campus Dr.
Weatherford, OK 73096
(405)774-1040
Fax: (405)774-7091
Chuck Felz, Dir.

Oregon

Linn-Benton Community College
Small Business Development Center
6500 SW Pacific Blvd.
Albany, OR 97321
(541)917-4923
Fax: (541)917-4445
Dennis Sargent, Dir.

Southern Oregon State College/Ashland
Small Business Development Center
Regional Services Institute
Ashland, OR 97520
(541)482-5838
Fax: (541)482-1115
Liz Shelby, Dir.

Central Oregon Community College
Small Business Development Center
2600 NW College Way
Bend, OR 97701
(541)383-7290
Fax: (541)317-3445
Bob Newhart, Dir.

Southwestern Oregon Community
College
Small Business Development Center
2110 Newmark Ave.
Coos Bay, OR 97420
(541)888-7100
Fax: (541)888-7113
Jon Richards, Dir.

Columbia Gorge Community College

SBDC

400 E. Scenic Dr., Ste. 257
The Dalles, OR 97058
(541)298-3118
Fax: (541)298-3119
Mr. Bob Cole, Dir.

Lane Community College

Oregon SBDC

44 W. Broadway, Ste. 501
Eugene, OR 97401-3021
(541)726-2250
Fax: (541)345-6006
Dr. Edward Cutler, State Dir.

Rogue Community College

Small Business Development Center

214 SW 4th St.
Grants Pass, OR 97526
(541)471-3515
Fax: (541)471-3589
Lee Merritt, Dir.

Mount Hood Community College

Small Business Development Center

323 NE Roberts St.
Gresham, OR 97030
(503)667-7658
Fax: (503)666-1140
Don King, Dir.

Oregon Institute of Technology

Small Business Development Center

3201 Campus Dr. S. 314
Klamath Falls, OR 97601
(541)885-1760
Fax: (541)885-1855
Jamie Albert, Dir.

Eastern Oregon State College

Small Business Development Center

Regional Services Institute
1410 L Ave.
La Grande, OR 97850
(541)962-3391
800-452-8639
Fax: (541)962-3668
John Prosnik, Dir.

Oregon Coast Community College

Small Business Development Center

4157 NW Hwy. 101, Ste. 123
PO Box 419
Lincoln City, OR 97367
(541)994-4166
Fax: (541)996-4958
Guy Faust, Contact

Southern Oregon State College/Medford

Small Business Development Center

Regional Services Institute
332 W. 6th St.
Medford, OR 97501
(541)772-3478
Fax: (541)734-4813
Liz Shelby, Dir.

Clackamas Community College

Small Business Development Center

7616 SE Harmony Rd.
Milwaukie, OR 97222
(503)656-4447
Fax: (503)652-0389
Jan Stennick, Dir.

Treasure Valley Community College

Small Business Development Center

650 College Blvd.
Ontario, OR 97914
(541)889-6493
Fax: (541)881-2743
Kathy Simko, Dir.

Blue Mountain Community College

Small Business Development Center

37 SE Dorion
Pendleton, OR 97801
(541)276-6233
Fax: (541)276-6819
Gerald Wood, Dir.

Portland Community College

Small Business Development Center

2701 NW Vaughn St., No. 499
Portland, OR 97209
(503)978-5080
Fax: (503)228-6350
Robert Keyser, Dir.

Portland Community College

Small Business International Trade Program

121 SW Salmon St., Ste. 210
Portland, OR 97204
(503)274-7482
Fax: (503)228-6350
Tom Niland, Dir.

Umpqua Community College

Small Business Development Center

744 SE Rose
Roseburg, OR 97470
(541)672-2535
Fax: (541)672-3679
Terry Swagerty, Dir.

Chemeketa Community College

Small Business Development Center

365 Ferry St. SE
Salem, OR 97301
(503)399-5088
Fax: (503)581-6017
Tom Nelson, Dir.

Clatsop Community College

Small Business Development Center

1761 N. Holladay
Seaside, OR 97138
(503)738-3347
Fax: (503)738-7843
Lori Martin, Dir.

Tillamook Bay Community College

Small Business Development Center

401 B Main St.
Tillamook, OR 97141
(503)842-2551
Fax: (503)842-2555
Kathy Wilkes, Dir.

Pennsylvania

Lehigh University

Small Business Development Center

Rauch Business Ctr., No. 37
621 Taylor St.
Bethlehem, PA 18015
(610)758-3980
Fax: (610)758-5205
Dr. Larry A. Strain, Dir.

Clarion University of Pennsylvania

Small Business Development Center

Dana Still Bldg., Rm. 102
Clarion, PA 16214
(814)226-2060
Fax: (814)226-2636
Dr. Woodrow Yeaney, Dir.

Bucks County SBDC Outreach Center

2 E. Court St.
Doylestown, PA 18901
(215)230-7150
Bruce Love, Dir.

Gannon University

Small Business Development Center

120 W. 9th St.
Erie, PA 16501
(814)871-7714
Fax: (814)871-7383
Ernie Post, Dir.

Kutztown University

Small Business Development Center

2986 N. 2nd St.
Harrisburg, PA 17110

(717)720-4230
Fax: (717)720-4262
Katherine Wilson, Dir.

Indiana University of Pennsylvania SBDC
208 Eberly College of Business
Indiana, PA 15705
(412)357-7915
Fax: (412)357-5985
Dr. Tony Palamone, Dir.

St. Vincent College
Small Business Development Center
Alfred Hall, 4th Fl.
300 Fraser Purchase Rd.
Latrobe, PA 15650
(412)537-4572
Fax: (412)537-0919
Jack Fabean, Dir.

Bucknell University
Small Business Development Center
126 Dana Engineering Bldg., 1st Fl.
Lewisburg, PA 17837
(717)524-1249
Fax: (717)524-1768
Charles Knisely, Dir.

St. Francis College
Small Business Development Center
Business Resource Center
Loretto, PA 15940
(814)472-3200
Fax: (814)472-3202
Edward Huttenhower, Dir.

LaSalle University
Small Business Development Center
1900 W. Olney Ave.
Box 365
Philadelphia, PA 19141
(215)951-1416
Fax: (215)951-1597
Andrew Lamas, Dir.

Temple University
Small Business Development Center
1510 Cecil B. Moore Ave.
Philadelphia, PA 19121
(215)204-7282
Fax: (215)204-4554
Geraldine Perkins, Dir.

University Of Pennsylvania
Pennsylvania SBDC
The Wharton School
423 Vance Hall
3733 Spruce St.
Philadelphia, PA 19104-6374

(215)898-1219
Fax: (215)573-2135
E-mail:
ghiggins@sec1.wharton.upenn.edu
Gregory L. Higgins Jr.

Duquesne University
Small Business Development Center
Rockwell Hall, Rm. 10, Concourse
600 Forbes Ave.
Pittsburgh, PA 15282
(412)396-6233
Fax: (412)396-5884
Dr. Mary T. McKinney, Dir.

University of Pittsburgh
Small Business Development Center
The Joseph M. Katz Graduate School
of Business
208 Bellefield Hall
315 S. Bellefield Ave.
Pittsburgh, PA 15213
(412)648-1544
Fax: (412)648-1636
Ann Dugan, Dir.

University of Scranton
Small Business Development Center
St. Thomas Hall, Rm. 588
Scranton, PA 18510
(717)941-7588
Fax: (717)941-4053
Elaine M. Tweedy, Dir.

West Chester University
SBDC
319 Anderson Hall
211 Carter Dr.
West Chester, PA 19383
(610)436-2162
Fax: (610)436-2577

Wilkes University
Small Business Development Center
Hollenback Hall
192 S. Franklin St.
Wilkes Barre, PA 18766-0001
(717)831-4340
800-572-4444
Fax: (717)824-2245
Jeffrey Alves, Dir.

Puerto Rico

Small Business Development Center
Edificio Union Plaza, Ste. 701
416 Ponce de Leon Ave.
Hato Rey, PR 00918
(787)763-6811
Fax: (787)763-4629
Carmen Marti, State Dir.

Rhode Island

Northern Rhode Island Chamber of Commerce SBDC
6 Blackstone Valley Pl., Ste. 105
Lincoln, RI 02865-1105
(401)334-1000
Fax: (401)334-1009
Shelia Hoogeboom, Program Mgr.

Newport County Chamber of Commerce
E. Bay Small Business Development Center
45 Valley Rd.
Middletown, RI 02842-6377
(401)849-6900
Fax: (401)841-0570
Samuel Carr, Program Mgr.

Fishing Community Program Office SBDC
PO Box 178
Narragansett, RI 02882
(401)783-2466
Angela Caporelli, Program Mgr.

South County SBDC
QP/D Industrial Park
35 Belver Ave., Rm. 212
North Kingstown, RI 02852-7556
(401)294-1227
Fax: (401)294-6897
Elizabeth Kroll, Program Mgr.

Bryant College
Small Business Development Center
30 Exchange Terrace, 4th Fl.
Providence, RI 02903-1793
(401)831-1330
Fax: (401)274-5410
Ann Marie Marshall, Case Mgr.

Enterprise Community SBDC/BIC
550 Broad St.
Providence, RI 02907
(401)272-1083
Fax: (401)272-1186
Simon Goudiaby, Program Mgr.

Bell Atlantic Telecommunications Center
1150 Douglas Pke.
Smithfield, RI 02917-1284
(401)232-0220
Fax: (401)232-0242
Kate Dolan, Managing Dir.

Bryant College
Export Assistance Center
SBDC
1150 Douglas Pike
Smithfield, RI 02917

(401)232-6407
Fax: (401)232-6416
Raymond Fogarty, Dir.

Bryant College
Rhode Island SBDC
1150 Douglas Pike
Smithfield, RI 02917-1284
(401)232-6111
Fax: (401)232-6933
Douglas H. Jobling, State Dir.

Entrepreneurship Training Program
Bryant College
SBDC
1150 Douglas Pike
Smithfield, RI 02917-1284
(401)232-6115
Fax: (401)232-6933
Sydney Okashige, Program Mgr.

Bristol County Chamber of Commerce
SBDC
PO Box 250
Warren, RI 02885-0250
(401)245-0750
Fax: (401)245-0110
Samuel Carr, Program Mgr.

Central Rhode Island Chamber
of Commerce
SBDC
3288 Post Rd.
Warwick, RI 02886-7151
(401)732-1100
Fax: (401)732-1107
Mr. Elizabeth Kroll, Program Mgr.

South Carolina

University of South Carolina at Aiken
Aiken Small Business Development
Center
171 University Pkwy.
Box 9
Aiken, SC 29801
(803)641-3646
Fax: (803)641-3647
Jackie Moore, Area Mgr.

University of South Carolina
at Beaufort
Small Business Development Center
800 Carteret St.
Beaufort, SC 29902
(803)521-4143
Fax: (803)521-4142
Martin Goodman, Area Mgr.

Clemson University
Small Business Development Center
College of Business and Public Affairs
425 Sirrine Hall
Box 341392
Clemson, SC 29634-1392
(803)656-3227
Fax: (803)656-4869
Becky Hobart, Regional Dir.

University of South Carolina
College of Business Administration
South Carolina SBDC
Hipp Bldg.
1710 College St.
Columbia, SC 29208
(803)777-4907
Fax: (803)777-4403
John Lenti, State Director

University of South Carolina
Small Business Development Center
College of Business Administration
Columbia, SC 29208
(803)777-5118
Fax: (803)777-4403
James Brazell, Dir.

Coastal Carolina College
Small Business Development Center
School of Business Administration
PO Box 261954
Conway, SC 29526-6054
(803)349-2170
Fax: (803)349-2455
Tim Lowery, Area Mgr.

Florence-Darlington Technical College
Small Business Development Center
PO Box 100548
Florence, SC 29501-0548
(803)661-8256
Fax: (803)661-8041
David Raines, Area Mgr.

Greenville Manufacturing Field Office
SBDC
53 E. Antrim Dr.
Greenville, SC 29607
(803)271-3005

University Center
Upstate Area Office Small Business
Development Center
216 S. Pleasantburg Dr., Rm. 140
Greenville, SC 29607
(864)250-8894
Fax: (864)250-8897

Upper Savannah Council
of Government
Small Business Development Center
Exchange Building
222 Phoenix St., Ste. 200
PO Box 1366
Greenwood, SC 29648
(803)941-8071
Fax: (803)941-8090
George Long, Area Mgr.

University of South Carolina at Hilton
Head
Small Business Development
Center
1 College Center Dr.
10 Office Park Rd.
Hilton Head, SC 29928-7535
(803)785-3995
Fax: (803)785-3995
Pat Cameron, Consultant

Charleston SBDC
5900 Core Dr., Ste. 104
North Charleston, SC 29406
(803)740-6160
Fax: (803)740-1607
Merry Boone, Area Mgr.

South Carolina State College
Small Business Development Center
School of Business Administration
Algernon Belcher Hall
300 College Ave.
Campus Box 7176
Orangeburg, SC 29117
(803)536-8445
Fax: (803)536-8066
John Gadson, Regional Dir.

Winthrop University
Winthrop Regional Small Business
Development Center
College of Business Administration
118 Thurmond Bldg.
Rock Hill, SC 29733
(803)323-2283
Fax: (803)323-4281
Nate Barber, Regional Dir.

Spartanburg Chamber
of Commerce
Small Business Development Center
105 Pine St.
PO Box 1636
Spartanburg, SC 29304
(803)594-5080
Fax: (803)594-5055
John Keagle, Area Mgr.

South Dakota

Aberdeen Small Business Development Center (Northeast Region)
620 15th Ave., SE
Aberdeen, SD 57401
(605)626-2565
Fax: (605)626-2667
Belinda Engelhart, Regional Dir.

Pierre Small Business Development Center
105 S. Euclid, Ste. C
Pierre, SD 57501
(605)773-5941
Fax: (605)773-5942
Greg Sund, Dir.

Rapid City Small Business Development Center (Western Region)
444 N. Mount Rushmore Rd., Rm. 208
Rapid City, SD 57701
(605)394-5311
Fax: (605)394-6140
Carl Gustafson, Regional Dir.

Sioux Falls Region
SBDC
405 S. 3rd Ave., Ste. 101
Sioux Falls, SD 57104
(605)367-5757
Fax: (605)367-5755
Wade Bruin, Regional Dir.

University of South Dakota
South Dakota SBDC
School of Business
414 E. Clark
Vermillion, SD 57069
(605)677-5498
Fax: (605)677-5272
E-mail: sbdc@sundance.usd.edu
Robert E. Ashley. Jr.

Watertown Small Business Development Center
124 1st. Ave., NW
PO Box 1207
Watertown, SD 57201
(605)886-7224
Fax: (605)882-5049
Belinda Engelhart, Regional Dir.

Tennessee

Chattanooga State Technical Community College
SBDC
100 Cherokee Blvd., No. 202
Chattanooga, TN 37405-3878
(423)752-1774

Fax: (423)752-1925
Donna Marsh, Specialist

Southeast Tennessee Development District
Small Business Development Center
25 Cherokee Blvd.
PO Box 4757
Chattanooga, TN 37405-0757
(423)266-5781
Fax: (423)267-7705
Sherri Bishop, Dir.

Austin Peay State University
Small Business Development Center
College of Business
Clarksville, TN 37044
(615)648-7764
Fax: (615)648-5985
John Volker, Dir.

Cleveland State Community College
Small Business Development Center
PO Box 3570
PO Box 3570
Cleveland, TN 37320-3570
(423)478-6247
Fax: (423)478-6251
Don Green, Dir.

Small Business Development Center (Columbia)
Maury County Chamber of Commerce Bldg.
106 W. 6th St.
PO Box 8069
Columbia, TN 38402-8069
(615)898-2745
Fax: (615)893-7089
Eugene Osekowsky, Small Business Specialist

Tennessee Technological University
SBDC
College of Business Administration
PO Box 5023
Cookeville, TN 38505
(931)372-3648
Fax: (931)372-6249
Dorothy Vaden, Senior Small Bus. Specialist

Dyersburg State Community College
Small Business Development Center
1510 Lake Rd.
Dyersburg, TN 38024-2450
(901)286-3201
Fax: (901)286-3271
Bob Wylie

Four Lakes Regional Industrial Development Authority
SBDC
PO Box 63
Hartsville, TN 37074-0063
(615)374-9521
Fax: (615)374-4608
Dorothy Vaden, Senior Small Bus. Specialist

Jackson State Community College
Small Business Development Center
McWherter Center, Rm. 213
2046 N. Parkway St.
Jackson, TN 38301-3797
(901)424-5389
Fax: (901)425-2641
David L. Brown

Lambuth University
SBDC
705 Lambuth Blvd.
Jackson, TN 38301
(901)425-3326
Fax: (901)425-3327
Phillip Ramsey, SB Specialist

East Tennessee State University
College of Business
SBDC
PO Box 70625
Johnson City, TN 37614-0625
(423)929-5630
Fax: (423)461-7080
Bob Justice, Dir.

Knoxville Area Chamber Partnership
International Trade Center
SBDC
Historic City Hall
601 W. Summit Hill Dr.
Knoxville, TN 37902-2011
(423)632-2990
Fax: (423)521-6367
Richard Vogler, IT Specialist

Pellissippi State Technical Community College
Small Business Development Center
Historic City Hall
601 W. Summit Hill Dr.
Knoxville, TN 37902-2011
(423)632-2980
Fax: (423)971-4439
Teri Brahams, Consortium Dir.

University of Memphis
International Trade Center
SBDC
320 S. Dudley St.
Memphis, TN 38152-0001

(901)678-4174
Fax: (901)678-4072
Philip Johnson, Dir.

University of Memphis
Tennessee SBDC
320 S. Dudley St.
Building No. 1
Memphis, TN 38152
(901)678-2500
Fax: (901)678-4072
Dr. Kenneth J. Burns, State Dir.

Walters State Community College
Tennessee Small Business Development Center
500 S. Davy Crockett Pkwy.
Morristown, TN 37813
(423)585-2675
Fax: (423)585-2679
Jack Tucker, Dir.

Middle Tennessee State University
Small Business Development Center
Chamber of Commerce Bldg.
501 Memorial Blvd.
PO Box 487
Murfreesboro, TN 37129-0001
(615)898-2745
Fax: (615)890-7600
Patrick Geho, Dir.

Tennessee State University
Small Business Development Center
College of Business
330 10th Ave. N.
Nashville, TN 37203-3401
(615)963-7179
Fax: (615)963-7160
Billy E. Lowe, Dir.

Texas

Abilene Christian University
Small Business Development Center
College of Business Administration
648 E. Hwy. 80
Abilene, TX 79601
(915)670-0300
Fax: (915)670-0311
Judy Wilhelm, Dir.

Sul Ross State University
Big Bend SBDC Satellite
PO Box C-47, Rm. 319
Alpine, TX 79832
(915)837-8694
Fax: (915)837-8104
Michael Levine, Dir.

Alvin Community College
Small Business Development Center
3110 Mustang Rd.
Alvin, TX 77511-4898
(713)388-4686
Fax: (713)388-4903
Gina Mattei, Dir.

West Texas A&M University
Small Business Development Center
T. Boone Pickens School of Business
1800 S. Washington, Ste. 209
Amarillo, TX 79102
(806)372-5151
Fax: (806)372-5261
Don Taylor, Dir.

Trinity Valley Community College
Small Business Development Center
500 S. Prairieville
Athens, TX 75751
(903)675-7403
800-335-7232
Fax: (903)675-5199
Judy Loden, Dir.

Lower Colorado River Authority
Small Business Development Center
3701 Lake Austin Blvd.
PO Box 220
Austin, TX 78703
(512)473-3510
Fax: (512)473-3285
Larry Lucero, Dir.

Lee College
Small Business Development Center
Rundell Hall
PO Box 818
Baytown, TX 77522-0818
(281)425-6309
Fax: (713)425-6309
Tommy Hathaway, Dir.

Lamar University
Small Business Development Center
855 Florida Ave.
Beaumont, TX 77705
(409)880-2367
Fax: (409)880-2201
Gene Arnold, Dir.

Bonham Satellite
Small Business Development Center
SBDC
Sam Rayburn Library, Bldg. 2
1201 E. 9th St.
Bonham, TX 75418
(903)583-7565
Fax: (903)583-6706
Darroll Martin, Coordinator

Blinn College
Small Business Development Center
902 College Ave.
Brenham, TX 77833
(409)830-4137
Fax: (409)830-4135
Phillis Nelson, Dir.

Brazos Valley Small Business Development Center
Small Business Development Center
4001 E. 29th St., Ste. 175
PO Box 3695
Bryan, TX 77805-3695
(409)260-5222
Fax: (409)260-5229
Sam Harwell, Dir.

Greater Corpus Christi Business Alliance
Small Business Development Center
1201 N. Shoreline
Corpus Christi, TX 78401
(512)881-1847
Fax: (512)882-4256
Rudy Ortiz, Dir.

Navarro Small Business Development Center
120 N. 12th St.
Corsicana, TX 75110
(903)874-0658
800-320-7232
Fax: (903)874-4187
Leon Allard, Dir.

Dallas County Community College
North Texas SBDC
1402 Corinth St.
Dallas, TX 75215
800-350-7232
Fax: (214)860-5813
Elizabeth (Liz) Klimback, Regional Dir.

International Assistance Center
SBDC
2050 Stemmons Fwy.
PO Box 420451
Dallas, TX 75258
(214)747-1300
800-337-7232
Fax: (214)748-5774
Beth Huddleston, Dir.

Bill J. Priest Institute for Economic Development
North Texas-Dallas Small Business Development Center
1402 Corinth St.
Dallas, TX 75215

(214)860-5842
800-348-7232
Fax: (214)860-5881
Pamela Speraw, Dir.

Technology Assistance Center
SBDC
1402 Corinth St.
Dallas, TX 75215
800-355-7232
Fax: (214)860-5881
Pamela Speraw, Dir.

Texas Center for Government
Contracting and Technology Assistance
Small Business Development Center
1402 Corinth St.
Dallas, TX 75215
(214)860-5841
Fax: (214)860-5881
Gerald Chandler, Dir.

Grayson County College
Small Business Development Center
6101 Grayson Dr.
Denison, TX 75020
(903)463-8787
800-316-7232
Fax: (903)463-5437
Cynthia Flowers-Whitfield, Dir.

Denton Small Business Development
Center
PO Drawer P
Denton, TX 76201
(254)380-1849
Fax: (254)382-0040
Carolyn Birkhead, Coordinator

Best Southwest
SBDC
214 S, Main, Ste. 102A
Duncanville, TX 75116
(214)709-5878
800-317-7232
Fax: (214)709-6089
Herb Kamm, Dir.

Best Southwest Small Business
Development Center
214 S. Main, Ste. 102A
Duncanville, TX 75116
(972)709-5878
800-317-7232
Fax: (972)709-6089
Neil Small, Dir.

University of Texas–Pan American
Small Business Development Center
1201 W. University Dr., Rm. BA-124
Center for Entrepreneurship & Economic
Development

Edinburg, TX 78539-2999
(956)316-2610
Fax: (956)316-2612
Juan Garcia, Dir.

El Paso Community College
Small Business Development Center
103 Montana Ave., Ste. 202
El Paso, TX 79902-3929
(915)831-4410
Fax: (915)831-4625
Roque R. Segura, Dir.

Small Business Development Center
for Enterprise Excellence
SBDC
7300 Jack Newell Blvd., S.
Fort Worth, TX 76118
(817)272-5930
Fax: (817)272-5932
Jo An Weddle, Dir.

Tarrant County Junior College
Small Business Development Center
Mary Owen Center, Rm. 163
1500 Houston St.
Ft. Worth, TX 76102
(817)871-2068
Fax: (817)871-0031
David Edmonds, Dir.

North Central Texas College
Small Business Development Center
1525 W. California
Gainesville, TX 76240
(254)668-4220
800-351-7232
Fax: (254)668-6049
Cathy Keeler, Dir.

Galveston College
Small Business Development Center
4015 Avenue Q
Galveston, TX 77550
(409)740-7380
Fax: (409)740-7381
Georgette Peterson, Dir.

Western Bank and Trust Satellite
SBDC
PO Box 461545
Garland, TX 75046
(214)860-5850
Fax: (214)860-5857
Al Salgado, Dir.

Grand Prairie Satellite
SBDC
Chamber of Commerce
900 Conover Dr.
Grand Prairie, TX 75053

(214)860-5850
Fax: (214)860-5857
Al Salgado, Dir.

Houston Community College System
Small Business Development Center
10450 Stancliff, Ste. 100
Houston, TX 77099
(281)933-7932
Fax: (281)568-3690
Joe Harper, Dir.

Houston International Trade Center
Small Business Development Center
1100 Louisiana, Ste. 500
Houston, TX 77002
(713)752-8404
Fax: (713)756-1500
Mr. Carlos Lopez, Dir.

North Harris Montgomery Community
College District
Small Business Development Center
250 N. Sam Houston Pkwy. E.
Houston, TX 77060
(281)260-3174
Fax: (713)591-3513
Kay Hamilton, Dir.

University of Houston
Southeastern Texas SBDC
1100 Louisiana, Ste. 500
Houston, TX 77002
(713)752-8444
Fax: (713)756-1500
J.E. "Ted" Cadou, Reg. Dir.

University of Houston
Texas Information Procurement
Service
Small Business Development Center
1100 Louisiana, Ste. 500
Houston, TX 77002
(713)752-8477
Fax: (713)756-1515
Jacqueline Taylor, Dir.

University of Houston
Texas Manufacturing Assistance Center
(Gulf Coast)
1100 Louisiana, Ste. 500
Houston, TX 77002
(713)752-8440
Fax: (713)756-1500
Roy Serpa, Regional Dir.

Sam Houston State University
Small Business Development Center
843 S. Sam Houston Ave.
PO Box 2058

Huntsville, TX 77341-3738
(409)294-3737
Fax: (409)294-3612
Bob Barragan, Dir.

Kingsville Chamber of Commerce
Small Business Development Center
635 E. King
Kingsville, TX 78363
(512)595-5088
Fax: (512)592-0866
Marco Garza, Dir.

Brazosport College
Small Business Development Center
500 College Dr.
Lake Jackson, TX 77566
(409)266-3380
Fax: (409)265-3482
Patricia Leyendecker, Dir.

Laredo Development Foundation
Small Business Development Center
Division of Business Administration
616 Leal St.
Laredo, TX 78041
(956)722-0563
Fax: (956)722-6247
Araceli Lozano, Acting Dir.

Kilgore College
SBDC
Triple Creek Shopping Plaza
110 Triple Creek Dr., Ste. 70
Longview, TX 75601
(903)757-5857
800-338-7232
Fax: (903)753-7920
Brad Bunt, Dir.

Texas Tech University
Northwestern Texas SBDC
Spectrum Plaza
2579 S. Loop 289, Ste. 114
Lubbock, TX 79423
(806)745-3973
Fax: (806)745-6207
E-mail: odbea@ttacs.ttu.edu
Craig Bean, Regional Dir.

Angelina Community College
Small Business Development Center
Hwy. 59 S.
PO Box 1768
Lufkin, TX 75902
(409)639-1887
Fax: (409)639-3863
Brian McClain, Dir.

Midlothian SBDC
330 N. 8th St., Ste. 203
Midlothian, TX 76065-0609

(214)775-4336
Fax: (214)775-4337

Northeast Texarkana
Small Business Development Center
PO Box 1307
Mt. Pleasant, TX 75455
(903)572-1911
800-357-7232
Fax: (903)572-0598
Bob Wall, Dir.

University of Texas–Permian Basin
Small Business Development Center
College of Management
4901 E. University Blvd.
Odessa, TX 79762
(915)552-2455
Fax: (915)552-2433
Arthur L. Connor III

Paris Junior College
Small Business Development Center
2400 Clarksville St.
Paris, TX 75460
(903)784-1802
Fax: (903)784-1801
Pat Bell, Dir.

Courtyard Center for Professional and Economic Development
Collin Small Business Development Center
4800 Preston Park Blvd., Ste. A126
Box 15
Plano, TX 75093
(972)985-3770
Fax: (972)985-3775
Chris Jones, Dir.

Angelo State University
Small Business Development Center
2610 West Ave. N.
Campus Box 10910
San Angelo, TX 76909
(915)942-2098
Fax: (915)942-2096
Harlan Bruha, Dir.

University of Texas (Downtown San Antonio)
South Texas Border SBDC
1222 N. Main, Ste. 450
San Antonio, TX 78212
(210)458-2450
Fax: (210)458-2464
E-mail: rmckinle@utsadt.utsa.edu
Robert McKinley, Regional Dir.

University of Texas at San Antonio
International Trade Center
SBDC
1222 N. Main, Ste. 450
San Antonio, TX 78212
(210)458-2470
Fax: (210)458-2464
Sara Jackson, Dir.

Houston Community College System
Small Business Development Center
13600 Murphy Rd.
Stafford, TX 77477
(713)499-4870
Fax: (713)499-8194
Ted Charlesworth, Acting Dir.

Tarleton State University
Small Business Development Center
College of Business Administration
Box T-0650
Stephenville, TX 76402
(817)968-9330
Fax: (817)968-9329
Jim Choate, Dir.

College of the Mainland
Small Business Development Center
1200 Amburn Rd.
Texas City, TX 77591
(409)938-1211
800-246-7232
Fax: (409)938-7578
Elizabeth Boudreau, Dir.

Tyler Junior College
Small Business Development Center
1530 South SW Loop 323, Ste. 100
Tyler, TX 75701
(903)510-2975
Fax: (903)510-2978
Frank Viso, Dir.

Middle Rio Grande Development Council
Small Business Development Center
209 N. Getty St.
Uvalde, TX 78801
(830)278-2527
Fax: (830)278-2929
Sheri Rutledge, Dir.

University of Houston–Victoria
Small Business Development Center
700 Main Center, Ste. 102
Victoria, TX 77901
(512)575-8944
Fax: (512)575-8852
Carole Parks, Dir.

McLennan Community College

Small Business Development Center

401 Franklin
Waco, TX 76708
(254)714-0077
800-349-7232
Fax: (254)714-1668
Lu Billings, Dir.

LCRA Coastal Plains

SBDC

PO Box 148
Wharton, TX 77488
(409)532-1007
Fax: (409)532-0056
Lynn Polson, Dir.

Midwestern State University

Small Business Development Center

3410 Taft Blvd.
Wichita Falls, TX 76308
(817)397-4373
Fax: (817)397-4374
Tim Thomas, Dir.

Utah

Southern Utah University

Small Business Development Center

351 W. Center
Cedar City, UT 84720
(435)586-5400
Fax: (435)586-5493
Derek Snow, Dir.

Snow College

Small Business Development Center

345 West 100 North
Ephraim, UT 84627
(435)283-7472
Fax: (435)283-6913
Russell Johnson, Dir.

Utah State University

Small Business Development Center

East Campus Bldg., Rm. 124
Logan, UT 84322
(435)797-2277
Fax: (435)797-3317
Franklin C. Prante, Dir.

Weber State University

Small Business Development Center

School of Business and Economics
Ogden, UT 84408-3815
(435)626-6070
Fax: (435)626-7423
Bruce Davis, Dir.

Utah Valley State College

Utah Small Business Development Center

800 West 200 South
Orem, UT 84058
(435)222-8230
Fax: (435)225-1229
Chuck Cozzens, Contact

South Eastern Utah AOG

Small Business Development Center

Price Center
PO Box 1106
Price, UT 84501
(435)637-5444
Fax: (435)637-7336
Dennis Rigby, Dir.

Utah State University Extension Office

SBDC

987 E. Lagoon St.
Roosevelt, UT 84066
(435)722-2294
Fax: (435)789-3689
Mark Holmes, Dir.

Dixie College

Small Business Development Center

225 South 700 East
St. George, UT 84770-3876
(435)652-7751
Fax: (435)652-7870
Jill Ellis, Dir.

Salt Lake Community College

SBDC

1623 S. State St.
Salt Lake City, UT 84115
(801)957-3480
Fax: (801)957-3489
Mike Finnerty, State Dir.

Salt Lake Community College

Sandy SBDC

8811 South 700 East
Sandy, UT 84070
(435)255-5878
Fax: (435)255-6393
Barry Bartlett, Dir.

Vermont

Brattleboro Development Credit Corp.

SBDC

72 Cotton Mill Hill
PO Box 1177
Brattleboro, VT 05301-1177
(802)257-7731
Fax: (802)258-3886
William McGrath, Executive V. P.

Greater Burlington Industrial Corp.

Northwestern Vermont Small Business Development Center

PO Box 786
Burlington, VT 05402-0786
(802)658-9228
Fax: (802)860-1899
Thomas D. Schroeder, Specialist

Addison County Economic Development Corp.

SBDC

RD4, Box 1309A
Middlebury, VT 05753
(802)388-7953
Fax: (802)388-8066
James Stewart, Exec. Dir.

Central Vermont Economic Development Center

SBDC

PO Box 1439
Montpelier, VT 05601-1439
(802)223-4654
Fax: (802)223-4655
Donald Rowan, Exec. Dir.

Lamoille Economic Development Corp.

SBDC

Sunset Dr.
PO Box 455
Morrisville, VT 05661-0455
(802)888-4542
Chris D'Elia, Executive Dir.

Bennington County Industrial Corp.

SBDC

PO Box 357
North Bennington, VT 05257-0357
(802)442-8975
Fax: (802)442-1101
Chris Hunsinger, Executive Dir.

Lake Champlain Islands Chamber of Commerce

SBDC

PO Box 213
North Hero, VT 05474-0213
(802)372-5683
Fax: (802)372-6104
Barbara Mooney, Exec. Dir.

Vermont Technical College

Small Business Development Center

PO Box 422
Randolph Center, VT 05060-0422
(802)728-9101
800-464-7232
Fax: (802)728-3026
Donald L. Kelpinski, State Dir.

Rutland Economic Development Corp.
Southwestern Vermont Small Business
Development Center
256 N. Main St.
Rutland, VT 05701-0039
(802)773-9147
Fax: (802)773-2772
Wendy Wilton, Regional Dir.

Franklin County Industrial
Development Corp.
SBDC
PO Box 1099
St. Albans, VT 05478-1099
(802)524-2194
Fax: (802)527-5258
Timothy J. Soule, Executive Dir.

Northeastern Vermont Small Business
Development Center
44 Main St.
PO Box 630
St. Johnsbury, VT 05819-0630
(802)748-1014
Fax: (802)748-1223
Charles E. E. Carter, Exec. Dir.

Springfield Development Corp.
Southeastern Vermont Small Business
Development Center
PO Box 58
Springfield, VT 05156-0058
(802)885-2071
Fax: (802)885-3027
Steve Casabona, Specialist

Green Mountain Economic
Development Corporation
SBDC
PO Box 246
White River Jct., VT 05001-0246
(802)295-3710
Fax: (802)295-3779
Lenae Quillen-Blume, SBDC Specialist

Virgin Islands

University of the Virgin Islands
(Charlotte Amalie)
Small Business Development Center
8000 Nisky Center, Ste. 202
Charlotte Amalie, VI 00802-5804
(809)776-3206
Fax: (809)775-3756
Ian Hodge, Assoc. State Dir.

University of the Virgin Islands
Small Business Development Center
Sunshine Mall
No.1 Estate Cane, Ste. 104

Frederiksted, VI 00840
(809)692-5270
Fax: (809)692-5629
Chester Williams, State Dir.

Virginia

Virginia Highlands SBDC
Rte. 382
PO Box 828
Abingdon, VA 24212
(540)676-5615
Fax: (540)628-7576
Jim Tilley, Dir.

Arlington Small Business Development
Center
George Mason University, Arlington
Campus
4001 N. Fairfax Dr., Ste. 450
Arlington, VA 22203-1640
(703)993-8129
Fax: (703)430-7293
Paul Hall, Dir.

Virginia Eastern Shore Corp.
SBDC
36076 Lankford Hwy.
PO Box 395
Belle Haven, VA 23306
(757)442-7179
Fax: (757)442-7181

Mount Empire Community College
Southwest Small Business Development
Center
Drawer 700, Rte. 23, S.
Big Stone Gap, VA 24219
(540)523-6529
Fax: (540)523-2400
Tim Blankenbecler, Dir.

Central Virginia Small Business
Development Center
918 Emmet St., N., Ste. 200
Charlottesville, VA 22903-4878
(804)295-8198
Fax: (804)295-7066
Robert A. Hamilton Jr.

Hampton Roads Chamber
of Commerce
SBDC
400 Volvo Pkwy.
PO Box 1776
Chesapeake, VA 23320
(757)664-2590
Fax: (757)548-1835
William J. Holoran Jr.

George Mason University
Northern Virginia Small Business
Development Center
4031 University Dr., Ste. 200
Fairfax, VA 22030
(703)277-7700
Fax: (703)993-2126
Michael Kehoe, Exec. Dir.

Longwood College (Farmville)
Small Business Development Center
515 Main St.
Farmville, VA 23909
(804)395-2086
Fax: (804)395-2359
Gerald L. Hughes Jr.

Rappahannock Region Small Business
Development Center
1301 College Ave.
Seacobeck Hall, Rm. 102
Fredericksburg, VA 22401
(540)654-1060
Fax: (540)654-1070
Jeffrey R. Sneddon, Exec. Dir.

Hampton Roads Inc.
Small Business Development Center
525 Butler Farm Rd., Ste. 102
Hampton, VA 23666
(757)825-2957
Fax: (757)825-2960
James Carroll, Dir.

James Madison University
Small Business Development Center
College of Business
Zane Showker Hall, Rm. 527
PO Box MSC 0206
Harrisonburg, VA 22807
(540)568-3227
Fax: (540)568-3106
Karen Wigginton, Dir.

Lynchburg Regional Small Business
Development Center
147 Mill Ridge Rd.
Lynchburg, VA 24502-4341
(804)582-6170
800-876-7232
Fax: (804)582-6106
Barry Lyons, Dir.

Flory Small Business Development
Center
10311 Sudley Manor Dr.
Manassas, VA 20109-2962
(703)335-2500
Linda Decker, Dir.

SBDC Satellite Office of Longwood
PO Box 709
115 Broad St.
Martinsville, VA 24114
(540)632-4462
Fax: (540)632-5059
Ken Copeland, Dir.

Lord Fairfax Community College
SBDC
173 Skirmisher Ln.
PO Box 47
Middletown, VA 22645
(540)869-6649
Fax: (540)868-7002
Robert Crosen, Dir.

Small Business Development Center
of Hampton Roads, Inc. (Norfolk)
420 Bank St.
PO Box 327
Norfolk, VA 23501
(757)664-2528
Fax: (757)622-5563
Warren Snyder, Dir.

New River Valley
SBDC
600-H Norwood St.
PO Box 3726
Radford, VA 24141
(540)831-6056

Southwest Virginia Community
College
Southwest Small Business Development
Center
PO Box SVCC, Rte. 19
Richlands, VA 24641
(540)964-7345
Fax: (540)964-5788
Jim Boyd, Dir.

Department of Business Assistance
Virginia SBDC
707 E. Main St., Ste. 300
Richmond, VA 23219
(804)371-8253
Fax: (804)225-3384
Bob Wilburn, State Dir.

Greater Richmond Small Business
Development Center
1 N. 5th St., Ste. 510
Richmond, VA 23219
(804)648-7838
800-646-SBDC
Fax: (804)648-7849
Charlie Meacham, Dir.

Regional Chamber Small Business
Development Center
Western Virginia SBDC Consortium
212 S. Jefferson St.
Roanoke, VA 24011
(540)983-0717
Fax: (540)983-0723
Ian Webb, Dir.

South Boston Satellite Office
of Longwood
Small Business Development Center
515 Broad St.
PO Box 1116
South Boston, VA 24592
(804)575-0044
Fax: (804)572-1762
Vincent Decker, Dir.

Loudoun County Small Business
Development Center
Satellite Office of Northern Virginia
207 E. Holly Ave., Ste. 214
Sterling, VA 20164
(703)430-7222
Fax: (703)430-7258
Ted London, Dir.

Warsaw Small Business Development
Center
Satellite Office of Rappahannock
5559 W. Richmond Rd.
PO Box 490
Warsaw, VA 22572
(804)333-0286
800-524-8915
Fax: (804)333-0187
John Clickener, Dir.

Wytheville Community College
Wytheville Small Business
Development Center
1000 E. Main St.
Wytheville, VA 24382
(540)223-4798
800-468-1195
Fax: (540)223-4716
Rob Edwards, Dir.

Washington

Bellevue Small Business Development
Center
Bellevue Community College
3000 Landerholm Circle SE
Bellevue, WA 98007-6484
(425)643-2888
Fax: (425)649-3113
Bill Huenefeld, Business Dev. Specialist

Western Washington University
Small Business Development Center
College of Business and Economics
308 Parks Hall
Bellingham, WA 98225-9073
(360)650-4831
Fax: (360)650-4844
Tom Dorr, Business Dev. Specialist

Centralia Community College
Small Business Development Center
600 W. Locust St.
Centralia, WA 98531
(360)736-9391
Fax: (360)730-7504
Joanne Baria, Business Dev. Specialist

Columbia Basin College–TRIDEC
Small Business Development Center
901 N. Colorado
Kennewick, WA 99336
(509)735-6222
Fax: (509)735-6609
Blake Escudier, Business Dev. Specialist

Edmonds Community College
Small Business Development Center
20000 68th Ave. W.
Lynnwood, WA 98036
(425)640-1435
Fax: (425)640-1532
Jack Wicks, Business Dev. Specialist

Big Bend Community College
Small Business Development Center
7662 Chanute St.
Moses Lake, WA 98837-3299
(509)762-6306
Fax: (509)762-6329
Ed Baroch, Business Dev. Specialist

Skagit Valley College
Small Business Development Center
2405 College Way
Mount Vernon, WA 98273
(360)428-1282
Fax: (360)336-6116
Peter Stroosma, Business Dev.
Specialist

Wenatchee Valley College
SBDC
PO Box 741
Okanogan, WA 98840
(509)826-5107
Fax: (509)826-1812
John Rayburn, Business Dev.
Specialist

Organizations, Agencies, & Consultants

South Puget Sound Community College
Small Business Development Center
721 Columbia St. SW
Olympia, WA 98501
(360)753-5616
Fax: (360)586-5493
Douglas Hammel, Business Dev.
Specialist

Washington State University (Pullman)
Small Business Development Center
501 Johnson Tower
PO Box 644851
Pullman, WA 99164-4727
(509)335-1576
Fax: (509)335-0949
Carol Riesenberg, State Dir.

International Trade Institute
North Seattle Community College
Small Business Development Center
2001 6th Ave., Ste. 650
Seattle, WA 98121
(206)553-0052
Fax: (206)553-7253
Ann Tamura, IT Specialist

South Seattle Community College
Duwamish Industrial Education Center
Small Business Development Center
6770 E. Marginal Way S
Seattle, WA 98108-3405
(206)768-6855
Fax: (206)764-5838
Henry Burton, Business Dev. Specialist

Washington Small Business
Development Center (Seattle)
180 Nickerson, Ste. 207
Seattle, WA 98109
(206)464-5450
Fax: (206)464-6357
Warner Wong, Business Dev. Specialist

Washington State University (Spokane)
Small Business Development Center
665 North Riverpoint Blvd.
Spokane, WA 99202
(509)358-7894
Fax: (509)358-7896
Richard Thorpe, Business Dev. Specialist

Washington Small Business
Development Center (Tacoma)
950 Pacific Ave., Ste. 300
PO Box 1933
Tacoma, WA 98401-1933
(253)272-7232
Fax: (253)597-7305
Neil Delisanti, Business Dev. Specialist

Columbia River Economic
Development Council
Small Business Development Center
217 SE 136th Ave., Ste. 105
Vancouver, WA 98660
(360)260-6372
Fax: (360)260-6369
Janet Harte, Business Dev. Specialist

Port of Walla Walla SBDC
500 Tausick Way
Rte. 4, Box 174
Walla Walla, WA 99362
(509)527-4681
Fax: (509)525-3101
Rich Monacelli, Business Dev. Specialist

Quest Small Business Development
Center
37 S. Wenatchee Ave., Ste. C
Industrial Bldg. 2, Ste. D.
Wenatchee, WA 98801-2443
(509)662-8016
Fax: (509)663-0455
Rich Reim, Business Dev. Specialist

Yakima Valley College
Small Business Development Center
PO Box 1647
Yakima, WA 98907
(509)454-3608
Fax: (509)454-4155
Audrey Rice, Business Dev. Specialist

West Virginia

College of West Virginia
SBDC
PO Box AG
Beckley, WV 25802
(304)252-7885
Fax: (304)252-9584
Tom Hardiman, Program Mgr.

West Virginia Department Office
West Virginia SBDC
950 Kanawha Blvd. E., Ste. 200
Charleston, WV 25301
(304)558-2960
(888)WVA-SBDC
Fax: (304)348-0127
Dr. Hazel Kroesser-Palmer, State-Dir.

Fairmont State College (Elkins Satellite)
SBDC
10 Eleventh St., Ste. 1
Elkins, WV 26241
(304)637-7205
Fax: (304)637-4902
James Martin, Business Analyst

Fairmont State College
Small Business Development Center
1000 Technology Dr., Ste. 1120
Fairmont, WV 26554
(304)367-2712
Fax: (304)367-2717
Jack Kirby, Program Mgr.

Marshall University
Small Business Development Center
1050 4th Ave.
Huntington, WV 25755-2126
(304)696-6246
Fax: (304)696-6277
Edna McClain, Program Mgr.

West Virginia Institute of Technology
Small Business Development Center
Engineering Bldg., Rm. 102
Montgomery, WV 25136
(304)442-5501
Fax: (304)442-3307
James Epling, Program Mgr.

West Virginia University
Fairmont State College Satellite
Small Business Development Center
PO Box 6025
Morgantown, WV 26506-6025
(304)293-5839
Fax: (304)293-7061
Sharon Stratton, Business Analyst

West Virginia University (Parkersburg)
Small Business Development Center
Rte. 5, Box 167-A
Parkersburg, WV 26101
(304)424-8277
Fax: (304)424-8315
Greg Hill, Program Mgr.

Shepherd College
Small Business Development Center
120 N. Princess St.
Shepherdstown, WV 25443
(304)876-5261
Fax: (304)876-5467
Fred Baer, Program Mgr.

West Virginia Northern Community
College
Small Business Development Center
1701 Market St.
College Sq.
Wheeling, WV 26003
(304)233-5900
Fax: (304)232-0965
Ron Trevellini, Program Mgr.

Wisconsin

University of Wisconsin–Eau Claire
Small Business Development Center
Schneider Hall, Rm. 113
PO Box 4004
Eau Claire, WI 54702-4004
(715)836-5811
Fax: (715)836-5263
Fred Waedt, Dir.

University of Wisconsin–Green Bay
Small Business Development Center
Wood Hall, Rm. 480
2420 Nicolet Dr.
Green Bay, WI 54311
(920)465-2089
Fax: (920)465-2552
Jan Thornton, Dir.

University of Wisconsin–Parkside
Small Business Development Center
Tallent Hall, Rm. 284
900 Wood Rd.
Kenosha, WI 53141-2000
(414)595-2189
Fax: (414)595-2471
Patricia Deutsch, Dir.

University of Wisconsin–La Crosse
Small Business Development Center
North Hall, Rm. 120
1701 Farwell St.
La Crosse, WI 54601
(608)785-8782
Fax: (608)785-6919
Jan Gallagher, Dir.

University of Wisconsin
Wisconsin SBDC
432 N. Lake St., Rm. 423
Madison, WI 53706
(608)263-7794
Fax: (608)263-7830
Erica McIntire, State Dir.

University of Wisconsin–Madison
Small Business Development Center
975 University Ave., Rm. 3260 Grainger
Hall
Madison, WI 53706
(608)263-2221
Fax: (608)263-0818
Neil Lerner, Dir.

University of Wisconsin–Milwaukee
Small Business Development Center
161 W. Wisconsin Ave., Ste. 600
Milwaukee, WI 53203
(414)227-3240
Fax: (414)227-3142
Sara Thompson, Dir.

University of Wisconsin–Oshkosh
Small Business Development Center
800 Algoma Blvd.
Oshkosh, WI 54901
(920)424-1453
Fax: (920)424-7413
John Mozingo, Dir.

University of Wisconsin–Stevens
Point
Small Business Development Center
Old Main Bldg., Rm. 103
Stevens Point, WI 54481
(715)346-3838
Fax: (715)346-4045
Vicki Lobermeier, Acting Dir.

University of Wisconsin–Superior
Small Business Development Center
1800 Grand Ave.
Superior, WI 54880-2898
(715)394-8352
Fax: (715)394-8592
Laura Urban, Dir.

University of Wisconsin
at Whitewater
Wisconsin Innovation Service Center
SBDC
416 McCutchen Hall
Whitewater, WI 53190
(414)472-1365
Fax: (414)472-1600
E-mail: malewicd@uwwvax.uww.edu
Debra Malewicki, Dir.

Wyoming

Casper Small Business Development
Center
Region III
111 W. 2nd St., Ste. 502
Casper, WY 82601
(307)234-6683
800-348-5207
Fax: (307)577-7014
Leonard Holler, Dir.

Cheyenne SBDC
Region IV
1400 E. College Dr.
Cheyenne, WY 82007-3298
(307)632-6141
800-348-5208
Fax: (307)632-6061
Arlene Soto, Regional Dir.

Northwest Community College
Small Business Development Center
Region II
146 South Bent St.
John Dewitt Student Center
Powell, WY 82435
(307)754-2139
800-348-5203
Fax: (307)754-0368
Dwane Heintz, Dir.

Rock Springs Small Business
Development Center
Region I
PO Box 1168
Rock Springs, WY 82902
(307)352-6894
800-348-5205
Fax: (307)352-6876

SERVICE CORPS OF RETIRED EXECUTIVES (SCORE) OFFICES

This section contains a listing of all SCORE offices organized alphabetically by state/U.S. territory, then by city, then by agency name.

Alabama

SCORE Office (Northeast Alabama)
1330 Quintard Ave.
Anniston, AL 36202
(256)237-3536

SCORE Office (North Alabama)
901 South 15th St, Rm. 201
Birmingham, AL 35294-2060
(205)934-6868
Fax: (205)934-0538

SCORE Office (Baldwin County)
29750 Larry Dee Cawyer Dr.
Daphne, AL 36526
(334)928-5838

SCORE Office (Shoals)
Florence, AL 35630
(256)760-9067

SCORE Office (Mobile)
600 S Court St.
Mobile, AL 36104
(334)240-6868
Fax: (334)240-6869

SCORE Office (Alabama Capitol City)
600 S. Court St.
Montgomery, AL 36104
(334)240-6868
Fax: (334)240-6869

SCORE Office (East Alabama)
601 Ave. A
Opelika, AL 36801
(334)745-4861
E-mail: score636@hotmail.com
Website: http://www.angelfire.com/sc/
score636/

SCORE Office (Tuscaloosa)
2200 University Blvd.
Tuscaloosa, AL 35402
(205)758-7588

Alaska

SCORE Office (Anchorage)
222 W. 8th Ave.
Anchorage, AK 99513-7559
(907)271-4022
Fax: (907)271-4545

Arizona

SCORE Office (Lake Havasu)
10 S. Acoma Blvd.
Lake Havasu City, AZ 86403
(520)453-5951
E-mail: SCORE@ctaz.com
Website: http://www.scorearizona.org/
lake_havasu/

SCORE Office (East Valley)
Federal Bldg., Rm. 104
26 N. MacDonald St.
Mesa, AZ 85201
(602)379-3100
Fax: (602)379-3143
E-mail: 402@aol.com
Website: http://www.scorearizona.org/
mesa/

SCORE Office (Phoenix)
2828 N. Central Ave., Ste. 800
Central & One Thomas
Phoenix, AZ 85004
(602)640-2329
Fax: (602)640-2360
E-mail: e-mail@SCORE-phoenix.org
Website: http://www.score-phoenix.org/

SCORE Office (Prescott Arizona)
1228 Willow Creek Rd., Ste. 2
Prescott, AZ 86301
(520)778-7438
Fax: (520)778-0812
E-mail: score@northlink.com
Website: http://www.scorearizona.org/
prescott/

SCORE Office (Tucson)
110 E. Pennington St.
Tucson, AZ 85702

(520)670-5008
Fax: (520)670-5011
E-mail: score@azstarnet.com
Website: http://www.scorearizona.org/
tucson/

SCORE Office (Yuma)
281 W. 24th St., Ste. 116
Yuma, AZ 85364
(520)314-0480
E-mail: score@C2i2.com
Website: http://www.scorearizona.org/
yuma

Arkansas

SCORE Office (South Central)
201 N. Jackson Ave.
El Dorado, AR 71730-5803
(870)863-6113
Fax: (870)863-6115

SCORE Office (Ozark)
Fayetteville, AR 72701
(501)442-7619

SCORE Office (Northwest Arkansas)
Glenn Haven Dr., No. 4
Ft. Smith, AR 72901
(501)783-3556

SCORE Office (Garland County)
Grand & Ouachita
PO Box 6012
Hot Springs Village, AR 71902
(501)321-1700

SCORE Office (Little Rock)
2120 Riverfront Dr., Rm. 100
Little Rock, AR 72202-1747
(501)324-5893
Fax: (501)324-5199

SCORE Office (Southeast Arkansas)
121 W. 6th
Pine Bluff, AR 71601
(870)535-7189
Fax: (870)535-1643

California

SCORE Office (Golden Empire)
1706 Chester Ave., No. 200
Bakersfield, CA 93301
(805)322-5881
Fax: (805)322-5663

SCORE Office (Greater Chico Area)
1324 Mangrove St., Ste. 114
Chico, CA 95926
(916)342-8932
Fax: (916)342-8932

SCORE Office (Concord)
2151-A Salvio St., Ste. B
Concord, CA 94520
(510)685-1181
Fax: (510)685-5623

SCORE Office (Covina)
935 W. Badillo St.
Covina, CA 91723
(818)967-4191
Fax: (818)966-9660

SCORE Office (Rancho Cucamonga)
8280 Utica, Ste. 160
Cucamonga, CA 91730
(909)987-1012
Fax: (909)987-5917

SCORE Office (Culver City)
PO Box 707
Culver City, CA 90232-0707
(310)287-3850
Fax: (310)287-1350

SCORE Office (Danville)
380 Diablo Rd., Ste. 103
Danville, CA 94526
(510)837-4400

SCORE Office (Downey)
11131 Brookshire Ave.
Downey, CA 90241
(310)923-2191
Fax: (310)864-0461

SCORE Office (El Cajon)
109 Rea Ave.
El Cajon, CA 92020
(619)444-1327
Fax: (619)440-6164

SCORE Office (El Centro)
1100 Main St.
El Centro, CA 92243
(619)352-3681
Fax: (619)352-3246

SCORE Office (Escondido)
720 N. Broadway
Escondido, CA 92025
(619)745-2125
Fax: (619)745-1183

SCORE Office (Fairfield)
1111 Webster St.
Fairfield, CA 94533
(707)425-4625
Fax: (707)425-0826

SCORE Office (Fontana)
17009 Valley Blvd., Ste. B
Fontana, CA 92335

(909)822-4433
Fax: (909)822-6238

SCORE Office (Foster City)
1125 E. Hillsdale Blvd.
Foster City, CA 94404
(415)573-7600
Fax: (415)573-5201

SCORE Office (Fremont)
2201 Walnut Ave., Ste. 110
Fremont, CA 94538
(510)795-2244
Fax: (510)795-2240

SCORE Office (Central California)
2719 N. Air Fresno Dr., Ste. 200
Fresno, CA 93727-1547
(559)487-5605
Fax: (559)487-5636

SCORE Office (Gardena)
1204 W. Gardena Blvd.
Gardena, CA 90247
(310)532-9905
Fax: (310)515-4893

SCORE Office (Lompoc)
330 N. Brand Blvd., Ste. 190
Glendale, CA 91203-2304
(818)552-3206
Fax: (818)552-3323

SCORE Office (Los Angeles)
330 N. Brand Blvd., Ste. 190
Glendale, CA 91203-2304
(818)552-3206
Fax: (818)552-3323

SCORE Office (Glendora)
131 E. Foothill Blvd.
Glendora, CA 91740
(818)963-4128
Fax: (818)914-4822

SCORE Office (Grover Beach)
177 S. 8th St.
Grover Beach, CA 93433
(805)489-9091
Fax: (805)489-9091

SCORE Office (Hawthorne)
12477 Hawthorne Blvd.
Hawthorne, CA 90250
(310)676-1163
Fax: (310)676-7661

SCORE Office (Hayward)
22300 Foothill Blvd., Ste. 303
Hayward, CA 94541
(510)537-2424

SCORE Office (Hemet)
1700 E. Florida Ave.
Hemet, CA 92544-4679
(909)652-4390
Fax: (909)929-8543

SCORE Office (Hesperia)
16367 Main St.
PO Box 403656
Hesperia, CA 92340
(619)244-2135

SCORE Office (Holloster)
321 San Felipe Rd., No. 11
Hollister, CA 95023

SCORE Office (Hollywood)
7018 Hollywood Blvd.
Hollywood, CA 90028
(213)469-8311
Fax: (213)469-2805

SCORE Office (Indio)
82503 Hwy. 111
PO Drawer TTT
Indio, CA 92202
(619)347-0676

SCORE Office (Inglewood)
330 Queen St.
Inglewood, CA 90301
(818)552-3206

SCORE Office (La Puente)
218 N. Grendanda St. D.
La Puente, CA 91744
(818)330-3216
Fax: (818)330-9524

SCORE Office (La Verne)
2078 Bonita Ave.
La Verne, CA 91750
(909)593-5265
Fax: (714)929-8475

SCORE Office (Lake Elsinore)
132 W. Graham Ave.
Lake Elsinore, CA 92530
(909)674-2577

SCORE Office (Lakeport)
PO Box 295
Lakeport, CA 95453
(707)263-5092

SCORE Office (Lakewood)
5445 E. Del Amo Blvd., Ste. 2
Lakewood, CA 90714
(213)920-7737

SCORE Office (Long Beach)
1 World Trade Center
Long Beach, CA 90831

SCORE Office (Los Alamitos)
901 W. Civic Center Dr., Ste. 160
Los Alamitos, CA 90720

SCORE Office (Los Altos)
321 University Ave.
Los Altos, CA 94022
(415)948-1455

SCORE Office (Manhattan Beach)
PO Box 3007
Manhattan Beach, CA 90266
(310)545-5313
Fax: (310)545-7203

SCORE Office (Merced)
1632 N. St.
Merced, CA 95340
(209)725-3800
Fax: (209)383-4959

SCORE Office (Milpitas)
75 S. Milpitas Blvd., Ste. 205
Milpitas, CA 95035
(408)262-2613
Fax: (408)262-2823

SCORE Office (Yosemite)
1012 11th St., Ste. 300
Modesto, CA 95354
(209)521-9333

SCORE Office (Montclair)
5220 Benito Ave.
Montclair, CA 91763

SCORE Office (Monterey Bay)
380 Alvarado St.
PO Box 1770
Monterey, CA 93940-1770
(408)649-1770

SCORE Office (Moreno Valley)
25480 Alessandro
Moreno Valley, CA 92553

SCORE Office (Morgan Hill)
25 W. 1st St.
PO Box 786
Morgan Hill, CA 95038
(408)779-9444
Fax: (408)778-1786

SCORE Office (Morro Bay)
880 Main St.
Morro Bay, CA 93442
(805)772-4467

SCORE Office (Mountain View)
580 Castro St.
Mountain View, CA 94041
(415)968-8378
Fax: (415)968-5668

SCORE Office (Napa)
1556 1st St.
Napa, CA 94559
(707)226-7455
Fax: (707)226-1171

SCORE Office (North Hollywood)
5019 Lankershim Blvd.
North Hollywood, CA 91601
(818)552-3206

SCORE Office (Northridge)
8801 Reseda Blvd.
Northridge, CA 91324
(818)349-5676

SCORE Office (Novato)
807 De Long Ave.
Novato, CA 94945
(415)897-1164
Fax: (415)898-9097

SCORE Office (East Bay)
519 17th St.
Oakland, CA 94612
(510)273-6611
Fax: (510)273-6015
E-mail: webmaster@eastbayscore.org
Website: http://www.eastbayscore.org

SCORE Office (Oceanside)
928 N. Coast Hwy.
Oceanside, CA 92054
(619)722-1534

SCORE Office (Ontario)
121 West B. St.
Ontario, CA 91762
Fax: (714)984-6439

SCORE Office (Oxnard)
PO Box 867
Oxnard, CA 93032
(805)385-8860
Fax: (805)487-1763

SCORE Office (Pacifica)
450 Dundee Way, Ste. 2
Pacifica, CA 94044
(415)355-4122

SCORE Office (Palm Desert)
72990 Hwy. 111
Palm Desert, CA 92260
(619)346-6111
Fax: (619)346-3463

SCORE Office (Palm Springs)
650 E. Tahquitz Canyon Way Ste. D
Palm Springs, CA 92262-6706
(760)320-6682
Fax: (760)323-9426

SCORE Office (Lakeside)
2150 Low Tree
Palmdale, CA 93551
(805)948-4518
Fax: (805)949-1212

SCORE Office (Palo Alto)
325 Forest Ave.
Palo Alto, CA 94301
(415)324-3121
Fax: (415)324-1215

SCORE Office (Pasadena)
117 E. Colorado Blvd., Ste. 100
Pasadena, CA 91105
(818)795-3355
Fax: (818)795-5663

SCORE Office (Paso Robles)
1225 Park St.
Paso Robles, CA 93446-2234
(805)238-0506
Fax: (805)238-0527

SCORE Office (Petaluma)
799 Baywood Dr., Ste. 3
Petaluma, CA 94954
(707)762-2785
Fax: (707)762-4721

SCORE Office (Pico Rivera)
9122 E. Washington Blvd.
Pico Rivera, CA 90660

SCORE Office (Pittsburg)
2700 E. Leland Rd.
Pittsburg, CA 94565
(510)439-2181
Fax: (510)427-1599

SCORE Office (Pleasanton)
777 Peters Ave.
Pleasanton, CA 94566
(510)846-9697

SCORE Office (Monterey Park)
485 N. Garey
Pomona, CA 91769

SCORE Office (Pomona)
485 N. Garey Ave.
Pomona, CA 91766
(909)622-1256

SCORE Office (Antelope Valley)
4511 West Ave. M-4
Quartz Hill, CA 93536
(805)272-0087
E-mail: avscore@ptw.com
Website: http://
www.score.av.org/

SCORE Office (Shasta)
737 Auditorium Dr.
Redding, CA 96099
(916)225-2770

SCORE Office (Redwood City)
1675 Broadway
Redwood City, CA 94063
(415)364-1722
Fax: (415)364-1729

SCORE Office (Richmond)
3925 MacDonald Ave.
Richmond, CA 94805

SCORE Office (Ridgecrest)
PO Box 771
Ridgecrest, CA 93555
(619)375-8331
Fax: (619)375-0365

SCORE Office (Riverside)
3685 Main St., Ste. 350
Riverside, CA 92501
(909)683-7100

SCORE Office (Sacramento)
9845 Horn Rd., 260-B
Sacramento, CA 95827
(916)361-2322
Fax: (916)361-2164
E-mail: sacchapter@directcon.net

SCORE Office (Salinas)
PO Box 1170
Salinas, CA 93902
(408)424-7611
Fax: (408)424-8639

SCORE Office (Inland Empire)
777 E. Rialto Ave.
Purchasing
San Bernardino, CA 92415-0760
(909)386-8278

SCORE Office (San Carlos)
San Carlos Chamber of Commerce
PO Box 1086
San Carlos, CA 94070
(415)593-1068
Fax: (415)593-9108

SCORE Office (Encinitas)
550 W. C St., Ste. 550
San Diego, CA 92101-3540
(619)557-7272
Fax: (619)557-5894

SCORE Office (San Diego)
550 West C. St., Ste. 550
San Diego, CA 92101-3540

(619)557-7272
Fax: (619)557-5894
Website: http://www.score-sandiego.org

SCORE Office (Menlo Park)
1100 Merrill St.
San Francisco, CA 94105
(415)325-2818
Fax: (415)325-0920

SCORE Office (San Francisco)
455 Market St., 6th Fl.
San Francisco, CA 94105
(415)744-6827
Fax: (415)744-6750
E-mail: sfscore@sfscore.
Website: http://www.sfscore.com

SCORE Office (San Gabriel)
401 W. Las Tunas Dr.
San Gabriel, CA 91776
(818)576-2525
Fax: (818)289-2901

SCORE Office (San Jose)
Deanza College
208 S. 1st St., Ste. 137
San Jose, CA 95113
(408)288-8479
Fax: (408)535-5541

SCORE Office (Santa Clara County)
280 S. 1st St., Rm. 137
San Jose, CA 95113
(408)288-8479
Fax: (408)535-5541
E-mail: svscore@Prodigy.net
Website: http://www.svscore.org

SCORE Office (San Luis Obispo)
3566 S. Hiquera, No. 104
San Luis Obispo, CA 93401
(805)547-0779

SCORE Office (San Mateo)
1021 S. El Camino, 2nd Fl.
San Mateo, CA 94402
(415)341-5679

SCORE Office (San Pedro)
390 W. 7th St.
San Pedro, CA 90731
(310)832-7272

SCORE Office (Orange County)
200 W. Santa Anna Blvd., Ste. 700
Santa Ana, CA 92701
(714)550-7369
Fax: (714)550-0191
Website: http://www.score114.org

SCORE Office (Santa Barbara)
3227 State St.
Santa Barbara, CA 93130
(805)563-0084

SCORE Office (Central Coast)
509 W. Morrison Ave.
Santa Maria, CA 93454
(805)347-7755

SCORE Office (Santa Maria)
614 S. Broadway
Santa Maria, CA 93454-5111
(805)925-2403
Fax: (805)928-7559

SCORE Office (Santa Monica)
501 Colorado, Ste. 150
Santa Monica, CA 90401
(310)393-9825
Fax: (310)394-1868

SCORE Office (Santa Rosa)
777 Sonoma Ave., Rm. 115E
Santa Rosa, CA 95404
(707)571-8342
Fax: (707)541-0331
Website: http://www.pressdemo.com/community/score/score.html

SCORE Office (Scotts Valley)
4 Camp Evers Ln.
Scotts Valley, CA 95066
(408)438-1010
Fax: (408)438-6544

SCORE Office (Simi Valley)
40 W. Cochran St., Ste. 100
Simi Valley, CA 93065
(805)526-3900
Fax: (805)526-6234

SCORE Office (Sonoma)
453 1st St. E
Sonoma, CA 95476
(707)996-1033

SCORE Office (Los Banos)
222 S. Shepard St.
Sonora, CA 95370
(209)532-4212

SCORE Office (Tuolumne County)
39 North Washington St.
Sonora, CA 95370
(209)588-0128
E-mail: score@mlode.com

SCORE Office (South San Francisco)
445 Market St., Ste. 6th Fl.
South San Francisco, CA 94105

(415)744-6827
Fax: (415)744-6812

SCORE Office (Stockton)
401 N. San Joaquin St., Rm. 215
Stockton, CA 95202
(209)946-6293

SCORE Office (Taft)
314 4th St.
Taft, CA 93268
(805)765-2165
Fax: (805)765-6639

SCORE Office (Conejo Valley)
625 W. Hillcrest Dr.
Thousand Oaks, CA 91360
(805)499-1993
Fax: (805)498-7264

SCORE Office (Torrance)
3400 Torrance Blvd., Ste. 100
Torrance, CA 90503
(310)540-5858
Fax: (310)540-7662

SCORE Office (Truckee)
PO Box 2757
Truckee, CA 96160
(916)587-2757
Fax: (916)587-2439

SCORE Office (Visalia)
113 S. M St,
Tulare, CA 93274
(209)627-0766
Fax: (209)627-8149

SCORE Office (Upland)
433 N. 2nd Ave.
Upland, CA 91786
(909)931-4108

SCORE Office (Vallejo)
2 Florida St.
Vallejo, CA 94590
(707)644-5551
Fax: (707)644-5590

SCORE Office (Van Nuys)
14540 Victory Blvd.
Van Nuys, CA 91411
(818)989-0300
Fax: (818)989-3836

SCORE Office (Ventura)
5700 Ralston St., Ste. 310
Ventura, CA 93001
(805)658-2688
Fax: (805)658-2252
E-mail: scoreven@jps.net
Website: http://www.jps.net/scoreven

SCORE Office (Vista)
201 E. Washington St.
Vista, CA 92084
(619)726-1122
Fax: (619)226-8654

SCORE Office (Watsonville)
PO Box 1748
Watsonville, CA 95077
(408)724-3849
Fax: (408)728-5300

SCORE Office (West Covina)
811 S. Sunset Ave.
West Covina, CA 91790
(818)338-8496
Fax: (818)960-0511

SCORE Office (Westlake)
30893 Thousand Oaks Blvd.
Westlake Village, CA 91362
(805)496-5630
Fax: (818)991-1754

Colorado

SCORE Office (Colorado Springs)
2 N. Cascade Ave., Ste. 110
Colorado Springs, CO 80903
(719)636-3074
Website: http://www.cscc.org/score02/index.html

SCORE Office (Denver)
US Custom's House, 4th Fl.
721 19th St.
Denver, CO 80201-0660
(303)844-3985
Fax: (303)844-6490
E-mail: score62@csn.net
Website: http://www.sni.net/score62

SCORE Office (Tri-River)
1102 Grand Ave.
Glenwood Springs, CO 81601
(970)945-6589

SCORE Office (Grand Junction)
2591 B & 3/4 Rd.
Grand Junction, CO 81503
(970)243-5242

SCORE Office (Gunnison)
608 N. 11th
Gunnison, CO 81230
(303)641-4422

SCORE Office (Montrose)
1214 Peppertree Dr.
Montrose, CO 81401
(970)249-6080

SCORE Office (Pagosa Springs)
PO Box 4381
Pagosa Springs, CO 81157
(970)731-4890

SCORE Office (Rifle)
0854 W. Battlement Pky., Apt. C106
Parachute, CO 81635
(970)285-9390

SCORE Office (Pueblo)
302 N. Santa Fe
Pueblo, CO 81003
(719)542-1704
Fax: (719)542-1624
E-mail: mackey@iex.net
Website: http://www.pueblo.org/score

SCORE Office (Ridgway)
143 Poplar Pl.
Ridgway, CO 81432

SCORE Office (Silverton)
PO Box 480
Silverton, CO 81433
(303)387-5430

SCORE Office (Minturn)
PO Box 2066
Vail, CO 81658
(970)476-1224

Connecticut

SCORE Office (Greater Bridgeport)
230 Park Ave.
Bridgeport, CT 06601-0999
(203)576-4369
Fax: (203)576-4388

SCORE Office (Bristol)
10 Main St. 1st. Fl.
Bristol, CT 06010
(203)584-4718
Fax: (203)584-4722

SCORE office (Greater Danbury)
246 Federal Rd.
Unit LL2, Ste. 7
Brookfield, CT 06804
(203)775-1151

SCORE Office (Greater Danbury)
246 Federal Rd., Unit LL2, Ste. 7
Brookfield, CT 06804
(203)775-1151

SCORE Office (Eastern Connecticut)
Administration Bldg., Rm. 313
PO 625
61 Main St. (Chapter 579)
Groton, CT 06475
(203)388-9508

SCORE Office (Greater Hartford County)
330 Main St.
Hartford, CT 06106
(860)548-1749
Fax: (860)240-4659
Website: http://www.score56.org

SCORE Office (Manchester)
20 Hartford Rd.
Manchester, CT 06040
(203)646-2223
Fax: (203)646-5871

SCORE Office (New Britain)
185 Main St., Ste. 431
New Britain, CT 06051
(203)827-4492
Fax: (203)827-4480

SCORE Office (New Haven)
25 Science Pk., Bldg. 25, Rm. 366
New Haven, CT 06511
(203)865-7645

SCORE Office (Fairfield County)
24 Beldon Ave., 5th Fl.
Norwalk, CT 06850
(203)847-7348
Fax: (203)849-9308

SCORE Office (Old Saybrook)
146 Main St.
Old Saybrook, CT 06475
(860)388-9508

SCORE Office (Simsbury)
Box 244
Simsbury, CT 06070
(203)651-7307
Fax: (203)651-1933

SCORE Office (Torrington)
23 North Rd.
Torrington, CT 06791
(203)482-6586

Delaware

SCORE Office (Dover)
Treadway Towers
PO Box 576
Dover, DE 19903
(302)678-0892
Fax: (302)678-0189

SCORE Office (Lewes)
PO Box 1
Lewes, DE 19958
(302)645-8073
Fax: (302)645-8412

SCORE Office (Milford)
204 NE Front St.
Milford, DE 19963
(302)422-3301

SCORE Office (Wilmington)
824 Market St., Ste. 610
Wilmington, DE 19801
(302)573-6652
Fax: (302)573-6092
Website: http://www.scoredelaware.com

District of Columbia

SCORE Office (George Mason University)
409 3rd St. SW, 4th Fl.
Washington, DC 20024
800-634-0245

SCORE Office (Washington DC)
1110 Vermont Ave. NW, 9th Fl.
Washington, DC 20043
(202)606-4000
Fax: (202)606-4225
E-mail: dcscore@hotmail.com
Website: http://www.scoredc.org/

Florida

SCORE Office (Desota County Chamber of Commerce)
16 South Velucia Ave.
Arcadia, FL 34266
(941)494-4033

SCORE Office (Suncoast/Pinellas)
Airport Business Ctr.
4707 - 140th Ave. N, No. 311
Clearwater, FL 33755
(813)532-6800
Fax: (813)532-6800

SCORE Office (DeLand)
336 N. Woodland Blvd.
DeLand, FL 32720
(904)734-4331
Fax: (904)734-4333

SCORE Office (South Palm Beach)
1050 S. Federal Hwy., Ste. 132
Delray Beach, FL 33483
(561)278-7752
Fax: (561)278-0288

SCORE Office (Ft. Lauderdale)
Federal Bldg., Ste. 123
299 E. Broward Blvd.
Ft. Lauderdale, FL 33301
(954)356-7263
Fax: (954)356-7145

SCORE Office (Southwest Florida)
The Renaissance
8695 College Pky., Ste. 345 & 346
Ft. Myers, FL 33919
(941)489-2935
Fax: (941)489-1170

SCORE Office (Treasure Coast)
Professional Center, Ste. 2
3220 S. US, No. 1
Ft. Pierce, FL 34982
(561)489-0548

SCORE Office (Gainesville)
101 SE 2nd Pl., Ste. 104
Gainesville, FL 32601
(904)375-8278

SCORE Office (Hialeah Dade Chamber)
59 W. 5th St.
Hialeah, FL 33010
(305)887-1515
Fax: (305)887-2453

SCORE Office (Daytona Beach)
921 Nova Rd., Ste. A
Holly Hills, FL 32117
(904)255-6889
Fax: (904)255-0229
E-mail: score87@dbeach.com

SCORE Office (South Broward)
3475 Sheridian St., Ste. 203
Hollywood, FL 33021
(305)966-8415

SCORE Office (Citrus County)
5 Poplar Ct.
Homosassa, FL 34446
(352)382-1037

SCORE Office (Jacksonville)
7825 Baymeadows Way, Ste. 100-B
Jacksonville, FL 32256
(904)443-1911
Fax: (904)443-1980
E-mail: scorejax@juno.com
Website: http://www.scorejax.org/

SCORE Office (Jacksonville Satellite)
3 Independent Dr.
Jacksonville, FL 32256
(904)366-6600
Fax: (904)632-0617

SCORE Office (Central Florida)
5410 S. Florida Ave., No. 3
Lakeland, FL 33801
(941)687-5783
Fax: (941)687-6225

SCORE Office (Lakeland)
100 Lake Morton Dr.
Lakeland, FL 33801
(941)686-2168

SCORE Office (St. Petersburg)
800 W. Bay Dr., Ste. 505
Largo, FL 33712
(813)585-4571

SCORE Office (Leesburg)
9501 US Hwy. 441
Leesburg, FL 34788-8751
(352)365-3556
Fax: (352)365-3501

SCORE Office (Cocoa)
1600 Farno Rd., Unit 205
Melbourne, FL 32935
(407)254-2288

SCORE Office (Melbourne)
Melbourne Professional Complex
1600 Sarno, Ste. 205
Melbourne, FL 32935
(407)254-2288
Fax: (407)245-2288

SCORE Office (Merritt Island)
1600 Sarno Rd., Ste. 205
Melbourne, FL 32935
(407)254-2288
Fax: (407)254-2288

SCORE Office (Space Coast)
Melbourn Professional Complex
1600 Sarno, Ste. 205
Melbourne, FL 32935
(407)254-2288
Fax: (407)254-2288

SCORE Office (Dade)
49 NW 5th St.
Miami, FL 33128
(305)371-6889
Fax: (305)374-1882
E-mail: score@netrox.net
Website: http://www.netrox.net/~score/

SCORE Office (Naples of Collier)
International College
2654 Tamiami Trl. E
Naples, FL 34112
(941)417-1280
Fax: (941)417-1281
E-mail: score@naples.net
Website: http://www.naples.net/clubs/score/index.htm

SCORE Office (Pasco County)
6014 US Hwy. 19, Ste. 302
New Port Richey, FL 34652
(813)842-4638

SCORE Office (Southeast Volusia)
115 Canal St.
New Smyrna Beach, FL 32168
(904)428-2449
Fax: (904)423-3512

SCORE Office (Ocala)
110 E. Silver Springs Blvd.
Ocala, FL 34470
(352)629-5959

Clay County SCORE Office
Clay County Chamber of Commerce
1734 Kingsdey Ave.
PO Box 1441
Orange Park, FL 32073
(904)264-2651
Fax: (904)269-0363

SCORE Office (Orlando)
80 N. Hughey Ave.
Rm. 445 Federal Bldg.
Orlando, FL 32801
(407)648-6476
Fax: (407)648-6425

SCORE Office (Emerald Coast)
19 W. Garden St., No. 325
Pensacola, FL 32501
(904)444-2060
Fax: (904)444-2070

SCORE Office (Charlotte County)
201 W. Marion Ave., Ste. 211
Punta Gorda, FL 33950
(941)575-1818
E-mail: score@gls3c.com
Website: http://www.charlotte-florida.com/
business/scorepg01.htm

SCORE Office (St. Augustine)
1 Riberia St.
St. Augustine, FL 32084
(904)829-5681
Fax: (904)829-6477

SCORE Office (Bradenton)
2801 Fruitville, Ste. 280
Sarasota, FL 34237
(813)955-1029

SCORE Office (Manasota)
2801 Fruitville Rd., Ste. 280
Sarasota, FL 34237
(941)955-1029
Fax: (941)955-5581

E-mail: score116@gte.net
Website: http://www.score-
suncoast.org/

SCORE Office (Tallahassee)
200 W. Park Ave.
Tallahassee, FL 32302
(850)487-2665

SCORE Office (Hillsborough)
4732 Dale Mabry Hwy. N, Ste. 400
Tampa, FL 33614-6509
(813)870-0125

SCORE Office (Lake Sumter)
122 E. Main St.
Tavares, FL 32778-3810
(352)365-3556

SCORE Office (Titusville)
2000 S. Washington Ave.
Titusville, FL 32780
(407)267-3036
Fax: (407)264-0127

SCORE Office (Venice)
257 N. Tamiami Trl.
Venice, FL 34285
(941)488-2236
Fax: (941)484-5903

SCORE Office (Palm Beach)
500 Australian Ave. S, Ste. 100
West Palm Beach, FL 33401
(561)833-1672
Fax: (561)833-1712

SCORE Office (Wildwood)
103 N. Webster St.
Wildwood, FL 34785

Georgia

SCORE Office (Atlanta)
Harris Tower, Suite 1900
233 Peachtree Rd., NE
Atlanta, GA 30309
(404)347-2442
Fax: (404)347-1227

SCORE Office (Augusta)
3126 Oxford Rd.
Augusta, GA 30909
(706)869-9100

SCORE Office (Columbus)
School Bldg.
PO Box 40
Columbus, GA 31901
(706)327-3654

SCORE Office
(Dalton-Whitfield)
305 S. Thorton Ave.
Dalton, GA 30720
(706)279-3383

SCORE Office (Gainesville)
PO Box 374
Gainesville, GA 30503
(770)532-6206
Fax: (770)535-8419

SCORE Office (Macon)
711 Grand Bldg.
Macon, GA 31201
(912)751-6160

SCORE Office (Brunswick)
4 Glen Ave.
St. Simons Island, GA 31520
(912)265-0620
Fax: (912)265-0629

SCORE Office (Savannah)
111 E. Liberty St., Ste. 103
Savannah, GA 31401
(912)652-4335
Fax: (912)652-4184
E-mail: info@scoresav.org
Website: http://www.coastalempire.com/
score/index.htm

Guam

SCORE Office (Guam)
Pacific News Bldg.,
Rm. 103
238 Archbishop Flores St.
Agana, GU 96910-5100
(671)472-7308

Hawaii

SCORE Office (Hawaii, Inc.)
1111 Bishop St., Ste. 204
PO Box 50207
Honolulu, HI 96813
(808)522-8132
Fax: (808)522-8135
E-mail: hnlscore@juno.com

SCORE Office (Kahului)
250 Alamaha, Unit N16A
Kahului, HI 96732
(808)871-7711

SCORE Office (Maui, Inc.)
590 E. Lipoa Pkwy., Ste. 227
Kihei, HI 96753
(808)875-2380

Idaho

SCORE Office (Treasure Valley)
1020 Main St., No. 290
Boise, ID 83702
(208)334-1696
Fax: (208)334-9353

SCORE Office (Eastern Idaho)
2300 N. Yellowstone, Ste. 119
Idaho Falls, ID 83401
(208)523-1022
Fax: (208)528-7127

Illinois

SCORE Office (Fox Valley)
40 W. Downer Pl.
PO Box 277
Aurora, IL 60506
(630)897-9214
Fax: (630)897-7002

SCORE Office (Greater Belvidere)
419 S. State St.
Belvidere, IL 61008
(815)544-4357
Fax: (815)547-7654

SCORE Office (Bensenville)
1050 Busse Hwy. Suite 100
Bensenville, IL 60106
(708)350-2944
Fax: (708)350-2979

SCORE Office (Central Illinois)
402 N. Hershey Rd.
Bloomington, IL 61704
(309)644-0549
Fax: (309)663-8270
E-mail: webmaster@central-illinois-score.org
Website: http://www.central-illinois-score.org/

SCORE Office (Southern Illinois)
150 E. Pleasant Hill Rd.
Box 1
Carbondale, IL 62901
(618)453-6654
Fax: (618)453-5040

SCORE Office (Chicago)
Northwest Atrium Ctr.
500 W. Madison St.,
No. 1250
Chicago, IL 60661
(312)353-7724
Fax: (312)886-5688
Website: http://www.mcs.net/~bic/

SCORE Office (Chicago–Oliver Harvey College)
Pullman Bldg.
1000 E. 11th St., 7th Fl.
Chicago, IL 60628
Fax: (312)468-8086

SCORE Office (Danville)
28 W. N. Street
Danville, IL 61832
(217)442-7232
Fax: (217)442-6228

SCORE Office (Decatur)
Milliken University
1184 W. Main St.
Decatur, IL 62522
(217)424-6297
Fax: (217)424-3993
E-mail: charding@mail.millikin.edu
Website: http://www.millikin.edu/
academics/Tabor/score.html

SCORE Office (Downers Grove)
925 Curtis
Downers Grove, IL 60515
(708)968-4050
Fax: (708)968-8368

SCORE Office (Elgin)
24 E. Chicago, 3rd Fl.
PO Box 648
Elgin, IL 60120
(847)741-5660
Fax: (847)741-5677

SCORE Office (Freeport Area)
26 S. Galena Ave.
Freeport, IL 61032
(815)233-1350
Fax: (815)235-4038

SCORE Office (Galesburg)
292 E. Simmons St.
PO Box 749
Galesburg, IL 61401
(309)343-1194
Fax: (309)343-1195

SCORE Office (Glen Ellyn)
500 Pennsylvania
Glen Ellyn, IL 60137
(708)469-0907
Fax: (708)469-0426

SCORE Office (Greater Alton)
Alden Hall
5800 Godfrey Rd.
Godfrey, IL 62035-2466
(618)467-2280
Fax: (618)466-8289
Website: http://www.altonweb.com/score/

SCORE Office (Grayslake)
19351 W. Washington St.
Grayslake, IL 60030
(708)223-3633
Fax: (708)223-9371

SCORE Office (Harrisburg)
303 S. Commercial
Harrisburg, IL 62946-1528
(618)252-8528
Fax: (618)252-0210

SCORE Office (Joliet)
100 N. Chicago
Joliet, IL 60432
(815)727-5371
Fax: (815)727-5374

SCORE Office (Kankakee)
101 S. Schuyler Ave.
Kankakee, IL 60901
(815)933-0376
Fax: (815)933-0380

SCORE Office (Macomb)
216 Seal Hall, Rm. 214
Macomb, IL 61455
(309)298-1128
Fax: (309)298-2520

SCORE Office (Matteson)
210 Lincoln Mall
Matteson, IL 60443
(708)709-3750
Fax: (708)503-9322

SCORE Office (Mattoon)
1701 Wabash Ave.
Mattoon, IL 61938
(217)235-5661
Fax: (217)234-6544

SCORE Office (Quad Cities)
622 19th St.
Moline, IL 61265
(309)797-0082
Fax: (309)757-5435
E-mail: score@qconline.com
Website: http://www.qconline.com/
business/score/

SCORE Office (Naperville)
131 W. Jefferson Ave.
Naperville, IL 60540
(708)355-4141
Fax: (708)355-8355

SCORE Office (Northbrook)
2002 Walters Ave.
Northbrook, IL 60062
(847)498-5555
Fax: (847)498-5510

SCORE Office (Palos Hills)
10900 S. 88th Ave.
Palos Hills, IL 60465
(847)974-5468
Fax: (847)974-0078

SCORE Office (Peoria)
124 SW Adams, Ste. 300
Peoria, IL 61602
(309)676-0755
Fax: (309)676-7534

SCORE Office (Prospect Heights)
1375 Wolf Rd.
Prospect Heights, IL 60070
(847)537-8660
Fax: (847)537-7138

SCORE Office (Quincy Tri-State)
300 Civic Center Plz., Ste. 245
Quincy, IL 62301
(217)222-8093
Fax: (217)222-3033

SCORE Office (River Grove)
2000 5th Ave.
River Grove, IL 60171
(708)456-0300
Fax: (708)583-3121

SCORE Office (Northern Illinois)
515 N. Court St.
Rockford, IL 61103
(815)962-0122
Fax: (815)962-0122

SCORE Office (St. Charles)
103 N. 1st Ave.
St. Charles, IL 60174-1982
(847)584-8384
Fax: (847)584-6065

SCORE Office (Springfield)
511 W. Capitol Ave., Ste. 302
Springfield, IL 62704
(217)492-4416
Fax: (217)492-4867

SCORE Office (Sycamore)
112 Somunak St.
Sycamore, IL 60178
(815)895-3456
Fax: (815)895-0125

SCORE Office (University)
Hwy. 50 & Stuenkel Rd.
Ste. C3305
University Park, IL 60466
(708)534-5000
Fax: (708)534-8457

Indiana

SCORE Office (Anderson)
205 W. 11th St.
Anderson, IN 46015
(317)642-0264

SCORE Office (Bloomington)
Star Center
216 W. Allen
Bloomington, IN 47403
(812)335-7334
E-mail: wtfische@indiana.edu
Website: http://
www.brainfreezemedia.com/score527/

SCORE Office (South East Indiana)
500 Franklin St.
Box 29
Columbus, IN 47201
(812)379-4457

SCORE Office (Corydon)
310 N. Elm St.
Corydon, IN 47112
(812)738-2137
Fax: (812)738-6438

SCORE Office (Crown Point)
Old Courthouse Sq. Ste. 206
PO Box 43
Crown Point, IN 46307
(219)663-1800

SCORE Office (Elkhart)
418 S. Main St.
Elkhart, IN 46515
(219)293-1531
Fax: (219)294-1859

SCORE Office (Evansville)
1100 W. Lloyd Expy., Ste. 105
Evansville, IN 47708
(812)426-6144

SCORE Office (Fort Wayne)
1300 S. Harrison St.
Ft. Wayne, IN 46802
(219)422-2601
Fax: (219)422-2601

SCORE Office (Gary)
973 W. 6th Ave., Rm. 326
Gary, IN 46402
(219)882-3918

SCORE Office (Hammond)
7034 Indianapolis Blvd.
Hammond, IN 46324
(219)931-1000
Fax: (219)845-9548

SCORE Office (Indianapolis)
429 N. Pennsylvania St., Ste. 100
Indianapolis, IN 46204-1873
(317)226-7264
Fax: (317)226-7259
E-mail: inscore@indy.net
Website: http://
www.score-indianapolis.org/

SCORE Office (Jasper)
PO Box 307
Jasper, IN 47547-0307
(812)482-6866

SCORE Office (Kokomo/Howard Counties)
106 N. Washington St.
Kokomo, IN 46901
(765)457-5301
Fax: (765)452-4564

SCORE Office (Logansport)
300 E. Broadway, Ste. 103
Logansport, IN 46947
(219)753-6388

SCORE Office (Madison)
301 E. Main St.
Madison, IN 47250
(812)265-3135
Fax: (812)265-2923

SCORE Office (Marengo)
Rt. 1 Box 224D
Marengo, IN 47140
Fax: (812)365-2793

SCORE Office (Marion/Grant Counties)
215 S. Adams
Marion, IN 46952
(765)664-5107

SCORE Office (Merrillville)
255 W. 80th Pl.
Merrillville, IN 46410
(219)769-8180
Fax: (219)736-6223

SCORE Office (Michigan City)
200 E. Michigan Blvd.
Michigan City, IN 46360
(219)874-6221
Fax: (219)873-1204

SCORE Office (South Central Indiana)
4100 Charleston Rd.
New Albany, IN 47150-9538
(812)945-0066

SCORE Office (Rensselaer)
104 W. Washington
Rensselaer, IN 47978

SCORE Office (Salem)
210 N. Main St.
Salem, IN 47167
(812)883-4303
Fax: (812)883-1467

SCORE Office (South Bend)
300 N. Michigan St.
South Bend, IN 46601
(219)282-4350
E-mail: chair@southbend-score.org
Website: http://www.southbend-score.org/

SCORE Office (Valparaiso)
150 Lincolnway
Valparaiso, IN 46383
(219)462-1105
Fax: (219)469-5710

SCORE Office (Vincennes)
27 N. 3rd
PO Box 553
Vincennes, IN 47591
(812)882-6440
Fax: (812)882-6441

SCORE Office (Wabash)
PO Box 371
Wabash, IN 46992
(219)563-1168
Fax: (219)563-6920

Iowa

SCORE Office (Burlington)
Federal Bldg.
300 N. Main St.
Burlington, IA 52601
(319)752-2967

SCORE Office (Cedar Rapids)
Lattner Bldg., Ste. 200
215-4th Avenue, SE, No. 200
Cedar Rapids, IA 52401-1806
(319)362-6405
Fax: (319)362-7861

SCORE Office (Illowa)
333 4th Ave. S
Clinton, IA 52732
(319)242-5702

SCORE Office (Council Bluffs)
7 N. 6th St.
Council Bluffs, IA 51502
(712)325-1000

SCORE Office (Northeast Iowa)
3404 285th St.
Cresco, IA 52136
(319)547-3377

SCORE Office (Des Moines)
Federal Bldg., Rm. 749
210 Walnut St.
Des Moines, IA 50309-2186
(515)284-4760

SCORE Office (Ft. Dodge)
Federal Bldg., Rm. 436
205 S. 8th St.
Ft. Dodge, IA 50501
(515)955-2622

SCORE Office (Independence)
110 1st. St. east
Independence, IA 50644
(319)334-7178
Fax: (319)334-7179

SCORE Office (Iowa City)
210 Federal Bldg.
PO Box 1853
Iowa City, IA 52240-1853
(319)338-1662

SCORE Office (Keokuk)
401 Main St.
Pierce Bldg., No. 1
Keokuk, IA 52632
(319)524-5055

SCORE Office (Central Iowa)
Fisher Community College
709 S. Center
Marshalltown, IA 50158
(515)753-6645

SCORE Office (River City)
15 West State St.
Mason City, IA 50401
(515)423-5724

SCORE Office (South Central)
SBDC, Indian Hills Community College
525 Grandview Ave.
Ottumwa, IA 52501
(515)683-5127
Fax: (515)683-5263

SCORE Office (Dubuque)
10250 Sundown Rd.
Peosta, IA 52068
(319)556-5110

SCORE Office (Southwest Iowa)
614 W. Sheridan
Shenandoah, IA 51601
(712)246-3260

SCORE Office (Sioux City)
Federal Bldg.
320 6th St.
Sioux City, IA 51101
(712)277-2324
Fax: (712)277-2325

SCORE Office (Iowa Lakes)
122 W. 5th St.
Spencer, IA 51301
(712)262-3059

SCORE Office (Vista)
119 W. 6th St.
Storm Lake, IA 50588
(712)732-3780

SCORE Office (Waterloo)
215 E. 4th
Waterloo, IA 50703
(319)233-8431

Kansas

SCORE Office (Southwest Kansas)
501 W. Spruce
Dodge City, KS 67801
(316)227-3119

SCORE Office (Emporia)
811 Homewood
Emporia, KS 66801
(316)342-1600

SCORE Office (Golden Belt)
1307 Williams
Great Bend, KS 67530
(316)792-2401

SCORE Office (Hays)
PO Box 400
Hays, KS 67601
(913)625-6595

SCORE Office (Hutchinson)
1 E. 9th St.
Hutchinson, KS 67501
(316)665-8468
Fax: (316)665-7619

SCORE Office (Southeast Kansas)
404 Westminster Pl.
PO Box 886
Independence, KS 67301
(316)331-4741

SCORE Office (McPherson)
306 N. Main
PO Box 616
McPherson, KS 67460
(316)241-3303

SCORE Office (Salina)
120 Ash St.
Salina, KS 67401
(785)243-4290
Fax: (785)243-1833

SCORE Office (Topeka)
1700 College
Topeka, KS 66621
(785)231-1010

SCORE Office (Wichita)
100 E. English, Ste. 510
Wichita, KS 67202
(316)269-6273
Fax: (316)269-6499

SCORE Office (Ark Valley)
205 E. 9th St.
Winfield, KS 67156
(316)221-1617

Kentucky

SCORE Office (Ashland)
PO Box 830
Ashland, KY 41105
(606)329-8011
Fax: (606)325-4607

SCORE Office (Bowling Green)
812 State St.
PO Box 51
Bowling Green, KY 42101
(502)781-3200
Fax: (502)843-0458

SCORE Office (Tri-Lakes)
508 Barbee Way
Danville, KY 40422-1548
(606)231-9902

SCORE Office (Glasgow)
301 W. Main St.
Glasgow, KY 42141
(502)651-3161
Fax: (502)651-3122

SCORE Office (Hazard)
B & I Technical Center
100 Airport Gardens Rd.
Hazard, KY 41701
(606)439-5856
Fax: (606)439-1808

SCORE Office (Lexington)
410 W. Vine St., Ste. 290, Civic C
Lexington, KY 40507
(606)231-9902
Fax: (606)253-3190
E-mail: scorelex@uky.campus.mci.net

SCORE Office (Louisville)
188 Federal Office Bldg.
600 Dr. Martin L. King Jr. Pl.
Louisville, KY 40202
(502)582-5976

SCORE Office (Madisonville)
257 N. Main
Madisonville, KY 42431
(502)825-1399
Fax: (502)825-1396

SCORE Office (Paducah)
Federal Office Bldg.
501 Broadway, Rm. B-36
Paducah, KY 42001
(502)442-5685

Louisiana

SCORE Office (Central Louisiana)
802 3rd St.
Alexandria, LA 71309
(318)442-6671

SCORE Office (Baton Rouge)
564 Laurel St.
PO Box 3217
Baton Rouge, LA 70801
(504)381-7130
Fax: (504)336-4306

SCORE Office (North Shore)
2 W. Thomas
Hammond, LA 70401
(504)345-4457
Fax: (504)345-4749

SCORE Office (Lafayette)
804 St. Mary Blvd.
Lafayette, LA 70505-1307
(318)233-2705
Fax: (318)234-8671
E-mail: score302@aol.com

SCORE Office (Lake Charles)
120 W. Pujo St.
Lake Charles, LA 70601
(318)433-3632

SCORE Office (New Orleans)
365 Canal St., Ste. 3100
New Orleans, LA 70130
(504)589-2356
Fax: (504)589-2339

SCORE Office (Shreveport)
400 Edwards St.
Shreveport, LA 71101
(318)677-2536
Fax: (318)677-2541

Maine

SCORE Office (Augusta)
40 Western Ave.
Augusta, ME 04330
(207)622-8509

SCORE Office (Bangor)
Peabody Hall, Rm. 229
One College Cir.
Bangor, ME 04401
(207)941-9707

SCORE Office (Central & Northern Arroostock)
111 High St.
Caribou, ME 04736
(207)492-8010
Fax: (207)492-8010

SCORE Office (Penquis)
South St.
Dover Foxcroft, ME 04426
(207)564-7021

SCORE Office (Maine Coastal)
Mill Mall
Box 1105
Ellsworth, ME 04605-1105
(207)667-5800
E-mail: score@arcadia.net

SCORE Office (Lewiston-Auburn)
BIC of Maine-Bates
Mill Complex
35 Canal St.
Lewiston, ME 04240-7764
(207)782-3708
Fax: (207)783-7745

SCORE Office (Portland)
66 Pearl St., Rm. 210
Portland, ME 04101
(207)772-1147
Fax: (207)772-5581
E-mail: Score53@score.maine.org
Website: http://www.score.maine.org/chapter53/

SCORE Office (Western Mountains)
255 River St.
PO Box 252
Rumford, ME 04257-0252
(207)369-9976

SCORE Office (Oxford Hills)
166 Main St.
South Paris, ME 04281
(207)743-0499

Maryland

SCORE Office (Southern Maryland)
2525 Riva Rd., Ste. 110
Annapolis, MD 21401
(410)266-9553
Fax: (410)573-0981
E-mail: score390@aol.com
Website: http://members.aol.com/
score390/index.htm

SCORE Office (Baltimore)
The City Crescent Bldg., 6th Fl.
10 S. Howard St.
Baltimore, MD 21201
(410)962-2233
Fax: (410)962-1805

SCORE Office (Bel Air)
108 S. Bond St.
Bel Air, MD 21014
(410)838-2020
Fax: (410)893-4715

SCORE Office (Bethesda)
7910 Woodmont Ave., Ste. 1204
Bethesda, MD 20814
(301)652-4900
Fax: (301)657-1973

SCORE Office (Bowie)
6670 Race Track Rd.
Bowie, MD 20715
(301)262-0920
Fax: (301)262-0921

SCORE Office (Dorchester County)
203 Sunburst Hwy.
Cambridge, MD 21613
(410)228-3575

SCORE Office (Upper Shore)
210 Marlboro Ave.
Easton, MD 21601
(410)822-4606
Fax: (410)822-7922

SCORE Office (Frederick County)
43A S. Market St.
Frederick, MD 21701
(301)662-8723
Fax: (301)846-4427

SCORE Office (Gaithersburg)
9 Park Ave.
Gaithersburg, MD 20877
(301)840-1400
Fax: (301)963-3918

SCORE Office (Glen Burnie)
103 Crain Hwy. SE
Glen Burnie, MD 21061

(410)766-8282
Fax: (410)766-9722

SCORE Office (Hagerstown)
111 W. Washington St.
Hagerstown, MD 21740
(301)739-2015
Fax: (301)739-1278

SCORE Office (Laurel)
7901 Sandy Spring Rd. Ste. 501
Laurel, MD 20707
(301)725-4000
Fax: (301)725-0776

SCORE Office (Salisbury)
300 E. Main St.
Salisbury, MD 21801
(410)749-0185
Fax: (410)860-9925

Massachusetts

SCORE Office (NE Massachusetts)
100 Cummings Ctr., Ste. 101 K
Beverly, MA 01923
(978)922-9441
Website: http://www1.shore.net/~score/

SCORE Office (Boston)
10 Causeway St., Rm. 265
Boston, MA 02222-1093
(617)565-5591
Fax: (617)565-5598
E-mail: boston-score-
20@worldnet.att.net
Website: http://www.scoreboston.org/

SCORE office (Bristol/Plymouth County)
53 N. 6th St., Federal Bldg.
Bristol, MA 02740
(508)994-5093

SCORE Office (SE Massachusetts)
60 School St.
Brockton, MA 02401
(508)587-2673
Fax: (508)587-1340
Website: http://
www.metrosouthchamber.com/score.html

SCORE Office (North Adams)
820 N. State Rd.
Cheshire, MA 01225
(413)743-5100

SCORE Office (Clinton Satellite)
1 Green St.
Clinton, MA 01510
Fax: (508)368-7689

SCORE Office (Greenfield)
PO Box 898
Greenfield, MA 01302
(413)773-5463
Fax: (413)773-7008

SCORE Office (Haverhill)
87 Winter St.
Haverhill, MA 01830
(508)373-5663
Fax: (508)373-8060

SCORE Office (Hudson Satellite)
PO Box 578
Hudson, MA 01749
(508)568-0360
Fax: (508)568-0360

SCORE Office (Cape Cod)
Independence Pk., Ste. 5B
270 Communications Way
Hyannis, MA 02601
(508)775-4884
Fax: (508)790-2540

SCORE Office (Lawrence)
264 Essex St.
Lawrence, MA 01840
(508)686-0900
Fax: (508)794-9953

SCORE Office (Leominster Satellite)
110 Erdman Way
Leominster, MA 01453
(508)840-4300
Fax: (508)840-4896

SCORE Office (Bristol/Plymouth Counties)
53 N. 6th St., Federal Bldg.
New Bedford, MA 02740
(508)994-5093

SCORE Office (Newburyport)
29 State St.
Newburyport, MA 01950
(617)462-6680

SCORE Office (Pittsfield)
66 West St.
Pittsfield, MA 01201
(413)499-2485

SCORE Office (Haverhill-Salem)
32 Derby Sq.
Salem, MA 01970
(508)745-0330
Fax: (508)745-3855

SCORE Office (Springfield)
1350 Main St.
Federal Bldg.

Springfield, MA 01103
(413)785-0314

SCORE Office (Carver)
12 Taunton Green, Ste. 201
Taunton, MA 02780
(508)824-4068
Fax: (508)824-4069

SCORE Office (Worcester)
33 Waldo St.
Worcester, MA 01608
(508)753-2929
Fax: (508)754-8560

Michigan

SCORE Office (Allegan)
PO Box 338
Allegan, MI 49010
(616)673-2479

SCORE Office (Ann Arbor)
425 S. Main St., Ste. 103
Ann Arbor, MI 48104
(313)665-4433

SCORE Office (Battle Creek)
34 W. Jackson Ste. 4A
Battle Creek, MI 49017-3505
(616)962-4076
Fax: (616)962-6309

SCORE Office (Cadillac)
222 Lake St.
Cadillac, MI 49601
(616)775-9776
Fax: (616)768-4255

SCORE Office (Detroit)
477 Michigan Ave., Rm. 515
Detroit, MI 48226
(313)226-7947
Fax: (313)226-3448

SCORE Office (Flint)
708 Root Rd., Rm. 308
Flint, MI 48503
(810)233-6846

SCORE Office (Grand Rapids)
111 Pearl St. NW
Grand Rapids, MI 49503-2831
(616)771-0305
Fax: (616)771-0328
E-mail: scoreone@iserv.net
Website: http://www.iserv.net/~scoreone/

SCORE Office (Holland)
480 State St.
Holland, MI 49423
(616)396-9472

SCORE Office (Jackson)
209 East Washington
PO Box 80
Jackson, MI 49204
(517)782-8221
Fax: (517)782-0061

SCORE Office (Kalamazoo)
345 W. Michigan Ave.
Kalamazoo, MI 49007
(616)381-5382
Fax: (616)384-0096
E-mail: score@nucleus.net

SCORE Office (Lansing)
117 E. Allegan
PO Box 14030
Lansing, MI 48901
(517)487-6340
Fax: (517)484-6910

SCORE Office (Livonia)
15401 Farmington Rd.
Livonia, MI 48154
(313)427-2122
Fax: (313)427-6055

SCORE Office (Madison Heights)
26345 John R
Madison Heights, MI 48071
(810)542-5010
Fax: (810)542-6821

SCORE Office (Monroe)
111 E. 1st
Monroe, MI 48161
(313)242-3366
Fax: (313)242-7253

SCORE Office (Mt. Clemens)
58 S/B Gratiot
Mt. Clemens, MI 48043
(810)463-1528
Fax: (810)463-6541

SCORE Office (Muskegon)
PO Box 1087
230 Terrace Plz.
Muskegon, MI 49443
(616)722-3751
Fax: (616)728-7251

SCORE Office (Petoskey)
401 E. Mitchell St.
Petoskey, MI 49770
(616)347-4150

SCORE Office (Pontiac)
Executive Office Bldg.
1200 N. Telegraph Rd.
Pontiac, MI 48341
(810)975-9555

SCORE Office (Pontiac)
PO Box 430025
Pontiac, MI 48343
(810)335-9600

SCORE Office (Port Huron)
920 Pinegrove Ave.
Port Huron, MI 48060
(810)985-7101

SCORE Office (Rochester)
71 Walnut Ste. 110
Rochester, MI 48307
(810)651-6700
Fax: (810)651-5270

SCORE Office (Saginaw)
901 S. Washington Ave.
Saginaw, MI 48601
(517)752-7161
Fax: (517)752-9055

SCORE Office (Upper Peninsula)
2581 I-75 Business Spur
Sault Ste. Marie, MI 49783
(906)632-3301

SCORE Office (Southfield)
21000 W. 10 Mile Rd.
Southfield, MI 48075
(810)204-3050
Fax: (810)204-3099

SCORE Office (Traverse City)
202 E. Grandview Pkwy.
PO Box 387
Traverse City, MI 49685
(616)947-5075
Fax: (616)946-2565

SCORE Office (Warren)
30500 Van Dyke, Ste. 118
Warren, MI 48093
(810)751-3939

Minnesota

SCORE Office (Aitkin)
Aitkin, MN 56431
(218)741-3906

SCORE Office (Albert Lea)
202 N. Broadway Ave.
Albert Lea, MN 56007
(507)373-7487

SCORE Office (Austin)
PO Box 864
Austin, MN 55912
(507)437-4561
Fax: (507)437-4869

SCORE Office (South Metro)
Ames Business Ctr.
2500 W. County Rd., No. 42
Burnsville, MN 55337
(612)898-5645
Fax: (612)435-6972
E-mail: southmetro@scoreminn.org
Website: http://www.scoreminn.org/
southmetro/

SCORE Office (Duluth)
1717 Minnesota Ave.
Duluth, MN 55802
(218)727-8286
Fax: (218)727-3113
E-mail: duluth@scoreminn.org
Website: http://www.scoreminn.org

SCORE Office (Fairmont)
PO Box 826
Fairmont, MN 56031
(507)235-5547
Fax: (507)235-8411

SCORE Office (Southwest Minnesota)
112 Riverfront St.
Box 999
Mankato, MN 56001
(507)345-4519
Fax: (507)345-4451
Website: http://www.scoreminn.org/

SCORE Office (Minneapolis)
North Plaza Bldg., Ste. 51
5217 Wayzata Blvd.
Minneapolis, MN 55416
(612)591-0539
Fax: (612)544-0436
Website: http://www.scoreminn.org/

SCORE Office (Owatonna)
PO Box 331
Owatonna, MN 55060
(507)451-7970
Fax: (507)451-7972

SCORE Office (Red Wing)
2000 W. Main St., Ste. 324
Red Wing, MN 55066
(612)388-4079

SCORE Office (Southeastern Minnesota)
220 S. Broadway, Ste. 100
Rochester, MN 55901
(507)288-1122
Fax: (507)282-8960
Website: http://www.scoreminn.org/

SCORE Office (Brainerd)
St. Cloud, MN 56301

SCORE Office (Central Area)
1527 Northway Dr.
St. Cloud, MN 56301
(320)240-1332
Fax: (320)255-9050
Website: http://www.scoreminn.org/

SCORE Office (St. Paul)
350 St. Peter St., No. 295
Lowry Professional Bldg.
St. Paul, MN 55102
(651)223-5010
Fax: (651)223-5048
Website: http://www.scoreminn.org/

SCORE Office (Winona)
Box 870
Winona, MN 55987
(507)452-2272
Fax: (507)454-8814

SCORE Office (Worthington)
1121 3rd Ave.
Worthington, MN 56187
(507)372-2919
Fax: (507)372-2827

Mississippi

SCORE Office (Delta)
915 Washington Ave.
PO Box 933
Greenville, MS 38701
(601)378-3141

SCORE Office (Gulfcoast)
1 Government Plaza
2909 13th St., Ste. 203
Gulfport, MS 39501
(228)863-0054

SCORE Office (Jackson)
1st Jackson Center, Ste. 400
101 W. Capitol St.
Jackson, MS 39201
(601)965-5533

SCORE Office (Meridian)
5220 16th Ave.
Meridian, MS 39305
(601)482-4412

Missouri

SCORE Office (Lake of the Ozark)
University Extension
113 Kansas St.
PO Box 1405
Camdenton, MO 65020
(573)346-2644
Fax: (573)346-2694

E-mail: score@cdoc.net
Website: http://sites.cdoc.net/score/

Chamber of Commerce (Cape Girardeau)
PO Box 98
Cape Girardeau, MO 63702-0098
(314)335-3312

SCORE Office (Mid-Missouri)
1705 Halstead Ct.
Columbia, MO 65203
(573)874-1132

SCORE Office (Ozark-Gateway)
1486 Glassy Rd.
Cuba, MO 65453-1640
(573)885-4954

SCORE Office (Kansas City)
323 W. 8th St., Ste. 104
Kansas City, MO 64105
(816)374-6675
Fax: (816)374-6692
E-mail: SCOREBIC@AOL.COM
Website: http://www.crn.org/score/

SCORE Office (Sedalia)
Lucas Place
323 W. 8th St., Ste.104
Kansas City, MO 64105
(816)374-6675

SCORE office (Tri-Lakes)
PO Box 1148
Kimberling, MO 65686
(417)739-3041

SCORE Office (Tri-Lakes)
HCRI Box 85
Lampe, MO 65681
(417)858-6798

SCORE Office (Mexico)
111 N. Washington St.
Mexico, MO 65265
(314)581-2765

SCORE Office (Southeast Missouri)
Rte. 1, Box 280
Neelyville, MO 63954
(573)989-3577

SCORE office (Poplar Bluff Area)
806 Emma St.
Poplar Bluff, MO 63901
(573)686-8892

SCORE Office (St. Joseph)
3003 Frederick Ave.
St. Joseph, MO 64506
(816)232-4461

SCORE Office (St. Louis)
815 Olive St., Rm. 242
St. Louis, MO 63101-1569
(314)539-6970
Fax: (314)539-3785
E-mail: info@stlscore.org
Website: http://www.stlscore.org/

SCORE Office (Lewis & Clark)
425 Spencer Rd.
St. Peters, MO 63376
(314)928-2900
Fax: (314)928-2900
E-mail: score01@mail.win.org

SCORE Office (Springfield)
620 S. Glenstone, Ste. 110
Springfield, MO 65802-3200
(417)864-7670
Fax: (417)864-4108

SCORE office (Southeast Kansas)
1206 W. First St.
Webb City, MO 64870
(417)673-3984

Montana

SCORE Office (Billings)
815 S. 27th St.
Billings, MT 59101
(406)245-4111

SCORE Office (Bozeman)
1205 E. Main St.
Bozeman, MT 59715
(406)586-5421

SCORE Office (Butte)
1000 George St.
Butte, MT 59701
(406)723-3177

SCORE Office (Great Falls)
710 First Ave. N
Great Falls, MT 59401
(406)761-4434
E-mail: scoregtf@in.tch.com

SCORE Office (Havre, Montana)
518 First St.
Havre, MT 59501
(406)265-4383

SCORE Office (Helena)
Federal Bldg.
301 S. Park
Helena, MT 59626-0054
(406)441-1081

SCORE Office (Kalispell)
2 Main St.
Kalispell, MT 59901

(406)756-5271
Fax: (406)752-6665

SCORE Office (Missoula)
723 Ronan
Missoula, MT 59806
(406)327-8806
E-mail: score@safeshop.com
Website: http://missoula.bigsky.net/score/

Nebraska

SCORE Office (Columbus)
Columbus, NE 68601
(402)564-2769

SCORE Office (Fremont)
92 W. 5th St.
Fremont, NE 68025
(402)721-2641

SCORE Office (Hastings)
Hastings, NE 68901
(402)463-3447

SCORE Office (Lincoln)
8800 O St.
Lincoln, NE 68520
(402)437-2409

SCORE Office (Panhandle)
150549 CR 30
Minatare, NE 69356
(308)632-2133
Website: http://www.tandt.com/SCORE

SCORE Office (Norfolk)
3209 S. 48th Ave.
Norfolk, NE 68106
(402)564-2769

SCORE Office (North Platte)
3301 W. 2nd St.
North Platte, NE 69101
(308)532-4466

SCORE Office (Omaha)
11145 Mill Valley Rd.
Omaha, NE 68154
(402)221-3606
Fax: (402)221-3680
E-mail: infoctr@ne.uswest.net
Website: http://www.tandt.com/score/

Nevada

SCORE Office (Incline Village)
969 Tahoe Blvd.
Incline Village, NV 89451
(702)831-7327
Fax: (702)832-1605

SCORE Office (Carson City)
301 E. Stewart
PO Box 7527
Las Vegas, NV 89125
(702)388-6104

SCORE Office (Las Vegas)
300 Las Vegas Blvd. S, Ste. 1100
Las Vegas, NV 89101
(702)388-6104

SCORE Office (Northern Nevada)
SBDC, College of Business
Administration
Univ. of Nevada
Reno, NV 89557-0100
(702)784-4436
Fax: (702)784-4337

New Hampshire

SCORE Office (North Country)
PO Box 34
Berlin, NH 03570
(603)752-1090

SCORE Office (Concord)
143 N. Main St., Rm. 202A
PO Box 1258
Concord, NH 03301
(603)225-1400
Fax: (603)225-1409

SCORE Office (Dover)
299 Central Ave.
Dover, NH 03820
(603)742-2218
Fax: (603)749-6317

SCORE Office (Monadnock)
34 Mechanic St.
Keene, NH 03431-3421
(603)352-0320

SCORE Office (Lakes Region)
67 Water St., Ste. 105
Laconia, NH 03246
(603)524-9168

SCORE Office (Upper Valley)
Citizens Bank Bldg., Rm. 310
20 W. Park St.
Lebanon, NH 03766
(603)448-3491
Fax: (603)448-1908
E-mail: billt@valley.net
Website: http://www.valley.net/~score/

SCORE Office (Merrimack Valley)
275 Chestnut St., Rm. 618
Manchester, NH 03103
(603)666-7561
Fax: (603)666-7925

SCORE Office (Mt. Washington Valley)
PO Box 1066
North Conway, NH 03818
(603)383-0800

SCORE Office (Seacoast)
195 Commerce Way, Unit-A
Portsmouth, NH 03801-3251
(603)433-0575

New Jersey

SCORE Office (Somerset)
Paritan Valley Community College, Rte. 28
Branchburg, NJ 08807
(908)218-8874
E-mail: nj-score@grizbiz.com.
Website: http://www.nj-score.org/

SCORE Office (Chester)
5 Old Mill Rd.
Chester, NJ 07930
(908)879-7080

SCORE Office (Greater Princeton)
4 A George Washington Dr.
Cranbury, NJ 08512
(609)520-1776

SCORE Office (Freehold)
36 W. Main St.
Freehold, NJ 07728
(908)462-3030
Fax: (908)462-2123

SCORE Office (North West)
Picantinny Innovation Ctr.
3159 Schrader Rd.
Hamburg, NJ 07419
(973)209-8525
Fax: (973)209-7252
E-mail: nj-score@grizbiz.com
Website: http://www.nj-score.org/

SCORE Office (Monmouth)
765 Newman Springs Rd.
Lincroft, NJ 07738
(908)224-2573
E-mail: nj-score@grizbiz.com
Website: http://www.nj-score.org/

SCORE Office (Manalapan)
125 Symmes Dr.
Manalapan, NJ 07726
(908)431-7220

SCORE Office (Jersey City)
2 Gateway Ctr., 4th Fl.
Newark, NJ 07102
(973)645-3982
Fax: (973)645-2375

SCORE Office (Newark)
2 Gateway Center, 15th Fl.
Newark, NJ 07102-5553
(973)645-3982
Fax: (973)645-2375
E-mail: nj-score@grizbiz.com
Website: http://www.nj-score.org

SCORE Office (Bergen County)
327 E. Ridgewood Ave.
Paramus, NJ 07652
(201)599-6090
E-mail: nj-score@grizbiz.com
Website: http://www.nj-score.org/

SCORE Office (Pennsauken)
4900 Rte. 70
Pennsauken, NJ 08109
(609)486-3421

SCORE Office (Southern New Jersey)
4900 Rte. 70
Pennsauken, NJ 08109
(609)486-3421
E-mail: nj-score@grizbiz.com
Website: http://www.nj-score.org/

SCORE Office (Greater Princeton)
216 Rockingham Row
Princeton Forrestal Village
Princeton, NJ 08540
(609)520-1776
Fax: (609)520-9107
E-mail: nj-score@grizbiz.com
Website: http://www.nj-score.org/

SCORE Office (Shrewsbury)
Hwy. 35
Shrewsbury, NJ 07702
(908)842-5995
Fax: (908)219-6140

SCORE Office (Ocean County)
33 Washington St.
Toms River, NJ 08754
(732)505-6033
E-mail: nj-score@grizbiz.com
Website: http://www.nj-score.org/

SCORE Office (Wall)
2700 Allaire Rd.
Wall, NJ 07719
(908)449-8877

SCORE Office (Wayne)
2055 Hamburg Tpke.
Wayne, NJ 07470
(201)831-7788
Fax: (201)831-9112

New Mexico

SCORE Office (Albuquerque)
525 Buena Vista, SE
Albuquerque, NM 87106
(505)272-7999
Fax: (505)272-7963

SCORE Office (Las Cruces)
Loretto Towne Center
505 S. Main St., Ste. 125
Las Cruces, NM 88001
(505)523-5627
Fax: (505)524-2101
E-mail: score.397@zianet.com

SCORE Office (Roswell)
Federal Bldg., Rm. 237
Roswell, NM 88201
(505)625-2112
Fax: (505)623-2545

SCORE Office (Santa Fe)
Montoya Federal Bldg.
120 Federal Place,
Rm. 307
Santa Fe, NM 87501
(505)988-6302
Fax: (505)988-6300

New York

SCORE Office (Northeast)
1 Computer Dr. S
Albany, NY 12205
(518)446-1118
Fax: (518)446-1228

SCORE Office (Auburn)
30 South St.
PO Box 675
Auburn, NY 13021
(315)252-7291

SCORE Office (South Tier Binghamton)
Metro Center, 2nd Fl.
49 Court St.
PO Box 995
Binghamton, NY 13902
(607)772-8860

SCORE Office (Queens County City)
12055 Queens Blvd., Rm. 333
Borough Hall, NY 11424
(718)263-8961

SCORE Office (Buffalo)
Federal Bldg., Rm. 1311
111 W. Huron St.
Buffalo, NY 14202

(716)551-4301
Website: http://www2.pcom.net/score/
buf45.html

SCORE Office (Canandaigua)
Chamber of Commerce Bldg.
113 S. Main St.
Canandaigua, NY 14424
(716)394-4400
Fax: (716)394-4546

SCORE Office (Chemung)
333 E. Water St., 4th Fl.
Elmira, NY 14901
(607)734-3358

SCORE Office (Geneva)
Chamber of Commerce Bldg.
PO Box 587
Geneva, NY 14456
(315)789-1776
Fax: (315)789-3993

SCORE Office (Glens Falls)
84 Broad St.
Glens Falls, NY 12801
(518)798-8463
Fax: (518)745-1433

SCORE Office (Orange County)
40 Matthews St.
Goshen, NY 10924
(914)294-8080
Fax: (914)294-6121

SCORE Office (Huntington Area)
151 W. Carver St.
Huntington, NY 11743
(516)423-6100

SCORE Office (Tompkins County)
904 E. Shore Dr.
Ithaca, NY 14850
(607)273-7080

SCORE Office (Long Island City)
120-55 Queens Blvd.
Jamaica, NY 11424
(718)263-8961
Fax: (718)263-9032

SCORE Office (Chatauqua)
101 W. 5th St.
Jamestown, NY 14701
(716)484-1103

SCORE Office (Westchester)
2 Caradon Ln.
Katonah, NY 10536
(914)948-3907
Fax: (914)948-4645
E-mail: score@w-w-w.com
Website: http://w-w-w.com/score/

SCORE Office (Queens County)
Queens Borough Hall
120-55 Queens Blvd. Rm. 333
Kew Gardens, NY 11424
(718)263-8961
Fax: (718)263-9032

SCORE Office (Brookhaven)
3233 Rte. 112
Medford, NY 11763
(516)451-6563
Fax: (516)451-6925

SCORE Office (Melville)
35 Pinelawn Rd., Rm. 207-W
Melville, NY 11747
(516)454-0771

SCORE Office (Nassau County)
400 County Seat Dr., No. 140
Mineola, NY 11501
(516)571-3303
E-mail: Counse1998@aol.com
Website: http://members.aol.com/
Counse1998/Default.htm

SCORE Office (Mt. Vernon)
4 N. 7th Ave.
Mt. Vernon, NY 10550
(914)667-7500

SCORE Office (New York)
26 Federal Plz., Rm. 3100
New York, NY 10278
(212)264-4507
Fax: (212)264-4963
E-mail: score1000@erols.com
Website: http://users.erols.com/
score-nyc/

SCORE Office (Newburgh)
47 Grand St.
Newburgh, NY 12550
(914)562-5100

SCORE Office (Owego)
188 Front St.
Owego, NY 13827
(607)687-2020

SCORE Office (Peekskill)
1 S. Division St.
Peekskill, NY 10566
(914)737-3600
Fax: (914)737-0541

SCORE Office (Penn Yan)
2375 Rte. 14A
Penn Yan, NY 14527
(315)536-3111

SCORE Office (Dutchess)
110 Main St.
Poughkeepsie, NY 12601
(914)454-1700

SCORE Office (Rochester)
601 Keating Federal Bldg., Rm. 410
100 State St.
Rochester, NY 14614
(716)263-6473
Fax: (716)263-3146
Website: http://www.ggw.org/score/

SCORE Office (Saranac Lake)
30 Main St.
Saranac Lake, NY 12983
(315)448-0415

SCORE Office (Suffolk)
286 Main St.
Setauket, NY 11733
(516)751-3886

SCORE Office (Staten Island)
130 Bay St.
Staten Island, NY 10301
(718)727-1221

SCORE Office (Ulster)
Clinton Bldg., Rm. 107
Stone Ridge, NY 12484
(914)687-5035
Fax: (914)687-5015
Website: http://www.scoreulster.org/

SCORE Office (Syracuse)
401 S. Salina, 5th Fl.
Syracuse, NY 13202
(315)471-9393

SCORE Office (Utica)
SUNY Institute of Technology, Route 12
Utica, NY 13504-3050
(315)792-7553

SCORE Office (Watertown)
518 Davidson St.
Watertown, NY 13601
(315)788-1200
Fax: (315)788-8251

North Carolina

SCORE office (Asheboro)
317 E. Dixie Dr.
Asheboro, NC 27203
(336)626-2626
Fax: (336)626-7077

SCORE Office (Asheville)
Federal Bldg., Rm. 259
151 Patton
Asheville, NC 28801-5770

(828)271-4786
Fax: (828)271-4009

SCORE Office (Chapel Hill)
104 S. Estes Dr.
PO Box 2897
Chapel Hill, NC 27514
(919)967-7075

SCORE Office (Coastal Plains)
PO Box 2897
Chapel Hill, NC 27515
(919)967-7075
Fax: (919)968-6874

SCORE Office (Charlotte)
200 N. College St., Ste. A-2015
Charlotte, NC 28202
(704)344-6576
Fax: (704)344-6769
E-mail: CharlotteSCORE47@AOL.com
Website: http://www.charweb.org/
business/score/

SCORE Office (Durham)
411 W. Chapel Hill St.
Durham, NC 27707
(919)541-2171

SCORE Office (Gastonia)
PO Box 2168
Gastonia, NC 28053
(704)864-2621
Fax: (704)854-8723

SCORE Office (Greensboro)
400 W. Market St., Ste. 103
Greensboro, NC 27401-2241
(910)333-5399

SCORE Office (Henderson)
PO Box 917
Henderson, NC 27536
(919)492-2061
Fax: (919)430-0460

SCORE Office (Hendersonville)
Federal Bldg., Rm. 108
W. 4th Ave. & Church St.
Hendersonville, NC 28792
(828)693-8702
E-mail: score@circle.net
Website: http://www.wncguide.com/
score/Welcome.html

SCORE Office (Unifour)
PO Box 1828
Hickory, NC 28603
(704)328-6111

SCORE Office (High Point)
1101 N. Main St.
High Point, NC 27262

(336)882-8625
Fax: (336)889-9499

SCORE Office (Outer Banks)
Collington Rd. and Mustain
Kill Devil Hills, NC 27948
(252)441-8144

SCORE Office (Down East)
312 S. Front St., Ste. 6
New Bern, NC 28560
(252)633-6688
Fax: (252)633-9608

SCORE Office (Kinston)
PO Box 95
New Bern, NC 28561
(919)633-6688

SCORE Office (Raleigh)
Century Post Office Bldg., Ste. 306
300 Federal St. Mall
Raleigh, NC 27601
(919)856-4739
E-mail: jendres@ibm.net
Website: http://www.intrex.net/score96/
score96.htm

SCORE Office (Sanford)
1801 Nash St.
Sanford, NC 27330
(919)774-6442
Fax: (919)776-8739

SCORE Office (Sandhills Area)
1480 Hwy. 15-501
PO Box 458
Southern Pines, NC 28387
(910)692-3926

SCORE Office (Wilmington)
Corps of Engineers Bldg.
96 Darlington Ave., Ste. 207
Wilmington, NC 28403
(910)815-4576
Fax: (910)815-4658

North Dakota

SCORE Office (Bismarck-Mandan)
700 E. Main Ave., 2nd Fl.
PO Box 5509
Bismarck, ND 58506-5509
(701)250-4303

SCORE Office (Fargo)
657 2nd Ave., Rm. 225
Fargo, ND 58108-3083
(701)239-5677

SCORE Office (Upper Red River)
4275 Technology Dr., Rm. 156
Grand Forks, ND 58202-8372
(701)777-3051

SCORE Office (Minot)
100 1st St. SW
Minot, ND 58701-3846
(701)852-6883
Fax: (701)852-6905

Ohio

SCORE Office (Akron)
1 Cascade Plz., 7th Fl.
Akron, OH 44308
(330)379-3163
Fax: (330)379-3164

SCORE Office (Ashland)
Gill Center
47 W. Main St.
Ashland, OH 44805
(419)281-4584

SCORE Office (Canton)
116 Cleveland Ave. NW, Ste. 601
Canton, OH 44702-1720
(330)453-6047

SCORE Office (Chillicothe)
165 S. Paint St.
Chillicothe, OH 45601
(614)772-4530

SCORE Office (Cincinnati)
Ameritrust Bldg., Rm. 850
525 Vine St.
Cincinnati, OH 45202
(513)684-2812
Fax: (513)684-3251
Website: http://
www.score.chapter34.org/

SCORE Office (Cleveland)
Eaton Center, Ste. 620
1100 Superior Ave.
Cleveland, OH 44114-2507
(216)522-4194
Fax: (216)522-4844

SCORE Office (Columbus)
2 Nationwide Plz., Ste. 1400
Columbus, OH 43215-2542
(614)469-2357
Fax: (614)469-2391
E-mail: info@scorecolumbus.org
Website: http://
www.scorecolumbus.org/

SCORE Office (Dayton)
Dayton Federal Bldg., Rm. 505
200 W. Second St.
Dayton, OH 45402-1430
(513)225-2887
Fax: (513)225-7667

SCORE Office (Defiance)
615 W. 3rd St.
PO Box 130
Defiance, OH 43512
(419)782-7946

SCORE Office (Findlay)
123 E. Main Cross St.
PO Box 923
Findlay, OH 45840
(419)422-3314

SCORE Office (Lima)
147 N. Main St.
Lima, OH 45801
(419)222-6045
Fax: (419)229-0266

SCORE Office (Mansfield)
55 N. Mulberry St.
Mansfield, OH 44902
(419)522-3211

SCORE Office (Marietta)
Thomas Hall
Marietta, OH 45750
(614)373-0268

SCORE Office (Medina)
County Administrative Bldg.
144 N. Broadway
Medina, OH 44256
(216)764-8650

SCORE Office (Licking County)
50 W. Locust St.
Newark, OH 43055
(614)345-7458

SCORE Office (Salem)
2491 State Rte. 45 S
Salem, OH 44460
(216)332-0361

SCORE Office (Tiffin)
62 S. Washington St.
Tiffin, OH 44883
(419)447-4141
Fax: (419)447-5141

SCORE Office (Toledo)
608 Madison Ave, Ste. 910
Toledo, OH 43624
(419)259-7598
Fax: (419)259-6460

SCORE Office (Heart of Ohio)
377 W. Liberty St.
Wooster, OH 44691
(330)262-5735
Fax: (330)262-5745

SCORE Office (Youngstown)
306 Williamson Hall
Youngstown, OH 44555
(330)746-2687

Oklahoma

SCORE Office (Anadarko)
PO Box 366
Anadarko, OK 73005
(405)247-6651

SCORE Office (Ardmore)
410 W. Main
Ardmore, OK 73401
(580)226-2620

SCORE Office (Northeast Oklahoma)
210 S. Main
Grove, OK 74344
(918)787-2796
Fax: (918)787-2796
E-mail: Score595@greencis.net

SCORE Office (Lawton)
4500 W. Lee Blvd., Bldg. 100, Ste. 107
Lawton, OK 73505
(580)353-8727
Fax: (580)250-5677

SCORE Office (Oklahoma City)
210 Park Ave., No. 1300
Oklahoma City, OK 73102
(405)231-5163
Fax: (405)231-4876
E-mail: score212@usa.net

SCORE Office (Stillwater)
439 S. Main
Stillwater, OK 74074
(405)372-5573
Fax: (405)372-4316

SCORE Office (Tulsa)
616 S. Boston, Ste. 406
Tulsa, OK 74119
(918)581-7462
Fax: (918)581-6908
Website: http://www.ionet.net/~tulscore/

Oregon

SCORE Office (Bend)
63085 N. Hwy. 97
Bend, OR 97701

(541)923-2849
Fax: (541)330-6900

SCORE Office (Willamette)
1401 Willamette St.
PO Box 1107
Eugene, OR 97401-4003
(541)465-6600
Fax: (541)484-4942

SCORE Office (Florence)
3149 Oak St.
Florence, OR 97439
(503)997-8444
Fax: (503)997-8448

SCORE Office (Southern Oregon)
33 N. Central Ave., Ste. 216
Medford, OR 97501
(541)776-4220
E-mail: pgr134f@prodigy.com

SCORE Office (Portland)
1515 SW 5th Ave., Ste. 1050
Portland, OR 97201
(503)326-3441
Fax: (503)326-2808
E-mail: gr134@prodigy.com

SCORE Office (Salem)
416 State St. (corner of Liberty)
Salem, OR 97301
(503)370-2896

Pennsylvania

SCORE Office (Altoona-Blair)
1212 12th Ave.
Altoona, PA 16601-3493
(814)943-8151

SCORE Office (Lehigh Valley)
Rauch Bldg. 37
Lehigh University
621 Taylor St.
Bethlehem, PA 18015
(610)758-4496
Fax: (610)758-5205

SCORE Office (Butler County)
100 N. Main St.
PO Box 1082
Butler, PA 16003
(412)283-2222
Fax: (412)283-0224

SCORE Office (Harrisburg)
4211 Trindle Rd.
Camp Hill, PA 17011
(717)761-4304
Fax: (717)761-4315

SCORE Office (Cumberland Valley)
75 S. 2nd St.
Chambersburg, PA 17201
(717)264-2935

SCORE Office (Monroe County-Stroudsburg)
556 Main St.
East Stroudsburg, PA 18301
(717)421-4433

SCORE Office (Erie)
120 W. 9th St.
Erie, PA 16501
(814)871-5650
Fax: (814)871-7530

SCORE Office (Bucks County)
409 Hood Blvd.
Fairless Hills, PA 19030
(215)943-8850
Fax: (215)943-7404

SCORE Office (Hanover)
146 Broadway
Hanover, PA 17331
(717)637-6130
Fax: (717)637-9127

SCORE Office (Harrisburg)
100 Chestnut, Ste. 309
Harrisburg, PA 17101
(717)782-3874

SCORE Office (East Montgomery County)
Baederwood Shopping Center
1653 The Fairways, Ste. 204
Jenkintown, PA 19046
(215)885-3027

SCORE Office (Kittanning)
2 Butler Rd.
Kittanning, PA 16201
(412)543-1305
Fax: (412)543-6206

SCORE Office (Lancaster)
118 W. Chestnut St.
Lancaster, PA 17603
(717)397-3092

SCORE Office (Westmoreland County)
300 Fraser Purchase Rd.
Latrobe, PA 15650-2690
(412)539-7505
Fax: (412)539-1850

SCORE Office (Lebanon)
252 N. 8th St.
PO Box 899

Lebanon, PA 17042-0899
(717)273-3727
Fax: (717)273-7940

SCORE Office (Lewistown)
3 W. Monument Sq., Ste. 204
Lewistown, PA 17044
(717)248-6713
Fax: (717)248-6714

SCORE Office (Delaware County)
602 E. Baltimore Pike
Media, PA 19063
(610)565-3677
Fax: (610)565-1606

SCORE Office (Milton Area)
112 S. Front St.
Milton, PA 17847
(717)742-7341
Fax: (717)792-2008

SCORE Office (Mon-Valley)
435 Donner Ave.
Monessen, PA 15062
(412)684-4277
Fax: (412)684-7688

SCORE Office (Monroeville)
William Penn Plaza
2790 Mosside Blvd., Ste. 295
Monroeville, PA 15146
(412)856-0622
Fax: (412)856-1030

SCORE Office (Airport Area)
986 Brodhead Rd.
Moon Township, PA 15108-2398
(412)264-6270
Fax: (412)264-1575

SCORE Office (Northeast)
8601 E. Roosevelt Blvd.
Philadelphia, PA 19152
(215)332-3400
Fax: (215)332-6050

SCORE Office (Philadelphia)
1315 Walnut St., Ste. 500
Philadelphia, PA 19107
(215)790-5050
Fax: (215)790-5057
E-mail: score46@bellatlantic.net
Website: http://www.pgweb.net/score46/

SCORE Office (Pittsburgh)
1000 Liberty Ave., Rm. 1122
Pittsburgh, PA 15222
(412)395-6560
Fax: (412)395-6562

SCORE Office (Tri-County)
801 N. Charlotte St.
Pottstown, PA 19464
(610)327-2673

SCORE Office (Reading)
601 Penn St.
Reading, PA 19601
(610)376-3497

SCORE Office (Scranton)
Oppenheim Bldg.
116 N. Washington Ave., Ste. 650
Scranton, PA 18503
(717)347-4611
Fax: (717)347-4611

SCORE Office (Central Pennsylvania)
200 Innovation Blvd., Ste. 242-B
State College, PA 16803
(814)234-9415
Fax: (814)238-9686
Website: http://countrystore.org/business/score.htm

SCORE Office (Monroe-Stroudsburg)
556 Main St.
Stroudsburg, PA 18360
(717)421-4433

SCORE Office (Uniontown)
Federal Bldg.
Pittsburg St.
PO Box 2065 DTS
Uniontown, PA 15401
(412)437-4222
E-mail: uniontownscore@lcsys.net

SCORE Office (Warren County)
315 2nd Ave.
Warren, PA 16365
(814)723-9017

SCORE Office (Waynesboro)
323 E. Main St.
Waynesboro, PA 17268
(717)762-7123
Fax: (717)962-7124

SCORE Office (Chester County)
Government Service Center, Ste. 281
601 Westtown Rd.
West Chester, PA 19382-4538
(610)344-6910
Fax: (610)344-6919
E-mail: score@locke.ccil.org

SCORE Office (Wilkes-Barre)
7 N. Wilkes-Barre Blvd.
Wilkes Barre, PA 18702-5241
(717)826-6502
Fax: (717)826-6287

SCORE Office (North Central Pennsylvania)
240 W. 3rd St., Rm. 227
PO Box 725
Williamsport, PA 17703
(717)322-3720
Fax: (717)322-1607
E-mail: score234@mail.csrlink.net
Website: http://www.lycoming.org/score/

SCORE Office (York)
Cyber Center
2101 Pennsylvania Ave.
York, PA 17404
(717)845-8830
Fax: (717)854-9333

Puerto Rico

SCORE Office (Puerto Rico & Virgin Islands)
PO Box 12383-96
San Juan, PR 00914-0383
(787)726-8040
Fax: (787)726-8135

Rhode Island

SCORE Office (Barrington)
281 County Rd.
Barrington, RI 02806
(401)247-1920
Fax: (401)247-3763

SCORE Office (Woonsocket)
640 Washington Hwy.
Lincoln, RI 02865
(401)334-1000
Fax: (401)334-1009

SCORE Office (Wickford)
8045 Post Rd.
North Kingstown, RI 02852
(401)295-5566
Fax: (401)295-8987

SCORE Office (J.G.E. Knight)
380 Westminster St.
Providence, RI 02903
(401)528-4571
Fax: (401)528-4539
E-mail: feedback@ch13.score.org.
Website: http://chapters.score.org/ch13

SCORE Office (Warwick)
3288 Post Rd.
Warwick, RI 02886
(401)732-1100
Fax: (401)732-1101

SCORE Office (Westerly)
74 Post Rd.
Westerly, RI 02891
(401)596-7761
800-732-7636
Fax: (401)596-2190

South Carolina

SCORE Office (Aiken)
PO Box 892
Aiken, SC 29802
(803)641-1111
800-542-4536
Fax: (803)641-4174

SCORE Office (Anderson)
Anderson Mall
3130 N. Main St.
Anderson, SC 29621
(864)224-0453

SCORE Office (Coastal)
284 King St.
Charleston, SC 29401
(803)727-4778
Fax: (803)853-2529

SCORE Office (Midlands)
Strom Thurmond Bldg., Rm. 358
1835 Assembly St., Rm 358
Columbia, SC 29201
(803)765-5131
Fax: (803)765-5962
Website: http://www.scoremidlands.org/

SCORE Office (Piedmont)
Federal Bldg., Rm. B-02
300 E. Washington St.
Greenville, SC 29601
(864)271-3638

SCORE Office (Greenwood)
PO Drawer 1467
Greenwood, SC 29648
(864)223-8357

SCORE Office (Hilton Head Island)
52 Savannah Trail
Hilton Head, SC 29926
(803)785-7107
Fax: (803)785-7110

SCORE Office (Grand Strand)
937 Broadway
Myrtle Beach, SC 29577
(803)918-1079
Fax: (803)918-1083
E-mail: score381@aol.com

SCORE Office (Spartanburg)
PO Box 1636
Spartanburg, SC 29304
(864)594-5000
Fax: (864)594-5055

South Dakota

SCORE Office (West River)
Rushmore Plz. Civic Ctr.
444 Mount Rushmore Rd., No. 209
Rapid City, SD 57701
(605)394-5311
E-mail: score@gwtc.net

SCORE Office (Sioux Falls)
First Financial Center
110 S. Phillips Ave., Ste. 200
Sioux Falls, SD 57104-6727
(605)330-4231
Fax: (605)330-4231

Tennessee

SCORE Office (Chattanooga)
Federal Bldg., Rm. 26
900 Georgia Ave.
Chattanooga, TN 37402
(423)752-5190
Fax: (423)752-5335

SCORE Office (Cleveland)
PO Box 2275
Cleveland, TN 37320
(423)472-6587
Fax: (423)472-2019

SCORE Office (Upper Cumberland Center)
1225 S. Willow Ave.
Cookeville, TN 38501
(615)432-4111
Fax: (615)432-6010

SCORE Office (Unicoi County)
PO Box 713
Erwin, TN 37650
(423)743-3000
Fax: (423)743-0942

SCORE Office (Greeneville)
115 Academy St.
Greeneville, TN 37743
(423)638-4111
Fax: (423)638-5345

SCORE Office (Jackson)
194 Auditorium St.
Jackson, TN 38301
(901)423-2200

SCORE Office (Northeast Tennessee)
1st Tennessee Bank Bldg.
2710 S. Roan St., Ste. 584
Johnson City, TN 37601
(423)929-7686
Fax: (423)461-8052

SCORE Office (Kingsport)
151 E. Main St.
Kingsport, TN 37662
(423)392-8805

SCORE Office (Greater Knoxville)
Farragot Bldg., Ste. 224
530 S. Gay St.
Knoxville, TN 37902
(423)545-4203
E-mail: scoreknox@ntown.com
Website: http://www.scoreknox.org/

SCORE Office (Maryville)
201 S. Washington St.
Maryville, TN 37804-5728
(423)983-2241
800-525-6834
Fax: (423)984-1386

SCORE Office (Memphis)
Federal Bldg., Ste. 390
167 N. Main St.
Memphis, TN 38103
(901)544-3588

SCORE Office (Nashville)
50 Vantage Way, Ste. 201
Nashville, TN 37228-1500
(615)736-7621

Texas

SCORE Office (Abilene)
2106 Federal Post Office and Court Bldg.
Abilene, TX 79601
(915)677-1857

SCORE Office (Austin)
2501 S. Congress
Austin, TX 78701
(512)442-7235
Fax: (512)442-7528

SCORE Office (Golden Triangle)
450 Boyd St.
Beaumont, TX 77704
(409)838-6581
Fax: (409)833-6718

SCORE Office (Brownsville)
3505 Boca Chica Blvd., Ste. 305
Brownsville, TX 78521
(210)541-4508

SCORE Office (Brazos Valley)
3000 Briarcrest, Ste. 302
Bryan, TX 77802
(409)776-8876
E-mail: 102633.2612@compuserve.com

SCORE Office (Cleburne)
Watergarden Pl., 9th Fl., Ste. 400
Cleburne, TX 76031
(817)871-6002

SCORE Office (Corpus Christi)
651 Upper North Broadway, Ste. 654
Corpus Christi, TX 78477
(512)888-4322
Fax: (512)888-3418

SCORE Office (Dallas)
6260 E. Mockingbird
Dallas, TX 75214-2619
(214)828-2471
Fax: (214)821-8033

SCORE Office (El Paso)
10 Civic Center Plaza
El Paso, TX 79901
(915)534-0541
Fax: (915)534-0513

SCORE Office (Bedford)
100 E. 15th St., Ste. 400
Ft. Worth, TX 76102
(817)871-6002

SCORE Office (Ft. Worth)
100 E. 15th St., No. 24
Ft. Worth, TX 76102
(817)871-6002
Fax: (817)871-6031
E-mail: fwbac@onramp.net

SCORE Office (Garland)
2734 W. Kingsley Rd.
Garland, TX 75041
(214)271-9224

SCORE Office (Granbury Chamber of Commerce)
416 S. Morgan
Granbury, TX 76048
(817)573-1622
Fax: (817)573-0805

SCORE Office (Lower Rio Grande Valley)
222 E. Van Buren, Ste. 500
Harlingen, TX 78550
(956)427-8533
Fax: (956)427-8537

SCORE Office (Houston)
9301 Southwest Fwy., Ste. 550
Houston, TX 77074

(713)773-6565
Fax: (713)773-6550

SCORE Office (Irving)
3333 N. MacArthur Blvd., Ste. 100
Irving, TX 75062
(214)252-8484
Fax: (214)252-6710

SCORE Office (Lubbock)
1205 Texas Ave., Rm. 411D
Lubbock, TX 79401
(806)472-7462
Fax: (806)472-7487

SCORE Office (Midland)
Post Office Annex
200 E. Wall St., Rm. P121
Midland, TX 79701
(915)687-2649

SCORE Office (Orange)
1012 Green Ave.
Orange, TX 77630-5620
(409)883-3536
800-528-4906
Fax: (409)886-3247

SCORE Office (Plano)
1200 E. 15th St.
PO Drawer 940287
Plano, TX 75094-0287
(214)424-7547
Fax: (214)422-5182

SCORE Office (Port Arthur)
4749 Twin City Hwy., Ste. 300
Port Arthur, TX 77642
(409)963-1107
Fax: (409)963-3322

SCORE Office (Richardson)
411 Belle Grove
Richardson, TX 75080
(214)234-4141
800-777-8001
Fax: (214)680-9103

SCORE Office (San Antonio)
Federal Bldg., Rm. A527
727 E. Durango
San Antonio, TX 78206
(210)472-5931
Fax: (210)472-5935

SCORE Office (Texarkana State College)
819 State Line Ave.
Texarkana, TX 75501
(903)792-7191
Fax: (903)793-4304

SCORE Office (East Texas)
RTDC
1530 SSW Loop 323, Ste. 100
Tyler, TX 75701
(903)510-2975
Fax: (903)510-2978

SCORE Office (Waco)
401 Franklin Ave.
Waco, TX 76701
(817)754-8898
Fax: (817)756-0776
Website: http://www.brc-waco.com/

SCORE Office (Wichita Falls)
Hamilton Bldg.
900 8th St.
Wichita Falls, TX 76307
(940)723-2741
Fax: (940)723-8773

Utah

SCORE Office (Northern Utah)
160 N. Main
Logan, UT 84321
(435)752-2161

SCORE Office (Ogden)
1701 E. Windsor Dr.
Ogden, UT 84604
(801)226-0881
E-mail: score158@netscape.net

SCORE Office (Central Utah)
1071 E. Windsor Dr.
Provo, UT 84604
(801)226-0881

SCORE Office (Southern Utah)
225 South 700 East
St. George, UT 84770
(801)652-7741

SCORE Office (Salt Lake)
169 E. 100 S.
Salt Lake City, UT 84111
(801)364-1331
Fax: (801)364-1310

Vermont

SCORE Office (Champlain Valley)
Winston Prouty Federal Bldg.
11 Lincoln St., Rm. 106
Essex Junction, VT 05452
(802)951-6762

SCORE Office (Montpelier)
87 State St., Rm. 205
PO Box 605

Montpelier, VT 05601
(802)828-4422
Fax: (802)828-4485

SCORE Office (Marble Valley)
256 N. Main St.
Rutland, VT 05701-2413
(802)773-9147

SCORE Office (Northeast Kingdom)
20 Main St.
PO Box 904
St. Johnsbury, VT 05819
(802)748-5101

Virgin Islands

SCORE Office (St. Croix)
United Plaza Shopping Center
PO Box 4010, Christiansted
St. Croix, VI 00822
(809)778-5380

SCORE Office (St. Thomas-St. John)
Federal Bldg., Rm. 21
Veterans Dr.
St. Thomas, VI 00801
(809)774-8530

Virginia

SCORE Office (Arlington)
2009 N. 14th St., Ste. 111
Arlington, VA 22201
(703)525-2400

SCORE Office (Blacksburg)
141 Jackson St.
Blacksburg, VA 24060
(540)552-4061

SCORE Office (Bristol)
20 Volunteer Pkwy.
Bristol, VA 24203
(540)989-4850

SCORE Office (Central Virginia)
1001 E. Market St., Ste. 101
Charlottesville, VA 22902
(804)295-6712
Fax: (804)295-7066

SCORE Office (Alleghany Satellite)
241 W. Main St.
Covington, VA 24426
(540)962-2178
Fax: (540)962-2179

SCORE Office (Central Fairfax)
3975 University Dr., Ste. 350
Fairfax, VA 22030
(703)591-2450

SCORE Office (Falls Church)
PO Box 491
Falls Church, VA 22040
(703)532-1050
Fax: (703)237-7904

SCORE Office (Glenns)
Glenns Campus
Box 287
Glenns, VA 23149
(804)693-9650

SCORE Office (Peninsula)
6 Manhattan Sq.
PO Box 7269
Hampton, VA 23666
(757)766-2000
Fax: (757)865-0339
E-mail: score100@seva.net

SCORE Office (Tri-Cities)
108 N. Main St.
Hopewell, VA 23860
(804)458-5536

SCORE Office (Lynchburg)
Federal Bldg.
1100 Main St.
Lynchburg, VA 24504-1714
(804)846-3235

SCORE Office (Greater Prince William)
8963 Center St
Manassas, VA 20110
(703)368-4813
Fax: (703)368-4733

SCORE Office (Martinsvile)
115 Broad St.
Martinsville, VA 24112-0709
(540)632-6401
Fax: (540)632-5059

SCORE Office (Hampton Roads)
Federal Bldg., Rm. 737
200 Grandby St.
Norfolk, VA 23510
(757)441-3733
Fax: (757)441-3733
E-mail: scorehr60@juno.com

SCORE Office (Norfolk)
Federal Bldg., Rm. 737
200 Granby St.
Norfolk, VA 23510
(757)441-3733
Fax: (757)441-3733

SCORE Office (Virginia Beach)
Chamber of Commerce
200 Grandby St., Rm 737

Norfolk, VA 23510
(804)441-3733

SCORE Office (Radford)
1126 Norwood St.
Radford, VA 24141
(540)639-2202

SCORE Office (Richmond)
Federal Bldg.
400 N. 8th St., Ste. 1150
PO Box 10126
Richmond, VA 23240-0126
(804)771-2400
Fax: (804)771-8018
E-mail: scorechapter12@yahoo.com
Website: http://www.cvco.org/score/

SCORE Office (Roanoke)
Federal Bldg., Rm. 716
250 Franklin Rd.
Roanoke, VA 24011
(540)857-2834
Fax: (540)857-2043
E-mail: scorerva@juno.com
Website: http://hometown.aol.com/
scorerv/Index.html

SCORE Office (Fairfax)
8391 Old Courthouse Rd., Ste. 300
Vienna, VA 22182
(703)749-0400

SCORE Office (Greater Vienna)
513 Maple Ave. West
Vienna, VA 22180
(703)281-1333
Fax: (703)242-1482

SCORE Office (Shenandoah Valley)
301 W. Main St.
Waynesboro, VA 22980
(540)949-8203
Fax: (540)949-7740
E-mail: score427@intelos.net

SCORE Office (Williamsburg)
201 Penniman Rd.
Williamsburg, VA 23185
(757)229-6511
E-mail: wacc@williamsburgcc.com

SCORE Office (Northern Virginia)
1360 S. Pleasant Valley Rd.
Winchester, VA 22601
(540)662-4118

Washington

SCORE Office (Gray's Harbor)
506 Duffy St.
Aberdeen, WA 98520

(360)532-1924
Fax: (360)533-7945

SCORE Office (Bellingham)
101 E. Holly St.
Bellingham, WA 98225
(360)676-3307

SCORE Office (Everett)
2702 Hoyt Ave.
Everett, WA 98201-3556
(206)259-8000

SCORE Office (Gig Harbor)
3125 Judson St.
Gig Harbor, WA 98335
(206)851-6865

SCORE Office (Kennewick)
PO Box 6986
Kennewick, WA 99336
(509)736-0510

SCORE Office (Puyallup)
322 2nd St. SW
PO Box 1298
Puyallup, WA 98371
(206)845-6755
Fax: (206)848-6164

SCORE Office (Seattle)
1200 6th Ave., Ste. 1700
Seattle, WA 98101
(206)553-7320
Fax: (206)553-7044
E-mail: score55@aol.com
Website: http://www.scn.org/civic/score-
online/index55.html

SCORE Office (Spokane)
801 W. Riverside Ave., No. 240
Spokane, WA 99201
(509)353-2820
Fax: (509)353-2600
E-mail: score@dmi.net
Website: http://www.dmi.net/score/

SCORE Office (Clover Park)
PO Box 1933
Tacoma, WA 98401-1933
(206)627-2175

SCORE Office (Tacoma)
1101 Pacific Ave.
Tacoma, WA 98402
(253)274-1288
Fax: (253)274-1289

SCORE Office (Fort Vancouver)
1701 Broadway, S-1
Vancouver, WA 98663
(360)699-1079

SCORE Office (Walla Walla)
500 Tausick Way
Walla Walla, WA 99362
(509)527-4681

SCORE Office (Mid-Columbia)
1113 S. 14th Ave.
Yakima, WA 98907
(509)574-4944
Fax: (509)574-2943
Website: http://www.ellensburg.com/
~score/

West Virginia

SCORE Office (Charleston)
1116 Smith St.
Charleston, WV 25301
(304)347-5463
E-mail: score256@juno.com

SCORE Office (Virginia Street)
1116 Smith St., Ste. 302
Charleston, WV 25301
(304)347-5463

SCORE Office (Marion County)
PO Box 208
Fairmont, WV 26555-0208
(304)363-0486

SCORE Office (Upper Monongahela Valley)
1000 Technology Dr., Ste. 1111
Fairmont, WV 26555
(304)363-0486
E-mail: score537@hotmail.com

SCORE Office (Huntington)
1101 6th Ave., Ste. 220
Huntington, WV 25701-2309
(304)523-4092

SCORE Office (Wheeling)
1310 Market St.
Wheeling, WV 26003
(304)233-2575
Fax: (304)233-1320

Wisconsin

SCORE Office (Fox Cities)
227 S. Walnut St.
Appleton, WI 54913
(920)734-7101
Fax: (920)734-7161

SCORE Office (Beloit)
136 W. Grand Ave., Ste. 100
PO Box 717
Beloit, WI 53511

(608)365-8835
Fax: (608)365-9170

SCORE Office (Eau Claire)
Federal Bldg., Rm. B11
510 S. Barstow St.
Eau Claire, WI 54701
(715)834-1573
E-mail: score@ecol.net
Website: http://www.ecol.net/~score/

SCORE Office (Fond du Lac)
207 N. Main St.
Fond du Lac, WI 54935
(414)921-9500
Fax: (414)921-9559

SCORE Office (Green Bay)
835 Potts Ave.
Green Bay, WI 54304
(414)496-8930
Fax: (414)496-6009

SCORE Office (Janesville)
20 S. Main St., Ste. 11
PO Box 8008
Janesville, WI 53547
(608)757-3160
Fax: (608)757-3170

SCORE Office (La Crosse)
712 Main St.
La Crosse, WI 54602-0219
(608)784-4880

SCORE Office (Madison)
505 S. Rosa Rd.
Madison, WI 53719
(608)441-2820

SCORE Office (Manitowoc)
1515 Memorial Dr.
PO Box 903
Manitowoc, WI 54221-0903
(414)684-5575
Fax: (414)684-1915

SCORE Office (Milwaukee)
310 W. Wisconsin Ave., Ste. 425
Milwaukee, WI 53203
(414)297-3942
Fax: (414)297-1377

SCORE Office (Central Wisconsin)
1224 Lindbergh Ave.
Stevens Point, WI 54481
(715)344-7729

SCORE Office (Superior)
Superior Business Center Inc.
1423 N. 8th St.
Superior, WI 54880

(715)394-7388
Fax: (715)393-7414

SCORE Office (Waukesha)
223 Wisconsin Ave.
Waukesha, WI 53186-4926
(414)542-4249

SCORE Office (Wausau)
300 3rd St., Ste. 200
Wausau, WI 54402-6190
(715)845-6231

SCORE Office (Wisconsin Rapids)
2240 Kingston Rd.
Wisconsin Rapids, WI 54494
(715)423-1830

Wyoming

SCORE Office (Casper)
Federal Bldg., No. 2215
100 East B St.
Casper, WY 82602
(307)261-6529
Fax: (307)261-6530

VENTURE CAPITAL & FINANCING COMPANIES

This section contains a listing of financing and loan companies in the United States and Canada. These listing are arranged alphabetically by country, then by state or province, then by city, then by organization name.

CANADA

Alberta

Launchworks Inc.
1902J 11th St., S.E.
Calgary, AB, Canada T2G 3G2
(403)269-1119
Fax: (403)269-1141
Website: http://www.launchworks.com
Investment Types: Start-up. Industry
Preferences: Diversified. Geographic
Preferences: Canada.

Native Venture Capital Company, Inc.
21 Artist View Point, Box 7
Site 25, RR 12
Calgary, AB, Canada T3E 6W3
(903)208-5380
Milt Pahl, President
Investment Types: Seed, startup, first
stage, second stage, and leveraged
buyout. Industry

Preferences: Diversified. Geographic
Preferences: Western Canada.

Miralta Capital Inc.
4445 Calgary Trail South
888 Terrace Plaza Alberta
Edmonton, AB, Canada T6H 5R7
(780)438-3535
Fax: (780)438-3129
Michael Welsh
Preferred Investment Size:
$1,000,000 minimum. Investment
Types: First and second stage,
and leveraged buyout. Industry
Preferences: Diversified
communications, computer
related, electronics, consumer
products, industrial products and
equipment. Geographic Preferences:
Canada.

Vencap Equities Alberta Ltd.
10180-101st St., Ste. 1980
Edmonton, AB, Canada T5J 3S4
(403)420-1171
Fax: (403)429-2541
Preferred Investment Size: $1,000,000
minimum. Investment Types: Start-up,
first and second stage, control-block
purchases, leveraged buyout, and
mezzanine. Industry Preferences:
Diversified. Geographic Preferences:
Northwest, Rocky Mountain region,
and Western Canada.

British Columbia

Discovery Capital
5th Fl., 1199 West Hastings
Vancouver, BC, Canada V6E 3T5
(604)683-3000
Fax: (604)662-3457
E-mail: info@discoverycapital.com
Website: http://
www.discoverycapital.com
Investment Types: Early stage and
start-up. Industry Preferences: Internet
related. Geographic Preferences:
Canada.

Greenstone Venture Partners
1177 West Hastings St.
Ste. 400
Vancouver, BC, Canada V6E 2K3
(604)717-1977
Fax: (604)717-1976
Website: http://www.greenstonevc.com
Investment Types: Diversified. Industry
Preferences: Diversified. Geographic
Preferences: Canada.

Growthworks Capital
2600-1055 West Georgia St.
Box 11170 Royal Centre
Vancouver, BC, Canada V6E 3R5
(604)895-7259
Fax: (604)669-7605
Website: http://www.wofund.com
Mike Philips
Preferred Investment Size: $330,000
to $3,300,000. Investment Types: Seed,
start-up, first and second stage,
balanced, joint ventures, mezzanine,
private placement, research and
development, and management
buyout. Industry Preferences:
Diversified. Geographic Preferences:
British Col

**MDS Discovery Venture Management,
Inc.**
555 W. Eighth Ave., Ste. 305
Vancouver, BC, Canada V5Z 1C6
(604)872-8464
Fax: (604)872-2977
E-mail: info@mds-ventures.com
David Scott, President
Investment Types: Seed, research and
development, startup, first and second
stages. Industry Preferences:
Biotechnology and communications.
Geographic Preferences: Western
Canada and Northwestern U.S.

Ventures West Management Inc.
1285 W. Pender St., Ste. 280
Vancouver, BC, Canada V6E 4B1
(604)688-9495
Fax: (604)687-2145
Website: http://www.ventureswest.com
Investment Types: Seed, research and
development, startup, first and second
stages. Industry Preferences:
Diversified technology. Geographic
Preferences: Northeast and Western
U.S., Canada.

Nova Scotia

ACF Equity Atlantic Inc.
Purdy's Wharf Tower II
Ste. 2106
Halifax, NS, Canada B3J 3R7
(902)421-1965
Fax: (902)421-1808
David Wilson
Investment Types: Seed, start-up, first
and second stage, balanced, mezzanine,
and leveraged buyout. Industry
Preferences: Diversified. Geographic
Preferences: Canada.

Montgomerie, Huck & Co.
146 Bluenose Dr.
PO Box 538
Lunenburg, NS, Canada B0J 2C0
(902)634-7125
Fax: (902)634-7130
Christopher Huck
Preferred Investment Size: $300,000
to $500,000. Investment Types: First
and second stage, leveraged buyout,
mezzanine, and special situation.
Industry Preferences: Diversified
communications, computer related,
and industrial machinery. Geographic
Preferences: Canada.

Ontario

IPS Industrial Promotion Services Ltd.
60 Columbia Way, Ste. 720
Markham, ON, Canada L3R 0C9
(905)475-9400
Fax: (905)475-5003
Azim Lalani
Preferred Investment Size: $500,000
minimum. Investment Types: Control-
block purchases, leveraged buyout, second
stage, and special situation. Industry
Preferences: Diversified. Geographic
Preferences: U.S. and Canada.

Betwin Investments Inc.
Box 23110
Sault Ste. Marie, ON, Canada P6A 6W6
(705)253-0744
Fax: (705)253-0744
D.B. Stinson
Preferred Investment Size: $500,000 to
$1,000,000. Investment Types: Second
stage. Industry Preferences: Diversified.
Geographic Preferences: U.S. and
Canada.

Bailey & Company, Inc.
594 Spadina Ave.
Toronto, ON, Canada M5S 2H4
(416)921-6930
Fax: (416)925-4670
Preferred Investment Size: $500,000 to
$1,000,000. Investment Types: Research
and development, first stage, and special
situations. Industry Preferences:
Diversified technology. Geographic
Preferences: No preference.

BCE Capital
(650)213-2500
Fax: (650)213-2222
Website: http://
www.accenturetechventures.com

Investment Types: Start-up, early
and later stage, balanced, expansion,
and mezzanine. Industry Preferences:
Internet and computer related, and
communications. Geographic
Preferences: Entire U.S.
200 Bay St.
South Tower, Ste. 3120
Toronto, ON, Canada M5J 2J2
(416)815-0078
Fax: (416)941-1073
Website: http://www.bcecapital.com
Preferred Investment Size: $350,000
to $2,000,000. Investment Types: Seed,
start-up, early stage, expansion, and
research and development. Industry
Preferences: Communications,
Internet related, electronics, and
computer software and services.
Geographic Preferences: Ontario
and West

Castlehill Ventures
55 University Ave., Ste. 500
Toronto, ON, Canada M5J 2H7
(416)862-8574
Fax: (416)862-8875
Investment Types: Start-up. Industry
Preferences: Telecommunications and
computer related. Geographic
Preferences: Ontario, Canada.

**CCFL Mezzanine Partners
of Canada**
70 University Ave.
Ste. 1450
Toronto, ON, Canada M5J 2M4
(416)977-1450
Fax: (416)977-6764
E-mail: info@ccfl.com
Website: http://www.ccfl.com
Paul Benson
Preferred Investment Size: $10,000,000.
Investment Types: Generalist PE.
Industry Preferences: Diversified.
Geographic Preferences: U.S. and
Canada.

Celtic House International
100 Simcoe St., Ste. 100
Toronto, ON, Canada M5H 3G2
(416)542-2436
Fax: (416)542-2435
Website: http://www.celtic-house.com
Investment Types: Early stage. Industry
Preferences: Computer software and
services, electronics, Internet related,
communications, and computer
hardware. Geographic Preferences: U.S.
and Canada.

Clairvest Group Inc.
22 St. Clair Ave. East
Ste. 1700
Toronto, ON, Canada M4T 2S3
(416)925-9270
Fax: (416)925-5753
Jeff Parr
Preferred Investment Size: $5,000,000
minimum. Investment Types: Balanced,
control-block purchases, later stage,
leveraged buyout, and special situation.
Industry Preferences: Diversified.
Geographic Preferences: U.S. and Canada.

Crosbie & Co., Inc.
One First Canadian Place
9th Fl.
PO Box 116
Toronto, ON, Canada M5X 1A4
(416)362-7726
Fax: (416)362-3447
E-mail: info@crosbieco.com
Website: http://www.crosbieco.com
Investment Types: Acquisition, distressed
debt, expansion, generalist PE, later stage,
leveraged and management buyouts,
mezzanine, private placement, recaps,
special situations, and turnarounds.
Industry Preferences: Diversified.
Geographic Preferences: Ontario, Canada.

Drug Royalty Corp.
Eight King St. East
Ste. 202
Toronto, ON, Canada M5C 1B5
(416)863-1865
Fax: (416)863-5161
Harry K. Loveys
Preferred Investment Size: $4,000,000 to
$5,000,000. Investment Types: Research
and development and special situation.
Industry Preferences: Biotechnology and
medical/health related. Geographic
Preferences: No preference.

Grieve, Horner, Brown & Asculai
8 King St. E, Ste. 1704
Toronto, ON, Canada M5C 1B5
(416)362-7668
Fax: (416)362-7660
Preferred Investment Size: $300,000 to
$500,000. Investment Types: Startup,
first and second stages. Industry
Preferences: Diversified. Geographic
Preferences: Entire U.S. and Canada.

Jefferson Partners
77 King St. West
Ste. 4010
PO Box 136

Toronto, ON, Canada M5K 1H1
(416)367-1533
Fax: (416)367-5827
Website: http://www.jefferson.com
Preferred Investment Size: $3,000,000 to
$10,000,000. Investment Types: Seed and
expansion. Industry Preferences:
Communications and media, software, and
Internet related. Geographic Preferences:
Northeastern U.S. and Canada.

J.L. Albright Venture Partners
Canada Trust Tower, 161 Bay St.
Ste. 4440
PO Box 215
Toronto, ON, Canada M5J 2S1
(416)367-2440
Fax: (416)367-4604
Website: http://www.jlaventures.com
Jon Prosser
Investment Types: First and second stage.
Industry Preferences: Internet related,
communications, and computer related.
Geographic Preferences: Canada.

McLean Watson Capital Inc.
One First Canadian Place
Ste. 1410
PO Box 129
Toronto, ON, Canada M5X 1A4
(416)363-2000
Fax: (416)363-2010
Website: http://www.mcleanwatson.com
Matt H. Lawton
Investment Types: First and second stage.
Industry Preferences: Diversified
communications, computer related, laser
related, and fiber optics. Geographic
Preferences: U.S. and Canada.

Middlefield Capital Fund
One First Canadian Place
85th Fl.
PO Box 192
Toronto, ON, Canada M5X 1A6
(416)362-0714
Fax: (416)362-7925
Website: http://www.middlefield.com
David Roode
Preferred Investment Size: $3,000,000
minimum. Investment Types: Second
stage, control-block purchases, industry
rollups, leveraged buyout, and mezzanine.
Industry Preferences: Diversified.
Geographic Preferences: U.S. and Canada.

Mosaic Venture Partners
24 Duncan St.
Ste. 300
Toronto, ON, Canada M5V 3M6

(416)597-8889
Fax: (416)597-2345
Investment Types: Early stage. Industry
Preferences: Internet related. Geographic
Preferences: U.S. and Canada.

Onex Corp.
161 Bay St.
PO Box 700
Toronto, ON, Canada M5J 2S1
(416)362-7711
Fax: (416)362-5765
Anthony Munk
Preferred Investment Size: $10,000,000
minimum. Investment Types: Control-
block purchases, leveraged buyout, and
special situations. Industry Preferences:
Diversified. Geographic Preferences: U.S.
and Canada.

Penfund Partners Inc.
145 King St. West
Ste. 1920
Toronto, ON, Canada M5H 1J8
(416)865-0300
Fax: (416)364-6912
Website: http://www.penfund.com
David Collins
Preferred Investment Size: $667,000 to
$4,670,000. Investment Types: Generalist
PE, leveraged and management buyouts,
and mezzanine. Industry Preferences:
Diversified. Geographic Preferences:
Canada.

Primaxis Technology Ventures Inc.
1 Richmond St. West, 8th Fl.
Toronto, ON, Canada M5H 3W4
(416)313-5210
Fax: (416)313-5218
Website: http://www.primaxis.com
Investment Types: Seed and early stage.
Industry Preferences: Telecommunications,
electronics, and manufacturing.
Geographic Preferences: Canada.

Priveq Capital Funds
240 Duncan Mill Rd., Ste. 602
Toronto, ON, Canada M3B 3P1
(416)447-3330
Fax: (416)447-3331
E-mail: priveq@sympatico.ca
Preferred Investment Size: $1,000,000
minimum. Investment Types: Industry
rollups, leveraged buyout, mezzanine,
recaps, second stage, and special
situation. Industry Preferences:
Diversified. Geographic Preferences: Mid
Atlantic, Midwest, Northeast, Northwest,
and Southeastern U.S.;

Roynat Ventures
40 King St. West, 26th Fl.
Toronto, ON, Canada M5H 1H1
(416)933-2667
Fax: (416)933-2783
Website: http://www.roynatcapital.com
Bob Roy
Investment Types: Early stage and
expansion. Industry Preferences:
Diversified. Geographic Preferences:
Canada.

Tera Capital Corp.
366 Adelaide St. East, Ste. 337
Toronto, ON, Canada M5A 3X9
(416)368-1024
Fax: (416)368-1427
Investment Types: Balanced. Industry
Preferences: Computer related and
biotechnology. Geographic Preferences:
U.S. and Canada.

Working Ventures Canadian Fund Inc.
250 Bloor St. East, Ste. 1600
Toronto, ON, Canada M4W 1E6
(416)934-7718
Fax: (416)929-0901
Website: http://www.workingventures.ca
Preferred Investment Size: $334,000
minimum. Investment Types: No
preference. Industry Preferences:
Diversified. Geographic Preferences:
Ontario and Western Canada.

Quebec

Altamira Capital Corp.
202 University
Niveau de Maisoneuve, Bur. 201
Montreal, QC, Canada H3A 2A5
(514)499-1656
Fax: (514)499-9570
Preferred Investment Size: $1,000,000
minimum. Investment Types: First stage.
Industry Preferences: Diversified.
Geographic Preferences: No preference.

Federal Business Development Bank
Venture Capital Division
Five Place Ville Marie, Ste. 600
Montreal, QC, Canada H3B 5E7
(514)283-1896
Fax: (514)283-5455
Preferred Investment Size: $1,000,000.
Investment Types: Seed, start-up, first
and second stage, mezzanine, research
and development, and leveraged buyout.
Industry Preferences: Biotechnology;
Internet related; computer software,

hardware, and services. Geographic
Preferences: Canada

Hydro-Quebec Capitech Inc.
75 Boul, Rene Levesque Quest
Montreal, QC, Canada H2Z 1A4
(514)289-4783
Fax: (514)289-5420
Website: http://www.hqcapitech.com
Investment Types: Seed, start-up, early,
first and second stage, balanced,
expansion, and mezzanine. Industry
Preferences: Diversified. Geographic
Preferences: U.S. and Canada.

Investissement Desjardins
2 complexe Desjardins
C.P. 760
Montreal, QC, Canada H5B 1B8
(514)281-7131
Fax: (514)281-7808
Website: http://www.desjardins.com/id
Preferred Investment Size: $5,000,000
minimum. Investment Types: Start-up,
first and second stage, control-block
purchases, mezzanine, and leveraged
buyout. Industry Preferences:
Diversified. Geographic Preferences:
Quebec, Canada.

Marleau Lemire Inc.
One Place Ville-Marie, Ste. 3601
Montreal, QC, Canada H3B 3P2
(514)877-3800
Fax: (514)875-6415
Jean Francois Perrault
Preferred Investment Size: $3,000,000
minimum. Investment Types: Second stage,
mezzanine, leveraged buyout, and special
situation. Industry Preferences: Diversified.
Geographic Preferences: Canada.

Speirs Consultants Inc.
365 Stanstead
Montreal, QC, Canada H3R 1X5
(514)342-3858
Fax: (514)342-1977
Derek Speirs
Preferred Investment Size: $1,000,000
minimum. Investment Types: Start-up,
first and second stage, control-block
purchases, industry rollups, leveraged
buyout, mezzanine, research and
development, and special situation.
Industry Preferences: Diversified.
Geographic Preferences: Canad

Tecnocap Inc.
4028 Marlowe
Montreal, QC, Canada H4A 3M2

(514)483-6009
Fax: (514)483-6045
Website: http://www.technocap.com
Preferred Investment Size: $1,000,000
minimum. Investment Types: Early stage
and expansion. Industry Preferences:
Diversified. Geographic Preferences:
Northeast and Southwest U.S., and Central
Canada.

Telsoft Ventures
1000, Rue de la Gauchetiere
Quest, 25eme Etage
Montreal, QC, Canada H3B 4W5
(514)397-8450
Fax: (514)397-8451
Investment Types: First and second stage,
and mezzanine. Industry Preferences:
Computer related. Geographic
Preferences: West Coast, and Western
Canada.

Saskatchewan

Saskatchewan Government Growth Fund
1801 Hamilton St., Ste. 1210
Canada Trust Tower
Regina, SK, Canada S4P 4B4
(306)787-2994
Fax: (306)787-2086
Rob M. Duguid, Vice President,
Investing
Investment Types: Startup, first stage,
second stage, and mezzanine. Industry
Preferences: Diversified. Geographic
Preferences: Western Canada.

UNITED STATES

Alabama

FHL Capital Corp.
600 20th Street North
Suite 350
Birmingham, AL 35203
(205)328-3098
Fax: (205)323-0001
Kevin Keck, Vice President
Preferred Investment Size: Between
$500,000 and $1,000,000. Investment
Types: Mezzanine, leveraged buyout, and
special situations. Geographic
Preferences: Southeast.

Harbert Management Corp.
One Riverchase Pkwy. South
Birmingham, AL 35244
(205)987-5500

Fax: (205)987-5707
Website: http://www.harbert.net
Charles Miller, Vice President
Preferred Investment Size: $5,000,000 to
$25,000,000. Investment Types:
Leveraged buyout, special situations and
industry roll ups. Industry Preferences:
Oil and gas not considered. Geographic
Preferences: Entire U.S.

Jefferson Capital Fund

PO Box 13129
Birmingham, AL 35213
(205)324-7709
Preferred Investment Size: From
$1,000,000. Investment Types: Leveraged
buyout, special situations and control
block purchases. Industry Preferences:
Telephone communications; consumer
leisure and recreational products;
consumer and industrial, medical and
catalog specialty distribut

Private Capital Corp.

100 Brookwood Pl., 4th Fl.
Birmingham, AL 35209
(205)879-2722
Fax: (205)879-5121
William Acker, Vice President
Preferred Investment Size: $1,000,000 to
$5,000,000. Investment Types: Startup, first
stage, second stage, mezzanine, leveraged
buyout, and special situations. Industry
Preferences: Communications; computer
related; industrial, and medical product
distribution; electronic components

21st Century Health Ventures

One Health South Pkwy.
Birmingham, AL 35243
(256)268-6250
Fax: (256)970-8928
W. Barry McRae
Preferred Investment Size: $5,000,000.
Investment Types: First stage, second
stage, and leveraged buyout. Industry
Preferences: Medical/Health related.
Geographic Preferences: Entire U.S.

FJC Growth Capital Corp.

200 W. Side Sq., Ste. 340
Huntsville, AL 35801
(256)922-2918
Fax: (256)922-2909
William B. Noojin, President
Preferred Investment Size: $300,000 and
$500,000. Investment Types: Mezzanine
and second stage. Industry Preferences:
Communications, electronics, hotels, and
resort. Geographic Preferences: Southeast.

Hickory Venture Capital Corp.

301 Washington St. NW
Suite 301
Huntsville, AL 35801
(256)539-1931
Fax: (256)539-5130
E-mail: hvcc@hvcc.com
Website: http://www.hvcc.com
J. Thomas Noojin, President
Preferred Investment Size: $1,000,000 -
$7,000,000. Investment Types: First stage,
late stage, and leverage buyout. Industry
Preferences: Communications, computer
and Internet-related, energy, consumer, and
biotechnology. Geographic Preferences:
Southeast, Midwest, and Texas.

Southeastern Technology Fund

7910 South Memorial Pkwy., Ste. F
Huntsville, AL 35802
(256)883-8711
Fax: (256)883-8558
Preferred Investment Size: $500,000 to
$5,000,000. Investment Types: Early, first
and second stage, and expansion.
Industry Preferences: Internet related,
computer related, and communications.
Geographic Preferences: Southeast.

Cordova Ventures

4121 Carmichael Rd., Ste. 301
Montgomery, AL 36106
(334)271-6011
Fax: (334)260-0120
Website: http://
www.cordovaventures.com
Teo F. Dagi
Investment Types: Startup, early, second
and late stage, and expansion. Industry
Preferences: Diversified. Geographic
Preferences: Southeast.

Small Business Clinic of Alabama/AG Bartholomew & Associates

PO Box 231074
Montgomery, AL 36123-1074
(334)284-3640
Preferred Investment Size: From
$2,000,000. Investment Types: Startup,
first stage, second stage, leveraged
buyout, and special situations. Industry
Preferences: Communications, computer
related, consumer, distribution,
industrial products and equipment,
medical/health related, educa

Arizona

Miller Capital Corp.

4909 E. McDowell Rd.
Phoenix, AZ 85008

(602)225-0504
Fax: (602)225-9024
Website: http://www.themillergroup.com
Rudy R. Miller, Chairman and President
Preferred Investment Size: $1,000,000 to
$20,000,000. Investment Types: First
stage, second stage, and recapitalizations.
Industry Preferences: Communications,
computer-related, electronics, financial
and business services, and consumer-
related. Geographic Preferences: Entire
U.S.

The Columbine Venture Funds

9449 North 90th St., Ste. 200
Scottsdale, AZ 85258
(602)661-9222
Fax: (602)661-6262
Preferred Investment Size: $300,000 -
$800,000. Investment Types: Seed,
research and development, startup, and
first stage. Industry Preferences:
Diversified technology. Geographic
Preferences: Southwest, Rocky
Mountains, and West Coast.

Koch Ventures

17767 N. Perimeter Dr., Ste. 101
Scottsdale, AZ 85255
(480)419-3600
Fax: (480)419-3606
Website: http://www.kochventures.com
Preferred Investment Size: $2,000,000 to
$10,000,000. Investment Types: Early
stage and expansion. Industry
Preferences: Electronics, Internet and
computer related, and communications.
Geographic Preferences: U.S.

McKee & Co.

7702 E. Doubletree Ranch Rd.
Suite 230
Scottsdale, AZ 85258
(480)368-0333
Fax: (480)607-7446
Mark Jazwin, Corporate Finance
Preferred Investment Size: From
$1,000,000. Investment Types: Second
stage, mezzanine, and leveraged buyout.
Industry Preferences: Communications,
computer related, consumer,
distribution, electronic components and
instrumentation, energy/natural
resources, biosensors, industrial pro

Merita Capital Ltd.

7350 E. Stetson Dr., Ste. 108-A
Scottsdale, AZ 85251
(480)947-8700
Fax: (480)947-8766

Investment Types: First and second stage, mezzanine, and special situation. Industry Preferences: Diversified. Geographic Preferences: Western U.S.

Valley Ventures/Arizona Growth Partners L.P.
6720 N. Scottsdale Rd., Ste. 208
Scottsdale, AZ 85253
(480)661-6600
Fax: (480)661-6262
Investment Types: Second stage, mezzanine, and leveraged buyout. Industry Preferences: Diversified. Geographic Preferences: Southwest and Rocky Mountains.

Estreetcapital.com
660 South Mill Ave., Ste. 315
Tempe, AZ 85281
(480)968-8400
Fax: (480)968-8480
Website: http://www.estreetcapital.com
Industry Preferences: Internet related. Geographic Preferences: Entire U.S.

Coronado Venture Fund
PO Box 65420
Tucson, AZ 85728-5420
(520)577-3764
Fax: (520)299-8491
Preferred Investment Size: $100,000 $500,000. Investment Types: Seed, startup, first and second stage. Industry Preferences: Communications, computer related, electronic components and instrumentation, genetic engineering, industrial products and equipment, medical and health related

Arkansas

Arkansas Capital Corp.
225 South Pulaski St.
Little Rock, AR 72201
(501)374-9247
Fax: (501)374-9425
Website: http://www.arcapital.com
Private firm investing own capital. Interested in financing expansion.

California

Sundance Venture Partners, L.P.
100 Clocktower Place, Ste. 130
Carmel, CA 93923
(831)625-6500
Fax: (831)625-6590

Preferred Investment Size: $800,000 minimum. Investment Types: First and second stage, mezzanine, leveraged buyout, and special situations. Industry Preferences: No preference. Geographic Preferences: Southwest and West Coast.

Westar Capital (Costa Mesa)
949 South Coast Dr., Ste. 650
Costa Mesa, CA 92626
(714)481-5160
Fax: (714)481-5166
E-mail: mailbox@westarcapital.com
Website: http://www.westarcapital.com
Alan Sellers, General Partner
Preferred Investment Size: $5,000,000 to $10,000,000. Investment Types: Leveraged buyouts, special situations, control block purchases, and industry roll ups. Industry Preferences: Diversified. Geographic Preferences: Northwest, Southwest, Rocky Mountains, and West Coast.

Alpine Technology Ventures
20300 Stevens Creek Boulevard, Ste. 495
Cupertino, CA 95014
(408)725-1810
Fax: (408)725-1207
Website: http://www.alpineventures.com
Investment Types: Seed, startup, research and development, first and second stage. Industry Preferences: Internet-related, communications, computer-related, distribution, electronic components and instrumentation, industrial products and equipment.

Bay Partners
10600 N. De Anza Blvd.
Cupertino, CA 95014-2031
(408)725-2444
Fax: (408)446-4502
Website: http://www.baypartners.com
Bob Williams, General Partner
Preferred Investment Size: $5,000,000 to $15,000,000. Investment Types: Seed and startup. Industry Preferences: Internet, communications, and computer related. Geographic Preferences: National.

Novus Ventures
20111 Stevens Creek Blvd., Ste. 130
Cupertino, CA 95014
(408)252-3900
Fax: (408)252-1713
Website: http://www.novusventures.com
Dan Tompkins, Managing General Partner

Preferred Investment Size: $500,000 to $1 Million. Investment Types: Start-up, first and early stage, expansion, and buyouts. Industry Preferences: Information technology. Geographic Preferences: Western U.S.

Triune Capital
19925 Stevens Creek Blvd., Ste. 200
Cupertino, CA 95014
(310)284-6800
Fax: (310)284-3290
Preferred Investment Size: $1,000,000 minimum. Investment Types: First, second, and late stage; mezzanine; control block; and special situations. Industry Preferences: Diversified technology. Geographic Preferences: West Coast.

Acorn Ventures
268 Bush St., Ste. 2829
Daly City, CA 94014
(650)994-7801
Fax: (650)994-3305
Website: http://www.acornventures.com
Preferred Investment Size: $250,000 minimum. Investment Types: Seed, first and second stage, and leveraged buyout. Industry Preferences: Diversified. Geographic Preferences: No preference.

Digital Media Campus
2221 Park Place
El Segundo, CA 90245
(310)426-8000
Fax: (310)426-8010
E-mail: info@thecampus.com
Website: http://www.digitalmediacampus.com
Investment Types: Seed and early stage. Industry Preferences: Entertainment and leisure, sports, and media. Geographic Preferences: U.S.

BankAmerica Ventures/BA Venture Partners
950 Tower Ln., Ste. 700
Foster City, CA 94404
(650)378-6000
Fax: (650)378-6040
Website: http://www.baventurepartners.com
George Rossman
Preferred Investment Size: $1,000,000 to $12,000,000. Investment Types: Startup, first and second stage. Industry Preferences: Computer and Internet related, communications, medical product distribution, electronic

components and instrumentation, genetic engineering, and medical/heal

Starting Point Partners
666 Portofino Lane
Foster City, CA 94404
(650)722-1035
Website: http://
www.startingpointpartners.com
Preferred Investment Size: $100,000 to
$1,000,000. Investment Types: Early
stage. Industry Preferences: Diversified.
Geographic Preferences: U.S.

Opportunity Capital Partners
2201 Walnut Ave., Ste. 210
Fremont, CA 94538
(510)795-7000
Fax: (510)494-5439
Website: http://www.ocpcapital.com
Peter Thompson, Managing Partner
Preferred Investment Size: $100,000 to
$1,500,000. Investment Types: Second stage,
late stage, mezzanine, leveraged buyout, and
industry roll ups. Industry Preferences:
Internet related, consumer related,
communications, computer, and medical/
health related. Geographic Preferences: E

Imperial Ventures Inc.
9920 S. La Cienega Boulevar, 14th Fl.
Inglewood, CA 90301
(310)417-5409
Fax: (310)338-6115
Preferred Investment Size: $500,000 to
$2,000,000. Investment Types: Second
stage and leveraged buyout. Industry
Preferences: Diversified. Geographic
Preferences: No preference.

Ventana Global (Irvine)
18881 Von Karman Ave., Ste. 1150
Irvine, CA 92612
(949)476-2204
Fax: (949)752-0223
Website: http://www.ventanaglobal.com
Scott A. Burri, Managing Director
Preferred Investment Size: $1,000,000
minimum. Investment Types: First and
second stage, seed, special situation, and
mezzanine. Industry Preferences:
Diversified technology. Geographic
Preferences: Southwest.

Integrated Consortium Inc.
50 Ridgecrest Rd.
Kentfield, CA 94904
(415)925-0386
Fax: (415)461-2726
Preferred Investment Size: $1,000,000.
Investment Types: First and second stage,

control-block purchases, industry
rollups, leveraged buyouts, and
mezzanine. Industry Preferences:
Entertainment and leisure, retail,
computer stores, franchises, food/
beverage, consumer products and ser

Enterprise Partners
979 Ivanhoe Ave., Ste. 550
La Jolla, CA 92037
(858)454-8833
Fax: (858)454-2489
Website: http://www.epvc.com
Preferred Investment Size: $1,000,000 to
$20,000,000. Investment Types: Early
stage. Industry Preferences: Diversified.
Geographic Preferences: Entire U.S.

Domain Associates
28202 Cabot Rd., Ste. 200
Laguna Niguel, CA 92677
(949)347-2446
Fax: (949)347-9720
Website: http://www.domainvc.com
Preferred Investment Size: $1,000,000 to
$20,000,000. Investment Types: Seed,
first stage and second stage, expansion,
private placement, research and
development, and balanced. Industry
Preferences: Electronics, computer,
biotechnology, and medical/health
related. Geographic Prefere

Cascade Communications Ventures
60 E. Sir Francis Drake Blvd., Ste. 300
Larkspur, CA 94939
(415)925-6500
Fax: (415)925-6501
Dennis Brush
Preferred Investment Size: $1,000,000 to
$5,000,000. Investment Types: Leveraged
buyout and special situations. Industry
Preferences: Communications and
franchises. Geographic Preferences:
Entire U.S and Canada.

Allegis Capital
One First St., Ste. Two
Los Altos, CA 94022
(650)917-5900
Fax: (650)917-5901
Website: http://www.allegiscapital.com
Robert R. Ackerman, Jr.
Investment Types: Seed and early stage.
Industry Preferences: Diversified.
Geographic Preferences: West Coast and
District of Columbia.

Aspen Ventures
1000 Fremont Ave., Ste. 200
Los Altos, CA 94024

(650)917-5670
Fax: (650)917-5677
Website: http://www.aspenventures.com
Alexander Cilento, Partner
Preferred Investment Size: $500,000 to
$3,500,000. Investment Policies: Equity.
Investment Types: Seed, and early stage.
Industry Preferences: Communications,
computer related, medical/health,
biotechnology, and electronics.
Geographic Preferences: West Coast.

AVI Capital L.P.
1 First St., Ste. 2
Los Altos, CA 94022
(650)949-9862
Fax: (650)949-8510
Website: http://www.avicapital.com
Brian J. Grossi, General Partner
Preferred Investment Size: $1,000,000 to
$2 million. Investment Policies: Equity
Only. Investment Types: Seed, startup,
first and second stage, and special
situations. Industry Preferences:
Computer hardware, software, and
services; Internet related;
communications; electronics; ener

Bastion Capital Corp.
1999 Avenue of the Stars, Ste. 2960
Los Angeles, CA 90067
(310)788-5700
Fax: (310)277-7582
E-mail: ga@bastioncapital.com
Website: http://www.bastioncapital.com
James Villanueva, Vice President
Preferred Investment Size: $10,000,000
minimum. Investment Types: Leveraged
buyout, special situations and control
block purchases. Industry Preferences:
Diversified. Geographic Preferences:
Entire U.S. and Canada.

Davis Group
PO Box 69953
Los Angeles, CA 90069-0953
(310)659-6327
Fax: (310)659-6337
Roger W. Davis, Chairman
Preferred Investment Size: $100,000
minimum. Investment Types: Early
stages, leveraged buyouts, and special
situations. Industry Preferences:
Diversified. Geographic Preferences:
International.

Developers Equity Corp.
1880 Century Park East, Ste. 211
Los Angeles, CA 90067
(213)277-0300

Investment Types: Seed, startup, and leverage buyout. Industry Preferences: Industrial products and machinery, transportation, and real estate.

Far East Capital Corp.
350 S. Grand Ave., Ste. 4100
Los Angeles, CA 90071
(213)687-1361
Fax: (213)617-7939
E-mail: free@fareastnationalbank.com
Preferred Investment Size: $100,000 to $300,000. Investment Types: First stage, second stage, mezzanine, and special situations. Industry Preferences: Communications, computer and Internet related, electronic components and instrumentation, genetic engineering, medical/health related

Kline Hawkes & Co.
11726 San Vicente Blvd., Ste. 300
Los Angeles, CA 90049
(310)442-4700
Fax: (310)442-4707
Website: http://www.klinehawkes.com
Robert M. Freiland, Partner
Preferred Investment Size: $4,000,000 to $10,000,000. Investment Types: Second and later stage, private placement, and expansion. Industry Preferences: Diversified technology. Geographic Preferences: West Coast.

Lawrence Financial Group
701 Teakwood
PO Box 491773
Los Angeles, CA 90049
(310)471-4060
Fax: (310)472-3155
Larry Hurwitz
Preferred Investment Size: $500,000 to $1,000,000. Investment Types: Second stage. Industry Preferences: Diversified. Geographic Preferences: West Coast.

Riordan Lewis & Haden
300 S. Grand Ave., 29th Fl.
Los Angeles, CA 90071
(213)229-8500
Fax: (213)229-8597
Jonathan Leach
Preferred Investment Size: $2,000,000 minimum. Investment Types: First and second stage, start-up, leveraged buyouts, and special situations. Industry Preferences: Diversified. Geographic Preferences: West Coast.

Union Venture Corp.
445 S. Figueroa St., 9th Fl.
Los Angeles, CA 90071
(213)236-4092
Fax: (213)236-6329
Preferred Investment Size: $300,000 to $500,000. Investment Types: Second stage, mezzanine, leveraged buyout, and special situations. Industry Preferences: Communications, computer related. Geographic Preferences: National.

Wedbush Capital Partners
1000 Wilshire Blvd.
Los Angeles, CA 90017
(213)688-4545
Fax: (213)688-6642
Website: http://www.wedbush.com
Preferred Investment Size: $500,000 minimum. Investment Types: Second stage, mezzanine, and leveraged buyouts. Industry Preferences: Diversified computer technology, consumer related, distribution, and healthcare. Geographic Preferences: West Coast.

Advent International Corp.
2180 Sand Hill Rd., Ste. 420
Menlo Park, CA 94025
(650)233-7500
Fax: (650)233-7515
Website: http://www.adventinternational.com
Preferred Investment Size: $1,000,000 minimum. Investment Types: Startup, first and second stage, mezzanine, leveraged buyout, special situations, recaps, and acquisitions. Industry Preferences: Diversified. Geographic Preferences: Entire U.S. and Canada.

Altos Ventures
2882 Sand Hill Rd., Ste. 100
Menlo Park, CA 94025
(650)234-9771
Fax: (650)233-9821
Website: http://www.altosvc.com
Investment Types: Start-up, seed, first and second stage. Industry Preferences: Internet and computer related, consumer related, medical/health. Geographic Preferences: West Coast.

Applied Technology
1010 El Camino Real, Ste. 300
Menlo Park, CA 94025
(415)326-8622
Fax: (415)326-8163
Ellie McCormack, Partner

Investment Types: Seed, startup, first and second stage, research and development. Industry Preferences: Diversified. Geographic Preferences: Entire U.S.

APV Technology Partners
535 Middlefield, Ste. 150
Menlo Park, CA 94025
(650)327-7871
Fax: (650)327-7631
Website: http://www.apvtp.com
Preferred Investment Size: $2,000,000 to $10,000,000. Investment Types: Early stage. Industry Preferences: Diversified. Geographic Preferences: Entire U.S.

August Capital Management
2480 Sand Hill Rd., Ste. 101
Menlo Park, CA 94025
(650)234-9900
Fax: (650)234-9910
Website: http://www.augustcap.com
Andrew S. Rappaport, General Partner
Preferred Investment Size: $1,000,000 to $5,000,000. Investment Types: Startup, first stage and special situations. Industry Preferences: Communications, computer related, distribution, and electronic components and instrumentation. Geographic Preferences: Northwest, Southwest, Rocky

Baccharis Capital Inc.
2420 Sand Hill Rd., Ste. 100
Menlo Park, CA 94025
(650)324-6844
Fax: (650)854-3025
Michelle von Roedelbronn
Preferred Investment Size: $1,000,000 minimum. Investment Types: Startup, first stage and second stage, mezzanine and special situations. Industry Preferences: Diversified. Geographic Preferences: West Coast.

Benchmark Capital
2480 Sand Hill Rd., Ste. 200
Menlo Park, CA 94025
(650)854-8180
Fax: (650)854-8183
E-mail: info@benchmark.com
Website: http://www.benchmark.com
Investment Types: Seed, research and development, startup, first and second stage, and special situations. Industry Preferences: Communications, computer related, and electronic components and instrumentation. Geographic Preferences: Southwest and West Coast.

Bessemer Venture Partners (Menlo Park)
535 Middlefield Rd., Ste. 245
Menlo Park, CA 94025
(650)853-7000
Fax: (650)853-7001
Website: http://www.bvp.com
Investment Types: Seed, research and development, start-up, first stages, leveraged buyout, special situations, and expansion. Industry Preferences: Communications, computer related, consumer products, distribution, and electronics. Geographic Preferences: Entire U.S.

The Cambria Group
1600 El Camino Real Rd., Ste. 155
Menlo Park, CA 94025
(650)329-8600
Fax: (650)329-8601
Website: http://www.cambriagroup.com
Paul L. Davies, III, Managing Principal
Preferred Investment Size: $3,000,000.
Investment Types: Second stage, mezzanine, leveraged buyout, special situations, and control block purchases. Industry Preferences: Diversified. Geographic Preferences: Entire U.S.

Canaan Partners
2884 Sand Hill Rd., Ste. 115
Menlo Park, CA 94025
(650)854-8092
Fax: (650)854-8127
Website: http://www.canaan.com
Preferred Investment Size: $5,00,000 to $20,000,000. Investment Types: First and second stage, and expansion. Industry Preferences: Diversified. Geographic Preferences: Entire U.S.

Capstone Ventures
3000 Sand Hill Rd., Bldg. One, Ste. 290
Menlo Park, CA 94025
(650)854-2523
Fax: (650)854-9010
Website: http://www.capstonevc.com
Eugene J. Fischer
Preferred Investment Size: $500,000 to $3,000,000. Investment Types: First and second stage, early, and expansion. Industry Preferences: Diversified high technology. Geographic Preferences: Diversified.

Comdisco Venture Group (Silicon Valley)
3000 Sand Hill Rd., Bldg. 1, Ste. 155
Menlo Park, CA 94025
(650)854-9484

Fax: (650)854-4026
Preferred Investment Size: $300,000 to $20,000,000. Investment Types: Seed, startup, first and second stage. Industry Preferences: Diversified. Geographic Preferences: No preference.

Commtech International
535 Middlefield Rd., Ste. 200
Menlo Park, CA 94025
(650)328-0190
Fax: (650)328-6442
Preferred Investment Size: $300,000 to $500,000. Investment Types: Seed and start-up. Industry Preferences: Diversified. Geographic Preferences: West Coast.

Compass Technology Partners
1550 El Camino Real, Ste. 275
Menlo Park, CA 94025-4111
(650)322-7595
Fax: (650)322-0588
Website: http://www.compasstechpartners.com
Leon Dulberger, General Partner
Investment Types: Mezzanine, leveraged buyout, and special situations. Industry Preferences: Diversified high technology. Geographic Preferences: National.

Convergence Partners
3000 Sand Hill Rd., Ste. 235
Menlo Park, CA 94025
(650)854-3010
Fax: (650)854-3015
Website: http://www.convergencepartners.com
Preferred Investment Size: $2,000,000 to $10,000,000. Investment Types: Seed, startup, research and development, early and late stage, and mezzanine. Industry Preferences: Communications, computer related, electronic components and instrumentation, and interactive media. Geographic P

The Dakota Group
PO Box 1025
Menlo Park, CA 94025
(650)853-0600
Fax: (650)851-4899
E-mail: info@dakota.com
Stephen A. Meyer, General Partner
Preferred Investment Size: $300,000 to $500,000. Investment Types: Early and later stages, and special situations. Industry Preferences: Diversified computer and communications technology, education, and publishing. Geographic Preferences: National.

Delphi Ventures
3000 Sand Hill Rd.
Bldg. One, Ste. 135
Menlo Park, CA 94025
(650)854-9650
Fax: (650)854-2961
Website: http://www.delphiventures.com
Preferred Investment Size: $500,000 minimum. Investment Types: Seed, startup, first and second stage. Industry Preferences: Medical/health related, Internet related, biotechnology, computer software and services. Geographic Preferences: Entire U.S.

El Dorado Ventures
2884 Sand Hill Rd., Ste. 121
Menlo Park, CA 94025
(650)854-1200
Fax: (650)854-1202
Website: http://www.eldoradoventures.com
Preferred Investment Size: $500,000 to $5,000,000. Investment Types: Seed, startup, first and second stage. Industry Preferences: Communications, computer and Internet related, electronics, and industrial products and equipment. Geographic Preferences: West Coast.

Glynn Ventures
3000 Sand Hill Rd., Bldg. 4, Ste. 235
Menlo Park, CA 94025
(650)854-2215
John W. Glynn, Jr., General Partner
Preferred Investment Size: $300,000 to $500,000. Investment Types: Start-up, first and second stage, leveraged buyout, and mezzanine. Industry Preferences: Diversified computer and communications technology, and medical/health. Geographic Preferences: East and West Coast.

Indosuez Ventures
2180 Sand Hill Rd., Ste. 450
Menlo Park, CA 94025
(650)854-0587
Fax: (650)323-5561
Website: http://www.indosuezventures.com
Preferred Investment Size: $250,000 to $1,500,000. Investment Types: Start-up, first and second stage, and mezzanine. Industry Preferences: Diversified. Geographic Preferences: West Coast.

Institutional Venture Partners
3000 Sand Hill Rd., Bldg. 2, Ste. 290
Menlo Park, CA 94025

(650)854-0132
Fax: (650)854-5762
Website: http://www.ivp.com
Preferred Investment Size: $500,000 minimum. Investment Types: Seed, startup, first and second stage, and special situations. Industry Preferences: Diversified. Geographic Preferences: International.

Interwest Partners (Menlo Park)

3000 Sand Hill Rd., Bldg. 3, Ste. 255
Menlo Park, CA 94025-7112
(650)854-8585
Fax: (650)854-4706
Website: http://www.interwest.com
Preferred Investment Size: $2,000,000 to $25,000,000. Investment Types: Seed, research and development, startup, first and second stage, expansion, and special situations. Industry Preferences: Diversified. Geographic Preferences: Entire U.S.

Kleiner Perkins Caufield & Byers (Menlo Park)

2750 Sand Hill Rd.
Menlo Park, CA 94025
(650)233-2750
Fax: (650)233-0300
Website: http://www.kpcb.com
Preferred Investment Size: $500,000. Investment Types: Seed, start-up, first and second stage. Industry Preferences: Diversified. Geographic Preferences: West Coast.

Magic Venture Capital LLC

1010 El Camino Real, Ste. 300
Menlo Park, CA 94025
(650)325-4149
Patrick Lynn
Preferred Investment Size: $100,000 to $1,000,000. Investment Types: Seed, start-up, first stage. Industry Preferences: Medical/health related. Geographic Preferences: West Coast.

Matrix Partners

2500 Sand Hill Rd., Ste. 113
Menlo Park, CA 94025
(650)854-3131
Fax: (650)854-3296
Website: http://www.matrixpartners.com
Andrew W. Verlahen, General Partner
Preferred Investment Size: $500,000 to $1,000,000. Investment Types: Startup, early, first and second stage, and leveraged buyout. Industry Preferences: Communications, computer related,

medical/health, and electronic components and instrumentation. Geographic Preferences: Entire U.S

Mayfield Fund

2800 Sand Hill Rd.
Menlo Park, CA 94025
(650)854-5560
Fax: (650)854-5712
Website: http://www.mayfield.com
Preferred Investment Size: $250,000 minimum. Investment Types: Seed, startup, first and second stage, and recapitalization. Industry Preferences: Diversified. Geographic Preferences: Northwest, Rocky Mountains, and West Coast.

McCown De Leeuw and Co. (Menlo Park)

3000 Sand Hill Rd., Bldg. 3, Ste. 290
Menlo Park, CA 94025-7111
(650)854-6000
Fax: (650)854-0853
Website: http://www.mdcpartners.com
Christopher Crosby, Principal
Preferred Investment Size: $40,000,000 minimum. Investment Types: Leveraged buyout and special situations. Industry Preferences: Diversified. Geographic Preferences: Entire U.S.

Menlo Ventures

3000 Sand Hill Rd., Bldg. 4, Ste. 100
Menlo Park, CA 94025
(650)854-8540
Fax: (650)854-7059
Website: http://www.menloventures.com
H. DuBose Montgomery, General Partner and Managing Director
Venture capital supplier. Provides start-up and expansion financing to companies with experienced management teams, distinctive product lines, and large growing markets. Primary interest is in technology-oriented, Internet, and computer related companies. Investments range from $5,00

Merrill Pickard Anderson & Eyre

2480 Sand Hill Rd., Ste. 200
Menlo Park, CA 94025
(650)854-8600
Fax: (650)854-0345
Preferred Investment Size: $1,000,000 maximum. Investment Types: Seed, startup, first and second stage. Industry Preferences: Diversified technology. Geographic Preferences: No preference.

New Enterprise Associates (Menlo Park)

2490 Sand Hill Rd.
Menlo Park, CA 94025
(650)854-9499
Fax: (650)854-9397
Website: http://www.nea.com
Ronald H. Kase, General Partner
Preferred Investment Size: $100,000 minimum. Investment Types: Seed, early, startup, first and second stage, and mezzanine. Industry Preferences: Diversified technology. Geographic Preferences: No preference.

Onset Ventures

2400 Sand Hill Rd., Ste. 150
Menlo Park, CA 94025
(650)529-0700
Fax: (650)529-0777
Website: http://www.onset.com
Preferred Investment Size: $100,000 minimum. Investment Types: Early stage. Industry Preferences: Communications, computer related, medical and health related. Geographic Preferences: West Coast.

Paragon Venture Partners

3000 Sand Hill Rd., Bldg. 1, Ste. 275
Menlo Park, CA 94025
(650)854-8000
Fax: (650)854-7260
Preferred Investment Size: $500,000 to $1,500,000. Investment Types: Start-up, seed, first and second stage, special situation. Industry Preferences: Diversified. Geographic Preferences: No preference.

Pathfinder Venture Capital Funds (Menlo Park)

3000 Sand Hill Rd., Bldg. 3, Ste. 255
Menlo Park, CA 94025
(650)854-0650
Fax: (650)854-4706
Jack K. Ahrens, II, Investment Officer
Preferred Investment Size: $2,00,000 minimum. Investment Types: Seed, startup, first and second stage, mezzanine, leveraged buyout, and special situations. Industry Preferences: Diversified technology. Geographic Preferences: Entire U.S. and Canada.

Rocket Ventures

3000 Sandhill Rd., Bldg. 1, Ste. 170
Menlo Park, CA 94025
(650)561-9100
Fax: (650)561-9183

Website: http://www.rocketventures.com
Preferred Investment Size: $100,000 to
$5,000,000. Investment Types: Seed,
start-up, and early stage. Industry
Preferences: Communications, software,
and Internet related. Geographic
Preferences: West Coast.

Sequoia Capital
3000 Sand Hill Rd., Bldg. 4, Ste. 280
Menlo Park, CA 94025
(650)854-3927
Fax: (650)854-2977
E-mail: sequoia@sequioacap.com
Website: http://www.sequoiacap.com
Investment Types: Early, seed, start-up,
first and second stage. Industry
Preferences: Diversified technology.
Geographic Preferences: Western U.S.
and international.

Sierra Ventures
3000 Sand Hill Rd., Bldg. 4, Ste. 210
Menlo Park, CA 94025
(650)854-1000
Fax: (650)854-5593
Website: http://www.sierraventures.com
Preferred Investment Size: $100,000
minimum. Investment Types: Seed,
startup, first and second stage,
recapitalization, and leveraged buyout.
Industry Preferences: Diversified.
Geographic Preferences: No preference.

Sigma Partners
2884 Sand Hill Rd., Ste. 121
Menlo Park, CA 94025-7022
(650)853-1700
Fax: (650)853-1717
E-mail: info@sigmapartners.com
Website: http://www.sigmapartners.com
Lawrence G. Finch, Partner
Investment Types: Seed, start-up, first
and second stage, special situation, recap,
and control block purchases. Industry
Preferences: Diversified technology.
Geographic Preferences: U.S.

Sprout Group (Menlo Park)
3000 Sand Hill Rd.
Bldg. 3, Ste. 170
Menlo Park, CA 94025
(650)234-2700
Fax: (650)234-2779
Website: http://www.sproutgroup.com
Investment Types: Seed, startup, first and
second stage, mezzanine, leveraged buyout,
and special situations. Industry Preferences:
Diversified technology. Geographic
Preferences: U.S. and foreign countries.

TA Associates (Menlo Park)
70 Willow Rd., Ste. 100
Menlo Park, CA 94025
(650)328-1210
Fax: (650)326-4933
Website: http://www.ta.com
Michael C. Child, Managing Director
Preferred Investment Size: $20,000,000 to
$60,000,000. Investment Types: Control-
block purchases, leveraged buyout, and
special situations. Industry Preferences:
Diversified. Geographic Preferences: No
preference.

Thompson Clive & Partners Ltd.
3000 Sand Hill Rd., Bldg. 1, Ste. 185
Menlo Park, CA 94025-7102
(650)854-0314
Fax: (650)854-0670
E-mail: mail@tcvc.com
Website: http://www.tcvc.com
Greg Ennis, Principal
Preferred Investment Size: $500,000 to
$1,000,000. Investment Types: Early
stage, management buyouts, and
special situations. Industry
Preferences: Diversified computer and
communications technology,
electronic instrumentation, genetic
engineering, and medical/health.
Geographic Pref

Trinity Ventures Ltd.
3000 Sand Hill Rd., Bldg. 1, Ste. 240
Menlo Park, CA 94025
(650)854-9500
Fax: (650)854-9501
Website: http://www.trinityventures.com
Lawrence K. Orr, General Partner
Preferred Investment Size: $5,000,000 to
$20,000,000. Investment Types: Early
stage. Industry Preferences:
Communications, computer and Internet
related, consumer products and services,
and electronics. Geographic Preferences:
Mid-Atlantic and Western U.S.

U.S. Venture Partners
2180 Sand Hill Rd., Ste. 300
Menlo Park, CA 94025
(650)854-9080
Fax: (650)854-3018
Website: http://www.usvp.com
William K. Bowes, Jr., Founding Partner
Preferred Investment Size: $500,000
minimum. Investment Types: Seed,
startup, first and second stage, and late
stage. Industry Preferences:
Communications, computer related,
consumer products and services,

distribution, electronics, and medical/
health related. Geographic Preferences:

USVP-Schlein Marketing Fund
2180 Sand Hill Rd., Ste. 300
Menlo Park, CA 94025
(415)854-9080
Fax: (415)854-3018
Website: http://www.usvp.com
Venture capital fund. Prefers specialty
retailing/consumer products companies.

Venrock Associates
2494 Sand Hill Rd., Ste. 200
Menlo Park, CA 94025
(650)561-9580
Fax: (650)561-9180
Website: http://www.venrock.com
Ted H. McCourtney, Managing General
Partner
Preferred Investment Size: $500,000
minimum. Investment Types: Seed,
research and development, startup, first
and second stage. Industry Preferences:
Diversified. Geographic Preferences: No
preference.

Brad Peery Capital Inc.
145 Chapel Pkwy.
Mill Valley, CA 94941
(415)389-0625
Fax: (415)389-1336
Brad Peery, Chairman
Preferred Investment Size: $100,000 to
$300,000. Investment Types: Second
stage financing. Industry Preferences:
Communications and media. Geographic
Preferences: Entire U.S.

Dot Edu Ventures
650 Castro St., Ste. 270
Mountain View, CA 94041
(650)575-5638
Fax: (650)325-5247
Website: http://
www.doteduventures.com
Investment Types: Early stage and seed.
Industry Preferences: Internet related.
Geographic Preferences: Entire U.S.

Forrest, Binkley & Brown
840 Newport Ctr. Dr., Ste. 480
Newport Beach, CA 92660
(949)729-3222
Fax: (949)729-3226
Website: http://www.fbbvc.com
Jeff Brown, Partner
Investment Policies: $1,000,000 to
$10,000,000. Investment Types: First
stage, second stage, expansion, and

balanced. Industry Preferences: Communications, computer and Internet related, consumer, electronic components and instrumentation, genetic engineering, industrial products and

Marwit Capital LLC
180 Newport Center Dr., Ste. 200
Newport Beach, CA 92660
(949)640-6234
Fax: (949)720-8077
Website: http://www.marwit.com
Thomas W. Windsor, Vice President
Preferred Investment Size: $250,000 minimum. Investment Types: Acquisition, control-block, leveraged buyout, and mezzanine. Industry Preferences: Software, transportation, distribution, and manufacturing. Geographic Preferences: Entire U.S.

Kaiser Permanente/National Venture Development
1800 Harrison St., 22nd Fl.
Oakland, CA 94612
(510)267-4010
Fax: (510)267-4036
Website: http://www.kpventures.com
Preferred Investment Size: $500,000 to $2,000,000. Investment Types: Balanced, first and second stage, expansion, joint ventures, and private placement. Industry Preferences: Diversified. Geographic Preferences: Entire U.S. and Canada.

Nu Capital Access Group, Ltd.
7677 Oakport St., Ste. 105
Oakland, CA 94621
(510)635-7345
Fax: (510)635-7068
Preferred Investment Size: $500,000 to $1,000,000. Investment Types: First and second stages, leveraged buyouts, industry rollups, and special situations. Industry Preferences: Diversified consumer products and services, food and industrial product distribution. Geographic Preference

Inman and Bowman
4 Orinda Way, Bldg. D, Ste. 150
Orinda, CA 94563
(510)253-1611
Fax: (510)253-9037
Preferred Investment Size: $1,000,000 minimum. Investment Types: Startup, first and second stage, leveraged buyout, and special situations. Industry Preferences: Diversified

technology. Geographic Preferences: West Coast.

Accel Partners (San Francisco)
428 University Ave.
Palo Alto, CA 94301
(650)614-4800
Fax: (650)614-4880
Website: http://www.accel.com
Preferred Investment Size: $1,000,000 minimum. Investment Types: Seed, startup, and early stage. Industry Preferences: Communications, computer related, medical/health, biotechnology, and electronic components and instrumentation. Geographic Preferences: No preference.

Accenture Technology Ventures
1661 Page Mill Rd.
Palo Alto, CA 94304
Preferred Investment Size: $100,000 minimum. Investment Types: Seed, startup, first and second stage. Industry Preferences: Diversified. Geographic Preferences: Entire U.S.

Advanced Technology Ventures
485 Ramona St., Ste. 200
Palo Alto, CA 94301
(650)321-8601
Fax: (650)321-0934
Website: http://www.atvcapital.com
Steven Baloff, General Partner
Investment Types: Startup, first stage, second stage, and balanced. Industry Preferences: Diversified. Geographic Preferences: National.

Anila Fund
400 Channing Ave.
Palo Alto, CA 94301
(650)833-5790
Fax: (650)833-0590
Website: http://www.anila.com
Investment Types: Early stage. Industry Preferences: Telecommunications and Internet related. Geographic Preferences: Entire U.S.

Asset Management Company Venture Capital
2275 E. Bayshore, Ste. 150
Palo Alto, CA 94303
(650)494-7400
Fax: (650)856-1826
E-mail: postmaster@assetman.com
Website: http://www.assetman.com
Preferred Investment Size: $750,000 minimum. Investment Types: Seed, startup,

and first stage. Industry Preferences: Diversified technology. Geographic Preferences: Northeast, West Coast.

BancBoston Capital/BancBoston Ventures
435 Tasso St., Ste. 250
Palo Alto, CA 94305
(650)470-4100
Fax: (650)853-1425
Website: http://www.bancbostoncapital.com
Preferred Investment Size: $1,000,000 to $10,000,000. Investment Types: Seed, early stage, acquisition, expansion, later stage, management buyouts, and recapitalizations. Industry Preferences: Diversified. Geographic Preferences: Entire U.S. and Eastern Canada.

Charter Ventures
525 University Ave., Ste. 1400
Palo Alto, CA 94301
(650)325-6953
Fax: (650)325-4762
Website: http://www.charterventures.com
Investment Types: Seed, startup, first and second stage, mezzanine, leveraged buyout, and special situations. Industry Preferences: Diversified. Geographic Preferences: No preference.

Communications Ventures
505 Hamilton Avenue, Ste. 305
Palo Alto, CA 94301
(650)325-9600
Fax: (650)325-9608
Website: http://www.comven.com
Clifford Higgerson, General Partner
Preferred Investment Size: $500,000 to $25,000,000. Investment Types: Seed, start-up, early, first, and second stage. Industry Preferences: Communications, Internet related, electronics, and computer related. Geographic Preferences: No preference.

HMS Group
2468 Embarcadero Way
Palo Alto, CA 94303-3313
(650)856-9862
Fax: (650)856-9864
Industry Preferences: Communications, computer related, electronics, and industrial products. Geographic Preferences: No preference.

New Vista Capital
540 Cowper St., Ste. 200
Palo Alto, CA 94301

(650)329-9333
Fax: (650)328-9434
E-mail: fgreene@nvcap.com
Website: http://www.nvcap.com
Frank Greene
Investment Types: Seed, startup, first
stage, second stage. Industry Preferences:
Communications, computer related,
electronics, and consumer related.
Geographic Preferences: Western U.S.,
Rocky Mountains.

Norwest Equity Partners (Palo Alto)
245 Lytton Ave., Ste. 250
Palo Alto, CA 94301-1426
(650)321-8000
Fax: (650)321-8010
Website: http://www.norwestvp.com
Charles B. Lennin, Partner
Preferred Investment Size: $1,000,000 to
$25,000,000. Investment Types: Seed,
early and later stage, and expansion.
Industry Preferences: Diversified.
Geographic Preferences: No preference.

Oak Investment Partners
525 University Ave., Ste. 1300
Palo Alto, CA 94301
(650)614-3700
Fax: (650)328-6345
Website: http://www.oakinv.com
Preferred Investment Size: $250,000 to
$5,000,000. Investment Types: Seed,
startup, first stage, leveraged buyout,
open market, control-block purchases,
and special situations. Industry
Preferences: communications, computer
related, consumer restaurants and
retailing, electronics, ge

**Patricof & Co. Ventures, Inc.
(Palo Alto)**
2100 Geng Rd., Ste. 150
Palo Alto, CA 94303
(650)494-9944
Fax: (650)494-6751
Website: http://www.patricof.com
Preferred Investment Size: $5,000,000
minimum. Investment Types: Seed,
startup, first and second stage,
mezzanine, and leveraged buyout.
Industry Preferences: Diversified.
Geographic Preferences: No preference.

RWI Group
835 Page Mill Rd.
Palo Alto, CA 94304
(650)251-1800
Fax: (650)213-8660
Website: http://www.rwigroup.com

Preferred Investment Size: $500,000 to
$4,000,000. Investment Types: Seed,
start-up, first and second stage. Industry
Preferences: Diversified. Geographic
Preferences: West Coast.

Summit Partners (Palo Alto)
499 Hamilton Ave., Ste. 200
Palo Alto, CA 94301
(650)321-1166
Fax: (650)321-1188
Website: http://
www.summitpartners.com
Christopher W. Sheeline
Preferred Investment Size: $1,500,000
minimum. Investment Types: First and
second stage, mezzanine, leveraged
buyout, special situations, and control
block purchases. Industry Preferences:
Diversified. Geographic Preferences:
Entire U.S. and Canada.

Sutter Hill Ventures
755 Page Mill Rd., Ste. A-200
Palo Alto, CA 94304
(650)493-5600
Fax: (650)858-1854
E-mail: shv@shv.com

Vanguard Venture Partners
525 University Ave., Ste. 600
Palo Alto, CA 94301
(650)321-2900
Fax: (650)321-2902
Website: http://
www.vanguardventures.com
Donald F. Wood, Partner
Preferred Investment Size: $500,000 to
$1,000,000. Investment Types: Early stages.
Industry Preferences: Diversified computer
and communications technology, genetic
engineering, and electronics. Geographic
Preferences: National.

Venture Growth Associates
2479 East Bayshore St., Ste. 710
Palo Alto, CA 94303
(650)855-9100
Fax: (650)855-9104
James R. Berdell, Managing Partner
Preferred Investment Size: $1,000,000 to
$5,000,000. Investment Types: First and
second stage, leveraged buyout, and
mezzanine. Industry Preferences:
Diversified technology, finance and
consumer related. Geographic
Preferences: West Coast.

Worldview Technology Partners
435 Tasso St., Ste. 120
Palo Alto, CA 94301

(650)322-3800
Fax: (650)322-3880
Website: http://www.worldview.com
Mike Orsak, General Partner
Investment Types: Seed, research and
development, startup, first stage, second
stage, mezzanine. Industry Preferences:
Diversified technology. Geographic
Preferences: National.

Jafco America Ventures, Inc.
505 Hamilton Ste. 310
Palto Alto, CA 94301
(650)463-8800
Fax: (650)463-8801
Website: http://www.jafco.com
Andrew P. Goldfarb, Senior Managing
Director
Preferred Investment Size: $500,000
minimum. Investment Types: First and
second stage and mezzanine. Industry
Preferences: Diversified technology.
Geographic Preferences: No preference.

**Draper, Fisher, Jurvetson/Draper
Associates**
400 Seaport Ct., Ste.250
Redwood City, CA 94063
(415)599-9000
Fax: (415)599-9726
Website: http://www.dfj.com
J.B. Fox
Preferred Investment Size: $1,000,000 to
$5,000,000. Investment Types: Seed,
startup, and first stage. Industry
Preferences: Communications, computer
and Internet related, electronic
components and instrumentation.
Geographic Preferences: No preference.

Gabriel Venture Partners
350 Marine Pkwy., Ste. 200
Redwood Shores, CA 94065
(650)551-5000
Fax: (650)551-5001
Website: http://www.gabrielvp.com
Preferred Investment Size: $500,000 to
$7,000,000. Investment Types: Seed, early
and first stage. Industry Preferences:
Internet and computer related,
communications, and electronics.
Geographic Preferences: West Coast and
Mid Atlantic.

Hallador Venture Partners, L.L.C.
740 University Ave., Ste. 110
Sacramento, CA 95825-6710
(916)920-0191
Fax: (916)920-5188
E-mail: chris@hallador.com

Chris L. Branscum, Managing Director Preferred Investment Size: $500,000 to $1,000,000. Investment Types: Early and later stages, and research and development. Industry Preferences: Diversified computer and communications technology, and electronic semiconductors. Geographic Preferences: Western U.S.

Emerald Venture Group
12396 World Trade Dr., Ste. 116
San Diego, CA 92128
(858)451-1001
Fax: (858)451-1003
Website: http://
www.emeraldventure.com
Cherie Simoni
Preferred Investment Size: $100,000 to $50,000,000. Investment Types: Start-up, seed, first and second stage, leveraged buyout, mezzanine, and research and development. Industry Preferences: Diversified. Geographic Preferences: No preference.

Forward Ventures
9255 Towne Centre Dr.
San Diego, CA 92121
(858)677-6077
Fax: (858)452-8799
E-mail: info@forwardventure.com
Website: http://
www.forwardventure.com
Standish M. Fleming, Partner
Preferred Investment Size: $500,000 to $10,000,000. Investment Types: Seed, research and development, startup, first and second stage, mezzanine, and private placement. Industry Preferences: Biotechnology, and medical/health related. Geographic Preferences: Entire U.S.

Idanta Partners Ltd.
4660 La Jolla Village Dr., Ste. 850
San Diego, CA 92122
(619)452-9690
Fax: (619)452-2013
Website: http://www.idanta.com
Preferred Investment Size: $500,000 minimum. Investment Types: Seed, startup, first and second stage. Industry Preferences: Diversified. Geographic Preferences: Entire U.S.

Kingsbury Associates
3655 Nobel Dr., Ste. 490
San Diego, CA 92122
(858)677-0600
Fax: (858)677-0800

Preferred Investment Size: $500,000 to $1,000,000. Investment Types: Start-up, first and second stage. Industry Preferences: Medical/health, biotechnology, computer and Internet related. Geographic Preferences: West Coast.

Kyocera International Inc.
Corporate Development
8611 Balboa Ave.
San Diego, CA 92123
(858)576-2600
Fax: (858)492-1456
Preferred Investment Size: $300,000 to $500,000. Investment Types: Second stage. Industry Preferences: Diversified. Geographic Preferences: Northeast, Northwest, West Coast.

Sorrento Associates, Inc.
4370 LaJolla Village Dr., Ste. 1040
San Diego, CA 92122
(619)452-3100
Fax: (619)452-7607
Website: http://
www.sorrentoventures.com
Vincent J. Burgess, Vice President
Preferred Investment Size: $500,000 to $7,000,000. Investment Policies: Equity only. Investment Types: Start-up, first and second stage, leveraged buyout, special situations, and control block purchases. Industry Preferences: Medicine, health, communications, electronics, special ret

Western States Investment Group
9191 Towne Ctr. Dr., Ste. 310
San Diego, CA 92122
(619)678-0800
Fax: (619)678-0900
Investment Types: Seed, research and development, startup, first stage, leveraged buyout. Industry Preferences: Computer related, consumer, electronic components and instrumentation, medical/health related. Geographic Preferences: Western U.S.

Aberdare Ventures
One Embarcadero Center, Ste. 4000
San Francisco, CA 94111
(415)392-7442
Fax: (415)392-4264
Website: http://www.aberdare.com
Preferred Investment Size: $500,000 to $7,000,000. Investment Types: Start-up, first and second stage. Industry Preferences: Diversified. Geographic Preferences: Entire U.S.

Acacia Venture Partners
101 California St., Ste. 3160
San Francisco, CA 94111
(415)433-4200
Fax: (415)433-4250
Website: http://www.acaciavp.com
Brian Roberts, Senior Associate
Preferred Investment Size: $2,000,000 to $10,000,000. Investment Types: Seed, startup, first and second stage, mezzanine and leveraged buyout. Industry Preferences: Computer, and medical/health related. Geographic Preferences: Entire U.S.

Access Venture Partners
319 Laidley St.
San Francisco, CA 94131
(415)586-0132
Fax: (415)392-6310
Website: http://
www.accessventurepartners.com
Robert W. Rees, II, Managing Director
Preferred Investment Size: $250,000 to $5 million. Investment Types: Seed, startup, and first stage. Industry Preferences: Internet related, biotechnology, communications, and computer software and services. Geographic Preferences: Southwest and Rocky Mountain region.

Alta Partners
One Embarcadero Center, Ste. 4050
San Francisco, CA 94111
(415)362-4022
Fax: (415)362-6178
E-mail: alta@altapartners.com
Website: http://www.altapartners.com
Jean Deleage, Partner
Preferred Investment Size: $1,000,000 to $10,000,000. Investment Types: Seed, startup, first and second stage, and mezzanine. Industry Preferences: Communications, computer related, distribution, electronic components and instrumentation, genetic engineering, industrial products and

Bangert Dawes Reade Davis & Thom
220 Montgomery St., Ste. 424
San Francisco, CA 94104
(415)954-9900
Fax: (415)954-9901
E-mail: bdrdt@pacbell.net
Lambert Thom, Vice President
Preferred Investment Size: $500,000 to $5,000,000. Investment Types: Second stage, mezzanine, leveraged buyout and special situations. Industry Preferences: Diversified. Geographic Preferences: No preference.

Berkeley International Capital Corp.
650 California St., Ste. 2800
San Francisco, CA 94108-2609
(415)249-0450
Fax: (415)392-3929
Website: http://www.berkeleyvc.com
Arthur I. Trueger, Chairman
Preferred Investment Size: $3,000,000 to
$15,000,000. Investment Types: Second
stage, mezzanine, leveraged buyout and
special situations. Industry Preferences:
Communications, computer related,
distribution, electronic components and
instrumentation, industrial products and
equipment

Blueprint Ventures LLC
456 Montgomery St., 22nd Fl.
San Francisco, CA 94104
(415)901-4000
Fax: (415)901-4035
Website: http://
www.blueprintventures.com
Preferred Investment Size: $3,000,000 to
$10,000,000. Investment Types: Early
stage. Industry Preferences:
Communications and Internet related.
Geographic Preferences: Entire U.S.

Blumberg Capital Ventures
580 Howard St., Ste. 401
San Francisco, CA 94105
(415)905-5007
Fax: (415)357-5027
Website: http://
www.blumberg-capital.com
Mark Pretorius, Principal
Preferred Investment Size: $500,000 to
$5,000,000. Investment Types: Seed,
start-up, first and early stage, and expansion.
Industry Preferences: Diversified.
Geographic Preferences: Entire U.S.

Burr, Egan, Deleage, and Co. (San Francisco)
1 Embarcadero Center, Ste. 4050
San Francisco, CA 94111
(415)362-4022
Fax: (415)362-6178
Private venture capital supplier. Invests
start-up, expansion, and acquisitions
capital nationwide. Principal concerns are
strength of the management team; large,
rapidly expanding markets; and unique
products for services. Past investments have
been made in the fields of biotechnolo

Burrill & Company
120 Montgomery St., Ste. 1370
San Francisco, CA 94104

(415)743-3160
Fax: (415)743-3161
Website: http://www.burrillandco.com
David Collier, Managing Director
Preferred Investment Size: $500,000 to
$5,000,000. Investment Types: Startup,
first and second stage, and mezzanine.
Industry Preferences: Diversified.
Geographic Preferences: No
preference.

CMEA Ventures
235 Montgomery St., Ste. 920
San Francisco, CA 94401
(415)352-1520
Fax: (415)352-1524
Website: http://www.cmeaventures.com
Thomas R. Baruch, General Partner
Preferred Investment Size: $100,000 to
$1,000,000. Investment Types: Seed,
startup, first and second stage. Industry
Preferences: Diversified high technology.
Geographic Preferences: No preference.

Crocker Capital
1 Post St., Ste. 2500
San Francisco, CA 94101
(415)956-5250
Fax: (415)959-5710
Investment Types: Second stage,
leveraged buyout, and start-up. Industry
Preferences: Communications, medical/
health related, consumer, retail, food/
beverage, education, industrial materials,
and manufacturing. Geographic
Preferences: West Coast.

Dominion Ventures, Inc.
44 Montgomery St., Ste. 4200
San Francisco, CA 94104
(415)362-4890
Fax: (415)394-9245
Preferred Investment Size: $1,000,000 to
$10,000,000. Investment Types: First and
second stage, and mezzanine. Industry
Preferences: Diversified. Geographic
Preferences: No preference.

Dorset Capital
Pier 1
Bay 2
San Francisco, CA 94111
(415)398-7101
Fax: (415)398-7141
Website: http://www.dorsetcapital.com
Preferred Investment Size: $1,000,000 to
$10,000,000. Investment Types: Second
and later stage, expansion, generalist PE,
leveraged and management buyouts.
Industry Preferences: Consumer retail,

food and beverage, and business services.
Geographic Preferences: Entire U.S.

Gatx Capital
Four Embarcadero Center, Ste. 2200
San Francisco, CA 94904
(415)955-3200
Fax: (415)955-3449
Preferred Investment Size: $500,000 to
$5,000,000. Investment Types: Early and
later stages, and leveraged buyouts.
Industry Preferences: Diversified
technologies, forestry, and agriculture.
Geographic Preferences: National and
Canada.

IMinds
135 Main St., Ste. 1350
San Francisco, CA 94105
(415)547-0000
Fax: (415)227-0300
Website: http://www.iminds.com
Preferred Investment Size: $500,000 to
$2,000,000. Investment Types: Seed,
start-up, and early stage. Industry
Preferences: Internet and computer
related. Geographic Preferences: West
Coast.

LF International Inc.
360 Post St., Ste. 705
San Francisco, CA 94108
(415)399-0110
Fax: (415)399-9222
Website: http://www.lfvc.com
Preferred Investment Size: $500,000 to
$1,000,000. Investment Types: Control-
block purchases, first and second stage,
expansion, industry rollups, management
buyouts, and special situations. Industry
Preferences: Consumer related, retail.
Geographic Preferences: Entire U.S.

Newbury Ventures
535 Pacific Ave., 2nd Fl.
San Francisco, CA 94133
(415)296-7408
Fax: (415)296-7416
Website: http://www.newburyven.com
Preferred Investment Size: $500,000 to
$1,000,000. Investment Types: Early and
later stages, and leveraged buyout.
Industry Preferences: Diversified high
technology. Geographic Preferences:
Eastern and Western U.S. and Canada.

Quest Ventures (San Francisco)
333 Bush St., Ste. 1750
San Francisco, CA 94104
(415)782-1414

Fax: (415)782-1415
E-mail: ruby@crownadvisors.com
Lucien Ruby, General Partner
Preferred Investment Size: $100,000
maximum. Investment Types: Seed and
special situations. Industry Preferences:
Diversified. Geographic Preferences: No
preference.

Robertson-Stephens Co.
555 California St., Ste. 2600
San Francisco, CA 94104
(415)781-9700
Fax: (415)781-2556
Website: http://
www.omegaadventures.com
Private venture capital firm. Considers
investments in any attractive merging-
growth area, including product and
service companies. Key preferences
include health care, communications and
technology, biotechnology, software, and
information services. Maximum
investment is $5 million.

Rosewood Capital, L.P.
One Maritime Plaza, Ste. 1330
San Francisco, CA 94111-3503
(415)362-5526
Fax: (415)362-1192
Website: http://www.rosewoodvc.com
Kevin Reilly, Vice President
Preferred Investment Size: $1,000,000 to
$3,000,000. Investment Policies: Equity.
Investment Types: Later stages, leveraged
buyout, and special situations. Industry
Preferences: Consumer and Internet
related. Geographic Preferences:
National.

Ticonderoga Capital Inc.
555 California St., No. 4950
San Francisco, CA 94104
(415)296-7900
Fax: (415)296-8956
Graham K Crooke, Partner
Preferred Investment Size: $5,000,000
maximum. Investment Types: Second
stage, mezzanine, leveraged buyout, and
consolidation strategies. Industry
Preferences: Diversified. Geographic
Preferences: Entire U.S. and Canada.

21st Century Internet Venture Partners
Two South Park
2nd Floor
San Francisco, CA 94107
(415)512-1221
Fax: (415)512-2650
Website: http://www.21vc.com

Shawn Myers
Preferred Investment Size: $5,000,000
maximum. Investment Types: Seed,
research and development, startup, first
and second stage, mezzanine, leveraged
buyout, and special situations. Industry
Preferences: Diversified. Geographic
Preferences: Entire U.S. and Canada.

VK Ventures
600 California St., Ste.1700
San Francisco, CA 94111
(415)391-5600
Fax: (415)397-2744
David D. Horwich, Senior Vice President
Preferred Investment Size: $100,000 to
$250,000. Investment Types: Second
stage, mezzanine, and leveraged buyout.
Industry Preferences: Diversified.
Geographic Preferences: West Coast.

Walden Group of Venture Capital Funds
750 Battery St., Seventh Floor
San Francisco, CA 94111
(415)391-7225
Fax: (415)391-7262
Arthur Berliner
Preferred Investment Size: $1,000,000 to
$7,000,000. Investment Types: Seed,
startup, first and second stage. Industry
Preferences: Diversified technology.
Geographic Preferences: Entire U.S.

Acer Technology Ventures
2641 Orchard Pkwy.
San Jose, CA 95134
(408)433-4945
Fax: (408)433-5230
James C. Lu, Managing Director
Preferred Investment Size: $500,000 to
$5,000,000. Investment Types: Seed,
startup, first and second stage. Industry
Preferences: Diversified. Geographic
Preferences: Entire U.S. and Canada.

Authosis
226 Airport Pkwy., Ste. 405
San Jose, CA 95110
(650)814-3603
Website: http://www.authosis.com
Investment Types: Seed, first and second
stage. Industry Preferences: Computer
software. Geographic Preferences: Entire
U.S.

Western Technology Investment
2010 N. First St., Ste. 310
San Jose, CA 95131
(408)436-8577

Fax: (408)436-8625
E-mail: mktg@westerntech.com
Investment Types: Seed, research and
development, startup, first stage, second
stage, mezzanine, leveraged buyout, and
special situations. Industry Preferences:
Diversified. Geographic Preferences:
National.

Drysdale Enterprises
177 Bovet Rd., Ste. 600
San Mateo, CA 94402
(650)341-6336
Fax: (650)341-1329
E-mail: drysdale@aol.com
George M. Drysdale, President
Preferred Investment Size: $500,000 to
$5,000,000. Investment Types: First and
second stage, mezzanine, leveraged
buyout, and special situations. Industry
Preferences: Diversified. Geographic
Preferences: West Coast.

Greylock
2929 Campus Dr., Ste. 400
San Mateo, CA 94401
(650)493-5525
Fax: (650)493-5575
Website: http://www.greylock.com
Preferred Investment Size: $250,000
minimum. Investment Types: Seed, start-up,
early and first stage, and expansion.
Industry Preferences: Diversified.
Geographic Preferences: Entire U.S.

Technology Funding
2000 Alameda de las Pulgas, Ste. 250
San Mateo, CA 94403
(415)345-2200
Fax: (415)345-1797
Peter F. Bernardoni, Partner
Small business investment corporation.
Provides primarily late first-stage, early
second-stage, and mezzanine equity
financing. Also offers secured debt with
equity participation to venture capital
backed companies. Investments range
from $250,000 to $500,000.

2M Invest Inc.
1875 S. Grant St.
Suite 750
San Mateo, CA 94402
(650)655-3765
Fax: (650)372-9107
E-mail: 2minfo@2minvest.com
Website: http://www.2minvest.com
Preferred Investment Size: $500,000 to $5
million. Investment Types: Startup.
Industry Preferences: Communications,

computer related, electronic components and instrumentation. Non-information technology companies not considered. Geographic Preferences: West Coast.

Phoenix Growth Capital Corp.
2401 Kerner Blvd.
San Rafael, CA 94901
(415)485-4569
Fax: (415)485-4663
E-mail: nnelson@phxa.com
Preferred Investment Size: $250,000 to $1,000,000. Investment Types: First and second stage, and mezzanine. Industry Preferences: Communications, computer related, consumer retailing, distribution, electronics, genetic engineering, medical/health related, education, publishing, and t

NextGen Partners LLC
1705 East Valley Rd.
Santa Barbara, CA 93108
(805)969-8540
Fax: (805)969-8542
Website: http://
www.nextgenpartners.com
Preferred Investment Size: $100,000 to $3,000,000. Investment Types: Seed, start-up, first and second stage, expansion, and research and development. Industry Preferences: Diversified. Geographic Preferences: Entire U.S. and Canada.

Denali Venture Capital
1925 Woodland Ave.
Santa Clara, CA 95050
(408)690-4838
Fax: (408)247-6979
E-mail: wael@denaliventurecapital.com
Website: http://
www.denaliventurecapital.com
Preferred Investment Size: $100,000 to $5,000,000. Investment Types: Early stage. Industry Preferences: Medical/health related. Geographic Preferences: West Coast.

Dotcom Ventures LP
3945 Freedom Circle, Ste. 740
Santa Clara, CA 95045
(408)919-9855
Fax: (408)919-9857
Website: http://
www.dotcomventuresatl.com
Investment Types: Early, first stage, and seed. Industry Preferences: Telecommunications and Internet related. Geographic Preferences: Entire U.S.

Silicon Valley Bank
3003 Tasman
Santa Clara, CA 95054
(408)654-7400
Fax: (408)727-8728
Investment Types: Startup, first stage, second stage, mezzanine. Industry Preferences: Diversified. Geographic Preferences: National.

Al Shugart International
920 41st Ave.
Santa Cruz, CA 95062
(831)479-7852
Fax: (831)479-7852
Website: http://www.alshugart.com
Investment Types: Seed, start-up, and early stage. Industry Preferences: Diversified. Geographic Preferences: U.S.

Leonard Mautner Associates
1434 Sixth St.
Santa Monica, CA 90401
(213)393-9788
Fax: (310)459-9918
Leonard Mautner
Preferred Investment Size: $100,000 to $300,000. Investment Types: Seed, start-up, first stage, and special situation. Industry Preferences: Diversified. Geographic Preferences: West Coast.

Palomar Ventures
100 Wilshire Blvd., Ste. 450
Santa Monica, CA 90401
(310)260-6050
Fax: (310)656-4150
Website: http://
www.palomarventures.com
Preferred Investment Size: $250,000 to $15,000,000. Investment Types: Seed, start-up, first and early stage, and expansion. Industry Preferences: Communications, Internet related, computer software and services. Geographic Preferences: West Coast and Southwest.

Medicus Venture Partners
12930 Saratoga Ave., Ste. D8
Saratoga, CA 95070
(408)447-8600
Fax: (408)447-8599
Website: http://www.medicusvc.com
Fred Dotzler, General Partner
Preferred Investment Size: $100,000 to $5,000,000. Investment Types: Early stages. Industry Preferences: Genetic engineering and healthcare industry. Geographic Preferences: Western U.S.

Redleaf Venture Management
14395 Saratoga Ave., Ste. 130
Saratoga, CA 95070
(408)868-0800
Fax: (408)868-0810
E-mail: nancy@redleaf.com
Website: http://www.redleaf.com
Robert von Goeben, Director
Preferred Investment Size: $1,000,000 to $4,000,000. Investment Policies: Equity. Investment Types: Early and late stage. Industry Preferences: Internet business related. Geographic Preferences: Northwest and Silicon Valley.

Artemis Ventures
207 Second St., Ste. E
3rd Fl.
Sausalito, CA 94965
(415)289-2500
Fax: (415)289-1789
Website: http://
www.artemisventures.com
Investment Types: Seed, first and second stage. Industry Preferences: Internet and computer related, electronics, and various products. Geographic Preferences: Northern U.S. and West Coast.

Deucalion Venture Partners
19501 Brooklime
Sonoma, CA 95476
(707)938-4974
Fax: (707)938-8921
Preferred Investment Size: $500,000 minimum. Investment Types: Seed, start-up, first and second stage. Industry Preferences: Computer software, biotechnology, education, energy conservation, industrial machinery, transportation, financial services, and publishing. Geographic Preferen

Windward Ventures
PO Box 7688
Thousand Oaks, CA 91359-7688
(805)497-3332
Fax: (805)497-9331
Investment Types: Seed, startup, first stage, second stage. Industry Preferences: Communications, computer related, electronic components and instrumentation, genetic engineering, industrial products and equipment, medical and health related. Geographic Preferences: West Coast.

National Investment Management, Inc.
2601 Airport Dr., Ste.210
Torrance, CA 90505

(310)784-7600
Fax: (310)784-7605
E-mail: robins621@aol.com
Preferred Investment Size: $1,000,000 to
$5,000,000. Investment Types: Leveraged
buyout. Industry Preferences: Consumer
products and retailing, distribution,
industrial products and equipment,
medical/health related, and publishing.
Real estate deals not considered.
Geographic Prefer

Southern California Ventures
406 Amapola Ave. Ste. 125
Torrance, CA 90501
(310)787-4381
Fax: (310)787-4382
Preferred Investment Size: $300,000 to
$1,000,000. Investment Types: Seed,
start-up, and first stage. Industry
Preferences: Communications, and
medical/health related. Geographic
Preferences: West Coast.

Sandton Financial Group
21550 Oxnard St., Ste. 300
Woodland Hills, CA 91367
(818)702-9283
Preferred Investment Size: $100,000 to
$250,000. Investment Types: Early and
later stages, and special situations. Industry
Preferences: No preference. Geographic
Preferences: National and Canada.

Woodside Fund
850 Woodside Dr.
Woodside, CA 94062
(650)368-5545
Fax: (650)368-2416
Website: http://www.woodsidefund.com
Matthew Bolton, Analyst
Investment Types: Seed, startup, first
stage, second stage, and special
situations. Industry Preferences:
Diversified technology. Geographic
Preferences: Western U.S.

Colorado

Colorado Venture Management
Ste. 300
Boulder, CO 80301
(303)440-4055
Fax: (303)440-4636
Preferred Investment Size: $250,000 to
$1,000,000. Investment Types: Seed,
start-up, early, and first and second stage.
Industry Preferences: Diversified.
Geographic Preferences: Midwest and
Rocky Mountain region.

Dean & Associates
4362 Apple Way
Boulder, CO 80301
Fax: (303)473-9900
Investment Types: First stage, second
stage, and mezzanine. Industry
Preferences: Internet related. Geographic
Preferences: Western U.S.

Roser Ventures LLC
1105 Spruce St.
Boulder, CO 80302
(303)443-6436
Fax: (303)443-1885
Website: http://www.roserventures.com
Steven T. Joanis, Associate
Investment Types: Startup, first stage,
second stage, and special situations.
Industry Preferences: Communications,
computer related, distribution, electronic
components and instrumentation,
energy/natural resources, industrial
products and equipment, medical and
health related. Geog

Sequel Venture Partners
4430 Arapahoe Ave., Ste. 220
Boulder, CO 80303
(303)546-0400
Fax: (303)546-9728
E-mail: tom@sequelvc.com
Website: http://www.sequelvc.com
Kinney Johnson, Partner
Preferred Investment Size: $100,000 to
$5,000,000. Investment Types: Seed,
startup, and early stage. Industry
Preferences: Diversified technology.
Geographic Preferences: Rocky
Mountains.

New Venture Resources
445C E. Cheyenne Mtn. Blvd.
Colorado Springs, CO 80906-4570
(719)598-9272
Fax: (719)598-9272
Jeffrey M. Cooper, Managing Director
Preferred Investment Size: $100,000 to
$250,000. Investment Types: Seed and
startup. Industry Preferences: Diversified
technology. Geographic Preferences:
Southwest, rocky mountains.

The Centennial Funds
1428 15th St.
Denver, CO 80202-1318
(303)405-7500
Fax: (303)405-7575
Website: http://www.centennial.com
Preferred Investment Size: $250,000 to
$5,000,000. Investment Types: Seed,

startup, first and second stage, and
national consolidations. Industry
Preferences: Diversified. Geographic
Preferences: No preference.

Rocky Mountain Capital Partners
1125 17th St., Ste. 2260
Denver, CO 80202
(303)291-5200
Fax: (303)291-5327
Investment Types: Mezzanine and
leveraged buyout. Industry Preferences:
Diversified. Communications, computer
related, consumer, distribution,
electronic components and
instrumentation, and industrial products
and equipment. Geographic Preferences:
Western U.S.

Sandlot Capital LLC
600 South Cherry St., Ste. 525
Denver, CO 80246
(303)893-3400
Fax: (303)893-3403
Website: http://www.sandlotcapital.com
Preferred Investment Size: $250,000 to
$20,000,000. Investment Types: Seed,
start-up, early and first stage, and special
situation. Industry Preferences:
Diversified. Geographic Preferences: U.S.

Wolf Ventures
50 South Steele St., Ste. 777
Denver, CO 80209
(303)321-4800
Fax: (303)321-4848
E-mail: businessplan@wolfventures.com
Website: http://www.wolfventures.com
David O. Wolf
Preferred Investment Size: $500,000 to
$3,000,000. Investment Types: First stage,
second stage, and special situations.
Industry Preferences: Diversified.
Geographic Preferences: Rocky mountains.

The Columbine Venture Funds
5460 S. Quebec St., Ste. 270
Englewood, CO 80111
(303)694-3222
Fax: (303)694-9007
Preferred Investment Size: $100,000 to
$250,000. Investment Types: Seed,
research and development, startup, and
first stage. Industry Preferences:
Diversified technology. Geographic
Preferences: Southwest, Rocky
Mountains, and West Coast.

Investment Securities of Colorado, Inc.
4605 Denice Dr.
Englewood, CO 80111

(303)796-9192
Preferred Investment Size: $100,000 to $300,000. Investment Types: Seed and startup. Industry Preferences: Electronic components, industrial controls and sensors, healthcare industry. Geographic Preferences: Rocky Mountain area.

Kinship Partners
6300 S. Syracuse Way, Ste. 484
Englewood, CO 80111
(303)694-0268
Fax: (303)694-1707
E-mail: block@vailsys.com
Preferred Investment Size: $250,000 to $1,000,000. Investment Types: Seed, startup, and early stage. Industry Preferences: Diversified computer and communication technology, specialty retailing, genetic engineering, and healthcare. Geographic Preferences: Within two hours of office.

Boranco Management, L.L.C.
1528 Hillside Dr.
Fort Collins, CO 80524-1969
(970)221-2297
Fax: (970)221-4787
Preferred Investment Size: $100,000. Investment Types: Early and late stage. Industry Preferences: Agricultural and animal biotechnology. Geographic Preferences: Within two hours of office.

Aweida Ventures
890 West Cherry St., Ste. 220
Louisville, CO 80027
(303)664-9520
Fax: (303)664-9530
Website: http://www.aweida.com
Investment Types: Seed and first and second stage. Industry Preferences: Software, Internet related, and medical/health related. Geographic Preferences: West Coast.

Access Venture Partners
8787 Turnpike Dr., Ste. 260
Westminster, CO 80030
(303)426-8899
Fax: (303)426-8828
E-mail: robert.rees@juno.com
Robert W. Rees, Managing Director
Investment Types: Seed, startup, first stage, and special situations. Industry Preferences: Diversified. Geographic Preferences: Western and Midwestern U.S.

Connecticut

Medmax Ventures LP
1 Northwestern Dr., Ste. 203
Bloomfield, CT 06002
(860)286-2960
Fax: (860)286-9960
Noam Karstaedt
Preferred Investment Size: $500,000 minimum. Investment Types: Seed, start-up, first and second stage, and research and development. Industry Preferences: Biotechnology and medical/health related. Geographic Preferences: Northeast.

James B. Kobak & Co.
Four Mansfield Place
Darien, CT 06820
(203)656-3471
Fax: (203)655-2905
Preferred Investment Size: $100,000 maximum. Investment Types: First stage. Industry Preferences: Publishing. Geographic Preferences: National.

Orien Ventures
1 Post Rd.
Fairfield, CT 06430
(203)259-9933
Fax: (203)259-5288
Anthony Miadich, Managing General Partner
Preferred Investment Size: $500,000 minimum. Investment Types: Start-up, seed, early and first stage. Industry Preferences: Diversified technology. Geographic Preferences: No preference.

ABP Acquisition Corporation
115 Maple Ave.
Greenwich, CT 06830
(203)625-8287
Fax: (203)447-6187
Preferred Investment Size: $10,000,000 to $30,000,000. Investment Types: Leveraged buyout and acquisition. Industry Preferences: Diversified. Geographic Preferences: Mid Atlantic, Northeast, Ontario, and Quebec.

Catterton Partners
9 Greenwich Office Park
Greenwich, CT 06830
(203)629-4901
Fax: (203)629-4903
Website: http://www.cpequity.com
Andrew C. Taub

Preferred Investment Size: $5,000,000 minimum. Investment Types: First stage, second stage, leveraged buyout, and special situations. Industry Preferences: Consumer products and services, Internet related, biotechnology. Geographic Preferences: U.S. and Canada.

Consumer Venture Partners
3 Pickwick Plz.
Greenwich, CT 06830
(203)629-8800
Fax: (203)629-2019
E-mail: lcummin@consumer-venture.com
Linda Cummin, Business Manager
Preferred Investment Size: $10,000,000 minimum. Investment Types: Startup, first and second stage, and leveraged buyout. Industry Preferences: Internet related, consumer related. Geographic Preferences: Entire U.S.

Insurance Venture Partners
31 Brookside Dr., Ste. 211
Greenwich, CT 06830
(203)861-0030
Fax: (203)861-2745
Preferred Investment Size: $500,000 to $50,000,000. Investment Types: First and second stage, and leveraged buyouts. Industry Preferences: Insurance. Geographic Preferences: U.S.

The NTC Group
Three Pickwick Plaza
Ste. 200
Greenwich, CT 06830
(203)862-2800
Fax: (203)622-6538
Preferred Investment Size: $1,000,000 minimum. Investment Types: Seed, first stage, control-block purchases, and leveraged buyout. Industry Preferences: Electronic components, factory automation, and machinery. Geographic Preferences: Entire U.S.

Regulus International Capital Co., Inc.
140 Greenwich Ave.
Greenwich, CT 06830
(203)625-9700
Fax: (203)625-9706
E-mail: lee@chaossystems.com
Preferred Investment Size: $100,000 minimum. Investment Types: Start-up, seed, research and development. Industry Preferences: Computer software, industrial materials and machinery, and publishing. Geographic Preferences: National.

Axiom Venture Partners

City Place II
185 Asylum St., 17th Fl.
Hartford, CT 06103
(860)548-7799
Fax: (860)548-7797
Website: http://www.axiomventures.com
Preferred Investment Size: $2,000,000 to
$5,000,000. Investment Types: Seed,
early and later stages, and expansion.
Industry Preferences: Communications,
computer and Internet related,
distribution, genetic engineering,
medical/health related. Geographic
Preferences: National.

Conning Capital Partners

City Place II
185 Asylum St.
Hartford, CT 06103-4105
(860)520-1289
Fax: (860)520-1299
E-mail: pe@conning.com
Website: http://www.conning.com
John B. Clinton, Executive Vice
President
Preferred Investment Size: $5,000,000 to
$35,000,000. Investment Types: Second
and late stage, and expansion. Industry
Preferences: Computer related,
consumer related, and medical/health
related. Geographic Preferences:
National.

First New England Capital L.P.

100 Pearl St.
Hartford, CT 06103
(860)293-3333
Fax: (860)293-3338
E-mail: info@firstnewenglandcapital.com
Website: http://
www.firstnewenglandcapital.com
Preferred Investment Size: $100,000 to
$1,000,000. Investment Types:
Mezzanine, expansion, and management
buyouts. Industry Preferences:
Communications, computer related,
electronics, consumer related, and
medical/health related. Geographic
Preferences: Northeastern U.S.

Northeast Ventures

One State St., Ste. 1720
Hartford, CT 06103
(860)547-1414
Fax: (860)246-8755
Preferred Investment Size: $1,000,000
minimum. Investment Types: Secondary.
Industry Preferences: Diversified.
Geographic Preferences: National.

Windward Holdings

38 Sylvan Rd.
Madison, CT 06443
(203)245-6870
Fax: (203)245-6865
Preferred Investment Size: $300,000
minimum. Investment Types: Leveraged
buyouts, mezzanine, recaps, and special
situations. Industry Preferences:
Electronics, food/beverage, and industrial
products. Geographic Preferences:
Northeastern U.S.

Advanced Materials Partners, Inc.

45 Pine St.
PO Box 1022
New Canaan, CT 06840
(203)966-6415
Fax: (203)966-8448
E-mail: wkb@amplink.com
Preferred Investment Size: $500,000 to
$25,000,000. Investment Types:
Seed, start-up, early and late stage,
leveraged buyout, research and
development, and special situations.
Industry Preferences: Diversified.
Geographic Preferences: National and
Canada.

RFE Investment Partners

36 Grove St.
New Canaan, CT 06840
(203)966-2800
Fax: (203)966-3109
Website: http://www.rfeip.com
James A. Parsons, General Partner
Preferred Investment Size: $15,000,000
minimum. Investment Policies: Prefer
equity investments. Investment Types:
Later stage, industry rollups, leveraged
buyout, mezzanine, and special
situations. Industry Preferences:
Diversified. Geographic Preferences:
Entire U.S.

Connecticut Innovations, Inc.

999 West St.
Rocky Hill, CT 06067
(860)563-5851
Fax: (860)563-4877
E-mail:
pamela.hartley@ctinnovations.com
Website: http://www.ctinnovations.com
Preferred Investment Size: $50,000
minimum to $1,000,000. Investment
Types: Start-up, first and second stage,
joint ventures, and mezzanine.
Industry Preferences: Diversified
technology. Geographic Preferences:
Northeast.

Canaan Partners

105 Rowayton Ave.
Rowayton, CT 06853
(203)855-0400
Fax: (203)854-9117
Website: http://www.canaan.com
Preferred Investment Size: $5,000,000 to
$20,000,000. Investment Types: Early,
first, and second stage; and expansion.
Industry Preferences: Diversified.
Geographic Preferences: National.

Landmark Partners, Inc.

10 Mill Pond Ln.
Simsbury, CT 06070
(860)651-9760
Fax: (860)651-8890
Website: http://
www.landmarkpartners.com
James P. McConnell, Partner
Preferred Investment Size: $500,000 to
$5,000,000. Investment Types: Seed,
start-up, first and second stage, and
special situations. Industry Preferences:
Diversified technology. Geographic
Preferences: U.S. and Canada.

Sweeney & Company

PO Box 567
Southport, CT 06490
(203)255-0220
Fax: (203)255-0220
E-mail: sweeney@connix.com
Preferred Investment Size: $1,000,000
minimum. Investment Types: Seed,
research and development, startup, first
stage, second stage, mezzanine, leveraged
buyout, and special situations. Industry
Preferences: Diversified. Geographic
Preferences: Northeast U.S. and Eastern
Canada.

Baxter Associates, Inc.

PO Box 1333
Stamford, CT 06904
(203)323-3143
Fax: (203)348-0622
Preferred Investment Size: $2,000,000
minimum. Investment Types: Seed,
start-up, first stage, research and
development, leveraged buyout, and
special situations. Industry Preferences:
Diversified. Geographic Preferences:
National.

Beacon Partners Inc.

6 Landmark Sq., 4th Fl.
Stamford, CT 06901-2792
(203)359-5776
Fax: (203)359-5876

Preferred Investment Size: $300,000 to $1,000,000. Investment Types: First stage, second stage, mezzanine, and leveraged buyout. Industry Preferences: Diversified. Geographic Preferences: Northeast.

Collinson, Howe, and Lennox, LLC
1055 Washington Blvd., 5th Fl.
Stamford, CT 06901
(203)324-7700
Fax: (203)324-3636
E-mail: info@chlmedical.com
Website: http://www.chlmedical.com
Investment Types: Seed, research and development, start-up, and first stage. Industry Preferences: Medical/health related, biotechnology, and Internet related. Geographic Preferences: National.

Prime Capital Management Co.
550 West Ave.
Stamford, CT 06902
(203)964-0642
Fax: (203)964-0862
Preferred Investment Size: $300,000 to $800,000. Investment Types: First and second stage, and recaps. Industry Preferences: Diversified. Geographic Preferences: Northeast.

Saugatuck Capital Co.
1 Canterbury Green
Stamford, CT 06901
(203)348-6669
Fax: (203)324-6995
Website: http://www.saugatuckcapital.com
Preferred Investment Size: $25,000,000 maximum. Investment Types: Leveraged buyout, acquisition, control-block purchases, expansion, later stage, and recaps. Industry Preferences: Diversified. Geographic Preferences: Entire U.S.

Soundview Financial Group Inc.
22 Gatehouse Rd.
Stamford, CT 06902
(203)462-7200
Fax: (203)462-7350
Website: http://www.sndv.com
Brian Bristol, Managing Director
Preferred Investment Size: $100,000 to $500,000. Investment Types: Second stage and mezzanine. Industry Preferences: Diversified information technology. Geographic Preferences: United States and Canada.

TSG Ventures, L.L.C.
177 Broad St., 12th Fl.
Stamford, CT 06901
(203)406-1500
Fax: (203)406-1590
Darryl Thompson
Preferred Investment Size: $30,000,000 minimum. Investment Types: Second stage and leveraged buyout. Industry Preferences: Diversified. Geographic Preferences: Entire U.S. and Canada.

Whitney & Company
177 Broad St.
Stamford, CT 06901
(203)973-1400
Fax: (203)973-1422
Website: http://www.jhwhitney.com
Preferred Investment Size: $1,000,000. Investment Types: Leveraged buyout and expansion. Industry Preferences: Diversified technology. Geographic Preferences: No preference.

Cullinane & Donnelly Venture Partners L.P.
970 Farmington Ave.
West Hartford, CT 06107
(860)521-7811
Fax: (860)521-7911
Preferred Investment Size: $300,000 to $1,000,000. Investment Types: Seed, first and second stage, and recaps. Industry Preferences: Diversified. Geographic Preferences: Northeast.

The Crestview Investment and Financial Group
431 Post Rd. E, Ste. 1
Westport, CT 06880-4403
(203)222-0333
Fax: (203)222-0000
Norman Marland, Pres.
Preferred Investment Size: $500,000 to $3,000,000. Investment Types: Seed, research and development, first stage, second stage, and mezzanine. Industry Preferences: Diversified. Geographic Preferences: U.S. and Canada.

Marketcorp Venture Associates, L.P. (MCV)
274 Riverside Ave.
Westport, CT 06880
(203)222-3030
Fax: (203)222-3033
E. Bulkeley Griswold, General Partner
Preferred Investment Size: $500,000 to $1,000,000. Investment Types: First and second stage, mezzanine, and leveraged

buyout. Industry Preferences: Consumer products and services, and computer services. Geographic Preferences: Entire U.S.

Oak Investment Partners (Westport)
1 Gorham Island
Westport, CT 06880
(203)226-8346
Fax: (203)227-0372
Website: http://www.oakinv.com
Preferred Investment Size: $250,000 to $5,000,000. Investment Types: Startup; early, first, second, and late stage; leveraged buyout; open market; control-block purchases; open market; and special situations. Industry Preferences: Diversified technology. Geographic Preferences: Natio

Oxford Bioscience Partners
315 Post Rd. W
Westport, CT 06880-5200
(203)341-3300
Fax: (203)341-3309
Website: http://www.oxbio.com
William Greenman
Preferred Investment Size: $500,000 to $5,000,000. Investment Types: Early and first stage, and research and development. Industry Preferences: Genetic engineering and medical/health related, computer related. Geographic Preferences: Entire U.S. and Canada.

Prince Ventures (Westport)
25 Ford Rd.
Westport, CT 06880
(203)227-8332
Fax: (203)226-5302
Preferred Investment Size: $500,000 to $1,000,000. Investment Types: Seed, startup, first and second stage, and leveraged buyout. Industry Preferences: Genetic engineering and medical/health related, computer software and services, industrial, and communications. Geographic Preferenc

LTI Venture Leasing Corp.
221 Danbury Rd.
Wilton, CT 06897
(203)563-1100
Fax: (203)563-1111
Website: http://www.ltileasing.com
Richard Livingston, Vice President
Preferred Investment Size: $500,000 to $2,000,000. Investment Types: Early, first, second, and late stage; mezzanine; and special situation. Industry

Preferences: Communications, computer related, consumer, electronic components and instrumentation, industrial products and equipment,

Delaware

Blue Rock Capital
5803 Kennett Pike, Ste. A
Wilmington, DE 19807
(302)426-0981
Fax: (302)426-0982
Website: http://
www.bluerockcapital.com
Preferred Investment Size: $250,000 to
$3,000,000. Investment Types: Seed,
start-up, and first stage. Industry
Preferences: Communication, Internet
related, computer, semiconductors, and
consumer related. Geographic
Preferences: Northeast, Middle Atlantic.

District of Columbia

Allied Capital Corp.
1919 Pennsylvania Ave. NW
Washington, DC 20006-3434
(202)331-2444
Fax: (202)659-2053
Website: http://www.alliedcapital.com
Tricia Daniels, Sales & Marketing
Preferred Investment Size: $5,000,000 to
$40,000,000. Investment Types:
Mezzanine, leveraged buyout, acquisition,
management buyouts, and recapitalization.
Industry Preferences: Diversified.
Geographic Preferences: No preference.

Atlantic Coastal Ventures, L.P.
3101 South St. NW
Washington, DC 20007
(202)293-1166
Fax: (202)293-1181
Website: http://www.atlanticcv.com
Preferred Investment Size: $300,000
minimum. Investment Types: Leveraged
buyout, mezzanine, and special
situations. Industry Preferences:
Communication and computer related,
and electronics. Geographic Preferences:
East Coast.

Columbia Capital Group, Inc.
1660 L St. NW, Ste. 308
Washington, DC 20036
(202)775-8815
Fax: (202)223-0544
Erica Batie, Director of Investments
Preferred Investment Size: $100,000 to
$250,000. Investment Types: First and

second stage, and mezzanine. Industry
Preferences: Communication and
computer related, electronics, and
biotechnology. Geographic Preferences:
Mid Atlanic.

Core Capital Partners
901 15th St., NW
9th Fl.
Washington, DC 20005
(202)589-0090
Fax: (202)589-0091
Website: http://www.core-capital.com
Preferred Investment Size: $1,000,000 to
$10,000,000. Investment Types: Start-up,
first and second stage, expansion, and
later stage. Industry Preferences:
Diversified. Geographic Preferences: Mid
Atlantic, Northeast, and Southeast.

Next Point Partners
701 Pennsylvania Ave. NW, Ste. 900
Washington, DC 20004
(202)661-8703
Fax: (202)434-7400
E-mail: mf@nextpoint.vc
Website: http://www.nextpointvc.com
Michael Faber, Managing General
Partner
Investment Types: First and second stage.
Industry Preferences: Communications,
computer related, and electronic
components. Geographic Preferences:
National.

**Telecommunications Development
Fund**
2020 K. St. NW
Ste. 375
Washington, DC 20006
(202)293-8840
Fax: (202)293-8850
Website: http://www.tdfund.com
Preferred Investment Size: $375,000 to
$1,000,000. Investment Types: Seed, early
stage, and expansion. Industry
Preferences: Internet related, computer
hardware/software and services, and
communications. Geographic
Preferences: Entire U.S.

Wachtel & Co., Inc.
1101 4th St. NW
Washington, DC 20005-5680
(202)898-1144
Preferred Investment Size: $100,000 to
$300,000. Investment Types: Start-up,
first and second stage, and recaps.
Industry Preferences: Diversified.
Geographic Preferences: East Coast.

Winslow Partners LLC
1300 Connecticut Ave. NW
Washington, DC 20036-1703
(202)530-5000
Fax: (202)530-5010
E-mail: winslow@winslowpartners.com
Robert Chartener, Partner
Investment Types: Later stage,
acquisition, control-block purchases,
expansion, management and leverage
buyouts. Industry Preferences:
Diversified. Geographic Preferences:
Entire U.S.

Women's Growth Capital Fund
1054 31st St., NW
Ste. 110
Washington, DC 20007
(202)342-1431
Fax: (202)341-1203
Website: http://www.wgcf.com
Preferred Investment Size: $500,000 to
$2,000,000. Investment Types: First,
second, and later stage. Industry
Preferences: Internet related,
communications, and computer software
and services. Geographic Preferences:
Entire U.S.

Florida

Sigma Capital Corp.
22668 Caravelle Circle
Boca Raton, FL 33433
(561)368-9783
Preferred Investment Size: $100,000 to
$300,000. Investment Types: Second
stage. Industry Preferences: Diversified
communication and computer,
consumer products and services,
distribution, electronics, genetic
engineering, finance, and real estate.
Geographic Preferences: Southeast.

**North American Business Development
Co., L.L.C.**
111 East Las Olas Blvd.
Ft. Lauderdale, FL 33301
(305)463-0681
Fax: (305)527-0904
Website: http://
www.northamericanfund.com
Robert Underwood
PIS $10,000,000 minimum. Investment
Types: Leveraged buyout, special
situations, control block purchases,
industry roll ups, and small business with
growth potential. Industry Preferences:
No preference. Geographic Preferences:
Southeast and Midwest.

Chartwell Capital Management Co. Inc.
1 Independent Dr., Ste. 3120
Jacksonville, FL 32202
(904)355-3519
Fax: (904)353-5833
E-mail: info@chartwellcap.com
Anthony Marinatos
Preferred Investment Size: $5,000,000 minimum. Investment Types: First stage, second stage and leveraged buyout. Industry Preferences: Diversified. Geographic Preferences: Northwest and Southeast.

CEO Advisors
1061 Maitland Center Commons
Ste. 209
Maitland, FL 32751
(407)660-9327
Fax: (407)660-2109
Preferred Investment Size: $300,000 to $500,000. Investment Types: Seed, start-up, first stage, and research and development. Industry Preferences: Diversified. Geographic Preferences: Southeast.

Henry & Co.
8201 Peters Rd., Ste. 1000
Plantation, FL 33324
(954)797-7400
June Knaudt
Preferred Investment Size: $500,000 to $1,000,000. Investment Types: First and second stage. Industry Preferences: Healthcare industry. Geographic Preferences: West Coast.

Avery Business Development Services
2506 St. Michel Ct.
Ponte Vedra, FL 32082
(904)285-6033
Preferred Investment Size: $2,000,000. Investment Types: Seed, research and development, startup, first stage, leveraged buyout, and special situations. Industry Preferences: Diversified. Geographic Preferences: National.

New South Ventures
5053 Ocean Blvd.
Sarasota, FL 34242
(941)358-6000
Fax: (941)358-6078
Website: http://www.newsouthventures.com
Preferred Investment Size: $300,000 to $3,000,000. Investment Types: Seed and early stage. Industry Preferences: Diversified. Geographic Preferences: Southeast.

Venture Capital Management Corp.
PO Box 2626
Satellite Beach, FL 32937
(407)777-1969
Preferred Investment Size: $100,000 to $300,000. Investment Types: First and second stage, and leveraged buyout. Industry Preferences: Diversified. Geographic Preferences: National.

Florida Capital Venture Ltd.
325 Florida Bank Plaza
100 W. Kennedy Blvd.
Tampa, FL 33602
(813)229-2294
Fax: (813)229-2028
Warren Miller
Preferred Investment Size: $500,000 minimum. Investment Types: Startup, first and second stage, leveraged buyout, and special situations. Industry Preferences: Diversified. Geographic Preferences: Southeast.

Quantum Capital Partners
339 South Plant Ave.
Tampa, FL 33606
(813)250-1999
Fax: (813)250-1998
Website: http://www.quantumcapitalpartners.com
Preferred Investment Size: $1,000,000 to $5,000,000. Investment Types: Expansion, later stage, and mezzanine. Industry Preferences: Diversified technology, medical/health, consumer, retail, financial and business services, and manufacturing. Geographic Preferences: Florida.

South Atlantic Venture Fund
614 W. Bay St.
Tampa, FL 33606-2704
(813)253-2500
Fax: (813)253-2360
E-mail: venture@southatlantic.com
Website: http://www.southatlantic.com
Donald W. Burton, Chairman and Managing Director
Preferred Investment Size: $1,500,000 minimum. Investment Types: First and second stage, special situations, expansion and control block purchases. Industry Preferences: Diversified. Geographic Preferences: Southeast, Middle Atlantic, and Texas.

LM Capital Corp.
120 S. Olive, Ste. 400
West Palm Beach, FL 33401

(561)833-9700
Fax: (561)655-6587
Website: http://www.lmcapitalsecurities.com
Preferred Investment Size: $5,000,000 minimum. Investment Types: Leveraged buyout. Industry Preferences: Diversified. Geographic Preferences: No preference.

Georgia

Venture First Associates
4811 Thornwood Dr.
Acworth, GA 30102
(770)928-3733
Fax: (770)928-6455
J. Douglas Mullins
Preferred Investment Size: $500,000 to $5,000,000. Investment Types: Seed, startup, first and second stage. Industry Preferences: Diversified technology and electronics. Geographic Preferences: Southeast.

Alliance Technology Ventures
8995 Westside Pkwy., Ste. 200
Alpharetta, GA 30004
(678)336-2000
Fax: (678)336-2001
E-mail: info@atv.com
Website: http://www.atv.com
Preferred Investment Size: $250,000 to $1,000,000. Investment Types: Seed, start-up, first and second stage. Industry Preferences: Diversified technology. Geographic Preferences: Southeast.

Cordova Ventures
2500 North Winds Pkwy., Ste. 475
Alpharetta, GA 30004
(678)942-0300
Fax: (678)942-0301
Website: http://www.cordovaventures.com
Teo F. Dagi
Preferred Investment Size: $250,000 to $4,000,000. Investment Policies: Equity and/or debt. Investment Types: Early and late stage, start-up, expansion, and balanced. Industry Preferences: Diversified. Geographic Preferences: Southeast.

Advanced Technology Development Fund
1000 Abernathy, Ste. 1420
Atlanta, GA 30328-5614
(404)668-2333
Fax: (404)668-2333

Preferred Investment Size: $500,000 to $1,500,000. Investment Types: Seed, start-up, first and second stage, and leveraged buyout. Industry Preferences: Diversified. Geographic Preferences: No preference.

CGW Southeast Partners
12 Piedmont Center, Ste. 210
Atlanta, GA 30305
(404)816-3255
Fax: (404)816-3258
Website: http://www.cgwlp.com
Garrison M. Kitchen, Managing Partner
Preferred Investment Size: $25,000,000 to $200,000,000. Investment Types: Management buyout. Industry Preferences: Diversified. Geographic Preferences: Entire U.S.

Cyberstarts
1900 Emery St., NW
3rd Fl.
Atlanta, GA 30318
(404)267-5000
Fax: (404)267-5200
Website: http://www.cyberstarts.com
Investment Types: Seed and start-up. Industry Preferences: Internet and financial services. Geographic Preferences: Entire U.S.

EGL Holdings, Inc.
10 Piedmont Center, Ste. 412
Atlanta, GA 30305
(404)949-8300
Fax: (404)949-8311
Salvatore A. Massaro, Partner
Preferred Investment Size: $1,000,000 minimum. Investment Types: Mezzanine, leveraged buyout, industry roll ups, recapitalization, and second stage. Industry Preferences: Diversified. Geographic Preferences: Southeast and East Coast, Midwest.

Equity South
1790 The Lenox Bldg.
3399 Peachtree Rd. NE
Atlanta, GA 30326
(404)237-6222
Fax: (404)261-1578
Douglas L. Diamond, Managing Director
Preferred Investment Size: $2,000,000 to $3,000,000. Investment Types: Mezzanine, leveraged buyout, recapitalization, and control block purchases. Industry Preferences: Diversified. Geographic Preferences: Northeast, Southeast, and Southwest.

Five Paces
3400 Peachtree Rd., Ste. 200
Atlanta, GA 30326
(404)439-8300
Fax: (404)439-8301
Website: http://www.fivepaces.com
Investment Types: Balanced. Industry Preferences: Diversified. Geographic Preferences: Entire U.S.

Frontline Capital, Inc.
3475 Lenox Rd., Ste. 400
Atlanta, GA 30326
(404)240-7280
Fax: (404)240-7281
Preferred Investment Size: $1,000,000 minimum. Investment Types: First stage. Industry Preferences: Diversified communication and computer technology, consumer products and services, distribution, electronics, business and financial services, and publishing. Geographic Preferences: S

Fuqua Ventures LLC
1201 W. Peachtree St. NW, Ste. 5000
Atlanta, GA 30309
(404)815-4500
Fax: (404)815-4528
Website: http://www.fuquaventures.com
Investment Types: Early stage. Industry Preferences: Internet related, biotechnology, communications, and computer software and services. Geographic Preferences: Entire U.S.

Noro-Moseley Partners
4200 Northside Pkwy., Bldg. 9
Atlanta, GA 30327
(404)233-1966
Fax: (404)239-9280
Website: http://www.noro-moseley.com
Preferred Investment Size: $1,000,000 to $5,000,000. Investment Types: Startup, first and second stage, mezzanine, leveraged buyout, special situations, and control block purchases. Industry Preferences: Diversified. Geographic Preferences: Southeast.

Renaissance Capital Corp.
34 Peachtree St. NW, Ste. 2230
Atlanta, GA 30303
(404)658-9061
Fax: (404)658-9064
Larry Edler
Preferred Investment Size: $300,000 minimum. Investment Types: Second stage, mezzanine, and leveraged buyout. Industry Preferences:

Diversified. Geographic Preferences: Southeast.

River Capital, Inc.
Two Midtown Plaza
1360 Peachtree St. NE, Ste. 1430
Atlanta, GA 30309
(404)873-2166
Fax: (404)873-2158
Jerry D. Wethington
Preferred Investment Size: $3,000,000 minimum. Investment Types: Mezzanine, recapitalization, and leveraged buyout. Industry Preferences: Diversified. Geographic Preferences: Southeast, Southwest, Midwest, and Middle Atlantic.

State Street Bank & Trust Co.
3414 Peachtree Rd. NE, Ste. 1010
Atlanta, GA 30326
(404)364-9500
Fax: (404)261-4469
Preferred Investment Size: $10,000,000 minimum. Investment Types: Leveraged buyout and special situations. Industry Preferences: Diversified technology. Geographic Preferences: National.

UPS Strategic Enterprise Fund
55 Glenlake Pkwy. NE
Atlanta, GA 30328
(404)828-8814
Fax: (404)828-8088
E-mail: jcacyce@ups.com
Website: http://www.ups.com/sef/sef_home
Preferred Investment Size: $1,000,000. Investment Types: Early and late stage. Industry Preferences: Diversified communication and computer technology. Geographic Preferences: United States and Canada.

Wachovia
191 Peachtree St. NE, 26th Fl.
Atlanta, GA 30303
(404)332-1000
Fax: (404)332-1392
Website: http://www.wachovia.com/wca
Preferred Investment Size: $5,000,000 to $15,000,000. Investment Types: Expansion, later stage, management buyouts, mezzanine, private placement, and recaps. Industry Preferences: Diversified. Geographic Preferences: Southeast.

Brainworks Ventures
4243 Dunwoody Club Dr.
Chamblee, GA 30341

(770)239-7447
Investment Types: Balanced and early and later stage. Industry Preferences: Telecommunications and computers. Geographic Preferences: Southeast.

First Growth Capital Inc.
Best Western Plaza, Ste. 105
PO Box 815
Forsyth, GA 31029
(912)781-7131
Fax: (912)781-0066
Preferred Investment Size: $100,000 to $300,000. Investment Types: Second stage and special situation. Industry Preferences: Diversified. Geographic Preferences: No preference.

Financial Capital Resources, Inc.
21 Eastbrook Bend, Ste. 116
Peachtree City, GA 30269
(404)487-6650
Preferred Investment Size: $5,000,000 minimum. Investment Types: Leveraged buyout. Industry Preferences: Machinery. Geographic Preferences: National.

Hawaii

HMS Hawaii Management Partners
Davies Pacific Center
841 Bishop St., Ste. 860
Honolulu, HI 96813
(808)545-3755
Fax: (808)531-2611
Preferred Investment Size: $500,000 to $1,500,000. Investment Types: Seed, start-up, first stage, and leveraged buyout. Industry Preferences: Internet related, communications, and consumer related. Geographic Preferences: Entire U.S.

Idaho

Sun Valley Ventures
160 Second St.
Ketchum, ID 83340
(208)726-5005
Fax: (208)726-5094
Preferred Investment Size: $5,000,000. Investment Types: Second stage, leveraged buyout, control-block purchases, and special situations. Industry Preferences: Diversified. Geographic Preferences: Entire U.S. and Canada.

Illinois

Open Prairie Ventures
115 N. Neil St., Ste. 209
Champaign, IL 61820

(217)351-7000
Fax: (217)351-7051
E-mail: inquire@openprairie.com
Website: http://www.openprairie.com
Dennis D. Spice, Managing Member
Preferred Investment Size: $250,000 to $2,500,000. Investment Types: Early stage. Industry Preferences: Diversified communication and computer technology, electronics, and genetic engineering. Geographic Preferences: Midwest.

ABN AMRO Private Equity
208 S. La Salle St., 10th Fl.
Chicago, IL 60604
(312)855-7079
Fax: (312)553-6648
Website: http://www.abnequity.com
David Bogetz, Managing Director
Preferred Investment Size: $10,000,000 maximum. Investment Types: Early stage and expansion. Industry Preferences: Diversified. Geographic Preferences: Entire U.S. and Canada.

Alpha Capital Partners, Ltd.
122 S. Michigan Ave., Ste. 1700
Chicago, IL 60603
(312)322-9800
Fax: (312)322-9808
E-mail: acp@alphacapital.com
William J. Oberholtzer, Vice President
Preferred Investment Size: $2,000,000 minimum. Investment Types: First and second stage, leveraged buyout, and special situations. Industry Preferences: Diversified. Geographic Preferences: Midwest.

Ameritech Development Corp.
30 S. Wacker Dr., 37th Fl.
Chicago, IL 60606
(312)750-5083
Fax: (312)609-0244
Craig Lee, Director
Preferred Investment Size: $5,000,000 minimum. Investment Types: Startup, first and second stage. Industry Preferences: Communications, computer related, and electronics. Geographic Preferences: Entire U.S.

Apex Investment Partners
225 W. Washington, Ste. 1450
Chicago, IL 60606
(312)857-2800
Fax: (312)857-1800
E-mail: apex@apexvc.com
Website: http://www.apexvc.com

Preferred Investment Size: $500,000 to $15,000,000. Investment Types: Early stage. Industry Preferences: Diversified communication and computer technology, consumer products and services, industrial/energy, and electronics. Geographic Preferences: Entire U.S.

Arch Venture Partners
8725 W. Higgins Rd., Ste. 290
Chicago, IL 60631
(773)380-6600
Fax: (773)380-6606
Website: http://www.archventure.com
Steven Lazarus, Managing Director
Preferred Investment Size: $100,000 to $1,000,000. Investment Types: Seed, start-up, early stage. Industry Preferences: Diversified communication and computer technology, electronics, and genetic engineering. Geographic Preferences: National.

The Bank Funds
208 South LaSalle St., Ste. 1680
Chicago, IL 60604
(312)855-6020
Fax: (312)855-8910
Investment Types: Control-block purchases, later stage, leveraged buyout, second stage, and special situation. Industry Preferences: Diversified. Geographic Preferences: No preference.

Batterson Venture Partners
303 W. Madison St., Ste. 1110
Chicago, IL 60606-3309
(312)269-0300
Fax: (312)269-0021
Website: http://www.battersonvp.com
Preferred Investment Size: $500,000 to $3,000,000. Investment Types: Seed, startup, first and second stage. Industry Preferences: Diversified. Geographic Preferences: Entire U.S.

William Blair Capital Partners, L.L.C.
222 W. Adams St., Ste. 1300
Chicago, IL 60606
(312)364-8250
Fax: (312)236-1042
E-mail: privateequity@wmblair.com
Website: http://www.wmblair.com
Maureen Naddy, Office Manager
Preferred Investment Size: $5,000,000 minimum. Investment Types: First and early stage, acquisition and leveraged buyout. Industry Preferences: Communications, computer related, consumer, electronics, energy/natural

resources, genetic engineering, and medical/health related. Geograph

Bluestar Ventures
208 South LaSalle St., Ste. 1020
Chicago, IL 60604
(312)384-5000
Fax: (312)384-5005
Website: http://www.bluestarventures.com
Preferred Investment Size: $1,000,000 to $3,000,000. Investment Types: Early, first, and second stage. Industry Preferences: Diversified. Geographic Preferences: Midwest.

The Capital Strategy Management Co.
233 S. Wacker Dr.
Box 06334
Chicago, IL 60606
(312)444-1170
Eric Von Bauer
Preferred Investment Size: $200,000 to $50,000,000. Investment Types: Various types. Industry Preferences: Diversified communication and computer technology, medical/health, industrial/energy, consumer products and services, distribution, electronics, and utilities. Geographic Prefer

DN Partners
77 West Wacker Dr., Ste. 4550
Chicago, IL 60601
(312)332-7960
Fax: (312)332-7979
Investment Types: Leveraged buyout. Industry Preferences: Communications, computer related, electronics, medical/health, consumer related, industrial products, transportation, financial services, publishing, and agriculture related. Geographic Preferences: U.S.

Dresner Capital Inc.
29 South LaSalle St., Ste. 310
Chicago, IL 60603
(312)726-3600
Fax: (312)726-7448
John Riddle
Preferred Investment Size: $500,000 to $1,000,000. Investment Types: Leveraged buyout, mezzanine, and second stage. Industry Preferences: Diversified. Geographic Preferences: No preference.

Eblast Ventures LLC
11 South LaSalle St., 5th Fl.
Chicago, IL 60603
(312)372-2600
Fax: (312)372-5621
Website: http://www.eblastventures.com
Preferred Investment Size: $100,000 to $500,000. Investment Types: Early, seed, start-up, and turnaround. Industry Preferences: Diversified. Geographic Preferences: Midwest.

Essex Woodlands Health Ventures, L.P.
190 S. LaSalle St., Ste. 2800
Chicago, IL 60603
(312)444-6040
Fax: (312)444-6034
Website: http://www.essexwoodlands.com
Marc S. Sandroff, General Partner
Preferred Investment Size: $1,000,000 to $12,000,000. Investment Types: Startup, early and second stage, private placement, and mezzanine. Industry Preferences: Healthcare, biotechnology, Internet related. Geographic Preferences: No preference.

First Analysis Venture Capital
233 S. Wacker Dr., Ste. 9500
Chicago, IL 60606
(312)258-1400
Fax: (312)258-0334
Website: http://www.firstanalysis.com
Bret Maxwell, CEO
Preferred Investment Size: $3,000,000 to $15,000,000. Investment Types: Early and later stage, and expansion. Industry Preferences: Diversified. Geographic Preferences: No preference.

Frontenac Co.
135 S. LaSalle St., Ste.3800
Chicago, IL 60603
(312)368-0044
Fax: (312)368-9520
Website: http://www.frontenac.com
Preferred Investment Size: $500,000 minimum. Investment Types: Start-up, first and second stage, leveraged buyout, special situation, and industry roll ups. Industry Preferences: Diversified. Geographic Preferences: Entire U.S.

GTCR Golder Rauner, LLC
6100 Sears Tower
Chicago, IL 60606
(312)382-2200
Fax: (312)382-2201
Website: http://www.gtcr.com
Bruce V. Rauner
Preferred Investment Size: $10,000,000 minimum. Investment Types: Leveraged buyout, acquisition, expansion,

management buyouts, and recapitalization. Industry Preferences: Diversified. Geographic Preferences: No preference.

High Street Capital LLC
311 South Wacker Dr., Ste. 4550
Chicago, IL 60606
(312)697-4990
Fax: (312)697-4994
Website: http://www.highstr.com
Preferred Investment Size: $2,000,000 to $10,000,000. Investment Types: Acquisition, control-block purchases, expansion, generalist PE, leveraged and management buyouts, recaps, and special situations. Industry Preferences: Diversified. Geographic Preferences: Entire U.S.

IEG Venture Management, Inc.
70 West Madison
Chicago, IL 60602
(312)644-0890
Fax: (312)454-0369
Website: http://www.iegventure.com
Preferred Investment Size: $100,000 to $500,000. Investment Types: Seed, startup, first and second stage. Industry Preferences: Diversified. Geographic Preferences: Midwest.

JK&B Capital
180 North Stetson, Ste. 4500
Chicago, IL 60601
(312)946-1200
Fax: (312)946-1103
E-mail: gspencer@jkbcapital.com
Website: http://www.jkbcapital.com
Preferred Investment Size: $5,000,000 to $20,000,000. Investment Types: Early and late stage, and expansion. Industry Preferences: Diversified. Geographic Preferences: National.

Kettle Partners L.P.
350 W. Hubbard, Ste. 350
Chicago, IL 60610
(312)329-9300
Fax: (312)527-4519
Website: http://www.kettlevc.com
Preferred Investment Size: $1,000,000 to $5,000,000. Investment Types: Early, first and second stage, seed, and start-up. Industry Preferences: Internet related, communications, computer related. Geographic Preferences: Entire U.S.

Lake Shore Capital Partners
20 N. Wacker Dr., Ste. 2807
Chicago, IL 60606
(312)803-3536

Fax: (312)803-3534
Preferred Investment Size: $1,000,000 to
$10,000,000. Investment Types: First and
second stage, mezzanine, and leveraged
buyout. Industry Preferences: Diversified.
Geographic Preferences: National.

LaSalle Capital Group Inc.
70 W. Madison St., Ste. 5710
Chicago, IL 60602
(312)236-7041
Fax: (312)236-0720
Anthony Pesavento
Preferred Investment Size: $1,000,000
minimum. Investment Types: Leveraged
buyout and special situation. Industry
Preferences: Entertainment and leisure,
consumer products, industrial products,
and machinery. Geographic Preferences:
No preference.

Linc Capital, Inc.
303 E. Wacker Pkwy., Ste. 1000
Chicago, IL 60601
(312)946-2670
Fax: (312)938-4290
E-mail: bdemars@linccap.com
Martin E. Zimmerman, Chairman
Preferred Investment Size: $500,000 to
$2,000,000. Investment Types: Seed,
start-up, early and late stage, mezzanine,
research and development, and special
situations. Industry Preferences:
Diversified communication and
computer technology, electronics, and
medical/health related. Ge

Madison Dearborn Partners, Inc.
3 First National Plz., Ste. 3800
Chicago, IL 60602
(312)895-1000
Fax: (312)895-1001
E-mail: invest@mdcp.com
Website: http://www.mdcp.com
Preferred Investment Size: $20,000,000
to $400,000,000. Investment Types:
Start-up, early stage, leveraged buyout,
special situations, and expansion.
Industry Preferences: Diversified.
Geographic Preferences: Entire U.S. and
Canada.

**Mesirow Private Equity Investments
Inc.**
350 N. Clark St.
Chicago, IL 60610
(312)595-6950
Fax: (312)595-6211
Website: http://
www.meisrowfinancial.com

Preferred Investment Size: $4,000,000
to $10,000,000. Investment Types:
Second stage, mezzanine, and leveraged
buyout. Industry Preferences:
Diversified. Geographic Preferences:
Entire U.S.

Mosaix Ventures LLC
1822 North Mohawk
Chicago, IL 60614
(312)274-0988
Fax: (312)274-0989
Website: http://
www.mosaixventures.com
Preferred Investment Size: $500,000 to
$3,000,000. Investment Types: Early and
later stage, and expansion. Industry
Preferences: Medical/health related.
Geographic Preferences: U.S.

Nesbitt Burns
111 West Monroe St.
Chicago, IL 60603
(312)416-3855
Fax: (312)765-8000
Website: http://www.harrisbank.com
I. David Burn
Investment Types: Control-block
purchases, leveraged buyout, and special
situation. Industry Preferences:
Diversified. Geographic Preferences: U.S.
and Canada.

Polestar Capital, Inc.
180 N. Michigan Ave., Ste. 1905
Chicago, IL 60601
(312)984-9090
Fax: (312)984-9877
E-mail: wl@polestarvc.com
Website: http://www.polestarvc.com
Preferred Investment Size: $250,000 to
$1,000,000. Investment Policies:
Primarily equity. Investment Types:
Start-up, first and second stage. Industry
Preferences: Communications, computer
related. Geographic Preferences: Entire
U.S.

Prince Ventures (Chicago)
10 S. Wacker Dr., Ste. 2575
Chicago, IL 60606-7407
(312)454-1408
Fax: (312)454-9125
Preferred Investment Size: $500,000 to
$1,000,000. Investment Types: Seed,
startup, first and second stage,
leveraged buyout. Industry Preferences:
Genetic engineering and medical/health
related. Geographic Preferences: No
preference.

Prism Capital
444 N. Michigan Ave.
Chicago, IL 60611
(312)464-7900
Fax: (312)464-7915
Website: http://www.prismfund.com
Investment Types: First and second stage,
mezzanine, leveraged buyout, and special
situations. Industry Preferences:
Diversified technology. Geographic
Preferences: National.

Third Coast Capital
900 N. Franklin St., Ste. 700
Chicago, IL 60610
(312)337-3303
Fax: (312)337-2567
E-mail: manic@earthlink.com
Website: http://
www.thirdcoastcapital.com
Preferred Investment Size: $2,000,000 to
$5,000,000. Industry Preferences:
Telecommunications and fiber optics.
Geographic Preferences: National.

Thoma Cressey Equity Partners
4460 Sears Tower, 92nd Fl.
233 S. Wacker Dr.
Chicago, IL 60606
(312)777-4444
Fax: (312)777-4445
Website: http://www.thomacressey.com
Investment Types: Early and later stage,
leveraged buyouts, and recapitalization.
Industry Preferences: Diversified.
Geographic Preferences: U.S. and
Canada.

Tribune Ventures
435 N. Michigan Ave., Ste. 600
Chicago, IL 60611
(312)527-8797
Fax: (312)222-5993
Website: http://
www.tribuneventures.com
Frances McCaughan
Preferred Investment Size: $1,000,000 to
$10,000,000. Investment Types: Early
stage, expansion, first and second stage,
seed, and start-up. Industry Preferences:
Diversified. Geographic Preferences:
Entire U.S.

Wind Point Partners (Chicago)
676 N. Michigan Ave., Ste. 330
Chicago, IL 60611
(312)649-4000
Website: http://www.wppartners.com
Preferred Investment Size: $10,000,000 to
$60,000,000. Investment Types: Later

stage, leveraged buyout, acquisition, expansion, and recapitalization. Industry Preferences: Diversified. Geographic Preferences: Midwest.

Marquette Venture Partners

520 Lake Cook Rd., Ste. 450
Deerfield, IL 60015
(847)940-1700
Fax: (847)940-1724
Website: http://
www.marquetteventures.com
Preferred Investment Size: $1,000,000 to $5,000,000. Investment Types: Startup, first and second stage. Industry Preferences: Diversified. Geographic Preferences: Mid Atlantic, Midwest, Rocky Mountain, and West Coast.

Duchossois Investments Limited, LLC

845 Larch Ave.
Elmhurst, IL 60126
(630)530-6105
Fax: (630)993-8644
Website: http://www.duchtec.com
Preferred Investment Size: $500,000 to $5,000,000. Investment Types: Early, first and second stage. Industry Preferences: Diversified. Communications and computer related. Geographic Preferences: National.

Evanston Business Investment Corp.

1840 Oak Ave.
Evanston, IL 60201
(847)866-1840
Fax: (847)866-1808
E-mail: t-parkinson@nwu.com
Website: http://www.ebic.com
Preferred Investment Size: $250,000 to $500,000. Investment Types: Early stages. Industry Preferences: Diversified communication and computer technology, consumer products and services, medical/health, electronics, and publishing. Geographic Preferences: Chicago metropolitan area.

Inroads Capital Partners L.P.

1603 Orrington Ave., Ste. 2050
Evanston, IL 60201-3841
(847)864-2000
Fax: (847)864-9692
Preferred Investment Size: $1,000,000 to $5,000,000. Investment Types: Expansion and later stage. Industry Preferences: Diversified. Geographic Preferences: Entire U.S.

The Cerulean Fund/WGC Enterprises

1701 E. Lake Ave., Ste. 170
Glenview, IL 60025
(847)657-8002
Fax: (847)657-8168
Walter G. Cornett, III, Managing Director
Preferred Investment Size: $5,000,000 minimum. Investment Types: Seed, start-up, leveraged buyout, special situations, control block purchases, and research and development. Industry Preferences: Diversified. Geographic Preferences: Midwest.

Ventana Financial Resources, Inc.

249 Market Sq.
Lake Forest, IL 60045
(847)234-3434
Preferred Investment Size: $5,000,000 minimum. Investment Types: Seed, start-up, first and second stage, research and development, leveraged buyout, and mezzanine. Industry Preferences: Diversified. Geographic Preferences: Midwest, Southeast, and Southwest.

Beecken, Petty & Co.

901 Warrenville Rd., Ste. 205
Lisle, IL 60532
(630)435-0300
Fax: (630)435-0370
E-mail: hep@bpcompany.com
Website: http://www.bpcompany.com
Preferred Investment Size: $2,000,000 to $12,000,000. Investment Types: Early, first, second, and late stage; expansion; management buyouts; private placement; recapitalization. Industry Preferences: Communications, computer related, genetic engineering, medical and health related. G

Allstate Private Equity

3075 Sanders Rd., Ste. G5D
Northbrook, IL 60062-7127
(847)402-8247
Fax: (847)402-0880
Preferred Investment Size: $5,000,000 minimum. Investment Types: Startup, first and second stage, mezzanine, leveraged buyout, and special situations. Industry Preferences: Diversified. Geographic Preferences: Entire U.S.

KB Partners

1101 Skokie Blvd., Ste. 260
Northbrook, IL 60062-2856
(847)714-0444
Fax: (847)714-0445

E-mail: keith@kbpartners.com
Website: http://www.kbpartners.com
Keith Bank, Managing Partner
Preferred Investment Size: $1,000,000 to $5,000,000. Investment Types: Seed, startup, and early, first and second stage. Industry Preferences: Diversified. Geographic Preferences: National.

Transcap Associates Inc.

900 Skokie Blvd., Ste. 210
Northbrook, IL 60062
(847)753-9600
Fax: (847)753-9090
Ira J. Ederson
Preferred Investment Size: $500,000 to $5,000,000. Investment Types: Mezzanine, second stage, and special situation. Industry Preferences: Diversified. Geographic Preferences: Entire U.S.

Graystone Venture Partners, L.L.C./Portage Venture Partners

One Northfield Plaza, Ste. 530
Northfield, IL 60093
(847)446-9460
Fax: (847)446-9470
Website: http://
www.portageventures.com
Mathew B. McCall, Vice President
Preferred Investment Size: $250,000 to $3,000,000. Investment Types: Early stage. Industry Preferences: Diversified communication and computer technology, consumer products and services, genetic engineering, and medical/health. Geographic Preferences: National.

Motorola Inc.

1303 E. Algonquin Rd.
Schaumburg, IL 60196-1065
(847)576-4929
Fax: (847)538-2250
Website: http://www.mot.com/mne
James Burke, New Business Development Manager
Investment Types: Startup, first and second stage. Industry Preferences: Diversified technology. Geographic Preferences: National.

Indiana

Irwin Ventures LLC

500 Washington St.
Columbus, IN 47202
(812)373-1434

Fax: (812)376-1709
Website: http://www.irwinventures.com
Preferred Investment Size: $750,000 to
$1,250,000. Investment Types: Early and
first stage. Industry Preferences: Internet
related and financial services.
Geographic Preferences: Northeast and
Northwest.

Cambridge Venture Partners
4181 East 96th St., Ste. 200
Indianapolis, IN 46240
(317)814-6192
Fax: (317)944-9815
Jean Wojtowicz, President
Preferred Investment Size: $100,000
maximum. Investment Types: Second
stage, mezzanine, and leveraged buyout.
Industry Preferences: No preference.
Geographic Preferences: Midwest, within
200 miles of office.

CID Equity Partners
One American Square, Ste. 2850
Box 82074
Indianapolis, IN 46282
(317)269-2350
Fax: (317)269-2355
Website: http://www.cidequity.com
Chris Gough, Associate
Preferred Investment Size: $1,000,000
minimum. Investment Types: Start-up,
early and first stage, industry rollups,
leveraged buyout, and special situations.
Industry Preferences: Diversified.
Geographic Preferences: Midwest and
Rocky Mountain region.

Gazelle Techventures
6325 Digital Way, Ste. 460
Indianapolis, IN 46278
(317)275-6800
Fax: (317)275-1101
Website: http://www.gazellevc.com
Preferred Investment Size: $2,000,000
maximum. Investment Types: Early and
later stage. Industry Preferences:
Diversified. Geographic Preferences:
Indiana.

Monument Advisors Inc.
Bank One Center/Circle
111 Monument Circle, Ste. 600
Indianapolis, IN 46204-5172
(317)656-5065
Fax: (317)656-5060
Website: http://www.monumentadv.com
Preferred Investment Size: $500,000 to
$7,000,000. Investment Types: Balanced,
leveraged buyout, management buyouts,

and mezzanine. Industry Preferences:
Business services, distribution, and
manufacturing. Geographic Preferences:
Midwest and Southeast.

MWV Capital Partners
201 N. Illinois St., Ste. 300
Indianapolis, IN 46204
(317)237-2323
Fax: (317)237-2325
Website: http://www.mwvcapital.com
Garth Dickey, Managing Director
Preferred Investment Size: $1,000,000 to
$5,000,000. Investment Types: Balanced,
second and later stage. Industry
Preferences: Diversified. Geographic
Preferences: Midwest.

First Source Capital Corp.
100 North Michigan St.
PO Box 1602
South Bend, IN 46601
(219)235-2180
Fax: (219)235-2227
Eugene L. Cavanaugh, Vice President
Preferred Investment Size: $300,000 to
$500,000. Investment Types: Second
stage, mezzanine, leveraged buyout, and
special situations. Industry Preferences:
Diversified. Geographic Preferences:
Midwest.

Iowa

Allsop Venture Partners
118 Third Ave. SE, Ste. 837
Cedar Rapids, IA 52401
(319)368-6675
Fax: (319)363-9515
Preferred Investment Size: $500,000
minimum. Investment Types: First stage,
industry rollups, leveraged buyout,
mezzanine, second stage, and special
situation. Industry Preferences:
Diversified. Geographic Preferences:
Entire U.S.

**InvestAmerica Investment Advisors,
Inc.**
101 2nd St. SE, Ste. 800
Cedar Rapids, IA 52401
(319)363-8249
Fax: (319)363-9683
Kevin F. Mullane, Vice President
Preferred Investment Size: $500,000 to
$1,000,000. Investment Types: First and
second stage, leveraged buyout, and
special situations. Industry Preferences:
Diversified. Geographic Preferences:
Entire U.S.

Pappajohn Capital Resources
2116 Financial Center
Des Moines, IA 50309
(515)244-5746
Fax: (515)244-2346
Website: http://www.pappajohn.com
Joe Dunham, President
Preferred Investment Size: $500,000 to
$1,000,000. Investment Policies: Equity.
Investment Types: Seed, start-up, first
and second stage, leveraged buyout, and
special situations. Industry Preferences:
Diversified communication and
computer technology, electronics, genetic
engineerin

**Berthel Fisher & Company Planning
Inc.**
701 Tama St.
PO Box 609
Marion, IA 52302
(319)497-5700
Fax: (319)497-4244
Investment Types: Later stage. Industry
Preferences: Diversified. Geographic
Preferences: Midwest.

Kansas

Enterprise Merchant Bank
7400 West 110th St., Ste. 560
Overland Park, KS 66210
(913)327-8500
Fax: (913)327-8505
Preferred Investment Size: $1,000,000
minimum. Investment Types: Second
stage, leveraged buyout, mezzanine, and
special situations. Geographic
Preferences: Midwest.

**Kansas Venture Capital, Inc. (Overland
Park)**
6700 Antioch Plz., Ste. 460
Overland Park, KS 66204
(913)262-7117
Fax: (913)262-3509
E-mail: jdalton@kvci.com
John S. Dalton, President
Preferred Investment Size: $1,000,000
minimum. Investment Types: First and
second stage, mezzanine, and leveraged
buyout. Industry Preferences:
Diversified. Geographic Preferences:
Midwest.

Child Health Investment Corp.
6803 W. 64th St., Ste. 208
Shawnee Mission, KS 66202
(913)262-1436
Fax: (913)262-1575

Website: http://www.chca.com
Investment Types: Balanced, early stage, first stage, seed, and start-up. Industry Preferences: Diversified. Geographic Preferences: Entire U.S.

Kansas Technology Enterprise Corp.

214 SW 6th, 1st Fl.
Topeka, KS 66603-3719
(785)296-5272
Fax: (785)296-1160
E-mail: ktec@ktec.com
Website: http://www.ktec.com
Preferred Investment Size: $300,000.
Investment Types: Seed, start-up, research and development. Industry Preferences: Diversified communication and computer technology, electronics, genetic engineering, and healthcare. Geographic Preferences: Within two hours of office.

Kentucky

Kentucky Highlands Investment Corp.

362 Old Whitley Rd.
London, KY 40741
(606)864-5175
Fax: (606)864-5194
Website: http://www.khic.org
Investment Types: Second stage, special situation, and start-up. Industry Preferences: Manufacturing. Geographic Preferences: Kentucky.

Chrysalis Ventures, L.L.C.

1850 National City Tower
Louisville, KY 40202
(502)583-7644
Fax: (502)583-7648
E-mail: bobsany@chrysalisventures.com
Website: http://
www.chrysalisventures.com
Preferred Investment Size: $3,000,000 to $5,000,000. Investment Types: Start-up, first and second stage. Industry Preferences: Diversified communication and computer technology. Geographic Preferences: Southeast and Midwest.

Humana Venture Capital

500 West Main St.
Louisville, KY 40202
(502)580-3922
Fax: (502)580-2051
E-mail: gemont@humana.com
George Emont, Director
Preferred Investment Size: $10,000,000 minimum. Investment Types: Seed, start-up, first and second stage, leveraged

buyout, mezzanine, and research and development. Industry Preferences: Medical/health related, Internet and computer related, and biotechnology. Geographic Preferences:

Summit Capital Group, Inc.

6510 Glenridge Park Pl., Ste. 8
Louisville, KY 40222
(502)332-2700
Preferred Investment Size: $10,000,000 to $40,000,000. Investment Types: Control-block purchases, expansion, leveraged and management buyouts. Industry Preferences: Diversified. Geographic Preferences: Southeast and Southwest.

Louisiana

Bank One Equity Investors, Inc.

451 Florida St.
Baton Rouge, LA 70801
(504)332-4421
Fax: (504)332-7377
Michael P. Kriby
Preferred Investment Size: $8,000,000 minimum. Investment Types: First and second stage, mezzanine, leveraged buyout, and special situations. Industry Preferences: Diversified. Geographic Preferences: Southeast and Southwest.

Advantage Capital Partners

LLE Tower
909 Poydras St., Ste. 2230
New Orleans, LA 70112
(504)522-4850
Fax: (504)522-4950
Website: http://www.advantagecap.com
Steven T. Stull, President
Preferred Investment Size: $1,000,000 to $10,000,000. Investment Types: Seed, start-up, early and second stage, and mezzanine. Industry Preferences: Diversified. Geographic Preferences: North and Southeast, and Midwest.

Maine

CEI Ventures / Coastal Ventures LP

2 Portland Fish Pier, Ste. 201
Portland, ME 04101
(207)772-5356
Fax: (207)772-5503
Website: http://www.ceiventures.com
Investment Types: No preference. Industry Preferences: Diversified. Geographic Preferences: Entire U.S.

Commwealth Bioventures, Inc.

4 Milk St.
Portland, ME 04101
(207)780-0904
Fax: (207)780-0913
E-mail: cbi4milk@aol.com
Investment Types: Seed. Industry Preferences: Biotechnology based start-ups. Geographic Preferences: No preference.

Maryland

Annapolis Ventures LLC

151 West St., Ste. 302
Annapolis, MD 21401
(443)482-9555
Fax: (443)482-9565
Website: http://
www.annapolisventures.com
Preferred Investment Size: $2,000,000 to $5,000,000. Investment Types: Later stage. Industry Preferences: Diversified. Geographic Preferences: Midwest, Northeast, and Southeast.

Delmag Ventures

220 Wardour Dr.
Annapolis, MD 21401
(410)267-8196
Fax: (410)267-8017
Website: http://
www.delmagventures.com
Preferred Investment Size: $250,000 to $1,000,000. Investment Types: Early stage and seed. Industry Preferences: Diversified. Geographic Preferences: Mid Atlantic.

Abell Venture Fund

111 S. Calvert St., Ste. 2300
Baltimore, MD 21202
(410)547-1300
Fax: (410)539-6579
Website: http://www.abell.org
Investment Types: Early stage, expansion, first and second stage, and private placement. Industry Preferences: Internet related, electronics, communications, and medical/health related. Geographic Preferences: Maryland.

ABS Ventures (Baltimore)

1 South St., Ste. 2150
Baltimore, MD 21202
(410)895-3895
Fax: (410)895-3899
Website: http://www.absventures.com
Preferred Investment Size: $500,000 maximum. Investment Types: Startup,

first and second stage, and mezzanine. Industry Preferences: Communications, computer related, genetic engineering, and medical/health related. Geographic Preferences: Entire U.S.

Anthem Capital, L.P.
16 S. Calvert St., Ste. 800
Baltimore, MD 21202-1305
(410)625-1510
Fax: (410)625-1735
Website: http://www.anthemcapital.com
Preferred Investment Size: $500,000 to $1,000,000. Investment Types: Early and later stage, mezzanine, and special situations. Industry Preferences: Diversified. Geographic Preferences: Middle Atlantic.

Catalyst Ventures
1119 St. Paul St.
Baltimore, MD 21202
(410)244-0123
Fax: (410)752-7721
Preferred Investment Size: $500,000 maximum. Investment Policies: Equity. Investment Types: Research and development, and early stage. Industry Preferences: Data communications, biotechnology, and medical related. Geographic Preferences: Middle Atlantic.

Maryland Venture Capital Trust
217 E. Redwood St., Ste. 2200
Baltimore, MD 21202
(410)767-6361
Fax: (410)333-6931
E-mail: rblank@mdbusiness.state.md.us
Preferred Investment Size: $1,000,000 to $5,000,000. Investment Types: Seed, startup, first and second stage. Industry Preferences: Diversified. Geographic Preferences: Maryland.

New Enterprise Associates (Baltimore)
1119 St. Paul St.
Baltimore, MD 21202
(410)244-0115
Fax: (410)752-7721
Website: http://www.nea.com
Frank A. Bonsal, Jr., Founding Partner
Preferred Investment Size: $100,000 minimum. Investment Types: Seed, startup, first and second stage, and mezzanine. Industry Preferences: Diversified. Geographic Preferences: Entire U.S.

T. Rowe Price Threshold Partnerships
100 E. Pratt St., 8th Fl.
Baltimore, MD 21202

(410)345-2000
Fax: (410)345-2800
Terral Jordan
Preferred Investment Size: $3,000,000 to $5,000,000. Investment Types: Mezzanine and special situations. Industry Preferences: Diversified. Geographic Preferences: Entire U.S.

Spring Capital Partners
16 W. Madison St.
Baltimore, MD 21201
(410)685-8000
Fax: (410)727-1436
E-mail: mailbox@springcap.com
Robert M. Stewart
Preferred Investment Size: $2,000,000 minimum. Investment Types: Second stage, acquisition, industry rollups, mezzanine, and leveraged buyout. Industry Preferences: Diversified. Geographic Preferences: Mid-Atlantic.

Arete Corporation
3 Bethesda Metro Ctr., Ste. 770
Bethesda, MD 20814
(301)657-6268
Fax: (301)657-6254
Website: http://www.arete-microgen.com
Jill Wilmoth
Investment Types: Seed, start-up, first stage, and research and development. Industry Preferences: Alternative energy. Geographic Preferences: Entire U.S. and Canada.

Embryon Capital
7903 Sleaford Place
Bethesda, MD 20814
(301)656-6837
Fax: (301)656-8056
Preferred Investment Size: $300,000 to $1,000,000. Investment Types: Diversified. Industry Preferences: Diversified. Geographic Preferences: Entire U.S.

Potomac Ventures
7920 Norfolk Ave., Ste. 1100
Bethesda, MD 20814
(301)215-9240
Website: http://www.potomacventures.com
Preferred Investment Size: $400,000 to $1,000,000. Investment Types: Early stage. Industry Preferences: Internet related. Geographic Preferences: Mid Atlantic.

Toucan Capital Corp.
3 Bethesda Metro Center, Ste. 700
Bethesda, MD 20814

(301)961-1970
Fax: (301)961-1969
Website: http://www.toucancapital.com
Preferred Investment Size: $1,000,000 to $1,000,000. Investment Types: Early stage, seed, and start-up. Industry Preferences: Diversified. Geographic Preferences: Entire U.S.

Kinetic Ventures LLC
2 Wisconsin Cir., Ste. 620
Chevy Chase, MD 20815
(301)652-8066
Fax: (301)652-8310
Website: http://www.kineticventures.com
Investment Types: Startup, first stage, second stage, and leveraged buyout. Industry Preferences: Diversified technology. Geographic Preferences: National.

Boulder Ventures Ltd.
4750 Owings Mills Blvd.
Owings Mills, MD 21117
(410)998-3114
Fax: (410)356-5492
Website: http://www.boulderventures.com
Preferred Investment Size: $2,000,000 to $5,000,000. Investment Types: Early stage, expansion, first stage, and start-up. Industry Preferences: Diversified. Geographic Preferences: Entire U.S.

Grotech Capital Group
9690 Deereco Rd., Ste. 800
Timonium, MD 21093
(410)560-2000
Fax: (410)560-1910
Website: http://www.grotech.com
Frank A. Adams, President and CEO
Preferred Investment Size: $1,000,000 to $5,000,000. Investment Types: First and second stage, start-up, mezzanine, leveraged buyouts, and special situations. Industry Preferences: Diversified. Geographic Preferences: Southeast and Middle Atlantic.

Massachusetts

Adams, Harkness & Hill, Inc.
60 State St.
Boston, MA 02109
(617)371-3900
Tim McMahan, Managing Director
Preferred Investment Size: $1,000,000 minimum. Investment Types: Second stage, balanced, mezzanine, and special

situation. Industry Preferences: Computer, consumer, electronics, business services, industrial products and equipment, and medical. Geographic Preferences: Northeast.

Advent International

75 State St., 29th Fl.
Boston, MA 02109
(617)951-9400
Fax: (617)951-0566
Website: http://
www.adventinernational.com
Will Schmidt, Managing Director
Preferred Investment Size: $1,000,000 minimum. Investment Types: Seed, first and second stage, mezzanine, leveraged buyout, special situations, research and development, and acquisitions. Industry Preferences: Diversified. Geographic Preferences: Entire U.S. and Canada.

American Research and Development

30 Federal St.
Boston, MA 02110-2508
(617)423-7500
Fax: (617)423-9655
Maureen A. White, Administrative Manager
Preferred Investment Size: $100,000 minimum. Investment Types: Seed, startup, first and second stage. Industry Preferences: Diversified technology. Geographic Preferences: Northeast.

Ascent Venture Partners

255 State St., 5th Fl.
Boston, MA 02109
(617)270-9400
Fax: (617)270-9401
E-mail: info@ascentvp.com
Website: http://www.ascentvp.com
Leigh E. Michl, Managing Director
Investment Types: First stage and acquisition. Industry Preferences: Diversified. Geographic Preferences: Northeast.

Atlas Venture

222 Berkeley St.
Boston, MA 02116
(617)488-2200
Fax: (617)859-9292
Website: http://www.atlasventure.com
Preferred Investment Size: $500,000 to $20,000,000. Investment Types: Seed, start-up, research and development, first and second stage, mezzanine, and balanced. Industry Preferences: Communications, computer, genetic

engineering, electronics, medical and health related. Geographic Pr

Axxon Capital

28 State St., 37th Fl.
Boston, MA 02109
(617)722-0980
Fax: (617)557-6014
Website: http://www.axxoncapital.com
Preferred Investment Size: $300,000 to $2,500,000. Investment Types: Balanced. Industry Preferences: Communications and media. Geographic Preferences: Northeast.

BancBoston Capital/BancBoston Ventures

175 Federal St., 10th Fl.
Boston, MA 02110
(617)434-2509
Fax: (617)434-6175
Website: http://
www.bancbostoncapital.com
Frederick M. Fritz, President
Preferred Investment Size: $1,000,000 to $100,000,000. Investment Types: Seed, early stage, acquisition, recaps, later stage, management buyouts, expansion, and mezzanine. Industry Preferences: Diversified. Geographic Preferences: Entire U.S. and Eastern Canada.

Boston Capital Ventures

Old City Hall
45 School St.
Boston, MA 02108
(617)227-6550
Fax: (617)227-3847
E-mail: info@bcv.com
Website: http://www.bcv.com
Alexander Wilmerding
Preferred Investment Size: $250,000 to $8,000,000. Investment Types: Startup, first and second stage, recaps, and leveraged buyouts. Industry Preferences: Diversified. Geographic Preferences: Entire U.S.

Boston Financial & Equity Corp.

20 Overland St.
PO Box 15071
Boston, MA 02215
(617)267-2900
Fax: (617)437-7601
E-mail: debbie@bfec.com
Deborah J. Monosson, Senior Vice President
Preferred Investment Size: $500,000 to $1,000,000. Investment Types: Seed, start-up, first and second stage, leveraged

buyout, mezzanine, and research and development. Industry Preferences: Diversified. Geographic Preferences: National.

Boston Millennia Partners

30 Rowes Wharf
Boston, MA 02110
(617)428-5150
Fax: (617)428-5160
Website: http://
www.millenniapartners.com
Dana Callow, Managing General Partner
Preferred Investment Size: $5,000,000 to $25,000,000. Investment Policies: Equity. Investment Types: First and second stage, start-up, leveraged buyout, and mezzanine. Industry Preferences: Communication, computer related, consumer services, electronics, genetic engineering, medical,

Bristol Investment Trust

842A Beacon St.
Boston, MA 02215-3199
(617)566-5212
Fax: (617)267-0932
E-mail: bernardberkman@prodigy.net
Preferred Investment Size: $100,000 minimum. Investment Policies: Equity. Investment Types: First and second stage, and mezzanine. Industry Preferences: Restaurants, retailing, consumer distribution, medical/health, and real estate. Geographic Preferences: Northeast.

Brook Venture Management LLC

50 Federal St., 5th Fl.
Boston, MA 02110
(617)451-8989
Fax: (617)451-2369
Website: http://www.brookventure.com
Preferred Investment Size: $500,000 to $2,500,000. Investment Types: Early and first stage. Industry Preferences: Diversified. Geographic Preferences: Northeast.

Burr, Egan, Deleage, and Co. (Boston)

200 Clarendon St., Ste. 3800
Boston, MA 02116
(617)262-7770
Fax: (617)262-9779
Preferred Investment Size: $2,000,000. Investment Types: No preference. Industry Preferences: Communications, computer, and medical/health related. Geographic Preferences: Entire U.S.

Cambridge/Samsung Partners
One Exeter Plaza
Ninth Fl.
Boston, MA 02116
(617)262-4440
Fax: (617)262-5562
Aashish Kalra, Associate
Preferred Investment Size: $100,000
minimum. Investment Policies: Equity.
Investment Types: Early stage. Industry
Preferences: Diversified. Geographic
Preferences: National.

Chestnut Street Partners, Inc.
75 State St., Ste. 2500
Boston, MA 02109
(617)345-7220
Fax: (617)345-7201
E-mail: chestnut@chestnutp.com
Drew Zalkind, Senior Vice President
Preferred Investment Size: $100,000 to
$1,000,000. Investment Types: Seed,
research and development, startup, and
first stage. Industry Preferences: Diversified.
Geographic Preferences: No preference.

Claflin Capital Management, Inc.
10 Liberty Sq., Ste. 300
Boston, MA 02109
(617)426-6505
Fax: (617)482-0016
Website: http://www.claflincapital.com
William Wilcoxson, General Partner
Preferred Investment Size: $100,000
minimum. Investment Types: Seed,
startup, and first stage. Industry
Preferences: Diversified. Geographic
Preferences: Northeast.

Copley Venture Partners
99 Summer St., Ste. 1720
Boston, MA 02110
(617)737-1253
Fax: (617)439-0699
Preferred Investment Size: $1,000,000
minimum. Investment Types: First and
second stage, and start-up. Industry
Preferences: Diversified. Geographic
Preferences: No preference.

**Corning Capital/Corning Technology
Ventures**
121 High Street, Ste. 400
Boston, MA 02110
(617)338-2656
Fax: (617)261-3864
Website: http://
www.corningventures.com
Preferred Investment Size: $100,000 to
$500,000. Investment Policies: Equity.

Investment Types: Early stage. Industry
Preferences: Diversified technology.
Geographic Preferences: Northeast.

Downer & Co.
211 Congress St.
Boston, MA 02110
(617)482-6200
Fax: (617)482-6201
E-mail: cdowner@downer.com
Website: http://www.downer.com
Charles W. Downer
Preferred Investment Size: $300,000 to
$500,000. Investment Types: Start-up,
first and second stage, and mezzanine.
Industry Preferences: Diversified.
Geographic Preferences: Northeastern
U.S. and Canada.

Fidelity Ventures
82 Devonshire St.
Boston, MA 02109
(617)563-6370
Fax: (617)476-9023
Website: http://
www.fidelityventures.com
Neal Yanofsky, Vice President
Preferred Investment Size: $1,000,000 to
$10,000,000. Investment Types: Startup,
first and second stage, leveraged buyout,
and special situations. Industry
Preferences: Diversified. Geographic
Preferences: Northeast.

Greylock Management Corp. (Boston)
1 Federal St.
Boston, MA 02110-2065
(617)423-5525
Fax: (617)482-0059
Chris Surowiec
Preferred Investment Size: $250,000
minimum. Investment Types: Seed,
startup, first and early stage, and expansion.
Industry Preferences: Diversified.
Geographic Preferences: No preference.

Gryphon Ventures
222 Berkeley St., Ste.1600
Boston, MA 02116
(617)267-9191
Fax: (617)267-4293
E-mail: all@gryphoninc.com
Andrew J. Atkinson, Vice President
Preferred Investment Size: $1,000,000
minimum. Investment Types: Startup,
first stage, second stage. Industry
Preferences: Energy/natural resources,
genetic engineering, and industrial
products and equipment. Geographic
Preferences: National.

Halpern, Denny & Co.
500 Boylston St.
Boston, MA 02116
(617)536-6602
Fax: (617)536-8535
David P. Malm, Partner
Preferred Investment Size: $5,000,000
to $40,000,000. Investment Types:
First stage, second stage, control-black
purchases, and leveraged buyouts.
Industry Preferences: Consumer
related, Internet and computer
related, communications, industrial/
energy, and medical/health. Geographic

Harbourvest Partners, LLC
1 Financial Center, 44th Fl.
Boston, MA 02111
(617)348-3707
Fax: (617)350-0305
Website: http://www.hvpllc.com
Kevin Delbridge, Managing Partner
Preferred Investment Size: $5,000,000
minimum. Investment Types: All types.
Industry Preferences: Diversified.
Geographic Preferences: No preference.

Highland Capital Partners
2 International Pl.
Boston, MA 02110
(617)981-1500
Fax: (617)531-1550
E-mail: info@hcp.com
Website: http://www.hcp.com
Keith Benjamin, General Partner
Preferred Investment Size: $500,000 to
$5,000,000. Investment Types: Seed,
startup, and early, first and second stage.
Industry Preferences: Communications,
computer and Internet related, genetic
engineering, and medical/health related.
Geographic Preferences: Entire U.S. and
Canada.

Lee Munder Venture Partners
John Hancock Tower T-53
200 Clarendon St.
Boston, MA 02103
(617)380-5600
Fax: (617)380-5601
Website: http://www.leemunder.com
Investment Types: Early, first, second,
and later stage; expansion; mezzanine;
seed; start-up; and special situation.
Industry Preferences: Diversified.
Geographic Preferences: East Coast, Mid
Atlantic, Northeast, and Southeast.

M/C Venture Partners
75 State St., Ste. 2500
Boston, MA 02109

(617)345-7200
Fax: (617)345-7201
Website: http://
www.mcventurepartners.com
Matthew J. Rubins
Preferred Investment Size: $5,000,000 to
$20,000,000. Investment Types: Early
stage. Industry Preferences:
Communications, computer software
and services, Internet related.
Geographic Preferences: Entire U.S. and
Canada.

Massachusetts Capital Resources Co.
420 Boylston St.
Boston, MA 02116
(617)536-3900
Fax: (617)536-7930
William J. Torpey, Jr., President
Preferred Investment Size: $500,000 to
$1,000,000. Investment Policies: Equity.
Investment Types: Second stage,
leveraged buyout, and mezzanine.
Industry Preferences: No preference.
Geographic Preferences: Northeast.

**Massachusetts Technology
Development Corp. (MTDC)**
148 State St.
Boston, MA 02109
(617)723-4920
Fax: (617)723-5983
E-mail: jhodgman@mtdc.com
Website: http://www.mtdc.com
John F. Hodgman, President
Preferred Investment Size: $200,000 to
$1,000,000. Investment Types: Early,
seed, and startup. Industry Preferences:
Diversified. Geographic Preferences:
Massachusetts.

New England Partners
One Boston Place, Ste. 2100
Boston, MA 02108
(617)624-8400
Fax: (617)624-8999
Website: http://www.nepartners.com
Christopher P. Young
Preferred Investment Size: $1,000,000 to
$5,000,000. Investment Types: Balanced,
early, and first and second stage. Industry
Preferences: Diversified. Geographic
Preferences: Entire U.S.

North Hill Ventures
Ten Post Office Square
11th Fl.
Boston, MA 02109
(617)788-2112
Fax: (617)788-2152

Website: http://
www.northhillventures.com
Preferred Investment Size: $1,500,000 to
$7,000,000. Investment Types: Balanced,
expansion, and later and second stage.
Industry Preferences: Communications,
computer software, Internet related,
consumer and retail related, business
services, and financial services.
Geographic Prefer

OneLiberty Ventures
150 Cambridge Park Dr.
Boston, MA 02140
(617)492-7280
Fax: (617)492-7290
Website: http://www.oneliberty.com
Stephen J. McCullen, General Partner
Preferred Investment Size: $1,000,000 to
$8,000,000. Investment Policies: Equity.
Investment Types: Early and late stage.
Industry Preferences: Diversified
technology. Geographic Preferences:
Northeast.

Schroder Ventures
Life Sciences
60 State St., Ste. 3650
Boston, MA 02109
(617)367-8100
Fax: (617)367-1590
Website: http://
www.shroderventures.com
Preferred Investment Size: $250,000
minimum. Investment Types: Balanced,
first stage, leveraged buyout, mezzanine,
second stage, special situation, and
start-up. Industry Preferences:
Diversified. Geographic Preferences:
Entire U.S. and Canada.

Shawmut Capital Partners
75 Federal St., 18th Fl.
Boston, MA 02110
(617)368-4900
Fax: (617)368-4910
Website: http://
www.shawmutcapital.com
Daniel Doyle, Managing Director
Preferred Investment Size: $5,000,000
minimum. Investment Types: Startup,
first stage, second stage, mezzanine,
leveraged buyout, and special situations.
Industry Preferences: Financial services
and applications. Geographic
Preferences: Entire U.S. and Canada.

Solstice Capital LLC
15 Broad St., 3rd Fl.
Boston, MA 02109

(617)523-7733
Fax: (617)523-5827
E-mail: solticecapital@solcap.com
Henry Newman, Partner
Preferred Investment Size: $250,000 to
$1,000,000. Investment Types: Early and
seed. Industry Preferences: Diversified.
Geographic Preferences: Northeast, Rocky
Mountain, Southwest, West Coast.

Spectrum Equity Investors
One International Pl., 29th Fl.
Boston, MA 02110
(617)464-4600
Fax: (617)464-4601
Website: http://
www.spectrumequity.com
William Collatos, Managing General
Partner
Preferred Investment Size: $5,000,000
minimum. Investment Types: Balanced.
Industry Preferences: Communications
and computer related. Geographic
Preferences: U.S. and Canada.

Spray Venture Partners
One Walnut St.
Boston, MA 02108
(617)305-4140
Fax: (617)305-4144
Website: http://www.sprayventure.com
Preferred Investment Size: $50,000 to
$4,000,000. Investment Policies: Equity.
Investment Types: Seed, start-up, first
and second stage, and research and
development. Industry Preferences:
Medical and health related, and genetic
engineering. Geographic Preferences:
National.

The Still River Fund
100 Federal St., 29th Fl.
Boston, MA 02110
(617)348-2327
Fax: (617)348-2371
Website: http://www.stillriverfund.com
Preferred Investment Size: $300,000 to
$4,000,000. Investment Types: Early
stage, expansion, first and second stage,
seed, and start-up. Industry Preferences:
Diversified. Geographic Preferences:
Entire U.S.

Summit Partners
600 Atlantic Ave., Ste. 2800
Boston, MA 02210-2227
(617)824-1000
Fax: (617)824-1159
Website: http://
www.summitpartners.com

Christopher W. Sheeline
Preferred Investment Size: $1,500,000 minimum. Investment Types: First and second stage, mezzanine, leveraged buyout, special situations, and control block purchases. Industry Preferences: Diversified. Geographic Preferences: Entire U.S. and Canada.

TA Associates, Inc. (Boston)
High Street Tower
125 High St., Ste. 2500
Boston, MA 02110
(617)574-6700
Fax: (617)574-6728
Website: http://www.ta.com
Brian Conway, Managing Director
Preferred Investment Size: $60,000,000 maximum. Investment Types: Leveraged buyout, special situations, control block purchases. Industry Preferences: Diversified. Geographic Preferences: No preference.

TVM Techno Venture Management
101 Arch St., Ste. 1950
Boston, MA 02110
(617)345-9320
Fax: (617)345-9377
E-mail: info@tvmvc.com
Website: http://www.tvmvc.com
Helmut Schuehsler, Partner
Investment Types: Seed, start-up, first and early stage. Industry Preferences: Diversified. Geographic Preferences: Entire U.S.

UNC Ventures
64 Burough St.
Boston, MA 02130-4017
(617)482-7070
Fax: (617)522-2176
Preferred Investment Size: $500,000 to $1,000,000. Investment Types: Leveraged buyout, mezzanine, and second stage. Industry Preferences: Radio and television broadcasting, environmental related, and financial services. Geographic Preferences: Entire U.S.

Venture Investment Management Company (VIMAC)
177 Milk St.
Boston, MA 02190-3410
(617)292-3300
Fax: (617)292-7979
E-mail: bzeisig@vimac.com
Website: http://www.vimac.com
Preferred Investment Size: $1,000,000 to $7,000,000. Investment Types: Seed,

startup, first and second stage. Industry Preferences: Diversified technology. Geographic Preferences: Northeast U.S. and Eastern Canada.

MDT Advisers, Inc.
125 Cambridge Park Dr.
Cambridge, MA 02140-2314
(617)234-2200
Fax: (617)234-2210
Website: http://www.mdtai.com
Michael E.A. O'Malley
Preferred Investment Size: $500,000 to $5,000,000. Investment Types: Early stage and expansion. Industry Preferences: Diversified. Geographic Preferences: Northeast.

TTC Ventures
One Main St., 6th Fl.
Cambridge, MA 02142
(617)528-3137
Fax: (617)577-1715
E-mail: info@ttcventures.com
Investment Types: Seed, startup, first stage, second stage, and mezzanine. Industry Preferences: Computer related. Geographic Preferences: National.

Zero Stage Capital Co. Inc.
101 Main St., 17th Fl.
Cambridge, MA 02142
(617)876-5355
Fax: (617)876-1248
Website: http://www.zerostage.com
Paul Kelley, President
Preferred Investment Size: $10,000 to $15,000,000. Investment Types: Early and later stage. Industry Preferences: Diversified technology. Geographic Preferences: Entire U.S.

Atlantic Capital
164 Cushing Hwy.
Cohasset, MA 02025
(617)383-9449
Fax: (617)383-6040
E-mail: info@atlanticcap.com
Website: http://www.atlanticcap.com
Preferred Investment Size: $300,000 to $500,000. Investment Types: Startup and first stage. Industry Preferences: Diversified. Geographic Preferences: National.

Seacoast Capital Partners
55 Ferncroft Rd.
Danvers, MA 01923
(978)750-1300
Fax: (978)750-1301
E-mail: gdeli@seacoastcapital.com

Website: http://www.seacoastcapital.com
Gregory A. Hulecki
Preferred Investment Size: $3,000,000 minimum. Investment Policies: Loans and equity investments. Investment Types: Second stage, industry rollups, leveraged buyout, mezzanine, and special situations. Industry Preferences: Diversified. Geographic Preferences: National.

Sage Management Group
44 South Street
PO Box 2026
East Dennis, MA 02641
(508)385-7172
Fax: (508)385-7272
E-mail: sagemgt@capecod.net
Charles Bauer
Preferred Investment Size: $500,000 to $1,000,000. Investment Policies: Equity. Investment Types: First and second stage, leveraged buyout, mezzanine, and special situations. Industry Preferences: Diversified technology. Geographic Preferences: National.

Applied Technology
1 Cranberry Hill
Lexington, MA 02421-7397
(617)862-8622
Fax: (617)862-8367
Ellie McCormack, Analyst
Preferred Investment Size: $100,000 to $2,000,000. Investment Types: Seed, startup, first and second stage, leveraged buyout, and research and development. Industry Preferences: Diversified. Geographic Preferences: Entire U.S.

Royalty Capital Management
5 Downing Rd.
Lexington, MA 02421-6918
(781)861-8490
Preferred Investment Size: $100,000 to $300,000. Investment Types: Startup, first stage, second stage, leveraged buyout, and special situations. Industry Preferences: Diversified. Geographic Preferences: Northeast.

Argo Global Capital
210 Broadway, Ste. 101
Lynnfield, MA 01940
(781)592-5250
Fax: (781)592-5230
Website: http://www.gsmcapital.com
Investment Types: Balanced and expansion. Industry Preferences: Communications, computer, and

Internet related. Geographic Preferences: No preference.

Industry Ventures
6 Bayne Lane
Newburyport, MA 01950
(978)499-7606
Fax: (978)499-0686
Website: http://
www.industryventures.com
Preferred Investment Size: $250,000 to $2,000,000. Investment Types: Early, first, and second stage; seed, start-up. Industry Preferences: Wireless communications, computer software, Internet related, retail, and media. Geographic Preferences: Mid Atlantic, Northeast, West Coast.

Softbank Capital Partners
10 Langley Rd., Ste. 202
Newton Center, MA 02459
(617)928-9300
Fax: (617)928-9305
E-mail: clax@bvc.com
Gary Rieschel
Investment Types: Seed, startup, first stage, second stage, mezzanine, leveraged buyout, and special situations. Industry Preferences: Communications and Internet. Geographic Preferences: Entire U.S. and Canada.

Advanced Technology Ventures (Boston)
281 Winter St., Ste. 350
Waltham, MA 02451
(781)290-0707
Fax: (781)684-0045
E-mail: info@atvcapital.com
Website: http://www.atvcapital.com
Preferred Investment Size: $15,000,000 to $35,000,000. Investment Types: Startup, first stage, second stage, and balanced. Industry Preferences: Diversified. Geographic Preferences: No preference.

Castile Ventures
890 Winter St., Ste. 140
Waltham, MA 02451
(781)890-0060
Fax: (781)890-0065
Website: http://www.castileventures.com
Preferred Investment Size: $100,000 to $15,000,000. Investment Types: Early, first, and second stage; seed; and start-up. Industry Preferences: Communications and media, and Internet related. Geographic Preferences: Mid Atlantic, Northeast, and Southeast.

Charles River Ventures
1000 Winter St., Ste. 3300
Waltham, MA 02451
(781)487-7060
Fax: (781)487-7065
Website: http://www.crv.com
Richard M. Burnes, Jr., General Partner
Preferred Investment Size: $1,000,000 to $20,000,000. Investment Types: Seed, startup, first and second stage. Industry Preferences: Diversified. Geographic Preferences: No preference.

Comdisco Venture Group (Waltham)
Totton Pond Office Center
400-1 Totten Pond Rd.
Waltham, MA 02451
(617)672-0250
Fax: (617)398-8099
Preferred Investment Size: $300,000 to $20,000,000. Investment Types: Seed, startup, first and second stage. Industry Preferences: Diversified. Geographic Preferences: National.

Marconi Ventures
890 Winter St., Ste. 310
Waltham, MA 02451
(781)839-7177
Fax: (781)522-7477
Website: http://www.marconi.com
Preferred Investment Size: $1,000,000 to $10,000,000. Investment Types: Balanced; first, second, and later stage; and start-up. Industry Preferences: Diversified. Geographic Preferences: U.S. and Canada.

Matrix Partners
Bay Colony Corporate Center
1000 Winter St., Ste.4500
Waltham, MA 02451
(781)890-2244
Fax: (781)890-2288
Website: http://www.matrixpartners.com
Andrew Marcuvitz, General Partner
Preferred Investment Size: $500,000 to $1,000,000. Investment Types: Startup, first and second stage, and leveraged buyout. Industry Preferences: Diversified. Geographic Preferences: Entire U.S.

North Bridge Venture Partners
950 Winter St. Ste. 4600
Waltham, MA 02451
(781)290-0004
Fax: (781)290-0999
E-mail: eta@nbvp.com
Preferred Investment Size: $2,000,000 to $3,000,000. Investment Types: Seed,

research and development, startup, first and second stage. Industry Preferences: Communications, computer related, medical/health, and electronics. Geographic Preferences: Entire U.S. and Canada.

Polaris Venture Partners
Bay Colony Corporate Ctr.
1000 Winter St., Ste. 3500
Waltham, MA 02451
(781)290-0770
Fax: (781)290-0880
E-mail: partners@polarisventures.com
Website: http://
www.polarisventures.com
Michael Hirschland
Preferred Investment Size: $250,000 to $15,000,000. Investment Types: Seed, startup, first and second stages. Industry Preferences: Information technology, medical and health related. Geographic Preferences: National.

Seaflower Ventures
Bay Colony Corporate Ctr.
1000 Winter St. Ste. 1000
Waltham, MA 02451
(781)466-9552
Fax: (781)466-9553
E-mail: moot@seaflower.com
Website: http://www.seaflower.com
Alexander Moot, Partner
Investment Types: Seed, research and development, startup, first and second stage, recaps, and strategic alliances. Industry Preferences: Diversified technology. Geographic Preferences: Eastern U.S. and Midwest.

Ampersand Ventures
55 William St., Ste. 240
Wellesley, MA 02481
(617)239-0700
Fax: (617)239-0824
E-mail: info@ampersandventures.com
Website: http://
www.ampersandventures.com
Paul C. Zigman, Partner
Preferred Investment Size: $5,000,000 to $15,000,000. Investment Types: All types. Industry Preferences: Diversified. Geographic Preferences: No preference.

Battery Ventures (Boston)
20 William St., Ste. 200
Wellesley, MA 02481
(781)577-1000

Fax: (781)577-1001
Website: http://www.battery.com
David A. Hartwig
Preferred Investment Size: $3,000,000 to $35,000,000. Investment Types: Seed, startup, first and second stage, mezzanine, and leveraged buyout. Industry Preferences: Communications, computer, computer and communications distribution. Geographic Preferences: No preference.

Commonwealth Capital Ventures, L.P.
20 William St., Ste.225
Wellesley, MA 02481
(781)237-7373
Fax: (781)235-8627
Website: http://www.ccvlp.com
Preferred Investment Size: $500,000 to $5,000,000. Investment Policies: Equity. Investment Types: Seed, start-up, first stage, leveraged buyout, mezzanine, and special situation. Industry Preferences: Diversified communication and computer technology, consumer products and services,

Fowler, Anthony & Company
20 Walnut St.
Wellesley, MA 02481
(781)237-4201
Fax: (781)237-7718
Preferred Investment Size: $4,000,000 to $5,000,000. Investment Types: All types. Industry Preferences: Diversified. Geographic Preferences: Entire U.S. and Canada.

Gemini Investors
20 William St.
Wellesley, MA 02481
(781)237-7001
Fax: (781)237-7233
C. Redington Barrett, III, Managing Director
Investment Types: Second stage, mezzanine, leveraged buyout, and special situations. Industry Preferences: Diversified. Geographic Preferences: National.

Grove Street Advisors Inc.
20 William St., Ste. 230
Wellesley, MA 02481
(781)263-6100
Fax: (781)263-6101
Website: http://
www.grovestreetadvisors.com
Preferred Investment Size: $1,000,000 to $7,500,000. Investment Types: First stage,

mezzanine, second stage, special situation, and start-up. Industry Preferences: Diversified. Geographic Preferences: U.S.

Mees Pierson Investeringsmaat B.V.
20 William St., Ste. 210
Wellesley, MA 02482
(781)239-7600
Fax: (781)239-0377
Dennis P. Cameron
Investment Types: First and second stage, and start-up. Industry Preferences: Diversified technology. Geographic Preferences: Entire U.S. and Canada.

Norwest Equity Partners
40 William St., Ste. 305
Wellesley, MA 02481-3902
(781)237-5870
Fax: (781)237-6270
Website: http://www.norwestvp.com
Charles B. Lennin
Preferred Investment Size: $1,000,000 to $25,000,000. Investment Types: Seed, early and later stage, and expansion. Industry Preferences: Diversified. Geographic Preferences: National.

Bessemer Venture Partners (Wellesley Hills)
83 Walnut St.
Wellesley Hills, MA 02481
(781)237-6050
Fax: (781)235-7576
E-mail: travis@bvpny.com
Website: http://www.bvp.com
Preferred Investment Size: $100,000 to $15,000,000. Investment Types: Seed, start-up, early stage, first and second stage, and expansion. Industry Preferences: Communications, computer related, consumer products, distribution, and electronics. Geographic Preferences: National.

Venture Capital Fund of New England
20 Walnut St., Ste. 120
Wellesley Hills, MA 02481-2175
(781)239-8262
Fax: (781)239-8263
E-mail: kjdvcfne3@aol.com
Kevin J. Dougherty, General Partner
Preferred Investment Size: $750,000 to $3,000,000. Investment Types: Startup, first and second stage. Industry Preferences: Diversified. Geographic Preferences: Northeast.

Prism Venture Partners
100 Lowder Brook Dr., Ste. 2500
Westwood, MA 02090
(781)302-4000
Fax: (781)302-4040
E-mail: dwbaum@prismventure.com
Preferred Investment Size: $2,000,000 to $10,000,000. Investment Types: Startup, first stage, second stage, and mezzanine. Industry Preferences: Communications, computer and Internet related, electronic components and instrumentation, medical and health. Geographic Preferences: U.S.

Palmer Partners LP
200 Unicorn Park Dr.
Woburn, MA 01801
(781)933-5445
Fax: (781)933-0698
John Shane
Preferred Investment Size: $250,000 to $1,000,000. Investment Types: Startup, first and second stage, and special situations. Industry Preferences: Communications, computer, energy/ natural resources, industrial, education, finance, and publishing. Geographic Preferences: Northeast, S

Michigan

Arbor Partners, L.L.C.
130 South First St.
Ann Arbor, MI 48104
(734)668-9000
Fax: (734)669-4195
Website: http://www.arborpartners.com
Preferred Investment Size: $250,000 minimum. Investment Policies: Equity. Investment Types: Early and expansion. Industry Preferences: Diversified technology. Geographic Preferences: Midwest.

EDF Ventures
425 N. Main St.
Ann Arbor, MI 48104
(734)663-3213
Fax: (734)663-7358
E-mail: edf@edfvc.com
Website: http://www.edfvc.com
Mary Campbell, Partner
Preferred Investment Size: $500,000 to $10,000,000. Investment Types: Seed, startup, first stage, second stage, expansion, and research and development. Industry Preferences: Diversified technology. Geographic Preferences: Midwest.

White Pines Management, L.L.C.
2401 Plymouth Rd., Ste. B
Ann Arbor, MI 48105
(734)747-9401
Fax: (734)747-9704
E-mail: ibund@whitepines.com
Website: http://www.whitepines.com
Preferred Investment Size: $1,000,000 to
$4,000,000. Investment Types: Second
stage, mezzanine, leveraged buyout, and
special situations. Industry Preferences:
Diversified. Geographic Preferences:
Southeast and Midwest.

Wellmax, Inc.
3541 Bendway Blvd., Ste. 100
Bloomfield Hills, MI 48301
(248)646-3554
Fax: (248)646-6220
Preferred Investment Size: $100,000 to
$1,000,000. Investment Policies: Equity.
Investment Types: Start-up, early and
late stage, leveraged buyout, and special
situations. Industry Preferences:
Diversified. Geographic Preferences:
Midwest, Southeast.

Venture Funding, Ltd.
Fisher Bldg.
3011 West Grand Blvd., Ste. 321
Detroit, MI 48202
(313)871-3606
Fax: (313)873-4935
Monis Schuster, Vice President
Preferred Investment Size: $1,000,000
minimum. Investment Policies: Equity.
Investment Types: Startup, seed,
leveraged buyout, research and
development, and special situations.
Industry Preferences: Diversified.
Geographic Preferences: National.

Investcare Partners L.P./GMA Capital LLC
32330 W. Twelve Mile Rd.
Farmington Hills, MI 48334
(248)489-9000
Fax: (248)489-8819
E-mail: gma@gmacapital.com
Website: http://www.gmacapital.com
Malcolm Moss, Managing Director
Investment Types: Second stage and
leveraged buyout. Industry Preferences:
Medical and health related. Geographic
Preferences: National.

Liberty Bidco Investment Corp.
30833 Northwestern Highway, Ste. 211
Farmington Hills, MI 48334

(248)626-6070
Fax: (248)626-6072
James Zabriskie, Vice President
Preferred Investment Size: $500,000
minimum. Investment Types: Second
stage, leveraged buyout, mezzanine,
and special situations. Industry
Preferences: Diversified. Geographic
Preferences: Midwestern U.S. and
Ontario, Canada.

Seaflower Ventures
5170 Nicholson Rd.
PO Box 474
Fowlerville, MI 48836
(517)223-3335
Fax: (517)223-3337
E-mail: gibbons@seaflower.com
Website: http://www.seaflower.com
M. Christine Gibbons, Partner
Investment Types: Seed, research and
development, startup, recaps, strategic
alliances, first and second stage. Industry
Preferences: Genetic engineering,
industrial products and equipment,
medical and health related. Geographic
Preferences: Midwest, Northeast, and
Mid Atlantic.

Ralph Wilson Equity Fund LLC
15400 E. Jefferson Ave.
Gross Pointe Park, MI 48230
(313)821-9122
Fax: (313)821-9101
Website: http://
www.RalphWilsonEquityFund.com
J. Skip Simms, President
Preferred Investment Size: $200,000 to
$1,000,000. Investment Types: Balanced,
early stage, expansion, and first and second
stage. Industry Preferences: Diversified.
Geographic Preferences: Entire U.S.

Minnesota

Development Corp. of Austin
1900 Eighth Ave., NW
Austin, MN 55912
(507)433-0346
Fax: (507)433-0361
E-mail: dca@smig.net
Website: http://www.spamtownusa.com
Preferred Investment Size: $100,000.
Investment Types: Startup, seed, and first
stage. Industry Preferences: Diversified.
Geographic Preferences: No preference.

Northeast Ventures Corp.
802 Alworth Bldg.
Duluth, MN 55802

(218)722-9915
Fax: (218)722-9871
Greg Sandbulte, President
Preferred Investment Size: $100,000 to
$500,000. Investment Policies: Equity.
Investment Types: Startup, early and late
stage, mezzanine, leveraged buyout, and
research and development. Industry
Preferences: No preference. Geographic
Preferences: Midwest.

Medical Innovation Partners, Inc.
6450 City West Pkwy.
Eden Prairie, MN 55344-3245
(612)828-9616
Fax: (612)828-9596
Mark B. Knudson, Ph.D., Managing
Partner
Preferred Investment Size: $100,000 to
$5,000,000. Investment Types: Seed,
startup, and first stage. Industry
Preferences: Medical technology and
healthcare, and communications.
Geographic Preferences: Northwest and
Midwest.

St. Paul Venture Capital, Inc.
10400 Vicking Dr., Ste. 550
Eden Prairie, MN 55344
(612)995-7474
Fax: (612)995-7475
Website: http://www.stpaulvc.com
Preferred Investment Size: $500,000
minimum. Investment Types: Early
stage. Industry Preferences:
Diversified. Geographic Preferences:
California, Massachusetts, and
Minnesota.

Cherry Tree Investments, Inc.
7601 France Ave. S, Ste. 150
Edina, MN 55435
(612)893-9012
Fax: (612)893-9036
Website: http://www.cherrytree.com
Sandy Trump
Preferred Investment Size: $100,000
minimum. Investment Types: Balanced
and early second stage. Industry
Preferences: Diversified. Geographic
Preferences: Midwest.

Shared Ventures, Inc.
6550 York Ave. S
Edina, MN 55435
(612)925-3411
Howard Weiner
Preferred Investment Size: $100,000 to
$300,000. Investment Types: First and
second stage, start-up, leveraged buyout,

control-block purchases, and special situations. Industry Preferences: Consumer, electronics, distribution, energy/natural resources, industrial products and equipme

Sherpa Partners LLC
5050 Lincoln Dr., Ste. 490
Edina, MN 55436
(952)942-1070
Fax: (952)942-1071
Website: http://www.sherpapartners.com
Preferred Investment Size: $250,000 to $5,000,000. Investment Types: Early stage. Industry Preferences: Telecommunications, computer software, and Internet related. Geographic Preferences: Midwest.

Affinity Capital Management
901 Marquette Ave., Ste. 1810
Minneapolis, MN 55402
(612)252-9900
Fax: (612)252-9911
Website: http://www.affinitycapital.com
Edson W. Spencer
Preferred Investment Size: $250,000 to $1,100,000. Investment Types: Seed, startup, first and second stage. Industry Preferences: Medical/Health related, Internet and computer related. Geographic Preferences: Midwest.

Artesian Capital
1700 Foshay Tower
821 Marquette Ave.
Minneapolis, MN 55402
(612)334-5600
Fax: (612)334-5601
E-mail: artesian@artesian.com
Frank B. Bennett, President
Preferred Investment Size: $300,000 to $500,000. Investment Types: Seed, research and development, leveraged buyout, and startup. Industry Preferences: Diversified. Geographic Preferences: Midwest.

Coral Ventures
60 S. 6th St., Ste. 3510
Minneapolis, MN 55402
(612)335-8666
Fax: (612)335-8668
Website: http://www.coralventures.com
Preferred Investment Size: $1,000,000 to $11,000,000. Investment Types: Seed, startup, first and second stage. Industry Preferences: Diversified technology. Geographic Preferences: No preference.

Crescendo Venture Management, L.L.C.
800 LaSalle Ave., Ste. 2250
Minneapolis, MN 55402
(612)607-2800
Fax: (612)607-2801
Website: http://www.crescendoventures.com
Jeffrey R. Tollefson, Partner
Preferred Investment Size: $1,000,000 to $5,000,000. Investment Types: Startup, seed, early and late stage. Industry Preferences: Diversified information technology. Geographic Preferences: U.S. and Canada.

Gideon Hixon Venture
1900 Foshay Tower
821 Marquette Ave.
Minneapolis, MN 55402
(612)904-2314
Fax: (612)204-0913
E-mail: bkwhitney@gideonhixon.com
Preferred Investment Size: $300,000 to $500,000. Investment Policies: Equity. Investment Types: Startup, seed, early and late stage. Industry Preferences: Diversified communication and computer technology, medical/health, and electronics. Geographic Preferences: West Coast.

Norwest Equity Partners
3600 IDS Center
80 S. 8th St.
Minneapolis, MN 55402
(612)215-1600
Fax: (612)215-1601
Website: http://www.norwestvp.com
Charles B. Lennin, Partner
Preferred Investment Size: $1,000,000 to $25,000,000. Investment Policies: Equity. Investment Types: Seed, expansion, early and later stage. Industry Preferences: Diversified. Geographic Preferences: National.

Oak Investment Partners (Minneapolis)
4550 Norwest Center
90 S. 7th St.
Minneapolis, MN 55402
(612)339-9322
Fax: (612)337-8017
Website: http://www.oakinv.com
Preferred Investment Size: $250,000 to $5,000,000. Investment Types: Startup, first stage, second and late stage, leveraged buyout, control-block purchases, open market, and special situations. Industry Preferences: Diversified. Geographic Preferences: Entire U.S.

Pathfinder Venture Capital Funds (Minneapolis)
7300 Metro Blvd., Ste. 585
Minneapolis, MN 55439
(612)835-1121
Fax: (612)835-8389
E-mail: jahrens620@aol.com
Jack K. Ahrens, II, Investment Officer
Preferred Investment Size: $2,000,000 minimum. Investment Types: Seed, startup, first and second stage, mezzanine, leveraged buyouts, and special situations. Industry Preferences: Diversified. Geographic Preferences: Entire U.S. and Canada.

U.S. Bancorp Piper Jaffray Ventures, Inc.
800 Nicollet Mall, Ste. 800
Minneapolis, MN 55402
(612)303-5686
Fax: (612)303-1350
Website: http://www.paperjaffreyventures.com
Preferred Investment Size: $250,000 minimum. Investment Types: Early and late stage, and mezzanine. Industry Preferences: Diversified. Geographic Preferences: Entire U.S.

The Food Fund, Ltd. Partnership
5720 Smatana Dr., Ste. 300
Minnetonka, MN 55343
(612)939-3950
Fax: (612)939-8106
John Trucano, Managing General Partner
Preferred Investment Size: $800,000 minimum. Investment Types: Startup, first and second stage, leveraged buyout, and special situations. Industry Preferences: Consumer related, industrial and energy, and electronics. Geographic Preferences: Entire U.S.

Mayo Medical Ventures
200 First St. SW
Rochester, MN 55905
(507)266-4586
Fax: (507)284-5410
Website: http://www.mayo.edu
Preferred Investment Size: $1,000,000 minimum. Investment Types: Early stage. Industry Preferences: Diversified. Geographic Preferences: Entire U.S.

Missouri

Bankers Capital Corp.
3100 Gillham Rd.
Kansas City, MO 64109

(816)531-1600
Fax: (816)531-1334
Lee Glasnapp, Vice President
Preferred Investment Size: $100,000
minimum. Investment Types: Leveraged
buyout. Industry Preferences: Consumer
product and electronics distribution,
and industrial equipment and
machinery. Geographic Preferences:
Midwest.

Capital for Business, Inc. (Kansas City)
1000 Walnut St., 18th Fl.
Kansas City, MO 64106
(816)234-2357
Fax: (816)234-2952
Website: http://
www.capitalforbusiness.com
Hollis A. Huels
Preferred Investment Size: $500,000 to
$5,000,000. Investment Types:
Expansion, leveraged and management
buyouts, and later stage. Industry
Preferences: Diversified. Geographic
Preferences: Midwest.

De Vries & Co. Inc.
800 West 47th St.
Kansas City, MO 64112
(816)756-0055
Fax: (816)756-0061
Preferred Investment Size: $500,000
minimum. Investment Types:
Acquisition, expansion, later stage,
leveraged and management buyout,
mezzanine, private placement, recaps,
and second stage. Industry Preferences:
Diversified. Geographic Preferences: No
preference.

**InvestAmerica Venture Group Inc.
(Kansas City)**
Commerce Tower
911 Main St., Ste. 2424
Kansas City, MO 64105
(816)842-0114
Fax: (816)471-7339
Kevin F. Mullane, Vice President
Preferred Investment Size: $500,000 to
$1,000,000. Investment Types: First and
second stage, leveraged buyout, and
special situations. Industry Preferences:
Diversified. Geographic Preferences:
Entire U.S.

Kansas City Equity Partners
233 W. 47th St.
Kansas City, MO 64112
(816)960-1771
Fax: (816)960-1777

Website: http://www.kcep.com
Preferred Investment Size: $2,000,000 to
$8,000,000. Investment Types: Start-up,
early stage, expansion, and joint
ventures. Industry Preferences:
Diversified. Geographic Preferences:
Midwest.

Bome Investors, Inc.
8000 Maryland Ave., Ste. 1190
St. Louis, MO 63105
(314)721-5707
Fax: (314)721-5135
Website: http://
www.gatewayventures.com
Gregory R. Johnson
Preferred Investment Size: $500,000 to
$1,000,000. Investment Types: Startup,
early and late stage. Industry Preferences:
Diversified. Geographic Preferences:
Midwest.

Capital for Business, Inc. (St. Louis)
11 S. Meramac St., Ste. 1430
St. Louis, MO 63105
(314)746-7427
Fax: (314)746-8739
Website: http://
www.capitalforbusiness.com
Hollis A. Huels
Preferred Investment Size: $500,000 to
$5,000,000. Investment Types:
Expansion, leveraged and management
buyouts, and later stage. Industry
Preferences: Diversified. Geographic
Preferences: Midwest.

Crown Capital Corp.
540 Maryville Centre Dr., Ste. 120
Saint Louis, MO 63141
(314)576-1201
Fax: (314)576-1525
Website: http://www.crown-cap.com
Investment Types: Control-block
purchases, first stage, leveraged buyout,
mezzanine, second stage, and special
situation. Industry Preferences:
Diversified. Geographic Preferences:
Entire U.S. and Canada.

Gateway Associates L.P.
8000 Maryland Ave., Ste. 1190
St. Louis, MO 63105
(314)721-5707
Fax: (314)721-5135
John S. McCarthy, Managing General
Partner
Preferred Investment Size: $1,000,000
minimum. Investment Types: Start-up,
second stage, mezzanine, leveraged

buyout, special situations, control block
purchases. Industry Preferences:
Communications, computer related,
electronics, and hospital and other
institutional management. Geo

Harbison Corp.
8112 Maryland Ave., Ste. 250
Saint Louis, MO 63105
(314)727-8200
Fax: (314)727-0249
Keith Harbison
Preferred Investment Size: $500,000
minimum. Investment Types: Control-
block purchases, leveraged buyout, and
special situation. Industry Preferences:
Diversified. Geographic Preferences: Mid
Atlantic and Southeast; Ontario and
Quebec, Canada.

Nebraska

Heartland Capital Fund, Ltd.
PO Box 642117
Omaha, NE 68154
(402)778-5124
Fax: (402)445-2370
Website: http://
www.heartlandcapitalfund.com
John G. Gustafson, Vice President
Preferred Investment Size: $500,000 to
$3,000,000. Investment Policies: Equity.
Investment Types: First and second stage,
and expansion. Industry Preferences:
Diversified technology. Geographic
Preferences: Southwest and Midwest.

Odin Capital Group
1625 Farnam St., Ste. 700
Omaha, NE 68102
(402)346-6200
Fax: (402)342-9311
Website: http://www.odincapital.com
Preferred Investment Size: $1,000,000 to
$5,000,000. Investment Types: Early,
first, and second stage, and expansion.
Industry Preferences: Internet related and
financial services. Geographic
Preferences: U.S.

Nevada

Edge Capital Investment Co. LLC
1350 E. Flamingo Rd., Ste. 3000
Las Vegas, NV 89119
(702)438-3343
E-mail: info@edgecapital.net
Website: http://www.edgecapital.net
Preferred Investment Size: $500,000 to
$15,000,000. Investment Types: Seed,

startup, first stage, second stage, mezzanine, leveraged buyout, and special situations. Industry Preferences: Diversified technology. Geographic Preferences: U.S. and Canada.

The Benefit Capital Companies Inc.
PO Box 542
Logandale, NV 89021
(702)398-3222
Fax: (702)398-3700
Robert Smiley
Preferred Investment Size: $2,500,000 minimum. Investment Types: Leveraged buyout and mezzanine. Industry Preferences: Diversified. Geographic Preferences: Entire U.S.

Millennium Three Venture Group LLC
6880 South McCarran Blvd., Ste. A-11
Reno, NV 89509
(775)954-2020
Fax: (775)954-2023
Website: http://www.m3vg.com
Preferred Investment Size: $500,000 to $2,000,000. Investment Types: Early stage, expansion, first stage, mezzanine, second stage, and seed. Industry Preferences: Diversified. Geographic Preferences: West Coast.

New Jersey

Alan I. Goldman & Associates
497 Ridgewood Ave.
Glen Ridge, NJ 07028
(973)857-5680
Fax: (973)509-8856
Alan Goldman
Preferred Investment Size: $500,000 minimum. Investment Types: Control-block purchases, leveraged buyout, mezzanine, second stage, and special situation. Industry Preferences: Diversified. Geographic Preferences: Entire U.S. and Canada.

CS Capital Partners LLC
328 Second St., Ste. 200
Lakewood, NJ 08701
(732)901-1111
Fax: (212)202-5071
Website: http://www.cs-capital.com
Preferred Investment Size: $500,000 to $3,000,000. Investment Types: Distressed debt, early stage, expansion, first and second stage, and turnaround. Industry Preferences: Internet and computer related, communications, and medical/health related. Geographic Preferences: Entire U.S. a

Edison Venture Fund
1009 Lenox Dr., Ste. 4
Lawrenceville, NJ 08648
(609)896-1900
Fax: (609)896-0066
E-mail: info@edisonventure.com
Website: http://www.edisonventure.com
John H. Martinson, Managing Partner
Preferred Investment Size: $1,000,000 to $6,000,000. Investment Types: Early and later stage, expansion, and management buyouts. Industry Preferences: Diversified. Geographic Preferences: Northeast and Middle Atlantic.

Tappan Zee Capital Corp. (New Jersey)
201 Lower Notch Rd.
PO Box 416
Little Falls, NJ 07424
(973)256-8280
Fax: (973)256-2841
Jeffrey Birnberg, President
Preferred Investment Size: $100,000 to $250,000. Investment Types: Leveraged buyout. Industry Preferences: Diversified. Geographic Preferences: No preference.

The CIT Group/Venture Capital, Inc.
650 CIT Dr.
Livingston, NJ 07039
(973)740-5429
Fax: (973)740-5555
Website: http://www.cit.com
Preferred Investment Size: $3,000,000 minimum. Investment Types: First and second stage, mezzanine, and leveraged buyout. Industry Preferences: Diversified. Geographic Preferences: Entire U.S.

Capital Express, L.L.C.
1100 Valleybrook Ave.
Lyndhurst, NJ 07071
(201)438-8228
Fax: (201)438-5131
E-mail: niles@capitalexpress.com
Website: http://www.capitalexpress.com
Niles Cohen
Preferred Investment Size: $300,000 to $500,000. Investment Policies: Equity. Investment Types: Start-up, first and second stage, and recaps. Industry Preferences: Internet and consumer related, and publishing. Geographic Preferences: East Coast.

Westford Technology Ventures, L.P.
17 Academy St.
Newark, NJ 07102

(973)624-2131
Fax: (973)624-2008
Preferred Investment Size: $300,000 to $500,000. Investment Types: Startup, first and second stage. Industry Preferences: Diversified communication and computer technology, electronics, industrial products and equipment. Geographic Preferences: No preference.

Accel Partners
1 Palmer Sq.
Princeton, NJ 08542
(609)683-4500
Fax: (609)683-4880
Website: http://www.accel.com
Preferred Investment Size: $1,000,000 minimum. Investment Types: Seed, start-up and early stage. Industry Preferences: Diversified. Geographic Preferences: National.

Cardinal Partners
221 Nassau St.
Princeton, NJ 08542
(609)924-6452
Fax: (609)683-0174
Website: http://www.cardinalhealthpartners.com
Lisa Skeete Tatum, Associate
Preferred Investment Size: $1,000,000 to $8,000,000. Investment Types: Seed, startup, first and second stage. Industry Preferences: Diversified. Geographic Preferences: U.S. and Canada.

Domain Associates L.L.C.
One Palmer Sq., Ste. 515
Princeton, NJ 08542
(609)683-5656
Fax: (609)683-9789
Website: http://www.domainvc.com
Preferred Investment Size: $1,000,000 to $20,000,000. Investment Types: Seed, start-up, first and second stage, balanced, expansion, mezzanine, private placement, research and development, and late stage. Industry Preferences: Electronic components and instrumentation, genetic engine

Johnston Associates, Inc.
181 Cherry Valley Rd.
Princeton, NJ 08540
(609)924-3131
Fax: (609)683-7524
E-mail: jaincorp@aol.com

Preferred Investment Size: $500,000 to $5,000,000. Investment Types: Start-up and early stage. Industry Preferences: Science and healthcare industry. Geographic Preferences: Northeast.

Kemper Ventures
Princeton Forrestal Village
155 Village Blvd.
Princeton, NJ 08540
(609)936-3035
Fax: (609)936-3051
Richard Secchia, Partner
Investment Types: Seed, research and development, startup, first and second stage. Industry Preferences: Computer related, medical and health related, financial services. Geographic Preferences: National.

Penny Lane Parnters
One Palmer Sq., Ste. 309
Princeton, NJ 08542
(609)497-4646
Fax: (609)497-0611
Preferred Investment Size: $1,000,000. Investment Types: Recaps, second stage, and leveraged buyouts. Industry Preferences: Computer related, genetic engineering, medical/health related, and electronics. Geographic Preferences: Eastern U.S.

Early Stage Enterprises L.P.
995 Route 518
Skillman, NJ 08558
(609)921-8896
Fax: (609)921-8703
Website: http://www.esevc.com
Ronald R. Hahn, Managing Director
Preferred Investment Size: $250,000 to $1,000,000. Investment Types: Seed, start-up, and early stage. Industry Preferences: Diversified. Geographic Preferences: Mid Atlantic.

MBW Management Inc.
1 Springfield Ave.
Summit, NJ 07901
(908)273-4060
Fax: (908)273-4430
Preferred Investment Size: $1,000,000 minimum. Investment Types: First stage, leveraged buyout, second stage, special situation, and start-up. Industry Preferences: Diversified. Geographic Preferences: No preference.

BCI Advisors, Inc.
Glenpointe Center W.
Teaneck, NJ 07666
(201)836-3900
Fax: (201)836-6368
E-mail: info@bciadvisors.com
Website: http://www.bcipartners.com
Thomas J. Cusick, General Partner
Preferred Investment Size: $5,000,000 to $25,000,000. Investment Types: Expansion. Industry Preferences: Diversified. Geographic Preferences: Entire U.S.

Demuth, Folger & Wetherill / DFW Capital Partners
Glenpointe Center E., 5th Fl.
300 Frank W. Burr Blvd.
Teaneck, NJ 07666
(201)836-2233
Fax: (201)836-5666
Website: http://www.dfwcapital.com
Donald F. DeMuth, General Partner
Preferred Investment Size: $500,000 minimum. Investment Policies: Equity. Investment Types: Acquisition, control-block purchases, later stage, leveraged buyout, management buyout, recaps, and speical situations. Industry Preferences: Healthcare, computer, communication, diversified.

First Princeton Capital Corp.
189 Berdan Ave., No. 131
Wayne, NJ 07470-3233
(973)278-3233
Fax: (973)278-4290
Website: http://www.lytellcatt.net
Michael Lytell
Preferred Investment Size: $200,000 minimum. Investment Types: First and second stage, mezzanine, recaps, control-block purchases, and leveraged buyout. Industry Preferences: Diversified. Geographic Preferences: Northeast and East Coast.

Edelson Technology Partners
300 Tice Blvd.
Woodcliff Lake, NJ 07675
(201)930-9898
Fax: (201)930-8899
Website: http://www.edelsontech.com
Harry Edelson, Managing Partner
Preferred Investment Size: $500,000 to $1,000,000. Investment Types: Seed, startup, first and second stage, leveraged buyout, and mezzanine. Industry Preferences: Diversified. Geographic Preferences: No preference.

New Mexico

Bruce F. Glaspell & Associates
10400 Academy Rd. NE, Ste. 313
Albuquerque, NM 87111
(505)292-4505
Fax: (505)292-4258
Bruce Glaspell
Preferred Investment Size: $100,000 to $5,000,000. Investment Types: Seed, startup, first stage, second stage, late stage, private placement, and expansion. Industry Preferences: Diversified. Geographic Preferences: Entire U.S. and Canada.

High Desert Ventures, Inc.
6101 Imparata St. NE, Ste. 1721
Albuquerque, NM 87111
(505)797-3330
Fax: (505)338-5147
E-mail: zilenziger@aol.com
Preferred Investment Size: $500,000 to $2,500,000. Investment Types: Startup and early stage. Industry Preferences: Diversified. Geographic Preferences: Northeast and Southwest.

New Business Capital Fund, Ltd.
5805 Torreon NE
Albuquerque, NM 87109
(505)822-8445
Preferred Investment Size: $100,000. Investment Policies: Equity. Investment Types: Seed, startup, and first stage. Industry Preferences: Diversified. Geographic Preferences: No preference.

SBC Ventures
10400 Academy Rd. NE, Ste. 313
Albuquerque, NM 87111
(505)292-4505
Fax: (505)292-4528
Viviana Cloninger, General Partner
Preferred Investment Size: $300,000 to $3,000,000. Investment Types: Seed, research and development, startup, and first stage. Industry Preferences: Diversified. Geographic Preferences: Entire U.S. and Canada.

Technology Ventures Corp.
1155 University Blvd. SE
Albuquerque, NM 87106
(505)246-2882
Fax: (505)246-2891
Beverly Bendicksen
Investment Types: Seed, startup, first and second stage. Industry Preferences: Diversified. Geographic Preferences: Southwest.

New York

New York State Science & Technology Foundation
Small Business Technology Investment Fund
99 Washington Ave., Ste. 1731
Albany, NY 12210
(518)473-9741
Fax: (518)473-6876
E-mail: jvanwie@empire.state.ny.us
Preferred Investment Size: $100,000 to $300,000. Investment Types: Seed, startup, first and second stage. Industry Preferences: Diversified technology. Geographic Preferences: Northeast.

Rand Capital Corp.
2200 Rand Bldg.
Buffalo, NY 14203
(716)853-0802
Fax: (716)854-8480
Website: http://www.randcapital.com
Allen F. Grum, President and CEO
Preferred Investment Size: $25,000 to $500,000. Investment Types: Second stage. Industry Preferences: Diversified. Geographic Preferences: Northeast and Ontario, Canada.

Seed Capital Partners
620 Main St.
Buffalo, NY 14202
(716)845-7520
Fax: (716)845-7539
Website: http://www.seedcp.com
Investment Types: Early stage. Industry Preferences: Diversified technology, communications, and other products. Geographic Preferences: Northeast.

Coleman Venture Group
5909 Northern Blvd.
PO Box 224
East Norwich, NY 11732
(516)626-3642
Fax: (516)626-9722
Preferred Investment Size: $100,000 to $1,000,000. Investment Types: First stage, recaps, seed, start-up, and special situation. Industry Preferences: Electronics and consumer products. Geographic Preferences: Northeast and West Coast, and Canada.

Vega Capital Corp.
45 Knollwood Rd.
Elmsford, NY 10523
(914)345-9500
Fax: (914)345-9505

Ronald Linden
Preferred Investment Size: $300,000 minimum. Investment Types: Second stage, mezzanine, leveraged buyout, and special situations. Industry Preferences: Diversified. Geographic Preferences: Northeast, Southeast, and Middle Atlantic.

Herbert Young Securities, Inc.
98 Cuttermill Rd.
Great Neck, NY 11021
(516)487-8300
Fax: (516)487-8319
Herbert D. Levine, President
Preferred Investment Size: $1,000,000 minimum. Investment Types: First and second stage, leveraged buyout, mezzanine, and special situation. Industry Preferences: Diversified communications and computer technology, consumer products and services, electronics, genetic engineering, hea

Sterling/Carl Marks Capital, Inc.
175 Great Neck Rd., Ste. 408
Great Neck, NY 11021
(516)482-7374
Fax: (516)487-0781
E-mail: stercrlmar@aol.com
Website: http://www.serlingcarlmarks.com
Preferred Investment Size: $1,000,000 to $2,000,000. Investment Types: Second stage, expansion, management buyouts, and mezzanine. Industry Preferences: Consumer related; distribution of electronics equipment, food and industrial products; and industrial equipment and machinery. Geog

Impex Venture Management Co.
PO Box 1570
Green Island, NY 12183
(518)271-8008
Fax: (518)271-9101
Jay Banker
Preferred Investment Size: $1,000,000 minimum. Investment Types: First stage, leveraged buyout, second stage, special situation, and start-up. Industry Preferences: Diversified. Geographic Preferences: Mid Atlantic and Northeast, and Quebec, Canada.

Corporate Venture Partners L.P.
200 Sunset Park
Ithaca, NY 14850
(607)257-6323

Fax: (607)257-6128
Preferred Investment Size: $500,000 to $1,000,000. Investment Types: First stage. Industry Preferences: Diversified. Geographic Preferences: Northeast.

Arthur P. Gould & Co.
One Wilshire Dr.
Lake Success, NY 11020
(516)773-3000
Fax: (516)773-3289
Andrew Gould, Vice President
Preferred Investment Size: $5,000,000 minimum. Investment Types: Seed, research and development, startup, first stage, second stage, mezzanine, and leveraged buyout. Industry Preferences: Diversified. Geographic Preferences: National.

Dauphin Capital Partners
108 Forest Ave.
Locust Valley, NY 11560
(516)759-3339
Fax: (516)759-3322
Website: http://www.dauphincapital.com
Preferred Investment Size: $1,000,000 to $3,000,000. Investment Types: Balanced; and early, first, second, and later stage. Industry Preferences: Diversified technology, education, and business services. Geographic Preferences: Entire U.S.

550 Digital Media Ventures
555 Madison Ave., 10th Fl.
New York, NY 10022
Website: http://www.550dmv.com
Investment Types: Early stage. Industry Preferences: Entertainment and leisure, and media. Geographic Preferences: Entire U.S.

Aberlyn Capital Management Co., Inc.
500 Fifth Ave.
New York, NY 10110
(212)391-7750
Fax: (212)391-7762
Lawrence Hoffman, Chairman and CEO
Preferred Investment Size: $25,000,000 minimum. Investment Types: Startup, first and second stage, leveraged buyout, and special situation. Industry Preferences: Diversified computer technology, food and beverage products, genetic engineering, and healthcare. Geographic Preferences:

Adler & Company
342 Madison Ave., Ste. 807
New York, NY 10173

(212)599-2535
Fax: (212)599-2526
Jay Nickse, Treasurer & Chief Financial
Officer
Investment Types: Startup, first and
second stage, leveraged buyout, and
control-block purchases. Industry
Preferences: Diversified. Geographic
Preferences: National.

Alimansky Capital Group, Inc.
605 Madison Ave., Ste. 300
New York, NY 10022-1901
(212)832-7300
Fax: (212)832-7338
Howard Duby, Managing Director
Preferred Investment Size: $2,000,000.
Investment Types: First stage, second
stage, mezzanine, leveraged buyout, and
special situations. Industry Preferences:
Diversified. Geographic Preferences:
Entire U.S. and Canada.

Allegra Partners
515 Madison Ave., 29th Fl.
New York, NY 10022
(212)826-9080
Fax: (212)759-2561
Preferred Investment Size: $1,000,000
minimum. Investment Types: First stage,
leveraged buyout, recaps, second stage,
and special situation. Industry
Preferences: Communications, computer
related, and consumer related.
Geographic Preferences: Mid Atlantic,
and Eastern and Western U.S

The Argentum Group
The Chyrsler Bldg.
405 Lexington Ave.
New York, NY 10174
(212)949-6262
Fax: (212)949-8294
Website: http://
www.argentumgroup.com
Walter H. Barandiaran, Managing Dir.
Preferred Investment Size: $10,000,000
minimum. Investment Types: Second
stage, mezzanine, leveraged buyout, and
special situations. Industry Preferences:
Diversified. Geographic Preferences:
Entire U.S.

Axavision Inc.
14 Wall St., 26th Fl.
New York, NY 10005
(212)619-4000
Fax: (212)619-7202
Preferred Investment Size: $100,000 to
$300,000. Investment Types: Seed and

start-up. Industry Preferences: Computer
services and software, Internet related,
and financial services. Geographic
Preferences: No preference.

Bedford Capital Corp.
18 East 48th St., Ste. 1800
New York, NY 10017
(212)688-5700
Fax: (212)754-4699
E-mail: info@bedfordnyc.com
Website: http://www.bedfordnyc.com
Nathan Bernstein
Preferred Investment Size: $100,000 to
$300,000. Investment Types: First and
second stage, industry rollups, recaps,
and leveraged buyout. Industry
Preferences: Diversified. Geographic
Preferences: Midwest.

Bloom & Co.
950 Third Ave.
New York, NY 10022
(212)838-1858
Fax: (212)838-1843
Jack S. Bloom, President
Preferred Investment Size: $3,000,000
minimum. Investment Types: Startup,
first and second stage, control-block
purchases, leveraged buyout, mezzanine,
and special situation. Industry
Preferences: No preference. Geographic
Preferences: No preference.

Bristol Capital Management
300 Park Ave., 17th Fl.
New York, NY 10022
(212)572-6306
Fax: (212)705-4292
Investment Types: Leveraged buyout,
mezzanine, second stage, and special
situation. Industry Preferences:
Communications, computer related,
electronics, medical/health related,
entertainment and leisure, retail, food/
beverage, consumer services, machinery,
and publishing. Geographic

**Citicorp Venture Capital Ltd. (New
York City)**
399 Park Ave., 14th Fl.
Zone 4
New York, NY 10043
(212)559-1127
Fax: (212)888-2940
Preferred Investment Size: $5,000,000.
Investment Types: Leveraged buyout,
second stage, and special situations.
Industry Preferences: Diversified.
Geographic Preferences: No preference.

CM Equity Partners
135 E. 57th St.
New York, NY 10022
(212)909-8428
Fax: (212)980-2630
Preferred Investment Size: $2,000,000
minimum. Investment Types: First and
second stage, start-up, mezzanine,
leveraged buyout, special situations, and
industry rollups. Industry Preferences:
Diversified. Geographic Preferences: No
preference.

Cohen & Co., L.L.C.
800 Third Ave.
New York, NY 10022
(212)317-2250
Fax: (212)317-2255
E-mail: nlcohen@aol.com
Neil L. Cohen, President
Preferred Investment Size: $10,000,000
minimum. Investment Types: Startup,
seed, early and late stage, mezzanine,
leveraged buyout, control-block
purchases, and special situations.
Industry Preferences:
Communications, consumer,
distribution, electronics, energy, and
healthcare. Geog

Cornerstone Equity Investors, L.L.C.
717 5th Ave., Ste. 1100
New York, NY 10022
(212)753-0901
Fax: (212)826-6798
Website: http://www.cornerstone-
equity.com
Mark Rossi, Senior Managing Director
Preferred Investment Size: $50,000,000
maximum. Investment Types: Leveraged
buyout, and special situations. Industry
Preferences: Diversified. Geographic
Preferences: No preference.

CW Group, Inc.
1041 3rd Ave., 2nd fl.
New York, NY 10021
(212)308-5266
Fax: (212)644-0354
Website: http://www.cwventures.com
Christopher Fenimore
Preferred Investment Size: $100,000 to
$5,000,000. Investment Types: Seed,
research and development, startup, first
and second stage, leveraged buyout,
special situations, and control block
purchases. Industry Preferences:
Specialize in the medical/health business
and biotechnology.

DH Blair Investment Banking Corp.
44 Wall St., 2nd Fl.
New York, NY 10005
(212)495-5000
Fax: (212)269-1438
J. Morton Davis, Chairman
Preferred Investment Size: $100,000.
Investment Types: Research and
development, startup, first stage, and
leveraged buyout. Industry Preferences:
Diversified. Geographic Preferences: No
preference.

Dresdner Kleinwort Capital
75 Wall St.
New York, NY 10005
(212)429-3131
Fax: (212)429-3139
Website: http://www.dresdnerkb.com
Richard Wolf, Partner
Preferred Investment Size: $5,000,000
minimum. Investment Types: Early and
second stage, expansion, mezzanine, and
leveraged buyout. Industry Preferences:
Diversified. Geographic Preferences:
National.

East River Ventures, L.P.
645 Madison Ave., 22nd Fl.
New York, NY 10022
(212)644-2322
Fax: (212)644-5498
Montague H. Hackett
Preferred Investment Size: $500,000 to
$5,000,000. Investment Types: Early and
late stage, and mezzanine. Industry
Preferences: Diversified communication
and computer technology, consumer
services, and medical. Geographic
Preferences: National.

Easton Hunt Capital Partners
641 Lexington Ave., 21st Fl.
New York, NY 10017
(212)702-0950
Fax: (212)702-0952
Website: http://www.eastoncapital.com
Investment Types: First stage, mezzanine,
and special situations. Industry
Preferences: Diversified. Geographic
Preferences: Entire U.S.

Elk Associates Funding Corp.
747 3rd Ave., Ste. 4C
New York, NY 10017
(212)355-2449
Fax: (212)759-3338
Gary C. Granoff, Pres.
Preferred Investment Size: $100,000 to
$300,000. Investment Types: Second

stage and leveraged buyout. Industry
Preferences: Radio and TV, consumer
franchise businesses, hotel and resort
areas, and transportation. Geographic
Preferences: Southeast and Midwest.

EOS Partners, L.P.
320 Park Ave., 22nd Fl.
New York, NY 10022
(212)832-5800
Fax: (212)832-5815
E-mail: mfirst@eospartners.com
Website: http://www.eospartners.com
Mark L. First, Managing Director
Preferred Investment Size: $3,000,000.
Investment Policies: Equity and equity-
oriented debt. Investment Types:
Industry rollups, leveraged buyout,
mezzanine, second stage, and special
situation. Industry Preferences:
Diversified. Geographic Preferences:
Entire United States and Canad

Euclid Partners
45 Rockefeller Plaza, Ste. 3240
New York, NY 10111
(212)218-6880
Fax: (212)218-6877
E-mail: graham@euclidpartners.com
Website: http://www.euclidpartners.com
Preferred Investment Size: $500,000 to
$5,000,000. Investment Types: Startup,
first and second stage. Industry
Preferences: Internet related, computer
software and services, genetic
engineering, and medical/health related.
Geographic Preferences: No preference.

Evergreen Capital Partners, Inc.
150 East 58th St.
New York, NY 10155
(212)813-0758
Fax: (212)813-0754
E-mail: rysmith@evergreencapital.com
Preferred Investment Size: $1,000,000 to
$300,000,000. Investment Types: No
preference. Industry Preferences:
Diversified. Geographic Preferences:
National.

Exeter Capital L.P.
10 E. 53rd St.
New York, NY 10022
(212)872-1172
Fax: (212)872-1198
E-mail: exeter@usa.net
Karen J. Watai, Partner
Preferred Investment Size: $1,000,000
minimum. Investment Policies: Loans
and equity investments. Investment

Types: Leveraged buyout, mezzanine,
second stage, and special situation.
Industry Preferences: Diversified.
Geographic Preferences: National.

Financial Technology Research Corp.
518 Broadway
Penthouse
New York, NY 10012
(212)625-9100
Fax: (212)431-0300
E-mail: fintek@financier.com
Neal Bruckman, President
Preferred Investment Size: $300,000 to
$500,000. Investment Types: Seed,
research and development, startup, first
stage, second stage, and special
situations. Industry Preferences:
Diversified. Geographic Preferences:
Entire U.S. and Canada.

4C Ventures
237 Park Ave., Ste. 801
New York, NY 10017
(212)692-3680
Fax: (212)692-3685
Website: http://www.4cventures.com
Ted Hobart, Partner
Preferred Investment Size: $500,000 to
$1,000,000. Investment Types: Seed,
research and development, startup, first
and second stage. Industry Preferences:
Communications, computer related, and
consumer. Geographic Preferences:
Entire U.S. and Canada.

Fusient Ventures
99 Park Ave., 20th Fl.
New York, NY 10016
(212)972-8999
Fax: (212)972-9876
E-mail: info@fusient.com
Website: http://www.fusient.com
Preferred Investment Size: $500,000 to
$3,000,000. Investment Types: Early and
first stage, and seed. Industry
Preferences: Internet, entertainment and
leisure, and media. Geographic
Preferences: U.S.

Generation Capital Partners
551 Fifth Ave., Ste. 3100
New York, NY 10176
(212)450-8507
Fax: (212)450-8550
Website: http://www.genpartners.com
Preferred Investment Size: $5,000,000.
Investment Types: Startup, early and late
stage, and leveraged buyout. Industry
Preferences: Diversified communications

and computer technology, consumer products and services, and industrial products and equipment. Geographic Preferences: Unite

Golub Associates, Inc.
555 Madison Ave.
New York, NY 10022
(212)750-6060
Fax: (212)750-5505
Evelyn Mordechai, Vice President
Preferred Investment Size: $1,000,000 to $10,000,000. Investment Types: Second stage, mezzanine, leveraged buyout, recaps, and special situations. Industry Preferences: Diversified. Geographic Preferences: Eastern U.S.

Hambro America Biosciences Inc.
650 Madison Ave., 21st Floor
New York, NY 10022
(212)223-7400
Fax: (212)223-0305
Preferred Investment Size: $2,500,000 to $5,000,000. Investment Types: First and second stage, and special situations. Industry Preferences: Genetic engineering, chemicals and materials, and medical/health related. Geographic Preferences: Entire U.S.

Hanover Capital Corp.
505 Park Ave., 15th Fl.
New York, NY 10022
(212)755-1222
Fax: (212)935-1787
Michael Wainstein
Preferred Investment Size: $300,000 minimum. Investment Types: Leveraged buyout, mezzanine, and second stage. Industry Preferences: Diversified. Geographic Preferences: Entire U.S.

Harvest Partners, Inc.
280 Park Ave, 33rd Fl.
New York, NY 10017
(212)559-6300
Fax: (212)812-0100
Website: http://www.harvpart.com
Harvey Mallement
Preferred Investment Size: $15,000,000 to $100,000,000. Investment Types: Acquisition, leveraged buyout, management buyouts, private placements, special situations, and turnaround. Industry Preferences: Consumer products and services, communications, distribution, fiberoptics, and me

Holding Capital Group, Inc.
10 E. 53rd St., 30th Fl.
New York, NY 10022
(212)486-6670
Fax: (212)486-0843
James W. Donaghy, President
Preferred Investment Size: $5,000,000.
Investment Types: Leveraged buyout.
Industry Preferences: No preference.
Geographic Preferences: Entire U.S.

Hudson Venture Partners
660 Madison Ave., 14th Fl.
New York, NY 10021-8405
(212)644-9797
Fax: (212)644-7430
Website: http://www.hudsonptr.com
Marilyn Adler
Preferred Investment Size: $500,000 to $2,800,000. Investment Types: Seed, start-up, first and early stages, and expansion. Industry Preferences: Diversified. Geographic Preferences: Entire U.S.

IBJS Capital Corp.
1 State St., 9th Fl.
New York, NY 10004
(212)858-2018
Fax: (212)858-2768
George Zombeck, Chief Operating Officer
Preferred Investment Size: $2,000,000.
Investment Types: Mezzanine, leveraged buyout, and special situations. Industry Preferences: Consumer products and services, and chemicals and materials. Geographic Preferences: Entire U.S.

InterEquity Capital Partners, L.P.
220 5th Ave.
New York, NY 10001
(212)779-2022
Fax: (212)779-2103
Website: http://www.interequity-capital.com
Preferred Investment Size: $1,000,000 to $3,000,000. Investment Types: First and second stage, mezzanine, leveraged buyout, and special situations. Industry Preferences: Diversified. Geographic Preferences: Entire U.S.

The Jordan Edmiston Group Inc.
150 East 52nd St., 18th Fl.
New York, NY 10022
(212)754-0710
Fax: (212)754-0337
Scott Peters
Preferred Investment Size: $1,000,000.
Investment Types: Leveraged buyout,

mezzanine, second stage, and special situation. Industry Preferences: Publishing. Geographic Preferences: No preference.

Josephberg, Grosz and Co., Inc.
633 3rd Ave., 13th Fl.
New York, NY 10017
(212)974-9926
Fax: (212)397-5832
Richard Josephberg
Preferred Investment Size: $1,000,000 to $30,000,000. Investment Types: Many types including seed, research and development, startup, first and second stage, mezzanine, and leveraged buyout. Industry Preferences: Diversified. Geographic Preferences: Entire U.S.

J.P. Morgan Capital Corp.
60 Wall St.
New York, NY 10260-0060
(212)648-9000
Fax: (212)648-5002
Website: http://www.jpmorgan.com
Lincoln E. Frank, Chief Operating Officer
Preferred Investment Size: $10,000,000 to $20,000,000. Investment Types: Second stage and special situations. Industry Preferences: Diversified. Geographic Preferences: Entire U.S. and Canada.

The Lambda Funds
380 Lexington Ave., 54th Fl.
New York, NY 10168
(212)682-3454
Fax: (212)682-9231
Preferred Investment Size: $200,000 to $500,000. Investment Types: Early stage, expansion, first and second stage, and management buyout. Industry Preferences: Diversified. Geographic Preferences: Mid Atlantic, Northeast, and West Coast.

Lepercq Capital Management Inc.
1675 Broadway
New York, NY 10019
(212)698-0795
Fax: (212)262-0155
Michael J. Connelly
Preferred Investment Size: $1,000,000 to $10,000,000. Investment Types: Control-block purchases, leveraged buyout, and second stage. Industry Preferences: Diversified. Geographic Preferences: No preference.

Loeb Partners Corp.
61 Broadway, Ste. 2400
New York, NY 10006
(212)483-7000
Fax: (212)574-2001
Preferred Investment Size: $100,000.
Investment Types: Early stage,
acquisition, expansion, leveraged and
management buyout. Industry
Preferences: Diversified. Geographic
Preferences: National.

Madison Investment Partners
660 Madison Ave.
New York, NY 10021
(212)223-2600
Fax: (212)223-8208
Preferred Investment Size: $5,000,000.
Investment Types: Second stage,
leveraged buyout, and industry roll ups.
Industry Preferences: Diversified.
Geographic Preferences: National.

MC Capital Inc.
520 Madison Ave., 16th Fl.
New York, NY 10022
(212)644-0841
Fax: (212)644-2926
Shunichi Maeda
Preferred Investment Size: $1,000,000 to
$30,000,000. Investment Types:
Acquisition, expansion, first stage, fund
of funds, generalist PE, joint ventures,
later stage, leveraged buyout, private
placement, second stage, special
situation, and turnaround. Industry
Preferences: Communic

McCown, De Leeuw and Co. (New York)
65 E. 55th St., 36th Fl.
New York, NY 10022
(212)355-5500
Fax: (212)355-6283
Website: http://www.mdcpartners.com
Christopher Crosby, Principal
Preferred Investment Size: $40,000,000
minimum. Investment Types: Leveraged
buyout and special situations. Industry
Preferences: Diversified. Geographic
Preferences: Entire U.S.

Morgan Stanley Venture Partners
1221 Avenue of the Americas, 33rd Fl.
New York, NY 10020
(212)762-7900
Fax: (212)762-8424
E-mail: msventures@ms.com
Website: http://www.msvp.com

Preferred Investment Size: $2,000,000.
Investment Types: Second stage,
mezzanine, leveraged buyout, and
industry roll ups. Industry
Preferences: Diversified technology.
Geographic Preferences: Entire U.S.
and Canada.

Nazem and Co.
645 Madison Ave., 12th Fl.
New York, NY 10022
(212)371-7900
Fax: (212)371-2150
E-mail: nazem@msn.com
Fred F. Nazem, Managing General
Partner
Preferred Investment Size: $1,000,000
minimum. Investment Types: Seed,
startup, first and second stage,
mezzanine, leveraged buyout, and special
situations. Industry Preferences:
Diversified. Geographic Preferences: No
preference.

Needham Capital Management, L.L.C.
445 Park Ave.
New York, NY 10022
(212)371-8300
Fax: (212)705-0299
Website: http://www.needhamco.com
Joseph Abramoff
Preferred Investment Size: $1,000,000 to
$10,000,000. Investment Policies: Equity.
Investment Types: Expansion, later stage,
leveraged buyout, management buyout,
and mezzanine. Industry Preferences:
Diversified technology. Geographic
Preferences: National.

Norwood Venture Corp.
1430 Broadway, Ste. 1607
New York, NY 10018
(212)869-5075
Fax: (212)869-5331
E-mail: nvc@mail.idt.net
Website: http://www.norven.com
Mark Littell
Preferred Investment Size: $500,000 to
$1,000,000. Investment Types:
Mezzanine, leveraged buyout, and special
situations. Industry Preferences:
Diversified. Geographic Preferences:
National.

Noveltek Venture Corp.
521 Fifth Ave., Ste. 1700
New York, NY 10175
(212)286-1963
Preferred Investment Size: $1,000,000
minimum. Investment Types:

Control-block purchases, first stage,
mezzanine, second stage, special
situation, and start-up. Industry
Preferences: Diversified. Geographic
Preferences: Entire U.S. and Canada.

Paribas Principal, Inc.
787 7th Ave.
New York, NY 10019
(212)841-2005
Fax: (212)841-3558
Gary Binning
Preferred Investment Size: $50,000,000.
Investment Types: Leveraged buyout,
special situations, and control block
purchases. Industry Preferences:
Diversified. Geographic Preferences:
Entire U.S.

Patricof & Co. Ventures, Inc. (New York)
445 Park Ave.
New York, NY 10022
(212)753-6300
Fax: (212)319-6155
Website: http://www.patricof.com
Preferred Investment Size: $500,000
minimum. Investment Types: Seed,
startup, first and second stage,
mezzanine, and leveraged buyout.
Industry Preferences: Diversified.
Geographic Preferences: No
preference.

The Platinum Group, Inc.
350 Fifth Ave, Ste. 7113
New York, NY 10118
(212)736-4300
Fax: (212)736-6086
Website: http://
www.platinumgroup.com
Michael Grant, Analyst
Investment Types: Startup, first stage,
second stage, and leveraged buyout.
Industry Preferences: Diversified.
Geographic Preferences: National.

Pomona Capital
780 Third Ave., 28th Fl.
New York, NY 10017
(212)593-3639
Fax: (212)593-3987
Website: http://www.pomonacapital.com
Karen Macleod
Preferred Investment Size: $1,000,000
minimum. Investment Types: Various
investment types. Industry Preferences:
Diversified. Geographic Preferences:
Entire U.S.

Prospect Street Ventures
10 East 40th St., 44th Fl.
New York, NY 10016
(212)448-0702
Fax: (212)448-9652
E-mail: wkohler@prospectstreet.com
Website: http://www.prospectstreet.com
Edward Ryeom, Vice President
Preferred Investment Size: $1,000,000 minimum. Investment Types: First and second stage, start-up, control-block purchases, recaps, and special situations. Industry Preferences: Internet related, computer software and services, computer hardware, and communications. Geographic Prefer

Regent Capital Management
505 Park Ave., Ste. 1700
New York, NY 10022
(212)735-9900
Fax: (212)735-9908
E-mail: ninamcle@aol.com
Richard Hochman, Managing Director
Preferred Investment Size: $3,500,000 minimum. Investment Types: Second stage, mezzanine, and leveraged buyout. Industry Preferences: Communications, consumer products and services. Geographic Preferences: National.

Rothschild Ventures, Inc.
1251 Avenue of the Americas, 51st Fl.
New York, NY 10020
(212)403-3500
Fax: (212)403-3652
Website: http://www.nmrothschild.com
Preferred Investment Size: $500,000 to $5,000,000. Investment Types: Seed, research and development, startup, first and second stage, mezzanine, and leveraged buyout. Industry Preferences: Diversified. Geographic Preferences: Entire U.S. and Canada.

Sandler Capital Management
767 Fifth Ave., 45th Fl.
New York, NY 10153
(212)754-8100
Fax: (212)826-0280
Preferred Investment Size: $20,000,000 minimum. Investment Policies: Equity. Investment Types: Seed, start-up, first and second stage, control-block purchases, leveraged buyout, mezzanine, research and development, and special situation. Industry Preferences: Diversified communicatio

Siguler Guff & Company
630 Fifth Ave., 16th Fl.
New York, NY 10111
(212)332-5100
Fax: (212)332-5120
Maria Boyazny, Associate
Investment Types: Startup, first stage, second stage, control-block purchases, mezzanine, leveraged buyout, and special situations. Industry Preferences: Diversified. Geographic Preferences: National.

Spencer Trask Ventures Inc.
535 Madison Ave.
New York, NY 10022
(212)355-5565
Fax: (212)751-3362
Website: http://www.spencertrask.com
A. Emerson Martin, II, Senior Managing Director
Preferred Investment Size: $3,000,000 minimum. Investment Types: Startup, first stage, second stage, and special situations. Industry Preferences: Diversified. Geographic Preferences: National.

Sprout Group (New York City)
277 Park Ave.
New York, NY 10172
(212)892-3600
Fax: (212)892-3444
E-mail: info@sproutgroup.com
Website: http://www.sproutgroup.com
Patrick J. Boroian, General Partner
Preferred Investment Size: $5,000,000 to $50,000,000. Investment Types: Seed, startup, first and second stage, mezzanine, leveraged buyout, and special situations. Industry Preferences: Diversified technology. Geographic Preferences: Entire U.S.

US Trust Private Equity
114 W.47th St.
New York, NY 10036
(212)852-3949
Fax: (212)852-3759
Website: http://www.ustrust.com/privateequity
Jim Ruler
Preferred Investment Size: $5,000,000 minimum. Investment Types: Early, first stage, and second stage. Industry Preferences: Diversified. Geographic Preferences: National.

Vencon Management Inc.
301 West 53rd St., Ste. 10F
New York, NY 10019

(212)581-8787
Fax: (212)397-4126
Website: http://www.venconinc.com
Ingrid Yang
Preferred Investment Size: $500,000 to $10,000,000. Investment Types: First and second stage, leveraged buyout, seed, special situation, and start-up. Industry Preferences: Diversified. Geographic Preferences: Entire U.S. and Canada.

Venrock Associates
30 Rockefeller Plaza, Ste. 5508
New York, NY 10112
(212)649-5600
Fax: (212)649-5788
Website: http://www.venrock.com
Preferred Investment Size: $500,000 minimum. Investment Types: Seed, research and development, startup, first and second stages. Industry Preferences: Diversified. Geographic Preferences: National.

Venture Capital Fund of America, Inc.
509 Madison Ave., Ste. 812
New York, NY 10022
(212)838-5577
Fax: (212)838-7614
E-mail: mail@vcfa.com
Website: http://www.vcfa.com
Dayton T. Carr, General Partner
Preferred Investment Size: $500,000 to $100,000,000. Investment Types: Secondary partnership interests. Industry Preferences: Does not consider tax shelters, real estate, or direct investments in companies. Geographic Preferences: Entire U.S.

Venture Opportunities Corp.
150 E. 58th St.
New York, NY 10155
(212)832-3737
Fax: (212)980-6603
E-mail: jerryvoc@aol.com
Jerry March
Preferred Investment Size: $2,000,000 minimum. Investment Types: Startup, first and second stage, mezzanine, leveraged buyout, and special situations. Industry Preferences: Diversified. Geographic Preferences: Entire U.S.

Warburg Pincus Ventures, Inc.
466 Lexington Ave., 11th Fl.
New York, NY 10017
(212)878-9309
Fax: (212)878-9200
Website: http://www.warburgpincus.com

Preferred Investment Size: $1,000,000 to $500,000,000. Investment Types: Many types including seed, startup, first and second stage, mezzanine, leveraged buyouts, private placements, recaps, and special situations. Industry Preferences: Diversified. Geographic Preferences: U.S. and C

Wasserstein, Perella & Co. Inc.
31 W. 52nd St., 27th Fl.
New York, NY 10019
(212)702-5691
Fax: (212)969-7879
Perry W. Steiner
Investment Types: Leveraged buyout. Industry Preferences: Diversified. Geographic Preferences: National.

Welsh, Carson, Anderson, & Stowe
320 Park Ave., Ste. 2500
New York, NY 10022-6815
(212)893-9500
Fax: (212)893-9575
Patrick J. Welsh, General Partner
Preferred Investment Size: $25,000,000 minimum. Investment Types: Leveraged buyout and special situations. Industry Preferences: Computer related and medical/health related. Geographic Preferences: Entire U.S.

Whitney and Co. (New York)
630 Fifth Ave. Ste. 3225
New York, NY 10111
(212)332-2400
Fax: (212)332-2422
Website: http://www.jhwitney.com
Preferred Investment Size: $1,000,000. Investment Types: Leveraged buyout and expansion. Industry Preferences: Diversified technology. Geographic Preferences: No preference.

Winthrop Ventures
74 Trinity Place, Ste. 600
New York, NY 10006
(212)422-0100
Cyrus Brown
Preferred Investment Size: $1,000,000 minimum. Investment Types: Startup, early and late stage, and leveraged buyout. Industry Preferences: Diversified. Geographic Preferences: National.

The Pittsford Group
8 Lodge Pole Rd.
Pittsford, NY 14534
(716)223-3523

Preferred Investment Size: $100,000 to $300,000. Investment Types: Startup, first and second stage, and control-block purchases. Industry Preferences: Diversified technology. Geographic Preferences: Eastern U.S. and Canada.

Genesee Funding
70 Linden Oaks, 3rd Fl.
Rochester, NY 14625
(716)383-5550
Fax: (716)383-5305
Preferred Investment Size: $200,000. Investment Types: Second stage, mezzanine, and leveraged buyout. Industry Preferences: Diversified. Geographic Preferences: Northeast.

Gabelli Multimedia Partners
One Corporate Center
Rye, NY 10580
(914)921-5395
Fax: (914)921-5031
E-mail: fsommer@gabelli.com
Preferred Investment Size: $250,000 to $500,000. Investment Policies: Equity. Investment Types: Seed, startup, first and second stage. Industry Preferences: Diversified communications. Geographic Preferences: Northeast.

Stamford Financial
108 Main St.
Stamford, NY 12167
(607)652-3311
Fax: (607)652-6301
Website: http://www.stamfordfinancial.com
Alexander C. Brosda
Preferred Investment Size: $1,000,000 to $2,500,000. Investment Types: Expansion and mezzanine. Industry Preferences: Diversified. Geographic Preferences: Entire U.S.

Northwood Ventures LLC
485 Underhill Blvd., Ste. 205
Syosset, NY 11791
(516)364-5544
Fax: (516)364-0879
E-mail: northwood@northwood.com
Website: http://www.northwoodventures.com
Paul Homer, Associate
Preferred Investment Size: $1,000,000 to $10,000,000. Investment Types: First and second stage, acquisition, expansion, leveraged buyout, private placement, special situations, and industry roll ups. Industry Preferences: Diversified.

Geographic Preferences: Entire U.S. and Canada.

Exponential Business Development Co.
216 Walton St.
Syracuse, NY 13202-1227
(315)474-4500
Fax: (315)474-4682
E-mail: dirksonn@aol.com
Website: http://www.exponential-ny.com
Dirk E. Sonneborn, Partner
Preferred Investment Size: $100,000 to $600,000. Investment Types: Early and first stage. Industry Preferences: No preference. Geographic Preferences: New York.

Onondaga Venture Capital Fund Inc.
714 State Tower Bldg.
Syracuse, NY 13202
(315)478-0157
Fax: (315)478-0158
Irving Schwartz
Preferred Investment Size: $100,000 to $250,000. Investment Types: Expansion, later stage, and mezzanine. Industry Preferences: Diversified. Geographic Preferences: Mid Atlantic and Northeast.

Bessemer Venture Partners (Westbury)
1400 Old Country Rd., Ste. 109
Westbury, NY 11590
(516)997-2300
Fax: (516)997-2371
E-mail: bob@bvpny.com
Website: http://www.bvp.com
Investment Types: Seed, research and development, start-up, first stages, leveraged buyout, special situations, and expansion. Industry Preferences: Communications, computer related, consumer products, distribution, and electronics. Geographic Preferences: Entire U.S.

Ovation Capital Partners
120 Bloomingdale Rd., 4th Fl.
White Plains, NY 10605
(914)258-0011
Fax: (914)684-0848
Website: http://www.ovationcapital.com
Preferred Investment Size: $500,000 to $4,000,000. Investment Types: Early stage. Industry Preferences: Internet related. Geographic Preferences: Northeast.

North Carolina

Carolinas Capital Investment Corp.
1408 Biltmore Dr.
Charlotte, NC 28207

(704)375-3888
Fax: (704)375-6226
E-mail: ed@carolinacapital.com
Edward Goode
Preferred Investment Size: $200,000 to
$1,000,000. Investment Types: Seed,
research and development, leveraged
buyout, startup, first and second stages.
Industry Preferences: Communications,
electronic components and
instrumentation. Geographic
Preferences: No preference.

First Union Capital Partners
1st Union Center, 12th Fl.
301 S. College St.
Charlotte, NC 28288-0732
(704)383-0000
Fax: (704)374-6711
Website: http://www.fucp.com
L. Watts Hamrick, III, Partner
Preferred Investment Size: $5,000,000
minimum. Investment Types: Seed, start-
up, first and second stage, mezzanine,
expansion, leveraged buyout, special
situations, and control block purchases.
Industry Preferences: Diversified.
Geographic Preferences: No preference.

Frontier Capital LLC
525 North Tryon St., Ste. 1700
Charlotte, NC 28202
(704)414-2880
Fax: (704)414-2881
Website: http://www.frontierfunds.com
Preferred Investment Size: $500,000 to
$3,000,000. Investment Types: Early stage
and expansion. Industry Preferences:
Telecommunications, computer related,
electronics, and energy. Geographic
Preferences: Mid Atlantic and Southeast.

Kitty Hawk Capital
2700 Coltsgate Rd., Ste. 202
Charlotte, NC 28211
(704)362-3909
Fax: (704)362-2774
Website: http://
www.kittyhawkcapital.com
Stephen W. Buchanan, General Partner
Preferred Investment Size: $1,000,000 to
$7,000,000. Investment Types:
Expansion, first and early stage. Industry
Preferences: Diversified. Geographic
Preferences: Southeast.

Piedmont Venture Partners
One Morrocroft Centre
6805 Morisson Blvd., Ste. 380
Charlotte, NC 28211

(704)731-5200
Fax: (704)365-9733
Website: http://www.piedmontvp.com
Preferred Investment Size: $250,000 to
$5,000,000. Investment Types: Early
stage. Industry Preferences:
Diversified. Geographic Preferences:
Southeast.

Ruddick Investment Co.
1800 Two First Union Center
Charlotte, NC 28282
(704)372-5404
Fax: (704)372-6409
Richard N. Brigden, Vice President
Preferred Investment Size: $500,000 to
$1,000,000. Investment Types: First and
second stage, and mezzanine. Industry
Preferences: Diversified. Geographic
Preferences: Southeast.

The Shelton Companies Inc.
3600 One First Union Center
301 S. College St.
Charlotte, NC 28202
(704)348-2200
Fax: (704)348-2260
Preferred Investment Size: $1,000,000 to
$10,000,000. Investment Types: Control-
block purchases, leveraged buyouts,
recaps, and second stage. Industry
Preferences: Diversified. Geographic
Preferences: Mid Atlantic, Midwest,
Southeast, and Southwest.

Wakefield Group
1110 E. Morehead St.
PO Box 36329
Charlotte, NC 28236
(704)372-0355
Fax: (704)372-8216
Website: http://
www.wakefieldgroup.com
Anna Nelson, Partner
Preferred Investment Size: $1,000,000 to
$5,000,000. Investment Types: Early
stage. Industry Preferences: Diversified.
Geographic Preferences: Southeast.

Aurora Funds, Inc.
2525 Meridian Pkwy., Ste. 220
Durham, NC 27713
(919)484-0400
Fax: (919)484-0444
Website: http://www.aurorafunds.com
Preferred Investment Size: $250,000 to
$1,500,000. Investment Types: Startup,
seed, early and first stage. Industry
Preferences: Diversified. Geographic
Preferences: Eastern United States.

Intersouth Partners
3211 Shannon Rd., Ste. 610
Durham, NC 27707
(919)493-6640
Fax: (919)493-6649
E-mail: info@intersouth.com
Website: http://www.intersouth.com
Jonathan Perl
Preferred Investment Size: $2,000,000
to $10,000,000. Investment Types:
Seed, startup, first and early stages.
Industry Preferences: Diversified.
Geographic Preferences: Southeast and
Southwest.

Geneva Merchant Banking Partners
PO Box 21962
Greensboro, NC 27420
(336)275-7002
Fax: (336)275-9155
Website: http://
www.genevamerchantbank.com
Preferred Investment Size: $1,000,000 to
$7,000,000. Investment Types: Balanced,
distressed debt, expansion, leveraged and
management buyout, mezzanine, second
stage, and special situation. Industry
Preferences: Diversified. Geographic
Preferences: Mid Atlantic, Midwest, and
Southeas

**The North Carolina Enterprise Fund,
L.P.**
3600 Glenwood Ave., Ste. 107
Raleigh, NC 27612
(919)781-2691
Fax: (919)783-9195
Website: http://www.ncef.com
Charles T. Closson, President and CEO
Preferred Investment Size: $2,000,000
minimum. Investment Policies: Equity.
Investment Types: Startup, first stage,
and mezzanine. Industry Preferences:
Diversified. Geographic Preferences:
North Carolina and Southeast.

Ohio

Senmend Medical Ventures
4445 Lake Forest Dr., Ste. 600
Cincinnati, OH 45242
(513)563-3264
Fax: (513)563-3261
Preferred Investment Size: $500,000 to
$1,000,000. Investment Types: Second
stage and mezzanine. Industry
Preferences: Genetic engineering,
medical and health related. Geographic
Preferences: National.

The Walnut Group
312 Walnut St., Ste. 1151
Cincinnati, OH 45202
(513)651-3300
Fax: (513)929-4441
Website: http://
www.thewalnutgroup.com
Preferred Investment Size: $500,000 to
$5,000,000. Investment Types: Balanced.
Geographic Preferences: Northeast.

Brantley Venture Partners
20600 Chagrin Blvd., Ste. 1150
Cleveland, OH 44122
(216)283-4800
Fax: (216)283-5324
Kevin J. Cook, Associate
Preferred Investment Size: $1,000,000 to
$5,000,000. Investment Types: Industry
rollups, seed, start-up, and first stage.
Industry Preferences: Diversified.
Geographic Preferences: Entire U.S.

Clarion Capital Corp.
1801 E. 9th St., Ste. 1120
Cleveland, OH 44114
(216)687-1096
Fax: (216)694-3545
Preferred Investment Size: $250,000 to
$500,000. Investment Types: Early, first
and second stage. Industry Preferences:
Diversified. Geographic Preferences: East
Coast, Midwest, and West Coast.

Crystal Internet Venture Fund, L.P.
1120 Chester Ave., Ste. 418
Cleveland, OH 44114
(216)263-5515
Fax: (216)263-5518
E-mail: jf@crystalventure.com
Website: http://www.crystalventure.com
Daniel Kellog, Partner
Preferred Investment Size: $1,000,000 to
$6,000,000. Investment Policies: Equity.
Investment Types: Balanced and early
stage. Industry Preferences: Diversified
communications and computer
technology. Geographic Preferences:
National.

Key Equity Capital Corp.
127 Public Sq., 28th Fl.
Cleveland, OH 44114
(216)689-3000
Fax: (216)689-3204
Website: http://www.keybank.com
Cindy J. Babitt
Preferred Investment Size: $1,000,000
minimum. Investment Policies: Willing
to make equity investments. Investment

Types: Expansion, industry rollups,
leveraged buyout, second stage, and
special situation. Industry Preferences:
Diversified. Geographic Preferences:
National.

Morgenthaler Ventures
Terminal Tower
50 Public Square, Ste. 2700
Cleveland, OH 44113
(216)416-7500
Fax: (216)416-7501
Website: http://www.morgenthaler.com
Robert C. Belles, Jr., General Partner
Preferred Investment Size: $500,000
minimum. Investment Types: Startup,
first and second stage, acquisition,
leveraged and management buyout,
special situations, and expansion.
Industry Preferences: Diversified.
Geographic Preferences: Entire U.S. and
Ontario, Canada.

National City Equity Partners Inc.
1965 E. 6th St.
Cleveland, OH 44114
(216)575-2491
Fax: (216)575-9965
E-mail: nccap@aol.com
Website: http://www.nccapital.com
Carl E. Baldassarre, Managing Director
Preferred Investment Size: $1,000,000 to
$20,000,000. Investment Types: Second
stage, mezzanine, leveraged buyout,
special situations, recaps, management
buyouts, and expansion. Industry
Preferences: Diversified. Geographic
Preferences: Entire U.S.

Primus Venture Partners, Inc.
5900 LanderBrook Dr., Ste. 2000
Cleveland, OH 44124-4020
(440)684-7300
Fax: (440)684-7342
E-mail: info@primusventure.com
Website: http://www.primusventure.com
Jeffrey J. Milius, Investment Manager
Preferred Investment Size: $5,000,000
minimum. Investment Types: Early stage,
startup, expansion and balanced.
Industry Preferences: Diversified.
Geographic Preferences: Entire U.S.

Banc One Capital Partners (Columbus)
150 East Gay St., 24th Fl.
Columbus, OH 43215
(614)217-1100
Fax: (614)217-1217
Suzanne B. Kriscunas, Managing
Director

Preferred Investment Size: $1,000,000
minimum. Investment Types: Later
stage, leveraged buyout, mezzanine,
industry rollups, and special
situations. Industry Preferences:
Diversified. Geographic Preferences:
Entire U.S.

Battelle Venture Partners
505 King Ave.
Columbus, OH 43201
(614)424-7005
Fax: (614)424-4874
Preferred Investment Size: $500,000 to
$1,000,000. Investment Types: Startup,
first and second stage. Industry
Preferences: Energy/natural resources,
industrial products and equipment.
Geographic Preferences: National.

Ohio Partners
62 E. Board St., 3rd Fl.
Columbus, OH 43215
(614)621-1210
Fax: (614)621-1240
E-mail: mcox@ohiopartners.com
Investment Types: Startup, first and
second stage. Industry Preferences:
Computer related. Geographic
Preferences: Western U.S. and
Midwest.

Capital Technology Group, L.L.C.
400 Metro Place North, Ste. 300
Dublin, OH 43017
(614)792-6066
Fax: (614)792-6036
E-mail: info@capitaltech.com
Website: http://www.capitaltech.com
Preferred Investment Size: $250,000 to
$1,000,000. Investment Types: Seed, early
and start-up. Industry Preferences:
Diversified electronics, alternative
energy, and Internet related. Geographic
Preferences: National.

Northwest Ohio Venture Fund
4159 Holland-Sylvania R., Ste. 202
Toledo, OH 43623
(419)824-8144
Fax: (419)882-2035
E-mail: bwalsh@novf.com
Barry P. Walsh, Managing Partner
Preferred Investment Size: $250,000
minimum. Investment Types: Seed,
early and late stage, leveraged
buyout, mezzanine, research and
development. Industry Preferences:
Diversified. Geographic Preferences:
Midwest.

Oklahoma

Moore & Associates
1000 W. Wilshire Blvd., Ste. 370
Oklahoma City, OK 73116
(405)842-3660
Fax: (405)842-3763
Preferred Investment Size: $500,000 minimum. Investment Types: Startup, first and second stage, mezzanine, and leveraged buyout. Industry Preferences: Diversified technology. Geographic Preferences: National.

Chisholm Private Capital Partners
100 West 5th St., Ste. 805
Tulsa, OK 74103
(918)584-0440
Fax: (918)584-0441
Website: http://www.chisholmvc.com
James Bode, General Partner
Preferred Investment Size: $1,000,000 to $4,000,000. Investment Types: Startup, early and late stage. Industry Preferences: Diversified communications and computer, consumer products and retailing, electronics, alternative energy, and medical. Geographic Preferences: Entire U.S.

Davis, Tuttle Venture Partners (Tulsa)
320 S. Boston, Ste. 1000
Tulsa, OK 74103-3703
(918)584-7272
Fax: (918)582-3404
Website: http://www.davistuttle.com
Preferred Investment Size: $5,000,000 minimum. Investment Types: First and second stage, mezzanine, and leveraged buyout. Industry Preferences: Diversified. Geographic Preferences: Southwest.

RBC Ventures
2627 E. 21st St.
Tulsa, OK 74114
(918)744-5607
Fax: (918)743-8630
K.Y. Vargas, Vice President
Preferred Investment Size: $2,000,000 minimum. Investment Policies: Equity. Investment Types: Control-block purchases, leveraged buyout, mezzanine, second stage, and special situations. Industry Preferences: Diversified transportation. Geographic Preferences: Southwest.

Oregon

Utah Ventures II LP
10700 SW Beaverton-Hillsdale Hwy., Ste. 548

Beaverton, OR 97005
(503)574-4125
E-mail: adishlip@uven.com
Website: http://www.uven.com
Preferred Investment Size: $1,000,000 to $7,000,000. Investment Types: Early stages. Industry Preferences: Diversified technology. Geographic Preferences: Northwest and Rocky Mountains.

Orien Ventures
14523 SW Westlake Dr.
Lake Oswego, OR 97035
(503)699-1680
Fax: (503)699-1681
Anthony Miadich, Managing General Partner
Preferred Investment Size: $500,000 minimum. Investment Types: Start-up, seed, early and first stage. Industry Preferences: Diversified technology. Geographic Preferences: No preference.

OVP Venture Partners (Lake Oswego)
340 Oswego Pointe Dr., Ste. 200
Lake Oswego, OR 97034
(503)697-8766
Fax: (503)697-8863
E-mail: info@ovp.com
Website: http://www.ovp.com
Preferred Investment Size: $1,000,000 to $10,000,000. Investment Types: Seed, startup, and early stage. Industry Preferences: Communications, computer and Internet related, electronics, genetic engineering, and medical health related. Geographic Preferences: Western U.S. and Western

Oregon Resource and Technology Development Fund
4370 NE Halsey St., Ste. 233
Portland, OR 97213-1566
(503)282-4462
Fax: (503)282-2976
Preferred Investment Size: $100,000 to $300,000. Investment Types: Seed, start-up, research and development. Industry Preferences: Biotechnology, electronics, computer software and services, and medical/health related. Geographic Preferences: West Coast.

Shaw Venture Partners
400 SW 6th Ave., Ste. 1100
Portland, OR 97204-1636
(503)228-4884
Fax: (503)227-2471
Website: http://www.shawventures.com

Preferred Investment Size: $250,000 to $3,000,000. Investment Types: Seed, startup, first and second stage, leveraged buyout, and special situations. Industry Preferences: Diversified. Geographic Preferences: Northwest.

Pennsylvania

Mid-Atlantic Venture Funds
125 Goodman Dr.
Bethlehem, PA 18015
(610)865-6550
Fax: (610)865-6427
Website: http://www.mavf.com
Thomas A. Smith
Preferred Investment Size: $500,000 to $8,000,000. Investment Types: Seed, research and development, first and second stage, leveraged buyout. Industry Preferences: Diversified. Geographic Preferences: Middle Atlantic and Northeast.

Newspring Ventures
100 W. Elm St., Ste. 101
Conshohocken, PA 19428
(610)567-2380
Fax: (610)567-2388
Website: http://www.newsprintventures.com
Preferred Investment Size: $1,000,000 minimum. Investment Types: Early stage and expansion. Industry Preferences: Communications, computer related, medical products, industrial products, and business services. Geographic Preferences: Mid Atlantic.

Patricof & Co. Ventures, Inc.
455 S. Gulph Rd., Ste. 410
King of Prussia, PA 19406
(610)265-0286
Fax: (610)265-4959
Website: http://www.patricof.com
Preferred Investment Size: $500,000 minimum. Investment Types: Seed, startup, first and second stage, mezzanine, and leveraged buyout. Industry Preferences: Diversified. Geographic Preferences: No preference.

Loyalhanna Venture Fund
527 Cedar Way, Ste. 104
Oakmont, PA 15139
(412)820-7035
Fax: (412)820-7036
James H. Knowles, Jr.
Preferred Investment Size: $300,000 to $1,000,000. Investment Types: First and

second stage, and leveraged buyout. Industry Preferences: No preference. Geographic Preferences: Entire U.S.

Innovest Group Inc.

2000 Market St., Ste. 1400
Philadelphia, PA 19103
(215)564-3960
Fax: (215)569-3272
Richard Woosnam
Preferred Investment Size: $500,000 to $1,000,000. Investment Types: First stage, leveraged buyout, recaps, second stage, special situation, and start-up. Industry Preferences: Diversified. Geographic Preferences: Mid Atlantic, Midwest, Northeast, and Southeast.

Keystone Venture Capital Management Co.

1601 Market St., Ste. 2500
Philadelphia, PA 19103
(215)241-1200
Fax: (215)241-1211
Website: http://www.keystonevc.com
Peter Ligeti
Preferred Investment Size: $2,000,000 to $5,000,000. Investment Types: First and second stage, balanced, and expansion. Industry Preferences: Diversified. Geographic Preferences: Middle Atlantic.

Liberty Venture Partners

2005 Market St., Ste. 200
Philadelphia, PA 19103
(215)282-4484
Fax: (215)282-4485
E-mail: info@libertyvp.com
Website: http://www.libertyvp.com
Thomas Morse
Preferred Investment Size: $3,000,000 to $7,000,000. Investment Types: Early stage and expansion. Industry Preferences: Diversified technology. Geographic Preferences: National.

Penn Janney Fund, Inc.

1801 Market St., 11th Fl.
Philadelphia, PA 19103
(215)665-4447
Fax: (215)557-0820
William Rulon-Miller
Preferred Investment Size: $1,000,000 minimum. Investment Types: Second stage, mezzanine, leveraged buyout, and special situations. Industry Preferences: Diversified. Geographic Preferences: Northeast, West Coast, and Middle Atlantic.

Philadelphia Ventures, Inc.

The Bellevue
200 S. Broad St.
Philadelphia, PA 19102
(215)732-4445
Fax: (215)732-4644
Walter M. Aikman, Managing Director
Preferred Investment Size: $500,000 maximum. Investment Types: Startup, first and second stage, mezzanine, and leveraged buyout. Industry Preferences: Diversified technology. Geographic Preferences: Entire U.S.

Birchmere Ventures Inc.

2000 Technology Dr.
Pittsburgh, PA 15219-3109
(412)803-8000
Fax: (412)687-8139
Website: http://www.birchmerevc.com
Investment Types: Early stage, expansion, first and later stage, and start-up. Industry Preferences: Diversified. Geographic Preferences: Mid Atlantic.

CEO Venture Fund

2000 Technology Dr., Ste. 160
Pittsburgh, PA 15219-3109
(412)687-3451
Fax: (412)687-8139
E-mail: ceofund@aol.com
Website: http://www.ceoventurefund.com
Ned Renzi, General Partner
Preferred Investment Size: $1,000,000 to $2,000,000. Investment Types: Startup, first stage, second stage, leveraged buyout, and special situations. Industry Preferences: Diversified technology. Geographic Preferences: Middle Atlantic states.

Innovation Works Inc.

2000 Technology Dr., Ste. 250
Pittsburgh, PA 15219
(412)681-1520
Fax: (412)681-2625
Website: http://www.innovationworks.org
Preferred Investment Size: $100,000 to $500,000. Investment Types: Early and first stage, seed, and start-up. Industry Preferences: Diversified technology. Geographic Preferences: Pennsylvania.

Keystone Minority Capital Fund L.P.

1801 Centre Ave., Ste. 201
Williams Sq.
Pittsburgh, PA 15219
(412)338-2230

Fax: (412)338-2224
Earl Hord, General Partner
Preferred Investment Size: $500,000 minimum. Investment Types: Startup, first stage, second stage, mezzanine, and leveraged buyout. Industry Preferences: Diversified. Geographic Preferences: Middle Atlantic states.

Mellon Ventures, Inc.

One Mellon Bank Ctr., Rm. 3500
Pittsburgh, PA 15258
(412)236-3594
Fax: (412)236-3593
Website: http://www.mellonventures.com
Preferred Investment Size: $2,000,000 to $25,000,000. Investment Types: Mezzanine, leveraged buyout, and special situations. Industry Preferences: Diversified. Geographic Preferences: National.

Pennsylvania Growth Fund

5850 Ellsworth Ave., Ste. 303
Pittsburgh, PA 15232
(412)661-1000
Fax: (412)361-0676
Barry Lhormer, Partner
Preferred Investment Size: $500,000 minimum. Investment Types: Leveraged buyout, mezzanine, second stage, and special situation. Industry Preferences: Diversified. Geographic Preferences: Middle Atlantic, Midwest, Northeast, and Southeast.

Point Venture Partners

The Century Bldg.
130 Seventh St., 7th Fl.
Pittsburgh, PA 15222
(412)261-1966
Fax: (412)261-1718
Kent Engelmeier, General Partner
Preferred Investment Size: $2,000,000. Investment Types: Startup, first stage, second stage, mezzanine, recaps, and leveraged buyout. Industry Preferences: Diversified. Geographic Preferences: Eastern and Midwestern U.S.

Cross Atlantic Capital Partners

5 Radnor Corporate Center, Ste. 555
Radnor, PA 19087
(610)995-2650
Fax: (610)971-2062
Website: http://www.xacp.com
Preferred Investment Size: $1,000,000 to $10,000,000. Investment Types: Balanced, early stage, expansion, seed, and start-up.

Industry Preferences: Diversified.
Geographic Preferences: Entire U.S.

Meridian Venture Partners (Radnor)
The Radnor Court Bldg., Ste. 140
259 Radnor-Chester Rd.
Radnor, PA 19087
(610)254-2999
Fax: (610)254-2996
E-mail: mvpart@ix.netcom.com
Kenneth E. Jones
Preferred Investment Size: $1,000,000 to
$2,000,000. Investment Types: Second stage,
leveraged buyout, and special situations.
Industry Preferences: Diversified.
Geographic Preferences: Entire U.S.

TDH
919 Conestoga Rd., Bldg. 1, Ste. 301
Rosemont, PA 19010
(610)526-9970
Fax: (610)526-9971
J.B. Doherty, Managing General Partner
Preferred Investment Size: $1,500,000
minimum. Investment Types: Startup,
first and second stage, mezzanine, recaps,
and leveraged buyout. Industry
Preferences: Diversified. Geographic
Preferences: Eastern U.S. and Midwest.

Adams Capital Management
500 Blackburn Ave.
Sewickley, PA 15143
(412)749-9454
Fax: (412)749-9459
Website: http://www.acm.com
Joel Adams, General Partner
Investment Types: Early and first stages.
Industry Preferences: Diversified
technology. Geographic Preferences:
National.

S.R. One, Ltd.
Four Tower Bridge
200 Barr Harbor Dr., Ste. 250
W. Conshohocken, PA 19428
(610)567-1000
Fax: (610)567-1039
Barbara Dalton, Vice President
Preferred Investment Size: $500,000 to
$5,000,000. Investment Types: Start-up,
first and second stage, and late stage.
Industry Preferences: Healthcare and
genetic engineering, and computer
software and services. Geographic
Preferences: No preference.

**Greater Philadelphia Venture Capital
Corp.**
351 East Conestoga Rd.
Wayne, PA 19087

(610)688-6829
Fax: (610)254-8958
Fred Choate, Manager
Preferred Investment Size: $100,000 to
$300,000. Investment Types: First and
second stage, leveraged buyout,
mezzanine, and special situations.
Industry Preferences: Diversified.
Geographic Preferences: Middle Atlantic.

PA Early Stage
435 Devon Park Dr., Bldg. 500, Ste. 510
Wayne, PA 19087
(610)293-4075
Fax: (610)254-4240
Website: http://www.paearlystage.com
Preferred Investment Size: $100,000 to
$10,000,000. Investment Types: Early,
first, and second stage; seed; and start-
up. Industry Preferences: Diversified.
Geographic Preferences: Mid Atlantic.

The Sandhurst Venture Fund, L.P.
351 E. Constoga Rd.
Wayne, PA 19087
(610)254-8900
Fax: (610)254-8958
Preferred Investment Size: $500,000 to
$1,000,000. Investment Types: Second
stage, recaps, and leveraged buyout.
Industry Preferences: Computer stores,
disposable medical/health related, and
industrial products. Geographic
Preferences: East Coast and Middle
Atlantic.

TL Ventures
700 Bldg.
435 Devon Park Dr.
Wayne, PA 19087-1990
(610)975-3765
Fax: (610)254-4210
Website: http://www.tlventures.com
Pam Strisofsky,
pstrisofsky@tlventures.com
Preferred Investment Size: $2,000,000
minimum. Investment Types: Seed and
early stage. Industry Preferences:
Diversified technology. Geographic
Preferences: National.

Rockhill Ventures, Inc.
100 Front St., Ste. 1350
West Conshohocken, PA 19428
(610)940-0300
Fax: (610)940-0301
E-mail: chuck@rockhillventures.com
Preferred Investment Size: $1,000,000 to
$2,000,000. Investment Types: Seed,
research and development, startup, first

and second stage, leveraged buyout, and
recaps. Industry Preferences: Genetic
engineering and medical/health related.
Geographic Preferences: Eastern U.S.

Puerto Rico

Advent-Morro Equity Partners
Banco Popular Bldg.
206 Tetuan St., Ste. 903
San Juan, PR 00902
(787)725-5285
Fax: (787)721-1735
Cyril L. Meduna, General Partner
Preferred Investment Size: $500,000 to
$3,000,000. Investment Types: No
preference. Industry Preferences:
Diversified. Geographic Preferences:
Puerto Rico.

North America Investment Corp.
Mercantil Plaza, Ste. 813
PO Box 191831
San Juan, PR 00919
(787)754-6178
Fax: (787)754-6181
Marcelino D. Pastrana-Torres, President
Preferred Investment Size: $25,000 to
$250,000. Investment Types: Early stage
and expansion. Industry Preferences:
Consumer products and retailing,
consumer distribution, industrial
equipment, therapeutic equipment, real
estate, and business services. Geographic
Preferences: Puerto R

Rhode Island

Manchester Humphreys, Inc.
40 Westminster St., Ste. 900
Providence, RI 02903
(401)454-0400
Fax: (401)454-0403
Preferred Investment Size: $500,000
minimum. Investment Types: Leveraged
and management buyouts. Industry
Preferences: Diversified. Geographic
Preferences: National.

Navis Partners
50 Kennedy Plaza, 12th Fl.
Providence, RI 02903
(401)278-6770
Fax: (401)278-6387
Website: http://www.navispartners.com
Rory B. Smith, General Partner
Preferred Investment Size: $20,000,000 to
$75,000,000. Investment Policies: Equity.
Investment Types: Acquisition, early and
later stage, leveraged and management

buyouts, recaps, and expansion. Industry Preferences: Diversified. Geographic Preferences: U.S. and Canada.

South Carolina

Capital Insights, L.L.C.
PO Box 27162
Greenville, SC 29616-2162
(864)242-6832
Fax: (864)242-6755
E-mail: jwarner@capitalinsights.com
Website: http://www.capitalinsights.com
Preferred Investment Size: $500,000 to $5,000,000. Investment Policies: Equity. Investment Types: Early and late stage. Industry Preferences: Communications and consumer-related services. Geographic Preferences: Southeast.

Transamerica Mezzanine Financing
7 N. Laurens St., Ste. 603
Greenville, SC 29601
(864)232-6198
Fax: (864)241-4444
J. Phillip Falls, Investment Officer
Investment Types: Seed, startup, first stage, second stage, and mezzanine. Industry Preferences: Diversified technology. Geographic Preferences: Southeast.

Tennessee

Valley Capital Corp.
Krystal Bldg.
100 W. Martin Luther King Blvd., Ste. 212
Chattanooga, TN 37402
(423)265-1557
Fax: (423)265-1588
Faye Robinson
Preferred Investment Size: $200,000 minimum. Investment Types: Second stage, mezzanine, and leveraged buyout. Industry Preferences: Diversified. Geographic Preferences: Southeast.

Coleman Swenson Booth Inc.
237 2nd Ave. S
Franklin, TN 37064-2649
(615)791-9462
Fax: (615)791-9636
Website: http://www.colemanswenson.com
Larry H. Coleman, Ph.D., Managing Partner
Preferred Investment Size: $1,000,000 to $7,000,000. Investment Types: Seed, startup, first and second stage, and

mezzanine. Industry Preferences: Diversified. Geographic Preferences: No preference.

Capital Services & Resources, Inc.
5159 Wheelis Dr., Ste. 106
Memphis, TN 38117
(901)761-2156
Fax: (907)767-0060
Charles Y. Bancroft, Treasurer
Preferred Investment Size: $300,000 minimum. Investment Policies: Equity. Investment Types: Second stage, leveraged buyout, and special situations. Industry Preferences: Diversified. Geographic Preferences: United States and Canada.

Paradigm Capital Partners LLC
6410 Poplar Ave., Ste. 395
Memphis, TN 38119
(901)682-6060
Fax: (901)328-3061
Preferred Investment Size: $500,000 to $6,000,000. Investment Types: First and second stage, and seed. Industry Preferences: Diversified. Geographic Preferences: Southeast.

SSM Ventures
845 Crossover Ln., Ste. 140
Memphis, TN 38117
(901)767-1131
Fax: (901)767-1135
Website: http://www.ssmventures.com
R. Wilson Orr, III
Preferred Investment Size: $2,000,000 to $10,000,000. Investment Types: Startup, leveraged buyout, and expansion. Industry Preferences: Diversified. Geographic Preferences: Southeast and Southwest U.S.

Capital Across America L.P.
501 Union St., Ste. 201
Nashville, TN 37219
(615)254-1414
Fax: (615)254-1856
Website: http://www.capitalacrossamerica.com
Investment Types: Balanced. Industry Preferences: Diversified; women/minority-owned businesses. Geographic Preferences: Entire U.S.

Equitas L.P.
2000 Glen Echo Rd., Ste. 101
PO Box 158838
Nashville, TN 37215-8838
(615)383-8673

Fax: (615)383-8693
Preferred Investment Size: $500.000. Investment Types: Second stage, leveraged buyout, mezzanine, recaps, and special situation. Industry Preferences: Diversified. Geographic Preferences: Southeast and Midwest.

Massey Burch Capital Corp.
One Burton Hills Blvd., Ste. 350
Nashville, TN 37215
(615)665-3221
Fax: (615)665-3240
E-mail: tcalton@masseyburch.com
Website: http://www.masseyburch.com
Lucious E. Burch, IV, Partner
Preferred Investment Size: $1,000,000 to $5,000,000. Investment Types: Seed, startup, early and first stage. Industry Preferences: Communication and computer related. Geographic Preferences: Southeast.

Nelson Capital Corp.
3401 West End Ave., Ste. 300
Nashville, TN 37203
(615)292-8787
Fax: (615)385-3150
Preferred Investment Size: $500,000 minimum. Investment Types: First and second stage, leveraged buyout, and mezzanine. Industry Preferences: Diversified. Geographic Preferences: Southeast.

Texas

Phillips-Smith Specialty Retail Group
5080 Spectrum Dr., Ste. 805 W
Addison, TX 75001
(972)387-0725
Fax: (972)458-2560
E-mail: pssrg@aol.com
Website: http://www.phillips-smith.com
G. Michael Machens, General Partner
Preferred Investment Size: $1,000,000 minimum. Investment Types: Seed, startup, first and second stage, mezzanine, and leveraged buyout. Industry Preferences: Retail and Internet related. Geographic Preferences: Entire U.S.

Austin Ventures, L.P.
701 Brazos St., Ste. 1400
Austin, TX 78701
(512)485-1900
Fax: (512)476-3952
E-mail: info@ausven.com
Website: http://www.austinventures.com

Joseph C. Aragona, General Partner Preferred Investment Size: $1,000,000 to $15,000,000. Investment Types: Seed, startup, first and second stage, leveraged buyout, and special situations. Industry Preferences: Diversified. Geographic Preferences: Southwest and Texas.

The Capital Network
3925 West Braker Lane, Ste. 406
Austin, TX 78759-5321
(512)305-0826
Fax: (512)305-0836
Preferred Investment Size: $100,000 to $500,000. Investment Types: Seed, early and late stage, leveraged buyout, mezzanine, research and development, and special situations. Industry Preferences: Diversified. Geographic Preferences: United States and Canada.

Techxas Ventures LLC
5000 Plaza on the Lake
Austin, TX 78746
(512)343-0118
Fax: (512)343-1879
E-mail: bruce@techxas.com
Website: http://www.techxas.com
Bruce Ezell, General Partner
Preferred Investment Size: $500,000 to $5,000,000. Investment Types: Seed, startup, first stage, second stage, balanced, joint ventures, and special situations. Industry Preferences: Diversified technology. Geographic Preferences: Texas.

Alliance Financial of Houston
218 Heather Ln.
Conroe, TX 77385-9013
(936)447-3300
Fax: (936)447-4222
Preferred Investment Size: $300,000 to $500,000. Investment Types: Second stage, mezzanine, leveraged buyout, and special situations. Industry Preferences: Sales, distribution, and manufacturing. Geographic Preferences: Gulf states.

Amerimark Capital Corp.
1111 W. Mockingbird, Ste. 1111
Dallas, TX 75247
(214)638-7878
Fax: (214)638-7612
E-mail: amerimark@amcapital.com
Website: http://www.amcapital.com
Preferred Investment Size: $500,000 minimum. Investment Types: Second stage, mezzanine, and leveraged buyout.

Industry Preferences: Diversified. Geographic Preferences: National.

AMT Venture Partners/AMT Capital Ltd.
5220 Spring Valley Rd., Ste. 600
Dallas, TX 75240
(214)905-9757
Fax: (214)905-9761
Website: http://www.amtcapital.com
Preferred Investment Size: $100,000 to $500,000. Investment Types: First and second stages, and expanion. Industry Preferences: Industrial products and equipment, electronic components and instruments. Geographic Preferences: National.

Arkoma Venture Partners
5950 Berkshire Lane, Ste. 1400
Dallas, TX 75225
(214)739-3515
Fax: (214)739-3572
E-mail: joelf@arkomavp.com
Joel Fontenot, Executive Vice President
Preferred Investment Size: $250,000 to $2,500,000. Investment Policies: Equity. Investment Types: Seed, start-up, early and second stage, and expansion. Industry Preferences: Communications, computer, and electronics. Geographic Preferences: Southwest.

Capital Southwest Corp.
12900 Preston Rd., Ste. 700
Dallas, TX 75230
(972)233-8242
Fax: (972)233-7362
Website: http://www.capitalsouthwest.com
Howard Thomas, Investment Associate
Preferred Investment Size: $1,000,000 to $6,000,000. Investment Types: First and second stage, leveraged buyout, acquisition, expansion, management buyout, and late stage. Industry Preferences: Diversified. Geographic Preferences: Entire U.S.

Dali, Hook Partners
One Lincoln Center, Ste. 1550
5400 LBJ Freeway
Dallas, TX 75240
(972)991-5457
Fax: (972)991-5458
E-mail: dhook@hookpartners.com
Website: http://www.hookpartners.com
David J. Hook
Preferred Investment Size: $100,000 to $5,000,000. Investment Types: Balanced,

first, and second stage. Industry Preferences: Diversified. Geographic Preferences: Southwest and West Coast.

HO2 Partners
Two Galleria Tower
13455 Noel Rd., Ste. 1670
Dallas, TX 75240
(972)702-1144
Fax: (972)702-8234
Website: http://www.ho2.com
Preferred Investment Size: $750,000 to $3,000,000. Investment Types: First and second stage, and seed. Industry Preferences: Diversified technology. Geographic Preferences: Texas.

Interwest Partners (Dallas)
2 Galleria Tower
13455 Noel Rd., Ste. 1670
Dallas, TX 75240
(972)392-7279
Fax: (972)490-6348
Website: http://www.interwest.com
Preferred Investment Size: $2,000,000 to $25,000,000. Investment Types: Seed, research and development, startup, first and second stage, expansion, and special situations. Industry Preferences: Diversified. Geographic Preferences: Entire U.S.

Kahala Investments, Inc.
8214 Westchester Dr., Ste. 715
Dallas, TX 75225
(214)987-0077
Fax: (214)987-2332
Lee R. Slaughter, Jr., President
Preferred Investment Size: $10,000,000 minimum. Investment Types: Mezzanine, leveraged buyout, special situations, control block purchases, and industry roll ups. Industry Preferences: Diversified. Geographic Preferences: Southeast and Southwest.

MESBIC Ventures Holding Co.
2435 North Central Expressway, Ste. 200
Dallas, TX 75080
(972)991-1597
Fax: (972)991-4770
Website: http://www.mvhc.com
Jeff Schaefer
Preferred Investment Size: $1,000,000 minimum. Investment Policies: Loans and/or equity. Investment Types: Leveraged buyout, mezzanine, and second stage. Industry Preferences: Diversified. Geographic Preferences: Southeast and Southwest.

North Texas MESBIC, Inc.

9500 Forest Lane, Ste. 430
Dallas, TX 75243
(214)221-3565
Fax: (214)221-3566
Preferred Investment Size: $300,000
minimum. Investment Types: Second
stage, mezzanine, and leveraged buyout.
Industry Preferences: Consumer food and
beverage products, restaurants, retailing,
consumer and food distribution.
Geographic Preferences: Southwest.

Richard Jaffe & Company, Inc,

7318 Royal Cir.
Dallas, TX 75230
(214)265-9397
Fax: (214)739-1845
E-mail: rjaffe@pssi.net
Richard R. Jaffe, President
Preferred Investment Size: $100,000 to
$300,000. Investment Types: Startup,
first stage, leveraged buyouts, and special
situations. Industry Preferences:
Diversified. Geographic Preferences:
Southwest.

Sevin Rosen Management Co.

13455 Noel Rd., Ste. 1670
Dallas, TX 75240
(972)702-1100
Fax: (972)702-1103
E-mail: info@srfunds.com
Website: http://www.srfunds.com
John V. Jaggers, Partner
Preferred Investment Size: $500,000
minimum. Investment Types: Start-up,
early and first stage. Industry Preferences:
Diversified technology. Geographic
Preferences: Entire U.S.

Stratford Capital Partners, L.P.

300 Crescent Ct., Ste. 500
Dallas, TX 75201
(214)740-7377
Fax: (214)720-7393
E-mail: stratcap@hmtf.com
Michael D. Brown, Managing Partner
Preferred Investment Size: $1,000,000
minimum. Investment Policies: Equity,
sub debt with equity. Investment Types:
Expansion, later stage, acquisition,
leveraged and management buyout,
mezzanine, and recaps. Industry
Preferences: Diversified. Geographic
Preferences: National.

Sunwestern Investment Group

12221 Merit Dr., Ste. 935
Dallas, TX 75251

(972)239-5650
Fax: (972)701-0024
Preferred Investment Size: $500,000 to
$1,000,000. Investment Types: Second
stage, leveraged buyout, and special
situations. Industry Preferences:
Diversified. Geographic Preferences:
Southwest and West Coast.

Wingate Partners

750 N. St. Paul St., Ste. 1200
Dallas, TX 75201
(214)720-1313
Fax: (214)871-8799
Preferred Investment Size: $20,000,000
minimum. Investment Types: Leveraged
buyout and control block purchases.
Industry Preferences: Diversified.
Geographic Preferences: Entire U.S. and
Canada.

Buena Venture Associates

201 Main St., 32nd Fl.
Fort Worth, TX 76102
(817)339-7400
Fax: (817)390-8408
Website: http://www.buenaventure.com
Preferred Investment Size: $1,000,000 to
$50,000,000. Investment Types: Early,
first and second stage; seed; and start-up.
Industry Preferences: Diversified
technology, and health services.
Geographic Preferences: Entire U.S.

The Catalyst Group

3 Riverway, Ste. 770
Houston, TX 77056
(713)623-8133
Fax: (713)623-0473
E-mail: herman@thecatalystgroup.net
Website: http://
www.thecatalystgroup.net
Rick Herman, Partner
Preferred Investment Size: $1,000,000
minimum. Investment Types: Second
stage, mezzanine, leveraged buyout, and
control block purchases. Industry
Preferences: Diversified. Geographic
Preferences: No preference.

Cureton & Co., Inc.

1100 Louisiana, Ste. 3250
Houston, TX 77002
(713)658-9806
Fax: (713)658-0476
Stewart Cureton, Jr., President
Preferred Investment Size: $10,000,000
minimum. Investment Types: First and
second stage, leveraged buyout, and
special situations. Industry Preferences:

Diversified. Geographic Preferences:
Southwest.

Davis, Tuttle Venture Partners (Dallas)

8 Greenway Plaza, Ste. 1020
Houston, TX 77046
(713)993-0440
Fax: (713)621-2297
Website: http://www.davistuttle.com
Phillip Tuttle, Partner
Preferred Investment Size: $5,000,000
minimum. Investment Types: First and
second stage, mezzanine, and leveraged
buyout. Industry Preferences:
Diversified. Geographic Preferences:
Southwest.

Houston Partners

401 Louisiana, 8th Fl.
Houston, TX 77002
(713)222-8600
Fax: (713)222-8932
Preferred Investment Size: $500,000 to
$1,000,000. Investment Types: Start-up,
first and second stage, and expansion.
Industry Preferences: Diversified
industry preference. Geographic
Preferences: Entire U.S.

Southwest Venture Group

10878 Westheimer, Ste. 178
Houston, TX 77042
(713)827-8947
(713)461-1470
David M. Klausmeyer, Partner
Preferred Investment Size: $50,000,000
minimum. Investment Types:
Diversified. Industry Preferences:
Diversified. Geographic Preferences: U.S.
and Canada.

Triad Ventures

AM Fund

4600 Post Oak Place, Ste. 100
Houston, TX 77027
(713)627-9111
Fax: (713)627-9119
David Mueller
Preferred Investment Size: $800,000
maximum. Investment Types: First and
second stage, and mezzanine. Industry
Preferences: Medical, consumer,
computer-related. Geographic
Preferences: Southwest and Texas.

Ventex Management, Inc.

3417 Milam St.
Houston, TX 77002-9531
(713)659-7870
Fax: (713)659-7855

Preferred Investment Size: $1,000,000 to $5,000,000. Investment Types: Second stage, mezzanine, leveraged buyout, and special situations. Industry Preferences: Diversified. Geographic Preferences: Southwest.

MBA Venture Group

1004 Olde Town Rd., Ste. 102
Irving, TX 75061
(972)986-6703
John Mason
Preferred Investment Size: $1,000,000 minimum. Investment Types: First stage, leveraged buyout, mezzanine, research and development, second stage, seed, start-up. Industry Preferences: Diversified. Geographic Preferences: Entire U.S.

First Capital Group Management Co.

750 East Mulberry St., Ste. 305
PO Box 15616
San Antonio, TX 78212
(210)736-4233
Fax: (210)736-5449
Jeffrey P. Blanchard, Managing Partner
Preferred Investment Size: $1,000,000 minimum. Investment Types: First and second stage, mezzanine, leveraged buyout, and special situations. Industry Preferences: Diversified. Geographic Preferences: Southwest.

The Southwest Venture Partnerships

16414 San Pedro, Ste. 345
San Antonio, TX 78232
(210)402-1200
Fax: (210)402-1221
E-mail: swvp@aol.com
Preferred Investment Size: $500,000 to $5,000,000. Investment Types: Startup, first and second stage, and leveraged buyout. Industry Preferences: Diversified. Geographic Preferences: Southwest.

Medtech International Inc.

1742 Carriageway
Sugarland, TX 77478
(713)980-8474
Fax: (713)980-6343
Dave Banker
Preferred Investment Size: $100,000 to $500,000. Investment Types: First stage, leveraged buyout, mezzanine, research and development, second stage, seed, special situation, and start-up. Industry Preferences: Diversified. Geographic Preferences: No preference.

Utah

First Security Business Investment Corp.

15 East 100 South, Ste. 100
Salt Lake City, UT 84111
(801)246-5737
Fax: (801)246-5740
Preferred Investment Size: $300,000 to $800,000. Investment Policies: Loans and/or equity. Investment Types: Leveraged buyout, mezzanine, and second stage. Industry Preferences: Diversified. Geographic Preferences: West Coast, Rocky Mountains.

Utah Ventures II, L.P.

423 Wakara Way, Ste. 206
Salt Lake City, UT 84108
(801)583-5922
Fax: (801)583-4105
Website: http://www.uven.com
James C. Dreyfous, Managing General Partner
Preferred Investment Size: $1,000,000 to $7,000,000. Investment Types: Early stage. Industry Preferences: Diversified technology. Geographic Preferences: Northwest and Rocky Mountain region.

Wasatch Venture Corp.

1 S. Main St., Ste. 1400
Salt Lake City, UT 84133
(801)524-8939
Fax: (801)524-8941
E-mail: mail@wasatchvc.com
Todd Stevens, Manager
Preferred Investment Size: $500,000 to $2,000,000. Investment Policies: Equity and debt. Investment Types: Early stage. Industry Preferences: High technology. Geographic Preferences: Western U.S.

Vermont

North Atlantic Capital Corp.

76 Saint Paul St., Ste. 600
Burlington, VT 05401
(802)658-7820
Fax: (802)658-5757
Website: http://www.northatlanticcapital.com
Preferred Investment Size: $1,500,000 minimum. Investment Types: First and second stage, mezzanine, and leveraged buyout. Industry Preferences: Diversified technology. Geographic Preferences: Northeast.

Green Mountain Advisors Inc.

PO Box 1230
Quechee, VT 05059
(802)296-7800
Fax: (802)296-6012
Website: http://www.gmtcap.com
Michael Sweatman, President
Preferred Investment Size: $100,000 to $500,000. Investment Types: Second stage, expansion, and mezzanine. Industry Preferences: Technology, communications. Geographic Preferences: Entire U.S.

Virginia

Oxford Financial Services Corp.

Alexandria, VA 22314
(703)519-4900
Fax: (703)519-4910
E-mail: oxford133@aol.com
J. Alden Philbrick
Preferred Investment Size: $1,000,000. Investment Types: Seed, research and development, startup, first stage, second stage, and mezzanine. Industry Preferences: Diversified technology. Geographic Preferences: National.

Continental SBIC

4141 N. Henderson Rd.
Arlington, VA 22203
(703)527-5200
Fax: (703)527-3700
Michael W. Jones, Senior Vice President
Preferred Investment Size: $300,000 to $5,000,000. Investment Types: No preference. Industry Preferences: Diversified. Geographic Preferences: Northeast, Southeast, Middle Atlantic, and Central Canada.

Novak Biddle Venture Partners

1750 Tysons Blvd., Ste. 1190
McLean, VA 22102
(703)847-3770
Fax: (703)847-3771
E-mail: roger@novakbiddle.com
Website: http://www.novakbiddle.com
Roger Novak, General Partner
Preferred Investment Size: $1,000,000 to $5,000,000. Investment Types: Seed and early stage. Industry Preferences: Communications and computer related. Geographic Preferences: Eastern U.S.

Spacevest

11911 Freedom Dr., Ste. 500
Reston, VA 20190
(703)904-9800

Fax: (703)904-0571
E-mail: spacevest@spacevest.com
Website: http://www.spacevest.com
Roger P. Widing, Managing Director
Preferred Investment Size: $250,000 to
$10,000,000. Investment Policies: Equity.
Investment Types: Early and late stage,
expansion, and mezzanine. Industry
Preferences: Diversified. Geographic
Preferences: U.S. and Canada.

Virginia Capital

1801 Libbie Ave., Ste. 201
Richmond, VA 23226
(804)648-4802
Fax: (804)648-4809
E-mail: webmaster@vacapital.com
Website: http://www.vacapital.com
Thomas E. Deardorff, Vice President
Investment Types: Acquisition, balanced,
expansion, and leveraged and
management buyouts. Industry
Preferences: Communications,
consumer, medical and health related.
Geographic Preferences: Mid Atlantic.

Calvert Social Venture Partners

402 Maple Ave. W
Vienna, VA 22180
(703)255-4930
Fax: (703)255-4931
E-mail: calven2000@aol.com
John May, Managing General Partner
Preferred Investment Size: $100,000 to
$700,000. Investment Types: First stages.
Industry Preferences: Diversified.
Geographic Preferences: Middle Atlantic
states.

Fairfax Partners

8000 Towers Crescent Dr., Ste. 940
Vienna, VA 22182
(703)847-9486
Fax: (703)847-0911
E-mail: bgouldey@fairfaxpartners.com
Bruce K. Gouldey, Managing Director
Investment Types: Startup, first stage,
second stage, and leveraged buyout.
Industry Preferences: Computer related,
Medical and health related. Geographic
Preferences: Middle Atlantic States.

Global Internet Ventures

8150 Leesburg Pike, Ste. 1210
Vienna, VA 22182
(703)442-3300
Fax: (703)442-3388
Website: http://www.givinc.com
Preferred Investment Size: $500,000 to
$3,000,000. Investment Types: Early stage.

Industry Preferences: Communications,
computer, and Internet related.
Geographic Preferences: Entire U.S.

Walnut Capital Corp. (Vienna)

8000 Towers Crescent Dr., Ste. 1070
Vienna, VA 22182
(703)448-3771
Fax: (703)448-7751
Preferred Investment Size: $300,000 to
$500,000. Investment Types: Startup,
first and second stage, mezzanine, and
leveraged buyout. Industry Preferences:
Diversified. Geographic Preferences: No
preference.

Washington

Encompass Ventures

777 108th Ave. NE, Ste. 2300
Bellevue, WA 98004
(425)486-3900
Fax: (425)486-3901
E-mail: info@evpartners.com
Website: http://
www.encompassventures.com
Preferred Investment Size: $300,000 to
$3,000,000. Investment Types: Research
and development, startup, first and
second stages. Industry Preferences:
Computer related, medical and health
related. Geographic Preferences: Western
U.S. and Canada.

Fluke Venture Partners

11400 SE Sixth St., Ste. 230
Bellevue, WA 98004
(425)453-4590
Fax: (425)453-4675
E-mail: gabelein@flukeventures.com
Website: http://www.flukeventures.com
Dennis Weston, Managing Director
Preferred Investment Size: $250,000 to
$2,500,000. Investment Types: Startup,
seed, first stage, second stage, expansion,
and mezzanine. Industry Preferences:
Diversified. Geographic Preferences:
Northwest.

Pacific Northwest Partners SBIC, L.P.

15352 SE 53rd St.
Bellevue, WA 98006
(425)455-9967
Fax: (425)455-9404
Preferred Investment Size: $500,000
minimum. Investment Policies: Private
equity investments. Investment Types:
Seed, start-up, and early and first stage.
Industry Preferences: Diversified.
Geographic Preferences: Entire U.S.

Materia Venture Associates, L.P.

3435 Carillon Pointe
Kirkland, WA 98033-7354
(425)822-4100
Fax: (425)827-4086
Preferred Investment Size: $500,000 to
$1,000,000. Investment Types: Startup,
first and second stage, and mezzanine.
Industry Preferences: Advanced
industrial products and equipment.
Geographic Preferences: Entire U.S.

OVP Venture Partners (Kirkland)

2420 Carillon Pt.
Kirkland, WA 98033
(425)889-9192
Fax: (425)889-0152
E-mail: info@ovp.com
Website: http://www.ovp.com
Preferred Investment Size: $1,000,000 to
$10,000,000. Investment Types: Seed,
startup, early stage. Industry Preferences:
Diversified technology. Geographic
Preferences: Western U.S. and Canada.

Digital Partners

999 3rd Ave., Ste. 1610
Seattle, WA 98104
(206)405-3607
Fax: (206)405-3617
Website: http://www.digitalpartners.com
Preferred Investment Size: $250,000 to
$3,000,000. Investment Types: Early, first
and second stage, and seed. Industry
Preferences: Diversified technology.
Geographic Preferences: Northwest and
Western Canada.

Frazier & Company

601 Union St., Ste. 3300
Seattle, WA 98101
(206)621-7200
Fax: (206)621-1848
E-mail: jon@frazierco.com
Jon Gilbert, General Partner
Preferred Investment Size: $2,000,000 to
$3,000,000. Investment Types: No
preference. Industry Preferences:
Diversified. Geographic Preferences:
National.

Kirlan Venture Capital, Inc.

221 First Ave. W, Ste. 108
Seattle, WA 98119-4223
(206)281-8610
Fax: (206)285-3451
E-mail: bill@kirlanventure.com
Website: http://www.kirlanventure.com
Preferred Investment Size: $300,000 to
$500,000. Investment Types: First stage,

second stage, and mezzanine. Industry Preferences: Diversified technology. Geographic Preferences: Western U.S. and Canada.

Phoenix Partners

1000 2nd Ave., Ste. 3600
Seattle, WA 98104
(206)624-8968
Fax: (206)624-1907
E-mail: djohnsto@interserv.com
William B. Horne, Chief Financial Officer
Preferred Investment Size: $2,000,000 to $3,000,000. Investment Types: Seed, research and development, startup, first and second stage, and mezzanine. Industry Preferences: Diversified. Geographic Preferences: No preference.

Voyager Capital

800 5th St., Ste. 4100
Seattle, WA 98103
(206)470-1180
Fax: (206)470-1185
E-mail: info@voyagercap.com
Website: http://www.voyagercap.com
Erik Benson, Senior Associate
Preferred Investment Size: $5,000,000 to $10,000,000. Investment Policies: Equity. Investment Types: Startup, early and late stage. Industry Preferences: Diversified communications and computer related. Geographic Preferences: West Coast and Western Canada.

Northwest Venture Associates

221 N. Wall St., Ste. 628
Spokane, WA 99201
(509)747-0728
Fax: (509)747-0758

Website: http://www.nwva.com
Christopher Brookfield
Preferred Investment Size: $1,000,000 to $2,000,000. Investment Types: Seed, research and development, startup, first stage, second stage, and mezzanine. Industry Preferences: Diversified. Geographic Preferences: Northwest and Rocky Mountains.

Wisconsin

Venture Investors Management, L.L.C.

University Research Park
505 S. Rosa Rd.
Madison, WI 53719
(608)441-2700
Fax: (608)441-2727
E-mail: roger@ventureinvestors.com
Website: http://www.ventureinvesters.com
Scott Button, Partner
Preferred Investment Size: $250,000 to $1,000,000. Investment Types: Seed, startup, first and second stage, mezzanine, and special situations. Industry Preferences: Diversified. Geographic Preferences: Southeast and Midwest.

Capital Investments, Inc.

1009 West Glen Oaks Lane, Ste. 103
Mequon, WI 53092
(414)241-0303
Fax: (414)241-8451
E-mail: dmayer@capitalinvestmentsinc.com
Website: http:// www.capitalinvestmentsinc.com
Preferred Investment Size: $500,000 to $1,000,000. Investment Types: Second stage, mezzanine, and leveraged buyout. Industry

Preferences: Diversified. Geographic Preferences: Southwest and Midwest.

Future Value Venture, Inc.

2745 N. Martin Luther King Dr., Ste. 204
Milwaukee, WI 53212-2300
(414)264-2252
Fax: (414)264-2253
E-mail: fvvventures@aol.com
William Beckett, President
Preferred Investment Size: $100,000 to $300,000. Investment Types: First and second stage, start-up, and mezzanine. Industry Preferences: No preference. Geographic Preferences: Entire U.S.

Lubar and Co., Inc.

700 N. Water St., Ste. 1200
Milwaukee, WI 53202
(414)291-9000
Fax: (414)291-9061
David J. Lubar, Partner
Preferred Investment Size: $10,000,000 minimum. Investment Types: Second stage, leveraged buyout, special situations, and control block purchases. Industry Preferences: Diversified. Geographic Preferences: Midwest.

GCI

20875 Crossroads Cir., Ste. 100
Waukesha, WI 53186
(262)798-5080
Fax: (262)798-5087
Preferred Investment Size: $2,000,000 minimum. Investment Types: First stage, second stage, and leveraged buyout. Industry Preferences: Diversified technology. Geographic Preferences: National.

Glossary of Small Business Terms

Absolute liability
Liability that is incurred due to product defects or negligent actions. Manufacturers or retail establishments are held responsible, even though the defect or action may not have been intentional or negligent.

ACE
See Active Corps of Executives

Accident and health benefits
Benefits offered to employees and their families in order to offset the costs associated with accidental death, accidental injury, or sickness.

Account statement
A record of transactions, including payments, new debt, and deposits, incurred during a defined period of time.

Accounting system
System capturing the costs of all employees and/or machinery included in business expenses.

Accounts payable
See Trade credit

Accounts receivable
Unpaid accounts which arise from unsettled claims and transactions from the sale of a company's products or services to its customers.

Active Corps of Executives (ACE)
A group of volunteers for a management assistance program of the U.S. Small Business Administration; volunteers provide one-on-one counseling and teach workshops and seminars for small firms.

ADA
See Americans with Disabilities Act

Adaptation
The process whereby an invention is modified to meet the needs of users.

Adaptive engineering
The process whereby an invention is modified to meet the manufacturing and commercial requirements of a targeted market.

Adverse selection
The tendency for higher-risk individuals to purchase health care and more comprehensive plans, resulting in increased costs.

Advertising
A marketing tool used to capture public attention and influence purchasing decisions for a product or service. Utilizes various forms of media to generate consumer response, such as flyers, magazines, newspapers, radio, and television.

Age discrimination
The denial of the rights and privileges of employment based solely on the age of an individual.

Agency costs
Costs incurred to insure that the lender or investor maintains control over assets while allowing the borrower or entrepreneur to use them. Monitoring and information costs are the two major types of agency costs.

Agribusiness
The production and sale of commodities and products from the commercial farming industry.

America Online
An online service which is accessible by computer modem. The service features Internet access, bulletin boards, online periodicals, electronic mail, and other services for subscribers.

Americans with Disabilities Act (ADA)
Law designed to ensure equal access and opportunity to handicapped persons.

Annual report
Yearly financial report prepared by a business that adheres to the requirements set forth by the Securities and Exchange Commission (SEC).

Antitrust immunity
Exemption from prosecution under antitrust laws. In the transportation industry, firms with antitrust immunity are permitted under certain conditions to set schedules and sometimes prices for the public benefit.

Applied research
Scientific study targeted for use in a product or process.

Asians
A minority category used by the U.S. Bureau of the Census to represent a diverse group that includes Aleuts, Eskimos, American Indians, Asian Indians, Chinese, Japanese, Koreans, Vietnamese, Filipinos, Hawaiians, and other Pacific Islanders.

Assets
Anything of value owned by a company.

Audit
The verification of accounting records and business procedures conducted by an outside accounting service.

Average cost
Total production costs divided by the quantity produced.

Balance Sheet
A financial statement listing the total assets and liabilities of a company at a given time.

Bankruptcy
The condition in which a business cannot meet its debt obligations and petitions a federal district court either for reorganization of its debts (Chapter 11) or for liquidation of its assets (Chapter 7).

Basic research
Theoretical scientific exploration not targeted to application.

Basket clause
A provision specifying the amount of public pension funds that may be placed in investments not included on a state's legal list (see separate citation).

BBS
See Bulletin Board Service

BDC
See Business development corporation

Benefit
Various services, such as health care, flextime, day care, insurance, and vacation, offered to employees as part of a hiring package. Typically subsidized in whole or in part by the business.

BIDCO
See Business and industrial development company

Billing cycle
A system designed to evenly distribute customer billing throughout the month, preventing clerical backlogs.

Birth
See Business birth

Blue chip security
A low-risk, low-yield security representing an interest in a very stable company.

Blue sky laws
A general term that denotes various states' laws regulating securities.

Bond
A written instrument executed by a bidder or contractor (the principal) and a second party (the surety or sureties) to assure fulfillment of the principal's obligations to a third party (the obligee or government) identified in the bond. If the principal's obligations are not met, the bond assures payment to the extent stipulated of any loss sustained by the obligee.

Bonding requirements
Terms contained in a bond (see separate citation).

Bonus
An amount of money paid to an employee as a reward for achieving certain business goals or objectives.

Brainstorming
A group session where employees contribute their ideas for solving a problem or meeting a company objective without fear of retribution or ridicule.

Brand name
The part of a brand, trademark, or service mark that can be spoken. It can be a word, letter, or group of words or letters.

Bridge financing
A short-term loan made in expectation of intermediateterm or long-term financing. Can be used when a company plans to go public in the near future.

Broker
One who matches resources available for innovation with those who need them.

Budget
An estimate of the spending necessary to complete a project or offer a service in comparison to cash-on-hand and expected earnings for the coming year, with an emphasis on cost control.

Bulletin Board Service (BBS)
An online service enabling users to communicate with each other about specific topics.

Business and industrial development company (BIDCO)
A private, for-profit financing corporation chartered by the state to provide both equity and long-term debt capital to small business owners (see separate citations for equity and debt capital).

Business birth
The formation of a new establishment or enterprise. The appearance of a new establishment or enterprise in the Small Business Data Base (see separate citation).

Business conditions
Outside factors that can affect the financial performance of a business.

Business contractions
The number of establishments that have decreased in employment during a specified time.

Business cycle
A period of economic recession and recovery. These cycles vary in duration.

Business death
The voluntary or involuntary closure of a firm or establishment. The disappearance of an establishment or enterprise from the Small Business Data Base (see separate citation).

Business development corporation (BDC)
A business financing agency, usually composed of the financial institutions in an area or state, organized to assist in financing businesses unable to obtain assistance through normal channels; the risk is spread among various members of the business development corporation, and interest rates may vary somewhat from those charged by member institutions. A venture capital firm in which shares of ownership are publicly held and to which the Investment Act of 1940 applies.

Business dissolution
For enumeration purposes, the absence of a business that was present in the prior time period from any current record.

Business entry
See Business birth

Business ethics
Moral values and principles espoused by members of the business community as a guide to fair and honest business practices.

Business exit
See Business death

Business expansions
The number of establishments that added employees during a specified time.

Business failure
Closure of a business causing a loss to at least one creditor.

Business format franchising
The purchase of the name, trademark, and an ongoing business plan of the parent corporation or franchisor by the franchisee.

Business license
A legal authorization issued by municipal and state governments and required for business operations.

Business name
Enterprises must register their business names with local governments usually on a "doing business as" (DBA) form. (This name is sometimes referred to as a "fictional name.") The procedure is part of the business licensing process and prevents any other business from using that same name for a similar business in the same locality.

Business norms
See Financial ratios

Business permit
See Business license

Business plan
A document that spells out a company's expected course of action for a specified period, usually including a detailed listing and analysis of risks and uncertainties. For the small business, it should examine the proposed products, the market, the industry, the management policies, the marketing policies, production needs, and financial needs. Frequently, it is used as a prospectus for potential investors and lenders.

Business proposal
See Business plan

Business service firm
An establishment primarily engaged in rendering services to other business organizations on a fee or contract basis.

Business start
For enumeration purposes, a business with a name or similar designation that did not exist in a prior time period.

Cafeteria plan
See Flexible benefit plan

Capacity
Level of a firm's, industry's, or nation's output corresponding to full practical utilization of available resources.

Capital
Assets less liabilities, representing the ownership interest in a business. A stock of accumulated goods, especially at a specified time and in contrast to income

received during a specified time period. Accumulated goods devoted to production. Accumulated possessions calculated to bring income.

Capital expenditure
Expenses incurred by a business for improvements that will depreciate over time.

Capital gain
The monetary difference between the purchase price and the selling price of capital. Capital gains are taxed at a rate of 28% by the federal government.

Capital intensity
The relative importance of capital in the production process, usually expressed as the ratio of capital to labor but also sometimes as the ratio of capital to output.

Capital resource
The equipment, facilities and labor used to create products and services.

Caribbean Basin Initiative
An interdisciplinary program to support commerce among the businesses in the nations of the Caribbean Basin and the United States. Agencies involved include: the Agency for International Development, the U.S. Small Business Administration, the International Trade Administration of the U.S. Department of Commerce, and various private sector groups.

Catastrophic care
Medical and other services for acute and long-term illnesses that cost more than insurance coverage limits or that cost the amount most families may be expected to pay with their own resources.

CDC
See Certified development corporation

CD-ROM
Compact disc with read-only memory used to store large amounts of digitized data.

Certified development corporation (CDC)
A local area or statewide corporation or authority (for profit or nonprofit) that packages U.S. Small Business Administration (SBA), bank, state, and/or private money into financial assistance for existing business

capital improvements. The SBA holds the second lien on its maximum share of 40 percent involvement. Each state has at least one certified development corporation. This program is called the SBA 504 Program.

Certified lenders
Banks that participate in the SBA guaranteed loan program (see separate citation). Such banks must have a good track record with the U.S. Small Business Administration (SBA) and must agree to certain conditions set forth by the agency. In return, the SBA agrees to process any guaranteed loan application within three business days.

Champion
An advocate for the development of an innovation.

Channel of distribution
The means used to transport merchandise from the manufacturer to the consumer.

Chapter 7 of the 1978 Bankruptcy Act
Provides for a court-appointed trustee who is responsible for liquidating a company's assets in order to settle outstanding debts.

Chapter 11 of the 1978 Bankruptcy Act
Allows the business owners to retain control of the company while working with their creditors to reorganize their finances and establish better business practices to prevent liquidation of assets.

Closely held corporation
A corporation in which the shares are held by a few persons, usually officers, employees, or others close to the management; these shares are rarely offered to the public.

Code of Federal Regulations
Codification of general and permanent rules of the federal government published in the Federal Register.

Code sharing
See Computer code sharing

Coinsurance
Upon meeting the deductible payment, health insurance participants may be required to make additional health care cost-sharing payments.

Coinsurance is a payment of a fixed percentage of the cost of each service; copayment is usually a fixed amount to be paid with each service.

Collateral
Securities, evidence of deposit, or other property pledged by a borrower to secure repayment of a loan.

Collective ratemaking
The establishment of uniform charges for services by a group of businesses in the same industry.

Commercial insurance plan
See Underwriting

Commercial loans
Short-term renewable loans used to finance specific capital needs of a business.

Commercialization
The final stage of the innovation process, including production and distribution.

Common stock
The most frequently used instrument for purchasing ownership in private or public companies. Common stock generally carries the right to vote on certain corporate actions and may pay dividends, although it rarely does in venture investments. In liquidation, common stockholders are the last to share in the proceeds from the sale of a corporation's assets; bondholders and preferred shareholders have priority. Common stock is often used in firstround start-up financing.

Community development corporation
A corporation established to develop economic programs for a community and, in most cases, to provide financial support for such development.

Competitor
A business whose product or service is marketed for the same purpose/use and to the same consumer group as the product or service of another.

Computer code sharing
An arrangement whereby flights of a regional airline are identified by the two-letter code of a major carrier in the computer reservation system to help direct passengers to new regional carriers.

Consignment
A merchandising agreement, usually referring to secondhand shops, where the dealer pays the owner of an item a percentage of the profit when the item is sold.

Consortium
A coalition of organizations such as banks and corporations for ventures requiring large capital resources.

Consultant
An individual that is paid by a business to provide advice and expertise in a particular area.

Consumer price index
A measure of the fluctuation in prices between two points in time.

Consumer research
Research conducted by a business to obtain information about existing or potential consumer markets.

Continuation coverage
Health coverage offered for a specified period of time to employees who leave their jobs and to their widows, divorced spouses, or dependents.

Contractions
See Business contractions

Convertible preferred stock
A class of stock that pays a reasonable dividend and is convertible into common stock (see separate citation). Generally the convertible feature may only be exercised after being held for a stated period of time. This arrangement is usually considered second-round financing when a company needs equity to maintain its cash flow.

Convertible securities
A feature of certain bonds, debentures, or preferred stocks that allows them to be exchanged by the owner for another class of securities at a future date and in accordance with any other terms of the issue.

Copayment
See Coinsurance

Copyright
A legal form of protection available to creators and authors to safeguard their works from unlawful use or claim of ownership by others. Copyrights may be acquired for works of art, sculpture, music, and published or unpublished manuscripts. All copyrights should be registered at the Copyright Office of the Library of Congress.

Corporate financial ratios
The relationship between key figures found in a company's financial statement expressed as a numeric value. Used to evaluate risk and company performance. Also known as Financial averages, Operating ratios, and Business ratios.

Corporation
A legal entity, chartered by a state or the federal government, recognized as a separate entity having its own rights, privileges, and liabilities distinct from those of its members.

Cost containment
Actions taken by employers and insurers to curtail rising health care costs; for example, increasing employee cost sharing (see separate citation), requiring second opinions, or preadmission screening.

Cost sharing
The requirement that health care consumers contribute to their own medical care costs through deductibles and coinsurance (see separate citations). Cost sharing does not include the amounts paid in premiums. It is used to control utilization of services; for example, requiring a fixed amount to be paid with each health care service.

Cottage industry
Businesses based in the home in which the family members are the labor force and family-owned equipment is used to process the goods.

Credit Rating
A letter or number calculated by an organization (such as Dun & Bradstreet) to represent the ability and disposition of a business to meet its financial obligations.

Customer service
Various techniques used to ensure the satisfaction of a customer.

Cyclical peak
The upper turning point in a business cycle.

Cyclical trough
The lower turning point in a business cycle.

DBA
See Business name

Death
See Business death

Debenture
A certificate given as acknowledgment of a debt (see separate citation) secured by the general credit of the issuing corporation. A bond, usually without security, issued by a corporation and sometimes convertible to common stock.

Debt
Something owed by one person to another. Financing in which a company receives capital that must be repaid; no ownership is transferred.

Debt capital
Business financing that normally requires periodic interest payments and repayment of the principal within a specified time.

Debt financing
See Debt capital

Debt securities
Loans such as bonds and notes that provide a specified rate of return for a specified period of time.

Deductible
A set amount that an individual must pay before any benefits are received.

Demand shock absorbers
A term used to describe the role that some small firms play by expanding their output levels to accommodate a transient surge in demand.

Demographics
Statistics on various markets, including age, income, and education, used to target specific products or services to appropriate consumer groups.

Demonstration
Showing that a product or process has been modified sufficiently to meet the needs of users.

Deregulation
The lifting of government restrictions; for example, the lifting of government restrictions on the entry of new businesses, the expansion of services, and the setting of prices in particular industries.

Desktop Publishing
Using personal computers and specialized software to produce camera-ready copy for publications.

Disaster loans
Various types of physical and economic assistance available to individuals and businesses through the U.S. Small Business Administration (SBA). This is the only SBA loan program available for residential purposes.

Discrimination
The denial of the rights and privileges of employment based on factors such as age, race, religion, or gender.

Diseconomies of scale
The condition in which the costs of production increase faster than the volume of production.

Dissolution
See Business dissolution

Distribution
Delivering a product or process to the user.

Distributor
One who delivers merchandise to the user.

Diversified company
A company whose products and services are used by several different markets.

Doing business as (DBA)
See Business name

Dow Jones
An information services company that publishes the Wall Street Journal and other sources of financial information.

Dow Jones Industrial Average
An indicator of stock market performance.

Earned income
A tax term that refers to wages and salaries earned by the recipient, as opposed to monies earned through interest and dividends.

Economic efficiency
The use of productive resources to the fullest practical extent in the provision of the set of goods and services that is most preferred by purchasers in the economy.

Economic indicators
Statistics used to express the state of the economy. These include the length of the average work week, the rate of unemployment, and stock prices.

Economically disadvantaged
See Socially and economically disadvantaged

Economies of scale
See Scale economies

EEOC
See Equal Employment Opportunity Commission

8(a) Program
A program authorized by the Small Business Act that directs federal contracts to small businesses owned and operated by socially and economically disadvantaged individuals.

Electronic mail (e-mail)
The electronic transmission of mail via phone lines.

E-mail
See Electronic mail

Employee leasing
A contract by which employers arrange to have their workers hired by a leasing company and then leased back to them for a management fee. The leasing company typically assumes the administrative burden of payroll and provides a benefit package to the workers.

Employee tenure
The length of time an employee works for a particular employer.

Employer identification number
The business equivalent of a social security number. Assigned by the U.S. Internal Revenue Service.

Enterprise
An aggregation of all establishments owned by a parent company. An enterprise may consist of a single, independent establishment or include subsidiaries and other branches under the same ownership and control.

Enterprise zone
A designated area, usually found in inner cities and other areas with significant unemployment, where businesses receive tax credits and other incentives to entice them to establish operations there.

Entrepreneur
A person who takes the risk of organizing and operating a new business venture.

Entry
See Business entry

Equal Employment Opportunity Commission (EEOC)
A federal agency that ensures nondiscrimination in the hiring and firing practices of a business.

Equal opportunity employer
An employer who adheres to the standards set by the Equal Employment Opportunity Commission (see separate citation).

Equity
The ownership interest. Financing in which partial or total ownership of a company is surrendered in exchange for capital. An investor's financial return comes from dividend payments and from growth in the net worth of the business.

Equity capital
See Equity; Equity midrisk venture capital

Equity financing
See Equity; Equity midrisk venture capital

Equity midrisk venture capital
An unsecured investment in a company. Usually a purchase of ownership interest in a company that occurs in the later stages of a company's development.

Equity partnership
A limited partnership arrangement for providing start-up and seed capital to businesses.

Equity securities
See Equity

Equity-type
Debt financing subordinated to conventional debt.

Establishment
A single-location business unit that may be independent (a single-establishment enterprise) or owned by a parent enterprise.

Establishment and Enterprise Microdata File
See U.S. Establishment and Enterprise Microdata File

Establishment birth
See Business birth

Establishment Longitudinal Microdata File
See U.S. Establishment Longitudinal Microdata File

Ethics
See Business ethics

Evaluation
Determining the potential success of translating an invention into a product or process.

Exit
See Business exit

Experience rating
See Underwriting

Financial ratios
See Corporate financial ratios; Industry financial ratios

Financial statement
A written record of business finances, including balance sheets and profit and loss statements.

Financing
See First-stage financing; Second-stage financing; Thirdstage financing

First-stage financing
Financing provided to companies that have expended their initial capital, and require funds to start full-scale manufacturing and sales. Also known as First-round financing.

Fiscal year
Any twelve-month period used by businesses for accounting purposes.

504 Program
See Certified development corporation

Flexible benefit plan
A plan that offers a choice among cash and/or qualified benefits such as group term life insurance, accident and health insurance, group legal services, dependent care assistance, and vacations.

FOB
See Free on board

Format franchising
See Business format franchising; Franchising

401(k) plan
A financial plan where employees contribute a percentage of their earnings to a fund that is invested in stocks, bonds, or money markets for the purpose of saving money for retirement.

Four Ps
Marketing terms referring to Product, Price, Place, and Promotion.

Franchising
A form of licensing by which the owner-the franchisor-distributes or markets a product, method, or service through affiliated dealers called franchisees. The product, method, or service being marketed is identified by a brand name, and the franchisor maintains control over the marketing methods employed. The franchisee is often given exclusive access to a defined geographic area.

Export
A product sold outside of the country.

Export license
A general or specific license granted by the U.S. Department of Commerce required of anyone wishing to export goods. Some restricted articles need approval from the U.S. Departments of State, Defense, or Energy.

Failure
See Business failure

Fair share agreement
An agreement reached between a franchisor and a minority business organization to extend business ownership to minorities by either reducing the amount of capital required or by setting aside certain marketing areas for minority business owners.

Feasibility study
A study to determine the likelihood that a proposed product or development will fulfill the objectives of a particular investor.

Federal Trade Commission (FTC)
Federal agency that promotes free enterprise and competition within the U.S.

Federal Trade Mark Act of 1946
See Lanham Act

Fictional name
See Business name

Fiduciary
An individual or group that hold assets in trust for a beneficiary.

Financial analysis
The techniques used to determine money needs in a business. Techniques include ratio analysis, calculation of return on investment, guides for measuring profitability, and break-even analysis to determine ultimate success.

Financial intermediary
A financial institution that acts as the intermediary between borrowers and lenders. Banks, savings and loan associations, finance companies, and venture capital companies are major financial intermediaries in the United States.

Free on board (FOB)
A pricing term indicating that the quoted price includes the cost of loading goods into transport vessels at a specified place.

Frictional unemployment
See Unemployment

FTC
See Federal Trade Commission

Fulfillment
The systems necessary for accurate delivery of an ordered item, including subscriptions and direct marketing.

Full-time workers
Generally, those who work a regular schedule of more than 35 hours per week.

Garment registration number
A number that must appear on every garment sold in the U.S. to indicate the manufacturer of the garment, which may or may not be the same as the label under which the garment is sold. The U.S. Federal Trade Commission assigns and regulates garment registration numbers.

Gatekeeper
A key contact point for entry into a network.

GDP
See Gross domestic product

General obligation bond
A municipal bond secured by the taxing power of the municipality. The Tax Reform Act of 1986 limits the purposes for which such bonds may be issued and establishes volume limits on the extent of their issuance.

GNP
See Gross national product

Good Housekeeping Seal
Seal appearing on products that signifies the fulfillment of the standards set by the Good Housekeeping Institute to protect consumer interests.

Goods sector
All businesses producing tangible goods, including agriculture, mining, construction, and manufacturing businesses.

GPO
See Gross product originating

Gross domestic product (GDP)
The part of the nation's gross national product (see separate citation) generated by private business using resources from within the country.

Gross national product (GNP)
The most comprehensive single measure of aggregate economic output. Represents the market value of the total output of goods and services produced by a nation's economy.

Gross product originating (GPO)
A measure of business output estimated from the income or production side using employee

compensation, profit income, net interest, capital consumption, and indirect business taxes.

HAL
See Handicapped assistance loan program

Handicapped assistance loan program (HAL)
Low-interest direct loan program through the U.S. Small Business Administration (SBA) for handicapped persons. The SBA requires that these persons demonstrate that their disability is such that it is impossible for them to secure employment, thus making it necessary to go into their own business to make a living.

Health maintenance organization (HMO)
Organization of physicians and other health care professionals that provides health services to subscribers and their dependents on a prepaid basis.

Health provider
An individual or institution that gives medical care. Under Medicare, an institutional provider is a hospital, skilled nursing facility, home health agency, or provider of certain physical therapy services.

Hispanic
A person of Cuban, Mexican, Puerto Rican, Latin American (Central or South American), European Spanish, or other Spanish-speaking origin or ancestry.

HMO
See Health maintenance organization

Home-based business
A business with an operating address that is also a residential address (usually the residential address of the proprietor).

Hub-and-spoke system
A system in which flights of an airline from many different cities (the spokes) converge at a single airport (the hub). After allowing passengers sufficient time to make connections, planes then depart for different cities.

Human Resources Management
A business program designed to oversee recruiting, pay, benefits, and other issues related to the company's work force, including planning to determine the optimal use of labor to increase production, thereby increasing profit.

Idea
An original concept for a new product or process.

Import
Products produced outside the country in which they are consumed.

Income
Money or its equivalent, earned or accrued, resulting from the sale of goods and services.

Income statement
A financial statement that lists the profits and losses of a company at a given time.

Incorporation
The filing of a certificate of incorporation with a state's secretary of state, thereby limiting the business owner's liability.

Incubator
A facility designed to encourage entrepreneurship and minimize obstacles to new business formation and growth, particularly for high-technology firms, by housing a number of fledgling enterprises that share an array of services, such as meeting areas, secretarial services, accounting, research library, on-site financial and management counseling, and word processing facilities.

Independent contractor
An individual considered self-employed (see separate citation) and responsible for paying Social Security taxes and income taxes on earnings.

Indirect health coverage
Health insurance obtained through another individual's health care plan; for example, a spouse's employersponsored plan.

Industrial development authority
The financial arm of a state or other political subdivision established for the purpose of financing economic development in an area, usually through loans to nonprofit organizations, which in turn provide facilities for manufacturing and other industrial operations.

Glossary

Industry financial ratios
Corporate financial ratios averaged for a specified industry. These are used for comparison purposes and reveal industry trends and identify differences between the performance of a specific company and the performance of its industry. Also known as Industrial averages, Industry ratios, Financial averages, and Business or Industrial norms.

Inflation
Increases in volume of currency and credit, generally resulting in a sharp and continuing rise in price levels.

Informal capital
Financing from informal, unorganized sources; includes informal debt capital such as trade credit or loans from friends and relatives and equity capital from informal investors.

Initial public offering (IPO)
A corporation's first offering of stock to the public.

Innovation
The introduction of a new idea into the marketplace in the form of a new product or service or an improvement in organization or process.

Intellectual property
Any idea or work that can be considered proprietary in nature and is thus protected from infringement by others.

Internal capital
Debt or equity financing obtained from the owner or through retained business earnings.

Internet
A government-designed computer network that contains large amounts of information and is accessible through various vendors for a fee.

Intrapreneurship
The state of employing entrepreneurial principles to nonentrepreneurial situations.

Invention
The tangible form of a technological idea, which could include a laboratory prototype, drawings, formulas, etc.

IPO
See Initial public offering

Job description
The duties and responsibilities required in a particular position.

Job tenure
A period of time during which an individual is continuously employed in the same job.

Joint marketing agreements
Agreements between regional and major airlines, often involving the coordination of flight schedules, fares, and baggage transfer. These agreements help regional carriers operate at lower cost.

Joint venture
Venture in which two or more people combine efforts in a particular business enterprise, usually a single transaction or a limited activity, and agree to share the profits and losses jointly or in proportion to their contributions.

Keogh plan
Designed for self-employed persons and unincorporated businesses as a tax-deferred pension account.

Labor force
Civilians considered eligible for employment who are also willing and able to work.

Labor force participation rate
The civilian labor force as a percentage of the civilian population.

Labor intensity
The relative importance of labor in the production process, usually measured as the capital-labor ratio; i.e., the ratio of units of capital (typically, dollars of tangible assets) to the number of employees. The higher the capital-labor ratio exhibited by a firm or industry, the lower the capital intensity of that firm or industry is said to be.

Labor surplus area
An area in which there exists a high unemployment rate. In procurement (see separate citation), extra points are given to firms in counties that are

designated a labor surplus area; this information is requested on procurement bid sheets.

Labor union
An organization of similarly-skilled workers who collectively bargain with management over the conditions of employment.

Laboratory prototype
See Prototype

LAN
See Local Area Network

Lanham Act
Refers to the Federal Trade Mark Act of 1946. Protects registered trademarks, trade names, and other service marks used in commerce.

Large business-dominated industry
Industry in which a minimum of 60 percent of employment or sales is in firms with more than 500 workers.

LBO
See Leveraged buy-out

Leader pricing
A reduction in the price of a good or service in order to generate more sales of that good or service.

Legal list
A list of securities selected by a state in which certain institutions and fiduciaries (such as pension funds, insurance companies, and banks) may invest. Securities not on the list are not eligible for investment. Legal lists typically restrict investments to high quality securities meeting certain specifications. Generally, investment is limited to U.S. securities and investment-grade blue chip securities (see separate citation).

Leveraged buy-out (LBO)
The purchase of a business or a division of a corporation through a highly leveraged financing package.

Liability
An obligation or duty to perform a service or an act. Also defined as money owed.

License
A legal agreement granting to another the right to use a technological innovation.

Limited partnerships
See Venture capital limited partnerships

Liquidity
The ability to convert a security into cash promptly.

Loans
See Commercial loans; Disaster loans; SBA direct loans; SBA guaranteed loans; SBA special lending institution categories Local Area Network (LAN) Computer networks contained within a single building or small area; used to facilitate the sharing of information.

Local development corporation
An organization, usually made up of local citizens of a community, designed to improve the economy of the area by inducing business and industry to locate and expand there. A local development corporation establishes a capability to finance local growth.

Long-haul rates
Rates charged by a transporter in which the distance traveled is more than 800 miles.

Long-term debt
An obligation that matures in a period that exceeds five years.

Low-grade bond
A corporate bond that is rated below investment grade by the major rating agencies (Standard and Poor's, Moody's).

Macro-efficiency
Efficiency as it pertains to the operation of markets and market systems.

Managed care
A cost-effective health care program initiated by employers whereby low-cost health care is made available to the employees in return for exclusive patronage to program doctors.

Management Assistance Programs
See SBA Management Assistance Programs

Management and technical assistance
A term used by many programs to mean business (as opposed to technological) assistance.

Glossary

Mandated benefits
Specific treatments, providers, or individuals required by law to be included in commercial health plans.

Market evaluation
The use of market information to determine the sales potential of a specific product or process.

Market failure
The situation in which the workings of a competitive market do not produce the best results from the point of view of the entire society.

Market information
Data of any type that can be used for market evaluation, which could include demographic data, technology forecasting, regulatory changes, etc.

Market research
A systematic collection, analysis, and reporting of data about the market and its preferences, opinions, trends, and plans; used for corporate decision-making.

Market share
In a particular market, the percentage of sales of a specific product.

Marketing
Promotion of goods or services through various media.

Master Establishment List (MEL)
A list of firms in the United States developed by the U.S. Small Business Administration; firms can be selected by industry, region, state, standard metropolitan statistical area (see separate citation), county, and zip code.

Maturity
The date upon which the principal or stated value of a bond or other indebtedness becomes due and payable.

Medicaid (Title XIX)
A federally aided, state-operated and administered program that provides medical benefits for certain low income persons in need of health and medical care who are eligible for one of the government's welfare cash payment programs, including the aged, the blind, the disabled, and members of families with dependent children where one parent is absent, incapacitated, or unemployed.

Medicare (Title XVIII)
A nationwide health insurance program for disabled and aged persons. Health insurance is available to insured persons without regard to income. Monies from payroll taxes cover hospital insurance and monies from general revenues and beneficiary premiums pay for supplementary medical insurance.

MEL
See Master Establishment List

MESBIC
See Minority enterprise small business investment corporation

MET
See Multiple employer trust

Metropolitan statistical area (MSA)
A means used by the government to define large population centers that may transverse different governmental jurisdictions. For example, the Washington, D.C. MSA includes the District of Columbia and contiguous parts of Maryland and Virginia because all of these geopolitical areas comprise one population and economic operating unit.

Mezzanine financing
See Third-stage financing

Micro-efficiency
Efficiency as it pertains to the operation of individual firms.

Microdata
Information on the characteristics of an individual business firm.

Mid-term debt
An obligation that matures within one to five years.

Midrisk venture capital
See Equity midrisk venture capital

Minimum premium plan
A combination approach to funding an insurance plan aimed primarily at premium tax savings. The employer self-funds a fixed percentage of estimated monthly claims and the insurance company insures the excess.

Minimum wage
The lowest hourly wage allowed by the federal government.

Minority Business Development Agency
Contracts with private firms throughout the nation to sponsor Minority Business Development Centers which provide minority firms with advice and technical assistance on a fee basis.

Minority Enterprise Small Business Investment Corporation (MESBIC)
A federally funded private venture capital firm licensed by the U.S. Small Business Administration to provide capital to minority-owned businesses (see separate citation).

Minority-owned business
Businesses owned by those who are socially or economically disadvantaged (see separate citation).

Mom and Pop business
A small store or enterprise having limited capital, principally employing family members.

Moonlighter
A wage-and-salary worker with a side business.

MSA
See Metropolitan statistical area

Multi-employer plan
A health plan to which more than one employer is required to contribute and that may be maintained through a collective bargaining agreement and required to meet standards prescribed by the U.S. Department of Labor.

Multi-level marketing
A system of selling in which you sign up other people to assist you and they, in turn, recruit others to help them. Some entrepreneurs have built successful companies on this concept because the main focus of their activities is their product and product sales.

Multimedia
The use of several types of media to promote a product or service. Also, refers to the use of several different types of media (sight, sound, pictures, text) in a CD-ROM (see separate citation) product.

Multiple employer trust (MET)
A self-funded benefit plan generally geared toward small employers sharing a common interest.

NAFTA
See North American Free Trade Agreement

NASDAQ
See National Association of Securities Dealers Automated Quotations

National Association of Securities Dealers Automated Quotations
Provides price quotes on over-the-counter securities as well as securities listed on the New York Stock Exchange.

National income
Aggregate earnings of labor and property arising from the production of goods and services in a nation's economy.

Net assets
See Net worth

Net income
The amount remaining from earnings and profits after all expenses and costs have been met or deducted. Also known as Net earnings.

Net profit
Money earned after production and overhead expenses (see separate citations) have been deducted.

Net worth
The difference between a company's total assets and its total liabilities.

Network
A chain of interconnected individuals or organizations sharing information and/or services.

New York Stock Exchange (NYSE)
The oldest stock exchange in the U.S. Allows for trading in stocks, bonds, warrants, options, and rights that meet listing requirements.

Niche
A career or business for which a person is well-suited. Also, a product which fulfills one need of a particular market segment, often with little or no competition.

Glossary

Nodes
One workstation in a network, either local area or wide area (see separate citations).

Nonbank bank
A bank that either accepts deposits or makes loans, but not both. Used to create many new branch banks.

Noncompetitive awards
A method of contracting whereby the federal government negotiates with only one contractor to supply a product or service.

Nonmember bank
A state-regulated bank that does not belong to the federal bank system.

Nonprofit
An organization that has no shareholders, does not distribute profits, and is without federal and state tax liabilities.

Norms
See Financial ratios

North American Free Trade Agreement (NAFTA)
Passed in 1993, NAFTA eliminates trade barriers among businesses in the U.S., Canada, and Mexico.

NYSE
See New York Stock Exchange

Occupational Safety & Health Administration (OSHA)
Federal agency that regulates health and safety standards within the workplace.

Optimal firm size
The business size at which the production cost per unit of output (average cost) is, in the long run, at its minimum.

Organizational chart
A hierarchical chart tracking the chain of command within an organization.

OSHA
See Occupational Safety & Health Administration

Overhead
Expenses, such as employee benefits and building utilities, incurred by a business that are unrelated to the actual product or service sold.

Owner's capital
Debt or equity funds provided by the owner(s) of a business; sources of owner's capital are personal savings, sales of assets, or loans from financial institutions.

P & L
See Profit and loss statement

Part-time workers
Normally, those who work less than 35 hours per week. The Tax Reform Act indicated that part-time workers who work less than 17.5 hours per week may be excluded from health plans for purposes of complying with federal nondiscrimination rules.

Part-year workers
Those who work less than 50 weeks per year.

Partnership
Two or more parties who enter into a legal relationship to conduct business for profit. Defined by the U.S. Internal Revenue Code as joint ventures, syndicates, groups, pools, and other associations of two or more persons organized for profit that are not specifically classified in the IRS code as corporations or proprietorships.

Patent
A grant made by the government assuring an inventor the sole right to make, use, and sell an invention for a period of 17 years.

PC
See Professional corporation

Peak
See Cyclical peak

Pension
A series of payments made monthly, semiannually, annually, or at other specified intervals during the lifetime of the pensioner for distribution upon retirement. The term is sometimes used to denote the portion of the retirement allowance financed by the employer's contributions.

Pension fund
A fund established to provide for the payment of pension benefits; the collective contributions made by all of the parties to the pension plan.

Performance appraisal
An established set of objective criteria, based on job description and requirements, that is used to evaluate the performance of an employee in a specific job.

Permit
See Business license

Plan
See Business plan

Pooling
An arrangement for employers to achieve efficiencies and lower health costs by joining together to purchase group health insurance or self-insurance.

PPO
See Preferred provider organization

Preferred lenders program
See SBA special lending institution categories

Preferred provider organization (PPO)
A contractual arrangement with a health care services organization that agrees to discount its health care rates in return for faster payment and/or a patient base.

Premiums
The amount of money paid to an insurer for health insurance under a policy. The premium is generally paid periodically (e.g., monthly), and often is split between the employer and the employee. Unlike deductibles and coinsurance or copayments, premiums are paid for coverage whether or not benefits are actually used.

Prime-age workers
Employees 25 to 54 years of age.

Prime contract
A contract awarded directly by the U.S. Federal Government.

Private company
See Closely held corporation

Private placement
A method of raising capital by offering for sale an investment or business to a small group of investors (generally avoiding registration with the Securities and Exchange Commission or state securities registration

agencies). Also known as Private financing or Private offering.

Pro forma
The use of hypothetical figures in financial statements to represent future expenditures, debts, and other potential financial expenses.

Proactive
Taking the initiative to solve problems and anticipate future events before they happen, instead of reacting to an already existing problem or waiting for a difficult situation to occur.

Procurement
A contract from an agency of the federal government for goods or services from a small business.

Prodigy
An online service which is accessible by computer modem. The service features Internet access, bulletin boards, online periodicals, electronic mail, and other services for subscribers.

Product development
The stage of the innovation process where research is translated into a product or process through evaluation, adaptation, and demonstration.

Product franchising
An arrangement for a franchisee to use the name and to produce the product line of the franchisor or parent corporation.

Production
The manufacture of a product.

Production prototype
See Prototype

Productivity
A measurement of the number of goods produced during a specific amount of time.

Professional corporation (PC)
Organized by members of a profession such as medicine, dentistry, or law for the purpose of conducting their professional activities as a corporation. Liability of a member or shareholder is limited in the same manner as in a business corporation.

Profit and loss statement (P & L)
The summary of the incomes (total revenues) and costs of a company's operation during a specific period of time. Also known as Income and expense statement.

Proposal
See Business plan

Proprietorship
The most common legal form of business ownership; about 85 percent of all small businesses are proprietorships. The liability of the owner is unlimited in this form of ownership.

Prospective payment system
A cost-containment measure included in the Social Security Amendments of 1983 whereby Medicare payments to hospitals are based on established prices, rather than on cost reimbursement.

Prototype
A model that demonstrates the validity of the concept of an invention (laboratory prototype); a model that meets the needs of the manufacturing process and the user (production prototype).

Prudent investor rule or standard
A legal doctrine that requires fiduciaries to make investments using the prudence, diligence, and intelligence that would be used by a prudent person in making similar investments. Because fiduciaries make investments on behalf of third-party beneficiaries, the standard results in very conservative investments. Until recently, most state regulations required the fiduciary to apply this standard to each investment. Newer, more progressive regulations permit fiduciaries to apply this standard to the portfolio taken as a whole, thereby allowing a fiduciary to balance a portfolio with higher-yield, higher-risk investments. In states with more progressive regulations, practically every type of security is eligible for inclusion in the portfolio of investments made by a fiduciary, provided that the portfolio investments, in their totality, are those of a prudent person.

Public equity markets
Organized markets for trading in equity shares such as common stocks, preferred stocks, and warrants.

Includes markets for both regularly traded and nonregularly traded securities.

Public offering
General solicitation for participation in an investment opportunity. Interstate public offerings are supervised by the U.S. Securities and Exchange Commission (see separate citation).

Quality control
The process by which a product is checked and tested to ensure consistent standards of high quality.

Rate of return
The yield obtained on a security or other investment based on its purchase price or its current market price. The total rate of return is current income plus or minus capital appreciation or depreciation.

Real property
Includes the land and all that is contained on it.

Realignment
See Resource realignment

Recession
Contraction of economic activity occurring between the peak and trough (see separate citations) of a business cycle.

Regulated market
A market in which the government controls the forces of supply and demand, such as who may enter and what price may be charged.

Regulation D
A vehicle by which small businesses make small offerings and private placements of securities with limited disclosure requirements. It was designed to ease the burdens imposed on small businesses utilizing this method of capital formation.

Regulatory Flexibility Act
An act requiring federal agencies to evaluate the impact of their regulations on small businesses before the regulations are issued and to consider less burdensome alternatives.

Research
The initial stage of the innovation process, which includes idea generation and invention.

Research and development financing
A tax-advantaged partnership set up to finance product development for start-ups as well as more mature companies.

Resource mobility
The ease with which labor and capital move from firm to firm or from industry to industry.

Resource realignment
The adjustment of productive resources to interindustry changes in demand.

Resources
The sources of support or help in the innovation process, including sources of financing, technical evaluation, market evaluation, management and business assistance, etc.

Retained business earnings
Business profits that are retained by the business rather than being distributed to the shareholders as dividends.

Revolving credit
An agreement with a lending institution for an amount of money, which cannot exceed a set maximum, over a specified period of time. Each time the borrower repays a portion of the loan, the amount of the repayment may be borrowed yet again.

Risk capital
See Venture capital

Risk management
The act of identifying potential sources of financial loss and taking action to minimize their negative impact.

Routing
The sequence of steps necessary to complete a product during production.

S corporations
See Sub chapter S corporations

SBA
See Small Business Administration

SBA direct loans
Loans made directly by the U.S. Small Business Administration (SBA); monies come from funds appropriated specifically for this purpose. In general, SBA direct loans carry interest rates slightly lower than those in the private financial markets and are available only to applicants unable to secure private financing or an SBA guaranteed loan.

SBA 504 Program
See Certified development corporation

SBA guaranteed loans
Loans made by lending institutions in which the U.S. Small Business Administration (SBA) will pay a prior agreed-upon percentage of the outstanding principal in the event the borrower of the loan defaults. The terms of the loan and the interest rate are negotiated between theborrower and the lending institution, within set parameters.

SBA loans
See Disaster loans; SBA direct loans; SBA guaranteed loans; SBA special lending institution categories

SBA Management Assistance Programs
Classes, workshops, counseling, and publications offered by the U.S. Small Business Administration.

SBA special lending institution categories
U.S. Small Business Administration (SBA) loan program in which the SBA promises certified banks a 72-hour turnaround period in giving its approval for a loan, and in which preferred lenders in a pilot program are allowed to write SBA loans without seeking prior SBA approval.

SBDB
See Small Business Data Base

SBDC
See Small business development centers

SBI
See Small business institutes program

SBIC
See Small business investment corporation

SBIR Program
See Small Business Innovation Development Act of 1982

Scale economies
The decline of the production cost per unit of output (average cost) as the volume of output increases.

Scale efficiency
The reduction in unit cost available to a firm when producing at a higher output volume.

SCORE
See Service Corps of Retired Executives

SEC
See Securities and Exchange Commission

SECA
See Self-Employment Contributions Act

Second-stage financing
Working capital for the initial expansion of a company that is producing, shipping, and has growing accounts receivable and inventories. Also known as Second-round financing.

Secondary market
A market established for the purchase and sale of outstanding securities following their initial distribution.

Secondary worker
Any worker in a family other than the person who is the primary source of income for the family.

Secondhand capital
Previously used and subsequently resold capital equipment (e.g., buildings and machinery).

Securities and Exchange Commission (SEC)
Federal agency charged with regulating the trade of securities to prevent unethical practices in the investor market.

Securitized debt
A marketing technique that converts long-term loans to marketable securities.

Seed capital
Venture financing provided in the early stages of the innovation process, usually during product development.

Self-employed person
One who works for a profit or fees in his or her own business, profession, or trade, or who operates a farm.

Self-Employment Contributions Act (SECA)
Federal law that governs the self-employment tax (see separate citation).

Self-employment income
Income covered by Social Security if a business earns a net income of at least $400.00 during the year. Taxes are paid on earnings that exceed $400.00.

Self-employment retirement plan
See Keogh plan

Self-employment tax
Required tax imposed on self-employed individuals for the provision of Social Security and Medicare. The tax must be paid quarterly with estimated income tax statements.

Self-funding
A health benefit plan in which a firm uses its own funds to pay claims, rather than transferring the financial risks of paying claims to an outside insurer in exchange for premium payments.

Service Corps of Retired Executives (SCORE)
Volunteers for the SBA Management Assistance Program who provide one-on-one counseling and teach workshops and seminars for small firms.

Service firm
See Business service firm

Service sector
Broadly defined, all U.S. industries that produce intangibles, including the five major industry divisions of transportation, communications, and utilities; wholesale trade; retail trade; finance, insurance, and real estate; and services.

Set asides
See Small business set asides

Short-haul service
A type of transportation service in which the transporter supplies service between cities where the maximum distance is no more than 200 miles.

Short-term debt
An obligation that matures in one year.

SIC codes
See Standard Industrial Classification codes

Single-establishment enterprise
See Establishment

Small business
An enterprise that is independently owned and operated, is not dominant in its field, and employs fewer than 500 people. For SBA purposes, the U.S. Small Business Administration (SBA) considers various other factors (such as gross annual sales) in determining size of a business.

Small Business Administration (SBA)
An independent federal agency that provides assistance with loans, management, and advocating interests before other federal agencies.

Small Business Data Base
A collection of microdata (see separate citation) files on individual firms developed and maintained by the U.S. Small Business Administration.

Small business development centers (SBDC)
Centers that provide support services to small businesses, such as individual counseling, SBA advice, seminars and conferences, and other learning center activities. Most services are free of charge, or available at minimal cost.

Small business development corporation
See Certified development corporation

Small business-dominated industry
Industry in which a minimum of 60 percent of employment or sales is in firms with fewer than 500 employees.

Small Business Innovation Development Act of 1982
Federal statute requiring federal agencies with large extramural research and development budgets to allocate a certain percentage of these funds to small research and development firms. The program, called the Small Business Innovation Research (SBIR) Program, is designed to stimulate technological innovation and make greater use of small businesses in meeting national innovation needs.

Small business institutes (SBI) program
Cooperative arrangements made by U.S. Small Business Administration district offices and local colleges and universities to provide small business firms with graduate students to counsel them without charge.

Small business investment corporation (SBIC)
A privately owned company licensed and funded through the U.S. Small Business Administration and private sector sources to provide equity or debt capital to small businesses.

Small business set asides
Procurement (see separate citation) opportunities required by law to be on all contracts under $10,000 or a certain percentage of an agency's total procurement expenditure.

Smaller firms
For U.S. Department of Commerce purposes, those firms not included in the Fortune 1000.

SMSA
See Metropolitan statistical area

Socially and economically disadvantaged
Individuals who have been subjected to racial or ethnic prejudice or cultural bias without regard to their qualities as individuals, and whose abilities to compete are impaired because of diminished opportunities to obtain capital and credit.

Sole proprietorship
An unincorporated, one-owner business, farm, or professional practice.

Special lending institution categories
See SBA special lending institution categories

Standard Industrial Classification (SIC) codes
Four-digit codes established by the U.S. Federal Government to categorize businesses by type of economic activity; the first two digits correspond to major groups such as construction and manufacturing, while the last two digits correspond to subgroups such as home construction or highway construction.

Standard metropolitan statistical area (SMSA)
See Metropolitan statistical area

Start-up
A new business, at the earliest stages of development and financing.

Start-up costs
Costs incurred before a business can commence operations.

Start-up financing
Financing provided to companies that have either completed product development and initial marketing or have been in business for less than one year but have not yet sold their product commercially.

Stock
A certificate of equity ownership in a business.

Stop-loss coverage
Insurance for a self-insured plan that reimburses the company for any losses it might incur in its health claims beyond a specified amount.

Strategic planning
Projected growth and development of a business to establish a guiding direction for the future. Also used to determine which market segments to explore for optimal sales of products or services.

Structural unemployment
See Unemployment

Sub chapter S corporations
Corporations that are considered noncorporate for tax purposes but legally remain corporations.

Subcontract
A contract between a prime contractor and a subcontractor, or between subcontractors, to furnish supplies or services for performance of a prime contract (see separate citation) or a subcontract.

Surety bonds
Bonds providing reimbursement to an individual, company, or the government if a firm fails to complete a contract. The U.S. Small Business Administration guarantees surety bonds in a program much like the SBA guaranteed loan program (see separate citation).

Swing loan
See Bridge financing

Target market
The clients or customers sought for a business' product or service.

Targeted Jobs Tax Credit
Federal legislation enacted in 1978 that provides a tax credit to an employer who hires structurally unemployed individuals.

Tax number
A number assigned to a business by a state revenue department that enables the business to buy goods without paying sales tax.

Taxable bonds
An interest-bearing certificate of public or private indebtedness. Bonds are issued by public agencies to finance economic development.

Technical assistance
See Management and technical assistance

Technical evaluation
Assessment of technological feasibility.

Technology
The method in which a firm combines and utilizes labor and capital resources to produce goods or services; the application of science for commercial or industrial purposes.

Technology transfer
The movement of information about a technology or intellectual property from one party to another for use.

Tenure
See Employee tenure

Term
The length of time for which a loan is made.

Terms of a note
The conditions or limits of a note; includes the interest rate per annum, the due date, and transferability and convertibility features, if any.

Third-party administrator
An outside company responsible for handling claims and performing administrative tasks associated with health insurance plan maintenance.

Third-stage financing
Financing provided for the major expansion of a company whose sales volume is increasing and that is breaking even or profitable. These funds are used for further plant expansion, marketing, working capital, or development of an improved product. Also known as Third-round or Mezzanine financing.

Time deposit
A bank deposit that cannot be withdrawn before a specified future time.

Time management
Skills and scheduling techniques used to maximize productivity.

Trade credit
Credit extended by suppliers of raw materials or finished products. In an accounting statement, trade credit is referred to as "accounts payable."

Trade name
The name under which a company conducts business, or by which its business, goods, or services are identified. It may or may not be registered as a trademark.

Trade periodical
A publication with a specific focus on one or more aspects of business and industry.

Trade secret
Competitive advantage gained by a business through the use of a unique manufacturing process or formula.

Trade show
An exhibition of goods or services used in a particular industry. Typically held in exhibition centers where exhibitors rent space to display their merchandise.

Trademark
A graphic symbol, device, or slogan that identifies a business. A business has property rights to its trademark from the inception of its use, but it is still prudent to register all trademarks with the Trademark Office of the U.S. Department of Commerce.

Translation
See Product development

Treasury bills
Investment tender issued by the Federal Reserve Bank in amounts of $10,000 that mature in 91 to 182 days.

Treasury bonds
Long-term notes with maturity dates of not less than seven and not more than twenty-five years.

Treasury notes
Short-term notes maturing in less than seven years.

Trend
A statistical measurement used to track changes that occur over time.

Trough
See Cyclical trough

UCC
See Uniform Commercial Code

UL
See Underwriters Laboratories

Underwriters Laboratories (UL)
One of several private firms that tests products and processes to determine their safety. Although various firms can provide this kind of testing service, many local and insurance codes specify UL certification.

Underwriting
A process by which an insurer determines whether or not and on what basis it will accept an application for insurance. In an experience-rated plan, premiums are based on a firm's or group's past claims; factors other than prior claims are used for community-rated or manually rated plans.

Unfair competition
Refers to business practices, usually unethical, such as using unlicensed products, pirating merchandise, or misleading the public through false advertising, which give the offending business an unequitable advantage over others.

Unfunded accrued liability
The excess of total liabilities, both present and prospective, over present and prospective assets.

Unemployment
The joblessness of individuals who are willing to work, who are legally and physically able to work, and who are seeking work. Unemployment may represent the temporary joblessness of a worker between jobs (frictional unemployment) or the joblessness of a worker whose skills are not suitable for jobs available in the labor market (structural unemployment).

Uniform Commercial Code (UCC)
A code of laws governing commercial transactions across the U.S., except Louisiana. Their purpose is to bring uniformity to financial transactions.

Glossary

Uniform product code (UPC symbol)
A computer-readable label comprised of ten digits and stripes that encodes what a product is and how much it costs. The first five digits are assigned by the Uniform Product Code Council, and the last five digits by the individual manufacturer.

Unit cost
See Average cost

UPC symbol
See Uniform product code

U.S. Establishment and Enterprise Microdata (USEEM) File
A cross-sectional database containing information on employment, sales, and location for individual enterprises and establishments with employees that have a Dun & Bradstreet credit rating.

U.S. Establishment Longitudinal Microdata (USELM) File
A database containing longitudinally linked sample microdata on establishments drawn from the U.S. Establishment and Enterprise Microdata file (see separate citation).

U.S. Small Business Administration 504 Program
See Certified development corporation

USEEM
See U.S. Establishment and Enterprise Microdata File

USELM
See U.S. Establishment Longitudinal Microdata File

VCN
See Venture capital network

Venture capital
Money used to support new or unusual business ventures that exhibit above-average growth rates, significant potential for market expansion, and are in need of additional financing to sustain growth or further research and development; equity or equity-type financing traditionally provided at the commercialization stage, increasingly available prior to commercialization.

Venture capital company
A company organized to provide seed capital to a business in its formation stage, or in its first or second stage of expansion. Funding is obtained through public or private pension funds, commercial banks and bank holding companies, small business investment corporations licensed by the U.S. Small Business Administration, private venture capital firms, insurance companies, investment management companies, bank trust departments, industrial companies seeking to diversify their investment, and investment bankers acting as intermediaries for other investors or directly investing on their own behalf.

Venture capital limited partnerships
Designed for business development, these partnerships are an institutional mechanism for providing capital for young, technology-oriented businesses. The investors' money is pooled and invested in money market assets until venture investments have been selected. The general partners are experienced investment managers who select and invest the equity and debt securities of firms with high growth potential and the ability to go public in the near future.

Venture capital network (VCN)
A computer database that matches investors with entrepreneurs.

WAN
See Wide Area Network

Wide Area Network (WAN)
Computer networks linking systems throughout a state or around the world in order to facilitate the sharing of information.

Withholding
Federal, state, social security, and unemployment taxes withheld by the employer from employees' wages; employers are liable for these taxes and the corporate umbrella and bankruptcy will not exonerate an employer from paying back payroll withholding. Employers should escrow these funds in a separate account and disperse them quarterly to withholding authorities.

Workers' compensation
A state-mandated form of insurance covering workers injured in job-related accidents. In some

states, the state is the insurer; in other states, insurance must be acquired from commercial insurance firms. Insurance rates are based on a number of factors, including salaries, firm history, and risk of occupation.

Working capital
Refers to a firm's short-term investment of current assets, including cash, short-term securities, accounts receivable, and inventories.

Yield
The rate of income returned on an investment, expressed as a percentage. Income yield is obtained by dividing the current dollar income by the current market price of the security. Net yield or yield to maturity is the current income yield minus any premium above par or plus any discount from par in purchase price, with the adjustment spread over the period from the date of purchase to the date of maturity.

Glossary

Cumulative Index